Strategies of Contai

Strategies of Containment

A Critical Appraisal of American National
Security Policy during the Cold War

Revised and Expanded Edition

JOHN LEWIS GADDIS

OXFORD
UNIVERSITY PRESS

OXFORD
UNIVERSITY PRESS

Oxford University Press, Inc., publishes works that further
Oxford University's objective of excellence
in research, scholarship, and education.

Oxford   New York
Auckland   Cape Town   Dar es Salaam   Hong Kong   Karachi
Kuala Lumpur   Madrid   Melbourne   Mexico City   Nairobi
New Delhi   Shanghai   Taipei   Toronto

With offices in
Argentina   Austria   Brazil   Chile   Czech Republic   France   Greece
Guatemala   Hungary   Italy   Japan   Poland   Portugal   Singapore
South Korea   Switzerland   Thailand   Turkey   Ukraine   Vietnam

Copyright © 1982, 2005 by Oxford University Press, Inc.

First published by Oxford University Press, Inc., 1982
198 Madison Avenue, New York, New York 10016
www.oup.com

First issued as an Oxford University Press paperback, 1982
Published as a revised and expanded edition, 2005

Oxford is a registered trademark of Oxford University Press

Library of Congress Cataloging-in-Publication Data
Gaddis, John Lewis.
Strategies of containment : a critical appraisal of American national security policy during the cold
war / John Lewis Gaddis.—Rev. and expanded ed.
p.   cm.
Includes bibliographical references.
ISBN-13: 978-0-19-517448-9 ISBN-10: 0-19-517448-8
ISBN-13: 978-0-19-517447-2 (pbk.) ISBN-10: 0-19-517447-X (pbk.)
1. United States—Foreign relations—1945–1989.
2. United States—Foreign relations—1989–
3. National security—United States—History—20th century.
4. National security—United States—History—21st century.
I. Title
E744.G24   2005
327.73'009'045—dc22   2004065459

9 8 7 6 5 4 3 2 1
Printed in the United States of America on acid-free paper

For

WENDELL P. C. MORGENTHALER, JR.
Colonel, USMC (Ret.)

and

ALAN T. ISAACSON
Captain, USN

Strategy seminars, 1975–1977
U. S. Naval War College

Preface

Historians, it has been suggested, can be divided into two groups: "lumpers" and splitters."[1] "Lumpers" seek to impose order on the past: they deliver themselves of sweeping generalizations that attempt to make sense out of whole epochs; they seek to systematize complexity, to reduce the chaos, disorder, and sheer untidiness of history to neat patterns that fit precisely within the symmetrical confines of chapters of books, usually designed to be inflicted upon unsuspecting undergraduates. "Splitters," on the other hand, write mostly for each other—and their defenseless graduate students. They like to point out exceptions, qualifications, incongruities, paradoxes; in short, they elevate quibbling to a high historiographical art. Both approaches are necessary, even indispensable, to the writing of history, but they do not always occur in the same proportion at the same time with reference to the same topic. Establishing a balance between "lumpers" and "splitters" is no easy thing.

This has been especially true of a field some people are not yet prepared to regard as history—the record of United States involvement in the Cold War. Initial accounts, written during the 1950's and early 1960's, tended toward the particular—lengthy but not very analytical narratives of what happened, based usually on memoir material and published sources, sometimes also on inside information. One dipped into them at first fascinated but then quickly surfeited by the detail: the question "what does it all mean?" remained unanswered. An answer of sorts came in the late 1960's and early 1970's with that outbreak of "lumping" known as revisionism: it was general, analytical, breathtaking at times in its findings, but occasionally reminiscent as well of a trapeze artist in its leaps from one conclusion to another without visible means of support. Inevitably, reaction set in—the "splitters" appeared, gnawing away at the foundations of revisionism until many of its most impressive structures—though hardly all—came tumbling down. No comparably broad synthesis has emerged to take their place. Cold War studies in recent years have seen much careful monographic work, based on a wealth of new sources, but no overall pattern has emerged from it. That is unfortunate, because as important as absorption in the particular is, there is a certain value in stepping back at times to try to take in the larger picture, even if parts of it stick out of the frame in awkward places.

This book is an effort to redress the balance in favor of "lumping." It seeks to reinterpret, in the light of new evidence and recent research, the whole of United States national security policy since World War II. It approaches its subject, not from the more traditional diplomatic, economic, ideological, or military perspectives, but from an angle of vision that I think incorporates all of these: that of strategy. By "strategy," I mean quite simply the process by which ends are related to means, intentions to capabilities, objectives to resources. Every maker of policy consciously or unconsciously goes through such a process, but scholarly students of policy, in their fascination with regional, topical, or bureaucratic approaches, have paid curiously little attention to it. I should like to apply this "strategic" perspective to what seems to me to have been the central preoccupation of postwar national security policy—the idea of containment*—with a view toward explaining the successive mutations, incarnations, and transformations that concept has undergone through the years.

My approach to this subject has been influenced by the work of Alexander George, who has done a great deal to break down artificial methodological barriers separating the fields of contemporary history and political science. George has suggested that there exists, for political leaders, something he calls an "operational code"—a set of assumptions about the world, formed early in one's career, that tend to govern without much sub-

---

*The term "containment" poses certain problems, implying as it does a consistently defensive orientation in American policy. One can argue at length about whether Washington's approach to the world since 1945 has been primarily defensive—I tend to think it has—but the argument is irrelevant for the purposes of this book. What is important here is that American leaders consistently *perceived* themselves as responding to rather than initiating challenges to the existing international order. For this reason, it seems to me valid to treat the idea of containment as the central theme of postwar national security policy.

sequent variation the way one responds to crises afterward.[2] Building on this argument, I would suggest that there exist for presidential administrations certain "strategic" or "geopolitical" codes, assumptions about American interests in the world, potential threats to them, and feasible responses, that tend to be formed either before or just after an administration takes office, and barring very unusual circumstances tend not to change much thereafter. "It is an illusion," Henry Kissinger has written, "to believe that leaders gain in profundity while they gain experience. . . . the convictions that leaders have formed before reaching high office are the intellectual capital they will consume as long as they continue in office."[3]

There have been, I will argue, five distinct geopolitical codes in the postwar era: George Kennan's original strategy of containment, articulated between 1947 and 1949 and, I think, largely implemented by the Truman administration during that period; the assumptions surrounding NSC-68, put into effect between 1950 and 1953 as a result of the Korean War; the Eisenhower-Dulles "New Look," which lasted from 1953 to 1961; the Kennedy-Johnson "flexible response" strategy, which shaped the American approach to the world until Johnson left office in 1969; and that complex of ideas we now nostalgically associate with the term "détente," put forward by Nixon and Kissinger in the early 1970's, and continued in effect by both Ford and Carter until the invasion of Afghanistan late in 1979. Borrowing again from Alexander George, I propose to undertake here a modest "structured, focused comparison"[4] of these geopolitical codes, these successive approaches to containment, to see what patterns might emerge from them. My objective in all of this is to throw out a large, but I hope not too indigestible "lump," which should at least give the "splitters," who have been on a pretty thin diet lately, something to chew on.

A word is in order about the organization of this book. Chapters One and Eleven treat, in a general way, the World War II antecedents and the current status of containment. Chapters Two through Ten deal more rigorously with the approaches to containment outlined above. My procedure generally has been to describe each strategy in one chapter,* and to evaluate implementation in the one that follows. There are, however, two

---

*In line with George's call for systematic comparison, I have (I hope without being too obtrusive about it) asked the following questions of each strategy: (1) What conception did the administration in question have of American interests in the world? (2) How did it perceive threats to those interests? (3) What responses did it choose to make, in the light of those interests and threats? (4) How did it seek to justify those responses?

exceptions to this pattern. Because of the relatively brief period in which NSC-68 formed the basis of national strategy, Chapter Four, which deals with it, covers both content and implementation. Chapter Eight, on the implementation of "flexible response," takes the form of a detailed case study on the Vietnam War.

This book is a direct outgrowth of my having taught for two years at the United States Naval War College, an institution unique, I believe, in its concern for the relationship of history to policy. I am indebted to Admirals Stansfield Turner and Julien J. LeBourgeois and to Philip A. Crowl for having made that experience possible; also to former colleagues, notably James E. King, Thomas H. Etzold, David Schoenbaum, and Ned Lebow, with whom the ideas in this book have been much discussed; to a large number of students whose respectful but healthy skepticism was a valued corrective; and to two congenial teaching partners and officemates, whose patience and forbearance are commemorated on the dedication page.

Students and colleagues at Ohio University have also heard more about this book than they would ever have chosen to, and I am grateful to them for their comments, especially Charles C. Alexander, Alonzo L. Hamby, and David L. Williams. Karen Williams went beyond the call of duty to track down an elusive footnote reference, and Doris Dorr typed the manuscript with the efficiency history professors at Athens have come to appreciate.

George F. Kennan and W. W. Rostow took time to read carefully and answer questions about portions of the manuscript dealing with their years in Washington; I am grateful to them for their patience in considering arguments with which I suspect they did not always agree. Robert A. Divine put aside his own study of Eisenhower to give me cogent advice on Chapters Five and Six. And it has been a pleasure to work with Sheldon Meyer, Victoria Bijur, and the Oxford University Press in preparing the book for publication.

I have been fortunate in having been given forums in an unusual variety of places in which to develop some of the ideas that appear here. I should like to thank Professors Sadao Asada and Nobunao Matsuyama for arranging my participation in the 1978 Kyoto American Studies summer seminar, where the outline for this book was first worked out; Samuel F. Wells, Jr., for having organized fruitful sessions on the relationship of history to policy and on NSC-68 at the Woodrow Wilson International Center for Scholars; Dr. and Mrs. Gerald J. Bernath for having made possible the 1980 Stuart L. Bernath Memorial Lecture to the Society for Historians of

American Foreign Relations; Professor Arthur Funk for organizing the 1980 joint meeting of the British and American Committees on the History of the Second World War in London; and, finally, my colleagues in both the "mini-" and "maxi-Klubis" at the Historical Research and Documentation Institute, University of Helsinki.

This book is based heavily on archival materials, many of them recently opened. My thanks for their indispensable assistance to the staffs of the Harry S. Truman, Dwight D. Eisenhower, John F. Kennedy, and Lyndon B. Johnson libraries, as well as the Diplomatic and Modern Military branches of the National Archives; also to George F. Kennan for permission to use and quote from his private papers, and to the staff of the Seeley Mudd Library at Princeton University, where they are housed.

Grants from the Naval War College Advanced Research Center and the National Endowment for the Humanities helped to support the writing of this book, and are gratefully acknowledged. Brief portions of it have appeared, in slightly different forms, in *Foreign Affairs*, *International Security*, and the Society for Historians of American Foreign Relations *Newsletter*, and appear here by permission.

Family obligations come last, but hardly least. Michael and David showed uncommon restraint in not raiding (at least not often) their father's hoard of paper, notecards, paperclips, and tape. My wife Barbara (who dislikes sentimental acknowledgments) provided a sympathetic ear and a critical mind to help me over rough spots, but mostly would have preferred to be studying glaciers and peat bogs, or listening to Willie Nelson.

Helsinki, Finland   J. L. G.
January 1981

Preface to the Revised and Expanded Edition

When the first edition of *Strategies of Containment* came out, in 1982, Ronald Reagan had recently entered the White House, Leonid Brezhnev was still alive—although not well—inside the Kremlin, and it was not at all clear how, when, or even whether the Cold War would end. The book itself, for this reason, ended indecisively: it reached no firm conclusion as to how well containment had worked, or what its prospects might be. Whatever its utility in explaining the history of that strategy, the distinction I made between symmetrical and asymmetrical forms of containment offered little guidance for the future. My only suggestion echoed something Franklin D. Roosevelt once said about high tariffs and low tariffs: that there ought to be a way to "weave them together"—to draw upon the strengths of both approaches while rejecting their weaknesses.[1] In the absence of any further specification as to how that might be done, this was not a particularly helpful piece of advice. There is no evidence that anyone in the Reagan administration paid the slightest attention to it.

They did not need to, because the President and his advisers were well on the way, by then, to crafting a new strategy of containment that would resolve most of the contradictions I had identified in its predecessors. The Reagan strategy—for it was chiefly his own creation—was already in place by the time Mikhail Gorbachev came to power in Moscow in 1985. Whether it paved the way for his accession is still debated among historians; but that it created a basis for cooperation with the United States in changing the nature of the Soviet Union has long been obvious. It fell to Reagan, therefore, to complete the task of containment that George F.

Kennan had first set forth in the aftermath of World War II. And he did it in a way that Kennan himself had anticipated: by enlisting a Soviet leader in the task of altering his own regime.

Chapter Eleven—now much expanded from the original edition—tells this story. I have also taken this opportunity to revise and update all the preceding chapters, including their bibliographical references, and to add a new epilogue. My purpose is to complete a circle: to trace the history of containment all the way through to an end that was remarkably close to what Kennan envisaged at the beginning.

This new edition also completes a second, if less portentous, circle. As its original preface explains, *Strategies of Containment* grew out of the opportunity I had to teach the now legendary Strategy and Policy curriculum at the Naval War College during the mid-1970's. It has been my privilege since then, working with my colleagues Paul Kennedy and Charles Hill, to bring that curriculum to Yale University, where it now thrives as the highly popular "Studies in Grand Strategy" seminar. "And where did the Naval War College get the idea for its course?" I recently asked its originator, Admiral Stansfield Turner. "Oh, we got it from Yale," he replied, "back in the days when you used to teach that sort of thing." I am pleased that we teach that sort of thing at Yale once again.

It remains only to thank Susan Ferber of Oxford University Press for suggesting this new edition and for facilitating its preparation, Catherine Humphries for copy-editing, Patterson Lamb for proofreading—and Toni Dorfman, for copy-editing, proofreading, love, and life.

New Haven, Connecticut   J. L. G.
February 2005

Contents

Abbreviations

ABM	Anti-ballistic missile
CIA	Central Intelligence Agency
CPP	*Carter Public Papers*
DSB	*Department of State Bulletin*
EPP	*Eisenhower Public Papers*
FACC	Foreign Assistance Correlation Committee
FRUS	*Foreign Relations of the United States*
HASC	House Armed Services Committee
HFAC	House Foreign Affairs Committee
ICBM	Inter-continental ballistic missile
IRBM	Intermediate range ballistic missile
JCS	Joint Chiefs of Staff
JIC	Joint Intelligence Committee
JPP	*Johnson Public Papers*
KPP	*Kennedy Public Papers*
MAD	Mutual assured destruction
MIRV	Multiple independently targeted re-entry vehicle
MLF	Multilateral nuclear force
NATO	North Atlantic Treaty Organization
NPP	*Nixon Public Papers*
NSC	National Security Council
NSDD	National Security Decision Directive
NWC	National War College
OSS	Office of Strategic Services
PPS	Policy Planning Staff
RPP	*Reagan Public Papers*
SALT	Strategic Arms Limitation Talks
SDI	Strategic Defense Initiative
SFRC	Senate Foreign Relations Committee
SLBM	Submarine-launched ballistic missile
SNIE	Special National Intelligence Estimate
START	Strategic Arms Reduction Talks
SWNCC	State-War-Navy Coordinating Committee
TPP	*Truman Public Papers*

Strategies of Containment

Prologue:
Containment Before Kennan

"My children, it is permitted you in time of grave danger to walk with the devil until you have crossed the bridge." It was Franklin D. Roosevelt's version of an old Balkan proverb (sanctioned by the Orthodox Church, no less), and he liked to cite it from time to time during World War II to explain the use of questionable allies to achieve unquestionable objectives.[1] In all-out war, he believed, the ultimate end—victory—justified a certain broad-mindedness regarding means, nowhere more so than in reliance on Stalin's Soviet Union to help defeat Germany and Japan. Allies of any kind were welcome enough in London and Washington during the summer of 1941; still the U.S.S.R.'s sudden appearance in that capacity could not avoid setting off Faustian musings in both capitals. Winston Churchill's willingness to extend measured parliamentary accolades to the Devil if Hitler should invade Hell is well known;* less familiar is Roosevelt's paraphrase of his proverb to an old friend, Joseph Davies: "I can't take communism nor can you, but to cross this bridge I would hold hands with the Devil."[2]

The imagery, in the light of subsequent events, was apt. Collaboration with the Soviet Mephistopheles helped the United States and Great Britain achieve victory over their enemies in a remarkably short time and with surprisingly few casualties, given the extent of the fighting involved. The price, though, was the rise of an even more powerful and less

---

* "If Hitler invaded Hell I would make at least a favourable reference to the Devil in the House of Commons." (Winston S. Churchill, *The Grand Alliance* [Boston: 1950], pp. 370–71.)

fathomable totalitarian state, and, as a consequence, a Cold War that lasted ten times longer than the brief and uneasy alliance that won the world war.

"Containment," the term generally used to characterize American policy toward the Soviet Union during the postwar era, was a series of attempts to deal with the consequences of that wartime Faustian bargain: the idea was to prevent the Soviet Union from using the power and position it won as a result of that conflict to reshape the postwar international order, a prospect that seemed, in the West, no less dangerous than what Germany or Japan might have done had they had the chance. George F. Kennan coined the term in July 1947 when he called publicly for a "long-term, patient but firm and vigilant containment of Russian expansion tendencies,"[3]* but it would be an injustice to wartime policy-makers to imply, as has too often been done, that they were oblivious to the problem. In fact, "containment" was much on the minds of Washington officials from 1941 on; the difficulty was to mesh that long-term concern with the more immediate imperative of defeating the Axis. What Roosevelt, Harry S. Truman, and their advisers sought was a way to win the war without compromising the objectives for which it was being fought. It was out of their successive failures to square that circle that Kennan's concept of "containment" eventually emerged.

I

One way to have resolved the dilemma would have been to devise military operations capable of containing the Russians while at the same time enlisting their help in subduing the Germans. Truman himself had suggested a crude way of doing this after Hitler attacked the Soviet Union in June 1941: "If we see that Germany is winning the war we ought to help Russia, and if Russia is winning, we ought to help Germany and in that way let them kill as many as possible."[4]† But Truman at the time was an obscure Missouri senator. His momentary flash of geopolitical cynicism attracted little attention until he unexpectedly entered the White House four years later. By that time, and with increasing frequency in the months that fol-

---

* Kennan had used the term at least once previously, assuring a State Department audience in September 1946 that his recommendations "should enable us, if our policies are wise and non-provocative, to contain them [the Russians] both militarily and politically for a long time to come." (Quoted in George F. Kennan, *Memoirs: 1925–1950* [Boston: 1967], p. 304.)

† Truman added, though, that he did not want to see Hitler victorious under any circumstances.

lowed, questions were being raised as to whether the United States had not relied on the Russians too heavily to defeat the Germans too thoroughly. William C. Bullitt, former ambassador to the Soviet Union and now one of that country's most vociferous critics, said it best in a 1948 *Life* magazine article entitled: "How We Won the War and Lost the Peace."[5]

Bullitt himself had advocated an alternative strategy five years earlier in a series of top-secret memoranda to Roosevelt. Stalin's war aims were not those of the West, he had insisted: those who argued that participation in an anti-fascist coalition had purged the Soviet dictator of his autocratic and expansionist tendencies were assuming, on the basis of no evidence, a conversion "as striking as [that] of Saul on the road to Damascus." A Europe controlled from Moscow would be at least as dangerous as one ruled from Berlin, and yet "if Germany is to be defeated without such cost in American and British lives that victory might well prove to be a concealed defeat (like the French victory in the war of 1914), the continued participation of the Red Army in the war against Germany is essential." The problem, then, was to prevent "the domination of Europe by the Moscow dictatorship without losing the participation of the Red Army in the war against the Nazi dictatorship." Bullitt's answer, put forward long before Winston Churchill advocated a similar but better-known solution,* was to introduce Anglo-American forces into Eastern Europe and the Balkans, for the purpose, first, of defeating the Germans, but second, of barring the Red Army from the rest of Europe. "War is an attempt to achieve political objectives by fighting," Bullitt reminded Roosevelt in August 1943, "and political objectives must be kept in mind in planning operations."[6]

There are hints that Roosevelt considered using military forces to achieve something like the political results Bullitt had in mind. The President showed more than polite interest in Churchill's schemes for Anglo-American military operations in the Balkans, despite the horrified reactions of Secretary of War Henry Stimson and the Joint Chiefs of Staff.[7] He emphasized, at least twice in 1943, the need to get to Berlin as soon as the Russians did in the event of a sudden German collapse.[8] And in April 1945, less than a week before his death, he countered Churchill's complaints about Soviet behavior by pointing out that "our armies will in a very

---

* According to Forrest C. Pogue, Churchill did not explicitly propose to the Americans the idea of deploying Anglo-American forces in such a way as to contain the Russians until after the Yalta Conference in 1945. (*George C. Marshall: Organizer of Victory* [New York: 1973], p. 517.)

few days be in a position that will permit us to become 'tougher' than has heretofore appeared advantageous to the war effort."[9]

But Roosevelt generally resisted efforts to deploy forces for the dual purposes of defeating the Germans and containing the Russians. He did not do this, though, in a geopolitical vacuum: there were, in his mind, powerful reasons other than a single-minded concentration on victory for holding hands with the Devil to cross the bridge.

One had to do with Roosevelt's conception of the balance of power. American security, he thought, required preventing the coming together of potentially hostile states. He had extended diplomatic recognition to the Soviet Union in 1933 partly to counter-balance, and attempt to keep separate, the growing military power of Germany and Japan.[10] When Stalin rejected that role by authorizing the 1939 Nazi-Soviet Pact, Roosevelt carefully left the way open for an eventual reconciliation with Moscow, despite his intense personal revulsion at the Russians' behavior.[11] He moved swiftly when the German invasion in June 1941 made it possible to reconstitute his strategy, even though collaboration with the U.S.S.R. was more difficult to sell in a still ostensibly neutral United States than in embattled Britain.[12] One of his persistent concerns after Pearl Harbor was to prevent a new "deal" between Hitler and Stalin, and simultaneously to secure the latter's cooperation in the war against Japan.[13] The geopolitical requirements of keeping adversaries divided, therefore, constituted one powerful argument against military deployments directed against Russia as well as Germany.

Coupled with this was an appreciation of the nature of American power. Roosevelt was an early and firm believer in the "arsenal of democracy" concept—the idea that the United States could most effectively contribute toward the maintenance of international order by expending technology but not manpower. Long before Pearl Harbor, he had sought to enlist the productive energies of American industry in the anti-fascist cause: the United States, he thought, should serve as a privileged sanctuary, taking advantage of its geographical isolation and invulnerable physical plant to produce the goods of war, while leaving others to furnish the troops to fight it.[14] Even after belligerency became unavoidable, Roosevelt and his chief military strategist, General George C. Marshall, retained elements of this approach, limiting the American army to 90 divisions instead of the 215 that had been thought necessary to defeat both Germany and Japan. As Marshall admitted, though, this could not have been done without Soviet manpower.[15] The United States, in this sense, was as dependent on the Red Army as the Russians were on American Lend-Lease—perhaps more so. That fact, too, precluded military operations aimed at containing the Russians while defeating the Germans.

There was yet a third consideration, most often attributed to Churchill but very much present in Roosevelt's mind as well: the need to minimize casualties.* Averell Harriman best summarized the President's concern in this regard:

> Roosevelt was very much affected by World War I, which he had, of course, seen at close range. He had a horror of American troops landing again on the continent and becoming involved in the kind of warfare he had seen before—trench warfare with all its appalling losses. I believe he had in mind that if the great armies of Russia could stand up to the Germans, this might well make it possible for us to limit our participation largely to naval and air power.[16]

The United States was new at the business of being a world power, Roosevelt must have reasoned. If the sacrifices involved became too great, especially in a war in which its own territory did not seem directly threatened, then pressures for a reversion to a "fortress America" concept, if not outright isolationism, might still prevail. Letting allies bear the brunt of casualties was a way of ensuring internationalism for the future.

Finally, there was the fact that the United States had another war to wage in the Pacific, one in which it was bearing a far heavier share of the burden than in Europe. To be sure, American strategy even before Pearl Harbor had been to defeat Germany first. But Roosevelt recognized that support for military operations against Hitler also required progress in the war against Japan: the American people would not tolerate indefinite defeats in one ocean while arming to cross the other. Hence, F.D.R.'s strategy evolved by subtle stages into one of taking on Germany and Japan at the same time; the war in the Pacific became more than just the holding action that had originally been planned.[17] The effects were beneficial in one sense: few people would have anticipated that wars against both Germany and Japan could have been brought to almost simultaneous conclusions with so few casualties.[18] But the price, again, was reliance on Soviet manpower to carry the main burden of the struggle in Europe. Had the

---

* "I was very careful to send Mr. Roosevelt every few days a statement of our casualties," General Marshall later recalled. "I tried to keep before him all the time the casualty results because you get hardened to these things and you have to be very careful to keep them always in the forefront of your mind." (Pogue, *Marshall: Organizer of Victory*, p. 316.)

atomic bomb not worked, the Russians might have been called upon to play a similar role in the Pacific after Germany's surrender.

It will not do, then, to see Roosevelt's strategy as totally insulated from political considerations. A war plan aimed at making careful use of American resources to maintain a global balance of power without at the same time disrupting the fabric of American society hardly fits that characterization. It is true that Roosevelt did not orient wartime strategy toward the coming Cold War—he foresaw that possibility, but hoped, indeed trusted, that it would not arise. Instead he concentrated on winning the war the United States was in at the time as quickly as possible and at the least possible cost. Given those objectives, it would have been hard to improve on the strategy Roosevelt followed.

It is interesting, as a corrective to those who have criticized Roosevelt for ignoring political considerations, to see how the Russians—especially Stalin—viewed his conduct of the war. The emphasis here was on the wholly political nature of American strategy: one historical account has even claimed that F.D.R. explicitly adopted Truman's 1941 recommendation to let Russians and Germans kill each other off.[19] Certainly, on the basis of statistical indices, this would appear to have been the effect; for every American who died in the war, thirteen Germans and *ninety* Russians died.* It is worth asking whether something like this might not have been Roosevelt's intent all along: might his strategy in reality have been a crafty way of ensuring both full Russian participation in the war and the postwar containment of the Soviet Union, not by denying that country territory or resources, but by exhausting it?

With the elusive Roosevelt, one can never be sure. Few statesmen cloaked their intentions more carefully than the deceptively loquacious F.D.R.. If this had been his strategy, it is unlikely that he would have told anyone about it. There is, though, a more plausible and less sinister explanation. To have done what the Russians wanted—create an early second front—or what his domestic critics wanted—deploy forces against both Russians and Germans—would have violated Roosevelt's fundamental

---

* Gerhard Weinberg cites American casualties in World War II at 300,000, German casualties at over 4 million, and Soviet casualties at approximately 25 million. More recent research places the Soviet figure at 27 million. (Gerhard L. Weinberg, *A World at Arms: A Global History of World War II* [New York: 1994], p. 894; Vladimir O. Pechatnov and C. Carl Edmondson, "The Russian Perspective," in Ralph B. Levering, Vladimir O. Pechatnov, Verena Botzenhart-Viehe, and C. Carl Edmondson, *Debating the Origins of the Cold War: American and Russian Perspectives* [New York: 2002], p. 86.)

aversion to the use of American manpower in shaping world affairs. The President fully intended to have an impact, but he sought to do it in such a way as to neither demoralize nor debilitate the nation. In short, he wanted to keep means from corrupting ends. It is easy to write off this approach as naïve, as some of Roosevelt's American detractors have done, or as self-serving, as the Russians did. What seems more probable, though, is that Roosevelt's strategy reflected the rational balance of objectives and re-sources any wise statesman will try to achieve, *if he can*. It was Stalin's mis-fortune, largely as a result of his errors of strategy between 1939 and 1941, to have denied himself that opportunity.*

II

Another reason for doubting that Roosevelt set out deliberately to contain the Russians by exhausting them is that his postwar plans seemed to lean in a wholly different direction—that of containment by integration. F.D.R. sought to ensure a stable postwar order by offering Moscow a prominent place in it; by making it, so to speak, a member of the club. The assump-tion here—it is a critical one for understanding Roosevelt's policy—was that Soviet hostility stemmed from insecurity, but that the sources of that insecurity were external. They lay, the President thought, in the threats posed by Germany and Japan, in the West's longstanding aversion to Bol-shevism, and in the refusal, accordingly, of much of the rest of the world to grant the Russians their legitimate position in international affairs. "They didn't know us, that's the really fundamental difference," he commented in 1944. "They are friendly people. They haven't got any crazy ideas of conquest, and so forth; and now that they have got to know us, they are much more willing to accept us."[20] With the defeat of the Axis,† and with the West's willingness to make the Soviet Union a full partner in shaping the peace to come, the reasons for Stalin's suspicions, Roosevelt expected, would gradually drop away.

The President had never seen in the ideological orientation of the So-viet state a reason not to have cooperative relations at the interstate level.

---

* It is worth speculating as to whether Stalin would have ordered suicidal missions to rescue Great Britain or the United States had they been under severe attack. The precedent of 1939–1941 does not suggest so.

† One reason for Roosevelt's insistence on harsh treatment for Germany after the war was his desire to reassure the Soviet Union. (See, on this point, Robert Murphy, *Diplomat Among Warriors* [Garden City, N.Y.: 1964], p. 227.)

As a liberal, he lacked the visceral horror with which American conservatives regarded the use of state authority to bring about social change. As a self-confident patrician, he discounted the appeal communism might have inside the United States.[21] As a defender of the international balance of power, he distinguished between fascism's reliance on force to achieve its objectives and what he saw as communism's less dangerous use of subversion and propaganda.[22] But, most important, as an intelligent observer of the international scene, he sensed a trend in the evolution of the Soviet state that many experts on that country were only beginning to grasp: that, for the moment at least, considerations of national interest had come to overshadow those of ideology in determining Stalin's behavior.

It was within this context that Roosevelt developed his idea of integrating the Soviet Union into a common postwar security structure. F.D.R. had long advocated some form of great-power condominium to maintain world order. He was, it has been argued, a "renegade Wilsonian," seeking Wilson's goals by un-Wilsonian means.[23] Chief among these was his conviction that the peace-loving states should band together to deter aggression, first by isolating the perpetrators, and then, if necessary, by using force against them. As early as 1935, Roosevelt had spoken of an arrangement along those lines to blockade Nazi Germany; two years later he was proposing similar though vague plans for collective resistance against Japan.[24] Nothing came of either initiative, but it is worth noting that Roosevelt had counted on the Soviet Union's cooperation in both of them. It was not too surprising, then, that after June 1941, when Moscow was again in a position to cooperate with the West, F.D.R. should have revived his plan, this time in the form of the "Four Policemen"—the United States, Great Britain, the Soviet Union and China—who would, as the President described it, impose order on the rest of the postwar world, bombing anyone who would not go along.[25]

The "Four Policemen" concept appears, at first glance, to have reflected an unrealistic assumption on Roosevelt's part that the great powers would always agree, an expectation that seemed at odds with the obviously antagonistic nature of the international system. Again, though, surface manifestations are deceiving. "When there [are] four people sitting in a poker game and three of them [are] against the fourth," F.D.R. told Henry Wallace late in 1942, "it is a little hard on the fourth." Wallace took this to mean the possibility of American, Russian, and Chinese pressures against the British, and indeed the President did subsequently make efforts to impress both Stalin and Chiang Kai-shek with his own anti-imperial aspirations.[26] But Roosevelt was telling others, at roughly the same time, that he needed China as one of the "Four Policemen" to counter-balance Russia.[27] Certainly Churchill could have been counted upon to join in any such enterprise, should it become necessary. The picture is hardly one of anticipating harmony, therefore; rather, it is reminiscent, as much as anything else, of Bismarck's cold-blooded tactic of keeping potential rivals off balance by preventing them from aligning with each other.[28]

Roosevelt also used what a later generation would call "linkage" to ensure compliance with American postwar aims. His employment of economic and political pressure to speed the dismantling of the British Empire has been thoroughly documented.[29] No comparably blatant requirements were imposed on the Soviet Union, probably because Roosevelt feared that that relationship, unlike the one with London, was too delicate to stand the strain.[30] Still, he did keep certain cards up his sleeve for dealing with Moscow after the war, notably the prospect of reconstruction assistance either through Lend-Lease or a postwar loan, together with a generous flow of reparations from Western-occupied Germany, all of which Washington would have been able to control in the light of Soviet behavior.[31] Also, intriguingly, there was Roosevelt's refusal, even after learning they knew of it, to tell the Russians about the atomic bomb, perhaps with a view to postwar bargaining.[32] This combination of counterweights and linkages is not what one would expect from a statesman assuming a blissfully serene postwar environment. Although Roosevelt certainly hoped for such an outcome, he was too good a poker player to count on it.

But Roosevelt's main emphasis was on trying to make the Grand Alliance survive Hitler's defeat by creating relationships of mutual trust among its leaders. The focus of his concern—and indeed the only allied leader not already in some position of dependence on the United States—was Stalin. F.D.R. has been criticized for attempting to use his personal charm to "get through" to the Soviet autocrat, whose resistance to such blandishments was legendary.[33] As with so much of Roosevelt's diplomacy, though, what seems at first shallow and superficial becomes less so upon reflection. The President realized that Stalin was the only leader in the U.S.S.R. with the authority to modify past attitudes of hostility. However discouraging the prospect of "getting through," there was little point in dealing with anyone below him.[34] And it is worth noting that improvements in Soviet-American relations, when they occurred during the Cold War, generally did so when some basis of mutual respect, if not trust, existed at the top: examples include Eisenhower and Khrushchev after the 1955 Geneva summit, Kennedy and Khrushchev after the Cuban missile crisis, Nixon and Brezhnev during the early 1970's, and Reagan and Gorbachev during the late 1980's. Winning Stalin's trust may have been impossible—no one, with the curious exception of Hitler between 1939 and 1941, appears to have managed it. But making the attempt, given the uncertainties of postwar politics and diplomacy, was neither an unreasonable nor an ingenuous enterprise.

Like any statesman, Roosevelt was pursuing multiple objectives. Building a friendly peacetime relationship with the Soviet Union was only one of them, and as often happens, other priorities got in the way. For example, his second front strategy, designed not so much to weaken Russia as to avoid weakening the United States, could not help but create suspicions in Moscow that Washington was in fact seeking containment by exhaustion.[35] These dark misgivings survived even the D-Day landings: as late as April 1945 Stalin was warning subordinates that the Americans and British might yet make common cause with the Germans; that same month the Red Army began constructing *defensive* installations in Central Europe.[36]

Another of Roosevelt's priorities was to win domestic support for his postwar plans, and thereby to avoid Wilson's repudiation by his own countrymen in 1919–1920. To do this, F.D.R. moderated his own harsh approach to the task of peacekeeping: the country was not ready, Speaker of the House Sam Rayburn told him late in 1942, for a settlement to be enforced through blockades and bombing.[37] Roosevelt sought, accordingly, to integrate the great power condominium his strategic instincts told him would be necessary to preserve world order, on the one hand, with the ideals his political instincts told him would be needed at home to overcome objections to an "unjust" peace, on the other.[38] Idealism, in Roosevelt's mind, could serve eminently realistic ends.

It would be a mistake, then, to write off Roosevelt's concern for self-determination in Eastern Europe as mere window-dressing. Although prepared to see that part of the world fall within Moscow's sphere of influence, he expected as well that as fears of Germany subsided, the Russians would moderate the severity of the measures needed to maintain their position there. Otherwise, he was convinced, it would be impossible to "sell" the resulting settlement to the American people.* But, like Henry

---

* Ralph B. Levering has pointed out that presidents have a considerable capacity to shape public opinion: the implication is that Roosevelt could have "educated" the public to accept a settlement based on classic spheres of influence. (See his *American Opinion and the Russian Alliance, 1939–1945* [Chapel Hill: 1976], pp. 204–7.) But what is important here is not the

Kissinger in somewhat different circumstances thirty years later, Roosevelt found himself in a situation in which domestic support for what he had negotiated depended upon the exercise of discretion and restraint in the Kremlin. Those tendencies were no more prevalent then than later; as a consequence, a gap developed between what F.D.R. thought the public would tolerate and what the Russians would accept—a gap papered over, at Yalta, by fragile compromises.

Competing priorities therefore undercut Roosevelt's efforts to win Stalin's trust: to that extent, his strategy failed. Even if these had not existed, there is reason to wonder whether F.D.R.'s approach would have worked, given the balefully suspicious personality of the Soviet dictator. But there are, at times, justifications for directing flawed strategies at inauspicious targets, and World War II may have been one of these. Certainly alternatives to the policies actually followed contained difficulties as well. And there are grounds for thinking that Roosevelt might not have continued his open-handed approach once the war ended: his quiet incorporation of counter-weights and linkages into his strategy suggests that possibility.* One is left, then, where one began: with a surface impression of casual, even frivolous, superficiality, and yet with a growing realization that darker, more cynical, but more perceptive instincts lay not far beneath.

III

Whatever Roosevelt's intentions were for after the war, dissatisfaction with the strategy he was following during it had become widespread within the government by the end of 1944. American military chiefs and Lend-Lease administrators resented the Russians' increasingly importunate demands on their limited resources, made with little understanding of supply problems or logistics, and with infrequent expressions of gratitude.[39] Career diplomats had always maintained a certain coolness toward the U.S.S.R. Now, with the State Department excluded by Roosevelt from any top-level dealings with that country, they brooded in relative isolation over the gap they saw emerging between Stalin's postwar aims and the principles of

President's theoretical power to manipulate public opinion, but his actual perception of that power. And the evidence is strong that Roosevelt habitually underestimated his influence in that regard, as far as foreign affairs were concerned.
* "Averell [Harriman] is right," Roosevelt complained on March 23, 1945. "We can't do business with Stalin. He has broken every one of the promises made at Yalta." (W. Averell Harriman and Elie Abel, *Envoy to Churchill and Stalin, 1941–1946* [New York: 1975], p. 444.)

the Atlantic Charter.[40] But it was officials with direct experience of service in the Soviet Union who developed the strongest and most influential objections to Roosevelt's open-handedness. Attempts to win Stalin's trust through generosity and goodwill would not work, they argued: the Soviet dictator was too apt to confuse those qualities with weakness. What was needed instead was recognition of the fact that the Soviet Union was going neither to leave nor to lose the war, and that if its Western allies did not soon begin to apply such leverage as they had available, the Kremlin would shape its own peace settlement, without regard to their aspirations or interests.

The argument came most forcefully from W. Averell Harriman, United States ambassador in Moscow since 1943, and from General John R. Deane, head of the American military mission there. Both men had gone to the Soviet Union convinced that Roosevelt's strategy of unconditional aid was wise; both had been determined to make it work. Within a year, though, both had developed reservations about that strategy, on the grounds that trusting the Russians had produced few if any reciprocal benefits. Thus, Deane found his efforts to coordinate military activities foundering on the Russians' unwillingness to share information or facilities, while Harriman grew increasingly angry at Moscow's tendency to impose unilateral political settlements in Eastern Europe as its armies moved into that region. Both men had expressed their frustrations in strong terms by the end of 1944: "We must make clear what we expect of them as the price of our goodwill," Harriman wrote in September of that year. "Unless we take issue with the present policy there is every indication [that] the Soviet Union will become a world bully wherever their interests are involved." "Gratitude cannot be banked in the Soviet Union," Deane added three months later, in what became almost a slogan for those seeking a revision of Roosevelt's policy. "Each transaction is complete in itself without regard to past favors. The party of the second part is either a shrewd trader to be admired or a sucker to be despised."[41]

Harriman and Deane did not advocate giving up attempts to win postwar Soviet cooperation; in this respect, their position differed from that of a third influential American in Moscow, George F. Kennan, at that time minister-counselor of the embassy there. Kennan, one of the State Department's first trained Russian experts, saw little possibility of resolving differences with the U.S.S.R. on any other basis than a frank acknowledgment of respective spheres of influence. The Soviet Union intended to dominate its surroundings, he argued; there was no reason the United States or its democratic allies should sanction, or even appear to sanction, the grisly procedures that would be necessary to accomplish that goal.[42] Harriman and Deane, together with Charles E. Bohlen, another State Department Russian expert then serving in Washington, were not prepared to go that far. The American public would never accept a settlement based on spheres of influence, they insisted; it was important to have made the effort to secure Stalin's cooperation, however discouraging the prospects. But that objective did not preclude taking a blunter and harder line than in the past. The idea, Harriman emphasized, should be to "strengthen the hand of those around Stalin who want to play the game along our lines and to show Stalin that the advice of the counselors of a tough policy is leading him into difficulties." What was needed was "a firm but friendly *quid pro quo* attitude."[43]

Roosevelt was not averse to this idea. He had been careful, in his handling of Lend-Lease, reparations, a postwar loan, and the atomic bomb, to hold out both the "sticks" and "carrots" needed to make a *quid pro quo* strategy work. But he was unwilling to resort to them while the war was still on: this was his major disagreement with Harriman, Deane, and a growing number of his other advisers. They thought it imperative to act while the fighting was under way because American leverage, primarily in the form of Lend-Lease, would be greater than after victory, and because if the United States waited until the end of the war to act, it might find the issues with which it was concerned already settled to Moscow's satisfaction. Roosevelt's priority, to the end, was to win the war: *quid pro quo* bargaining might follow, but it would not precede that accomplishment.

F.D.R.'s death, in April 1945, cleared the way for a revision of strategy he himself would probably have carried out, although not in as abrupt and confused a manner as was actually done. Truman, totally unbriefed as to what Roosevelt had been trying to do, consulted the late President's advisers. But those most directly associated with Soviet affairs, notably Harriman, had been trying to stiffen Roosevelt's position; now, with a new and untutored chief executive in the White House, they redoubled their efforts at "education." Eager to appear decisive and in command, Truman accepted this instruction with an alacrity that unsettled even those providing it, lecturing Soviet Foreign Minister Vyacheslav Molotov in person, and his distant master by cable, in a manner far removed from the graceful ambiguities of F.D.R.[44] The result was ironic: Truman embraced a *quid pro quo* approach in the belief that he was implementing Roosevelt's policy, but in doing so he convinced the Russians that he had changed it. F.D.R.'s elusiveness continued to bedevil Soviet-American relations, even beyond the grave.

In fact (and despite his 1941 remark about letting Germans and Russians kill each other off), Truman was no more prepared to abandon the possibility of an accommodation with Moscow than were Harriman and Deane. He firmly rejected Churchill's advice to deploy Anglo-American military forces in such a way as to keep the Russians out of as much of Germany as possible. He sent Harry Hopkins to Moscow in May of 1945, in part to repair the damage his own brusqueness had done. Long after relations with Stalin went sour, he continued to seek the counsel of Soviet sympathizers, notably Henry A. Wallace and Joseph E. Davies. The new President harbored a healthy skepticism toward all totalitarian states: ideology, he thought, whether communist or fascist, was simply an excuse for dictatorial rule. But, like Roosevelt, he did not see totalitarianism in itself as precluding normal relations. Not surprisingly in the light of his background, the analogy of big city political bosses in the United States came most easily to mind: their methods might not be delicate or fastidious, but one could work with them, so long as they kept their word.[45]

Truman found a kindred spirit in James F. Byrnes, whom he appointed Secretary of State shortly after taking office. An individual of vast experience in domestic affairs but almost none in diplomacy, Byrnes believed in practicing what had worked well for him at home. Nations, he thought, like individuals or interest groups, could always reach agreement on difficult issues if a sufficient willingness to negotiate and compromise existed on both sides. A *quid pro quo* strategy was as natural for Byrnes, then, as for Truman. Dealing with the Russians, the new Secretary of State observed, was just like managing the United States Senate: "You build a post office in their state and they'll build a post office in our state."[46]

The new administration thought it had leverage over the Russians in several respects. Harriman himself had stressed the importance of postwar reconstruction assistance, which the United States would be able to control, whether through Lend-Lease, a rehabilitation loan, or reparations shipments from its occupation zone in Germany. Roosevelt had been leaning toward using this leverage at the time of his death; Truman quickly confirmed that unconditional aid would not be extended past the end of the fighting. Lend-Lease would be phased out, and postwar loans and reparations shipments would be tied, at least implicitly, to future Soviet political cooperation.[47]* Publicity was another form of leverage: the ad-

---

*The Potsdam protocol, upon American insistence, specified that the Soviet Union was to receive 10 percent of such industrial equipment as was "unnecessary" for the functioning of the postwar German economy, but the Western powers would make the determination as to what

ministration assumed that the Kremlin was still sensitive to "world opinion," and that by calling attention openly to instances of Soviet unilateralism, it could get the Russians to back down.[48] Then there was the ultimate sanction of the atomic bomb: Byrnes, though not all his colleagues in the administration, believed that the simple presence of this awesome weapon in the American arsenal would make the Russians more manageable than in the past. At a minimum, he wanted to hold back commitments to seek the international control of atomic energy as a bargaining chip for use in future negotiations.[49]

None of these attempts to apply leverage worked out as planned. The Russians were never dependent enough on American economic aid to make substantial concessions to get it: intelligence reports had long indicated that such aid, if extended, would have speeded reconstruction by only a matter of months. Another difficulty was that key Congressmen, whose support would have been necessary for the passage of any loan, made it clear that they would demand in return nothing less than free elections and freedom of speech inside the Soviet Union, and the abandonment of its sphere of influence in Eastern Europe.[50] Publicity, directed against Soviet violations of the Yalta agreements in that part of the world, produced no greater success: when Byrnes warned that he might have to release a report on conditions in Romania and Bulgaria prepared by the American publisher Mark Ethridge, Stalin, with understandable self-confidence, threatened to have his own "impartial" observer, the Soviet journalist Ilya Ehrenburg, issue his report on those countries.[51] The Russians dealt effectively with the atomic bomb by simply appearing to ignore it, except for a few heavy-handed cocktail party jokes by a tipsy Molotov. In the meantime, domestic pressures had forced Truman to commit the United States to the principle of international control before Byrnes had even attempted to extract a *quid pro quo* from Moscow.[52]

By the time of the Moscow foreign ministers' conference in December 1945, Byrnes had come to much the same conclusion that Roosevelt had a year earlier: that the only way to reconcile the American interest in self-determination with the Soviet interest in security was to negotiate thinly disguised agreements designed to cloak the reality of Moscow's control behind a façade of democratic procedures.* But that approach, manifested

was necessary and what was not. (*Foreign Relations of the United States* [hereafter *FRUS*]: *The Conference of Berlin (The Potsdam Conference), 1945* [Washington: 1960], II, 1485–86.)
* The Russians, in return, extracted a token concession from the United States which appeared to broaden, but in fact did not, their role in the occupation of Japan.

in the form of token concessions by the Russians on Bulgaria and Romania, came across at home as appeasement. As a result, Byrnes found himself under attack from both the President and Congress, upon his return, for having given up too much.[53] The *quid pro quo* strategy, by early 1946, had not only failed to produce results. It had become a domestic political liability as well.

Quid pro quo proved unsuccessful for several reasons. One was the difficulty of making "sticks" and "carrots" commensurate with concessions to be demanded from the other side. The "sticks" the United States had available were either unimpressive, as was the case with publicity, or unusable, as in the instance of the atomic bomb. The major "carrot," economic aid, was important to the Russians, but not to the point of justifying the concessions that would have been required to obtain it. Another difficulty was the problem of coordination. Bargaining implies the ability to control the combination of pressures and inducements to be applied, but that in turn requires central direction, not easy in a democracy in the best of circumstances, and certainly not during the first year of an inexperienced and badly organized administration. Extraneous influences—Congress, the press, public opinion, bureaucracies, personalities—tended to intrude upon the bargaining process, making the alignment of conditions to be met with incentives to be offered awkward, to say the least.

But the major difficulty was simply the Soviet Union's imperviousness to external influences. The *quid pro quo* strategy had assumed, as had Roosevelt's, that Soviet behavior could be affected from the outside: the only differences had been over method and timing. In fact, though, there was not much the West could do, in the short term, to shape Stalin's decisions. The Soviet dictator maintained tight control in a mostly self-sufficient country, with little knowledge or understanding of, much less susceptibility to, events in the larger world. It was this realization of impermeability—of the fact that neither trust nor pressure had made any difference—that paved the way for the revision of strategy set off by George Kennan's "long telegram" of February 1946.

IV

Rarely in the course of diplomacy does an individual manage to express, within a single document, ideas of such force and persuasiveness that they immediately change a nation's foreign policy. That was the effect, though, of the 8,000-word telegram dispatched from Moscow by Kennan on February 22, 1946. Prodded by a puzzled State Department to explain the increasingly frequent anti-Western statements in the speeches of Soviet leaders, and by a Treasury Department wanting to know why the U.S.S.R. had refused to join the International Monetary Fund and the World Bank, Kennan, with a mixture of exhilaration at having been asked and exasperation at having until then been ignored, composed a primer on Soviet foreign policy with all the speed and intensity that comes from direct experience and passionate conviction. As was once said of another career diplomat in another country at another time whose ideas had a similar impact, "there was . . . such a heat in his spirit that knowledge of history and contemporary politics, acute judgment and power of exposition ran together with a kind of incandescence which lit up everything on which his mind and feeling and words were directed."*

The thesis of Kennan's "long telegram" was that the whole basis of American policy toward the Soviet Union during and after World War II had been wrong. That policy, whether in the form of Roosevelt's emphasis on integration or Harriman's on bargaining, had assumed the existence of no structural impediments to normal relations within the Soviet Union itself; the hostility Stalin had shown toward the West, rather, had been the result of insecurities bred by external threats. These could be overcome, it had been thought, either by winning Stalin's trust through openhandedness, or by commanding his respect through a *quid pro quo* approach. In either case, the choice as to whether cooperation would continue was believed to be up to the United States: if Washington chose the right approach, then the Russians would come along.†

Kennan insisted that Soviet foreign policy bore little relationship to what the West did or did not do: the "party line is not based on any objective analysis of [the] situation beyond Russia's borders; . . . it arises mainly from basic inner-Russian necessities which existed before [the] recent war and exist today." Kremlin leaders were too unsophisticated to know how to

* Sir Owen O'Malley writing of Eyre Crowe, Senior Clerk in the British Foreign Office, whose January 1907 "Memorandum on the present state of British relations with France and Germany" had similar, if less dramatic, repercussions. (Quoted in Zara S. Steiner, *The Foreign Office and Foreign Policy, 1898–1914* [London: 1969], p. 117.)

† The extent to which Soviet behavior would be determined by Western attitudes was the most consistent single theme in wartime analyses of Soviet-American relations undertaken by the Office of Strategic Services. See especially Research and Analysis reports 523, 959, 1109, 2073, 2284, and 2669, all in the Office of Intelligence Research Files, Department of State records, Record Group 59, Diplomatic Branch, National Archives.

govern by any means other than repression: they therefore needed excuses "for the dictatorship without which they did not know how to rule, for cruelties they did not dare not to inflict, for sacrifices they felt bound to demand." Picturing the outside world "as evil, hostile and menacing" provided such a justification. "A hostile international environment is the breath of life for [the] prevailing internal system in this country," Kennan argued in another dispatch to the State Department the following month. "[W]e are faced here with a tremendous vested interest dedicated to [the] proposition that Russia is a country walking a dangerous path among implacable enemies. [The] disappearance of Germany and Japan (which were the only real dangers) from [the] Soviet horizon left this vested interest no choice but to build up [the] US and United Kingdom to fill this gap."[54]

There could be, then, no permanent resolution of differences with such a government, since it relied on the fiction of external threat to maintain its internal legitimacy. "Some of us here have tried to conceive the measures our country would have to take if it really wished to pursue, at all costs, [the] goal of disarming Soviet suspicions," Kennan noted in March.

> We have come to [the] conclusion that nothing short of complete disarmament, delivery of our air and naval forces to Russia and resigning of [the] powers of government to American Communists would even dent this problem: and even then we believe—and this is not facetious—that Moscow would smell a trap and would continue to harbor [the] most baleful misgivings.

"We are thus up against the fact," Kennan continued, "that suspicion in one degree or another is an integral part of [the] Soviet system, and will not yield entirely to any form of rational persuasion or assurance. . . . To this climate, and not to wishful preconceptions, we must adjust our diplomacy."[55]

Within days of its receipt the "long telegram" and Kennan's other dispatches had been circulated, read, commented upon, and for the most part accepted in Washington as the most plausible explanation of Soviet behavior, past and future. "If none of my previous literary efforts had seemed to evoke even the faintest tinkle from the bell at which they were aimed," he recalled, "this one, to my astonishment, struck it squarely and set it vibrating with a resonance that was not to die down for many months." Why, though, did the Truman administration attach such importance to the views of a still relatively junior Foreign Service officer? What accounted for the fact, as Kennan later put it, that "official Washington, whose states of receptivity or the opposite are determined by subjective emotional currents as intricately imbedded in the subconscious as those of the most complicated of Sigmund Freud's erstwhile patients, was ready to receive the given message"?[56]

The reason was a growing awareness in Washington that the *quid pro quo* strategy had not worked, but that nothing had yet arisen to take its place. Kennan's analyses did not, in themselves, provide such a strategy: they were devoted primarily to an elucidation of the Soviet threat. Such positive recommendations as they contained were limited to the need for candor, courage, and self-confidence in dealing with the Russians.[57] But there were more specific conclusions that seemed to emerge from Kennan's argument, and the Truman administration was quick to seize on these as the basis for yet another approach to the problem of Soviet power in the postwar world, a strategy best characterized by Secretary of State Byrnes (with all of the enthusiasm of a recent convert) as one of "patience and firmness."[58]

The new strategy contained several departures from past practice: (1) No further efforts would be made to conceal disagreements with the Russians; rather, these would be aired openly, frankly, but in a non-provocative manner. (2) There would be no more concessions to the Soviet Union: the United States would, in effect, "draw the line," defending all future targets of Soviet expansion, but without any attempt to "liberate" areas already under Moscow's control. (3) To facilitate this goal, United States military strength would be reconstituted and requests from allies for economic and military aid would be favorably considered. (4) Negotiations with the Soviet Union would continue, but only for the purpose of registering Moscow's acceptance of American positions or of publicizing Soviet intransigence in order to win allies abroad and support at home.[59] The idea, in all of this, was that, confronted by Western firmness, Stalin would see Western patience as the more desirable alternative, and would begin to exercise the restraint necessary to bring it about. Or, as Clark Clifford's top secret report to President Truman on Soviet-American relations put it in September: "it is our hope that they will change their minds and work out with us a fair and equitable settlement when they realize that we are too strong to be beaten and too determined to be frightened."[60]

"Patience and firmness" became the watchword for dealings with the Soviet Union over the next year—if anything, the emphasis, as the Joint Chiefs of Staff had recommended, was primarily on the "firmness."[61] The new approach showed up in the Eastern Mediterranean and the Near East, where the administration not only induced the U.S.S.R. to withdraw troops from Iran and to give up demands for boundary concessions and base rights from Turkey, but in addition committed itself to support the government of Greece against an externally supplied communist insurgency and to station the Sixth Fleet indefinitely in the waters surrounding the latter two countries.[62] It showed up in East Asia, where Washington continued to resist any substantive role for the Russians in the occupation of Japan, while at the same time making clear its determination to prevent a Soviet takeover of all of Korea.[63] It showed up in Germany, where the United States cut off reparations shipments from its zone and began moving toward consolidating it with those of the British and the French, while at the same time offering the Russians a four-power treaty guaranteeing the disarmament of Germany for twenty-five years.[64] It showed up in the Council of Foreign Ministers, where Byrnes firmly resisted Soviet bids to take over former Italian territories along the southern Mediterranean coastline, while at the same time patiently pursuing negotiations on peace treaties for former German satellites.[65] Finally, and most dramatically, the new strategy manifested itself in the Truman Doctrine, in which the administration generalized its obligations to Greece and Turkey into what appeared to be a world-wide commitment to resist Soviet expansionism wherever it appeared.

Truman's March 12, 1947, proclamation that "it must be the policy of the United States to support free peoples who are resisting attempted subjugation by armed minorities or outside pressures" has traditionally been taken as having marked a fundamental point of departure for American foreign policy in the Cold War. In fact, it can more accurately be seen as the ultimate expression of the "patience and firmness" strategy that had been in effect for the past year. Decisions to aid Greece and Turkey, as well as other nations threatened by the Soviet Union, had been made months before.[66] What was new, in early 1947, was Great Britain's abrupt notice of intent to end its own military and financial support to those two countries, together with the need for quick Congressional action to replace it. It was that requirement, in turn, that forced the Truman administration to justify its request in globalist terms; even so, that rhetoric was consistent with the assumption, underlying the "patience and firmness" strategy for almost a year, that the United States could allow no further gains in territory or influence for the Soviet Union anywhere.[67]

No strategy can be effective, though, if it fails to match means with ends: what is striking, in retrospect, about the "patience and firmness" approach is the extent to which ends were decided upon without reference to means. No serious attempt had been made to reverse the headlong rush toward demobilization in the light of the Soviet threat: the armed forces of the United States, which had stood at 12 million at the end of the war with Germany, were down to 3 million by July 1946, and to 1.6 million a year later.[68] Defense expenditures, which had been $83.0 billion in fiscal 1945, the last full year of war, went down to $42.7 billion for fiscal 1946 and $12.8 billion for fiscal 1947.[69] Nor, with the election of an economy-minded Republican Congress in November 1946, did there seem to be much chance of reversing this trend.[70] The Truman Doctrine implied an open-ended commitment to resist Soviet expansionism, therefore, at a time when the means to do so had almost entirely disappeared.

This obvious deficiency made it clear that something more than "patience and firmness" would be required: either means would have to be expanded to fit interests—an unlikely prospect, given the political and economic circumstances of the time*—or, more likely, interests would have to be contracted to fit means. The latter is what in fact took place during the spring of 1947. That period was significant, not as one in which the United States took on new commitments, but rather as the point at which it began to differentiate between the ones it already had. The blunt reality of limited means had once again, as during World War II, forced the making of distinctions between vital and peripheral interests. But that task demanded more than just a set of attitudes, which is what "patience and firmness" had largely boiled down to. It required a strategy, based, as all successful strategies must be, on the calculated relationship of resources to objectives. It was within this context that the concept of "containment" began to develop—and with it the career of its chief architect, George F. Kennan.

---

* That option would be undertaken, though, in 1950. See Chapter Four.

George F. Kennan and the Strategy of Containment

Kennan's abrupt transition from career diplomat to Cold War strategist grew out of more than just an "outrageous encumberment of the telegraphic process."[1] By the time the "long telegram" had won him the reputation of being the government's foremost Soviet expert, there was already in his writing and thinking a depth of strategic vision—a knack for seeing relationships between objectives and capabilities, aspirations and interests, long-term and short-term priorities—rarely found in harried bureaucracies. It was this quality that commended him to Secretary of the Navy James V. Forrestal, a man of similar concerns, as the ideal "deputy for foreign affairs" at the newly established National War College in Washington, the nation's first institution devoted to the study of political-military affairs at the highest level. Kennan's success there in turn attracted the attention of George C. Marshall, who, upon becoming Secretary of State early in 1947, resolved to impart greater coherence to American diplomacy by organizing a "Policy Planning Staff," charged with "formulating and developing . . . long-term programs for the achievement of U.S. foreign policy objectives." In May of that year, Kennan left the war college to become the staff's first director.[2] His place in Washington was by that time unique: he alone among top officials combined knowledge of and experience in Soviet affairs, exposure to what would be called "national security" studies, and a position of responsibility from which to make recommendations for action.

In the summer of 1947, Kennan inadvertently added fame or notoriety to this list, depending on one's point of view, with the publication in *Foreign Affairs* of "The Sources of Soviet Conduct," the article that introduced the term "containment" to the world.[3] Attributed only to a "Mr. X" to preserve Kennan's anonymity, the essay nonetheless quickly fell victim to the reportorial enterprise of Arthur Krock, who revealed its authorship and thereby imparted to it something of the character of an official policy pronouncement. This revelation in turn provoked the critical zeal of Walter Lippmann, who dissected the piece in a series of articles far exceeding the length of the original.[4] The result was confusion that has persisted ever since. Because Kennan never intended the "X" article as a comprehensive statement of national strategy in the first place, it reflected only imperfectly his thinking on that subject. Careless drafting moreover produced passages that appeared to contradict positions Kennan had been advocating within the government, so much so that he found himself in places agreeing more with Lippmann's critique than with his own article. And Kennan's official status precluded public clarification of his views, which had to wait until his memoirs were published twenty years later.[5]

As a consequence, there has developed a kind of cottage industry among Cold War scholars, devoted to elucidating "what Kennan really meant to say."[6] All of this attention suggests Kennan's importance as well as his elusiveness, for although his role was by no means decisive in shaping the Truman administration's approach to the world, his ideas, more than those of anyone else, did provide the intellectual rationale upon which it was based. As Henry Kissinger would later put it, "George Kennan came as close to authoring the diplomatic doctrine of his era as any diplomat in our history."[7] What follows is an attempt to reconstruct that doctrine, based not simply on the "X" article or Kennan's other rare published pronouncements from the late 1940's, but also on the Policy Planning Staff studies produced under his direction, the off-the-record and at times classified lectures he continued to deliver at the National War College and elsewhere within the government after assuming his State Department responsibilities, and his own surviving notes, memoranda, and recorded extemporaneous comments. Subsequent chapters will examine the extent to which the Truman administration actually implemented that strategy, and to which succeeding administrations modified it in the years to come.

I

Definitions of national interest in international affairs tend toward the bland and unexceptionable: they all seem to boil down, in one form or another, to the need to create an international environment conducive to the survival and prospering of the nation's domestic institutions. Certainly the definition Kennan wrote down in the summer of 1948 did not depart from this pattern. "The fundamental objectives of our foreign policy," he asserted, "must always be":

1. to protect the security of the nation, by which is meant the continued ability of this country to pursue the development of its internal life without serious interference, or threat of interference, from foreign powers; and

2. to advance the welfare of its people, by promoting a world order in which this nation can make the maximum contribution to the peaceful and orderly development of other nations and derive maximum benefit from their experiences and abilities.

Kennan cautioned that "complete security or perfection of international environment will never be achieved." Any such statement of objectives could be at best "an indication of direction, not of final destination."[8] Still, this was as close as Kennan came to identifying the nation's irreducible interest in world affairs; few people, one suspects, would have questioned his formulation. The more difficult task was to specify precisely what was required to enhance the security of the nation and the congeniality of the international environment.

Americans traditionally had answered this question, Kennan argued, in two ways. One was what he called the "universalistic" approach, which assumed "that if all countries could be induced to subscribe to certain standard rules of behavior, the ugly realities—the power of aspirations, the national prejudices, the irrational hatreds and jealousies—would be forced to recede behind the protecting curtain of accepted legal restraint, and . . . the problems of our foreign policy could thus be reduced to the familiar terms of parliamentary procedures and majority decision." Universalism assumed the possibility of harmony in international affairs, sought to achieve it through the creation of artificial structures like the League of Nations or the United Nations, and depended for its success on the willingness of nations to subordinate their own security requirements to those of the international community.

The alternative Kennan described as the "particularized" approach. It was "skeptical of any scheme for compressing international affairs into legalist concepts. It holds that the content is more important than the form, and will force its way through any formal structure which is placed upon it. It considers that the thirst for power is still dominant among so many peoples that it cannot be assuaged or controlled by anything but counterforce." Particularism would not reject the idea of joining with other governments to preserve world order, but to be effective such alliances would have to be based "upon real community of interest and outlook, which is to be found only among limited groups of governments, and not upon the abstract formalism of universal international law or international organization."[9]

Kennan considered universalism an inappropriate framework for American interests because it assumed "that men everywhere are basically like ourselves, that they are animated by substantially the same hopes and inspirations, that they all react in substantially the same way in given circumstances." For him the most notable characteristic of the international environment was its diversity, not its uniformity. To make national security contingent upon the worldwide diffusion of American institutions would be to exceed national capabilities, thereby endangering those institutions. "We are great and strong; but we are not great enough or strong enough to conquer or to change or to hold in subjugation by ourselves all . . . hostile or irresponsible forces. To attempt to do so would mean to call upon our own people for sacrifices which would in themselves completely alter our way of life and our political institutions, and would lose the real objectives of our policy in trying to defend them."[10]

Universalism would also involve committing the United States to a goal Kennan thought neither possible nor desirable: the elimination of armed conflict from international life. It could only be done, he thought, by freezing the status quo—"people don't depart from the status quo peacefully when it is in their interest to maintain it"—that in turn meant ensnaring the nation "in such bewildering and confining commitments as to prevent us from employing our influence in world affairs in ways which would be beneficial to world security and world stability." The fact was that war might not always be evil; peace might not always be good: "There is 'peace' behind the walls of a prison, if you like that. There is 'peace' in present-day Czechoslovakia."

> Unpleasant as this may be, we may have to face up to the fact that there may be instances where violence somewhere in the world on a limited scale is more desirable than the alternatives, because those alternatives would be global wars in which we ourselves would be involved, in which no one would win, and in which all civilization would be dragged down. I think we have to face the fact [that] there may be arrangements of peace less acceptable to the security of this country than isolated recurrences of violence.

"Perhaps the whole idea of world peace has been a premature, unworkable, grandiose form of day-dreaming," Kennan argued in June 1947, "and that we should have held up as our goal: 'Peace if possible, and insofar as it effects our interest.' "[11]

Finally, universalism risked bogging the country down "in the meshes of a sterile and cumbersome international parliamentarianism" that might inhibit action necessary in defense of the national interest. Kennan attached little significance to the United Nations; it was an illusion, he insisted, to assume that positions taken there had much actual influence on world affairs. Rather, they resembled "a contest of *tableaux morts*: there is a long period of preparation in relative obscurity; then the curtain is lifted; the lights go on for a brief moment; the posture of the group is recorded for posterity by the photography of voting; and whoever appears in the most graceful and impressive position has won." If somehow this "parliamentary shadow-boxing" could be given practical recognition, "this would indeed be a refined and superior manner of settling international differences." But since that was not likely, the only effect was to distract the American people from the real issues, and to render the international organization itself, in the long run, ridiculous.[12]

It followed, then, that the national interest would best be served not by trying to restructure the international order—the "universalistic" solution—but through the "particularist" approach of trying to maintain equilibrium within it, so that no one country, or group of countries, could dominate it. "Our safety depends," Kennan told a National War College audience in December 1948,

> on our ability to establish a balance among the hostile or undependable forces of the world: To put them where necessary one against the other; to see that they spend in conflict with each other, if they must spend it at all, the intolerance and violence and fanaticism which might otherwise be directed against us, that they are thus compelled to cancel each other out and exhaust themselves in internecine conflict in order that the constructive forces, working for world stability, may continue to have the possibility of life.[13]

Harmony might be unlikely—hardly a surprising conclusion given Kennan's pessimistic view of human nature—but security could be attained nonetheless through a careful balancing of power, interests, and antagonisms.

Several corollaries proceeded logically from this argument. One was that not all parts of the world were equally vital to American security. "We should select first," Kennan wrote in August 1948, "those areas of the world which . . . we cannot permit . . . to fall into hands hostile to us, and . . . we [should] put forward, as the first specific objective of our policy and as an irreducible minimum of national security, the maintenance of political regimes in those areas at least favorable to the continued power and independence of our nation." Kennan's list of such areas included:

A. The nations and territories of the Atlantic community, which include Canada, Greenland and Iceland, Scandinavia, the British Isles, western Europe, the Iberian Peninsula, Morocco and the west coast of Africa down to the bulge, and the countries of South America from the bulge north;
B. The countries of the Mediterranean and the Middle East as far east as, and including, Iran; and
C. Japan and the Philippines.

The creation in these regions of "political attitudes favorable to our concepts of international life . . . will tax the full power and ingenuity of our diplomacy for some time to come. To create such conditions and attitudes in the world as a whole is clearly beyond our power at this time, and for many decades to come."[14]

Kennan further refined this concept the following month. In what he acknowledged was an oversimplification—"what I am trying to get at is the heart of the problem here, and I will concede to you that you can argue about the details of it"—Kennan told students at the National War College that there were "only five centers of industrial and military power in the world which are important to us from the standpoint of national security." These were the United States, Great Britain, Germany and central Europe, the Soviet Union, and Japan. Only in these locations "would [you] get the requisite conditions of climate, of industrial strength, of population and of tradition which would enable people there to develop and launch the type of amphibious power which would have to be launched if our national security were seriously affected." Only one of these power centers was in hostile hands; the primary interest of the United States in world affairs, therefore, was to see to it that no others fell under such control."[15]

This concept of five vital power centers was not intended to represent the only interests the United States had in the world. As his earlier list had indicated, Kennan recognized the need for a secure sphere of influence in the Western hemisphere, as well as access to centers of industrial power, sources of raw materials, and defensive strongpoints elsewhere in the world. What he was saying was that of the varieties of power that existed

on the international scene, industrial-military power was the most dangerous, and hence primary emphasis should be placed on keeping it under
control.

Kennan was also making the point that because capabilities were limited, priorities of interest had to be established. He elaborated on this in
an unusual public address late in 1949:

> The problems of this world are deeper, more involved, and more stubborn
> than many of us realize. The limitations on [what] this nation, or any other
> single nation, can accomplish with that margin of its energies and material
> production which it can afford to devote to outside affairs are greater than
> we are often inclined to remember. It is imperative, therefore, that we econ-
> omize with our limited resources and that we apply them where we feel that
> they will do the most good.

What was required was the identification of "certain categories of needs to
which we will be able to respond less promptly and less fully than to others." Such a procedure should not be taken as suggesting either inconsistency or the absence of policy; rather, it was simply a recognition of the
fact that "no global policy which has reality in deeds as well as in words can
fail to be primarily a policy of priorities—a policy of wise economy in the
use of our own strength."[16]

A second corollary of Kennan's argument was that the internal organization of states was not, in and of itself, a proper matter of concern for
American foreign policy. "It is a traditional principle of this Government,"
he wrote in late 1948, "to refrain from interference in the internal affairs
of other countries. . . . Whoever proposes or urges such intervention
should properly bear the burden of proof (A) that there is sufficiently powerful national interest to justify our departure . . . from a rule of international conduct which has been proven sound by centuries of experience, . . . and (B) that we have the means to conduct such intervention
successfully and can afford the cost in terms of the national effort it involves."[17] The United States could coexist with, even benefit from, diversity; what was dangerous was the combination of hostility with the ability
to do something about it.

Principles like non-intervention were of course not infallible guides to
action in all situations, but they did reflect certain internal priorities distinctive to the American system of government and could not be disregarded without in some way diminishing those priorities. "I think there is
a close connection between foreign policy and internal policy," Kennan

observed, "and a change in one cannot take place without a change in the other. I have a feeling if we ever get to the point . . . where we cease having ideals in the field of foreign policy, something very valuable will have gone out of our internal political life." In times of uncertainty the best the nation could do was "to see that the initial lines of its policy are as close as possible to the principles dictated by its traditions and its nature, and that where it is necessary to depart from these lines, people are aware that this is a departure and understand why it is necessary."[18]

A third and related corollary was that there need be no conflict between the demands of security and those of principle, provided the first were understood as necessarily preceding the second. "Our country has made the greatest effort in modern times . . . to treat questions of international life from the standpoint of principles and not of power," Kennan told students at the Naval Academy in May 1947, "but even we in the end are compelled to consider the security of our people, . . . because . . . unless they can enjoy that security they will never be able to make any useful contribution to a better and more peaceful world."[19] No set of ideals could survive anarchy, or even chronic insecurity; certain minimal standards of stability had to be established before principles could be put into effect.* This reasoning led Kennan back to the concept of the balance of power as the most appropriate way of reconciling national aspirations with the national interest.

Kennan's was, then, a conception of interests based on a pessimistic view of the international order, but on a degree of measured optimism as to the possibilities for restraining rivalries within it. This could be done, not by relying on artificial sanctions and constraints, but by making use of the equilibrium maintained by the very tensions inherent in the system. It was a view conscious of the fact that because capabilities are finite, interests must be also; distinctions had to be made between what was vital and what was not. It was also sensitive to the need to subordinate means to ends; to the danger that lack of discrimination in methods employed could corrupt objectives sought. Finally, it insisted on using this perception of interests as a standard against which to evaluate threats, not the other way around: threats had no meaning, Kennan insisted, except with reference to and in terms of one's concepts of interests.

---

* Kennan's views on this point paralleled those of Reinhold Niebuhr. See, for a sampling, Rex Harry Davis and Robert Crocker Good, eds., *Reinhold Niebuhr on Politics* (New York: 1960), especially pp. 65, 107, 182, 245, and 280–81.

II

The only nation that met Kennan's test of combining hostility with capability was, of course, the Soviet Union. Despite his reservations about the possibility of postwar cooperation, Kennan had had no quarrel with the wartime strategy of reliance on the Russians to help defeat Nazi Germany: there had been no basis for coexistence with Hitler.* "We had to use [the Soviet Union] although we should have known that it was devoted and consecrated to our destruction." But the effect of victory had been to place the Red Army in a dominant position throughout Eastern Europe and parts of East Asia, bringing it within striking distance of the devastated but still revivable industrial centers of Germany and Japan. This circumstance, together with the presence throughout much of the rest of the world of communist parties subservient to Moscow's will, seemed to place the Russians in a position to obtain what the war had been fought to prevent: control of two or more world power centers by forces hostile to the United States and its democratic allies.[20]

Moscow's antipathy for the West, Kennan argued, grew out of both historical and ideological circumstances. Russian history afforded ample evidence to sustain the impression of a hostile outside world; it also provided precedents for the concept of the state "as an ideological entity destined eventually to spread to the utmost limits of the earth." Marxism-Leninism reinforced those tendencies, as did the conspiratorial habits Soviet leaders had picked up during years in the underground and the predictably unsympathetic responses their post-1917 policies had provoked in the West. There was, thus, "a highly intimate and subtle connection between traditional Russian habits of thought and the ideology which has now become official for the Soviet regime."[21]

Kennan regarded that ideology as fulfilling several functions. It served to legitimize an illegitimate government: if one could not rule by the will of God, as had the Russian tsars, then ruling by an appropriately tailored

---

* Kennan acknowledged that "there was a great deal in Hitler's so-called new order which would have made sense if the guiding spirit behind it had not been Hitler. But we had to recognize that this was a force which was trying to seize Western Europe, although it emerged from inside Western Europe. It was a force with which we could never have lived at peace, a force which if successful could have come to dominate the eastern power center, too. To have mobilized those two forces together in this way would have been just about as dangerous to us, perhaps not quite, as though it had been the other way around and the Russians had come into possession of the West." (National War College lecture, September 17, 1948, Kennan Papers, Box 17.)

historical imperative was the next best thing. It excused the repression without which unimaginative Soviet leaders did not know how to act: as long as the rest of the world was capitalist, harsh measures could be justified to protect the leading communist state. It associated the U.S.S.R. with the aspirations and frustrations of discontented elements in other countries, thereby creating in the international communist movement an instrument with which to project influence beyond Soviet borders.[22]

But Kennan did not see the ideological writings of Marx and Lenin as a reliable guide with which to anticipate Soviet behavior. "Ideology," he wrote in January 1947, "is a product and not a determinant of social and political reality. . . . [I]ts bearing is on coloration of background, on form of expression, and on method of execution, rather than on basic aim." Furthermore, Marxism-Leninism was so amorphous an ideology that, like many others, it required intermediaries—in this case the Soviet government—to apply it to the real world. This circumstance placed Stalin in a position to say what communism was at any given moment. "The leadership is at liberty," Kennan wrote in a little-noticed portion of the "X" article, "to put forward for tactical purposes any particular thesis it finds useful . . . and to require the faithful and unquestioning acceptance of that thesis by the members of the movement as a whole. This means that truth is not a constant but is actually created, for all intents and purposes, by the Soviet leaders themselves. . . . It is nothing absolute and immutable."[23]

Ideology, then, was not so much a guide to action as a justification for action already decided upon. Stalin might not feel secure until he had come to dominate the entire world, but this would be because of his own unfathomable sense of insecurity, not any principled commitment to the goal of an international classless society. It followed, therefore, that the objective of containment should be to limit Soviet expansionism, and that communism posed a threat only to the extent that it was the instrument of that expansion.

Kennan did not expect the Soviet Union to risk war to gain its desired ends. Neither the Russian economy nor the Russian people were in any condition to stand another conflict so soon after the last. Nor could Kremlin leaders feel confident of their ability to sustain offensive military operations beyond their borders—experiences with Finland in 1939–40 and Japan in 1904–05 could hardly have been encouraging in this respect. Stalin was no Hitler; he had no fixed timetable for aggression and would prefer, if possible, to make gains by political rather than military means. Miscalculation, of course, remained a danger: "War must therefore be regarded, if not as a probability, at least as a possibility, and one serious enough to be taken account of fully in our military and political planning." But "we do not think the Russians, since the termination of the war, have had any serious intentions of resorting to arms."[24]

More serious was the possibility of conquest by psychological means: the danger that the people of Western Europe and Japan, two of the five vital centers of industrial power, might become so demoralized by the combined dislocations of war and reconstruction as to make themselves vulnerable, through sheer lack of self-confidence, to communist-led coups, or even to communist victories in free elections. Since both European and Japanese communists were, at that time, reliable instruments of the Kremlin, such developments would have meant in effect the extension of Moscow's control over Europe and much of East Asia as well. It was against this contingency that the strategy of containment was primarily aimed—not Soviet military attack, not international communism, but rather the psychological malaise in countries bordering on Moscow's sphere of influence that made them, and hence the overall balance of power, vulnerable to Soviet expansive tendencies. As Kennan reminded students at the National War College in June 1947: "it is the shadows rather than the substance of things that move the hearts, and sway the deeds, of statesmen."[25]

Ultimately, Kennan believed, these shadows, if not dispelled, would demoralize American society as well. Democracy at home might not require the existence of a completely democratic world, but neither could it survive in one that was completely totalitarian: the United States did have a vital interest in the continued independence of at least some nations resembling it. "The fact of the matter is," Kennan argued, "that there is a little bit of the totalitarian buried somewhere, way down deep, in each and every one of us." The Soviet threat lay not in the area of military potential, but rather "in the terrible truths which the Russians have discovered about the vulnerability of liberal democratic society to organizational and propaganda techniques totally cynical in concept and based on the exploitation of the evil, rather than the good, in human nature." The progressive subjugation of nations lying between the United States and the center of world communism could, if unresisted, reduce Americans "to a position of helplessness and loneliness and ignominy among the nations of mankind."[26]

But the challenge was not without its compensations, and at times Kennan even appeared to welcome it. "To avoid destruction," he noted in the

"X" article, "the United States need only measure up to its own best traditions and prove itself worthy of preservation as a great nation. Surely, there was never a fairer test of national quality than this." Two-and-a-half years later, he told students at the National War College that the real problem of Western democracy was "the crisis produced by the growing disproportion between man's moral nature and the forces subject to [his] control."

> For us in this country the problem boils down to one of obtaining a social mastery over the runaway horse of technology; of confining and bending to our will these forces . . . ; of creating here at home a stable balance between consumption and resources, between men and nature; in producing here institutions which would demonstrate that a free society can govern without tyrannizing and that man can inhabit a good portion of the earth without devastating it . . . ; and then, armed with this knowledge, . . . going forth to see what we can do in order that stability may be given to all of the non-communist world.

Communism was not the disease; it was only a complication. "We will not cure the disease by treating the complication alone." Nor, Kennan added, "should [we] get too violently indignant over the fact that such a complication exists. As one of my associates recently said: 'If it had never existed, we would have had to invent it, to create the sense of urgency we need to bring us to the point of decisive action.' "[27]

III

Because Kennan saw the Soviet challenge as largely psychological in nature, his recommendations for dealing with it tended to take on a psychological character as well: the goal was to produce in the minds of potential adversaries, as well as potential allies and the American people, attitudes that would facilitate the emergence of an international order more favorable to the interests of the United States. By the end of 1948, Kennan had come to regard three steps as necessary to accomplish this objective: (1) restoration of the balance of power through the encouragement of self-confidence in nations threatened by Soviet expansionism; (2) reduction, by exploiting tension between Moscow and the international communist movement, of the Soviet Union's ability to project influence beyond its borders; and (3) modification, over time, of the Soviet concept of international relations, with a view to bringing about a negotiated settlement of outstanding differences.[28]*

"All in all," Kennan wrote late in 1947, "our policy must be directed toward restoring a balance of power in Europe and Asia." The best means of accomplishing this "would . . . seem to be the strengthening of the natural forces of resistance within the respective countries which the communists are attacking and that has been, in essence, the basis of our policy." What had sapped resistance in areas vulnerable to Soviet expansion was not so much the threat of a new war as the persisting effects of the last: "the profound exhaustion of physical plant and of spiritual vigor." What was needed was action dramatic enough to make an immediate psychological impression, and yet substantial enough to begin to deal with the underlying problems involved. It was to economic aid that Kennan primarily looked to produce this effect.[29]

The public announcement of a long-term program of American economic assistance would in itself do much to restore self-confidence in Western Europe, Kennan believed, so long as it treated that region as a whole, and allowed recipients considerable responsibility for planning and implementation. This emphasis on European initiative had several motivations behind it. It was consistent with the principle of minimizing interference in the internal affairs of other countries. It also took into account American capabilities—given Washington's limited experience at that time with administering large foreign aid programs, it is questionable whether the United States could have done anything other than leave implementation largely up to the Europeans.[30] But, most important, it would provide a test of the extent to which "natural forces of resistance" still existed in Europe. "With the best of will, the American people cannot really help those who are not willing to help themselves. And if the requested initiative and readiness to bear public responsibility are not forthcoming from the European governments, then that will mean that *rigor mortis* has already set in on the body public of Europe as we have known it and that it may be already too late for us to change decisively the course of events."[31]†

---

* Kennan did not always list these steps in the same order, and at one point he listed as the third step "to see that the power of Europe, as Europe revives, does not again fall into the hands of people like the German Nazis, who did not know how to use it, who would do stupid things with it, and who would turn it against ourselves and who would eventually probably destroy it." (Naval War College lecture, October 11, 1948, Kennan Papers, Box 17.)

† Kennan later pointed out that European initiative did not mean abdication of overall American control: "It doesn't work if you just send the stuff over and relax. It has to be played polit-

Kennan's insistence on treating Western Europe as a unit* reflected the obvious point that together the states of that region could better withstand Soviet pressure than if they acted separately, but it was also an indirect means of integrating Germany into European society. If aid could be directed to Western Europe as a whole, Kennan reasoned, then the British, French, and American zones of occupation in Germany could be included. It was crucial to keep German industry, located primarily within these zones, out of the hands of the Russians. Full-scale occupation could not continue indefinitely, both because of its expense and because of the hostility the long-term presence of foreign troops would generate. Rearming the Germans themselves would only alarm their former victims, both to the west and the east. If the German economy could be interwoven with that of Western Europe, though, this might lead the Germans "out of their collective egocentrism and [encourage them] to see things in larger terms, to have interests elsewhere in Europe and elsewhere in the world, and to learn to think of themselves as world citizens and not just Germans." Such a policy would require eliminating the more punitive aspects of the occupation; it would also necessitate careful coordination with Germany's West European neighbors. "Yet without the Germans, no real European federation is thinkable. And without federation, the other countries of Europe can have no protection against a new attempt at foreign domination."[32]

In Japan as well, American occupation authorities had initially emphasized the punishment of former adversaries. Kennan favored instead, as in Germany, organizing centers of resistance to potential new ones. Hence, he recommended shifting the goal of Japanese occupation policy from control to rehabilitation, and delaying the signing of a peace treaty that would end the occupation until the basis for a stable, self-confident society had been established. This willingness to transform erstwhile enemies into allies reflected Kennan's concern with global equilibrium: "Any world balance of power means first and foremost a balance on the Eurasian land mass. That balance is unthinkable as long as Germany and Japan remain power vacuums." What had to be done was "to bring back the strength and the will of those peoples to a point where they could play their part in the

ically, when it gets over. It has to be dangled, sometimes withdrawn, sometimes extended. It has to be a skillful operation." (NWC lecture, December 18, 1947, Kennan Papers, Box 17.)
* Kennan's original proposal called for extending aid to Eastern Europe and the Soviet Union as well, but this was a tactic for straining the relationship between Moscow and its satellites, not a serious plan to undertake the rehabilitation of those areas. See below, p. 65.

Eurasian balance of power, and yet to a point not so far advanced as to permit them again to threaten the interests of the maritime world of the West."[33]

Kennan fully acknowledged the importance of military forces in maintaining this balance: "You have no idea," he told students at the National War College in 1946, "how much it contributes to the general politeness and pleasantness of diplomacy when you have a little quiet armed force in the background." The mere existence of such forces, he wrote two years later, "is probably the most important single instrumentality in the conduct of U.S. foreign policy." A Policy Planning Staff study done under Kennan's direction in the summer of 1948 concluded that armed strength was essential as a means of making political positions credible, as a deterrent to attack, as a source of encouragement to allies, and, as a last resort, as a means of waging war successfully should war come.[34] And Kennan himself advocated maintaining and at several points considered the possibility of using small, highly trained mobile forces, capable of acting swiftly in local situations to restore the balance of power.*

But military forces had their distinct limitations as well, especially for a democracy: "It cannot use them as an offensive threat. It cannot manipulate them tactically, on any extensive scale, for the accomplishment of measures short of war. They therefore constitute, for the most part, a fixed, rather than a mobile, factor in the conduct of foreign policy." Moreover, recent history had demonstrated that military victories brought with them as many problems as they solved:

> We may defeat an enemy, but life goes on. The demands and aspirations of people, the compulsions that worked on them before they were defeated, begin to operate again after the defeat, unless you can do something to remove them. No victory can really be complete unless you eradicate the people against you were fighting or change basically the whole compulsions under which they live. For that reason I am suspicious of military force as a means of countering the political offensive which we face with the Russians today.

---

* Kennan is on record as having at least considered the possibility of U.S. military intervention in Greece in 1947, in Italy in 1948, and on Taiwan (for the purpose of ejecting the Chinese Nationalists) in 1949. (See *FRUS: 1947*, V, 468–69; *FRUS: 1948*, III, 848–49; and *FRUS: 1949*, IX, 356–59.) None of these instances reflected positions consistently advocated, however, and their importance has at times been exaggerated. (See, for example, C. Ben Wright, "Mr. 'X' and Containment," *Slavic Review*, XXXV [March 1976], 29; Eduard Mark, "The Question of Containment: A Reply to John Lewis Gaddis," *Foreign Affairs*, LVI [January 1978], 435.) It should also be noted that Kennan, like most Washington officials, supported the use of United States troops in 1950 to defend South Korea.

"Remember," Kennan told a National War College audience in October 1947, in a point he would emphasize repeatedly during the next several years, "that . . . as things stand today, it is not Russian military power which is threatening us, it is Russian political power. . . . If it is not entirely a military threat, I doubt that it can be effectively met entirely by military means."[35]

Implicit in this warning about excessive reliance on the military was the assumption that weapons and troop levels were not the only determinants of power on the international scene—politics, psychology, and economics also played a role. And it was in this last area that the United States possessed a particular advantage: through loans and outright grants of aid it alone was in a position to affect the rate at which other countries reconstructed or modernized their economies. It should not be surprising, then, that Kennan seized on this instrument as the primary (but not the only) means of restoring the world balance of power; significantly, his plans for aid to Europe envisaged no formal military commitment to the defense of that region.[36] Rather, his idea was one reminiscent of an earlier period when the European balance of power had been threatened—the "arsenal of democracy" concept of 1939–41, with its assumption that the most effective contribution the United States could make toward stabilization of the international order lay in the area of technology, not military manpower.[37]

This program of attempting to strengthen "natural forces of resistance" was not to be applied indiscriminately. By the end of 1947, Kennan had worked out three specific criteria to govern the dispensing of American aid: (1) "Whether there are any local forces of resistance worth strengthening." Where strong traditions of representative government existed, there was no problem, but where the choice was between a communist regime and some other variety of totalitarianism no less repressive, "we have to be careful not to lend moral prestige to unworthy elements by extending American aid." (2) "The importance of the challenged areas to our own security." What would a communist takeover of the country in question mean for the safety of the United States? Could that country's resources be combined with those of the Soviet Union to produce significant military power? (3) "The probable costs of our action and their relation to the results to be achieved." There had to be a kind of "business accounting procedure in political terms" to see whether the expenses likely to be incurred outweighed the expected benefits. "Our opposition to communist expansion is not an absolute factor," Kennan stressed. "It . . . must be taken in relation to American security and American objectives. We are not necessarily always against the expansion of communism, and certainly not always against it to the same degree in every area. It all depends on the circumstances."[38]*

As vital but vulnerable industrial centers, Western Europe and Japan, of course, had first priority: the idea, Kennan wrote in 1949, was "that we can continue to make it . . . overly risky for Russians to attack as long as they have only their own power base." But the defense of these areas also required safeguarding selected non-industrial regions around them. Hence, Kennan strongly supported the Truman administration's request for aid to Greece and Turkey early in 1947; he was also an early advocate of what came to be known as the "defensive perimeter" concept in East Asia—the idea that U.S. interests in the Western Pacific could best be secured through the defense of such island strongholds as Okinawa and the Philippines, while avoiding mainland commitments. But Kennan objected vigorously to the notion that the United States had to resist communism wherever it appeared. Such an approach would cause "everybody in the world [to start] coming to you with his palm out and saying, 'We have some communists—now come across.' . . . That obviously won't work." China specifically was an area the United States should avoid: "If I thought for a moment that the precedent of Greece and Turkey obliged us to try to do the same thing in China, I would throw up my hands and say we had better have a whole new approach to the affairs of the world."[39]

The ultimate goal was not a division of the world into Soviet and American spheres of influence, but rather the emergence over the long term of independent centers of power in Europe and Asia. "Our objective," Kennan told students at the National War College, "is . . . to make it possible for all the European countries to lead again an independent national existence without fear of being crushed by their neighbor to the east." The emphasis in Japanese occupation policy, he stressed, "should lie in the achievement of maximum stability of Japanese society, in order that Japan

---

* Kennan put forward a similar but less elaborate set of criteria in discussing aid to Greece before a National War College audience on March 28, 1947: "(A) The problem at hand is one within our economic, technical, and financial capabilities; (B) If we did not take such action, the resulting situation might redound very decidedly to the advantage of our political adversaries; (C) If, on the other hand, we do take the action in question, there is good reason to hope that the favorable consequences will carry far beyond the limits of Greece itself." (Quoted in *Memoirs: 1925–1950*, p. 320.)

may best be able to stand on her own feet when the protecting hand is withdrawn." These arguments had in common the assumption that Russians and Americans could not indefinitely confront one another across World War II truce lines; at some point a mutual withdrawal from these artificial positions would have to occur. To replace them, Kennan hoped for a world order based not on superpower hegemony, but on the natural balance only diverse concentrations of authority, operating independently of one another, could provide.[40]

The second stage in Kennan's strategy, once the balance of power had been restored, was to seek to reduce the Soviet Union's ability in the future to project influence beyond its borders. That influence had been extended in two ways: (1) through the installation, primarily in Eastern Europe, of communist governments subservient to Moscow; and (2) through the use, elsewhere in the world, of communist parties which at that time were still reliable instruments of Soviet foreign policy. The United States should try to counter these initiatives, Kennan argued, by encouraging and where possible exploiting tension between the Kremlin leadership and the international communist movement.[41]

This strategy would work, he thought, because of the Russians' chronic inability to tolerate diversity. As a Policy Planning Staff study done in the summer of 1948 noted: "[T]he history of the Communist International is replete with . . . instances of the difficulty non-Russian individuals and groups have encountered in trying to be the followers of Moscow doctrines. The Kremlin leaders are so inconsiderate, so relentless, so overbearing and so cynical in the discipline they impose on their followers that few can stand their authority for very long." It was this tendency of the Kremlin "to leave in its train a steady backwash of disillusioned former followers" that created opportunities for the United States and its allies.[42]

The temptations of disaffection would intensify, the Policy Planning Staff suggested, as communist parties outside the Soviet Union assumed the responsibilities of government: "the actions of people in power are often controlled far more by the circumstances in which they are obliged to exercise that power than by the ideas and principles which animated them when they were in opposition." As long as they were only revolutionaries seeking power, communists outside the Soviet Union had little choice but to look to Moscow for leadership and support, whatever the frustrations involved. "But now that they have the appearance and considerable of the substance of power, subtle new forces come into play. Power, even the taste of it, is as likely to corrupt communist as bourgeois leaders. Considerations of national as well as personal interest materialize and come into conflict with the colonial policy pursued by the Soviet interests."[43]*

The most obvious place for this to happen, of course, was Eastern Europe, the only area outside the U.S.S.R. (and Mongolia) where communists actually controlled governments, even if by virtue of Soviet military power. The problem of maintaining authority there, Kennan thought, would become an increasingly difficult one for Moscow: "It is unlikely that approximately one hundred million Russians will succeed in holding down permanently, in addition to their own minorities, some ninety millions of Europeans with a higher cultural level and with long experience in resistance to foreign rule." Kennan predicted accurately late in 1947 that the Russians would not long tolerate the existence of an independent Czechoslovakia. When the Yugoslav schism appeared in the summer of 1948, he welcomed it as confirming his analysis, and as a precedent for what might happen elsewhere.[44]

"I can't say to you today whether Titoism is going to spread in Europe," Kennan told an audience at the Naval War College in October 1948, "[but] I am almost certain that it is going to spread in Asia." Kennan had been predicting for the past year and a half that the Soviet Union would not be able to control communism in China, should it come to power: "The men in the Kremlin," he had observed in February 1947, "would suddenly discover that this fluid and subtle oriental movement which they thought they held in the palm of their hand had quietly oozed away between their fingers and that there was nothing left there but a ceremonious Chinese bow and a polite and inscrutable Chinese giggle." Kennan even suggested at one point that a communist-dominated China might pose more of a threat to the security of the Soviet Union and to Moscow's control over the international communist movement than it would to the United States, since such a China would lack for many years an industrial base capable of producing the instruments of amphibious and air warfare.[45]

Kennan also expected splits to develop between the Kremlin and local communists in Western Europe and the Mediterranean countries. "Here

---

* Kennan had noted in a paper produced in May 1945 that "He who holds that national salvation can come only through bondage to a greater nation may be, in some cases, a far seeing man. It is not easy for him to be a popular figure." ("Russia's International Position at the Close of the War with Germany," May 1945, printed in Kennan, *Memoirs: 1925–1950*, p. 536.)

we have the weakest and most vulnerable points in the Kremlin armor," he noted in May 1947. "These Communist Parties do not yet have behind them the bayonets of the Soviet secret police power. . . . Their fate may still be influenced by the electorates of those countries or by the governments there in power, or by the actions of other free governments such as our own." If conditions that made the communist appeal popular in the European democracies could be successfully dealt with by other means, then these parties would never come to power. And even if they did, this would be no calamity for the United States so long as the government in question remained independent of Soviet police or military power:

> A communist regime in power in some such country which either failed to meet its responsibilities and discredited itself in the eyes of the people or which turned on its masters, repudiated the Kremlin's authority, and bit the hand which had reared it, might be more favorable to the interests of this country and of world peace in the long run than an unscrupulous opposition party spewing slander from the safe vantage point of irresponsibility and undermining the prestige of this country in the eyes of the world.[46]

The United States had the power to accelerate fissiparous tendencies within the international communist movement, Kennan thought, but only by indirect methods. Blanket condemnations of communism everywhere would not work because they focused attention only on the symptoms, not the disease itself. Nor could much be expected from issuing ultimatums to Moscow, since the Russians did not control all communists and might not be able to call them off, in certain parts of the world, even if they wanted to. Direct military intervention to prevent communist takeovers would only propel the United States into a series of civil wars from which it would be difficult to extricate itself. And if the intervention was directed against a communist government that had come into power through democratic processes—a very real possibility in Western Europe in 1947 and 1948, Kennan believed—this "would constitute a precedent which, in my opinion, might have a demoralizing influence on our whole foreign policy and corrupt that basic decency of purpose which, despite all our blunders and our shortsightedness, still makes us a great figure among the nations of the world."[47]

One thing the United States could do, though, was to make the economic rehabilitation of Western Europe succeed. This would have the advantage, not only of restoring the balance of power, but of removing or at least mitigating the conditions that had made indigenous communism popular there in the first place. Moreover, the example would severely strain Moscow's control over Eastern Europe, since the Soviet Union was so much less equipped than the United States to emulate it. "It has been our conviction," Kennan commented late in 1948, "that if economic recovery could be brought about and public confidence restored in western Europe—if western Europe, in other words, could be made the home of a vigorous, prosperous and forward-looking civilization—the communist regime in eastern Europe . . . would never be able to stand the comparison, and the spectacle of a happier and more successful life just across the fence . . . would be bound in the end to have a disintegrating and eroding effect on the communist world."[48]

The retention of American military forces in key areas could also be used to promote tension between European communists and the Kremlin. Kennan believed that Moscow had given its followers permission to try to seize power in their respective countries, but only if the result was not to bring an American military presence closer to that of the Red Army. Should the price of a communist victory in Italy or Greece be an increase in American air or naval strength in the Mediterranean, then the Russians would not be prepared to pay it. American forces could best be employed, therefore, not by trying to oppose indigenous communists within their own countries, something Kennan considered a "risky and profitless undertaking, apt to do more harm than good," but by showing that "the continuation of communist activities has a tendency to attract U.S. armed power to the vicinity of the affected areas, and that if these areas are ones from which the Kremlin would definitely wish U.S. power excluded," then Moscow would have to "exert a restraining influence on local communist forces." The effect would be to produce a conflict "between the interests of the Third Internationale, on the one hand, and those of the sheer military security of the Soviet Union, on the other. In conflicts of this sort, the interests of narrow Soviet nationalism usually win."[49]

The United States could also work to encourage Titoism within the communist bloc. It was important to do this discreetly, though, because one of the few things Kennan thought the Russians might risk war for would be to maintain their sphere of influence in Eastern Europe. "They are not so dumb," he commented in September 1948; "they realize what is going to happen to them once that process sets in." Hence, the United States should not openly call for the overthrow of Soviet-controlled governments in that part of the world. As a 1949 Policy Planning Staff study put it: "Proposed operations directed at the satellites must . . . be measured against the kind and degree of retaliation which they are likely to provoke from the Kremlin. They must not exceed in provocative effect what is calculated suitable in the given situation." The United States should not, of course, forget that its ultimate aim in Eastern Europe was the establishment of governments free from all forms of totalitarianism. But since such regimes were a distant prospect at best, given the absence of democratic traditions in the region, "strong tactical considerations . . . argue against setting up this goal as an immediate objective." Rather, the objective should be "to foster a heretical drifting-away process on the part of the satellite states" without assuming responsibility for it. And for the moment that meant being willing to tolerate, and even cooperate with, East European communist governments independent of the Soviet Union for the purpose of containing the Soviet Union.[50]

Interestingly, Kennan saw no comparable possibilities of working with a Chinese Communist government, should one come to power: "We have . . . no reason to believe that the Chinese communist leaders would be inclined to pay serious heed to the views of the United States people, whose motives and aspirations they have been maliciously maligning and distorting for years." The best policy for the United States in China would be one of "hands-off" rather than "the kind of meddling in which we have indulged to date." Fortunately, though, the Russians could expect as much or more difficulty in trying to establish their own authority in Beijing, even if Washington did nothing. "Events have borne out [the] view," Kennan wrote early in 1950, "that the projection of Moscow's political power over further parts of Asia would encounter impediments, resident in the nature of the area, which would be not only not of our making but would actually be apt to be weakened by any attempts on our part to intervene directly." As a result, the overall situation in Asia, "while serious, is neither unexpected nor necessarily catastrophic."[51]*

---

* Kennan's reservations about dealing with the Chinese communists did not imply sympathy for Chiang Kai-shek. In July 1949 he suggested (but immediately withdrew) a proposal to use American forces to eject the Chinese Nationalists from Formosa, which he preferred to leave under Japanese (and hence American) control for the time being. (Policy Planning Staff 53, "United States Policy Toward Formosa and the Pescadores," July 6, 1949, *FRUS: 1949*, IX, 356–60.) He elaborated on his views in a September 1951 memorandum: "As for China, I have no use for either of the two regimes, one of which has intrigued in this country in a manner scarcely less disgraceful to it than to ourselves, while the other has committed itself to a program of hostility to us as savage and arrogant as anything we have ever faced. The tie to the Chiang regime I hold to be both fateful and discreditable, and feel it should be severed at once, at the cost, if need be, of a real domestic political showdown. After that, the less we Americans have to do with China the better. We need neither covet the favor, nor fear the enmity, of any Chinese regime. China is not the great power of the Orient; and we Americans

"[I]t has often been alleged," Kennan told a Pentagon audience in November 1948, "that our policy, usually referred to . . . as the policy of 'containment', was a purely negative policy, which precluded any forward action. . . . That is entirely untrue." For reasons of discretion the United States could not openly acknowledge that it was seeking to fragment the international communist movement. "[W]e have no need to make a gratuitous contribution to the Soviet propaganda effort by assuming responsibility for a process of disintegration which communism had brought upon itself and for which it had no one but itself to blame."[52] But such public acknowledgment was hardly necessary, because in this case little positive action was needed to gain the objective. The breakup of international communism was an irreversible trend, certain to proceed regardless of what the United States did. Washington need only align its policies with it.

Kennan based this conclusion on what one might call an "imperial analogue"—the idea that international communism, whatever its surface manifestations, in fact differed little from and was subject to many of the same self-destructive tendencies of classical imperialism. He liked to quote Edward Gibbon's proposition that "there is nothing more contrary to nature than the attempt to hold in obedience distant provinces." The very process of trying to maintain an empire would, sooner or later, generate resistance sufficient to undermine it. "[T]here is a possibility," Kennan commented in September 1949, "that Russian Communism may some day be destroyed by its own children in the form of the rebellious Communist parties of other countries. I can think of no development in which there would be greater logic and justice." Failing that, there might at least develop opposing blocs within the communist world. "A situation of this description," a Policy Planning Staff study noted, "might eventually provide us with an opportunity to operate on the basis of a balance in the communist world and to foster the tendencies toward accommodation with the West implicit in such a state of affairs." Nationalism, then, would prove the most durable of ideologies; it would be through the encouragement of nationalism, whether in areas threatened by communism or within the communist bloc itself, that the objectives of containment would largely be achieved.[53]

But because Kennan believed Moscow's hostility toward the West to be rooted in forces deep within Russian society, he did not expect "tenden-

have certain subjective weaknesses that make us ill-equipped to deal with the Chinese." ("Summary by George F. Kennan on points of difference between his views and those of the Department of State," September 1951, Kennan Papers, Box 24.)

cies toward accommodation" to emerge until a fundamental change had taken place in the Soviet concept of international relations. The third step in his strategy was to bring about such a change: to effect a shift in the thinking of Kremlin leaders away from their own version of universalism—the conviction that security required restructuring the outside world along Soviet lines—to particularism—to toleration and even the encouragement of diversity.[54]

One conceivable way to achieve this objective, of course, would be to go to war, but Kennan repeatedly warned against such measures as inconsistent with the desired end. A war with the Soviet Union would not resemble World War II, he pointed out; the United States and its allies could hardly expect to conquer and occupy the entire territory of the U.S.S.R., or to impose unconditional surrender on its government. And even if that were possible, no one could guarantee that whatever successor regimes might arise would be any less difficult to deal with. Atomic bombs and other weapons of mass destruction were useful only for destroying an adversary, not for changing his attitudes. Finally, such an all-out war could well imperil the very society it was supposed to defend:

> It would be useful, in my opinion, if we were to recognize that the real purposes of the democratic society cannot be achieved by large-scale violence and destruction; that even in the most favorable circumstances war between great powers spells a dismal deterioration of world conditions from the standpoint of the liberal-democratic tradition; and that the only positive function it can fulfill for us—a function, the necessity and legitimacy of which I do not dispute—is to assure that we survive physically as an independent nation when our existence and independence might otherwise be jeopardized and that the catastrophe which we and our friends suffer, if cataclysm is unavoidable, is at least less than that suffered by our enemies.*

---

* Much has been made of the transcript of a lecture Kennan gave at the Air War College on April 10, 1947 (Kennan Papers, Box 17), which reports him as having said in answer to a question that the United States might be justified in considering a preventive war against the Soviet Union. (See, for example, Wright, "Mr. 'X' and Containment," p. 19.) But the full context of Kennan's transcribed remarks makes it clear that he discussed preventive war only as a last resort, to be considered if Soviet war-making potential was exceeding that of the United States and if opportunities for peaceful solutions had been exhausted, situations which, he believed, did not exist at that time. And by January 1949 Kennan was appearing to rule out preventive war altogether: "[A] democratic society cannot plan a preventive war. Democracy leaves no room for conspiracy in the great matters of state. But even if it were possible for democracy to lay its course deliberately toward war, I would question whether that would be the right answer. . . . [W]e are condemned, I think, to define our objectives here in terms of what can be accomplished by measures short of war. And, while this is a matter of personal philosophy rather than of objective observation, I for one am deeply thankful that Providence has placed

Not surprisingly, then, Kennan concluded: "I would rather wait thirty years for a defeat of the Kremlin brought about by the tortuous and exasperatingly slow devices of diplomacy than to see us submit to the test of arms a difference so little susceptible to any clear and happy settlement by those means."[55]

At the opposite end of the scale was the possibility of changing the Soviet concept of international relations through negotiations. Mere exposure to the American point of view was not likely to have much effect, Kennan warned: "[T]hey are [not] going to turn around and say: 'By George, I never thought of that before. We will go right back and change our policies.' . . . They aren't that kind of people." But if self-confidence in Western Europe could be restored, and the vacuum left by Germany's collapse filled, then the Russians might indeed be willing to "talk turkey," at least regarding a lowering of tensions in Europe; certainly the United States should be prepared for that eventuality. That day would come "when they have arrived at the conclusion that they cannot have what they want without talking to us. It has been our endeavor to assist them to that conclusion."[56]

But the most effective means of modifying Soviet behavior lay in a combination of deterrents and inducements that Kennan called "counter-pressure." "The shape of Soviet power," he explained in February 1947, "is like that of a tree which has been bent in infancy and twisted into a certain pattern. It can be caused to grow back into another form; but not by any sudden or violent application of force. This effect can be produced only by the exertion of steady pressure over a period of years in the right direction." Later that year, Kennan shifted to the analogy to chess to clarify how "counter-pressure" was to be achieved: "It is through the way in which you marshall all the forces at your disposal on the world chess-board. I mean not only the military forces you have, although that is very important, but all the political forces. You just have to dispose of your pawns, your queens and kings in such a way that the Russian sees it is going to be in his interests to do what you want him to do, and then he will go ahead and do it."* NSC 20/1, the comprehensive overview of the U.S. policy toward the Soviet Union that Kennan supervised in the summer of 1948, used more

that particular limitation on us." (Lecture to Foreign Service Institute, January 19, 1949, Kennan Papers, Box 17.)

* Kennan used the term "counterforce" instead of "counter-pressure" in the "X" article, but failed to clarify its meaning—a fact which, he admits, has given rise to much confusion. (Kennan, *Memoirs: 1925–1950*, pp. 359–60.)

general terminology to express the same idea: "[T]he Soviet leaders are prepared to recognize situations, if not arguments. If, therefore, situations can be created in which it is clearly not to the advantage of their power to emphasize the elements of conflict in their relations with the outside world, then their actions, and even the tenor of their propaganda to their own people, can be modified."[57]

Americans could hasten this process, Kennan thought, simply by being themselves: "The United States . . . must demonstrate by its own self-confidence and patience, but particularly by the integrity and dignity of its example, that the true glory of Russian national effort can find its expression only in peaceful and friendly association with other peoples and not in attempts to subjugate and dominate those peoples." This emphasis on the force of example reflected Kennan's identification with the architects of late eighteenth- and early nineteenth-century American foreign policy, who thought in similar terms; it was also a manifestation of his belief in the importance of "good form" in both private and public affairs:

> [I]f we wish our relations with Russia to be normal and serene, the best thing we can do is to see that on our side, at least, they are given the outward aspect of normalcy and serenity. Form means a great deal in international life. . . . What is important, in other words, is not so much what is done as how it is done. And in this sense, good form in outward demeanor becomes more than a means to an end, more than a subsidiary attribute: it becomes a value in itself, with its own validity and its own effectiveness, and perhaps— human nature being what it is—the greatest value of all.

Soviet-American relations therefore boiled down, Kennan told students at the Naval Academy in May 1947, "to a sort of long-range fencing match in which the weapons are not only the development of military power but the loyalties and convictions of hundreds of millions of people and the control or influence over their forms of political organization. . . . It may be the strength and health of our respective systems which is decisive and which will determine the issue. This may be done—and probably will be done— without a war."[58]

IV

Kennan gave relatively little thought to the problems of explaining containment to Congress, the bureaucracy, or the general public, all of whose support would be necessary to implement it. This was partly because as a planner of policy he did not consider it his responsibility to devote much time to justifying it, partly also because he never succeeded in reconciling in his own mind the need for precision and flexibility in diplomacy with a constitutional framework that seemed at best inhospitable to those qualities:

> The pursuit of power by diplomatic means—like the pursuit of power by military means—calls for discipline, security, and the ability to move your forces swiftly and surely, taking full advantage of the concealment of your own thoughts and the element of your surprise. . . . [C]an you conduct a modern foreign policy where one great part of your action can be determined on a day-to-day basis . . . by persons subject to professional discipline in matters of security and other matters, whereas another great part of your action has to be determined in bodies which meet only periodically and take their decisions under the peculiar pressures of public debate and compromise?[59]

The complaint embraced problems of both bureaucracy and democracy. With regard to the first, Kennan saw professionalism and discipline as the solution: "The understanding of governmental policies in the field of foreign affairs cannot be readily acquired by people who are new to that field," he noted in 1948, "even when they are animated by the best will in the world. . . . It is a matter of educating and training, for which years are required." And once policy had been established, the bureaucracy had a responsibility to carry it out faithfully. "I think we must not fear the principle of indoctrination within the government service," he wrote two years later. "The Secretary of State is charged personally by the President with the conduct of foreign affairs, and there is no reason why he should not insist that his views and interpretations be those of the entire official establishment."[60]

But the task of combining professionalism with discipline was not an easy one. The very act of transforming expertise into policy guidelines distorted that expertise, Kennan believed. It was misleading to assume it possible "to describe in a few pages a program designed to achieve U.S. objectives with respect to the U.S.S.R." Documents of this nature produced oversimplification and rigidity when what was needed were sophisticated assessments of changing situations, together with the flexibility to act on the basis of them. And even if usable guidelines could be devised, there was no guarantee that the bureaucracy would follow them:

> [T]he operating units—the geographical and functional units—will not take interference from any unit outside the line of command. They insist on an effective voice in policy determination; if one of them cannot make its voice

alone valid, it insists on the right to water down any recommendation going to the Secretary to a point where it may be meaningless but at least not counter to its own view. If an unwelcome recommendation does find the Secretary's approval, they will perhaps give it perfunctory recognition, but they will pursue basically their own policies anyway, secure in the knowledge that no one can really survey their entire volume of work, that the issues which agitate the present will soon be outdated, and that the people who are trying to force their hand will soon be gone.

The simple fact was that "no policy and no concept . . . will . . . stick in our government unless it can be drummed into the minds of a very large number of persons, including quite a few whose mental development has not advanced very far beyond the age which is said to be the criterion for the production of movies in Hollywood."[61]

The problem of how to win support for policy without distorting it also came up in dealings with Congress and the general public. The government had an obligation to lead, Kennan acknowledged: "I think we would be very poor representatives of our country indeed if we were to sit back passively, knowing all we know, and to say: 'Our own views don't come into the question, and we do just do what the people tell us to do.'" But leadership too often took the form of exaggerated rhetoric, not education. The prime example was President Truman's March 1947 speech to Congress on aid to Greece and Turkey—an employment of universalist rhetoric for particularist purposes that deeply offended Kennan's sense of the proper relationship between ends and means. He also despaired of the administration's willingness to modify carefully formulated policies in order to placate Congressional critics: "my specialty," he noted angrily in January 1948, "was the defense of US interests against others, not against our own representatives."[62]

It was not Kennan's allegiance to democracy that was in question here; on the contrary, he relied heavily, as has been seen, on the force of the democratic example to attract the uncommitted, reassure the allied, and discomfit the hostile. Nor was it logical, if as he asserted the aim of strategy was to protect the nation's domestic institutions, to abandon those institutions in the interest of furthering that strategy. What Kennan did question was the extent to which the requirements of democracy, like those of bureaucracy, required generalizing about the particular:

There are very few general observations which can be made about the conduct of states which have any absolute validity at all times and in all cases. The few that might have such validity are almost invariably to be found in the realm of platitude. If this absolute validity is lacking, the chances are that the utterance in question will some day rise to haunt us in a context where it is no longer fully applicable. If, on the other hand, the utterance remains in the realm of platitude, then there is all the more reason why we should not associate ourselves with it.

"It is simply not given to human beings to know the totality of truth," he concluded. "Similarly, no one can see in its totality anything so fundamental and so unlimited in all its implications as the development of our people in their relation to their world environment." And yet without some confidence that strategies chosen for surviving in that environment would work, there would be little support for them. This was the central dilemma for which Kennan never developed a satisfactory answer. It would account for many of the difficulties he encountered in seeking to implement his strategy of containment.[63]

Implementing Containment

Attempts to establish relationships between individuals, ideas, and events are hazardous in the best of circumstances—all the more so when the individual involved expresses himself eloquently but elliptically, when he resists any systematic exposition of his ideas, and when there is a vigorous debate over how those ideas affected the events associated with them. These problems all exist in attempting to evaluate Kennan's influence on the foreign and military policies of the Truman administration. Kennan himself has underestimated his role: with a degree of modesty unusual in writers of memoirs, he has insisted that the views he put forward during the late 1940's "made only a faint and wholly inadequate impression on official Washington."[1]* Others have overestimated his influence but have misunderstood his views, relying too heavily on the conspicuous but misleading "X" article.[2] Still others have pointed out that Kennan was only one of several key advisers on international affairs during the Truman administration, and that it is easy to be beguiled by the gracefulness of his prose into an exaggerated impression of its actual influence.[3]

To insist that Kennan's thinking either shaped or reflected that of the administration would be to oversimplify, for in fact it did both. Kennan himself acknowledges having played a decisive role in certain areas: the

* "I met with [Truman] once or twice during this period. . . . I suspect he was vaguely aware that there was a young fellow over in the State Department who had written a good piece on the Russians—I doubt whether Truman ever really read anything I wrote, though. Certainly I don't think he grasped my position." (Interview with George F. Kennan, Washington, D.C., October 31, 1974.)

emphasis placed on European initiative and German rehabilitation in the Marshall Plan, the offer to extend aid under that plan to the Soviet Union and its East European satellites, the reorientation of Japanese occupation policy.[4] One might add to this list as well Kennan's explanation of the roots of Soviet behavior, his skepticism regarding Moscow's willingness to risk war, and his anticipation of polycentrism within the international communist movement. But Kennan's overall strategic concept, as presented in the previous chapter, did not emerge fully formed in 1947; it was as much a rationalization for (and, at times, a critique of) what the administration did during the next three years as it was an impetus to those actions.* What can be said with certainty is that Kennan did more than anyone else in the administration to articulate containment as a strategy—that is, as a process by which available means could be made to serve desired ends. Nor should this be surprising, since it was Kennan's function as director of the Policy Planning Staff to do just that.

Kennan's thinking and that of the administration he served paralleled each other from 1947 until well into 1949.[5] Differences existed, to be sure, and these grew more pronounced as time passed. But Kennan's was hardly a voice crying in the wilderness, as his *Memoirs* sometimes imply. Rather, a comparison of his recommendations with the administration's actions during this period suggests that his ideas can be taken as a guide, not only to the intellectual origins of containment, but to much of its early implementation as well.

I

The first stage of Kennan's strategy, it will be recalled, had been to restore the balance of power left unstable by the defeats of Germany and Japan, and by the simultaneous expansion of Soviet influence in Europe and Asia.

* Charles P. Kindleberger, chief of the State Department's Division of German and Austrian Economic Affairs, described something of this process in a July 1948 memorandum, although his account does less than full justice to the extent of Kennan's contribution: "As I reconstruct the plot, [James] Reston would have lunch with [Under-Secretary of State Dean] Acheson. Mr. Acheson, as many of his warmest admirers are prepared to concede, converses with a broad brush. Reston would get him started on European recovery, and Mr. Acheson would allude to plans under consideration. The following day invariably Reston would have a first-page story in the *New York Times* referring to big planning going on in the State Department. This would give Mr. Kennan, who had just been appointed to the newly created planning staff in February [*sic*], the jim-jams. If there was public talk of all this planning in the Department, and the planning staff had received so much publicity, maybe this was where the effort should be applied." (Kindleberger memorandum, "Origins of the Marshall Plan," July 22, 1948, *FRUS: 1947*, III, 242.)

Kennan had based that prescription on a particularist rather than a universalist conception of American security interests: what was required was not to remake the world in the image of the United States, but rather to preserve its diversity against attempts to remake it in the image of others. He had also stressed the necessity, imposed by limited means, of establishing hierarchies of interests, of differentiating between the vital and the peripheral. And he had insisted that if competition was to take place, it do so on terrain and with instruments best calculated to apply American strengths against Soviet weaknesses, thereby preserving the initiative while minimizing costs. The ultimate objective was to build an international order made up of independent centers of power, in which nations subject to Soviet pressure would have both the means and the will to resist it themselves.

Abandoning universalism was not without its difficulties. The official position of the United States government since the middle of World War II had been that postwar security could be achieved only through a fundamental restructuring of the international system, involving the disarmament of past and potential adversaries, maximum application of the principle of self-determination, the lowering of barriers to trade and investment, and, most important, the creation of a new collective security organization to keep the peace. It was to be, as Wendell Willkie had said, "one world"; not surprisingly its institutions were to resemble closely those of the United States. The energies Washington officials put into implementing this program testify to the existence of uneasy consciences over the aloof, some said irresponsible, role the United States had played during the years preceding the war, and to the intimations of omnipotence many Americans felt as that conflict neared its end. That this Wilsonian vision was never unanimously held within the government—Franklin D. Roosevelt himself had been a notable, if discreet, skeptic—did not lessen the difficulties of departing from it once it had been publicly articulated.[6] Throughout the Truman administration a residue of universalist thinking remained at the level of long-term aspirations—not least in the mind of the Chief Executive himself.*

By 1947, though, even dedicated advocates of universalism had been forced to admit that their goals could not be implemented in the foreseeable

---

*Truman for years carried in his wallet a copy of the portion of Tennyson's poem "Locksley Hall" that predicted a "Parliament of Man, the Federation of the world." "We're going to have that someday," he insisted, "I guess that's what I've really been working for ever since I first put that poetry in my pocket." (John Hersey, "Mr. President," New Yorker, XXVII [April 7, 1951], 49–50.)

future—primarily because the Soviet Union seemed to have its own universalist security requirements, incompatible with those of the United States. The Joint Chiefs of Staff put the matter bluntly in April of that year: "faith in the ability of the United Nations as presently constituted to protect, now or hereafter, the security of the United States would mean only that the faithful have lost sight of the vital security interest of the United States and could quite possibly lead to results fatal to that strategy." Or, as Kennan's friend and fellow Soviet expert Charles E. Bohlen observed: "There are, in short, two worlds instead of one." However reluctantly arrived at, this conclusion made the administration receptive to Kennan's call for a strategy of balancing power within the existing international order rather than persisting in what were sure to be futile efforts to achieve "one world." "[T]he objective of our policy from this point on," Secretary of State Marshall announced after reading a Kennan memorandum on the subject to the President and his cabinet in November 1947, "would be the restoration of [a] balance of power in both Europe and Asia and . . . all actions would be viewed in the light of this objective."[7]

There soon developed a line of reasoning reminiscent of Sir Halford Mackinder's geopolitics, with its assumption that none of the world's "rimlands" could be secure if the European "heartland" was under the domination of a single hostile power.[8] One of the first papers drafted by the staff of the new National Security Council warned, in March 1948, that "between the United States and the U.S.S.R. there are in Europe and Asia areas of great potential power which if added to the existing strength of the Soviet world would enable the latter to become so superior in manpower, resources and territory that the prospect for the survival of the United States as a free nation would be slight." Eight months later, following that body's first comprehensive review of policy toward the U.S.S.R., the President approved NSC 20/4, which concluded that "Soviet domination of the potential power of Eurasia, whether achieved by armed aggression or by political and subversive means, would be strategically and politically unacceptable to the United States."[9]

But there were at least two ways to defend the "rimlands," and hence preserve global equilibrium. One way, which might be called the "perimeter defense" concept, assumed all "rimlands" to be of equal importance, and called for resistance to aggression wherever along the periphery of the "heartland" it occurred. This approach had been implied in the "patience and firmness" strategy and in the Truman Doctrine; it appeared even more explicitly in Kennan's "X" article, which spoke of the need "to confront the Russians with unalterable counter-force at every point where they show signs of encroaching upon the interests of a peaceful and stable world."[10] By the time that article was published in July 1947, though, Kennan had begun to move toward the alternative of "strongpoint defense"— concentration on the defense of particular regions and means of access to them, rather than on the defense of fixed lines. The Policy Planning Staff's criticisms of the Truman Doctrine reflected this viewpoint; so too did Kennan's emphasis on the rehabilitation of Western Europe and Japan, and, ultimately, his concept of the five vital centers of industrial and war-making capacity, along with the need to keep the four not then under Soviet control from becoming so.

Kennan's evolving commitment to "strongpoint" rather than "perimeter" defense at once responded to and refined official thinking. In one sense, his pronouncements were nothing more than articulations of and rationalizations for moves the administration was already making in that direction, and would have continued to make even if Kennan had not been present. But articulation and rationalization can, in themselves, stimulate further action: they provide otherwise myopic bureaucracies with a sense of perspective, visible goals, and, most important, standards against which to detect contradictions and anomalies. It is in this latter sense that Kennan's ideas reinforced and at times redirected existing trends; for this reason it is important to understand the attractions his advocacy of "strongpoint" defense had for the Truman administration as the most appropriate method of reconstituting the balance of power.

One such attraction was consistency with the prevailing perception of means available. A striking characteristic of both administration and Congressional attitudes during the early Cold War years was the conviction that, no matter how dangerous the external peril, the country had only limited resources with which to fight it. Unrestrained military spending, it was feared, would set off either unacceptable inflation through persistent peacetime budget deficits, or confiscatory taxes and economic controls. Reinforcing this concern was the belief that the Russians had set out deliberately to drive the United States into bankruptcy by forcing it to disperse resources in an ever-widening circle of commitments. Given this situation, the defense of points rather than lines seemed best calculated to achieve needed economies. The objective, Secretary of State Marshall noted, should be to avoid "dispersal of our forces when concentration appears to be the wisest cause, especially in view of our present limitations."[11]

It is true that in his March 1947 speech to Congress on aid to Greece and Turkey the President had suggested something approaching an obligation to aid victims of aggression everywhere. But administration spokesmen had gone out of their way in subsequent Congressional hearings to emphasize that the Truman Doctrine established no precedents for specific action elsewhere. Future requests for aid would be evaluated individually on the basis of need, American self-interest, and the likelihood that assistance, if extended, would be effective.[12] "Our resources are not unlimited," Truman was pointing out by September of that year. "We must apply them where they can serve the most effectively to bring production, freedom, and confidence back to the world." Under-Secretary of State Robert Lovett put the matter even more forcefully in the summer of 1948:

> [T]he line must be drawn somewhere or the United States would find itself in the position of underwriting the security of the whole world. . . . [W]e must be careful not to over-extend ourselves. We lack sufficient financial and economic resources simultaneously to finance the economic recovery of Europe, to furnish arms and equipment to all individual countries or groups of countries which request them, and to build up our own military strength.[13]

Kennan found little resistance, then, to his insistence on the need to distinguish vital from peripheral interests: for a nation confronting expanding commitments with what appeared to be fixed, or even dwindling, resources, such an approach seemed prudent, even inevitable.

A second advantage of the strongpoint defense concept was that it allowed the United States to choose the most favorable terrain upon which to confront the Soviet Union. A "perimeter" defense would have required readiness to act along its entire extent, whether local conditions favored resistance or not. The "strongpoint" concept permitted concentration on areas that were both defensible and vital, without worrying too much about the rest. The assumption was that not all interests were of equal importance; that the United States could tolerate the loss of peripheral areas provided this did not impair its ability to defend those that were vital.

Kennan's principal criterion for differentiating vital from peripheral interests was, of course, the presence of industrial-military capacity, together with necessary sources of raw materials and secure lines of communication. The Truman administration never explicitly endorsed this approach, but its actions between 1947 and 1949 suggest that it viewed the world in much the same way. The major foreign policy initiative during this period, the European Recovery Program, was aimed at rebuilding war-shattered industrial economies as bulwarks against Soviet expansion.

Similar considerations transformed the mission of occupation authorities in Germany and Japan from that of repression to rehabilitation. War plans from the period attached high priority to the defense of Western Europe, the Mediterranean, the Middle East and Japan, both as centers of industrial (and in the case of the Middle East raw material) power to be kept out of the hands of the Russians, and (except for Japan) as base areas from which to launch counter-offensives once the initial attack had been repelled.[14]

The administration also shared Kennan's view of those areas whose loss to Soviet control, however regrettable, would not immediately endanger American security. These comprised primarily the mainland of Asia, from Afghanistan around to Korea.* The area lacked war-making capabilities that could be of use to the Soviet Union anytime soon; moreover, the task of defending it, given the distances and logistical problems involved, would be immense. Nor would the Russians find it easy to retain control there should they get it, both because of the same problems of distance and logistics, and because of the rising tide of nationalism among the people of those regions.[15] The idea of maintaining a "defensive perimeter" in the western Pacific—which gained wide currency in Washington in 1948 and 1949[16]—was in fact misleading: what that strategy implied was not the defense of a perimeter at all, but rather the safeguarding of selected island strongpoints—Japan, Okinawa, the Philippines—while avoiding potentially debilitating commitments on the mainland.

It is in this sense that the administration can be said to have shared Kennan's assumption that threats, to be serious, had to combine hostility with capability. Hostility in and of itself posed no danger. Only where it coupled with, or significantly reinforced, industrial war-making potential was there legitimate cause for concern. The coming to power of communist regimes on the non-industrialized Asian mainland might not be a pleasant prospect, but neither was it one grave enough to require preventive action, considering the costs involved. Rather, the United States had to be selective in its choice of terrain upon which to resist, with a view both to the importance of the interests at stake there, and to the ease (and economy) with which they could be defended, given the instruments at hand.

A third advantage of strongpoint over perimeter defense was that it allowed the United States to choose these instruments. One of the most

---

* Other regions, notably Latin America and Africa, were obviously considered important to U.S. security, but were under no immediate threat of attack.

persistent ideas in American thinking about international affairs in the twentieth century had been that of using economic and technological resources, but not manpower, to maintain the balance of power overseas. The idea appeared as early as the turn of the century in the Open Door policy; it certainly existed in the minds of Woodrow Wilson and his advisers between 1914 and 1917; it was also behind the "arsenal of democracy" concept in the early 1940's. And although the principle failed to keep the United States out of World Wars I and II, it did affect the way in which the nation fought those wars, with dollars and hardware expended more generously than manpower.[17] Fundamental to this approach was the notion of *asymmetrical* response—of applying one's own strengths against adversary weaknesses, rather than attempting to match the adversary in all of his capabilities. And, of course, economic and technological prowess was throughout this period the particular strength of the United States, never more so than at the end of World War II. Kennan's emphasis on achieving containment primarily through the economic rehabilitation of Western Europe and Japan was, therefore, very much in the mainstream of official thinking at the time.

It was in line with this tradition that the Truman administration made the decision in 1947 to concentrate on economic recovery overseas, even if this meant deferring military preparedness. The objectives, Secretary of Defense Forrestal explained in December, were "economic stability, political stability and military stability . . . in about that order."

> At the present time we are keeping our military expenditures below the levels which our military leaders must in good conscience estimate as the minimum which would in themselves ensure national security. By so doing we are able to increase our expenditures to assist in European recovery. In other words, we are taking a calculated risk in order to follow a course which offers a prospect of eventually achieving national security and also long-term world stability.

"We are moving toward our goal of world peace in many ways," Truman told the Congress early in 1948. "But the most important efforts which we are now making are those which support world economic reconstruction."[18]

This "calculated risk" of assigning priority to the economic instruments of containment was based on several assumptions. One was the belief, strongly held by Kennan, that the Soviet Union had no immediate intention of starting a war. Intelligence reports between 1947 and 1949 generally confirmed that assessment, both because the Russians lacked the means of countering the American atomic bomb, and because they appeared to be capable of getting what they wanted in Europe—subservience to Moscow—without resort to military force. These estimates did acknowledge the ever-present possibility of miscalculation, and warned that if present tactics should stop paying off, the Kremlin might be more willing to risk war. But, as Forrestal put it, "as long as we can outproduce the world, can control the sea and can strike inland with the atomic bomb, we can assume certain risks otherwise unacceptable. . . . The years before any possible power can achieve the capability effectively to attack us with weapons of mass destruction are our years of opportunity."[19]

Another assumption was that economic aid would produce greater benefits per dollar expended than would a military buildup. "Which is better for the country," Truman asked, "to spend twenty or thirty billion dollars [over the next four years] to keep the peace or to do as we did in 1920 and then have to spend 100 billion dollars for four years to fight a war?"[20] Moreover there were definite limits to what military forces could accomplish in peacetime. These became particularly evident in the spring of 1948 when suggestions surfaced in the State Department regarding the possibility of sending American ground troops into Italy and Greece. The Joint Chiefs of Staff effectively discouraged whatever inclinations existed to dispatch such forces by insisting that "no military involvement should be made unless preceded by mobilization"—a requirement not likely to be met short of war.[21] It is significant that even after the decision had been made to form a military alliance with the nations of Western Europe and to grant military assistance to them (decisions about which Kennan had reservations, as will be seen), the priorities of economic rehabilitation remained. "Recovery is the first objective," Secretary of State Dean Acheson told the Senate Foreign Relations Committee in April 1949, "and therefore the new military production, the military efforts we are talking about here, are all limited and controlled by the prior necessity for recovery in Europe."[22]

This is not to say that the administration excluded from its calculations, any more than Kennan did, the use of non-economic instruments of containment. Washington officials relied heavily on the atomic bomb as the ultimate deterrent to aggression, although they differed over how it would be used if war came with the Soviet Union, or whether it would be effective.[23] Naval forces were employed from 1946 on to maintain an American "presence" in the Mediterranean with a view to discouraging Soviet aspirations in that part of the world. The administration's unsuccessful campaign for Universal Military Training was intended largely as a show of "resolve" to impress Moscow.[24] Covert action was also an instrument of containment; indeed Kennan specifically endorsed it as such, provided strict controls were maintained. Propaganda and psychological warfare techniques attracted increasing attention and funding as time went on.[25] Still, the Truman administration's primary emphasis between 1947 and 1949 was much as Kennan said it should be—on the economic instrument as the cheapest and most effective way to achieve containment.

Finally, there was the assumption that American interests—and global equilibrium generally—would best be served by the emergence of independent and self-confident centers of power overseas rather than spheres of influence subservient to Washington, and that economic rehabilitation would most effectively contribute to that objective. The idea in Europe, as one State Department official put it, had been to create "a third force . . . strong enough to say 'no' both to the Soviet Union and the United States, if our actions should seem so to require."[26] To be sure, this toleration of diversity was never sufficiently broad to accommodate communist governments in Western Europe or Japan, but the assumption was that such governments, whether they came to power by legal or illegal means, could only be instruments of the Kremlin and hence not truly independent.[27]* Within these limits, Washington did not insist on ideological compatibility as a prerequisite for aid. "We should give support to political parties that offer Europeans a positive program suited to Europe's political needs and development," Assistant Secretary of State Willard Thorp argued, "rather than looking for parties and individuals who seem to represent most exactly the political and economic ideology that has been successful in America." A State Department analysis of Japanese occupation policy concluded that "the U.S. can neither impose nor enforce a pro-western orien-

---

* "I remember when it was accepted doctrine to say in the United States, 'We don't care if another country wants to be communist, that is all right, that is an internal matter, that is a matter for them to decide,'" Dean Acheson told students at the National War College in December 1947. "It was only as we had more and more experience with communism that we learned it was not a doctrine which people picked up and looked over and either adopted or rejected. . . . As that came home to us we began to see it wasn't true that it was no concern of ours whether the Greeks, the Italians or some other people were communists or not, because those people were not having a choice about it. They were being coerced either by an internal organization financed by other countries, or by external pressure to adopt a system of government which had the inescapable consequence of inclusion in the system of the Russian power." (Acheson National War College lecture, "Formulation of Foreign Policy in the United States," December 16, 1947, copy in Naval War College Archives, RG 15.)

tation on any foreign people, including the Japanese." The effort should be, rather, toward "the development within that country of indigenous resistance to Communism and of spontaneous orientation toward the west, while at the same time making sure that our essential military requirements with respect to Japan are provided for."[28]

The objective of strongpoint defense, then, was not so much control as denial: the American interest was not to dominate other power centers, but to see to it that no one else did either. This was a goal consistent with the principle of non-intervention in the internal affairs of other nations, and with the fact that the United States had only limited capabilities to bring to bear in their defense. It did not mean insistence on particular forms of government; only that governments not be changed arbitrarily in such a way as to upset the world balance of power. And it was in this context that the operative language of the Truman Doctrine, at first glance so inconsistent with the principle of strongpoint defense, came to be viewed. As one of the committees charged with drafting Truman's speech had put it:

> The present power relationships of the great states preclude the domination of the world by any one of them. Those power relationships cannot be substantially altered by the unilateral action of any one great state without profoundly disturbing the whole structure of the United Nations. Though the *status quo* is not sacred and unchangeable, we cannot overlook a unilateral gnawing away at the *status quo*.[29]

Rephrased positively, and somewhat more expansively, this became: "It must be the policy of the United States to support free peoples who are resisting attempted subjugation by armed minorities or by outside pressures." The actual policies the Truman administration followed during the next three years suggest that, as was the case with Kennan's "X" article, rhetoric overleaped intent by a considerable degree.

In general, the Truman administration can be said to have implemented the first stage of Kennan's strategy with remarkable fidelity. Universalism was abandoned; perimeter defense was, for the moment, deferred; economic and technological means were employed selectively and asymmetrically to establish at least a degree of self-confidence, if not self-sufficiency, in those centers of industrial-military power not controlled by the Russians. This was no insignificant achievement, for an additional point upon which Kennan and the administration agreed was that the balance of power was ultimately a psychological phenomenon: that relatively small expenditures of effort, if applied in the right places and in the right manner, would suffice to overcome the exhaustion and disillusionment that had swept the West in the wake of the war, and to throw Moscow, for a change, on the defensive. One need only compare the configuration of power in Europe and Northeast Asia at the end of the Cold War with that established four decades earlier to realize the impressive success this particular strategy of containment attained.

II

The second stage in Kennan's strategy had been to try to bring about fragmentation within the international communist movement. At first glance this recommendation, based as it was on the assumption that communism was not, or need not be, a monolith, would appear to have met with an unfavorable response on the part of the Truman administration. The general impression is that Washington officials saw all communism as a threat, not just the Soviet variety; that when the President referred in his speech on Greece and Turkey to the existence of "two ways of life," he had in mind the distinction between that ideology and its capitalist rival.[30] Again, though, closer examination reveals more complex patterns.

The only specific mention of communism in the Truman Doctrine speech had to do with the leadership of the Greek insurgents: it is clear from the context that the "two ways of life" referred to were totalitarianism and democracy, not communism and capitalism. It was "totalitarian regimes imposed upon free peoples" that undermined "the foundations of international peace and hence the security of the United States"—the same issue posed by Germany and Japan during World War II. "There isn't any difference in totalitarian states," Truman liked to argue. "I don't care what you call them—you call them Nazi, Communist or Fascist, or Franco, or anything else—they are all alike." The assumption was that arbitrary rule itself, whether of the Right or the Left, contributed to instability in the world. As Truman put it in the summer of 1947, "the stronger the voice of a people in the formulation of national policies, the less the danger of aggression."[31]*

---

*A letter Truman wrote to his daughter the day after delivering his speech on Greece and Turkey is revealing, both of his view of totalitarianism and of his domestic critics: "The attempt of Lenin, Trotsky, Stalin, et al., to fool the world and the American Crackpots Association, represented by Jos. Davies, Henry Wallace, Claude Pepper and the actors and artists in immoral Greenwich Village, is just like Hitler's and Mussolini's so-called socialist states. Your pop had to tell the world just that in polite language." (Truman to Margaret Truman, March 13, 1947, quoted in Margaret Truman, *Harry S. Truman* [New York: 1973], p. 343. See also pp. 359–60.)

The administration did not see itself at that point, therefore, as setting out on an anti-communist crusade. "That is not what the President is talking about," Acheson told the Senate Foreign Relations Committee later in March. "He is talking about the fact that where a free people is being coerced to give up its free institutions, we are interested." Special efforts were made that spring to keep references to "communism" out of the public speeches of administration officials and to encourage instead use of the term "totalitarianism." As a member of the White House staff noted, "this leaves the Soviet no opening for complaint for if they charge that the reference is to them then the reply could be that they admit they are totalitarian." It was important, another adviser observed, to convince the world "that we have something positive and attractive to offer, and not just anti-communism."[32]

This point of view made the administration receptive to Kennan's suggestion that Marshall Plan aid be offered to the Soviet Union and its Eastern European satellites as well as to the non-communist states of Europe. The objective here was to do one of two things: to place responsibility for the division of Europe squarely on the Russians if, as expected, they rejected the offer; or, alternatively, in the unlikely event that they accepted it, to use aid as a means of forcing the East Europeans to "abandon near-exclusive Soviet orientation of their economies."[33] There was in this latter alternative the implied possibility of aiding some communist regimes in order to contain others—a stratagem more fully developed the following year in response to events in Yugoslavia. Neither the White House nor the State Department explicitly sanctioned Kennan's idea of attempting by this device to strain the relationship between Moscow and its satellites, but it was clear, however the Russians responded to the aid offer, that this would be the effect.

Kennan had also recommended tying the level of American military activity in the Eastern Mediterranean to levels of communist activity in Italy and Greece, again with a view to promoting antagonism between the Soviet Union and its ideological followers in those countries. It is clear that the Truman administration had at least the first part of this approach in mind late in 1947 and early in 1948: National Security Council studies from that period did call for increasing American forces there in response to escalations in communist activity, up to and including the possibility of intervention with ground troops if necessary.[34] But there is no specific evidence that these plans, which never had to be implemented, had as their objective the encouragement of tension within the international communist movement; rather the prevailing assumption seems to have been that the Greek and Italian communists would remain loyal to Moscow whatever happened, and would have to be dealt with accordingly.*

That view had to be modified, though, following the surprising events of June 1948. Tito's Yugoslavia had hitherto been regarded as one of Moscow's most reliable (and reprehensible) satellites. "I am told that Tito murdered more than four hundred thousand of the opposition in Yugoslavia before he got himself firmly established there as a dictator," Truman commented in April of that year. And yet, once Belgrade's break with Moscow was confirmed, the administration quickly endorsed the Policy Planning Staff's recommendation that the United States not let the internal character of Tito's regime stand in the way of a normal diplomatic and economic relationship.[35] It was in the "obvious interest" of the United States, Acheson observed early in 1949, "that 'Titoism' continue [to] exist as [an] erosive and disintegrating force in [the] Sov[iet] sphere." A major debate erupted between the State and Defense Departments later that year over the export of a steel blooming mill to Yugoslavia, but the decision in the end was that the need to bolster Tito's government against a possible Soviet attack outweighed whatever security risks were involved. And by the end of the year Truman had made it clear publicly that the United States would regard such an attack as an act of aggression, thereby implying something more than a passive response.[36]

Moreover, the administration agreed with Kennan that Titoism should not be regarded as an isolated phenomenon, but rather as a precedent to be encouraged elsewhere. "The United States must take advantage of the present situation," a Moscow embassy intelligence report argued in April 1949, "not only to 'contain' the Soviet sphere but to reduce it, seizing and maintaining the initiative in all fields." One tempting target was, of course, the rest of Eastern Europe, where Tito's heresy had had a distinctly unsettling effect. Despite indications that the Russians were tightening their control there, the administration devoted much time and thought during 1949 to ways of encouraging further dissidence in the satellites, ranging from Voice of America broadcasts and human rights campaigns in the United Nations to economic pressures and covert action. And in December 1949, Truman approved NSC 58/2, based on an earlier Policy Plan-

---

* The State Department did use the Soviet Union's rejection of aid to Eastern Europe to try to persuade Italian voters that aid to their country would not continue under a communist government. See Marshall's speech at Berkeley, California, March 19, 1948, *Department of State Bulletin* (hereafter DSB), XVIII (March 28, 1948), 424.

ning Staff study, which called for efforts "to bring about the elimination of Soviet power from the satellite states" even if this meant cooperation, for the moment, with "schismatic communist regimes."[37]

Still more promising opportunities for encouraging Titoism appeared to exist in China, where by 1949 Mao Zedong's Communists had virtually routed Chiang Kai-shek and the Nationalists. The possibility that Mao might follow in Tito's footsteps was widely discussed in the State Department and especially at the American Embassy in Moscow, which in October recommended recognizing the new Chinese Communist government as a means of facilitating that process.[38] This line of reasoning coincided with the long-standing belief of the Department's China specialists that Mao's movement had evolved independently of the Russians, that Moscow did not control it, and might, for that reason, have reservations about its coming to power.[39] Acheson found these arguments convincing—so much so that in order to avoid doing anything that might drive the Chinese communists to align themselves permanently with the Russians he favored allowing the continuation of trade in non-strategic items with the mainland and opposed aiding Chiang's regime on Taiwan, despite the fact that such aid would have been consistent with the strategy of defending island strongholds.[40]

A group of consultants appointed by Acheson to review East Asian policy approved that approach in November 1949 and advised preparing for eventual recognition of the Chinese Communist government. The Secretary of State presented these conclusions to the President on November 17, and in his memorandum of the discussion provided a succinct overview of the emerging strategy:

> Broadly speaking, there were two objectives of policy: One might be to oppose the Communists' regime, harass it, needle it, and if an opportunity appeared to attempt to overthrow it. Another objective of policy would be to attempt to detach it from subservience to Moscow and over a period of time encourage those vigorous influences which might modify it. I pointed out that this second alternative did not mean a policy of appeasement any more than it had in the case of Tito. . . . I said the Consultants were unanimous in their judgment that the second course was the preferable one.
>
> The President thought that in the broad sense in which I was speaking that this was the correct analysis.

On December 30, 1949, after extensive discussions in the National Security Council, Truman approved NSC 48/2, which concluded that "The United States should exploit, through appropriate political, psychological and economic means, any rifts between the Chinese Communists and the U.S.S.R. and between Stalinists and other elements in China, while scrupulously avoiding the appearance of intervention. Where appropriate, covert as well as overt means should be utilized to achieve these objectives."[41]*

There were anomalies and inconsistencies in all of this, to be sure. As both Acheson's memorandum and NSC 48/2 suggest, administration officials were not always clear on whether the Chinese Communists themselves would repudiate Moscow's leadership, or whether the Chinese people would overthrow them once their ties to the Russians had become obvious. Acheson was not optimistic about prospects for Titoism elsewhere in Asia, particularly Indochina.[42] Kennan, although convinced that Sino-Soviet hostility existed, had little sympathy with Acheson's strategy of giving up Taiwan as a means of encouraging it—his preference would have been to deny the island to *both* the Nationalists and the Communists.[43] The public rhetoric of administration spokesmen became more vociferous in its denunciations of "communism," not just the Soviet Union, during 1949, and there was increasing emphasis as well on the importance of ideology as a means of predicting the behavior of communist states.[44]

But the President's approval of NSC 48/2 and NSC 58/2 within three weeks of each other in December 1949 was no anomaly: it reflected a carefully thought-out strategy of using Titoism to roll back Soviet influence in the communist world. It was based on the proposition, as former ambassador to the Soviet Union Walter Bedell Smith had put it in March of that year, "that the United States does not fear communism if it is not controlled by Moscow and not committed to aggression." It proceeded with an expectation set out in a widely circulated dispatch from the embassy in Belgrade the following month:

> [T]hat wherever a set of circumstances involving a Communist Party which has largely by its own efforts achieved victory and consolidated its power, a leadership more or less continuous and isolated in some degree from direct Soviet experience, a mass membership new, uneducated, and bound to the leadership by ties of emotion and nationalism, and an attempt by Moscow to

* In response to a letter from Maury Maverick recommending recognition of the Chinese Communists, Truman wrote on November 22, 1949: "Your letter of the nineteenth is the most sensible letter I've seen on the China situation. . . . There are so many crackpots who know all about what to do and who really know nothing about what to do, it is a pleasure to hear from somebody who has a little common sense in the matter." (Truman Papers, PSF, Box 173, Subject File: Foreign Affairs: China, 1949.)

alter policies which are fundamentally organizational—wherever such a set of circumstances, or some combination of them, is to be found, there at least a presumption of the possibility of Titoism may exist.

Truman's policy assumed, as the American chiefs of mission in Eastern Europe had put it in October, that "Any and all movements within world communism which tend to weaken and disrupt the Kremlin's control within the communist world represent forces which are operating in the interests of the West and therefore should be encouraged and assisted."[45]

One should not conclude from this that the administration was prepared to welcome the coming to power of communist governments where they did not already exist, or that it had abandoned its hostility toward totalitarianism in general. But the President's decisions of December 1949 did constitute acceptance of Kennan's "imperial analogue"—the idea, as the Belgrade embassy had put it, that the Russians were "ill-fitted to the management of empire," and that the United States could take advantage of that weakness to reduce Moscow's power and influence in the world.[46] Viewed in this context, the strategy can be seen as a logical complement to the administration's (and Kennan's) other strategy of seeking to build self-confident centers of power along the periphery of the Soviet sphere: the goal, in both cases, was to align United States interests with the forces of nationalism as instruments with which to contain Soviet imperialism.

III

The third stage of Kennan's strategy had been to try to bring about changes, over time, in the Soviet concept of international relations: to convince Russian leaders that their interests could better be served by learning to live with a diverse world than by trying to remake it in their image. Kennan had rejected both war and appeasement as a means of accomplishing this. It could only be done, he thought, through a long-term process of what might be called "behavior modification"—responding positively to whatever conciliatory initiatives emanated from the Kremlin, while firmly countering those that were not. And indeed NSC 20/4, approved by President Truman in November 1948, did proclaim it as the U.S. policy: "To create situations which will compel the Soviet Government to recognize the practical undesirability of acting on the basis of its present concepts and the necessity of behaving in accordance with precepts of international conduct, as set forth in the purposes and principles of the UN Charter."[47]

But here the correspondence between Kennan's views and those of the Truman administration ended. Kennan took the position that modifying Soviet behavior required *both* positive and negative reinforcement: it was as important to reward the Kremlin for conciliatory gestures as it was to resist aggressive ones. This meant being prepared to engage in such negotiations as seemed likely to produce mutually acceptable results. The administration conveyed the appearance of being willing to discuss outstanding issues with Moscow,[48] but Kennan regarded several of its major actions between 1948 and 1950—the formation of the North Atlantic Treaty Organization, the creation of an independent West German state, the insistence on retaining American forces in post-occupation Japan, and the decision to build the hydrogen bomb—as certain to reinforce Soviet feelings of suspicion and insecurity, and, hence, to narrow opportunities for negotiations. Kennan's position, in each of these cases, had support elsewhere in the government, but it was not strong enough to prevent the decisions made on these issues from going against his recommendations.

The initiative for the North Atlantic Treaty came from the West Europeans themselves, and reflected the uneasiness they felt over the disparity in military power on the European continent: the Red Army had, at that time, thirty divisions in Eastern and Central Europe alone; combined U.S., British, and French forces came to less than ten divisions. Intelligence estimates credited the Russians with the ability to sweep to the English Channel and the Pyrenees in a matter of weeks if war came.[49] Concern over this situation led Great Britain, France, and the Benelux countries to form their own military alliance, the Western Union, in March 1948 and to seek to associate the United States with it. The State Department was sympathetic: by June it had secured the Senate's authorization to engage in such discussions, and by September the Western Union countries, together with the United States and Canada, had agreed on the outlines of a treaty providing that an attack on any one of them or on any other nations that might be included within its terms would be regarded as an attack upon all.[50]

Because of a trip to Japan and a subsequent period of hospitalization, Kennan had not been involved in the initial discussions regarding European security early in 1948, but upon his return he quickly made clear his reservations about the course the administration had chosen to follow. These boiled down to three points: (1) That the Europeans had mistaken what was essentially a political threat for a military one, and that they risked, as a result, "a general preoccupation with military affairs, to the detriment of economic recovery." (2) That outside the immediate North Atlantic area, "which embraces a real community of defense interest firmly rooted in geography and tradition," any alliance extended only to some countries would render the rest all the more vulnerable, while an alliance including all friendly countries would render itself meaningless. "[T]here is no logical stopping point in the development of a system of anti-Russian alliances," Kennan warned, "until that system has circled the globe and has embraced all the non-communist countries of Europe, Asia and Africa." (3) That an alliance made up of nations receiving Marshall Plan aid would amount "to a final militarization of the present dividing-line through Europe," and that "no alternation, or obliteration, of that line could take place without having an accentuated military significance." Such a development might be unavoidable, "but our present policy is still directed . . . toward the eventual peaceful withdrawal of both the United States and the U.S.S.R. from the heart of Europe, and accordingly toward the encouragement of the growth of a third force which can absorb and take over the territory between the two."[51]

These were not isolated concerns. There was worry in Washington that emphasis on rearmament would delay recovery; indeed one of the conditions attached to the administration's military assistance program for Western Europe was that economic revival would continue to have first priority.[52] The question of how to include some countries without appearing to write off others also caused a great deal of agonizing: in the end the administration stretched the concept of "North Atlantic" to encompass Italy, but refused to extend it to Greece, Turkey, or Iran, or to form a comparable pact with the non-communist countries of the Western Pacific.[53]* There was less concern about Kennan's third point—that an alliance might freeze the existing division of Europe—because most observers already regarded that division as an accomplished fact. It should be noted, though, that in its original configuration NATO was consistent with the idea of building up Europe as a "third force"—it concentrated on strengthening European, not American, defenses; it did not provide, at that time, for the permanent stationing of U.S. ground troops in Europe.[54]

Despite its reservations, the administration went on to conclude a North Atlantic Treaty and initiate a program of military assistance to its members. Kennan came to see, regretfully, that there were few alternatives. "The basic cause of insecurity in the minds of the western

* Greece and Turkey finally joined NATO in 1952.

Europeans," he concluded, "is . . . really a lack of confidence in them-selves. . . . They are scared, tired people today and they don't really want to face the realities." The United States had demanded on the part of its European allies a willingness to run risks:

> By asking the Europeans to go in for economic recovery before achieving military security, we were in effect asking them to walk a sort of tightrope and telling them that if they concentrated on their own steps and did not keep looking down into the chasm of their own military helplessness we thought there was a good chance that they would arrive safely on the other side. And on this basis we made our economic aid available.
>
> Now the first of the snags we have struck has been the fact that a lot of people have not been able to refrain from looking down.

The effect was to cause too many Europeans and Americans to "spend their time worrying and trembling about a Soviet military attack on the West which probably no one in Moscow has thus far had any serious in-tention of launching." It was all "understandable and at the same time it is really a mistake." The question, though, was what to do about it:

> Is it better that we do alone what we think is right or that we do in company with others what we think is wrong and against, perhaps, all our own in-stincts and desires? We have faced that question more than once and we have come to the conclusion that come what may, we simply must hold with the French and the British, better to hold with them even though they are wrong rather than step apart with them if we are right, because if we let dis-unity creep in we may have lost the whole battle anyway.

"It is very simple to deal with an enemy," Kennan concluded; "simpler than dealing with a friend."[55]

The same gap between the desirable and the practicable existed with regard to Germany. Frustrated by the Soviet Union's refusal to accept re-unification on terms acceptable to the West, representatives of Great Britain, France, and the United States agreed at London in the spring of 1948 to allow the formation of a German government in their zones, while at the same time maintaining occupation controls. This "London Confer-ence" program, it was publicly insisted, would "in no way preclude and on the contrary should facilitate eventual 4-power agreement on the German problem." But reunification, in Washington's set of priorities, had long since taken second place to the need to integrate non-communist Ger-many into the economy of Western Europe. "This Gov[ernmen]t is deter-mined," Marshall had noted in February, "not to permit reestablishment of German economic and political unity under conditions which are likely

to bring about effective domination of all Germany by [the] Soviets."
There was little doubt, then, as to the actual effect the "London Conference" agreements were likely to have on prospects for reunification: as an
internal State Department memorandum put it later that summer, "Germany will probably remain divided."[56]

Kennan had at one point favored partitioning Germany,[57] but by 1948
he had begun to doubt the desirability of that approach. One problem, he
thought, was that the Germans themselves would never accept it. As a result, it would be impossible to find responsible leaders to whom to turn
over a government, and that in turn would mean the continuation of occupation controls, which were also alienating the German people. The economy of an independent West German state would not be self-sufficient; in
the absence of European federation, at best a distant prospect, the alternatives would be economic collapse or continued aid from the United
States. Finally, and most important, the creation of a West German state,
like the formation of NATO, would tend to freeze existing lines of division
in Europe, thereby preventing the withdrawal of Soviet and American
forces from the center of the continent and precluding as well attempts to
erode Moscow's control in Eastern Europe. "If we carry on along present
lines," Kennan wrote in August 1948, "Germany must divide into eastern
and western governments and western Europe must move toward a tight
military alliance with this country which can only complicate the eventual
integration of the satellites into a European community. From such a
trend of developments, it would be hard—harder than it is now—to find
'the road back' to a united and free Europe."[58]

With these considerations in mind, the Policy Planning Staff in November 1948 proposed "Program A"—a new approach to a four-power settlement in Germany calling for internationally supervised elections throughout the country, the establishment of a provisional German government,
the abolition of zonal boundaries, and the simultaneous withdrawal of occupation forces to specified garrison areas (which, in the case of the British,
Russians, and Americans, would be seaports, to avoid the need for overland
supply lines). Germany would continue to be disarmed and demilitarized,
but the economy would be encouraged to revive, and trade with both Eastern and Western Europe would be allowed. Kennan acknowledged that the
Russians were unlikely to accept "Program A" at once. But it would give the
United States the initiative in future negotiations; it would, like the Marshall Plan, place the onus for rejection on Moscow; and it might, he
thought, provide the basis for an eventual settlement should the Russians

ever decide to accept one. Insistence on the London Conference program would achieve none of these objectives.[59]

"Program A" produced a decidedly tepid response within the government. Robert D. Murphy, the United States Political Adviser for Germany, thought it a "worthwhile document" but, in a profusion of metaphor, commented that "the trouble with our good blue prints often seems to be that they get bloody noses bumping into Russian, French, and at times, British stone walls." Murphy later turned one of Kennan's own arguments against the proposal, suggesting that the creation of an independent West German state would in itself "exert an inevitable magnetic force on Eastern Germany and make even more difficult Soviet control of that area." Foy Kohler, the American *chargé* in Moscow, warned that Soviet acceptance of "Program A" would induce complacency in the West, eroding the public's willingness to be taxed in support of military preparedness. The Joint Chiefs of Staff argued that the advantages of a Soviet troop withdrawal would be illusory, since preparations for war could be conducted inside Poland or the U.S.S.R., where they would be less easily detected than in East Germany.* And, as the crowning blow, someone leaked the substance of "Program A" to the *New York Times* shortly before the Council of Foreign Ministers met in May 1949 to discuss the German question, forcing the State Department to deny that it had ever been seriously considered in the first place.[60]

Acheson himself may have had doubts about the London Conference program—he told Murphy in March 1949 that "he did not understand . . . how we ever arrived at the decision to see established a Western German government." One of his closest advisers, Philip C. Jessup, strongly endorsed Kennan's "Program A." But in the end the Secretary of State concluded that the London Conference approach would run fewer risks, both in terms of relations with the British and the French, who worried about a revival of German power, and in terms of preventing Soviet domination of the entire country. "We are concerned with the integration of Germany into a free and democratic Europe," he wrote in May. "We have made and are making progress to this end with the part of Germany which we con-

---

* "[We] were not envisaging that Russian troops would remain in Poland after ours had been withdrawn from the interior of Germany. Their stated purpose there was to assure the supply lines for their forces in the interior of Germany. Once these forces had been withdrawn, we would have expected the garrisons in Poland to be withdrawn; and there was nothing to prevent us from asking for this as part of the Soviet *quid pro quo*." (Kennan to the author, September 4, 1980.)

trol and we shall not jeopardize this progress by seeking a unified Germany as in itself good." The withdrawal of Soviet troops from Eastern Germany might be a desirable goal, but "the withdrawal of American and British troops from Germany would be too high a price." Kennan drew the appropriate conclusions: "the trend of our thinking . . . means . . . that we do not really want to see Germany reunified at this time, and that there are *no* conditions on which we would really find such a solution satisfactory."[61]

A similar pattern of events developed with respect to Japan. Despite resistance from the Pentagon and General Douglas MacArthur's headquarters, the administration had accepted Kennan's recommendation in 1948 that no peace treaty be signed until the goal of occupation policy had been shifted from punishment to reconstruction. As in the case of Germany his concern had been that continued emphasis on the repression of former adversaries would only create power vacuums into which the Soviet Union could move, by either internal subversion or external pressure.[62] By late 1949, though, a variety of considerations—the continued costs of the occupation, evidence of its increasing unpopularity with the Japanese, pressures from allies, concern that the Russians might themselves propose a treaty—had led Acheson to conclude that preparations for such a settlement should be initiated. And in May 1950, in a move designed as much to restore bipartisan cooperation on foreign policy as to secure expert advice, the President named John Foster Dulles, the leading Republican spokesman on international affairs, to take charge of those preparations.[63]

Planning proceeded on the assumption, with which Kennan had no quarrel, that under no circumstances was the Soviet Union to be allowed to gain control of Japan. As Acheson put it, in language that could well have been Kennan's, "were Japan added to the Communist bloc, the Soviets would acquire skilled manpower and industrial potential capable of significantly altering the balance of world power."[64] But, as had been the case with Germany, there were two ways to deny once hostile concentrations of industrial power to the Russians: one could negotiate their demilitarization and neutralization, or one could act unilaterally to bind them to the United States and its allies. Not surprisingly, given the positions he had taken on NATO and the creation of a West German state, Kennan leaned toward the first alternative—even to the point of suggesting in August 1950 that the United States agree to the demilitarization and neutralization of Japan in return for a Russian-arranged cease-fire and withdrawal of invading forces in Korea. Kennan did not push his views on Japan's future strongly, though, and there is no evidence that Acheson consulted him in any significant way on approaches to the Japanese peace treaty.[65]*

The option of demilitarization and neutralization did gain a hearing, nonetheless, through the exertions of an unlikely advocate—General MacArthur. Kennan and MacArthur shared several assumptions that led them to similar conclusions on Japan: both feared the tendency of prolonged military occupations to alienate the people occupied; both regarded bases on Japan proper as unnecessary so long as the United States retained military facilities on Okinawa and in the Philippines; both doubted the Russians' willingness to risk war and thought they could be relied upon to keep commitments that were in their own best interest. The United States and the Soviet Union, MacArthur pointed out, had virtually identical strategic objectives in Japan: "The United States does not wish Japan to enter the Soviet orbit or to become an armed ally of the Soviet Union; the Soviet Union, on the other had, does not wish Japan to be used by the United States as a base of operations against Russia." It would therefore be to the mutual advantage of both countries "to have a disarmed Japan, neutralized by common consent and guarantee of all the interested powers."[66]†

As had been the case with Germany, though, the State Department concluded that the risks of negotiating with the Russians on Japan outweighed the benefits. "[W]e were in favor of working out a Treaty soon," Acheson told the British and French foreign ministers in September 1949, but "our interests were so great in Japan that we could not get ourselves in a position in which we had to approve a treaty we did not like." Several months later, the Secretary of State complained that "neutrality is an illusion in the context of East-West tensions. Thus, while Western Powers honored their obligation to observe Japanese neutrality, the Soviets would continue to pursue infiltration tactics, permitting them ultimately to turn Japan into an aggressive military threat." Since Japanese rearmament was forbidden under the new constitution, and since there were no United Nations forces to protect the country, the only alternative was to arrange to keep United States troops in Japan even after the peace treaty went into

---

* Acheson requested that Kennan's August 21, 1950, memorandum on Japan not be circulated within the Department of State. (*FRUS: 1950*, VII, 623n.)

† Kennan had in 1948 disagreed with MacArthur on the desirability of a demilitarization treaty, but subsequently came to support it. (Kennan notes of conversation with MacArthur, March 25, 1948, enclosed in PPS 28, March 25, 1948, *FRUS: 1948*, VI, 713.)

effect. This would "rule out, in our opinion, any real prospect that the U.S.S.R. or Communist China would be a party to the treaty."[67]

Years later, Kennan would concede that arrangements for Germany and Japan had not worked out as badly as he had expected. The occupation was evidently not as distasteful to the inhabitants of those countries as it was to Kennan and, in any event, it was soon over; both states came in time to favor the continued presence of American military bases on their territory. The Germans did not react violently against partition, and both West Germany and Japan proved to be economically viable despite the territorial truncations imposed by war. But Kennan was appalled at the way in which policy had been formulated in these situations: as in the case of NATO the methods of containment had been allowed to overshadow its ultimate objective, which was to change the Soviet concept of international relations and thus make possible a negotiated settlement of outstanding differences. A strategy of encircling the U.S.S.R. with military alliances could hardly encourage that process. As Kennan noted with regard to West Germany, "what was conceived as an instrument became, little by little, an end in itself. What was supposed to have been the servant of policy became its determinant instead."[68]

In no area, though, did this question of process versus objective become more acute for Kennan than in the realm of military strategy following the Soviet Union's unexpectedly early detonation of an atomic bomb in August 1949. That event set off a debate in Washington over whether or not to respond by building the far more powerful hydrogen, or "super," bomb, and it was during the course of this debate that Kennan worked out, for the first time, his position on the use of nuclear weapons in war. Kennan considered the seventy-nine-page paper he drafted on this subject "to have been in its implications one of the most important, if not the most important, of all the documents I ever wrote in government."[69] And not surprisingly, because what Kennan called for in his long memorandum on "The International Control of Atomic Energy" was nothing less than an end to reliance on nuclear weapons as instruments of offensive warfare.

Kennan came to this position for reasons that went to the heart of the relationship between policy, strategy, and the instruments of war: there was no way, he argued, in which weapons of mass destruction could be made to serve rational ends beyond simply deterring the outbreak of hostilities. War, after all, was supposed to be a means to an end, not an end in itself; it might imply an end "marked by submission to a new political will and perhaps to a new regime of life, but an end which at least did not negate the principle of life itself." Weapons of mass destruction lacked these characteristics. "They reach beyond the frontiers of western civilization, to the concepts of warfare which were once familiar to the Asiatic hordes. They cannot really be reconciled with a political purpose directed to shaping, rather than destroying, the lives of the adversary. They fail to take account of the ultimate responsibility of men for one another." It was important "that we not fall into the error of initiating, or planning to initiate, the employment of these weapons and concepts, thus hypnotizing ourselves into the belief that they may ultimately serve some positive national purpose."[70]

Kennan was not arguing here for any unilateral relinquishment of nuclear weapons. In the absence of a foolproof system of international control, he thought, some such devices would have to be retained "for purposes of deterrence and retaliation." What he was advocating was (1) in peacetime, a posture of what would later come to be called "minimum deterrence"—restricting the number and power of weapons in the American nuclear arsenal strictly to "our estimate as to what it would take to make attack on this country or its allies by weapons of mass destruction a risky, probably unprofitable, and therefore irrational undertaking for any adversary," and (2) should war come, a strategy of "no first use." Such an approach, Kennan admitted, would require careful consultation with allies and a considerable upgrading of conventional military capabilities. But it might obviate the need to build a hydrogen bomb, and it would place the United States in a better position from which to negotiate seriously with the Soviet Union on the international control of all nuclear weapons. "It is we ourselves who have started the discussion [about the hydrogen bomb]," Kennan pointed out. "There are no grounds for concluding that the Russians, who do not require the mass destruction weapons for the establishment of an adequate military posture, are necessarily insincere in their stated desire to see them effectively proscribed from the conduct of warfare."[71]

There was considerable sympathy within the State Department and the Atomic Energy Commission for Kennan's point of view. The AEC's General Advisory Committee warned that "a super bomb might become a weapon of genocide"; the capacity to retaliate with large numbers of atomic bombs would, it thought, be sufficient to deter the Russians from launching even a hydrogen bomb attack. The chairman of the AEC, David E. Lilienthal, joined with two of the four other members of the commission to oppose development of the new bomb on the grounds that it was not "consistent with this country's program for world peace or our own long term security." Acheson himself argued at a Policy Planning Staff meeting in November 1949 that

> perhaps the best thing is an 18–24 month moratorium on the super-bomb—bilateral if possible, unilateral if necessary—during which time you do your best to ease the international situation, come to an agreement with the Russians, put your own economic house in order, get your people's minds set to do whatever is necessary to do, and if no agreement is in sight at the end of that time—instead of dropping a bomb on the Russians as one school advocates—then go ahead with overall production of both [hydrogen and atomic bombs], backed up by your economy and your people, having made your best effort to do otherwise.

A month later, he acknowledged that "we cannot . . . carry conviction . . . in advocating and directing the effort for international control and abolition of atomic weapons if at the same time our military reliance upon them is growing."[72]

But there were also strong countervailing pressures, notably from Congress and the military. Senator Brien MacMahon, chairman of the Joint Committee on Atomic Energy, gave some hint of the mood on Capitol Hill when he wrote Truman: "Any idea that American renunciation of the super would inspire hope in the world or that 'disarmament by example' would earn us respect is so suggestive of an appeasement psychology and so at variance with the bitter lessons learned before, during and after two recent world wars that I will comment no further." The Joint Chiefs of Staff cited the weapon's advantages, not only as a deterrent but as "an offensive weapon of the greatest known power possibilities"; these considerations, they concluded, "decisively outweigh the possible social, psychological and moral objections." Lewis L. Strauss, a dissenting member of the Atomic Energy Commission, thought it "unwise to renounce unilaterally any weapon which an enemy can reasonably be expected to possess." Nor, as Acheson himself had to admit, was there any assurance that the Russians would not develop their own "super," regardless of what the United States did*—and as the final report to the President by the secretaries of State and Defense and the chairman of the AEC acknowledged, "sole possession by the Soviet Union of this weapon would cause severe

---

* It is clear now that Soviet scientists had been working on their own hydrogen bomb since 1946. (See David Holloway, *Stalin and the Bomb: The Soviet Union and Atomic Energy, 1939–1956* [New Haven: 1994], pp. 294–99.)

damage not only to our military posture but to our foreign policy position."[73]

These considerations led the President, on January 31, 1950, to author-ize a determination of "the technical feasibility of a thermonuclear weapon"—since feasibility could not be determined without an actual demonstration, this was in fact tantamount to an authorization to build.[74] "There actually was no decision to make on the H bomb," Truman told his staff a few days later. "[W]e had . . . to do it—make the bomb—though no one wants to use it. But . . . we have got to have it if only for bargaining purposes with the Russians."[75] Kennan's point, of course, had been that the very decision to build the bomb would inhibit bargaining with the Rus-sians on international control, since the Kremlin was unlikely to negotiate from a position of weakness. But this was not the kind of "bargaining" Tru-man had in mind: rather his perception, and the perception of most of his advisers, was that it was the United States, as a technologically rich but manpower-poor country, that was operating from a position of weakness, since of necessity it relied more heavily than did the Soviet Union on weapons of mass destruction to maintain the balance of power. The Soviet atomic test had upset that balance; only by building the "super," it was thought, could equilibrium be regained.[76]

Kennan maintained in retrospect that his views on nuclear weapons had been received with a mixture of "bewilderment and pity for my naiveté," and that it would not be until the Kennedy administration that an aware-ness would begin to develop "of the basic unsoundness of a defense pos-ture based primarily on weapons indiscriminately destructive and suicidal in their implications."[77] This complaint does less than full justice to the Truman administration, for one of the key assumptions of NSC-68—the complete reexamination of national security policy ordered by the Presi-dent as part of his decision on the hydrogen bomb—would be the need to move away from almost total reliance on weapons of mass destruction; from the risk, as the document put it, "of having no better choice than to capitulate or precipitate a global war."[78] Ironically, though, the costs of im-plementing that shift in strategy far exceeded Kennan's perception of what the nation's interests or capabilities would allow—so much so that NSC-68 evolved into a new and fundamentally different strategy of containment from what Kennan had originally advocated.

The decisions on NATO, West Germany, Japan, and the hydrogen bomb all had in common a determination on the part of the Truman ad-ministration to bolster the position of the United States and its allies with respect to the Soviet Union, to build what Acheson liked to call "situations of strength." This approach was not intended to preclude eventual negotiations with the Russians, but it did seek to defer them until requisite levels of strength had been reached.[79] It left little room for efforts to alter the Soviet concept of international relations through positive as well as negative reinforcement. Rather, "strength" came to be viewed as an end in itself, not as a means to a larger end; the process of containment became more important than the objective that process was supposed to attain. "It was not 'containment' that failed," Kennan commented years later; "it was the intended follow-up that never occurred."[80]*

IV

By the time Kennan left the Policy Planning Staff at the end of 1949 it was clear that his recommendations no longer carried the weight they once had. Slowly but steadily the burden of proof—always a substantial encumbrance in a bureaucracy[81]—had shifted from Kennan's critics to Kennan himself: "my concept of the manner in which our diplomatic effort should be conducted is not shared by any of the other senior officials of the department," he noted in his diary in November of that year. "Even if [the Secretary of State] shared my views, he would have to operate through people whose philosophy of foreign affairs would necessarily be a different one."[82] It is worth asking how this happened—how an administration that had found Kennan's reasoning persuasive regarding the first two stages of containment came to reject, however regretfully, his advice concerning the third. The answer appears to lie in the increasing difficulty Truman and his other advisers had in accepting Kennan's assumptions (1) that the danger of war was remote; (2) that asymmetry could be tolerated indefinitely; (3) that negotiations, if in the interests of both sides, could be productive; and (4) that diplomacy should be flexible.

Intelligence estimates continued to confirm the assumption that the Russians would not deliberately risk total war, but the administration grew

---

* "The real moment of irremediable failure for my own efforts came when it became apparent that the Western governments, and notably our own, were incapable both of cultivating the military and economic strength essential as a background for any successful negotiation, and at the same time holding open for the Russians any reasonable prospect of negotiation. The best we could bring ourselves to offer them, at the crucial moments, was some form of unconditional capitulation of their own political interests. They were not so weak that they had to accept anything of this sort." (Kennan to the author, September 4, 1980.)

less and less comfortable with Kennan's corollary argument that it could therefore safely concentrate on the economic rather than the military instruments of containment. The problem was that Kennan's appeared to be an intuitive rather than a verifiable judgment. Soviet intentions, his critics argued, could not be measured as precisely as Soviet capabilities, and even if they could be, intentions, unlike capabilities, could shift overnight, thereby negating the value of the measurement. As Paul Nitze, Kennan's successor as director of the Policy Planning Staff, observed, "we are in the position of being unable to prove either that the Soviets would or would not use force."[83] For those seeking to minimize risks—always a majority in a bureaucracy—it seemed wiser to base decisions on measurable quantities than on what Kennan himself admitted was "the unfirm substance of the imponderables."[84] It is significant that during the drafting of NSC-68 in the spring of 1950, Acheson dismissed as irrelevant efforts by Kennan and his fellow Soviet expert Charles Bohlen to rank the Kremlin's foreign policy priorities—the important thing, Acheson thought, was the U.S.S.R.'s capacity for aggression, whatever its present intentions.[85]

In retrospect, it is not difficult to see the weaknesses in this line of reasoning. There was in the administration's emphasis on capabilities at the expense of intentions a tendency to equate the importance of information with the ease of measuring it*—an approach better suited to physics than to international relations. There was also a failure to grasp the fact that capabilities are a function of intentions, and vice versa: capabilities do not exist except as the result of decisions reflecting intentions (however imperfectly); intentions count for little if they neglect capabilities, both as they exist and as they are likely to. Nor is it all that clear that Soviet capabilities were in fact more "knowable" than Soviet intentions. There is a case to be made for the argument that changes in the instruments of power available to the Kremlin surprised the West more often during the Cold War than shifts in the objectives with which that power was wielded. These are arguments verified by the passage of time, though, an advantage obviously not available to the strategists of 1950.

A second and closely related problem had to do with the toleration of asymmetry. Kennan's concept of strongpoint defense, with its idea of applying one's own strengths against adversary weaknesses, assumed a hierarchy of interests in the world: not all interests could be of equal impor-

---

* David Hackett Fischer has described this as the "quantitative fallacy"—see his *Historians' Fallacies: Toward a Logic of Historical Thought* (New York: 1970), p. 90.

tance; not all threats need be of equal danger. But this meant being willing to tolerate situations in which Soviet strengths were directed against American weaknesses. The two most worrisome by 1950 were the "loss" of mainland China to communism, which appeared make the rest of Asia vulnerable, and the situation in Western Europe, where the deterrent effect of the American atomic bomb could no longer be relied upon to counter Soviet conventional force superiority. Kennan acknowledged these asymmetries of power, but had little to recommend other than to be of good cheer. As he later recalled arguing with respect to Europe:

> We are like a man who has let himself into a walled garden and finds himself alone there with a dog with very big teeth. The dog, for the moment, shows no signs of aggressiveness. The best thing for us to do is surely to try to establish, as between the two of us, the assumption that the teeth have nothing whatsoever to do with our mutual relationship—that they are neither here nor there. If the dog shows no disposition to assume that it is otherwise, why should we raise the subject and invite attention to the disparity?[86]

Since China was not a vital power center, Soviet control over it, even if it could be maintained (which Kennan doubted), would pose no significant threat to the West. Non-communist Europe was much more vital, but the Russians knew that they could not take it without a war, and that they were unlikely to risk, even with their own atomic weapons.

Succeeding years proved Kennan right in both of these calculations, but that reassurance was not available at the time. What seemed important then was not so much the nature of Soviet power or the intentions Kremlin leaders had for it—neither of which were subject to verification—but rather the undeniable and eminently verifiable fact that power had shifted to Moscow's advantage in those parts of the world in highly visible ways. It was this shift in the *perception* of power relationships that caused a sense of weakness in the West, and a consequent unwillingness to approach negotiations with the Russians before remedying it. Kennan had earlier acknowledged the demoralizing effects changes in the perception of power could have: the Marshall Plan, after all, had been developed to counter just such a shift. But he apparently felt no need to propose comparably sweeping measures to deal with the psychological "shocks" of China and the Soviet atomic bomb.

Another problem with Kennan's approach was the fact that it would have required a willingness to negotiate with the Russians at a time when there were few indications of reciprocal interest on their part. Whatever Stalin's motives in authorizing the Czech coup, the Berlin blockade, the campaign to eradicate Western influences inside the U.S.S.R., the purge of suspected "Titoist" elements in Eastern Europe, and a long series of vituperative tirades by Soviet representatives in the United Nations, the effect was not to produce the atmosphere conducive to negotiations. It is true that behind-the-scenes contacts had helped to defuse the Berlin crisis early in 1949, but these discussions did nothing to resolve the differences that had led to the blockade in the first place.[87] Kennan's point had been that despite their differences, the Soviet Union and the West still shared common interests in a mutual withdrawal of forces from central Europe, the reunification of Germany, the neutralization of Japan, and the international control of atomic energy. Were the United States and its allies to make serious offers on these matters, he thought, the Russians would have little choice but to respond with equal seriousness, since it would be in their own best interests to do so. If that was the case, though, Stalin's government did very little to indicate it at the time.

And even if it had, negotiations with the Russians would have raised serious difficulties for the Truman administration, which was increasingly coming to regard this option as a risky and profitless enterprise. Public and Congressional opinion would view such discussions either as a sign of a "thaw" in the Cold War, in which case support for needed defense and foreign aid programs might dry up, or as evidence of appeasement—a danger not to be brushed aside in a period when the word "Yalta" had taken on much of the opprobrium hitherto reserved for "Munich." Allies would demand to be consulted, thereby precluding secrecy and flexibility; any failure to take them into confidence would raise fears of a "sell-out" at their expense. The Russians themselves would probably regard willingness to negotiate as a sign of weakness, and would raise their price for a settlement accordingly. The issue, in a nutshell, was credibility: how could the American commitment to resist aggression be believed if at the same time the United States was engaged in negotiations with the most likely aggressor? It was simply easier not to negotiate.[88]

Finally, Kennan's strategy required flexibility: the capacity to shift direction, emphasis, and if necessary expenditures in response to the course of events, without losing sight of long-range objectives. The United States was not merely reacting to events in the external world, he repeatedly pointed out; its own actions would in fact shape that world to a considerable extent. There was a need, then, to monitor carefully the impact of American initiatives, and to modify them where required to keep them consistent with ultimate goals. Written statements of policy might be helpful in defining those goals, or in deciding upon an initial approach to them, but such documents could hardly foresee all contingencies and as a result tended to promote rigidity. Bureaucracies could not be trusted to monitor themselves—there were too many temptations to defend existing procedures, whether in the national interest or not. The best guarantee of both flexibility and far-sightedness, Kennan believed, was to grant qualified experts immediate access to decision-makers at the top, unencumbered by the obligation to clear their recommendations through subordinate bureaucracies, free to suggest reconsiderations or adjustments as required.[89]

But this arrangement would have been difficult to reconcile with the bureaucracy's need for direction, a clear requirement if coordinated operations were to be carried out. Kennan's approach, it has been pointed out, resisted attempts "to congeal and disseminate an esoteric skill"; it relied heavily on the "noncommunicable wisdom of the experienced career official" and had little patience with the "rigidities, simplifications, and artificialities" involved in administering large organizations.[90] Acheson saw only limited value in this kind of advice:

> I recognized and highly appreciated the personal and esoteric skill of our Foreign Service officers, but believed that insofar as their wisdom was "noncommunicable," its value, though great in operations abroad, was limited in Washington. There major foreign policies must be made by the man charged with that responsibility in the Constitution, the President. He rarely came to his task trained in foreign affairs, nor did his personal entourage. What he needed was communicable wisdom, not mere conclusions, however soundly based in experience or intuition, what the man in the street called "educated hunches." I saw my duty as gathering all the wisdom available and communicating it amid considerable competition.[91]

Reconsiderations require time, energy, and intellectual effort, commodities always in short supply. Preoccupied as they were with maintaining support for containment within the bureaucracy, the Congress, the informed public, and among allies overseas, the last thing Truman and Acheson wanted was quick shifts of direction, or grand reassessments of underlying assumptions. The famous rejoinder Acheson addressed to a group of Republican critics is applicable here as well: the farmer who pulled up his crops every morning to see how much their roots had grown during the night would not be very productive.[92]

The price of administrative effectiveness can be strategic shortsightedness, though: in retrospect one of the strongest criticisms that can be made of the Truman administration's conduct of foreign and national security policy is that it failed to maintain the proper subordination of means to ends. In its determined effort to restore Western economic and military strength, it lost sight of the objective that strength was supposed to serve: ending the Cold War. In a pattern that was to become familiar in years to come, process triumphed over policy, with results considerably different from what Kennan, or even the administration itself, would have thought desirable.

But Kennan's strategy, too, contained a fundamental flaw. It sought to achieve its objectives ultimately through psychological means—by instilling self-confidence, not just in nations directly threatened by Soviet expansion, but in the United States itself. It also depended, though, on the ability of national leaders to make and maintain rational distinctions between vital and peripheral interests, adversary capabilities and intentions, negotiations and appeasement, flexibility and direction. What Kennan failed to take into account was the possibility that insistence on rational distinctions might induce irrational fears, thereby undermining self-confidence. Psychology, after all, incorporates irrational as well as rational states of mind; dismissing irrational fears for what they were was not enough to make them go away. Kennan's tightrope analogy was indeed apt: it was an economical but risky way to cross the chasm, but even though the rope proved to be tougher and more resilient than anyone suspected at the time, it was still not easy to walk on it without looking down.

NSC-68 and the Korean War

It seems odd, at first glance, that George Kennan, the most graceful prose stylist to serve in Washington in modern times, never took the trouble while in an official capacity to write down his complete concept of containment. Much of his thinking found its way into policy papers, to be sure, and the Truman administration did implement many of Kennan's recommendations between 1947 and 1949. But one had to glean the elements of his strategy from pronouncements delivered in a variety of forms before a variety of audiences. Kennan undertook no systematic exposition of his program.

This aversion to written policy guidelines was no accident: "I had no confidence," Kennan later recalled, "in the ability of men to define hypothetically in any useful way, by means of general and legal phraseology, future situations which no one could really imagine or envisage."[1] Issues of international relations were too subtle and evanescent to be reduced to paper without oversimplification; once papers had been agreed upon it was too difficult to get bureaucracies to reconsider them in the light of changing circumstances. But because Kennan found it either impossible or unnecessary to convey to the bureaucracies charged with implementing his strategy the way in which its parts related to the whole, there never developed the sense of direction at all levels of government that ensures perpetuation. As a result, Kennan found the administration committing itself to moves that seemed reasonable enough in themselves—NATO, the creation of a West German state, the decision to retain military bases in post-occupation Japan, the development of a hydrogen bomb—but inconsistent with the ultimate objectives of his strategy. By the time he got around to detecting and pointing out the discrepancies, it was too late to make changes.

It was precisely this need for greater coherence in policy formulation following the shocks of 1949—the "loss" of China, the Soviet atomic bomb, persistent inter-service debates over strategy, and the dilemma of how to meet expanding responsibilities with what appeared to be limited resources—that caused President Truman, early in 1950, to authorize just the sort of study Kennan had resisted: a single, comprehensive statement of interests, threats, and feasible responses, capable of being communicated throughout the bureaucracy. But Kennan was not there to oversee it. He had resigned as director of the Policy Planning Staff at the end of 1949, and the task of drafting the new document, which came to be known as NSC-68, fell to a small *ad hoc* committee of State and Defense Department officials under the chairmanship of Kennan's successor, Paul H. Nitze.[2]

NSC-68 was not intended as a repudiation of Kennan. He was consulted at several stages in the drafting process and the final document—of some sixty-six single-spaced typed pages—reflected his views at several points. The objective rather was to systematize containment, and to find the means to make it work. But the very act of reducing the strategy to writing exposed the differences that had begun to develop between Kennan and the administration. The search for means, together with the generous way in which the drafting committee construed its mandate, accentuated these. The result, like that more prominent product of a broadly construed mandate, the United States Constitution,* was a document more sweeping in content and implications than its originators had intended.

I

The differences between Kennan's conception of United States interests and that of NSC-68 are not immediately apparent. The document proclaimed as the nation's "fundamental purpose" assuring the "the integrity and vitality of our free society which is founded on the dignity and worth of the individual." It went on to announce "our determination to create

---

*The drafting of NSC-68 also resembled the drafting of the Constitution in that both were done independently of the agencies nominally responsible for such matters—in the case of the latter, the Confederation Congress; in the former, the National Security Council.

conditions under which our free and democratic system can live and prosper." It associated American interests with diversity, not uniformity: "the prime reliance of the free society is on the strength and appeal of its idea, and it feels no compulsion sooner or later to bring all societies into conformity with it." And it appeared to rely on the balance of power as the means of ensuring that diversity: the opening paragraph recalled with apparent approval the international system that preceded World War I, in which "for several centuries it has proved impossible for any one nation to gain such preponderant strength that a coalition of other nations could not in time face it with greater strength."[3]

But there the similarity ended. Kennan had argued that all that was necessary to maintain the balance of power, and thereby safeguard diversity, was to keep centers of industrial-military capability out of hostile hands. Unfriendly regimes elsewhere, though not to be desired, posed little threat to global stability so long as they lacked means of manifesting their hostility. NSC-68 took a very different point of view: "any substantial further extension of the area under the domination of the Kremlin would raise the possibility that no coalition adequate to confront the Kremlin with greater strength could be assembled." And, again: "the assault on free institutions is worldwide now, and in the context of the present polarization of power a defeat of free institutions anywhere is a defeat everywhere."[4]* The implication was clear: Kennan's strategy of defending selected strongpoints would no longer suffice; the emphasis rather would have to be on perimeter defense, with all points along the perimeter considered of equal importance.

NSC-68's endorsement of perimeter defense suggests several major departures in underlying assumptions from Kennan. One of these had to do with the nature of effective power in international affairs. Kennan had taken the view that only industrial-military power could bring about significant changes in world politics, and that as long as it was kept in rough balance, international stability (though not necessarily all exposed positions) could be preserved. But Kennan himself had been forced to acknowledge, by 1949, that things were not that simple. Insecurity could manifest itself in psychological as well as physical terms, as the Western Europeans' demands for American military protection had shown. And psychological

---

* The wording here suggests that Kennan's strategy might have been considered appropriate for less trying times, but that the balance of power had swung so far in favor of the Soviet bloc that no further losses could be tolerated.

insecurity could as easily develop from the distant sound of falling dominoes as from the rattling of sabers next door. This was the major unresolved dilemma in Kennan's thinking—how could the self-confidence
upon which his strategy depended survive the making of distinctions between peripheral and vital interests? As far as the authors of NSC-68 were
concerned, it could not.

From their perspective, changes in the balance of power could occur
not only as the result of economic maneuvers or military action, but from
intimidation, humiliation, or even loss of credibility. The Soviet Union,
Nitze reminded his colleagues, made no distinction between military and
other forms of aggression; it was guided "by the simple consideration of
weakening the world power position of the US." NSC-68 added that
"[s]ince everything that gives us or others respect for our institutions is a
suitable object for attack, it also fits the Kremlin's design that where, with
impunity, we can be insulted and made to suffer indignity the opportunity
shall not be missed." The Soviet Union was out "to demonstrate to the free
world that force and the will to use it are on the side of the Kremlin [and]
that those who lack it are decadent and doomed."[5]

The implications were startling. World order, and with it American security, had come to depend as much on *perceptions* of the balance of
power as on what that balance actually was. And the perceptions involved
were not just those of statesmen customarily charged with making policy;
they also reflected mass opinion, foreign as well as domestic, informed as
well as uninformed, rational as well as irrational. Before such an audience
even the appearance of a shift in power relationships could have unnerv-
ing consequences. Judgments based on such traditional criteria as geography, economic capacity, or military potential now had to be balanced
against considerations of image, prestige, and credibility. The effect was
vastly to increase the number and variety of interests deemed relevant to
national security, and to blur distinctions between them.

But proliferating interests could be of little significance apart from the
means to defend them, and here NSC-68 challenged another of the assumptions that had informed Kennan's strategy of containment: the perception of limited resources, which had made distinctions between vital
and peripheral interests necessary in the first place. On this point there
had been no divergence of viewpoint between Kennan and the administration. President Truman had continued to insist on holding down defense expenditures in order to avoid either higher taxes or budget deficits.
His guidelines for the fiscal 1951 budget, drawn up in the summer of

1949, proposed increased spending for domestic programs as well, and hence limited the military to a ceiling of $13 billion. "We realize . . . that our Nation's economy under existing conditions can afford only a limited amount for defense," General Omar Bradley, chairman of the Joint Chiefs of Staff, had told the House Armed Services Committee later that year, "and that we must look forward to diminishing appropriations for the armed services." But Bradley added that his reference to existing conditions had been deliberate, "because obviously, if war is thrust upon us, the American people will spend the amount necessary to provide for national defense, and to carry out their international obligations."[6]

What NSC-68 did was to suggest a way to increase defense expenditures without war, without long-term budget deficits, and without crushing tax burdens. Only 6–7 percent of the gross national product was then being devoted to military expenditures, it pointed out;* adding investment in war-related industries brought the figure to around 20 percent. Comparable statistics for the Soviet Union were 13.8 percent and 40 percent. But the Soviet economy was operating at nearly full capacity; the American economy was not. The President's January 1950 economic report to the Congress had noted that with a higher level of economic activity, the gross national product could be raised from the 1949 level of $255 billion to as much as $300 billion in five years. This increment could be used to finance a substantial buildup in Western military and economic strength without decreasing the domestic standard of living. Civilian consumption might actually rise as a result, since such a program could well push the gross national product beyond what was required for new military and foreign assistance programs. "One of the most significant lessons of our World War II experience," NSC-68 pointed out, "was that the American economy, when it operates at a level approaching full efficiency, can provide enormous resources for purposes other than civilian consumption while simultaneously providing a higher standard of living."[7]

Despite their obvious implications for military spending, these ideas did not originate in the Pentagon, where doctrines of fiscal orthodoxy had become more strongly entrenched than usual with the appointment of Louis Johnson as Secretary of Defense. They came instead from a group of liberal civilian advisers eager to apply Keynesian techniques to the management of the domestic economy. The most influential of these was Leon Keyserling, soon to become chairman of the Council of Economic

---

* Actually, the figure was closer to 5 percent. See Appendix.

Advisers, who had begun to argue that the nation could sustain more vigorous growth rates if the government would stimulate the economy and tolerate short-term budget deficits until tax revenues from increased economic activity began to roll in. The idea, as Keyserling put it, should be to expand the pie, not argue over how to divide it. Keyserling had the President's domestic program in mind in advancing that argument, and to that end had persuaded Truman to endorse the eventual feasibility of a $300 billion gross national product.[8]

The committee drafting NSC-68 was thus able to incorporate Keyserling's viewpoint with some semblance of presidential sanction, but to adapt it to purposes very different from its original objectives. Nevertheless, after reading NSC-68, Keyserling expressed "full agreement" with its economic conclusions, warning only of the need to undertake educational efforts to correct the widespread impression that "increased defense must mean equivalently lowered living standards, higher taxes and a proliferation of controls."[9]* The implications were as startling as the idea that interests were indivisible: if the government would only take it upon itself to "manage" the economy, then the means of defense could be expanded as needed to protect those interests. As Robert A. Lovett, former Under-Secretary of State, Wall Street banker, and no Keynesian liberal, told the drafting committee, "there was practically nothing that the country could not do if it wanted to do it."[10] To its earlier assertion that there *should* not be distinctions between peripheral and vital interests, NSC-68 had shown with seductive logic that there *need* not be.

But if expandable means made possible larger ends, did it follow that these ends justified a larger *variety* of means than had previously been thought appropriate? The authors of NSC-68 took an ambivalent position on this point. On the one hand, they argued that "the responsibility of world leadership . . . demands that we make the attempt, and accept the risks inherent in it, to bring about order and justice by means consistent with the principles of freedom and democracy." They noted further that whereas "the Kremlin is able to select whatever means are expedient in seeking to carry out its fundamental design," democracies enjoyed no such freedom of choice:

---

* "Keyserling and I discussed these matters frequently; though he wanted to spend the money on other programs, he was convinced that the country could afford $40 billion for defense if necessary." (Paul Nitze, "The Development of NSC-68," *International Security,* IV [Spring, 1980], 169.)

> The resort to force, to compulsion, to the imposition of its will is . . . a diffi-
> cult and dangerous act for a free society, which is warranted only in the face
> of even greater dangers. The necessity of the act must be clear and com-
> pelling; the act must commend itself to the overwhelming majority as an in-
> escapable exception to the basic idea of freedom; or the regenerative capac-
> ity of free men after the act has been performed will be endangered.

But then they added:

> The integrity of our system will not be jeopardized by any measures, covert
> or overt, violent or non-violent, which serve the purpose of frustrating the
> Kremlin design, nor does the necessity for conducting ourselves so as to af-
> firm our values in actions as well as words forbid such measures, provided
> only they are appropriately calculated to that end and are not so excessive or
> misdirected as to make us enemies of the people instead of the evil men who
> have enslaved them.[11]

This was a sweeping mandate indeed, difficult to reconcile with the self-
denying ordinance that had just preceded it.

The reconciliation the authors of NSC-68 probably had in mind (although it is nowhere explicitly stated in the document) was this: that while
in principle a democracy should choose its methods selectively, when confronted with an absolute threat to its survival anything was fair game. The
same reasoning could be applied to the problems of differentiating interests and providing means as well: considerations of priority and economy
might be appropriate in normal times, but in the face of a threat such as
that posed by the Soviet Union, preoccupations of this sort had to go by
the board. The world crisis, as dangerous in its potential as anything confronted in World Wars I or II, rendered all interests vital, all means affordable, all methods justifiable. For the authors of NSC-68, American interests could not be defined apart from the threat the Soviet Union posed
to them: "frustrating the Kremlin design," as the document so frequently
put it, became an end it itself, not a means to a larger end.

II

But just what was the Kremlin design, and how did perceptions of it reflected in NSC-68 differ from Kennan's? "The fundamental design of
those who control the Soviet Union and the international communist
movement," the document argued, "is to retain and solidify their absolute
power, first in the Soviet Union and second in the areas now under their
control. In the minds of the Soviet leaders, however, achievement of this

design requires the dynamic extension of their authority and the ultimate elimination of any effective opposition to their authority." This much Kennan would have found unexceptionable. Nor did Nitze and his colleagues see Soviet expansion as motivated primarily by ideological considerations. Like Kennan they saw Marxism-Leninism as more the instrument than the determinant of Soviet policy: "the Kremlin's conviction of its own infallibility has made its devotion to theory so subjective that past or present pronouncements as to doctrine offer no reliable guide to future action." Rather, Soviet hostility stemmed simply from the inability of a totalitarian system to tolerate diversity: "The existence and persistence of the idea of freedom is a permanent and continuous threat to the foundations of the slave society; and it therefore regards as intolerable the long continued existence of freedom in the world."[12]

The authors of NSC-68 also agreed with Kennan that this inability to live with diversity was a weakness, certain eventually to create problems for the Kremlin, but they differed with him as to how soon. Kennan took the position that the U.S.S.R. was already overextended; that it was finding it difficult to control areas it had already absorbed; and that the resulting strains, revealed vividly in the Titoist heresy, offered opportunities the United States could exploit. NSC-68 took a more pessimistic view. Soviet expansion, it argued, had so far produced strength, not weakness; whatever the liabilities of Titoism they were more than counter-balanced by the victory of communism in China, the Soviet atomic bomb, and Moscow's continued military buildup at a time when the United States was rigorously limiting its own comparable expenditures. Given this situation, it seemed imprudent "to risk the future on the hazard that the Soviet Empire, because of over-extension or other reasons, will spontaneously destroy itself from within."[13]

Neither Kennan nor NSC-68 questioned the Russians' superiority in conventional forces or their ability, in time, to develop sufficient atomic weapons to neutralize the American advantage in that field as well. Rather, their conflicting assessments of the existing power balance hinged on the issue of whether or not the U.S.S.R. would deliberately risk war. Kennan, reasoning from an evaluation of Soviet intentions, argued that disparities in military power could be tolerated because the Russians had little to gain from exploiting them. The Soviet leadership was cautious, prone to seek its objectives at minimum cost and risk without reference to any fixed timetable. The United States could therefore content itself with an asymmetrical response—reinforcing its own strengths and those of its allies, but with no effort to duplicate Soviet force configurations. NSC-68, emphasizing Soviet capabilities, argued that the Russians had not provoked war so far only because they had lacked the assurance of winning it. Once their capabilities had expanded to the point where they could reasonably expect to win—NSC-68 estimated that this would occur in 1954, when the Russians would have enough atomic bombs to devastate the United States—then the intentions of Kremlin leaders, if Washington did nothing in the meantime to build up its own forces, might well be to risk war, probably in the form of a surprise attack.[14]

Until then, the most significant danger was that of war by proxy. Kennan himself had come to acknowledge the possibility that the Soviet Union might authorize limited military action by its satellites, but such maneuvers would be designed, he thought, to achieve Soviet objectives without setting off a general war. Since not all of its interests were equally vital, the United States could still choose whether and how to respond: "world realities have greater tolerances than we commonly suppose against ambitious schemes for world domination."[15] NSC-68, on the other hand, saw "piecemeal aggression" as an instrument of war, aimed at exploiting the Americans' unwillingness to use nuclear weapons unless directly attacked. Operating from the very different assumption that interests were indivisible, it warned that any failure to respond could lead to "a descending spiral of too little and too late, of doubt and recrimination, [of] ever narrower and more desperate alternatives." The result would be a series of "gradual withdrawals under pressure until we discover one day that we have sacrificed positions of vital interest."[16]

Even without war the Soviet Union could use its armed forces—which NSC-68 described as "far in excess of those necessary to defend its national territory"—to erode the position of the United States and its allies: such strength provided the U.S.S.R. "with great coercive power for use in time of peace . . . and serves as a deterrent to the victims of its aggression from taking any action in opposition to its tactics which would risk war." The objective was "to back up infiltration with intimidation." It was true that the United States itself had greater military forces than ever before in peacetime, but the measure of effectiveness in such matters was comparison with present adversaries, not past economies. When balanced against increasing Soviet military power and the commitments the United States had undertaken to contain it, "it is clear that our military strength is becoming dangerously inadequate."[17] If Kennan shared this concern, he said nothing about it. His sole recommendations for increasing peacetime military forces during this period were confined to the development of elite, highly mobile, compact units, capable of responding quickly and effectively to limited aggression, but in no way designed to counter Soviet capabilities he was convinced would not be used.[18]

At the heart of these differences between Kennan and the authors of NSC-68 was a simple inversion of intellectual procedure: where Kennan tended to look at the Soviet threat in terms of an independently established concept of irreducible interests, NSC-68 derived its view of American interests primarily from its perception of the Soviet threat. Kennan's insistence on the need to deter hostile combinations of industrial-military power could have applied as well to the adversaries of World Wars I and II as to the Soviet Union. No comparably general statement of fundamental interests appeared in NSC-68. The document paid obeisance to the balance of power, diversity, and freedom, but nowhere did it set out the minimum requirements necessary to secure those interests. Instead it found in the simple presence of a Soviet threat sufficient cause to deem the interest threatened vital.

The consequences of this approach were more than procedural: they were nothing less than to transfer to the Russians control over what United States interests were at any given point. To define interests in terms of threats is, after all, to make interests a function of threats—interests will then expand or contract as threats do. By applying pressure in particular areas Kremlin leaders could, if they were astute enough, force the United States and its allies to expend resources in parts of the world far removed from Kennan's original list of vital interests. The whole point of NSC-68 had been to generate additional means with which to defend existing interests. But by neglecting to define those interests apart from the threat to them, the document in effect expanded interests along with means, thereby vitiating its own intended accomplishment.

III

In its recommendations for action to meet the Soviet challenge, NSC-68 once again, as in its discussions of interests and threats, began from a position similar to Kennan's, but then departed from it. The document defined "containment" as an effort

> by all means short of war to (1) block further expansion of Soviet power, (2) expose the falsities of Soviet pretensions, (3) induce a retraction of the

Kremlin's control and influence and (4) in general, so foster the seeds of destruction within the Soviet system that the Kremlin is brought at least to the point of modifying its behavior to conform to generally accepted international standards.

It went on to note that "it was and continues to be cardinal in this policy that we possess superior overall power in ourselves or in dependable combination with other like-minded nations," but that at the same time "we always leave open the possibility of negotiation with the U.S.S.R." A "diplomatic freeze," it pointed out, "tends to defeat the very purposes of 'containment' because it raises tensions at the same time that it makes Soviet retractions and adjustments in the direction of moderated behavior more difficult." The idea should be "to exert pressure in a fashion which will avoid so far as possible directly challenging Soviet prestige, to keep open the possibility for the U.S.S.R. to retreat before pressure with a minimum loss of face and to secure political advantage from the failure of the Kremlin to yield or take advantage of the openings we leave it."[19]

But where Kennan had sought to block Soviet expansion by a variety of political, economic, psychological, and military measures, NSC-68 concentrated almost exclusively on the last of these: "Without superior aggregate military strength, in being and readily mobilizable, a policy of 'containment' . . . is no more than a policy of bluff." Where Kennan had emphasized reliance on existing forces of resistance—especially nationalism—NSC-68 stressed the need for the United States to be able to respond militarily when aggression took place. This would not require matching the Russians weapon for weapon, but it would necessitate "a build-up of military strength by the United States and its allies to a point at which the combined strength will be superior . . . to the forces that can be brought to bear by the Soviet Union and its satellites." And that strength would have to be sufficient "to provide an adequate defense against air attack on the United States and Canada and an adequate defense against air and surface attack on the United Kingdom and Western Europe, Alaska, the Western Pacific, Africa, and the Near and Middle East, and on the long lines of communication to those areas."[20]

NSC-68, by design, contained no estimate of what these forces would cost or how they would be used. Imprecision, its drafters believed, was necessary to gain action: debates over budget allocations and force deployments could only delay clearance of the document, especially in the Pentagon, where inter-service disputes over these issues had become both bitter and public. "The purpose of NSC-68," Acheson later recalled, "was to so bludgeon the mass mind of 'top government' that not only could the President make a decision but that the decision could be carried out."[21] It was in fact easier, as Keyserling had suggested, to expand the pie rather than argue over how to divide it. Nonetheless, informal estimates did circulate within the drafting committee: these agreed that the document's recommended programs would cost about $50 billion annually, or three and a half times the President's existing $13.5 billion ceiling on military expenditures.[22] The assumption was that the country could easily afford this amount—once psychological inhibitions about short-term budget deficits had been overcome.

It should be emphasized that the authors of NSC-68 saw this buildup as defensive in nature. They rejected preventive war as both unfeasible—since it would rely on atomic weapons which in themselves might not compel capitulation or deter attacks on allies—and morally repugnant. A "first blow" against the U.S.S.R. could be justified only if it was "demonstrably in the nature of a counter-attack to a blow which is on its way or about to be delivered."[23] Nor should a war with the Soviet Union, if one occurred, seek annihilation of the enemy:

> In the words of the *Federalist* (No. 28) "the means to be employed must be proportioned to the extent of the mischief." The mischief may be a global war or it may be a Soviet campaign for limited objectives. In either case we should take no avoidable initiative which would cause it to become a war of annihilation, and if we have the forces to defeat a Soviet drive for limited objectives it may well be to our interest not to let it become a global war. Our aim in applying force must be to compel the acceptance of our terms consistent with our objectives, and our capabilities for the application of force should, therefore, within the limits of what we can sustain over the long pull, be congruent to the range of tasks which we may encounter.[24]

The idea here, in short, was calibration: to do no less, but also no more, than was required to safeguard American interests.

As a corollary, NSC-68 endorsed Kennan's argument that the United States had come to rely too heavily on atomic weapons as an instrument of deterrence: "The only deterrent we can present to the Kremlin is the evidence we give that we may make any of the critical points which we cannot hold the occasion for a global war of annihilation." This left Washington with "no better choice than to capitulate or precipitate a global war." It was imperative, accordingly, "to increase as rapidly as possible our general air, ground and sea strength and that of our allies to a point where we are militarily not so heavily dependent on atomic weapons." But such measures would not involve any reduction in the American atomic arsenal—indeed NSC-68 specifically approved the decision to build the hydrogen bomb, in the expectation that the Russians would soon have one too. Nor did the document accept Kennan's concept of "no first use": such a declaration, it argued, "would be interpreted by the U.S.S.R. as an admission of great weakness and by allies as a clear indication that we intended to abandon them."[25] Rather, what was needed was the capacity for what would later be called "flexible response"—the ability to counter aggression at whatever level of violence it occurred, but without unnecessary escalation.

In a sense, both Kennan and the authors of NSC-68 favored "flexible response," but they conceived of it in different terms. NSC-68, assuming war to be a real possibility, argued for a kind of "vertical" flexibility up and down the spectrum of military capabilities, ranging from peacetime deterrence through nuclear war. Kennan, convinced that war with the Soviet Union was unlikely, wanted instead "horizontal" flexibility—the ability to employ limited military force where appropriate, but to be able to make at least equal if not greater use of the economic, diplomatic, and psychological instruments of containment. NSC-68, assuming the indivisibility of interests, thought of flexible response as symmetrical response—acting wherever the Russians chose to challenge interests. For Kennan it meant asymmetrical response—acting only when interests at stake were vital, conditions favorable, and means accessible. For NSC-68, flexible response implied the capacity to generate resources to match commitments. For Kennan, it suggested the need to restrict commitments to keep them in line with resources. These were subtle differences, but not insubstantial ones.

It is a reflection of NSC-68's preoccupation with the military balance of power that it said relatively little about Kennan's second stage of containment—the exploitation of tensions within the international communist movement. What it did say appeared, once again, to proceed from Kennan's premises but to arrive at different conclusions. NSC-68 noted the Soviet Union's vulnerability to nationalism, both within its borders and in its satellite empire. It concluded from this, as Kennan had, that "if a satellite feels able to effect its independence of the Kremlin, as Tito was able to do, it is likely to break away." As a result, "[i]t may even be said that the capabilities of the Soviet world, specifically the capabilities of the masses who have nothing to lose but their Soviet chains, are a potential which can be enlisted on our side."[26] There was implied here the same reasoning that had informed Kennan's strategy: that it was the Soviet Union, not international communism, which threatened American security, and that where communists independent of Moscow's control existed, the United States could well work with them to contain Moscow's expansionist ambitions.

But NSC-68 nowhere said this, nor did it suggest means by which fragmentation within the international communist movement might be encouraged. Instead it assumed continued Soviet control over Eastern Europe, and although it anticipated some economic problems for the Russians in China, it suggested that the difficulties faced by the noncommunist states of the region "present more than offsetting opportunities."[27] The omission of any strategy for promoting fragmentation is surprising since that goal remained very much alive elsewhere in the administration at the time NSC-68 was being drafted. In January 1950, for example, the Joint Chiefs of Staff had advocated continued military assistance to Yugoslavia "to insure continued resistance to Moscow control since such an example of successful opposition might encourage movements of resistance to Moscow control in other satellite states." "What we are concerned with in China," Secretary of State Acheson told the Senate Foreign Relations Committee in March, "is that whoever runs China, even if the devil himself runs China, that he is an independent devil. That is infinitely better than if he is a stooge of Moscow or China comes under Russia." NSC-68's reticence on this point was sufficiently noticeable for one of Acheson's subordinates to ask, after reading a preliminary draft: "Have we, in fact, adequately explored the question of whether there may not be a critical point in Soviet expansion beyond which the benefits to the U.S.S.R. will turn to disadvantage?"[28]

Several possible explanations for NSC-68's silence on this question suggest themselves. One has to do with timing: where Kennan and Acheson had seen fragmentation as a sufficiently immediate prospect to justify action at once, the drafters of NSC-68 tended to see it as a more remote possibility, too problematic to affect existing configurations of power.[29] NSC-68 also concerned itself more with appearances than did either Kennan or Acheson. A victory for communism in a particular country might not, in the long run, be a gain for the Soviet Union, but it was certain in the short run to *appear* as a loss for the United States. The Truman administration had done little publicly to explain that all communists were not equally dangerous; by 1950, given the fevered domestic political atmosphere generated by the Alger Hiss case and the rise of McCarthyism, any such educational effort would have produced more heat than light.* American interests, NSC-68 had argued, depended as much on the perception of power as on power itself; if the United States even seemed to be losing ground to its adversaries, the effects could be much the same as if that loss had actually occurred.

These dilemmas all manifested themselves with respect to Taiwan, where the administration by the spring of 1950 was developing second thoughts about its policy of not opposing a Chinese Communist takeover for fear of driving the Russians and the Chinese closer together. Among those influential in bringing about this reconsideration was John Foster Dulles, who had become a special consultant to the Department of State in April. Dulles argued, in a memorandum written the following month, that

> [i]f our conduct indicates a continuing disposition to fall back and allow doubtful areas to fall under Soviet Communist control, then many nations will feel confirmed in the impression, already drawn from the North Atlantic Treaty, that we do not expect to stand firm short of the North Atlantic area. . . . If our conduct seems to confirm that conclusion, then we can expect an accelerated deterioration of our influence in the Mediterranean, Near East, Asia and the Pacific.[30]

Dulles played no role in the drafting of NSC-68, but his thinking closely paralleled that document's concern with appearances. It was also sufficiently persuasive to set off a reassessment of Taiwan policy within the State Department which, though not complete at the time the Korean War broke out, had progressed sufficiently to suggest that any strategy of promoting fragmentation in the communist world would have to be weighed against the costs to the non-communist world of allowing even perceived shifts in the balance of power.[31]

With regard to Kennan's third stage of containment—changing the Soviet concept of international relations—NSC-68 again acknowledged the desirability of the objective but balked at the method. "[W]e can expect no lasting abatement of the crisis unless and until a change occurs in the nature of the Soviet system," the document noted, but the United States had it within its power to accelerate those changes:

---

* As Acheson found out in 1949 when he used the medium of a 1,054-page "white paper" to attempt to educate the American people on China. See his *Present at the Creation*, pp. 302–3, and David S. McLellan, *Dean Acheson: The State Department Years* (New York: 1976), pp. 194–98.

> By practically demonstrating the integrity and vitality of our system the free world widens the area of possible agreement and thus can hope gradually to bring about a Soviet acknowledgment of realities which in sum will eventually constitute a frustration of the Kremlin design. Short of this, however, it might be possible to create a situation which will induce the Soviet Union to accommodate itself, with or without the conscious abandonment of its design, to coexistence on tolerable terms with the non-Soviet world.

The Russian people were a potential ally in this enterprise: "clearly it will not only be less costly but more effective if this change occurs to a maximum extent as a result of internal forces in Soviet society." Accordingly, NSC-68 stressed the importance of doing nothing in war or peace that might "irrevocably unite the Russian people behind the regime that enslaves them."[32]

But, unlike Kennan, NSC-68 ruled out diplomacy as a means of altering the Soviet outlook: a negotiated settlement, it argued, could not take place until the Soviet system itself had changed. To be sure, public opinion in the West would require that the United States and its allies appear willing to discuss agreements with the Russians. A sound negotiating position, in this sense, was "an essential element in the ideological conflict." But "any offer of, or attempt at, negotiation of a general settlement . . . could only be a tactic." Negotiations would be useful, not in and of themselves, but as "a means of gaining support for a program of building strength." Ultimately, of course, the West would want to arrange with the Soviet government or its successor a permanent resolution of outstanding differences. But this kind of settlement was far in the future; if and when it occurred, it would be a record of "the progress which the free world will have made in creating a political and economic system so successful that the frustration of the Kremlin's design for world domination will be complete."[33]

This could hardly be described as a forthcoming negotiating posture. The more accurate characterization might be "devious," since the appearance conveyed was quite opposite to what was actually intended. But these strong inhibitions about negotiations did not originate with NSC-68. As has been seen, they played a prominent role in official thinking throughout 1949, and in fact constituted the first major point of disagreement between Kennan and the administration. What NSC-68 did was to clarify the assumptions upon which this reluctance to negotiate had been based.

One of these was the belief that American military strength, relative to that of the Soviet Union, was declining, and that the United States as a consequence should avoid negotiating with the Russians until it could do so from a position of strength.[34] But as one critic of NSC-68 pointed out,

> it is hard to accept a conclusion that the U.S.S.R. is approaching a straight-out military superiority over us when, for example (1) our Air Force is vastly superior qualitatively, is greatly superior numerically in the bombers, trained crews and other facilities necessary for offensive warfare; (2) our supply of fission bombs is much greater than that of the U.S.S.R., as is our thermonuclear potential; (3) our navy is so much stronger than that of the U.S.S.R. that they should not be mentioned in the same breath; (4) the economic health and military potential of our allies is, with our help, growing daily; and (5) while we have treaties of alliance with and are furnishing arms to countries bordering the U.S.S.R., the U.S.S.R. has none with countries within thousands of miles of us.[35]

What the authors of NSC-68 were concerned about, of course, were future trends, not existing balances: the argument was that the Soviet Union was devoting roughly twice the percentage of its gross national product to military expenditures as was the United States, and that if the United States did not increase its own spending proportionally, it would fall behind. But since NSC-68 itself pointed out that the total American gross national product in 1949 had been *four times* that of the Soviet Union,[36] it is difficult to avoid the conclusion that a double standard was being applied here: potential Soviet capabilities were being taken into account, but not those of the United States. It was on this questionable basis that NSC-68 derived its assessment of American weakness, and hence discouraged negotiations.

A second deterrent to negotiations was the belief that the Soviet Union would enjoy certain inherent advantages in conducting them. It would have the benefit of secrecy, and so could be expected to know more about its adversaries than they would know about it. It would not have to defer to public opinion, or consult in advance with allies. And, through the international communist movement, it could manipulate public opinion outside the U.S.S.R. while insulating its own people from external influences. "These are important advantages," NSC-68 argued; "together with the unfavorable trend of our power position, they militate . . . against successful negotiation of a general settlement at this time."[37] But NSC-68 failed to mention some of the disadvantages the Russians would face in negotiations with the West: the difficulty a totalitarian system has in assessing outside events objectively; the tendency of those who are insensitive to public opinion to alienate public opinion; the burden of holding together alliances based on coercion, not mutual interest. One wonders whether

NSC-68's list of Soviet "advantages" was not as much a veiled complaint about the frustrations facing American diplomats as it was an accurate evaluation of Soviet negotiating prowess.

But of course the most significant deterrent to negotiations was the fact that there appeared to be little to negotiate about. The years 1945-1949 had seen a protracted series of diplomatic contacts with the Russians, with painfully little to show for the effort expended. Moreover, if, as NSC-68 argued, all interests were now vital, then future negotiations could take place only on the basis of Soviet capitulations. Short of that, Moscow's willingness or lack of willingness to negotiate became irrelevant. The great weakness in this approach was its failure to allow for the very phenomenon both Kennan and the authors of NSC-68 had hoped eventually to bring about: a fundamental change in the Soviet concept of international relations.

NSC-68 was, then, a deeply flawed document, in the sense that the measures it recommended undercut the goals it was trying to achieve. A military buildup might enhance American security if American interests remained stable, but NSC-68 expanded interests. Fragmentation of the communist world might be a desirable objective, but treating communists everywhere as equally dangerous was not the way to achieve it. A more moderate Soviet attitude toward the outside world was certainly to be welcomed, but a negotiating posture that required Soviet capitulation could hardly hasten it. What all of these anomalies reflect is a failure of strategic vision: an inability to relate short-term to long-term considerations, to coordinate actions with interests. This failure probably resulted from the way in which NSC-68 was drafted—it was a committee product, not, as in the case of Kennan's strategy, the work of one man; it was also as much a work of advocacy as of analysis, a "bludgeon," as Acheson had put it. Whatever the case, NSC-68's recommendations for action provided less than adequate guidance as to how objectives and capabilities were to be combined to produce coherent strategy.

IV

One of the things most striking about NSC-68 was its rhetorical tone. Portions of it sounded as though they had been intended for the floor of Congress, or some other conspicuous public platform: "The idea of freedom is the most contagious idea in history. . . . Where the despot holds absolute power . . . all other wills must be subjugated in an act of willing submission, a degradation willed by the individual upon himself under the compulsion of a perverted faith. . . . The system becomes God, and submission to the will of God becomes submission to the will of the system."[38] This is not what one would expect in a top secret document destined not to be made public for a quarter of a century.* But it was only the details of NSC-68 that were sensitive; its principal conclusions were widely publicized at the time, although without attribution to their source. The whole point of the document had been to shake the bureaucracy, Congress, and the public into supporting more vigorous action; hence, it is not surprising that its drafters gave more thought than Kennan had to how that support might be generated.

Within the bureaucracy, the problem was largely taken care of by the unusual manner in which the document was drafted. Standard procedure would have been for the paper to emanate from one of the major departments or the National Security Council staff, to be coordinated with and cleared through all affected agencies, and then to be forwarded to the President through the National Security Council. But a small *ad hoc* committee made up of State and Defense Department representatives drafted NSC-68; it was forced on the economy-minded Secretary of Defense, Louis Johnson, as a virtual *fait accompli*; and it went directly to the President without further interdepartmental or National Security Council clearance. Only after the President had read it and, presumably, endorsed its general conclusions was it submitted formally to the National Security Council, but by then it carried the considerable weight of at least presidential sympathy, if not as yet explicit presidential approval.[39]

Securing the support of Congress and the general public was another matter, one to which the authors of NSC-68 gave considerable thought. The document's conclusions should be stated "simply, clearly, and in . . . 'Hemingway sentences,'" Robert Lovett told the drafting committee. "[I]f we can sell every useless article known to man in large quantities, we should be able to sell our very fine story in large quantities." Edward W. Barrett, the Assistant Secretary of State for Public Affairs, saw the campaign as proceeding in two stages: the first would be to "build up a full public awareness of the problem," the second would be for the government then "to come forward with positive steps to be taken just as soon as the atmosphere is right." But it was important to have "at least the broad proposals for action well in hand before the psychological 'scare campaign' is started."[40]

* NSC-68 was not declassified until 1975. It was first published in the *Naval War College Review*, XXVII (May–June, 1975), 51–108.

The term "scare campaign" may have been a bit strong for what was actually intended, but there is no question that the administration did seek to present the issues in dramatic, even exaggerated, terms. "If we made our points clearer than truth," Acheson later acknowledged, "we did not differ from most other educators and could hardly do otherwise."[41] In a series of public speeches and appearances before Congressional committees in the spring of 1950, the Secretary of State conveyed the essence of NSC-68, along with broad evocations of the need to defend "the free world": "We are children of freedom. We cannot be safe except in an environment of freedom. . . . We believe that all people in the world are entitled to as much freedom, to develop in their own way, as we want ourselves."[42] It had been Acheson, of course, who three years earlier had been instrumental in picturing the Truman Doctrine as part of the struggle between "democracy" and "totalitarianism"; NSC-68 simplified the distinction still further with its references to the "free" and the "slave" worlds.[43] The terms bothered James B. Conant, one of the consultants to the drafting committee: was the American objective then, he wondered, to "democratize everyone"? Nitze assured him that it was not, but pointed out that "if we had objectives only for the purpose of repelling invasion and not to create a better world, the will to fight would be lessened."[44]

The problem with terms like "free world," as Conant suggested, was that they confused perceptions of fundamental interest: was American security contingent on having a homogenous world modeled on itself, or did it require merely balanced diversity? Put in those terms, the authors of NSC-68 would not have hesitated to answer in favor of the latter. But the administration's public rhetoric—rhetoric now explicitly sanctioned by NSC-68—could not help but convey a very different impression: the administration appeared, as a consequence, to be sliding into the very universalism it had earlier rejected. The immediate tactical objective of winning public and Congressional support for increasing the military budget took precedence over the administration's long-term interest in having the public understand clearly the ultimate goals of American foreign policy, and the limitations on American power.

V

As it happened, NSC-68's advocates did not have to work as hard as anticipated to win support for it thanks to unexpected help from the Soviet Union. It is clear beyond doubt now that Stalin authorized the North Korean invasion of South Korea;[45] it is also clear that that event ensured the implementation of NSC-68. Indeed, this latter outcome was so serendipitous that some students of the subject have implied complicity on the part of American officials, either in Washington or Tokyo, in bringing it about.[46] There is no evidence to support this argument other than the dubious assumption that effects invariably proceed from conscious intent, but it is true that President Truman had not formally approved NSC-68 at the time the fighting broke out in Korea,* that his advisers had foreseen difficulties in getting Congress to fund it, and that the attack across the 38th parallel caused both of these things to happen.

The reason was the remarkable manner in which the Korean War appeared to validate several of NSC-68's most important conclusions. One of these was the argument that all interests had become equally vital, that any further shift in the balance of power, no matter how small, could upset the entire structure of postwar international relations. There was almost immediate agreement in Washington that Korea, hitherto regarded as a peripheral interest, had by the nature of the attack on it become vital if American credibility elsewhere was not to be questioned. "To sit by while Korea is overrun by unprovoked armed attack," Dulles warned, "would start [a] disastrous chain of events leading most probably to world war." Even Kennan acknowledged that "if these developments proceed in a way favorable to Soviet purposes and prestige and unfavorable to our own, there will scarcely be any theater of the east-west conflict which will not be adversely affected thereby." To a nation still recoiling from the "loss" of China, still brooding over the "lessons" of Munich, Korea quickly became a symbol of resolve regardless of its military-strategic significance. As the President told a national radio-television audience in September: "If aggression were allowed to succeed in Korea, it would be an open invitation to new acts of aggression elsewhere. . . . We cannot hope to maintain our own freedom if freedom elsewhere is wiped out."[47]

The North Korean attack also confirmed NSC-68's assumption— shared, in this case, by Kennan—that the Soviet Union might resort to war by proxy, even in the face of American nuclear superiority. Estimates of Soviet purposes in Korea varied. The objective could be simply to humiliate the United States in an area where the Russians had not expected a response. It could be a feint designed to lure American forces away from some more vital area, prior to an attack there. Or it could be intended as

---

* Truman's approval, by then a formality, came on September 30, 1950. (*FRUS: 1950,* I, 400.)

one of a series of actions designed to tie down American forces in peripheral theaters, thereby weakening Washington's ability to act where vital interests were at stake. Whatever the case, there was general agreement, as Acheson told the Cabinet in July, "that the present world situation is one of extreme danger and tension which, either by Soviet desire or by the momentum of events arising from the Korean situation . . . , could present the United States with new outbreaks of aggression possibly up to and including general hostilities."[48]

Finally, the fighting in Korea reinforced NSC-68's argument that existing U.S. forces were inadequate: atomic weapons alone would not deter limited aggression, and Washington lacked the conventional means necessary to cover all contingencies. "It is becoming apparent to the world that we do not have the capabilities to face the threat," Acheson warned his Cabinet colleagues; in Europe particularly questions were being raised about the American capacity to respond should a Soviet attack take place. The U.S. had been, after all, in a relatively favorable position to deal with the Korean crisis, since it had air, ground, and naval forces stationed close by. But that situation was unique: "If they had gone into Greece," Acheson admitted to the Senate Foreign Relations Committee, "we don't have any troops within a thousand miles of Greece. We couldn't have done anything about Iran; we would have a terrible time doing anything about Berlin." "What we have had to do," he later observed, "is to construct a defense with inadequate means, trying to guess where each play would come through the line. The result has been amazingly good, but no team can win a pennant this way."[49]

American strategy in Korea was consistent with the spirit of NSC-68, even to the point of duplicating some of that document's contradictions. NSC-68 had called for resisting aggression wherever it occurred, but without unnecessary escalation. Certainly the desire to keep the fighting limited was a prominent feature of the U.S. response in Korea. It influenced the geographical restrictions placed on the scope of the fighting, the decision not to use Chinese Nationalist troops, even the administration's rhetoric, which avoided characterizing the conflict as anything other than a "police action," or charging the Russians with direct responsibility for it.[50] War with the Soviet Union might come, Pentagon strategists acknowledged, but Korea was neither the time nor the place to fight it. As the Joint Chiefs of Staff noted in July, "it would be militarily unsound for the United States to commit large forces against the U.S.S.R. in an area of slight strategic importance, as well as one of Soviet choice."[51]

But the need to limit the fighting had to be weighed against the demands of "credibility," an equally prominent if not always consistent concern of NSC-68. The dilemma arose most keenly with regard to the 38th parallel, the artificial and politically sensitive boundary between North and South Korea. To confine military operations to the south of that line would not only be tactically difficult; it might also project to the world an appearance of weakness. It would be, warned John M. Allison, director of the State Department's Office of Northeast Asian Affairs, "a policy of appeasement . . . a timid, half-hearted policy designed not to provoke the Soviets to war. . . . I fail to see what advantage we gain by a compromise with clear moral principles and a shirking of our duty to make clear once and for all that aggression does not pay."[52] But to cross the line would be to risk either Soviet or Chinese intervention, thereby widening the war. Kennan, among others, warned repeatedly of this possibility, which he thought might occur even before United Nations forces moved into North Korea.[53]* In the end, though, the dictates of military necessity, the pressures of credibility, even, at one point, the fleeting hope that the "liberation" of North Korea might strain the relationship between Beijing and Moscow, caused the National Security Council to endorse and the President to approve military operations as far north of the 38th parallel as seemed prudent without setting off a Soviet or Chinese counteroffensive.[54] There were risks in this strategy, Acheson acknowledged, but "a greater risk would be incurred by showing hesitation and timidity."[55]

The gamble, of course, did not pay off, and the resulting Chinese intervention late in November 1950 imposed a harsh test on the administration's strategy of flexible but limited response. Official reactions ranged from consideration of total withdrawal to expansion of the war into Manchuria and China, and even the possible use of the atomic bomb. (General MacArthur appeared to favor all of these options simultaneously, somewhat to the confusion of his superiors in Washington.)[56] But an abandonment of South Korea, Acheson argued, "would make us the greatest appeasers of all time," while retaliation against China might bring in the Russians on terrain distinctly unfavorable to the United States: "Korea," the Joint Chiefs still insisted, "is not the place to fight a major war."[57] After much discussion, the decision was made to attempt to stabilize the front at or near the 38th parallel, but to make no further effort to "liberate" North

---

* Kennan had earlier not ruled out the possibility of U.S. military action north of the parallel, though. (See his *Memoirs: 1925–1950*, pp. 487–88, and *FRUS: 1950*, I, 326.)

Korea or to spread the war beyond its borders. Once that had been accomplished, the administration would consider negotiations leading toward a cease-fire.[58]

U.S. officials approached these negotiations with a wariness worthy of NSC-68. In January 1951 Acheson made a "murderous" decision to support a United Nations resolution calling for a cease-fire, in the "fervent hope," as he later put it, that the Chinese would reject it.[59] They did, thereby establishing precisely the appearance of American reasonableness and enemy recalcitrance NSC-68 had called for. Several months later, the military situation in Korea had stabilized to the point that the administration could regard itself as having attained a situation of parity, if not strength, so that when the Russians offered in June (after discreet prompting by the State Department, using Kennan as an intermediary) to try to arrange cease-fire negotiations, the U.S. again accepted, this time sincerely.[60] Both sides immediately took uncompromising positions and stuck to them, with the result that talks with the North Koreans and Chinese Communists were still dragging on at the Panmunjom truce tent when the Truman administration left office a year and a half later, as was the fighting. But the President and his advisers had demonstrated to their own satisfaction the capacity of the United States to resist both proxy aggression and the temptations of a wider war, and to that extent their strategy had been consistent with NSC-68.

The Korean War's impact extended far beyond the Korean peninsula, though, and in this wider sphere the influence of NSC-68 was substantial as well. The defense budget showed the effect most dramatically. Even after reading NSC-68 in April 1950, Truman had remained committed to his $13.5 billion ceiling on defense spending for the fiscal year 1951, which would begin on July 1, 1950. "The defense budget next year will be smaller than it is this year," he told a press conference early in May, "and we are continually cutting it by economies."[61]* Korea changed all of that, providing the shock necessary to shift the budgetary arguments of NSC-68 from the realm of theory to that of practical necessity. The President "must ask for money," Acheson told the Cabinet on July 14, "and if it is a question of asking for too little or too much, he should ask for too much."[62]

---

* Secretary of Defense Louis Johnson told Acheson as late as June 5, 1950, that he did not expect defense costs to be increased. (Lucius Battle memorandum, Acheson-Johnson telephone conversation, June 5, 1950, Acheson Papers, Box 65, "Memoranda of conversations: May–June, 1950.")

Truman showed little hesitation in accepting this advice. On July 19, he asked Congress for an additional $10 billion for defense; there followed in turn requests for a supplemental $4 billion for military assistance on August 1, another $1.6 billion for defense on August 4, and $16.8 billion more for that purpose on December 1. The final Congressional defense authorization for fiscal 1951 came to $48.2 billion, a 257 percent increase over the original White House request of $13.5 billion.[63] Projections made at the end of 1950 by the Council of Economic Advisers showed that if the proposed military buildup continued, defense expenditures within a year would be running at an annual rate of around $70 billion. Spending at this level would require cutbacks in the production of automobiles, houses, radios, and television sets, but even so, Keyserling emphasized, "the proposed programs could hardly be described as austere." They fell, he thought, "about half way between 'business as usual' and a really large scale dedication of our enormous economic resources to the defense of our freedoms."[64]

In their discussions of how to deploy this new military strength, Washington officials appeared to lean more toward Kennan's concept of asymmetrical response, with its concern for the conservation of limited resources and its implied distinction between vital and peripheral interests, than toward NSC-68's perception of interests as indivisible. "Our view is that we must not attempt to build up United States military power to defend all these areas where the Soviets in one guise or another might attack," the three service secretaries told Secretary of Defense Johnson on August 1: "We would badly dissipate our strength if we did so." A week earlier Acheson had even acknowledged before the Senate Foreign Relations Committee that the United States might have to cede additional areas to the Russians if it was not to find itself, in the words of his questioner, Senator Henry Cabot Lodge, "hopelessly committed all over the world." And on August 25, the National Security Council approved the conclusion that "The program for the increased military stature and preparedness of the U.S. should proceed without regard to possible temporary relaxation of international tension and without regard to isolated instances of aggression unless the latter provide evidence of the imminence of war."[65]

As had been the case in 1941, a decision had been made well before the fighting began to concentrate strength against the primary adversary in Europe, whatever happened in East Asia. "[T]he main center of our activity at the present time has got to be in Europe," Acheson had told the Senate Foreign Relations Committee early in May:

> We cannot scatter our shots equally all over the world. We just haven't got enough shots to do that. . . . If anything happens in Western Europe the whole business goes to pieces, and therefore our principal effort must be on building up the defenses, building up the economic strength of Western Europe, and so far as Asia is concerned, treating that as a holding operation. . . . This is not satisfying to a great many people who would like us to take vigorous steps everywhere at the same, but we just haven't got the power to do that.[66]

Korea, which could have been a distraction, became instead in the eyes of the administration an opportunity, not so much to build up military strength in Asia (though a moderate increase did, of necessity, take place there), but to bolster the obviously inadequate defenses of Western Europe.

This effort took two distinct, though interconnected, forms. One was the decision, made in September 1950, to send from four to six divisions of U.S. troops to Europe to participate in a NATO defense force to be commanded by an American—almost certain to be General Dwight D. Eisenhower.[67] (Eisenhower was in fact named to the post in December.) This was, Acheson told the British and French foreign ministers, "a complete revolution in American foreign policy and in the attitude of the American people."[68] But the decision had been made in the face of Pentagon opposition to the assumption of new obligations until U.S. military strength had substantially increased.[69] The Defense Department's price for going along was a second major American proposal: the rearmament of West Germany, and the incorporation of its forces into the NATO defense organization.[70] Much of the diplomacy of the next five years would revolve around the delicate question of how to subordinate the West Europeans' atavistic fears of the Germans to their all-too-contemporary fears of the Soviet Union. The underlying strategic concept remained consistent, though, even in the face of Chinese intervention in Korea. It was important to keep in mind, Acheson emphasized later in December, the fact that "our principal antagonist . . . was the Soviet Union and not China." Hence the necessity of defending Great Britain, Western Europe, and the Mediterranean, for "[i]f we did not . . . hold these parts of the world, then it seemed likely not only that we would have no platform from which to operate if we had to against the Soviet Union, but that we would turn great potential strength to the other side."[71]

As Acheson's statements had implied, though, this effort to maintain hierarchies of interests depended on a clear and parsimonious perception of the threat, and this the administration failed to maintain, most notably with regard to Communist China. Acheson himself had remained sensitive to the possibility of Sino-Soviet antagonism. He repeatedly sought to assure the Chinese of American peaceful intentions as MacArthur's forces were driving toward the Yalu (even to the point of invoking the American record in "the brotherly development of border waters"[72]—an example very much dependent, for its credibility, upon short memories), and to warn, along with other administration officials, of the dangers posed to China by Soviet imperialism. "Our objective, of course," one of his advisers noted on the eve of the all-out Chinese offensive in Korea, "is to destroy the basis for a durable alliance between the Soviet Union and China."[73]

But the administration had simultaneously been supporting actions that could only alienate the already suspicious Chinese. One of these had been the decision, announced on June 27, to send the Seventh Fleet to patrol the Taiwan Strait. The administration had justified this move as a military necessity imposed by the fighting in Korea, implying nothing as to the ultimate disposition of the island, but Beijing clearly saw it as confirming a long-standing American policy of supporting Chiang Kai-shek.[74] Another tactical move inconsistent with long-range strategy had been the administration's well-intentioned effort to avoid charging the Russians with direct responsibility for the North Korean invasion—oddly, though, it chose to do this by characterizing the aggression in Korea as "Communist" rather than "Soviet," thereby implying greater complicity than intended on the part of Beijing.[75] Finally, of course, the decision to send United Nations forces across the 38th parallel, made more for reasons of credibility and prestige than from any desire to get into a wider war, nonetheless had that effect. None of these actions was directed specifically against China— even the deployment of the Seventh Fleet had been motivated primarily by concern over the possibility of *Soviet* air bases on a Taiwan controlled by Beijing.[76] But their consequences, in retrospect, are clear: as Kennan had foreseen as early as August 1950, "our policy toward the rival Chinese regimes is one almost sure . . . to strengthen Peiping-Moscow solidarity rather than weaken it."[77]*

---

* It should be noted, though, that Kennan favored the decision to neutralize Taiwan.

China's entry into the Korean War in November put an abrupt end to any immediate hopes of trying to separate Moscow and Beijing. The Chinese had been involved in Korea all along, Acheson told the National Security Council on November 28, but behind them "there was always the Soviet Union which was a more somber consideration. We must consider Korea not in isolation but in the worldwide problem of confronting the Soviet Union as an antagonist."[78] The "wedge" strategy was, for the moment, moribund, but a remarkable post-mortem on it was conducted during the visit of British Prime Minister Clement Attlee to Washington early in December.

Attlee opened the discussion by venturing the suggestion that, despite Chinese intervention, significant differences remained between Beijing and Moscow which would, in time, produce hostility between them. "[I]t was quite true that the Chinese are hard-shelled Marxists," he pointed out, "but it was quite possible that they were not Soviet imperialists. There was a chance of Titoism." Was it wise, Attlee wondered, "to follow a policy which without being effective against China leaves her with Russia as her only friend?" Acheson acknowledged that few American officials would disagree with that analysis. He himself had been more "bloodied" by putting it forward than anyone else. But "the question was not whether this was a correct analysis but whether it was possible to act on it."

One difficulty, Acheson explained, was that the Sino-Soviet split was still a long-range prospect, while military problems in East Asia were immediate. "Perhaps in ten or fifteen years we might see a change in the Chinese attitude but we do not have that time available. . . . If in taking a chance on the long future of China we affect the security of the United States at once, that is a bad bargain." Moreover, the attitude of the American people had to be taken into account. No administration could expect support for a policy of resisting aggression in one part of the world and accepting it in another. "The public mind was not delicate enough to understand such opposing attitudes." Finally, events in East Asia could not be separated from those taking place in other parts of the world. European rearmament was lagging, Franco-German differences remained unresolved, NATO needed a supreme commander and troops in formation. Chinese intervention "would provide a better chance to get our people behind the effort and to draw on the power from the United States which is the only source of power. It is vitally important to hold the United States in this effort." Truman seconded Acheson's arguments, but with characteristic brevity. The Chinese, he told Attlee, "are satellites of Russia and will be satellites as long as the present Peiping regime is in power. . . . The Chinese do, of course, have national feelings. The Russians cannot dominate them forever, but that is a long-range view and does not help us just now."[79]

Here, in a nutshell, were the fundamental elements of NSC-68: the presumption of Western weakness; the fear that the coordinated short-term actions of adversaries were too dangerous to wait for inevitable strains to develop between them; the conviction that strengthening alliances should precede efforts to resolve differences with adversaries, and that adversary hostility could actually be helpful in that process; the belief that the American people were too unsophisticated to grasp distinctions between hierarchies of interest, varieties of aggression, or gradations of response; the pursuit of credibility for its own sake. Despite the fact that the administration had resolved not to let Korea become the occasion for getting bogged down in a peripheral war with a secondary adversary, this was precisely what happened. And it happened, one suspects, because of the extent to which the premises of NSC-68 had come to overshadow, and modify, the original strategy of containment.

VI

NSC-68's version of containment did not escape challenge, though, either within or outside the administration. Serious questions were raised about the strategy, most conspicuously by Republican "unilateralists"*—followers of General Douglas MacArthur, Senator Robert A. Taft, and former President Herbert Hoover—more effectively, as it turned out, by Republican "internationalists" centered around John Foster Dulles, but also, to a surprising extent, from inside the Truman administration itself. Despite differences on specifics, these criticisms all had in common concern over the loss of initiative implied in the administration's strategy, its apparently indefinite duration and mounting costs, and the implications posed thereby for the society the strategy was supposed to protect.

MacArthur's criticisms revolved around the administration's failure to share his view that Asia, not Europe, had become the decisive theater of

---

* I prefer this term to the more common "isolationists" or "neo-isolationists," since this particular form of "isolationism" might well have widened rather than restricted United States overseas involvement, especially in Asia. For the phenomenon in general, see Norman A. Graebner, *The New Isolationism: A Study in Politics and Foreign Policy Since 1950* (New York: 1956).

action in the Cold War. "This group of Europhiles," he complained in December 1950, "just will not recognize that it is Asia which has been selected for the test of Communist power and that if all Asia falls Europe would not have a chance—either with or without American assistance." He drew from this the conclusion that the United States should abandon its self-imposed restrictions on military action, blockade the Chinese mainland, make use of Chinese Nationalist manpower in Korea and elsewhere, bomb industrial targets inside China, and, if necessary, even withdraw from Korea in preparation for an offensive to be launched upon more favorable terrain. The Chinese, he insisted, were already engaged in all-out war; the Russians would fight only in defense of their own interests, which did not necessarily parallel those of the Chinese. Failure to choose this course would mean United States involvement in "an indecisive campaign with the cost of holding a position in Korea becoming, in the long run, infinitely greater than were we to fight back along conventional lines."[80]

It was, of course, the repeated public expression of these sentiments, against explicit official orders, that brought about MacArthur's abrupt relief from command in April 1951; the resulting Congressional hearings, conducted jointly by the Senate Foreign Relations and Armed Services Committees, provided a conspicuous forum both for the general and for the administration. In the course of his testimony, MacArthur made clear his conviction that Washington's strategy in Korea was subversive of the ends sought there: "the interests of this country are involved in saving the lives of its sons, rather than embarking upon an indefinite, indecisive campaign which will sacrifice thousands and thousands of additional American lives." War, the general insisted, had become a form of "mutual suicide"; the choice was "to let it go on indefinitely, destroying the fabric of society, or . . . to end it." What weakened MacArthur's argument was the fact that he was proposing to end the war by escalating it, a cure that seemed to many worse than the disease. In the single most memorable statement of the hearings, General Omar Bradley made the point with admirable precision: "this strategy would involve us in the wrong war, at the wrong place, at the wrong time, and with the wrong enemy." Acheson was even more succinct: "The whole effort of our policy is to prevent war and not have it occur."[81]

The administration succeeded with these arguments in discrediting MacArthur's recommendations, but not the fears of a costly and indecisive land war that had given rise to them. Instead these fears became the basis of a major Republican attack on the administration's foreign policy in 1951 and 1952. Former President Hoover set the tone late in December 1950, when he argued, in opposition to plans to send additional troops to Europe, that any attempt to engage communist armies on continental battlefields would not only strain limited economic resources; it "would be the graveyard of millions of American boys and would end in the exhaustion of this Gibraltar of Western Civilization." The alternative was to make use of American strengths—air and naval power—to control the Western hemisphere, the Atlantic and Pacific Oceans, and the island outposts of Great Britain, Japan, Formosa, and the Philippines; remaining non-communist mainland areas would have to rely primarily upon themselves for their defense. The implication was that the entire Eurasian continent could come under Soviet domination without significant harm to American security interests: "They can no more reach Washington in force than we can reach Moscow."[82]

A more moderate but more influential critique of administration policy came from Senator Taft, one of the most powerful Republicans in the Senate and a leading contender for the 1952 G.O.P. presidential nomination. In a series of speeches delivered during 1951, and in a book published at the end of that year, Taft too warned strongly of the dangers of protracted, limited wars, and of the loss of strategic initiative they entailed. "The first principle of military strategy," he pointed out, "is not to fight on the enemy's chosen battleground, where he has his greatest strength." Even more emphatically than Hoover, Taft stressed the economic and social costs of such a strategy: "there is a definite limit to what a government can spend in time of peace and still maintain a free economy, without inflation and with at least some elements of progress in standards of living and in education, welfare, housing, health, and other activities in which the people are vitally interested." No nation could "be constantly prepared to undertake a full-scale war at any moment and still hope to maintain any of the other purposes . . . for which nations are founded. . . . [A]n all-out war program in time of peace might mean the final and complete destruction of those liberties which it is the very purpose of the preparation to protect."

But there were major inconsistencies in Taft's program. Like Hoover, he opposed involvement in Eurasian land wars, called for greater reliance on air and naval power and less reliance on allies, and appeared to endorse an island stronghold concept. Yet he came, in the end, to support the administration's decision to send four additional divisions to NATO, and during the spring and summer of 1951 seemed to be moving toward MacArthur's prescriptions for widening the war in Asia. Very likely domestic political considerations had something to do with these inconsistencies: Taft was determined to attract the maximum possible support for his candidacy, and was not above bending principles occasionally in order to get it. Still, on one point Taft remained firm, and in it his views paralleled not only those of MacArthur and Hoover but also Kennan's: this was the need for a greater sensitivity than the Truman administration had shown so far to the relationship between ends and means. "An unwise and overambitious foreign policy," he wrote, "and particularly the effort to do more than we are able to do, is the one thing which might in the end destroy our armies and prove a real threat to the liberty of the people of the United States."[83]

The "unilateralism" of MacArthur, Hoover, and Taft coexisted uneasily inside the Republican party with the "internationalist" views held by followers of Governor Thomas E. Dewey of New York, the party's unsuccessful presidential candidate in 1944 and 1948, and Senator Arthur H. Vandenberg. This group also worried about loss of initiative and rising costs, but was unable to bring itself to write off whole sections of the Eurasian continent, or to give East Asia priority over Europe. By 1952, John Foster Dulles had emerged as its chief spokesman. He had been, in a way, a symbol of bipartisan cooperation on foreign policy, alternating service to his party during presidential campaigns with duties at the United Nations and in the State Department—most recently in connection with the Japanese peace treaty. But Dulles broke with the administration early in 1952, and in May of that year published a major critique of the Truman-Acheson approach to containment in a *Life* magazine article entitled "A Policy of Boldness."

Dulles began by echoing "unilateralist" complaints about the costs of existing policies. "[G]igantic expenditures" were unbalancing the budget, lowering the value of the dollar, and discouraging incentive; moreover, the resulting concentration on military matters threatened civil liberties at home and frightened valuable allies overseas. All of this might have been tolerable if the effort was producing results, but it was not: "Our present negative policies will never end the type of sustained offensive which Soviet Communism is mounting; they will never end the peril nor bring relief from the exertions which devour our economic, political and moral vitals. Ours are treadmill policies which, at best, might perhaps keep us in the same place until we drop exhausted." There was no question about the ultimate superiority of the United States and its allies in both material and moral capacity; the very repression communist leaders felt obliged to inflict upon their people reflected profound insecurity. But the Russians and their satellites (Dulles included China in this category) did have short-term advantages in terms of manpower and interior lines: "we cannot build a 20,000 mile Maginot Line or match the Red armies, man for man, gun for gun and tank for tank at any particular time or place their general staff selects. To attempt that would mean real strength nowhere and bankruptcy everywhere."

Dulles's solution was asymmetry, but of a particular kind: "the free world [must] develop the will and organize the means to retaliate instantly against open aggression by Red armies, so that, if it occurred anywhere, we could and would strike back where it hurts, by means of our own choosing." This could be done most efficiently by relying on atomic weapons, and on the strategic air and naval power necessary to deliver them. Such instruments had created "vast new possibilities of organizing a community power to stop open aggression before it starts and reduce, to the vanishing point, the risk of general war." Strategic weapons so far had been developed only for the purpose of fighting an all-out war; what had been overlooked was their potential, at far more reasonable cost than existing strategies, of preventing such a war. "If that catastrophe occurs, it will be because we have allowed these new and awesome forces to become the ordinary killing tools of the soldier when, in the hands of the statesmen, they could serve as effective political weapons in defense of the peace."[84]

Publicly, the Truman administration maintained its position in the face of these criticisms. "[T]he real threat to our security isn't the danger of bankruptcy," President Truman told a nationwide radio and television audience in March 1952:

> It's the danger of Communist aggression. If communism is allowed to absorb the free nations, one by one, then we would be isolated from our sources of supply and detached from our friends. Then we would have to take defense measures which might really bankrupt our economy, and change our way of life so that we wouldn't recognize it as American any longer. That's the very thing we're trying to keep from happening.

And, again, in April: "it is not true that our national security program costs so much that it will wreck the economy. On the contrary, the civilian side of our economy is stronger than it has ever been." Republican budget-cutting arguments, the President concluded with characteristic pungency, were "a bunch of hooey."[85]

But privately, administration officials had for some time shared many of their critics' concerns. As early as July 1950, Acheson had pointed out to Paul Nitze that while the United States had no choice but to hang on in Korea, even in the face of Chinese or Soviet intervention, the effort would be expensive, would tie down troops needed elsewhere, and would be difficult to justify domestically: "In other words, as the Virginians say, we have bought a colt." By November, Nitze himself was worrying over "the enormous cost" of providing the forces called for by NSC-68: "Is there anything which can be done, if necessary by radical measures, to reduce the extremely high cost of supporting combat units?" Acheson was painfully conscious of the dangers of being sucked into an indefinite land war in Asia—"there would be no end to it and it would bleed us dry," Truman recalls him saying at a National Security Council meeting on the day of full-scale Chinese intervention in Korea. And several days later, Acheson warned the Joint Chiefs of Staff that "the great trouble is that we are fighting the wrong nation. We are fighting the second team, whereas the real enemy is the Soviet Union."[86]

These concerns produced a major review of East Asian strategy in the spring of 1951 that brought the administration surprisingly close to MacArthur's recommendations just at the time it was seeking publicly to refute them. On May 17, 1951, while the MacArthur hearings were still underway, President Truman approved NSC-48/5, an overall restatement of Asian policy which endorsed existing limitations on the fighting in Korea but provided that, should Chinese aggression break out elsewhere, the United States would consider:

1. Imposing a blockade of the China coast by naval and air forces.
2. Military action against selected targets held by Communist China outside of Korea.
3. Participation defensively or offensively of the Chinese Nationalist forces, and the necessary operational assistance to make them effective.

Early in January 1952 Acheson carried this approach even further, informing British Prime Minister Winston Churchill that the United States was considering bombing Chinese military targets in the event the Korean armistice negotiations broke down, or if there should be a violation of an armistice agreement. It was not the American intention to use atomic bombs against China, General Bradley added, "since up to the present time no suitable targets were presented. If the situation changed in any way, so that suitable targets were presented, a new situation would arise."[87]*

The administration's flirtation with "MacArthurism" should not be exaggerated. It did not connote approval of the general's "Asia-first" strategy; rather, the intent was to get back to the more important business of containing the Russians in Europe by ending diversions of men and resources into inconclusive struggles with the Chinese. Nor was there any inclination to favor such measure over a negotiated cease-fire in Korea if that could be arranged. These were contingency plans, designed to deal either with a failure of negotiations or with an outbreak of aggression elsewhere. Still, they did reflect a nagging suspicion that Republican critics might be right in charging that the United States, by trying to respond symmetrically to proxy aggression, was losing control over the disposition of its own forces and over the expenditures necessary to sustain them.

Concern over limited resources also developed with respect to Europe during 1951, as it became apparent that the NATO alliance could not, without endangering economic recovery, support increases in military spending proportional to those taking place in the United States. The administration chose not to follow the advice of the Republican right to cut Europe adrift, though; instead it agreed to a scaling down of proposed force levels to bring them more into line with economic capabilities. The danger of a Soviet attack in Europe appeared to be declining anyway, Acheson told Churchill in January 1952; therefore it seemed logical "not to attempt to create forces beyond the capacity of ourselves and our allies to maintain, but to create sufficient force to make any action by the Soviet Union in Europe too dangerous to be attempted."[88]

Still, these intimations that means might not in fact be indefinitely expandable failed to shake the administration's faith in the fundamental validity of NSC-68, a fact that became clear in the summer of 1952 when the National Security Council undertook a complete review of that document. The resulting study, NSC-135/3, confirmed NSC-68's conclusion that the

*Curiously, NSC-48/5 and its accompanying staff study contained the most elaborate discussion yet of how to exploit tensions between Beijing and Moscow. (See *FRUS: 1951*, VI, 35, 47–52.) But as Acheson explained to Churchill, "Chinese intervention in Korea had made this hope seem very distant and impossible of attainment at the present. I did not think that over any period of time with which we could now be concerned it was possible to create a divergence between the two communist groups. Mr. Churchill and Mr. Eden agreed with this." (Acheson memorandum, conversation with Churchill and Anthony Eden, Washington, January 6, 1952, Acheson Papers, Box 66, "Memoranda of conversations, January, 1952.")

United States and its allies had the capacity to do whatever was required to resist Soviet expansion "for whatever length of time proves to be necessary." Indeed, even "acceleration and upward adjustment of our national security programs as a whole, if necessary, are well within our capacity and can be accomplished without serious adverse effects on the U.S. economy." Consequently, the ability of "the free world" to maintain its position would depend upon "(a) its capacity to stand firm against Soviet political warfare, which may be intensified by the increasing Soviet atomic capabilities, (b) a greater capability and greater willingness than have been demonstrated to commit appropriate forces and material for limited objectives, and (c) its ability to develop greater stability in peripheral or other unstable areas."[89]

Following the Republican victory at the polls in November, the administration refined the conclusions of NSC-135/3, tied them to specific recommendations for action, and presented them to the incoming Eisenhower administration as NSC-141. This was, of course, a valedictory, but it was an unrepentant one: NSC-141 was the most uncompromising expression yet of the interlocking logic of expandable means and symmetrical response. Existing programs, it acknowledged, were still not adequate to ensure American security: efforts were needed to bolster local forces of resistance in the Middle East and East Asia as well as Europe, to strengthen the continental defenses of the United States against air attack, and to initiate a large-scale civil defense program. NSC-141 made no cost estimates for these programs as a whole (the plan for continental defense alone was projected to cost an additional $8.5 billon through 1955), but it was clear that should they be implemented, Republican hopes for cutting the budget would have to be abandoned. "A capability for varied and flexible application of our striking power is essential," the document pointedly noted, "both because of the wide variety of situations which may confront us and because such a capability offers the best chance to convince the Soviets that they cannot hope to destroy our striking power by surprise attack."

NSC-141 was, in one sense, an admission of failure—after two-and-a-half years of strenuous effort, the nation still had not attained an adequate level of security. But it was also a staunch reaffirmation of the essential correctness of the Truman administration's strategy: the problem, it implied, had not been NSC-68, but the inconsistency with which it had been applied. There was in fact no distinction among European, Asian, and continental American interests; all were now equally threatened; all required a firm but non-provocative response. What the nation could not afford was a defense force capable only of restraining local aggression and fighting a nuclear war. The range of American interests in the world was much wider than that: "to the greatest possible extent, we must accordingly develop flexible, multi-purpose forces to meet the varied threats that confront us."[90]

VII

A year after leaving the State Department, Dean Acheson told a group of former colleagues gathered to reminisce about their years in Washington that "the thing to do was to get on and do what had to be done as quickly and effectively as you could, and if you stopped to analyze what you were doing . . . [a]ll you did was to weaken and confuse your will and not get anywhere." The topic under discussion was whether President Truman should have asked for Congressional authorization of military action in Korea, but the statement reflected Acheson's general proclivity for action almost as an end in itself, and his corresponding tendency to avoid reconsiderations, second thoughts, and above all self-doubt.[91] This had been largely the basis of his disagreements with Kennan, for whom such traits were a chronic affliction; it had also been one of the reasons for Acheson's excellent relationship with Harry S. Truman, a man of emphatically similar character. And it was, as well, a distinctive feature of NSC-68, and of the Truman administration's whole approach to national security policy after June 1950.

There was in the administration very much a sense of direction without destination—of marching forthrightly forward into unknown areas, without any clear sense of what the ultimate objective was, how long it would take to achieve it, or what it would cost. As one of Acheson's advisers put it, at the time of the decision to cross the 38th parallel, when "threatened by dark and menacing uncertainties, the part of both prudence and wisdom is to proceed confidently and quietly about one's own business." Acheson himself used a different but equally open-ended analogy a year later in a talk to students at the National War College:

> Collective security is like a bank account. It is kept alive by the resources which are put into it. In Korea the Russians presented a check which was drawn on the bank account of collective security. The Russians thought the check would bounce. . . . But to their great surprise, the teller paid it. The important thing was that the check was paid. The importance will be nothing

if the next check is not paid and if the bank account is not kept strong and sufficient to cover all checks which are drawn upon it.[92]

If it occurred to any of the Secretary of State's audience to wonder why the United States should be issuing blank checks to its adversaries in the first place, or how it proposed to keep its account balanced indefinitely in the face of such demands on it, they were too polite to ask.

"What we are trying to do," Acheson told the war college students, "is to find ways in which our power as a nation may match our responsibilities as a nation. . . . The job before all of us today is to learn the ins and outs of power and policy so that our nation's intentions and the capacities to achieve these intentions may be brought into balance." But this is just where the Truman administration failed. Beginning with a perception of implacable threat and expandable means, it derived a set of interests so vast as to be beyond the nation's political will, if not theoretical capacity, to sustain—as the election of 1952 showed. It was a fact that "ends always tend to outrun means," Acheson acknowledged belatedly in October 1952: "We are always forced to choose between a great many goals . . . all of which are good, and those which we can accomplish with the limited means at our command. . . . Then you come to this very, very difficult question of . . . choice: What to do first, what to defer until later, what to give up altogether."[93] It was precisely these choices that had been avoided since June of 1950, though; it would now be up to the Eisenhower administration to determine whether the "policy of boldness" of its new Secretary of State—John Foster Dulles—provided any better method.

Eisenhower, Dulles, and the New Look

Dwight D. Eisenhower did not run for president in 1952 out of any burning sense of dissatisfaction with the Truman administration's approach to containment. With the single exception of its China policy, about which he had had private reservations, Eisenhower had supported each of the administration's major diplomatic and strategic initiatives; indeed, since February 1951 he himself had been responsible for implementing its European strategy as NATO Supreme Commander. The general's reasons for allowing his name to be placed before the 1952 Republican national convention had more to do with his determination to keep the nomination out of the hands of Robert A. Taft, whom Eisenhower regarded as an isolationist; his concern over Truman's domestic programs, which he thought were leading to socialism; and his belief that survival of the two-party system required an end to twenty years of Democratic rule.[1]

Presidents are rarely made by endorsing their predecessors, though, and Eisenhower soon came under pressure to put "distance" between himself and the incumbent administration in the area of foreign affairs. To this end, he enlisted the aid of the Republican whose criticisms of containment he found least objectionable—the advocate of "boldness," John Foster Dulles. Certainly Dulles's promises of greater effectiveness at less cost appealed to Eisenhower, who had long nursed a vague sense of uneasiness about the country's ability to sustain indefinitely large military expenditures. He also shared Dulles's antipathy for the unilateralism of Hoover and Taft: "any thought of 'retiring within our own borders,'" he wrote, "will certainly lead to disaster for the U.S.A." Nor did he sympathize with those on the Republican Right who wanted to take military action against mainland China, thereby producing "a blundering, stumbling crash into a senseless war."[2]

But Eisenhower did have strong initial reservations about Dulles's theory of asymmetrical strategic deterrence (already coming to be known, confusingly, as the doctrine of "retaliation"). "I . . . was as deeply impressed as ever with the directness and simplicity of your approach to such complex problems," he wrote with artful artlessness after reading a preliminary draft of Dulles's *Life* magazine article.

> There is only one point that bothered me. . . . It is this: What should we do if Soviet political aggression, as in Czechoslovakia, successfully chips away exposed positions of the free world? So far as our resulting economic situation is concerned, such an eventuality would be just as bad for us as if the area had been captured by force. To my mind, this is the case where the theory of "retaliation" falls down.

"You put your finger on the weak point in my presentation," Dulles replied, and promised to remedy the deficiency in the final draft. The published article did not clarify the matter, though, and Eisenhower had to warn again that "exclusive reliance upon a mere power of retaliation is not a complete answer to the broad Soviet threat." When Dulles allowed the term "retaliatory striking power" to creep into the Republican platform, Eisenhower was furious—"I'll be damned if I run on that," he told amazed aides at the Chicago convention. The offending term was quickly removed but the idea, as subsequent events would reveal, remained firmly entrenched in Dulles's mind.[3]

Dulles had coupled his endorsement of strategic asymmetry with an appeal for "liberation" of the Soviet satellites, motivated more by determination to lure East European voting blocs away from the Democrats than from any realistic expectations of "rolling back" Moscow's sphere of influence. Eisenhower had misgivings about this, too. He reluctantly accepted language in the Republican platform condemning the "negative, futile and immoral policy of 'containment' which abandons countless human beings to a despotism and godless terrorism," but felt obliged to remind Dulles that "liberation" could only come by "peaceful means"—a point made clearly in Dulles's *Life* article but not in several of his speeches on behalf of the Republican ticket. Eisenhower kept Dulles at a distance during the rest of the campaign, and following his landslide victory over Adlai Stevenson in November, hesitated three weeks before naming his Secretary of

State, in the end selecting Dulles only after his advisers had warned him that the Taft wing of the party would accept no one else.[4]

It was largely politics, then, not intellectual affinity, that brought about the curious Eisenhower-Dulles "partnership."* Despite initial ambivalences it grew to be remarkably close, though never entirely free from the differences that had surfaced during the campaign. It was Dulles who primarily determined the *nature* of administration strategy—the selection of responses with which to counter threats. But the President possessed the keener *sense* of strategy of the two—of how responses were to be correlated with fundamental interests—and he also carefully retained ultimate authority, not hesitating to override his Secretary of State when he thought it appropriate to do so. Appearances to the contrary notwithstanding, therefore, Dulles never enjoyed the virtually free hand in foreign affairs that Truman had accorded Acheson after 1949.[5] Dulles was more tenacious than Eisenhower, though, and could at times get his way even in the face of presidential resistance through sheer pertinacity and repetition. The result was an amalgam: a strategy the product of two personally friendly but temperamentally very different men, reflecting strains and compromises as well as forbearance, cooperation, and mutual respect.

I

"Conceiving the defense of freedom, like freedom itself, to be one and indivisible, we hold all continents and peoples in equal regard and honor. We reject any insinuation that one race or another, one people or another, is in any sense inferior or expendable." So Dwight D. Eisenhower defined the range of American interests in his inaugural address on January 20, 1953. The statement served several functions. It was, first of all, a firm rejection of "fortress America" concepts that had been circulating within the Republican party in recent years, a position entirely appropriate for a man

---

* Emmet John Hughes recalls that in the period between the election and the inauguration, "Dulles apparently made one consistent impact upon Eisenhower: he bored him. Time after time, as Dulles spoke, I watched the all-too-expressive face of the President-elect and the gestures of impatience made almost more plain by the half-successful efforts to suppress them. His reactions were always the same—the brisk nodding of the head, in a manner designed to nudge a slow voice faster onward toward some obvious conclusion . . . the restless rhythm of the pencil tapping his knee . . . the slow glaze across the blue eyes, signaling the end of all mental contact . . . finally, the patient fixing of the eyes on the most distant corner of the ceiling, there to rest until the end of the Dulles dissertation." (*The Ordeal of Power: A Political Memoir of the Eisenhower Years* [New York: 1963], p. 51.)

who had run for president to save the party, and the country, from Robert A. Taft. It was as well, though, a reiteration of criticisms Taft and other Republicans had advanced against the Truman administration's "Europe-first" policy—an approach, they charged, that had led to the "loss" of China, the "no-win" strategy in Korea, and the relief of General MacArthur. Finally, Eisenhower's declaration served notice that his administration, like the authors of NSC-68, believed the world balance of power to be so delicately poised that no further victories for communism anywhere could be tolerated without upsetting it. As Eisenhower put it six months later, in language both his predecessor and successor in the White House could have endorsed: "As there is no weapon too small, no arena too remote, to be ignored, there is no free nation too humble to be forgotten."[6]

This did not mean that the United States had to dominate the world in order to be secure in it. Both Eisenhower and Dulles saw the capacity to tolerate diversity as a strength, one not shared by the Russians. "We do not assume that we have any mandate to run the world," the Secretary of State insisted. "Nothing indeed would be less in keeping with our traditions and our ideals." Eisenhower was particularly sensitive to the possibility that the United States might become too overbearing in its dealings with other countries. "We are [so] proud of our guarantees of freedom in thought and speech and worship," he wrote in a note to himself early in 1954, "that, unconsciously, we are guilty of one of the greatest errors that ignorance can make—we assume that our standard of values is shared by all other humans in the world." Later that year, he resorted to a military analogy to make the same point: "A platoon leader doesn't get his platoon to go that way by getting up and saying, 'I am smarter, I am bigger, I am stronger, I am the leader.' He gets men to go with him because they want to do it for him, because they believe in him." The Truman administration, he argued, had talked too loudly about world leadership. "This business of saying we are out in front, we know all the answers, you boys come along . . . they are just not going to do it, that I can tell you just from the knowledge of people I have."[7]

But toleration of diversity could not extend to those communist regimes that were puppets of Moscow, and hence the very negation of diversity. "Already one-third of the world is dominated by an imperialist brand of communism," Dulles had warned in 1952; "already the free world has been so shrunk that no further substantial parts of it can be lost without danger to the whole that remains." Eisenhower put this thought in more

memorable form two years later with his famous comparison of the Indochina situation to a row of dominoes, set up in such a way that if the first
one toppled, others followed. "Where in hell can you let the Communists
chip away any more?" he asked Congressional leaders in April 1954. "We
just can't stand it." Early in 1955, he expanded on the theme in a confidential letter to his old comrade-in-arms, Winston Churchill:

> We have come to the point where every additional backward step must be
> deemed a defeat for the Western world. In fact, it is a triple defeat. First, we
> lose a potential ally. Next, we give to an implacable enemy another recruit.
> Beyond this, every such retreat creates in the minds of neutrals the fear that
> we do not mean what we say when we pledge our support to people who
> want to remain free.

Two decades earlier, the world had entertained the "fatuous hope" that
Hitler, Mussolini, and the Japanese war lords might let it live in peace.
"We saw the result." Yet, "the Communist sweep over the world since
World War II has been much faster and much more relentless than the
1930['s] sweep of the dictators." It was necessary "to look some of these
unpleasant facts squarely in the face and meet them exactly as our Grand
Alliance of the 40's met our enemies and vanquished them."[8]*

The assumption behind these pronouncements was a familiar one: that
the United States could not, as Hoover and Taft had suggested, survive
with its institutions intact in a predominantly hostile world. But why not?
Precisely what would be the danger? For Dulles, it was the threat of moral
bankruptcy: "A United States which could be an inactive spectator while
the barbarians overran and desecrated the cradle of our Christian civilization would not be the kind of a United States which could defend itself."
There were, he thought, "certain basic moral concepts which all people
and nations can and do comprehend, and to which it is legitimate to appeal as providing some common standard of international conduct." A foreign policy framed without reference to those standards would be incapable of rallying support from the American people or their allies; the
result would be confusion and ultimate collapse. The role of power, Dulles
believed, was to give moral principles time to take root; once that had

---

* On January 7, 1955, Eisenhower approved a National Security Council paper containing the
statement that "As the lines between the Communist bloc and the Western coalition have
come to be more clearly drawn over the last few years, a situation has arisen in which any further Communist territorial gain would have an unfavorable impact within the free world that
might be out of all proportion to the strategic or economic significance of the territory lost."
(NSC-5501, "Basic National Security Policy," *FRUS: 1955–57*, XIX, 28.)

happened, force would not be necessary. "Where, however, there are many who do not accept moral principles, then that creates the need of force to protect those who do."[9]*

Eisenhower agreed that "we are a product and a representative of the Judaic-Christian civilization, and it does teach some concern for your brother. And I believe in that." But when asked to specify irreducible American interests in the world, the Chief Executive almost always emphasized economic rather than moral considerations. "The minimum requirement," he had written to Dulles in 1952, "is that we are able to trade freely, in spite of anything Russia may do, with those areas from which we obtain the raw materials that are vital to our economy." Press conference questions on this point regularly elicited presidential lectures on the critical importance of foreign manganese, cobalt, tin, and tungsten, in terms worthy of and gratifying to future New Left critics of American capitalism.[10] These divergent emphases produced the same effect, though: Eisenhower and Dulles could agree that the chief American interest in the world was access to the world, and that in turn required a world of at least minimal congeniality.

Up to this point, the Eisenhower administration's view of American interests differed little from that found in NSC-68: despite disclaimers of aspirations to world leadership, it was necessary to assume that role to protect the very diversity deemed vital to the nation's survival. But perceptions of means also shape perceptions of interests, and here there was a sharp departure from the practices of the previous administration. NSC-68 had argued that means could be expanded as needed to fit interests; the nation could afford whatever it took to achieve security. In spite of doubts raised within and outside the government, Truman and his principal advisers had remained committed to that proposition through the time they left

* During the 1952 campaign, Dulles had strongly criticized George Kennan's first book, *American Diplomacy: 1900–1950* (Chicago: 1951), which had condemned "legalistic-moralistic" tendencies in American foreign policy. Once again, though, Kennan's prose had failed to convey his meaning. "I have never felt, and trust I have never said, that moral concepts have no place in the conduct of the public affairs of the United States," Kennan wrote in a memorandum which he sent to Dulles. "Let us by all means conduct our national affairs at all times in what we conceive to be a decent, American manner—in a manner that does not represent a degradation of our own tradition or an abuse of our own national ideals—in such a manner that we can live easily with what we have done. . . . [But] let us keep our morality to ourselves. With regard to other nations let us not judge, that we not be judged. Let us not attempt to constitute ourselves the guardians of everyone else's virtue; we have enough trouble to guard our own." (Memorandum of August 18, 1952, enclosed in Kennan to Dulles, October 22, 1952, John Foster Dulles Papers, Box 61, "Kennan" folder.)

office. The new Republican administration found it strongly objection-able, though for several reasons.

First, there remained, in Eisenhower's mind, at least, the lurking fear that the American people might yet find the lures of isolationism irre-sistible if the price of internationalism seemed to be indefinite sacrifice. "[I]t is not easy," he noted in June 1953, "to convince an overwhelming majority of free people, everywhere, that they should pull in their belts, endure marked recessions in living standards, in order that we may at one and the same time develop backward countries and relieve starvation, while bearing the expenses and costs of battle in the more fortunate coun-tries." What made the situation worse was the possibility of prolonged, in-conclusive limited wars: "People grow weary of war, particularly when they see no decisive and victorious end to it." But in the case of Korea, where fighting was still going on, "victory would require such an expansion of the present conflict as to demand, practically, a general mobilization. This means regimentation—and the question arises as to the length of time that we could endure regimentation without losing important parts of our free system." The United States, he commented a year later, "cannot be strong enough to go to every spot in the world, where our enemies may use force or the threat of force, and defend those nations."[11]

Another problem was the unproductive nature of military expenditures in peacetime. The roots of communism, Dulles liked to argue, were not material in nature: "there are passions that cannot be . . . suppressed by foreign guns." Moreover, such spending diverted valuable resources from domestic priorities, as Eisenhower pointed out with unusual eloquence in April 1953:

> Every gun that is made, every warship launched, every rocket fired signi-fies, in the final sense, a theft from those who hunger and are not fed, those who are cold and are not clothed. . . .
>
> The cost of one modern heavy bomber is this: a modern brick school in more than 30 cities.
>
> It is two electric power plants, each serving a town of 60,000 population.
>
> It is two fine, fully equipped hospitals.
>
> It is some 50 miles of concrete highway.
>
> We pay for a single fighter plane with a half million bushels of wheat.
>
> We pay for a single destroyer with new homes that could have housed more than 8,000 people.

Later that year, the President told his budget director that he would like to see a slight increase in funding for housing, public works, and conservation, but "considerable over-all savings in [the Defense] Department." Tanks, guns, planes, and ships brought no lasting security, he insisted. "The most they can do is to protect you in what you have for the moment."[12]

But the most important reason for perceiving means as limited was the belief that unrestrained spending could alter the very nature of American society, either through the debilitating effects of inflation or through regimentation in the form of economic controls. This was probably the most persistent single theme of Eisenhower's public and private utterances while in the White House. It was based on the assumption that economic stability and military strength were inseparable, that if "these two are allowed to proceed in disregard for the other, you then create a situation either of doubtful military strength, or of such precarious economic strength that your military position is in constant jeopardy." No nation could defend itself unless it could make a living. But "how to make a living and bear this expense? . . . If you can't make a living in the long run, your people are ground down, and you have a new form of government." Dulles put it more bluntly: "If economic stability goes down the drain, everything goes down the drain."[13]

Keyserling's answer, of course, had been that government spending could stimulate the economy, thereby generating additional revenues and eventually overcoming whatever short-term budget deficits had been incurred. But to the fiscally conservative Eisenhower administration, this was not a persuasive argument. There was no way to determine in advance how much "inflationary borrowing" or "repressive taxation" an economic system could stand, a National Security Council study concluded in October 1953: "The higher the level of expenditures, the greater is the need for sound policies and the greater are the dangers of miscalculations and mischance. These dangers are now substantial." "I read . . . that . . . Mr. Keyserling has a plan for spending a good many more billion dollars, for reducing taxes, and balancing the budget at the same time," Eisenhower told a press conference in 1955. "That I would doubt was a good economic plan."[14]

The roots of this concern about means destroying ends varied. Certainly the Republican party was not hospitable to Keynesian ideas during this period—the situation it confronted, Representative Dewey Short told the President in 1953, was like "taking over a hussy who had spent all her husband's money and run up a lot of bills at the local department store." Nor were Eisenhower's friends in the business community, with whom he had formed comfortable ties since the war, sympathetic to such notions. Secretary of the Treasury George M. Humphrey's tireless devotion to balanced budgets reinforced these views: it was said of Humphrey that he feared deficits almost more than he feared the communists.[15] But it would be a mistake to see Eisenhower as merely reflecting the influences of those around him on this issue: he had strong convictions of his own on the proper relationship of ends and means, based on years of training and experience in the military.

Fundamental to these was Eisenhower's understanding of Clausewitz, whom he had studied during long languid years in Panama in the 1920's under the tutelage of a remarkable senior office, Fox Conner.[16] The major premise Eisenhower retained from reading the Prussian strategist was that in politics as well as in war, means had to be subordinated to ends; effort expended without purpose served no purpose, other than its own perpetuation. As President, Eisenhower regularly lectured press conferences on this point: "[W]e are now conducting a cold war. That cold war must have some objective, otherwise it would be senseless." And that objective had to be more than merely "victory," because a victory gained without regard to costs and effects, especially in a nuclear age, could be as devastating as defeat."* "Remember this: when you resort to force as the arbiter of human difficulty, you don't know where you are going; . . . if you get deeper and deeper, there is just no limit except what is imposed by the limitations of force itself."[17]

The whole idea was that "we must not destroy what we are attempting to defend." And what the United States was trying to defend was a way of life characterized by freedom of choice for individuals, democratic procedures for government, and private enterprise for the economy. An unthinking quest for absolute security could undermine all of these: "Should we have to resort to anything resembling a garrison state, then all that we are striving to defend would be weakened and, if long subjected to this kind of control, could disappear." It was no accident, then, that the

---

* "No matter how well prepared for war we may be, no matter how certain we are that within 24 hours we could destroy Kuibyshev and Moscow and Leningrad and Bakhu [*sic*] and all the other places that would allow the Soviets to carry on war, I want you to carry this question home with you: Gain such a victory, and what do you do with it? Here would be a great area from the Elbe to Vladivostok and down through Southeast Asia torn up and destroyed without government, without its communications, just an area of starvation and disaster. I ask you what would the civilized world do about it? I repeat there is no victory in any war except through our own imaginations, through our dedication and through our work to avoid it." (Eisenhower off-the-record statement to senior military officers, Quantico, Virginia, Hagerty diary, June 19, 1954, James Hagerty Papers, Box 1.)

National Security Council regularly came to list as "the basic objective of our national security policies: maintaining the security of the United States *and* the vitality of its fundamental values and institutions."[18]

The conjunction was significant. It reflected a tendency, not present in NSC-68, to equate security with the defense of permanent interests rather than with the repulsion of transitory threats. It implied the existence of interests distinct from threats, as well as a determination not to carry actions intended to counter threats so far that they endangered interests. And, to an extent surprising in an administration whose chief executive was long regarded as having had a "passive" approach to his responsibilities,[19] it was a concept of interests articulated and insisted on by the President himself.

II

But if Eisenhower largely defined the interests his administration sought, the prevailing perception of threat was chiefly that of John Foster Dulles. Given his long-standing efforts to apply standards of Christian morality to the conduct of international relations, it seems strange, at first glance, that the Secretary of State should have preoccupied himself more with threats than with interests. But Dulles, as a lawyer, had been trained to think in adversarial terms; interests, for him, could at times appear to be whatever was necessary to overwhelm the opponent.[20] Moreover, he had been much impressed by Arnold Toynbee's suggestion that without some kind of external challenge, civilizations withered and died.[21] It was not too difficult, then, for threats and interests to merge in Dulles's mind: to conclude that the United States *might actually have an interest in being threatened,* if through that process Americans could be goaded into doing what was required to preserve their way of life.

George Kennan, of course, had held a similar view, but he had insisted that hostile industrial-military power alone constituted the threat. No such precision restricted Dulles's vision. Instead he chose the occasion of his first televised address as Secretary of State to unveil a map showing the "vast area" from Berlin to Kamchatka filled with 800,000,000 people (thanks to events in China an increase of 600,000,000 since 1945, he pointedly noted) and controlled by "our proclaimed enemies." The implication was that adversaries, like interests, were indivisible; that when any nation went communist, regardless of its geographic location or strategic potential, American security was lessened thereby. "It is as simple as A, B, C," Dulles proclaimed some months later. "If Soviet communism is permitted to gobble up other parts of the world one by one, the day will come when the Soviet world will be so powerful that no corner of this world will be safe."[22]*

This "zero-sum" view of the world was consistent with the position taken in NSC-68, with one exception: whereas that document, like Kennan, had argued that communist ideology was more often the instrument, rather than the determinant, of Soviet policy, Dulles in his public utterances sought to convey the opposite impression. The objective of Soviet communism, he argued, was "to extend its system throughout the world and establish its 'one world' of state socialism." This would be done by overwhelming weak states through a combination of propaganda, subversion, and limited war, until the United States and its allies were encircled, exhausted, and ultimately forced either to yield voluntarily or be overthrown. It was all set out in Stalin's *Problems of Leninism*, "the present-day Communist bible, . . . [that] gives us the same preview that Hitler gave in *Mein Kampf*." The only difference was that Stalin, unlike Hitler, had no fixed timetable: his aims were implacable, but he was in no hurry to achieve them. War, then, was not inevitable, but conflict was, "until such time as the Communists so change their nature as to admit that those who wish to live by the moral law are free to do so without coercion by those who believe in enforced conformity to a materialistic standard."[23]

Whether Dulles actually believed in the *Mein Kampf* analogy is difficult to determine. He acknowledged that Russia had been an expansionist power long before it had become a communist power—by stretching history a bit, he was even able to claim that the United States had faced down an earlier Muscovite bid for world domination in 1823 by invoking the Monroe Doctrine against Tsar Alexander I.[24]† Dulles also appeared to agree with Kennan that insecurity might impel Soviet leaders to maintain a belligerent posture toward the outside world: "To Soviet Communists,

---

*There was an odd proclivity in the rhetoric of Dulles and several of his advisers for what might be called "gastronomic" imagery, with much talk of the communists "swallowing," "gobbling," and "digesting." I am indebted for this insight, the significance of which I am not quite sure of, to John F. Zeugner.

† Dulles of course exaggerated both the severity of the Russian "threat" to North America in the 1820's, and the extent to which the Monroe Doctrine was a direct response to it. (See, on this point, John Lewis Gaddis, *Russia, the Soviet Union, and the United States: An Interpretive History*, second edition [New York: 1990], pp. 8–11.)

freedom is frightening. To them it is inconsistent with order. That is why they feel that they will not be safe until they have liquidated freedom as a major force in world affairs." The Secretary of State even admitted at one point in 1956 that the Kremlin could change its ideological position whenever it found it convenient to do so: "Lenin wrote so voluminously that one can delve into his books and arrive at almost any conclusion you wish by picking and choosing."[25]

But in his public rhetoric, Dulles continued to stress ideology as the major determinant of Soviet policy. "It may be that Lenin and Stalin are dead," he observed in 1954. "So they are. But their doctrine is not dead. It continues to be taught to communists throughout the world, and they continue to practice it throughout the world." Asked in the wake of Nikita Khrushchev's 1956 denunciation of Stalin whether *Problems of Leninism* was still a reliable guide to Soviet behavior, Dulles replied: "I still have it on my desk both here and at my house because, in so far as I am aware, the Soviets, while they have attempted to disavow much of Stalin's program and many of his acts, have not themselves come up with any substitute." A close associate recalled how the Secretary of State would swivel in his chair, pick up Stalin's volume, locate with "surprising accuracy" what he was seeking, and then use it to prove his point. Dulles himself regarded his expertise in this area as one of his major contributions as Secretary of State: "I've done a great deal of reading on communist ideology," he noted immodestly. "This resulted in my understanding of the aims of international communism and produced a steadfast American policy in meeting that threat."[26]

On this subject, Dulles had an apt pupil in Eisenhower. The general had shown what some regarded as an unfortunate sluggishness in recognizing the seriousness of the Soviet threat after World War II. As late as December 1951 he had told C. L. Sulzberger that Kremlin leaders were either ideological fanatics or dictators "out to hang on to their jobs"—the latter, he thought, was the more likely alternative.[27] But by the spring of 1953, as president, he was sounding very much like Dulles. "Why shouldn't we, today, know what is going on?" he asked a press conference, citing the Secretary of State's *Mein Kampf* analogy. "How many of you have read Stalin's *Problems of Leninism?* How many of you have really studied Karl Marx and looked at the evolution of Marxian theory down to the present application?" Several months later, he proclaimed that "anyone who doesn't recognize that the great struggle of our time is an ideological one, . . . [is] not looking this question squarely in the face." And again, in 1954: "the central core of the great world problem is the aggressive intent of international communism."[28]

This concentration on the ideological roots of Soviet behavior had several effects. One was to legitimize an inclination the administration had already been driven toward by economic constraints: the tendency to focus more on Soviet intentions than capabilities. A central assumption of NSC-68 had been that adversary capabilities both determined and were more "knowable" than intentions; hence planning, to be safe, should stress the former. That argument had produced the "peak danger" concept, which had based U.S. military preparations on the assumption that war would come automatically once Soviet capabilities had reached the point at which Kremlin leaders could be reasonably confident of winning it. Eisenhower and his advisers disliked this approach because of its costs and the dislocations involved in crash planning (the year of peak danger was supposed to be 1954),[29] but it was difficult to justify abandoning it without some basis for regarding Soviet intentions as both discernible and significant. Emphasis on ideology did just that.*

The ideological writings of Marx, Lenin, and Stalin, Dulles believed, made Soviet intentions "knowable." Armed with this knowledge, the West could afford to ignore those Soviet capabilities not likely to be used. "We should always remember," he had noted in 1952, "that Soviet Communist doctrine has never taught primary reliance upon open war against the west." The danger was more subtle, as Eisenhower pointed out the following year: "by their military threat they have hoped to force upon America and the free world an unbearable security burden leading to economic disaster. They have plainly said that free people cannot preserve their way of life and at the same time provide enormous military establishments."[30] The implications were therefore clear: to attempt to match Soviet military capabilities in all respects would be to play into Moscow's hands, since it was unlikely that those capabilities would be employed for any purpose other than to frighten the West into exhausting itself. It further followed that if, as claimed, Soviet intentions were to achieve world revolution by means short of war, then that goal might be thwarted or at least deterred by a willingness on the part of the West to *threaten* war.

---

* This emphasis on Soviet intentions did not prevent top military officers from endorsing the traditional technique of concentrating on adversary capabilities. See speeches by Generals Matthew B. Ridgway, May 21, 1953, and Alfred M. Gruenther, February 22, 1955, DSB, XXVIII (June 22, 1953), 871, and XXXII (March 28, 1955), 516.

This preoccupation with ideology also led the administration to attribute to Kremlin leaders a clarity of strategic vision not possible in the Western democracies and, as a consequence, an extraordinary degree of tactical sophistication and flexibility. Moscow had, Dulles insisted, "a carefully prepared and superbly implemented program which, in a single generation, has brought a small Communist group into control over one-third of the world's population." The design for the future was to pick off countries one by one through subversion or indirect aggression until the United States and its allies had been encircled, isolated, and "strangled into submission." This combination of purposefulness, agility, and lack of scruple gave the Russians great advantages. "Wherever they lose," Assistant Secretary of State Walter Robertson complained, "they shift their ground. If they are balked in Europe, they switch to the Far East. If they are thrown back in battle, they turn to political maneuver, and vice versa." Communism was "adroit in its selection and use of every imaginable weapon to achieve its ends," Eisenhower warned in 1954. It is an indication of the seriousness with which he took his own argument that he had refused, the previous year, to commute the death sentence of Ethel Rosenberg because "from here on the Soviets would simply recruit their spies from among women."[31]

The President was particularly prone to see the diligent but subtle hand of the Kremlin at work in a variety of otherwise unrelated incidents around the world. There was little in the action of communist states that was not "deliberate and well thought out," he noted in 1954. While there might not be complete coordination, "I do say that when one of these governments permits anything to happen . . . , it does it deliberately and with a deliberate purpose." Three years later, he reviewed a succession of events—"the Korean invasion, the Huk activities in the Philippines, the determined effort to overrun all Viet Nam, the attempted subversion of Laos, Cambodia and Burma, the well-nigh successful attempt to take over Iran, the exploitation of the trouble spot of Trieste, and the penetration attempted in Guatemala"—all of which he insisted had been instances "of Soviet pressure designed to accelerate Communist conquest of every country where the Soviet government could make its influence felt."[32]

This perception of tactical virtuosity on the Russians' part made administration officials extremely wary of the surprisingly conciliatory gestures that began to emerge from the Kremlin after Stalin's death. "We must be constantly vigilant lest we fall into a trap," Dulles warned in May 1953. "Soviet Communists have constantly taught and practiced the art of deception, of making concessions merely in order to lure others into a false sense of security, which makes them the easier victims of ultimate aggression." And again, in 1954: "The death of Stalin has brought no basic change in Soviet policy." By 1955, the Secretary of State was prepared to acknowledge that there might be those in Moscow inclined to place national interests above those of world revolution. "We must not rebuff a change which might be that for which the world longs." But it was only prudent to remember that "Soviet Communist doctrine has persistently taught retreat and zigzag as a tactic of conquest. . . . We must not expose ourselves to what could be mortal danger." Taking note of Khrushchev's assertion that the Soviet Union would not abandon the teachings of Marx, Engels, and Lenin (Stalin was conspicuously absent) "until a shrimp learns to whistle," CIA Director Allen Dulles offered a slightly more tentative assessment: "This, I understand, is a Russian way of saying 'Never'—although I learn on good authority that in the deep reaches of the sea, as detected by modern science, . . . shrimp do make some gurgling noises."[33]

But the most dramatic manifestations of the administration's ideological fixation came in its public portrayal of international communism. It was a staple of official rhetoric during this period to refer, as Dulles did in April 1954, to "a vast monolithic system which, despite its power, believes that it cannot survive except as it succeeds in progressively destroying human freedom." Or, as Under-Secretary of State Walter Bedell Smith put it later that year: "Communism is a movement to bring all of the people in the world under one all-powerful central authority, and I define nationalism as the passionate desire of people to live their own lives in their own way. The two are incompatible, it seems to me." Walter Robertson noted early in 1955 that "these defiant imposters in Peiping come no closer to representing the true interests and aspirations of their country than do William Z. Foster and his cohorts in this country. . . . They are all part and parcel of the apparatus of the international communist conspiracy." That conspiracy, Allen Dulles asserted, had "its headquarters in Moscow, an affiliated organization in Peiping, and branch offices in Warsaw, Prague, and many other centers."[34]

Curiously, though, internal assessments of the Soviet threat assigned a lower priority to ideology than the administration's public rhetoric suggested. A National Security Council study early in 1955 concluded that "the Soviet leaders can be expected to seek constantly, by every means they find advantageous, to extend Communist power and to weaken those forces, especially U.S. power and influence, which they regard as inexorable enemies of their system." But Stalin's successors would "almost certainly avoid pursuing their long-term goals in ways which jeopardize the security of the regime or their control of the Communist bloc." Hence, Soviet objectives were, in order of importance:

A. The security of the regime and of the U.S.S.R..
B. Maintaining the Soviet hold on the European satellites, and keeping China within the Communist bloc.
C. Elimination of U.S. influence from Eurasia, and the isolation of the U.S.
D. Expansion of Soviet Communist power throughout Eurasia.
E. Elimination of the U.S. as a competing power center.
F. The spread of Communism throughout the world.

"These Communists are not early Christian martyrs," Eisenhower wrote privately a year and a half later. "I cannot see them starting a war merely for the opportunity that such a conflict might offer their successors to spread their doctrine."[35]

The administration also acknowledged to itself, in private, that communism and nationalism could be compatible. John Foster Dulles, like many others in Washington, had been strongly impressed by the "lessons" of Tito: "Insistence upon absolute conformity to a pattern made in Russia," he had written in 1949, "does not work in areas where the economic and social problems are different . . . and where there are deep-seated national and cultural loyalties." Despite the ideological orientation of Tito's regime, Dulles favored continuing aid to it in the hope that this example of independent communism might spread elsewhere in Eastern Europe and in China. That latter possibility was not considered far-fetched: a National Security Council study concluded in November 1953 that "there are major potentials for tension and discord in the Sino-Soviet partnership." And at a top-secret briefing for Eisenhower, Churchill, and French Foreign Minister Georges Bidault at Bermuda the following month, Dulles made the point even more explicitly:

> Mao Tse-tung was himself an outstanding Communist leader in his own right. It was natural, therefore, that there should be a certain unwillingness on the part of Mao to be dictated to by Moscow as had been possible with Stalin because of the latter's enormous prestige. . . . This was not the case with Malenkov. . . . The fact that this relationship exists is important and may eventually give us an opportunity for promoting division between the Soviet Union and Communist China in our own common interest.

"The basic change we need to look forward to isn't necessarily a change from communism to another form of government," Dulles told a close as-

sociate several years later. "The question is whether you can have communism in one country or whether it has to be for the world. If the Soviets
had national communism we could do business with their government."[36]

Why, then, did the administration seek to portray national communism
as impossible when it was secretly hoping to promote just that phenomenon? Dulles supplied one answer at Bermuda: "the best hope for intensi-
fying the strain and difficulties between Communist China and Russia
would be to keep the Chinese under maximum pressure rather than by relieving such pressure." There were, to be sure, those who thought that "by
being nice to the Communist Chinese we could wean them away from the
Soviets." But that would only produce competition with Russia for China's
favor, thus giving Beijing the best of both worlds. "Tito did not break with
Stalin because we were nice to Tito," Dulles pointed out. "On the contrary, we were very rough with Tito." Intelligence estimates generally reinforced Dulles's argument, stressing the limited leverage available to the
West in trying to bring about a Sino-Soviet split. Once manifestations of
independence did occur, Dulles was willing to recognize them publicly.
"The Chinese Communists exercise, I think, a measure of independence,"
he told a press conference in the wake of the first Quemoy-Matsu crisis in
1955; the following year, after Khrushchev's de-Stalinization speech, he
even admitted that "communism can be a national organization, not necessarily an international organization."[37] Evolution in that direction could
only be hastened by pressures, though, not inducements.[38]

Another difficulty in describing national communism as an acceptable
alternative was lack of assurance that a heretical communist regime would
be any more likely to respect U.S. interests than one loyal to Moscow. The
fact that a government was communist still seemed more important in determining its behavior than whether or not it took orders from the Kremlin. "Because of the uniform mold into which the masses [in Communist
countries] are pressed," career diplomat Robert Murphy commented in
1954, "we know what they will do and what they will say—regardless of na-
tionality or tongue." It is significant that Dulles, in acknowledging the relative autonomy of the Chinese Communist government, nonetheless went
out of his way to characterize it as more dangerous than its Soviet counterpart: "the Chinese were 'dizzy with success,'" he argued, seized by "an exaggerated sense of their own power," and possessed of an "aggressive fa-
naticism [that] presents a certain parallel to that of Hitler."[39] One could
have monolithic behavior, then, without having a monolith; the powerful
influence of ideology would ensure a communist regime's hostility toward

the West whatever its attitude toward the Soviet Union and whatever the logic of the international power balance.

Credibility was yet another problem. Like the authors of NSC-68, Eisenhower and his advisers attached great importance to appearances. Perceptions of power, they believed, could be as important as power itself. Victories even for independent communism could create the impression of a United States in retreat; the resulting loss in morale and will to resist could be devastating. "We [would] show ourselves fearful of the Communist brigands," Eisenhower wrote Churchill in 1955, "and create the impression that we are slinking along in the shadows, hoping that the beast will finally be satiated and cease his predatory tactics before he finally devours us." This, of course, had been the thought behind Eisenhower's "domino theory" in Indochina. Dulles subsequently carried it farther by appearing to hinge the security of the entire West upon the defense of Quemoy and Matsu—their loss, Dulles thought, would enable the Communists "to begin their objective of driving us out of the western Pacific, right back to Hawaii, and even to the United States!" Communists sought to foster the illusion that their triumph was inevitable. "We must have people on our side who believe that our way of life is the way of the future. They must also be tough, like the Communists."[40]

Finally, a coherent and credible external threat had the advantage of promoting one's own solidarity. The domestic benefits of crusading against "communism" were considerable at a time when both McCarthyism and unilateralism still had influence: "It's a fact, unfortunate though it be," Dulles admitted, "that in promoting our programs in Congress we have to make evident the international communist menace. Otherwise such programs . . . would be decimated." The same problem arose with allies: in the absence of such a threat, "they might feel that the danger was over and therefore they did not need to continue to spend large sums for defense." The Soviet Union, dependent neither on allies nor on the support of internal constituencies, had none of these difficulties. The moment of greatest danger for the West would come, Dulles liked to argue, when the perceived threat from the East had begun to fade—then allies would become quarrelsome, collective security arrangements would begin to seem outdated, neutralism would gain respectability. "Fear," he concluded, "makes easy the task of diplomats."[41]

It is odd that John Foster Dulles was in some ways more aware of the weaknesses of the Soviet regime and the constraints under which it operated than leading figures of the Truman administration had been. In his book *War or Peace*, published in the spring of 1950 just before the Korean War broke out, Dulles had discussed the subject in terms George Kennan would not have found unfamiliar:

> Dictatorships usually present a formidable exterior. They seem, on the outside, to be hard, glittering, and irresistible. Within, they are full of rottenness. They "are like unto whited sepulchers, which indeed appear beautiful outward, but are within full of dead men's bones, and of all uncleanness."[42]

Unlike Kennan, though, Dulles found it difficult to separate his assessment of the threat from the uses to which he sought to put it. Convinced that if the Soviet challenge disappeared, or even seemed to, so too would the unity of the anti-Soviet coalition at home and overseas, Dulles as Secretary of State played down what he knew of Soviet internal vulnerabilities and the tenuous nature of Moscow's control over the international communist movement. Instead he projected an image of undiminished danger, broadened now to include the entire communist world except for Tito. It was an effective argument for Dulles's purposes, so much so that he probably came to believe parts of it. But it was also a curious inversion of ends and means: the Soviet challenge, the removal or neutralization of which had been the original goal of containment, had now become a means by which that doctrine's instruments were to be perpetuated as ends in themselves.

III

In an effort to arrive at a strategy consistent with its perception of interests and threats (and to honor a pledge made during the campaign), the Eisenhower administration in the summer of 1953 went through an elaborate planning exercise known as "Operation Solarium,"* designed to consider all available options and decide upon the most appropriate course of action. At the President's request, three separate study groups were set up at the National War College, each charged with making the strongest possible case for its assigned option. These included: (1) continuation of the Truman strategy of "containment"—strangely enough, given the fact that Dulles had dropped him from the State Department the previous March, Kennan was asked to chair this group; (2) a strategy of "deterrence," which

---

* The term refers to the White House "solarium," where the initial meeting authorizing the exercise took place.

involved drawing lines around the periphery of the communist world, with the implied threat of nuclear retaliation against those who crossed them; and (3) "liberation"—the use of political, psychological, economic, and covert means to attempt to "roll back" existing areas of Soviet influence. A fourth alternative was proposed but not pursued, probably because Eisenhower ruled it out: preventive war to destroy U.S.S.R. nuclear capabilities before they grew to the point at which they could significantly threaten the United States. The risks of retaliation, it appeared, were already too great.[43]

Conventional wisdom has it that in the end, Eisenhower approved only the first of these options, with a slight modification in the direction of the second. Kennan recalls having been asked to the White House late that summer to brief the cabinet on the new approach: "At my feet, in the first row, sat Foster Dulles, silent and humble but outwardly respectful, and allowed himself to be thus instructed. If he then, in March, had triumphed by disembarrassing himself of my person, I, in August, had my revenge by saddling him, inescapably, with my policy."[44] But the "containment" option discussed in the "Solarium" study resembled NSC-68 more closely than it did Kennan's original strategy. And in practice the administration's strategic concept, which came to be known as the "New Look," managed to incorporate in one form or another all three of the alternatives considered in that exercise.

Central to this strategy was the idea of regaining the initiative while lowering costs. "No foreign policy really deserves the name," Eisenhower insisted in 1953, "if it is merely the reflex action from someone else's initiative." And again, early in 1954: "We can't afford to let the negative actions of the Communists force us into world-wide deployment. . . . We need to be free to decide where we can strike most effectively." The assumption here was that there was nothing contradictory about seeking both economy and the initiative. It had been the Truman administration's willingness to be sucked into wars it could neither win nor settle that had driven the defense budget to roughly $50 billion a year. Had the valedictory recommendations of NSC 141 been implemented, Eisenhower estimated, the deficit alone over the next five years would have come to $44 billion. Dulles made the same argument in his famous speech to the Council on Foreign Relations on January 12, 1954: Truman's strategy, he claimed, would have required readiness to fight "in the Arctic and in the Tropics; in Asia, the Near East, and in Europe; by sea, by land, and by air; with old weapons and with new weapons." It could not have been kept up for very long "without grave budgetary, economic, and social consequences."[45]

In that speech, Dulles revived the concept of strategic asymmetry he had first suggested in 1952, thereby providing the administration's most visible public explanation of how strategic initiative could be combined with budgetary restraint:

> We keep locks on our doors, but we do not have an armed guard in every home. We rely principally on a community security system so well equipped to punish any who break in and steal that, in fact, would-be aggressors are generally deterred. That is the modern way of getting maximum protection at bearable cost.

It could be done, Dulles insisted, by relying on the "deterrent of massive retaliatory power" to convince potential aggressors that they could not always prescribe conditions of competition to suit themselves. "The way to deter aggression is for the free community to be willing and able to respond vigorously at places and with means of its own choosing." Such an approach would allow shaping "our military establishment to fit what is *our* policy, instead of having to try to be ready to meet the enemy's many choices." The result would be "a selection of military means instead of a multiplication of means," and, as a consequence, "more basic security at less cost."[46]

Dulles's speech is best remembered for having publicized the term "massive retaliation," but it would be a mistake to view the Eisenhower administration's "New Look" strategy as revolving primarily around that concept, with its implied threat to use nuclear weapons upon minimal provocation. Rather, the central idea was that of asymmetrical response—of reacting to adversary challenges in ways calculated to apply one's strengths against the other side's weaknesses, even if this meant shifting the nature and location of the confrontation. The effect would be to regain the initiative while reducing costs. Nuclear weapons were a major component of that strategy, to be sure, but so too were such other elements as alliances, psychological warfare, covert action, and negotiations. All need to be considered to get a comprehensive picture of the administration's response to the perceived "Soviet-Communist" threat.

The Truman administration had never worked out a clear strategy for deriving political benefits from its possession of nuclear weapons. The devices figured prominently in war planning, to be sure, and their implied presence remained in the background of diplomacy during that period. But throughout most of the administration, the number of available weapons was so small that they could hardly have been used in peripheral conflicts—there were even doubts, as late as 1949, as to whether all of the atomic bombs in the American arsenal would be sufficient to compel Moscow's capitulation in the event of a full-scale war with the Soviet Union.[47] There was also sympathy for Kennan's view that nuclear and conventional weapons were sharply different in their characteristics and in the consequences of their use. It is significant that although Truman did authorize construction of the hydrogen bomb, his administration also attempted to move, in NSC-68, away from exclusive reliance on such weapons. Certainly the administration was at no point willing deliberately and publicly to threaten their use.*

All of this changed under Eisenhower. The number and variety of nuclear weapons had dramatically increased by the time he took office, both at the tactical and strategic level.[48] Intercontinental jet bombers were becoming operational. The new Chief Executive was determined to cut back on expensive ground force commitments—on "bottle washers and table waiters," as he put it. Overseas military bases were beginning to provoke anti-American sentiment in the countries where they were located; the governments concerned, Dulles warned, were coming to see such bases as "lightning rods rather than umbrellas." Together, these considerations made a powerful argument for greater emphasis on a U.S.-based airborne strategic nuclear deterrent: "It was agreed," Eisenhower noted after a conference with Dulles, Humphrey, and Secretary of Defense Charles E. Wilson in November 1953, "that the dependence that we are placing on new weapons would justify completely some reduction in conventional forces—that is, both ground troops and certain parts of the Navy."[49]

To make this strategy work, of course, the United States had to appear willing to use nuclear weapons wherever its interests were at stake. "Power," Dulles had observed in 1952, "never achieves its maximum possibility as a deterrent of crime unless those of criminal instincts have reason to fear that [it] will actually be used against them." Administration officials accordingly made a concerted public effort to blur the distinction

---

* Truman did, at one point, set off a major flurry by telling a press conference that use of the atomic bomb had always been under consideration in Korea. But the White House quickly issued a clarifying statement to the effect that only the President could authorize the bomb's use, and that no such authorization had been given. (Truman press conference and White House press release, November 30, 1950, *TPP: 1950*, p. 727.)

between nuclear and non-nuclear weapons that the previous administration had emphasized. "Atomic weapons have virtually achieved conventional status within our armed forces," the President told the United Nations in December 1953. NATO Supreme Commander General Alfred M. Gruenther argued in 1954 that "simply because atomic bombs do create casualties—and very heavy casualties against women and children—is no reason why we should become sentimental over . . . what weapons must be used. The chore is to make war itself impossible." Dulles argued that nuclear weapons were just another step in the increasing destructiveness of modern warfare, an advance roughly equivalent to that of gunpowder over the crossbow. "Where these things can be used on strictly military targets and for strictly military purposes," Eisenhower commented early in 1955, "I see no reason why they shouldn't be used just exactly as you would use a bullet or anything else."[50]

Internal documents from the early Eisenhower years suggest that this public position was not a bluff: the administration apparently was prepared to *consider* the use of nuclear weapons in a wide range of circumstances.* NSC-162/2, the top-secret statement of the "New Look" strategy approved by Eisenhower in October 1953, stipulated that in the event of hostilities with the Russians or the Chinese, "the United States will consider nuclear weapons to be as available for use as other munitions." The general idea, the President told Congressional leaders late in 1954, was "to blow hell out of them in a hurry if they start anything." Early in 1955, Eisenhower authorized an extension of this approach to limited wars as well: "the United States cannot afford to preclude itself from using nuclear weapons even in a local situation, if such use will bring the aggression to a swift and positive cessation, and if, on a balance of political and military consideration, such use will best advance U.S. security interests."[51]

---

* Preventive war continued to be one such option, despite its exclusion from the Solarium study. Eisenhower wrote Dulles in September 1953 that "we would have to be constantly ready, on an instantaneous basis, to inflict greater loss upon the enemy than he could reasonably hope to inflict upon us. This would be a deterrent—but if the contest to maintain this relative position should have to continue indefinitely, the cost would either drive us to war—or into some form of dictatorial government. In such circumstances, we would be forced to consider whether or not our duty to future generations did not require us to *initiate* war at the most propitious moment that we could designate." (Eisenhower to Dulles, September 8, 1953, *FRUS: 1952–54*, II, 461. Emphasis in the original.) But a year later, Eisenhower told a press conference: "A preventive war, to my mind, is an impossibility today. . . . [F]rankly, I wouldn't even listen to anyone seriously that came in and talked about such a thing." (Eisenhower press conference, August 11, 1954, *EPP: 1954*, p. 698.)

But to consider the use of such weapons was not routinely to sanction their use, and there is ample evidence of Eisenhower's caution in this regard. Although he had read and approved in advance Dulles's "massive retaliation" speech, its implied threat of automatic escalation to nuclear war clearly displeased him. "I don't think that big and bombastic talk is the thing that makes other people fear," he pointedly told a press conference the following month: "we fought a number of campaigns over in Europe, and I don't recall once issuing a precampaign statement that 'we are big and strong and mighty and tough and we are going to beat somebody's brains out.'" And again, in March 1954: "when it comes to saying that where on the fringe or the periphery of our interests . . . any kind of an act on the part of the enemy would justify that kind of thing, that I wouldn't hold for a moment. . . . Foster Dulles, by no stretch of the imagination, ever meant to be so specific and exact in stating what we would do." Later that year, the Chief Executive made a point of reminding the Secretary of State that "when we talk about . . . massive retaliation, we mean retaliation against an act that means irrevocable war."[52]

Dulles himself regretted the interpretation that had been placed on his speech and, in an elaboration of it published in *Foreign Affairs* the following April, he hastened to clarify his position: "massive atomic and thermonuclear retaliation is not the kind of power which could most usefully be evoked under all circumstances." What was necessary, rather, was "the flexibility and the facilities which make various responses available." For many kinds of communist aggression, the only feasible retaliation would be general war. But the West could not allow itself to rely only on that option: "the free world must have the means for responding effectively on a selective basis when it chooses." The important thing was "that a potential aggressor should know in advance that he can and will be made to suffer for his aggression more than he can possibly gain by it." The administration's strategy, the Secretary of State assured his young audience at a 4-H Clubs convention later that year, did not involve turning every local war into a general conflagration "with atomic bombs dropped all over the map."[53]

It is reasonable to ask, then, just what the administration's strategy was on the use of nuclear weapons, and how it differed from the recommendations put forward in NSC-68. The answer revolves largely around the question of symmetrical versus asymmetrical response. The Truman administration after 1950, of course, had emphasized symmetry: deterrence would work by creating certainty in the mind of the adversary both as to the inevitability and the limits of an American response—the United States would counter, but not exceed, the initial provocation. The Eisenhower administration, embracing asymmetry, sought to combine the certainty of a response with uncertainty as to its nature.* The idea was to open up a range of possible responses so wide that the Soviet Union would not be able to count on retaining the initiative; lacking that, it would come to see the risks of aggression as outweighing the benefits. All of this had to be done at tolerable cost, though; hence the attraction of threats to use nuclear weapons. As a top-secret statement of "Basic National Security Policy" put it early in 1955: "So long as the Soviets are uncertain of their ability to neutralize the U.S. nuclear-air retaliatory power, there is little reason to expect them to initiate general war or actions which they believe would . . . endanger the regime and the security of the U.S.S.R.."[54]

Admittedly there were dangers for the United States as well as the adversary in this procedure: miscalculation could always occur. But "you have to take chances for peace just as you have to take chances in war," Dulles insisted in a *Life* magazine interview early in 1956. "The ability to get to the verge without getting into the war is the necessary art. If you cannot master it, you inevitably get into a war. If you try to run away from it, if you are scared to go to the brink, you are lost."[55] The interview reflected the Secretary of State's chronic inability, having made his point, to subside; reporters quickly took advantage of his lapse to expatiate on the art of "brinkmanship," much to Dulles's discomfort. But the idea was not far off the mark as a characterization of what the Eisenhower administration was trying to do. There is no question that in its effort to lower the costs of containment it was willing to take on, through its reliance on nuclear weapons, greater risks than its predecessor had been willing to do.

Terms like "brinkmanship" and "massive retaliation" have tended to obscure the non-nuclear components of the "New Look" strategy. One of these was alliances. NSC-162/2 argued that the United States could not "meet its defense needs, even at exorbitant cost, without the support of allies." Overseas bases would continue for some years to be an important adjunct to the American strategic air capability; they would be vital should

---

* "Our deterrent striking power does not, today, have anywhere near the reassuring power of which it is capable because no one knows whether, when or where it would be used," Dulles had noted in 1952. "Complete precision on all of these matters is of course neither practical nor wise. There is reason for some calculated uncertainty and some flexibility, but there is never reason for the degree of political chaos which now involves this subject." (Dulles memorandum, June 25, 1952, Dulles Papers, Box 57, "Baldwin" folder.)

war break out on the Eurasian continent. The United States would also need the manpower reserves and economic resources of the major industrialized non-communist states. "Progressive loss to the Soviet bloc of these states would so isolate the United States and alter the world balance as to endanger the capacity of the United States to win in the event of general war or to maintain an adequate defense without undermining its fundamental institutions." It is significant that Dulles, in his 1954 *Foreign Affairs* article, listed alliances ahead even of nuclear deterrent capability as "the cornerstone of security for the free nations."[56]

Here there was no striking change from the practices of the Truman administration. Eisenhower and Dulles were at least as committed to NATO as their predecessors had been—given the new President's former association with that organization, this was hardly surprising. Nor was there any lessening of determination to incorporate Germany, reunified if possible, divided if necessary, into the Western alliance structure through the European Defense Community; if anything, Dulles stressed this point more heavily than Acheson had.[57] And with all of the Secretary of State's alleged susceptibility to "pactomania," it is interesting to note that the Eisenhower administration extended defense commitments by treaty to only four nations not already covered by alliances arranged during the Truman administration.*

But there were differences in tone, nuance, and function. Dulles was more inclined than Acheson had been to act without consulting allies; his frequent trips abroad were more often occasions for cajolery or self-justification than for a genuine exchange of views. Nor did the administration hesitate to apply pressure publicly on allies when it seemed necessary, as in the case of Dulles's threat to undertake an "agonizing reappraisal" of American security commitments if the French failed to join the European Defense Community, or Eisenhower's stern warnings to the British and

---

* By the time he left office, Truman's administration had concluded formal alliances with forty-one countries through the Rio Treaty (1947), the North Atlantic Treaty (1949), the ANZUS Treaty (1951), and the Japanese and Philippine security treaties (1951). The only additional countries given security commitments by treaty during the Eisenhower administration were Thailand and Pakistan through the SEATO Treaty (1955), and Korea (1953) and Taiwan (1955) through separate bilateral treaties. The United States never became a full member of the CENTO pact, but it did sign separate bilateral executive agreements with Turkey, Pakistan, and Iran in 1959, pledging American assistance in their defense. Because of Turkey's membership in NATO and Pakistan's in SEATO, though, only the pledge to Iran represented a new commitment.

the French to evacuate Egypt after the abortive Suez landings of 1956.*
There was also a difference in the objectives of Eisenhower's defense obligations from those Truman had authorized. The previous administration
had organized its coalitions primarily as war-fighting instruments: they
were restricted to nations whose geographical position made them vital to
the defense of the United States, and who could be expected to render significant assistance if a major war came. Eisenhower and Dulles emphasized more the deterrent power of alliances. The Secretary of State's aspiration was to encircle the Soviet Union and China with a ring of states
aligned with the United States either by treaty or unilateral declaration,[58]
not with any expectation that the countries involved could contribute directly to the defense of the United States, but rather with the hope that an
American security "umbrella" over them would discourage Russian or
Chinese attacks.

These alignments could be helpful in yet another way: they could provide manpower the United States itself could not afford to commit to deal
with local aggression. The idea, Eisenhower explained in 1957, had been
"to develop within the various areas and regions of the free world indigenous forces for the maintenance of order, the safeguarding of frontiers,
and the provision of the bulk of ground capability." The United States
would furnish technical assistance, and might even intervene with air and
naval forces if necessary. But it was important to remember that "the
United States could not maintain old-fashioned forces all around the
world." Asked whether the idea was to have other nationalities bearing the
brunt of any future fighting, the President replied that "that was the kernel
of the whole thing."[59]

There was a significant difference of opinion between the President
and the Secretary of State as to how far these alliances should be extended. Dulles had long held that in an ideological struggle as sharp as
the Cold War, there could be little room for middle ground: "neutrality,"
he announced in 1955, had become "an obsolete conception"; by 1956 it
was also "except under very exceptional circumstances . . . an immoral
and short-sighted conception." As was so often the case with Dulles, his
rhetoric cast his views into sharper relief than the facts justified: at no
point was he willing to write off as instruments of the Kremlin nations unwilling to align themselves formally with Washington. But he clearly had

*The British and the French had not consulted the United States prior to launching that
operation.

little sympathy for "neutrality," and considered it not in the best interests of the United States and the rest of the "free world."[60]

Eisenhower, interestingly, took a more tolerant view. Neutrality implied only a reluctance to join military alliances, he pointed out, not indifference to issues of right and wrong. The United States itself had been neutral during the first century and a half of its existence. Moreover, to pressure other nations into affiliating with such pacts could have unfortunate consequences, as the President noted in a confidential letter to his brother Edgar early in 1956:

> [F]or a long time, I have held that it is a very grave error to ask some of these nations to announce themselves as being on our side. . . . Such a statement on the part of a weak nation like Burma, or even India, would at once make them our all-out ally and we would have the impossible task of helping them arm for defense.
>
> Moreover, if a country would declare itself our military ally, then any attack made upon it by Communist groups would be viewed in most areas of the world as a more or less logical consequence. Since so much of the world thinks of the existing *ideological* struggle as a *power* struggle, the reaction to the kind of incident I talk about would be, "Well, they asked for it."
>
> On the other hand, if the Soviets attacked an avowed neutral, world opinion would be outraged.

It all went to show, Eisenhower concluded, "that over-simplified answers to the problems besetting the world today are extremely dangerous."[61]*

A third element in the "New Look" strategy was what the administration liked to call "psychological warfare." This could be, Eisenhower noted, anything "from the singing of a beautiful hymn up to the most extraordinary kind of physical sabotage."[62] The administration excluded none of these possibilities. Primarily, though, "psychological warfare" meant simply a robust faith in the efficacy of public posture: the belief that by merely making pronouncements and striking poses, the United States could increase the difficulties under which its adversaries operated.†

---

* "I want to wage the cold war in a militant, but reasonable, style," Eisenhower told Senator Styles Bridges in 1957, "whereby we appeal to the people of the world as a better group to hang with than the Communists. I am not concerned in buying friends or purchasing satellites or any other thing—that is all false. As a free country, the only ally we can have is a free ally, one that wants to be with us—that is what we are trying to develop." (Memorandum, Eisenhower-Bridges telephone conversation, May 21, 1957, Eisenhower Papers, Whitman File: DDE Diary, Box 13, "May 57 Misc (2).")

† Given the aura of Madison Avenue advertising techniques that surrounded this concept, it was appropriate that Eisenhower named as his first (and only) special assistant for "psychological warfare" C.D. Jackson, a former speechwriter and *Time* magazine executive.

The most conspicuous example of "psychological warfare" was Dulles's "liberation" strategy for Eastern Europe. Despite the future Secretary of State's vagueness on this point during the campaign, the Eisenhower administration never seriously considered actively trying to "roll back" Soviet influence in that part of the world. As NSC-162/2 noted: "The detachment of any major European satellite from the Soviet bloc does not now appear feasible except by Soviet acquiescence or war." Eisenhower and his advisers did not expect the former and were not prepared to risk the latter. Rhetoric, though, was another matter, and here the administration did everything it could to call attention to Soviet imperial vulnerabilities. "There is such a thing as indigestion," Dulles liked to argue, using his favorite gastronomic imagery. "People don't always get stronger by eating more." The Soviet Union was already overextended; should disorders break out in the satellites, the Kremlin might have to acknowledge "the futility of trying to hold captive so many peoples." Bringing this about would not require attempts to foment revolution from the outside, Dulles insisted, but merely a continued demonstration of the virtues of a free society, coupled with expressions of concern for those who did not enjoy its benefits.[63]

The administration's abortive proposal for a Congressional "captive nations" resolution early in 1953 was part of that strategy: off the record Dulles justified the measure as a "psychological weapon" intended "to try to get more initiative in the Cold War, to encourage what I have called 'indigestion' within the captive world, and to remove the fear which oppresses many of these captive peoples that we will, in the end, sell them out."[64]* So, too, were Dulles's running public commentaries on Soviet internal and international difficulties: "We know," he observed in 1954, "that the Soviet Communists' attempts to impose their absolute rule over 800 million captives involves them in what, in the long run, is an impossible task." Or, again, in 1956: "International communism is in a state of perplexity. . . . The weakness of Soviet imperialism is being made manifest." And in 1957: "how powerful must be the forces for change which are at work within Russia and how perplexed the rulers must be as to how to cope with these forces and at the same time maintain absolute power."[65] If there was in these statements some appearance of inconsistency with

---

* The administration allowed the proposal to die quietly after Republicans condemned it for failing specifically to repudiate the Yalta agreements, while Democrats opposed its implied criticisms of Roosevelt and Truman.

Dulles's portrayal of the adversary as dynamic, monolithic, and implacably dangerous, then it should probably be chalked up to the wish being father to the thought—which is, after all, the very nature of psychological warfare.

It is interesting to compare Dulles's approach to "liberation" with that of George Kennan, who also had seen possibilities for undermining Soviet rule in Eastern Europe. Kennan had sought to accomplish this, though, by exploiting latent but inescapable differences within the international communist movement. Dulles seemed more interested in having communism generally in that part of the world overthrown. To be sure, the administration's actual position was not that simple: as has been noted, it quietly continued to aid Tito's Yugoslavia and acknowledged, at times, the possibility of working with national communist regimes.[66] But the administration's public condemnations of communism everywhere overshadowed these nuances—a fact Dulles himself could justify on the grounds that pressure was more likely than inducement to bring fragmentation.

The psychological warfare counterpart of "liberation" in East Asia shows up in the administration's attitude toward China. As in the case of Eastern Europe, Washington officials had no illusions about who controlled the territory in question, or how difficult it would be to overthrow them: as NSC-162/2 noted late in 1953, "the Chinese Communist regime is firmly in control and is unlikely to be shaken in the foreseeable future by domestic forces or rival regimes, short of the occurrence of a major war." But there were things that could be done to make the task of ruling China more difficult. One was to remove the Seventh Fleet from the Taiwan Strait, thereby "unleashing" Chiang Kai-shek to attack the mainland; another was to continue withholding diplomatic recognition from Mao's regime, and to oppose to its seating in the United Nations. "You may have to recognize the fact of evil," Dulles commented, "but that doesn't mean that you have to clasp it to your bosom." Even the United States' refusal forcibly to repatriate Korean War prisoners had a psychological warfare dimension to it: knowing that in future wars defectors could expect and would get political asylum, Dulles argued, "the Red Armies become less dependable and there is far less risk that the Communists will be tempted to use these armies for aggression."[67]

Psychological warfare had other dimensions as well. It involved, of course, the constant use of propaganda, both printed and broadcast. It could involve such transparently self-serving gestures as the offer of one hundred thousand dollars to the first Soviet pilot to defect in a MIG, or such apparently sincere initiatives as Eisenhower's "open skies" inspection scheme, proposed at the Geneva summit conference in 1955. It could involve simply maintaining poise and self-confidence in the face of the enemy: "we even shook hands with some Communists," Vice President Richard Nixon acknowledged in a 1953 televised report on a trip to Southeast Asia. "[T]hey were picketing us, and we walked right among them, and met them, greeted them, talked to them, and as a result of doing that the Communist demonstration broke up."[68] It could involve impromptu episodes like Nixon's famous "debate" with Khrushchev in the kitchen of an American model home on exhibit in Moscow, or deliberate moves like the dispatch of Henry Cabot Lodge as a one man "truth squad" to follow the Soviet premier around the United States during his 1959 visit.[69] What all of these tactics had in common was a desire to "score points"—to make the United States look good, and to embarrass or discredit the other side.*

A fourth element in the "New Look" strategy, closely related to psychological warfare, was "covert operations," which the National Security Council defined in 1954 as "all activities . . . so planned and executed that any U.S. Government responsibility for them is not evident to unauthorized persons and that if uncovered the U.S. Government can plausibly disclaim any responsibility for them." The Central Intelligence Agency had been authorized to carry on such operations since 1948, in part on the basis of a suggestion made by Kennan. Nor had it been inactive: the budget for covert operations had mushroomed from $4.7 million in 1949 to $82 million by 1952, the personnel involved from 302 to 2,812 with an additional 3,142 overseas "contract personnel," the number of foreign stations from 7 to 47. Even so, covert operations did not really come into their own as an instrument of national strategy until the Eisenhower administration. One reason was bureaucratic: a merger of the CIA's clandestine collection and operations functions in August 1952 had given decided preference to the latter, both in terms of promotions and budget allocations.[70] Then, too, the new administration's emphasis on making containment work more efficiently at less cost tended to place a premium on covert activities which were, after all, relatively inexpensive. Finally,

---

* Still another example was the decision, in the summer of 1956, to release and publicize a covertly obtained version of Khrushchev's secret denunciation of Stalin before the Twentieth Party Congress the previous February.

Eisenhower chose as his new CIA director Allen W. Dulles, the Secretary of State's brother, thereby guaranteeing a closer coordination of intelligence operations with national strategy than had occurred heretofore.

The full dimensions of covert activity during the Eisenhower administration are still not completely known. Evidence is available regarding the kinds of activity involved, though: a 1954 National Security Council directive listed:

> propaganda, political action; economic warfare; escape and evasion and evacuation measures; subversion against hostile states or groups including assistance to underground resistance movements, guerrillas and refugee liberation groups; support of indigenous and anti-communist elements in threatened countries of the free world; deception plans and operations; and all activities compatible with this directive necessary to accomplish the foregoing.

It is also known that during this period the CIA organized the overthrow of two foreign governments (Iran in 1953, Guatemala in 1954), attempted unsuccessfully to overthrow two others (Indonesia in 1958, Cuba in 1960–61), infiltrated refugees into Eastern Europe to try to provoke disorders there, conducted guerrilla and paramilitary operations against China and North Vietnam from northern Burma and Laos, organized aerial reconnaissance missions over the Soviet Union and China, and at least considered—if it did not participate in—assassination plots against several foreign leaders (Zhou Enlai, Patrice Lumumba, Fidel Castro, and Rafael Trujillo). The agency also engaged in certain covert domestic activities, including mail and telecommunications surveillance, the infiltration of student, academic, journalistic, and cultural organizations, and financial subsidies to publishers and foundations.[71]

More difficult than establishing the fact that these and other operations took place is the task of determining which were carried out with the specific approval of the President, which were endorsed "in principle" but not monitored in detail, and which represented the agency's own initiatives. Eisenhower certainly knew of the CIA's major coup attempts, its counterinsurgency operations, and the reconnaissance overflights; the evidence regarding his knowledge of domestic covert activities is inconclusive, and no information has been found directly linking him or his successor with the agency's assassination plots.[72] What is clear, though, is that the administration gave the CIA an extraordinarily broad mandate, that it was willing to lie if necessary to maintain cover,[73] and that it did not consider such departures from conventional standards of official conduct to be inappropriate, given the circumstances. "I have come to the conclusion that some of our traditional ideas of international sportsmanship are scarcely applicable in the morass in which the world now flounders," the President wrote privately in 1955. "Truth, honor, justice, consideration of others, liberty for all—the problem is how to preserve them, nurture them and keep the peace—if this last is possible—when we are opposed by people who scorn . . . these values. I believe we can do it, but *we must not confuse these values with mere procedures, even though these last may have at one time held almost the status of moral concepts.*"[74]

If the Eisenhower administration was prepared to employ covert action on a broader scale than its predecessor, it was also more willing than the Truman administration had been to attempt negotiations with the U.S.S.R. and Communist China: these contacts, limited and unproductive though they were, constituted yet another component of the "New Look" strategy. The exchanges resulted in part from the moderate relaxation in international tensions that had followed Stalin's death, in part from the pressures of allies concerned more now about excessive rigidity on Washington's part than about any possibility of a "sell-out" to Moscow, in part from the greater latitude American politics tends to allow Republicans in dealing with "the enemy." But these initiatives were, as well, the product of Eisenhower's personal conviction that sooner or later progress would have to be made toward a resolution of Cold War differences.

Eisenhower stressed this point with such frequency and spontaneity that there is no reason to question his sincerity: "Every time that any opponent . . . is ready to say 'Let's wipe the slate clean and take a look at the present and the future', you will find me ready to do it." The proper approach was to "take at face value every offer that is made to us, until it is proved not to be worthy of being so taken." Distrust was a two-way street: it was fair to assume that the Russians "honestly, in certain instances, do question our intentions." Just because Moscow attached the adjective "peaceful" to the noun "coexistence" did not make it "appeasement": "coexistence is, in fact, a state of our being as long as we are not attempting to destroy the other side." Finally, "you don't promote the cause of peace by talking only to people with whom you agree. That is merely yes-man performance. You have got to meet face to face the people with whom you disagree at times, to determine whether or not there is a way of working out the differences and reaching a better understanding."[75]

Not surprisingly, these views did not always mesh well with those of John Foster Dulles, who tended to stress the risks more than the advantages of negotiations. "If Mr. Dulles and all his sophisticated advisers really mean that they can not talk peace seriously, then I am in the wrong pew," the President snapped in exasperation after encountering the State Department's resistance to an April 1953 speech extending conciliatory gestures to the new Soviet leadership. "For if it's war we should be talking about, I know the people to give me advice on that—and they're not in the State Department." Several months later, Eisenhower reminded Dulles that it would not do to give the impression "to our opponents or to our friends that we are merely concerned with showing that we have been very nice people, while the others have been very wicked indeed." The Secretary of State had "a lawyer's mind," the President acknowledged in 1958, and, as a result, an inclination to become "a sort of international prosecuting attorney."[76] Eisenhower, with his strategist's mind, tended to resist this approach, which in its search for immediate tactical advantage seemed at times to lose sight of the overall objective—a stable and congenial international order.

But Eisenhower respected and more often than not yielded to the Secretary of State's advice regarding the actual conduct of negotiations. And Dulles, deferential as always toward the President, never flatly opposed such contacts, admitting that they could at least clarify the position of the other side—sometimes he was even ahead of Eisenhower in encouraging them.[77] The result, then, was a compromise, the nature of which can be traced in the administration's successive statements of "Basic National Security Policy." NSC-162/2, of October 1953, acknowledged that the United States should keep open the possibility of negotiations with the U.S.S.R., both to pursue whatever opportunities for settlement might arise and to convince allies of American good faith in seeking them. "But, in doing so, we must not allow the possibility of such settlements to delay or reduce efforts to develop and maintain adequate free world strength, and thus enable the Soviets to increase their relative strength." It also had to be recognized that "the prospects for acceptable negotiated settlements are not encouraging." A year later NSC-5501, the successor to NSC-162/2, put the matter more simply: "The U.S. should be ready to negotiate with the U.S.S.R. whenever it clearly appears that U.S. security interests will be served thereby"—and it extended this approach to China as well, although without implying any change in nonrecognition policy. By the summer of 1957 one major qualification had been added: "The United States should not, however, make concessions in advance of similar action by the Soviets, in the hope of inspiring Soviet concessions."[78] But this was, on the whole, a more forthright—and forthcoming—negotiating posture than what had been advanced in NSC-68.

There were, to be sure, elements of inconsistency in the overall "New Look" strategy. Reliance on nuclear superiority could delay negotiations with the other side until it had made an effort to catch up; it could also unsettle allies who could see in it the possibility that they themselves might become targets in any future war, and that they could expect to bear the main burden of fighting at the conventional level. Psychological warfare and covert action measures could easily backfire, causing problems at home as well as with allies and adversaries. Negotiations, if carried too far, could impair the credibility of the deterrent and the solidity of alliances; their neglect, though, could lead to charges of inflexibility and intransigence.

Despite these anomalies, there was a common thread tying together nuclear deterrence, alliances, psychological warfare, covert action, and negotiations: they all had the advantage of being cheaper than the symmetrical response strategy of NSC-68. They implied a willingness to shift the nature and location of competition from the site of the original provocation, thereby admittedly risking escalation; but they also promised retention of the initiative, which is the key to minimizing costs. Given the conception of interests and threats under which the Eisenhower administration operated, the "New Look" was, therefore, an integrated and reasonably efficient adaptation of resources to objectives, of means to ends.

IV

However well integrated this strategy was, however, its public explanation certainly was not. There was a persistent gap between the Eisenhower administration's actions and the popular perception of them: the primary cause, it seems clear, was not the President's occasionally muddled syntax but rather an intractable case of pernicious hyperbole on the part of the Secretary of State. The record of the Eisenhower years is littered with examples of Dulles's penchant for overstatement (or reporters' abridgements of them)—"massive retaliation," "liberation," "agonizing reappraisal," the "immorality" of neutrality, "brinkmanship"—all of which conveyed in more forceful and dramatic terms than reality warranted what the administration was trying to do. The result was to confuse the public, alarm allies, and no doubt thoroughly bewilder adversaries.

This last effect was deliberate. Dulles believed firmly in the virtues of keeping the other side guessing about what the American response would be—although not on the likelihood of there being one. And, if the testimony of at least one eminent authority can be credited, he succeeded in this: "Dulles was a worthy adversary," Khrushchev later recalled. "It always kept us on our toes to match wits with him."[79] But Dulles found it difficult to separate the conduct of psychological warfare from the obligation to keep his own constituencies informed: the gains derived from unsettling adversaries hardly compensated for the damage Dulles's inflated rhetoric inflicted on alliance relationships, and on public presumptions of official common sense. One is forced to the conclusion that there were personal impulses as well as strategic designs behind the Secretary of State's weakness for histrionic pronouncement.

One of these, oddly enough, was an apparent need to "prove" his credentials as a Republican. Dulles was well aware of complaints from within his own party that he had collaborated too intimately with the previous administration; he seems to have felt the need to put a distinctively "Republican" stamp on policies whose novelty was not always immediately obvious from the outside. Rhetorical "packaging" was an easy way to do this. Mixed with it was an affinity for sonorous abstraction—the product, one gathers, of Dulles's legal experience—that caused him at times to express himself in terms that seemed insensitive to the personal or political realities with which he had to deal. Then there was, as well, the fact that Dulles's strengths were more those of the tactician than the strategist: he was resourceful in moving from one crisis to another, but he was not nearly as adept as Eisenhower in seeing how the individual parts of the administration's strategy related to the whole.[80]

The question arises, then, as to why Eisenhower, with his keen sense of the need to subordinate tactics to strategy, kept Dulles on. One reason, apparently, is that the President genuinely regarded their collaboration as a partnership, the continuation of which was of vital importance to the maintenance of world peace. There was never any question about where ultimate responsibility lay: "So far as Dulles is concerned, he has never made a serious pronouncement, agreement or proposal without complete and exhaustive consultation with me in advance and, of course, my approval." Still, "[t]here is probably no one [in the] world who has the technical competence of Foster Dulles in the diplomatic field. He has spent his life in this work in one form or another, and is a man of great intellectual capacity and moral courage. . . . Certainly if, with our standing in the world . . . , we are to be succeeded by individuals of less experience, lesser prestige and without the ties of acquaintanceships and even friendships that Foster and I have with many of the world leaders in many parts of the globe, then the question arises, 'What will happen?' "81*

Dulles was, in fact, a more subtle and skillful diplomat than his public rhetoric indicated. Nor is it true, as has often been charged, that Eisenhower delegated excessive authority to him. But power involves more than simply reserving the right to make final decisions—it requires as well the determination to monitor implementation closely to ensure correspondence with original intent, together with the ability to instill in subordinates some sense of what the strategy is so that where monitoring cannot take place, it need not. Eisenhower possessed neither of these characteristics in abundance: there was, in his approach to the office, a persistent failure to follow through on his usually quite sound initial instincts, a curious unwillingness to grasp the reins of power at all levels.82 As a result, Dulles could, at times, apply his own "stamp" on strategy; nowhere was this more true than in his strident and misleading public articulation of the "New Look."

---

* "Apparently with strangers his personality may not always be winning," Eisenhower wrote of Dulles early in 1958, "but with his friends he is charming and delightful." (Eisenhower to Hazlett, February 26, 1958, Eisenhower Papers, Whitman File: DDE Diaries, Box 18, "DDE Dictation Feb 58.")

Implementing the New Look

Criteria for judging the effectiveness of strategies vary, but Eisenhower's were clear enough: his goal was to achieve the maximum possible deterrence of communism at the minimum possible cost. In retrospect, the "New Look" strategy appears to have met these objectives. Despite the fact that his administration refrained from large-scale overseas military activity after the Korean armistice, the only countries "lost" to communism during its term were North Vietnam, already largely under Ho Chi Minh's control when Eisenhower entered the White House, and Cuba, whose communist orientation did not become clear until he was about to leave it. Expenditures for national defense remained remarkably stable, ranging from a low of $42.5 billion in fiscal 1956 to a high of $49.6 billion in fiscal 1961. More revealing are military expenditures as a percentage of the total budget—these figures actually declined, from 69.5 percent in 1954 to 50.8 percent in 1961. Defense spending as a percentage of gross domestic product also went down, from 13.1 percent in 1954 to 9.4 percent in 1961.[1] And yet, despite appearances to the contrary, these cuts produced no net reduction in American military strength relative to that of the Soviet Union—if anything, the United States was in a stronger posture vis-à-vis its major competitor at the end of Eisenhower's term than it was at the beginning.

Whether this was the result of luck or skill is difficult to say. Did the Eisenhower-Dulles strategy work because the administration had the good fortune to be in power at a time when its adversaries were planning no aggression, or did the sophistication and credibility of the "New Look" thwart such plans? The answer will require greater knowledge than we have, even now, of Soviet and Chinese intentions:[2] the successes of deterrence are always difficult to measure; the failures are plain enough. One thing is clear, though: historians of Eisenhower's presidency, aware of his successors' inability to achieve the same efficient adaptation of capabilities to objectives, have for the most part praised his conduct of national security affairs as reflecting a degree of prudence, restraint, and common sense not found in other early postwar administrations.[3]

Not many of Eisenhower's contemporaries would have shared that view during his final years in office. The prevailing judgment then in intellectual and political circles was that the "New Look" had failed, because it had: (1) relied excessively on nuclear weapons as the primary instrument of deterrence, thereby narrowing the range of feasible responses to aggression; (2) fumbled the handling of "third world" revolutions; (3) allowed a "missile gap" to develop, thus undermining the strategic balance with the Soviet Union; and (4) neglected opportunities for negotiations to lower Cold War tensions. These criticisms figured prominently in John F. Kennedy's successful campaign for the presidency in 1960. They also provide a convenient framework within which to reconsider both the accomplishments and the imperfections of the "New Look."

I

The first major charge against the Eisenhower administration was that in its efforts to achieve economy it had come to rely excessively on the use, or the threatened use, of nuclear weapons, thereby limiting its response, should aggression occur, to a choice between surrender and the risk of annihilation. The problem was the familiar one of "piece-meal" attacks: what assurance would there be as the Soviet Union began to deploy its own nuclear capabilities that the United States would reach into its nuclear arsenal for the means to counter every outward probe its adversaries launched, however insignificant? As a young Harvard political scientist named Henry Kissinger argued in 1957, it was impossible to combine "maximum horror and maximum certainty": "The greater the power, the greater the inhibitions against using it except in the most dire emergencies, and the more likely that no objective will seem important enough to justify resort to all-out war." If, moreover, the administration was willing to contemplate such an alternative, would it not be violating its own insistence that in strategic matters the cure ought not to be worse than the disease? It was, one critic noted, as if the local police had taken it upon themselves to use "block-buster" bombs against citizens who failed to shovel snow from their sidewalks.[4]

The administration's public reply, of course, was that nuclear weapons were only one of several feasible responses to aggression, and that it had no intention of concentrating exclusively on any one of them. "Undue reliance on one weapon or preparation for only one kind of warfare simply invites an enemy to resort to another," Eisenhower warned in 1955. "We must, therefore, keep in our armed forces balance and flexibility adequate for our purposes and objectives." The nuclear deterrent was essential, Dulles argued the following year, but that did not mean its invariable use against local aggression, or "nibblings": "We and our allies should, between us, have the capacity to deal with these without our action producing a general nuclear war." The idea was to keep potential adversaries guessing as to what the American response would be, so that they could never be sure that aggression would pay.[5]

Eisenhower and Dulles did insist, though, that the United States *itself* need not maintain the capability to respond at all levels: that was why one had allies. Instead, there should be a division of labor, with the Americans providing air and naval support, but relying on friends overseas for the manpower necessary to sustain a ground force response. Considerations of economy in part dictated this position—Eisenhower had cut $4.8 billion out of the fiscal 1955 defense budget by slashing $4.1 billion from the Army: land forces, he noted impatiently, could always "show a need for more and more."[6] But the President was also convinced that the advent of nuclear weapons had made it impossible to count on being able to move American troops abroad on a World War II scale. Had the Germans possessed atomic bombs, he pointed out, Allied forces could never even have crossed the Channel. And should nuclear war come, the Army would be needed to restore order and revive production at home, not to fight battles overseas.* The United States might deploy "a few Marine battalions or

---

* James Hagerty's diary provides some indication of Eisenhower's intensity of feeling on this point: "Suppose that attack were to occur tomorrow on fifteen of our cities. God damn it[!] It would be perfect rot to talk about shipping troops abroad when fifteen of our cities were in ruins. You would have disorder and almost complete chaos in the cities and on the roads around them. You would have to restore order and who is going to restore it? Do you think the police and fire departments of those cities could restore order? Nuts! That order is going to have to be restored by disciplined armed forces and by our Reserve. That's what our military is

Army units" for one or at most two "brushfire" wars, but "if it grew to anything like Korea proportions, the action would become one for the use of atomic weapons. Participation in small wars . . . is primarily a matter for Navy and Air."[7]

There would appear to have been, at first glance, a circularity in this reasoning: the United States would rely on nuclear weapons as an alternative to overseas ground force deployments, but in so doing it would risk the kind of confrontation that had made those deployments seem impracticable in the first place. Eisenhower calculated, though, that a convincing demonstration of willingness to use nuclear weapons would make aggression unlikely. If deterrence nonetheless failed, the limited employment of those weapons still would not invariably lead, the President claimed, to all-out war: "[T]he tactical use of atomic weapons against military targets would be no more likely to trigger off a big war than the use of twenty-ton 'block busters,'" he commented in 1956. The following year Eisenhower found much that was "interesting and worth reading" in Kissinger's "very provocative book," *Nuclear Weapons and Foreign Policy*, which argued that nuclear war could be kept limited and might even, under certain circumstances, produce less devastation than a conventional war.[8]*

The most important application of the principle that nuclear capabilities could deter and, if necessary, repel conventional aggression took place in Western Europe, where the administration as early as 1953 began to deploy tactical nuclear weapons to bolster NATO defenses. Although progress had been made in building up the alliance's ground forces, there were limits to how much more could be done without imposing unacceptable strains on West European economies. Even the addition of West German manpower through the European Defense Community would not, the administration thought, put NATO in a condition to resist a full-scale Soviet invasion. "The major deterrent to aggression against Western Europe," NSC 162/2 noted in October 1953, "is the manifest determination of the United States to use its atomic capability and massive retaliatory striking power if the area is attacked." American ground forces would stay in Western Europe as a contribution "to the strength and cohesion of the

going to be doing in the first days of an all-out atomic attack." (Hagerty Diary, February 1, 1955, Hagerty Papers, Box 1.)

* Eisenhower did object to the size of the military forces Kissinger wanted to maintain: "This would undoubtedly be a more expensive operation than we are carrying on at this time." (Eisenhower to Herter, July 31, 1957, Eisenhower Papers, Whitman File: DDE Diary, Box 14, "July 57 DDE Dictation.")

free world coalition," but if a Soviet attack came primary reliance would be on the use of nuclear weapons to repel it. Asked if this meant that the United States was taking upon itself the responsibility for starting a nuclear war, NATO Supreme Commander General Alfred Gruenther replied: "That is right. The West is taking the responsibility of defending itself, because we do not have the capability to defend ourselves . . . by purely conventional means."[9]

From this point on, U.S. strategy—and NATO strategy as well—was to compensate for manpower deficiencies by making credible the prospect of escalation to nuclear war if the Soviet Union attacked. This required a delicate balancing act, because what had to be deterred was not only a Red Army invasion but also the fears of the West Europeans that the Americans might abandon them, together with any temptations they might feel to deal with those fears by attempting to appease Moscow, or by developing nuclear weapons of their own.* The retention of American ground forces in Europe came to be seen, in time, as serving all of those functions: they provided a tangible sign of commitment—a "trip-wire" as the parlance of the day had it—to the Russians; they were also "hostages" to the West Europeans, since the U.S. could never evacuate them without at the same time defending Western Europe; and their access to nuclear weapons at the strategic and tactical levels could serve as a substitute for the national nuclear forces whose development Washington wished to avoid. It should be stressed, though, that the Eisenhower administration never intended to use these forces to fight a conventional war in Europe. As the President later commented with reference to the 1958–59 Berlin crisis: "If resort to arms should become necessary, our troops in Berlin would be quickly overrun, and the conflict would almost inevitably be global war. For this type of war our nuclear forces were more than adequate."[10]

The administration also relied heavily on nuclear capabilities to achieve its ends in more peripheral theaters, notably Korea. The Truman administration's strategy had been to exclude the use of such weapons there (though not necessarily elsewhere in Asia) [11] unless "our forces in the area would otherwise be faced with military disaster."[12] The Eisenhower administration was not sure whether nuclear strikes would in fact end the conflict, but it was willing to let it be known that the United States was contemplating them. "We were prepared for a much more intensive scale

---

* The British had tested an atomic bomb in 1952, but the French did not until 1960.

of warfare," Dulles later acknowledged. "We already had sent the means to the theater for delivering nuclear weapons. This became known to the Chinese Communists through their good intelligence and in fact we were not unwilling that they should find out."[13] It became an article of faith that this threat had been decisive in bringing about the July 1953 armistice. Should it be broken, Eisenhower told Congressional leaders early in 1954, the plan was "to hit them with everything we['ve] got."[14]*

Similarly, in the case of Indochina, the assumption was that if the United States became involved in the fighting, nuclear weapons would be "available for use as required by the tactical situation and as approved by the President." The National Security Council acknowledged that this might not be popular among the Indochinese, who would worry that their country might become "a battlefield of destruction on the Korean scale." It would also depress allies, because it "would remove the last hope that these weapons would not be used again in war." But if consulted, and persuaded that such action was essential "to keep Southeast Asia from falling under Communist control and to preserve the principle of collective security," they might be brought around to supporting such action, or at least not opposing it publicly.[15] In fact, of course, the occasion never arose, partly because Eisenhower insisted on having both British and Congressional support, which was not forthcoming, partly because the Army was able to demonstrate persuasively that the use of nuclear weapons in Indochina would not preclude the need for American ground troops;[16] and partly because the French, at whose invitation the United States had become involved in the first place, preferred to seek a negotiated settlement. But the Eisenhower administration's restraint in this regard had clearly been a function of circumstance, not of any principled opposition to the use of nuclear weapons in limited war.

The administration appears to have come closest to using nuclear weapons in the situation which, in the eyes of its critics, least called for them: the two crises over Quemoy and Matsu in 1954–55 and 1958. Eisenhower and Dulles worried about the security of these small Nationalist-held islands just off the China coast, not because they considered them vital to the defense of Taiwan, or because they agreed with Chiang

---

* It is clear now, however, that Chinese and North Korean exhaustion, together with Stalin's death in March 1953, brought about the armistice. The Eisenhower administration's nuclear threats were either misunderstood in Beijing, or disregarded. (See John Lewis Gaddis, *We Now Know: Rethinking Cold War History* [New York: 1997], pp. 108–9.)

Kai-shek's decision to build up his forces on them, but rather because they accepted the Nationalist leader's judgment that if the islands fell to the Communists, morale on Taiwan would crumble, leading to the loss of that more important position. That development in turn, Dulles argued, would impair the security of the entire Western pacific—Japan, Okinawa, and the Philippines—and would bring under Communist influence as well South Vietnam, Laos, Cambodia, Thailand, Burma, Malaya, and Indonesia. "The consequences in the Far East would be even more far-reaching and catastrophic than those which followed when the United States allowed the Chinese mainland to be taken over by the Chinese Communists, aided and abetted by the Soviet Union."[17]

The problem was that the islands were so close to the China mainland—a matter of a few miles—that conventional air and naval forces alone could not protect them. "If we defend Quemoy and Matsu," Dulles told Eisenhower in March 1954, "we'll have to use atomic weapons." Eisenhower agreed, and deliberately let it be known that the use of nuclear weapons was under consideration: "I hoped this answer would have some effect in persuading the Chinese Communists of the strength of our determination." Dulles noted in 1958 that although a conventional response might deter a Chinese attack in its initial stages, if it did not "our intervention would probably not be effective if it were limited to the use of conventional weapons." Should nuclear weapons be used, "there would be a strong popular revulsion against the US in most of the rest of the world," although if the weapons involved were small and the fall-out and civilian casualties light, the revulsion might not be long-lasting. "It is not certain, however, that the operation could be thus limited in scope or time, and the risk of a more extensive use of nuclear weapons, and even a risk of general war, would have to be accepted."[18]

At first glance, Dulles's handling of the two Quemoy-Matsu crises was impressive: Mao Zedong did back down, something he might not have done had it not been for the American nuclear threats.[19] But far from validating the administration's strategy, these incidents—particularly the one of 1958—in fact discredited it in the eyes of the American public and allies overseas by revealing how little it would take to push the U.S. into a war with China involving the probable use of nuclear weapons. It would be, Dean Acheson warned, "a war without friends or allies and over issues which the administration has not presented to the people, and which are not worth a single American life." Shaken by the depth of public and Congressional opposition, perhaps prodded by the ever-cautious Eisenhower,

Dulles himself quickly backtracked, denouncing Chiang's decision to deploy troops on the islands as "rather foolish" in the first place, and suggesting that if a cease-fire could be arranged, "it would not be wise or prudent to keep them there."[20] It was a strong indication that the limits of "brinkmanship" had been reached.

It is clear, in retrospect, that the Eisenhower administration was prepared to "go nuclear" in any of several contingencies—a Soviet conventional force attack in Europe, a violation of the Korean armistice, an escalation of the fighting in Indochina, or a Chinese Communist assault on Quemoy and Matsu. That it did not do so does not necessarily testify to the success of its strategy: in the absence of reliable insight into the intentions of those to be deterred, it is impossible to say with certainty whether there was anything to deter in the first place.[21] All that can be said is that the conventional military aggression the administration feared did not take place, whether because or in spite of what it did. It is possible, however, to evaluate the doctrine of "retaliation" in terms of its anticipated benefits over the symmetrical response strategy of NSC-68. Here the record is mixed.

There is no question that the new strategy achieved economies. In its budget for fiscal 1954, submitted just before it left office, the Truman administration had asked for new appropriations of $41.2 billion for the Department of Defense; Eisenhower quickly reduced this request to $35.8 billion, and sought only $30.9 billion for fiscal 1955. Most of this cut came from the Army, which shrank from 1.5 million to 1 million men between December 1953 and June 1955, but the other services also wound up with less than what the Truman administration had projected for them, even the Air Force. The latter service did, however, increase its share of actual defense spending from 34.2 percent in fiscal 1953, the last budget for which Truman was primarily responsible, to 46.2 percent by fiscal 1955. It remained at roughly that level throughout the rest of the Eisenhower administration.[22] Some reduction in defense spending would have occurred in any event once the fighting had stopped in Korea. But the extent of these reductions, together with the new "mix" of spending that so favored the Air Force, reflected the particular emphasis on nuclear deterrence that was basic to the "New Look."

Whether the new strategy regained the initiative, though, is another question: what was striking about the situations in which the administration sought to apply limited nuclear deterrence was the extent to which its range of choices was determined by allies.[23] By relying on them almost completely to carry out deterrence at the conventional level, Washington in effect relinquished control over that spectrum of response to aggression. Allies gained, as a result, the ability to manipulate the United States, either by doing too little, as in the case of the French in Indochina, or by doing too much, as Chiang Kai-shek did by concentrating his troops on the offshore islands.* Faced with these *faits acccomplis*, the administration had to choose between using nuclear weapons, which ran the risk of escalation, and not responding at all, thereby shaking allied "morale" and undermining the credibility of American commitments. For a strategy designed originally to increase the options open to American strategists, this was meager fruit indeed.

Nor was the strategy as impressive to adversaries as had been expected, because it failed to allow for differences between them. Deterrence worked well when the forces being deterred were under the control of a cautious central authority vulnerable to nuclear attack, as in the case of Warsaw Pact units in Eastern Europe, or Chinese Communist armies opposite Quemoy and Matsu. But the Korean armistice might well have been breached by the Koreans themselves, North or South: caution was not a habit in either Seoul or Pyongyang, nor was deference to the wishes of larger allies.† Had there been such a violation of the armistice, it is difficult to say how and against whom nuclear retaliation would have been carried out. And in Indochina, the French were half-heartedly confronting a totally committed revolutionary movement under little or no outside control: threats to use nuclear weapons could neither instill fighting spirit in the French, nor deter their adversaries from exploiting its absence. The

---

*James Hagerty traced the probable process of escalation in his diary: "We all believe that the Chi-Coms are building up an attack on Matsu and Quemoy and probably if that happens, it will be inevitable that our military units will be involved for this reason: If the Communists attack the islands in force, Chiang's Air Force on Formosa will immediately go into action. . . . The Communists['] Air Force will, in turn, go into action and sooner or later attack Formosan airports. Once this happens, under our Treaty obligations, the United States Air Force units go into action since an attack on Formosa would oblige us to do so. Once we go into action we will not stop our hot pursuit of Communist planes at any imaginary line but will be under orders to destroy them, either in the air or at their bases. That, of course, will do it." (Hagerty Diary, March 11, 1955, Hagerty Papers, Box 1.) But the original American position had been that Quemoy and Matsu were not vital to the defense of Taiwan in the first place; it was only Chiang's insistence that made them so.

†The South Koreans had almost torpedoed the armistice negotiations in June 1953 by releasing some 25,000 North Korean prisoners-of-war who had resisted repatriation to the North. For North Korean unpredictability, see Balázs Szalontai, "'You Have No Political Line of Your Own': Kim Il Sung and the Soviets, 1953–1964," Cold War International History Project *Bulletin*, #14/15 (Winter, 2003–Spring, 2004), pp. 87–137.

problem, in short, was that of fitting a single draconian solution to a diverse and varyingly tractable set of problems.

The most questionable aspect of the Eisenhower administration's strategy, however, was its apparent self-confidence that it could use nuclear weapons without setting off an all-out nuclear war. A limited nuclear conflict was possible, Kissinger had argued in *Nuclear Weapons and Foreign Policy*, but only if those participating in it had agreed beforehand on the boundaries beyond which it would not extend: "The limitation of war is established not only by our intentions but also by the manner in which the other side interprets them. Unless some concept of limitation of warfare is established in advance, miscalculation and misinterpretation . . . may cause the war to become all-out even should both sides intend to limit it."[24] Far from projecting certainty as to the limits and nature of its response, though, the administration deliberately cultivated unpredictability. "Let's keep the Reds guessing," Dulles had commented during the first Quemoy-Matsu crisis, "and not make any clearcut statement about them."[25] The assumption, somehow, was that the United States could with impunity escalate or even shift the location of the conflict, but that the other side would not.

It is also difficult to square Eisenhower's assurances that nuclear war could be kept limited with his profound skepticism regarding the utility of advance planning in war. "No war ever shows the characteristics that were expected," he told a press conference in 1954. It was simply not possible to generalize ahead of time about "an infinite variety of cases, under an infinite variety of provocations." Planning was important as training for emergencies, but plans would not be very much help when they actually occurred: "the very definition of an 'emergency' is that it is unexpected, therefore it is not going to happen the way you are planning. So, the first thing you do is to take all the plans off the top shelf and throw them out the window and start once more." "The only unchanging factor in war," Eisenhower added, "is the most changeable, uncertain, unpredictable element in war, and that is human nature."[26] Given the wholly unknown characteristics of even a limited nuclear conflict, it is not easy to see how Eisenhower could have retained as much confidence privately that it could be kept limited as his administration projected publicly.

In fact, he did not. "[L]et me tell you that if war comes, it will be horrible," he told a bellicose South Korean President Syngman Rhee in 1954. "Atomic war will destroy civilization. . . . There will be millions of people dead. . . . If the Kremlin and Washington ever lock up in a war, the results are too horrible to contemplate. I can't even imagine them." A year and a half later, he made notes on a top-secret briefing indicating that even though the Soviet Union would take three times the damage the United States did in a nuclear exchange, "something on the order of 65 percent of the [U.S.] population would require some kind of medical care, and in most instances, no opportunity whatsoever to get it. . . . It would literally be a business of digging ourselves out of the ashes, starting again." Even if the Russians tried to limit their attacks to American air bases, there would still be "no significant difference in the losses we would take."[27]*

Eisenhower's advisers—behind the scenes—had even less confidence that a nuclear war could be kept limited. Within months after taking office, Dulles himself had begun to worry that "the increased destructiveness of nuclear weapons and the approach of effective atomic parity are creating a situation in which general war would threaten the destruction of Western civilization." Talk of nuclear retaliation, he noted in 1954, was tending "to create 'peace at any price people' and might lead to an increase of appeasement sentiment in various countries. . . . Propaganda picturing us as warmongers on account of our atomic capabilities has done incalculable harm." It made sense, then, for the United States and its allies "to maintain sufficient flexible military capabilities, and firmness of policy, to convince the Communist rulers that the U.S. and its allies have the means to ensure that aggression will not pay and the will to use military force if the situation requires."[28]†

Over the next several years, Dulles persistently sought to achieve this flexibility by reducing the Eisenhower administration's reliance on nuclear deterrence—only to encounter resistance from Eisenhower himself. It was as if the two men had switched sides, with the President, who had been skeptical about Dulles's strategy during the 1952 campaign, having now embraced it, while Dulles himself had come to see the logic of Eisen-

---

* Eisenhower added that the only possible way to reduce American losses would be to launch a preventive attack on the Soviet Union. Strict constructionist to the end, though, he dismissed this option not only because of its inconsistency with American traditions, but also because of the difficulty of assembling Congress in secret session to vote the necessary declaration of war.
† Dulles was even speculating, by the end of 1954, about nuclear abolition as the only solution for expanding Soviet nuclear capabilities. "[A]tomic weapons are the only ones by which the U.S. can be virtually destroyed through a sudden attack, and if this danger of destruction should be removed by eliminating nuclear weapons this would help the U.S. by enabling retention intact of our industrial power which has acted both as a deterrent against total war and as a principal means of winning a war." (Notes, Dulles conversation with State Department advisers, December 29, 1954, *FRUS: 1952–54*, II, 1585–86.)

hower's earlier objections.[29] Part of the reason for Eisenhower's stubborn-
ness had to do with the perceptions of limited means that had dictated reliance on nuclear weapons in the first place. He had never lost his fear that
the United States could as easily defeat itself through excessive spending
as through a failure to deter Soviet and Chinese expansionism.[30] Support
for more "flexible" military capabilities, even if it came from his own Secretary of State, ran that risk—as had NSC-68.

But there was another more subtle reason for Eisenhower's objections.
He believed that the best way to avoid an all-out nuclear war was *to make
that the only military option available to the United States*.[31] His reasoning
was Clausewitzian: in his classic work, *On War*, the great Prussian strategist had coupled a vision of total and hence irrational violence with a
demonstration of how difficult—and how foolish—it would be to attempt
it. Clausewitz's "absolute war" was an abstraction, set up as a contrast to
what military force, in reality, could feasibly accomplish. By the 1950's,
though, "absolute war" had become an all too real possibility, a fact that
made his argument, from Eisenhower's perspective, all the more relevant.
The point was not to design a strategy, which implies getting from here to
there. It was rather to hold out a horror, in the interests of *not* getting
there. Apprised early in 1957 that the United States might suffer 50 million casualties in a nuclear war, Eisenhower's response was unequivocal:
"the only sensible thing for us to do was to put all our resources into our
SAC [Strategic Air Command] capability and into hydrogen bombs."[32]

Dulles was not the only adviser to recoil from this thinking. The military
services, sensing few opportunities for increasing appropriations or professional advancement, made clear their opposition. Even Eisenhower's
own National Security Council staff repeatedly turned out studies challenging his position.[33] But the President remained unmoved: he never
modified his private conviction that *any* war was bound to escalate to the
use of nuclear weapons. Not only was there no purpose in preparing for
anything else, it would be *dangerous* to prepare for anything else.

Eisenhower's aim, it seems clear now, was to avoid all wars, not simply
to deter nuclear war.[34] The "flexible capabilities" strategy Dulles had recommended was for the President no alternative at all because he saw it as
likely to lead to wars, not to prevent them. Its worst-case scenario would
substitute the use of many atomic for fewer thermonuclear bombs, but
this would hardly improve matters from an ecological or humanitarian
standpoint. It would increase conventional forces, running up great costs
and also great temptations to demonstrate the value of such forces—if

only to justify their costs. It would provide few safeguards if the Soviets or the Chinese should seek to strain American alliances and drain American resources through Korea-like entanglements: "We must now plan to fight peripheral wars on the same basis as we would fight a general war," Eisenhower insisted in 1956.[35] The logic of "massive retaliation," in short, was to convince *all* adversaries that *any* such conflict *might* escalate to a level at which *none* could hope to prevail. The term had been "scoffed at," the President acknowledged. But it was "likely to be the key to survival."[36]

His critics were right, then: Eisenhower did rely on nuclear weapons as the primary instrument of deterrence, thereby narrowing the range of feasible responses to aggression. His objective, though, was to make deterrence *more* credible to the Soviet Union and China, not less; it was also to deter his own advisers from placing American credibility at risk by involving the nation in costly and protracted limited wars. It reflected his extraordinary self-confidence: he "knew too much about the military to be fooled," he once observed.[37] But in this, he was unique: his successors were hardly likely to possess that quality. The result, then, was a strategy designed to make deterrence affordable over the "long haul," but surprisingly ill-suited to ensuring that result.

II

A second major criticism of the Eisenhower administration was that it had failed to deal successfully with the revolutionary movements that were becoming an increasingly prominent feature of life in Asia, the Middle East, Africa, and Latin America. These movements had arisen as European colonialism had declined (and, in Latin America, as resentment over the alleged neo-colonialism of the United States had grown). Despite their predictability, even inevitability, Washington officials more often than not seemed woefully unprepared for them. "[I]t is we, the American people, who should be marching at the head of this world-wide revolution, counseling it, helping it come to a healthy fruition," Senator John F. Kennedy charged, in what was to become a conspicuous theme of his 1960 campaign. "Yet we have allowed the Communists to evict us from our rightful estate. . . . We have been made to appear as the defenders of the status quo, while the Communists have portrayed themselves as the vanguard force, pointing the way to a better, brighter, and braver order of life." United Nations Ambassador Henry Cabot Lodge made the same point quietly within the councils of the administration: "the U.S. can win wars," he told the cabinet in November 1959, "but the question is can we win revolutions?"[38]

These failings stemmed from no lack of attention to the problem. Eisenhower and his advisers had from the beginning preoccupied themselves with the possibility that communists under Moscow's control might seek to take over "national liberation" movements, thereby expanding the sphere of Soviet authority and weakening, as a result, the position of the West.* "The Soviet leaders, in mapping their strategy for world conquest, hit on nationalism as a device for absorbing the colonial peoples," Dulles argued in 1953. "Stalin, in his classic lecture on the *Foundations of Leninism*, says that 'The road to victory of the revolution in the West lies through the revolutionary alliance with the liberation movement of the colonies and dependent countries.'"[39] Dulles's ideological literalism was off the mark as far as Stalin was concerned: in fact the Soviet autocrat did little to advance the interests of the proletarian revolution in the "third world." His more animated successors showed no such inhibitions, though, and over the next few years the Eisenhower administration was to find its fears confirmed, justifiably or not, in such diverse regions as Iran, Guatemala, Indochina, Egypt, Iraq, Lebanon, and Cuba. What it lacked was an appropriate strategy for frustrating what it perceived to be the Soviet "design" in these parts of the world.

The administration was sympathetic to nationalism as long as it took independent forms. Since his days at the Sorbonne as a student of Henri Bergson, Dulles had accepted the inevitability of change in international affairs: the task of statesmen, he thought, was to make the process as orderly as possible. "We and other nations must do all we can to see that this impulse results in viable countries, with constant betterment of their peoples, and not in chaos, bloodshed and impoverishment." Eisenhower argued that the colonial nations should "transform a necessity into a virtue"

* Eisenhower observed in a note to himself shortly before taking office: "Nationalism is on the march and world Communism is taking advantage of that spirit of nationalism to cause dissension in the free world. Moscow leads many misguided people to believe that they can count on Communist help to achieve and sustain nationalistic ambitions. Actually what is going on is that the Communists are hoping to take advantage of the confusion resulting from destruction of existing relationships and in the difficulties and uncertainties of disrupted trade, security and understandings, to further the aims of world revolution and the Kremlin's domination of all people." (Eisenhower diary note, January 6, 1953, Eisenhower Papers, Whitman File: DDE Diary, Box 5, "DDE Personal, 1953–4 [3].")

by granting independence gracefully.* The effect would be simultane-ously to provide the self-motivated indigenous forces needed to imple-ment the "New Look" in distant areas, and to undercut Moscow's claims to a "special relationship" with those parts of the world. "The United States cannot afford the loss to Communist extremism of constructive nationalist and reform movements in colonial areas of Asia and Africa," a National Se-curity Council study concluded in 1956. "The United States should seek (a) to work with, rather than against, such forces when convinced they are likely to remain powerful and grow in influence; and (b) to prevent the capture of such forces by Communism."[40]

But for the Eisenhower administration the means of channeling nation-alism into reliably anti-communist directions never quite seemed to be at hand. Covert action worked well enough as a short-term expedient in Iran and Guatemala, but the American role in such activities was impossible to conceal indefinitely. As it gradually became known, suspicions increased, making it all the more difficult to keep the next operation hidden under the cover of "plausible denial."[41] Psychological warfare measures required less, if any, secrecy, but their effects were slow, at times unpredictable, and subject to periodic Congressional pressures to economize. "Foster and I have long struggled with the Congress to get the kind of propaganda cam-paign established in [the Middle East] that could counteract anti-Western sentiment," Eisenhower wrote at the time of the 1958 Lebanon crisis. "We have never been able to get the money to do a good job, though today we are probably spending more by the month to solve this crisis than it would have cost us by the year to have been more effective in preventing it."[42]

Nuclear weapons were not much help either. Dulles had hoped that the doctrine of "massive retaliation" would discourage Moscow and Beijing from seeking to exploit "national liberation" movements, but by 1955 Eisenhower was admitting what he had probably known all along: that such a strategy "offers, of itself, no defense against the losses that we incur through the enemy's political and military nibbling. So long as he abstains from doing anything that he believes would provoke the free world to an open declaration of major war, he need not fear the 'deterrent.' "[43] More-over, whatever their impact on adversaries, threats to use nuclear weapons

---

* It says something about Eisenhower's militancy in this cause, though, that he thought a promise of self-rule after twenty-five years would be sufficient, and that the colonial powers would, in the end, be asked to remain, like the United States in Puerto Rico. (Eisenhower to Gruenther, November 30, 1954, Eisenhower Papers, Whitman File: DDE Diary, Box 5, "Nov. 54 [1].")

had the disconcerting effect of frightening friends, as the administration found out when it arranged a SEATO military exercise involving simulated atomic bomb blasts early in 1956. It is interesting to note that when American troops landed in Lebanon two years later, they did so without the nuclear weapons Eisenhower had earlier proclaimed to be an inseparable part of the modern military arsenal.[44]

But any widespread use of conventional forces on a protracted basis—in Lebanon the administration was fortunate enough to avoid this—would run the risk of repeating the "mistakes" of NSC-68. National Security Adviser Robert Cutler made the point firmly early in 1954, when the administration was considering coming to the aid of the French in Indochina. Even a complete victory by U.S. ground forces there would not eliminate communism elsewhere in Asia, he argued. Such operations would, however, range limited American manpower against the inexhaustible reserves of the Eurasian continent, while leaving Soviet and Chinese manpower unscathed. And they would so strain U.S. resources that it would be difficult to resist aggression anywhere else. "If the warfare must be localized in Indo-China," Cutler asked, "cannot there be imaginatively conceived a type of action which is *not* planned for decisive, old-style victory, with large U.S. forces committed against an immaterial enemy; but rather a warfare planned with slender forces to raise continuing, maximum unsettlement for the Communists?" Eisenhower thought not: "if we were to put one combat soldier into Indo China, then our entire prestige would be at stake, not only in that area but throughout the world." The United States might train indigenous forces, and might even use its own air and naval power to support them; but "I don't see any reason for American ground troops to be committed in Indo China."[45]

One could, of course, enlist the aid of allies to counter communism in the "third world." The effects, however, could as often be to constrict as to expand American opportunities to deal with these situations. To make allied cooperation a prerequisite for action, as the administration did in the case of Indochina in 1954, was to yield control over whether or not that action took place. "I am even yet spending days and hours trying to get a political climate established among the interested powers that would make it politically feasible within the United States to render the kind of help that our own interests and those of the free world would seem to require," Eisenhower wrote in June 1954. "But because we insist on treating everybody concerned as sovereign *equals*, it is extremely difficult to bring about the meeting of minds that is now so necessary." Another problem was that even close allies could, at times, take unilateral actions highly embarrassing to the United States, as the British and the French demonstrated by their unsuccessful attempt to seize the Suez Canal in October 1956. Those who began that adventure to secure oil supplies should be left to "boil in their own oil," a furious President commented. Finally, association with colonial or formerly colonial powers was not likely to enhance the reputation of the United States among peoples still convinced that imperialism was the greater danger than communism. "Let us remember," Dulles observed, "that while *we* think first of the danger that stems from international communism, many of *them* think first of possible encroachments from the West, for that is the rule they have actually known at first hand."[46]

The administration's preferred method of opposing "third world" communism was to build up local forces of resistance, capable of acting on their own if adequately supplied by the United States. This approach had the advantage of relative economy; it also reflected Eisenhower's conviction that "no Western power can go to Asia militarily, except as one of a concert of powers . . . includ[ing] local Asiatic peoples. To contemplate anything else is to lay ourselves open to the charge of imperialism and colonialism or—at the very least—of objectionable paternalism."[47] The idea was to strengthen indigenous forces by extending military and economic aid to such reliably anti-communist governments as the new one of Ngo Dinh Diem in South Vietnam, established with American support following the 1954 Geneva Conference, as well as older ones like South Korea, Taiwan, the Philippines, Pakistan, Iran, and Saudi Arabia. This aid would be coupled with bilateral and multilateral security pacts,* as well as with unilateral statements designed both to show American resolve and to deter external attack.

But these expedients had their own difficulties. Efforts to recruit members for SEATO and CENTO could appear as intrusive to the nations being recruited as anything the Russians or Chinese were doing, especially when linked to Dulles's inept pronouncements on the "immorality" of neutrality. Unilateral security guarantees could be taken as excuses for American intervention, as the hostile Arab reaction to the 1957 Eisenhower Doctrine showed. That single proclamation, pledging the United States to defend "the Middle East" against "overt armed aggression from any nation controlled by International Communism," dissipated almost

---

* Saudi Arabia was not included in the Central Treaty Organization, but did allow American air bases on its soil.

overnight the goodwill Washington had won in the Arab world by opposing the British-French-Israeli invasion of Egypt the year before.[48] And, of
course, none of this ensured that nations being protected by the United
States shared the administration's perception of interests and threats, or
that they would turn their nationalism against communism in the way
Washington wanted them to.

Much of the administration's difficulty in dealing with communism in
the "third world" stemmed from a chronic failure to distinguish deterrable
from non-deterrable phenomena. The theory of deterrence implies that
the behavior to be deterred represents something other than a total commitment on the part of the adversary, and that it is under reliable central
direction. Neither of these conditions could be assumed in East Asia, the
Middle East, or Latin America. It was all very well to threaten nuclear retaliation against the Chinese, whose determination to prolong the fighting
in Korea was not strong but whose control over the forces involved there
was. To apply the same tactic in Indochina, where the insurgents were totally committed but not as susceptible to outside control, was something
else again. NATO could well have deterred a Soviet attack in Europe if
one had ever been planned; there was no assurance, though, that alliances
patterned on that precedent would discourage autonomous but potentially
hostile revolutions in the arc of states running from Turkey to South
Korea. A Congressional resolution authorizing the defense of Taiwan
might carry weight with Beijing on the issues of Quemoy and Matsu; but
to attempt, through the Eisenhower Doctrine, to deter something as
vague as "communism" in an area as amorphous as "the Middle East" was
a wholly different proposition. Covert action might work with deceptive
smoothness to stage palace coups in Iran and Guatemala; its use as a
means of sparking broad popular uprisings against entrenched nationalist
regimes such as those of Sukarno in Indonesia or Castro in Cuba was another matter entirely. The administration, in short, was a victim of its own
successes and of its inability to see beyond them: it was not sufficiently
sensitive to the possibility that what worked in one context might not in a
wholly different one.[49]

Another difficulty was that the administration underestimated the "stay-
ing power" of nationalism. In a backhanded tribute to the organizational
abilities of the international communist movement, it fretted constantly
that newly independent states, if not securely aligned with Washington,
would eventually fall prey to the subtle but pervasive wiles of Moscow and
Beijing. "It is my personal conviction," Eisenhower wrote in March 1957,

"that almost any one of the new-born states of the world would far rather embrace Communism or any other form of dictatorship than to acknowledge the political domination of another government even though that brought to each citizen a far higher standard of living." Dulles made the same point in characteristically more dramatic tones the following month: "international communism is on the prowl to capture those nations whose leaders feel that newly acquired sovereign rights have to be displayed by flouting other independent nations. That kind of sovereignty is suicidal sovereignty."[50]*

This was a curious position for an administration prepared to acknowledge, if only to itself, that communism could take on national forms; for a Secretary of State convinced that the Soviet empire was a "whited sepulcher"; for a President persuaded that "when any dictatorship goes too far in its control, finally, whether it be the Roman Empire or Genghis Khan's or Napoleon's or anyone else's, just the very size of the thing begins to defeat them."[51] One reason for it may have been the fear that national communism might be as dangerous to the United States as its international counterpart. Another may have had to do with timing—it could take years for national tendencies to develop within communist states, and, in the interval, much damage might be done. The exigencies of domestic politics and psychological warfare suggest yet another explanation: even if the American public had been prepared to accept the view that there were multiple varieties of communism (and if anyone could have "sold" that view, it would surely have been Eisenhower and Dulles), there was still the question as to whether monolithic threats were not more effective in rallying public and allied support for Washington's strategy than fragmented ones. Still another possibility may have been simple inconsistency—a prosaic enough affliction, but one never to be entirely excluded from explanations of decisions made by human beings.

Whatever the cause, there was involved here a fundamental failure of strategic vision. The original concept of containment had called for enlisting the forces of nationalism, even where communist, to contain the expanding power of the Soviet Union. The Eisenhower administration should have had little difficulty embracing that approach: it did cooperate

---

*Vice President Nixon lectured a Filipino audience on this same point in July 1956: "I know there are those who feel that friendly neutrality toward the Kremlin and Peiping may spare them. But you know the proverb: He who sups with the devil must have a long spoon. . . . Those who feel that they can outmaneuver them are taking a fearful risk." (*DSB*, XXXV [July 16, 1956], 94.)

with Tito's Yugoslavia; it knew that national communism existed else-where; it could hardly have been accused of being "soft" on communism; it would have welcomed the economies such a self-executing strategy would have allowed. But because Dulles defined the threat as communism generally, not just the Soviet Union, the administration concentrated on opposing communism, even where it took on nationalist forms. Because the administration had so little faith in the ability of non-communist na-tionalism to sustain itself, it resorted to frantic and overbearing attempts to shore it up, in the process appearing to violate the very principles of sover-eignty and self-reliance it was trying to preserve. It is ironic that this fail-ure of vision—probably the administration's single most significant one—grew not so much out of inactivity, the sin with which it was charged at the time, as hyperactivity: given the durability nationalism had shown in the "third world," the administration would have been better advised to have applied in this area those qualities of patience, restraint, even benign neg-lect, that characterized its strategy elsewhere.

III

Like the problems of communism and nationalism in the "third world," another situation that seemed worse at the time than it does now was the so-called "missile gap." The crisis originated with the Soviet Union's launching of the first artificial earth satellite in October 1957. Khrushchev then intensified it through a deliberate effort to extract polit-ical advantages from the demonstration of long-range missile capability that that and other launchings provided.[52] The Eisenhower administra-tion was widely perceived, by 1959, to have done little to correct this ap-parent strategic imbalance: recently retired Army Chief of Staff General Maxwell D. Taylor spoke for a broad range of Congressional, academic, and military critics when he charged in his book *The Uncertain Trumpet* that "until about 1964 the United States is likely to be at a significant dis-advantage against the Russians in term of numbers and effectiveness of long-range missiles—*unless heroic measures are taken now*."[53] Eisen-hower refused to take those measures, and in retrospect it is clear that he and not his critics was right. The Russians did not in fact build the num-ber of ICBMs they had been expected to, and at no point during his pres-idency was the United States inferior to the Soviet Union in overall strategic capabilities. It did not look that way at the time, though, and as a consequence Eisenhower encountered on this issue his most strident and sustained opposition while President.

As a revelation of unexpected peril, the shock of Sputnik rivaled only Pearl Harbor and Korea. All at once the entire United States (and much of the rest of the world) appeared to be within range of a Soviet nuclear attack; warning time, a matter of hours when the means of delivery had been bombers, would now be at most thirty minutes. Worst of all, as Eisenhower publicly acknowledged, there was no known defense against a ballistic missile strike.[54] Official estimates had been that the U.S.S.R. would not have an operational ICBM capability until 1960 or 1961, by which time, it was thought, the U.S. would have one too.[55] Now it looked as if the nation would have to suffer through several years of dangerous vulnerability. Reminders of the difference between a weapon's demonstration and its operational use did little to allay public concern, nor did claims that Washington had regarded its own satellite program as a scientific, not military, enterprise, and that the U.S. was not in a "race" with the U.S.S.R.* It was ironic, Eisenhower commented, "that we should undertake something in good faith only to get behind the eight-ball in a contest which we never considered a contest."[56]

Both Pearl Harbor and Korea had provoked abrupt increases in American military expenditures; and, as it happened, the rationale for a somewhat more modest increase after Sputnik was conveniently at hand in the form of the Gaither Committee report,† a presidentially commissioned study of deterrence and defense, submitted to the White House early in November. It pointed out that with a gross national product only one-third that of the United States, the Soviet Union was matching American expenditures on both heavy industry and defense; if those trends continued, such Soviet spending might well double that of the United States by the end of the 1960's. The committee drew from this the conclusion that the United States could become vulnerable to a Soviet nuclear attack unless it took steps quickly: (1) to bolster its own offensive missile capabilities by

* If the administration did not regard itself as in a race with the Russians on satellite development, it clearly did on ICBMs. "The earliest development of ICBM capability is of vital importance to the security of the United States," Eisenhower wrote in September 1955. "We are determined . . . that nothing surmountable shall stand in the way of the most rapid progress on this program. . . . No other development program is now the subject of so urgent and emphatic a directive." (Eisenhower to Senator Clinton P. Anderson, September 13, 1955, Eisenhower Papers, Whitman File: DDE Diary, Box 6, "September 1955.")

† So called for the chairman of the group, H. Rowan Gaither, Jr., chairman of the board of the Ford Foundation.

accelerating the production of ICBMs and SLBMs (submarine-launched ballistic missiles) and by stationing IRBMs (intermediate-range ballistic missiles) in Europe; (2) to protect its own retaliatory forces by dispersing air bases, improving warning systems, and "hardening" missile launch sites; and (3) to construct fall-out shelters capable of safeguarding the nation's entire population should an attack occur. These programs, the committee estimated, would cost an additional $44 billion over the next five years and would require unbalanced budgets for the first four of those. But, in an argument reminiscent of NSC-68, it insisted that "these several defense measures are well within our economic capabilities. . . . The American people have always been ready to shoulder heavy costs for their defense when convinced of their necessity."[57]

Given the circumstances in which it appeared, the Gaither Committee report could have affected the American defense establishment almost as dramatically as NSC-68 had seven years earlier. Certainly it had no lack of supporters: when portions of the top-secret document leaked to the press, Congressional Democrats, concerned both with its national security implications and its domestic political possibilities, quickly endorsed its rumored conclusions and unsuccessfully demanded its official release. Several months later, a private study group commissioned by the Rockefeller Brothers Fund and headed by Henry Kissinger confirmed the committee's findings, thus suggesting that even among members of the President's own party its conclusions carried considerable weight. They emphatically did in the Pentagon, where the Army, Navy, and Air Force had all been clamoring for a share in the strategic deterrence mission. The Gaither Committee report offered something for everyone,* and the service chiefs did not hesitate to use the forum provided them by Congressional hearings to make their support for its recommendations known.[58] None of this would have much effect, though, without sympathy in the White House, and there the reaction was decidedly lukewarm.

Eisenhower did agree to increase the alert status of strategic bombers, disperse their bases, raise the number of ICBMs under development, and deploy IRBMs to Western Europe. But he firmly rejected the Gaither Committee's overall recommendations, for several reasons. He thought the group had neglected the advantages overseas bases gave to the United States, both in spreading out forces the Russians would have to hit in any

---

*The report even called for a modest increase in conventional force capabilities for fighting limited wars.

"first strike" and in complicating Moscow's own defense problems. He agreed with Dulles that fall-out shelters built for Americans but not allies would suggest a reversion to "fortress America" concepts—the United States, Dulles had argued, would thereby "just write off our friends in Europe." Economic advisers warned that the committee's projection of only mild budgetary deficits was excessively rosy: it depended on continued high employment and undiminished tax receipts, neither of which could be assumed. The more likely prospects, should the committee's program be put into effect, would be inflationary pressures, monetary and credit restrictions, and possibly even economic controls. These horrors alone were enough to damn the Gaither Committee report in the eyes of the President, whose personal definition of the much-feared "garrison state" was quite broad enough to include them.[59]

Hence, far from rising, military expenditures as a percentage of gross domestic product actually declined from 10.2 percent at the time of Sputnik to 10.0 percent for fiscal 1959, and 9.3 percent for fiscal 1960.[60]* In retrospect, these spending levels appear to have been entirely adequate: Soviet ICBM strength in 1961 turned out to be only a small fraction of what had been anticipated in 1959.[61] Eisenhower's steadfast opposition to a crash buildup of American strategic forces saved the country from an expensive effort to bring its actual capabilities into line with the rhetorical ones Khrushchev so loudly (and cheaply) claimed. That this was leadership there can be no question; whether it was leadership based on luck or skill, however, is another matter. Was Eisenhower's rejection of the Gaither Committee recommendations the result of a blind but fortuitous devotion to the principles of fiscal orthodoxy, or was it a precisely calibrated response to an accurately perceived threat, based on reason, imperturbability, and a sophisticated use of intelligence?

To be sure, Eisenhower's commitment to fiscal restraint had not weakened over the years. Alarmed by the projected size of the fiscal 1958 budget, he had taken the unusual step of asking the Congress to find places to cut it, a task the legislators set about in the summer of 1957 with greater zeal than he had intended. Sputnik reversed Congress's attitude, but not the President's. He acknowledged in the wake of the Soviet achievement that the country "would just have to do a little less 'buttering' and more 'gunning,'" but he at no point contemplated anything on the

---

* Actual expenditures for national defense went up modestly from $46.8 billion in fiscal 1958 to $49.0 billion in fiscal 1959, but then dropped to $48.1 billion in fiscal 1960.

order of what the Gaither Committee had recommended. "If the budget is too high," he lectured his new Secretary of Defense, Neil McElroy, "inflation occurs, which in effect cuts down the value of the dollar so that nothing is gained and the process is self-defeating." It was always possible, "by focusing simply on the military factor, to say that added funds will give added increments of military strength." But there was a point "at which the additions to military strengths resulting from additional funds diminish very rapidly." Sputnik had given "a surge to defense spending from which we have not recovered," the President complained two years later. If he had to approve another unbalanced budget, he "would be obliged to regard [the] Administration as discredited."[62]*

Eisenhower's restraint stemmed from more than just fiscal tightfistedness, though. He also had reasonably reliable information, on the basis of a major but unpublicizable intelligence coup, regarding the unexpectedly slow pace of Soviet ICBM construction. The CIA's U-2 overflights of the Soviet Union, which began in 1956, provided enough evidence of the absence of any large-scale ICBM program for the President to be able to assert with some confidence that the United States did not need one either. It is interesting to note that Eisenhower welcomed Sputnik as an unintentional Soviet recognition of "the freedom of international space"—an ambiguous reference whose significance was no doubt lost on most of his subordinates. A year and a half later, he suggested guardedly to his science advisers that the Russians might be having some of the same difficulties producing operational ICBMs that the United States was encountering. By January 1960 the CIA had put together enough information to begin basing its assessments not on Soviet capabilities but on "probable plans": these showed no indications of any crash ICBM program. The whole Soviet effort in this regard was so "leisurely and relaxed" that George Kistiakowsky, the President's special assistant for science and technology, wondered whether the U-2's had not missed an entire Soviet test range. That proved not to be the case, though, and Kistiakowsky noted years later that "without this [U-2] information, especially after Sputnik, the President probably could not have resisted the political pressures for massive expansion of our already large strategic arms programs."[63]

But even if U-2 intelligence had not been available, it seems unlikely that Eisenhower would have sought overwhelming numerical superiority

* Of the eight Eisenhower budgets, only three—those of fiscal 1956, 1957, and 1960—showed a surplus. The budget for fiscal 1959 was $12.4 billion in the red, largely because of the recession of 1958.

in missiles so long as the overall deterrent appeared sound. The President was an early believer in what would later become known as the doctrine of "sufficiency"—the idea that, beyond a certain point, the development of additional weapons did little good.* "[T]here comes a time . . . when a lead is not significant in the defensive arrangements of a country," he told a press conference in March 1955, more than a year before U-2 overflights began. "If you get enough of a particular type of weapon, I doubt that it is particularly important to have a lot more of it." Deterrence was a matter of judgment, not numbers; "if in the judgment of responsible officials the United States had adequate power to deter the Soviet from making an attack, . . . there was no justification for adding additional . . . weapons just for the purpose of trying to match in numbers those of the Soviet." It was better, after a certain point, to "put some of your money . . . in constructive things that tend to make people respectful of the great values we are supporting." How many times, Eisenhower asked impatiently, in 1958, "could [you] kill the same man"? Informed, two years later, that the nation would soon have the capacity of producing almost 400 Minuteman missiles per year, the President responded with a characteristic mixture of astonishment and exasperation: "Why don't we go completely crazy and plan on a force of 10,000?"[64]

Eisenhower's insistence on "sufficiency" was consistent with, indeed a direct outgrowth of, his belief in strategic asymmetry. It was important to pick "the phases of activity in which we should undertake to compete with the Soviets, and to beat them," he told his advisers in February 1958. But "we should not try to excel in everything." The Russians themselves had "done much better than we have in this matter": they had configured their forces on the basis of what the United States lacked rather than what it possessed. "They stopped their Bison and Bear [bomber] production, but we have kept on going, on the basis of incorrect estimates and at tremendous expense in a mistaken effort to be 100% secure." Soviet leaders, he suggested the following year, were "laughing at us for spending so much money on pointless armaments." It was foolish to "try to protect against everything imaginable"—there was no justification for "spending billions

---

* John Foster Dulles agreed with this concept, for reasons of public diplomacy. Care should be taken, he told the Cabinet in January 1958, to avoid emphasis on military "superiority" in the State of the Union address, because that concept could only lead to "invidious comparisons." He preferred "to stand on the concept of having sufficient military power to deter aggression." (Notes, cabinet meeting of January 3, 1958, Eisenhower Papers, Whitman File: DDE Diary, Box 18, "Staff Notes—Jan. 58.")

just to increase by a small percentage the performance of our current weapons system."[65] The better approach—the one Eisenhower fought so doggedly to impose on a recalcitrant Congress and military establishment—was to build on one's own strengths, match them against adversary weaknesses, and reap the benefits in both initiative and economy generated thereby.

This was a strategy, then, based not just on fiscal conservatism or secret intelligence, but also on the proposition, derived ultimately from Clausewitz, that one must have ends for all means. To maintain weapons irrelevant to the threat at hand—and Eisenhower put excess missile capacity in this category, as well as such other Pentagon favorites as the nuclear-powered aircraft carrier, any new manned bomber, and expanded ground forces—was to expend limited resources carelessly, with the result that the nation in the end would be unable to afford what really was necessary. Perhaps "a little too much" had been done even in the area of missiles after Sputnik, Eisenhower conceded in 1960, but that had been "because of an almost hysterical fear among some elements of the country." Decisions of such magnitude "should never be made under conditions of fear. . . . The important thing . . . was to remain true to our own beliefs and convictions."[66] This Eisenhower largely did, in the face of much opposition—and there is little evidence that national security suffered as a result.

IV

A fourth criticism of the Eisenhower administration, made more frequently after it left office than prior to 1961, was that in its preoccupation with security pacts, deterrence, and "brinkmanship," it had neglected the instruments of diplomacy in dealing with its adversaries. To be sure, Eisenhower and Dulles paid ample lip service to the need for negotiations with "the other side."[67] Nor were negotiators inactive during Eisenhower's presidency: there were three summits and five foreign ministers' meetings involving the Russians,* a protracted series of lower-level talks on arms control, agreements on cultural, educational, and technological cooperation with the U.S.S.R., and even arm's-length contacts with the People's Republic of China, first at the 1954 Geneva Conference on Korea and

---

* Eisenhower met with Soviet leaders at Geneva in 1955, Camp David in 1959, and abortively at Paris in 1960. There were foreign ministers' meetings in Berlin in 1954, Vienna and twice at Geneva in 1955, and again at Geneva in 1959.

Indochina, subsequently through informal ambassadorial-level discussions that took place intermittently beginning in 1955. This was, overall, a range of diplomatic activity more extensive than anything the Truman administration had attempted during its last years in office.

And yet, there persisted during most of the Eisenhower administration a vague feeling that these contacts with the communist world were somehow unnatural—a mood symbolized by Dulles's cold refusal to shake hands with Zhou Enlai at Geneva in 1954, and by his advice to Eisenhower to maintain "an austere countenance" when being photographed with Bulganin and Khrushchev at the Geneva summit the following year. It was, one observer later wrote, as if "the contaminating stigma of sin . . . attached to all acts and gestures of diplomacy that, by directly touching the unclean enemy, might give countenance to the damning offenses of his tyranny at home and his conquests abroad."[68] As a result, it has been argued, the Eisenhower administration missed opportunities to move toward détente with the Soviet Union and China—opportunities that would not come again until another Republican administration had taken office in 1969.[69]

Given the erratic nature of Khrushchev's and Mao's policies during this period, there are ample reasons now—on the basis of Soviet and Chinese sources—to doubt this claim.[70] This information was not available at the time, however, so it is worth appraising prospects for negotiations as they appeared then, the extent to which the administration responded to them, and the relative emphasis it placed on diplomacy as compared to the other instruments of containment—nuclear deterrence, alliances, psychological warfare, and covert action. What quickly becomes apparent is that Eisenhower and Dulles more often resorted to negotiations as a means of facilitating these other approaches to containment, rather than as a way of attempting to move beyond containment. They found it difficult to align opportunities for negotiations with their own willingness to participate in them.

In September 1953 John Foster Dulles sent Eisenhower a memorandum suggesting "a spectacular effort to relax world tensions on a global basis" by negotiating a mutual withdrawal of Soviet and American forces from Europe, together with an agreement on the limitation of conventional and nuclear arms. "The present is a propitious time for such a move, if it is ever to be made," he argued, "because we will be speaking from strength rather than weakness." The Korean armistice, the success of the Iranian coup, the apparent willingness of the French to act more vigorously in Indochina, Konrad Adenauer's recent electoral victory in West Germany, and the fact that Soviet advances in nuclear weaponry would not be felt for some time all made it a good moment to act, as did the fact that the new Eisenhower budget, with its dramatic cuts in defense expenditures, would not have to be made public until the end of the year. "I am in emphatic agreement that renewed efforts should be made to relax world tensions," Eisenhower replied. "Mutual withdrawals of Red Army Forces and of United States Forces could be suggested as a step toward relaxing these tensions. . . . Whatever move we make in this field should be done at a reasonably early date."[71]

But here the story ends. Neither the President, the Secretary of State, nor anyone else in the administration made any effort to pursue this remarkable idea, which went well beyond Kennan's controversial 1948 proposal for a mutual withdrawal of forces from *central* Europe.* The difficulties, of course, would have been substantial: Dulles had worried that the much less ambitious "New Look" strategy, with its conventional force reductions and upgraded continental defense capability, would appear in Europe as a "Fortress America" concept[72]—the withdrawal plan would have seemed all the more so. Moreover, the Secretary of State's instinct, when confronted with indications of weakness on the other side, was to press even harder: "This is the time to *crowd* the enemy—and maybe *finish* him, once and for all," he had told the Cabinet the previous July. By December of 1953, as Dulles was preparing for his first foreign ministers' meeting with the Russians, his attitude had become narrow and pessimistic. Little would come out of the talks, he told the President: "the question . . . is how do you get [it] over with . . . as little damage as possible."[73]

Eisenhower had at first leaned toward a conciliatory approach to the new Soviet leadership: over Dulles's objections he had delivered a speech in April 1953 distinguishing between Stalin and his successors and offering the latter negotiations with the West on "universal disarmament."[74] But the President resisted calls, most conspicuously from his old friend, Winston Churchill, for a summit conference. Dulles adamantly opposed any such meeting as long as West Germany's relationship to Western Europe remained unresolved, and Eisenhower worried that such a gathering might bolster the prestige of one or more members of the new Kremlin hierarchy. "That would . . . tend to minimize the struggles for power that are

* See above, pp. 73–74.

going on within Russia. We certainly don't want to do that."[75] In the end, the summit was delayed for two years: it took place only after the Western European Union had replaced the stillborn European Defense Community, West Germany had joined NATO, and the new Soviet leadership had demonstrated good faith by meeting American demands for a peace treaty with Austria.

By the time of the July 1955 Geneva summit, though, the U.S.S.R. was in a stronger position than it had been in the summer of 1953. New Kremlin leaders—Khrushchev first among them—were in place; the Soviet Union had achieved a rudimentary long-range bomber capability and was about to develop an operational hydrogen bomb; and the U.S. defense budget had been conspicuously cut. Apparently sensing this new strength, the Russians had by now withdrawn an offer Stalin had made in 1952 regarding the possibility of a unified but neutral German state; the alternatives from this point on were either a unified state under Soviet control or a permanently divided one. The prevailing view since the Truman administration had been that negotiations should proceed only from a position of "strength."[76] But in the process of bolstering particular constituents of strength—building up the Western alliance while imposing strains on the Russians—negotiations had been put off past the point at which Moscow might have felt the need to make concessions out of weakness.

Eisenhower's hopes for negotiations were highest in the area of arms control. "As of now the world is racing toward catastrophe," he wrote in a note to himself in December 1953: "something must be done to put a brake on." The President's "brake" was a plan by which nations possessing nuclear weapons would contribute materials needed to make them to an international atomic energy "bank," controlled by the United Nations, which would then put them to peaceful uses. This procedure would, Eisenhower thought, get the Russians accustomed to working with the United States in the field of atomic energy; it would at the same time preserve American security because "the US could unquestionably afford to reduce its atomic stock pile by two or three times the amounts that the Russians might contribute to the UN Agency, and still improve our relative position in the cold war and even in the event of the outbreak of war."[77]

Despite this element of self-interest, there is no reason to question Eisenhower's sincerity in seeking progress toward the control of nuclear armaments. Basic though they were to his strategy, the whole idea of such weapons offended his soldier's sense of the need for economy and purpose in war. "War implies a contest," he wrote privately in 1956; "when you get to the point that contest is no longer involved and the outlook comes close to destruction of the enemy and suicide for ourselves . . . then arguments as to the exact amount of available strength as compared to somebody else's are no longer the vital issues." Time and time again in years to come he would prod his advisers to come up with safe but constructive proposals in disarmament talks with the Russians: "we need some specific proposal in order to carry the disarmament struggle along" (March 1956); "planning and carrying out extensive [nuclear weapons] tests . . . while professing a readiness to suspend testing in a disarmament program . . . may bring accusations of bad faith" (August 1957); "in this terrific armament race we must . . . have some little bit of a hope. . . . in the long run [there] is nothing but war—if we give up all hope of a peaceful solution" (April 1959); "we say they are inflexible and they say we are inflexible . . . we must look for added or new subjects or possibilities on which to negotiate" (June 1959); "our real effort should go into making some meaningful move toward disarmament" (October 1959).[78]

But the actual course of negotiations between 1955 and 1959 saw an embarrassing series of American reversals of position that seemed to call into question precisely this sincerity. Hence, when the Russians in May 1955 accepted a long-standing U.S. demand by agreeing to the limited inspection of Soviet territory as a means of verifying disarmament, the United States instead of exploring this offer substituted Eisenhower's "open skies" inspection scheme, a plan whose propaganda advantages were considerable, but which, given the largely open nature of American society, could hardly be considered an even-handed approach to the problem. Nevertheless, the Russians did in 1957 accept the principle of aerial surveillance over portions of the U.S.S.R. and Eastern Europe (in return for reciprocal rights over Western Europe and the eastern United States), only to have Washington recall its excessively ardent negotiator, Harold Stassen, for having discussed counter-proposals with the Russians without consulting the British. Negotiations on disarmament having achieved little, the discussions shifted that year to the possibility of limiting nuclear tests, with verification to take place by atmospheric sampling and seismic means. Later in 1958, though, the administration backed away from this proposal as well, upon receipt of scientific evidence calling into question the reliability of seismic techniques in detecting underground nuclear tests. Nor could the administration agree on a clear set of proposals to be presented at a

Soviet-American conference that year on preventing surprise attacks. In the end, all that came out of these exchanges was an unenforced moratorium on nuclear testing, capable of being terminated at any time.[79]

These meager results, to be sure, were not all Washington's fault. Soviet inspection offers, whether aerial or ground, never covered more than a small portion of the territory from which an attack on the West could have been launched. Nor was Khrushchev above backing away from his own prior positions, as he showed by abruptly terminating negotiations following the successful Soviet ICBM test of August 1957, and in the wake of the notably unsuccessful Paris summit of 1960. Distrust, together with genuine uncertainties as to what would constitute adequate verification, combined to make neither side willing to take the risks that would have been necessary to reach an agreement at that time. But it is also fair to say that the Eisenhower administration accorded negotiations on arms control a lower priority than such other components of its strategy as the maintenance of a credible nuclear deterrent, the preservation of harmony among allies, and the determination to score "points" at the expense of the Russians in the arena of psychological warfare. The President's own personal commitment kept arms control negotiations going, but it was never sufficiently vigorous to gain them a status equal to the administration's other concerns.

The administration was also adamant in its refusal to enter into substantive negotiations with the People's Republic of China, despite the fact that Beijing's desire for an "opening" to the West, by the mid-1950's, was becoming obvious.[80] There was no absence of opportunity: following the Bandung Conference of April 1955, the Chinese began dropping persistent hints that Taiwan need not be "liberated" by military means, and that they would welcome an exchange of journalists and a lifting of the trade embargo. But beyond agreeing to ambassadorial-level talks at Geneva later that year, the U.S. made no effort to pursue these initiatives. And in June of 1957, Dulles effectively put an end to them with a firm restatement of U.S. support for Chiang Kai-shek and opposition both to recognizing the Beijing regime or admitting it to the United Nations.[81]

Historians have since criticized this stance on the grounds that it precluded any possibility of exploiting Sino-Soviet tension.[82] We now know, though, that the administration fully recognized the potential for discord between Moscow and Beijing, that it deliberately sought to intensify those antagonisms, and that its uncompromising support for Chiang Kai-shek, whatever its domestic political advantages, had the additional objective of doing just that. National Security Council studies done in 1953 had indicated that Washington could not, by itself, expect to split the two communist giants; Soviet behavior toward the Chinese would be more decisive. But by aiding the Chinese Nationalists, the United States could indirectly increase the difficulties under which the Moscow-Beijing axis operated. There were "some 400,000 Communist Chinese troops stationed opposite Formosa guarding against invasion," Dulles commented in December 1953. "This was another of the measures we liked to pursue on the theory of exerting maximum strain causing the Chinese Communists to demand more from Russia and thereby placing additional stress on Russian-Chinese relations."[83]

Dulles's statement provides an additional explanation for the administration's attachment to Chiang Kai-shek. It was not just a matter of ideological rigidity or political expediency; it was also a calculated effort to split a hostile alliance by exhausting its junior partner, forcing it to make demands its senior ally could not meet.[84] Eisenhower expressed doubt, during the first Quemoy-Matsu crisis, that the Russians would honor their military obligations to China if that country should get into a war with the United States; Moscow he thought, would restrain rather than support the Chinese.[85] And on the eve of the second offshore island crisis in 1958, the State Department provided an oblique public hint of Dulles's strategy by suggesting that diplomatic recognition, if extended, would only make Beijing officials "feel confirmed in the correctness of their policies and the advantages of continued close cooperation with Moscow"—presumably continued aloofness combined with pressure would have the opposite effect. Eisenhower clearly thought so: by November of that year he was wondering out loud whether "the Soviets were not really becoming concerned about Communist China as a possible threat to them in the future."[86]

One can argue, in a narrow sense, that Dulles's plan worked much as he thought it would. Historians of the Sino-Soviet split have in fact cited Moscow's reluctance to assist Beijing in the two Quemoy-Matsu crises as one of the causes of Mao's disillusionment with Moscow.[87]* These particular strains—there were, of course, many others—would not have developed had the United States refrained from so strongly supporting Chiang Kai-shek. Given the bitterness toward the United States that still persisted in China at that time, there is reason to question whether American

---

* Although more recent evidence suggests that Mao himself used the crises to consolidate his own domestic position and to unsettle both the Americans and the Russians. (Chen Jian, *Mao's China and the Cold War* [Chapel Hill: 2001], pp. 185–87; William Taubman, *Khrushchev: The Man and His Era* [New York: 2003], p. 392.)

attempts to conciliate Mao's regime would have produced a break with Moscow any sooner than Dulles's strategy of pressure did.

The difficulty with the Dulles approach was that it did not look beyond the immediate objective of splitting the two communist giants: it left the United States with two separate but roughly equally hostile adversaries, thus precluding opportunities to play off one against the other. General Matthew B. Ridgway had suggested as early as 1954 that if the objective was to split Beijing away from Moscow, then "the statesmanlike approach would seem to be to bring Red China to a realization that its long-range benefits derive from friendliness with America." But that would have required substantive diplomatic contacts, and these the administration resisted because of the problems they would pose with allies and with the American public. "[T]he purpose of creating divisive rather than unifying influences between China and the Soviets is obviously a correct one," Eisenhower wrote to Henry A. Wallace in 1957. "The problem is to discover ways of doing this without weakening our own ties with numerous Allies—particularly in the Far East." Recognition of Mao's government, he admitted three years later, "would destroy Chiang Kai-shek, our ally of long standing." Moreover, the American people were "emotional" about China—they tended to look at Beijing's record on Korea, American prisoners of war, Indochina and Taiwan, and to say "to hell with that." Eisenhower himself refused to say "never" at least with regard to mainland China's admission to the United Nations, but before that could happen the Chinese would have to "cease their aggressive intent, release our prisoners, and abandon their professed intention of taking Formosa by force."[88]*

The Eisenhower administration did begin moving in its final years toward a more forthcoming position on negotiations with the Soviet Union than it had previously demonstrated. Dulles's handling of Khrushchev's November 1958 ultimatum on access to West Berlin was a textbook demonstration of how combinations of threats and inducements could defuse a crisis. Convinced that the Russians had acted out of a sincere if misplaced fear of the West Germans, the Secretary of State sought to extend reassurances and even minor concessions through diplomatic channels while at the same time acting to strengthen the Western alliance and reaffirm Western rights in the divided city.[89] These initiatives led,

---

* Eisenhower meant here not Korean War prisoners, who had been released after the 1953 armistice, but several pilots subsequently shot down over China while flying reconnaissance missions for the Central Intelligence Agency.

shortly after Dulles's death in the spring of 1959, to another Soviet-American summit, this time in the United States.* The idea, as the President put it, was "to try to get Khrushchev committed to negotiations as a principle in the conduct of our relations."[90]

The Camp David summit of September 1959 failed to live up to the President's hopes (although, to be sure, Khrushchev's American visit more than fulfilled those of reporters in search of colorful copy). The only specifics to emerge from it were an agreement to hold a four-power summit in Paris the following spring, Eisenhower's acceptance of an invitation to visit the Soviet Union, and an indication from Khrushchev that he would not press the matter of Berlin until those meetings had been held. But the Camp David talks, together with other diplomatic contacts with the Russians initiated during the last years of the Eisenhower administration, did have one important effect not immediately obvious at the time: they served to legitimize the idea that negotiations were an appropriate means of dealing with Moscow, and that they could be undertaken without risking the unraveling of alliances or the appearance of appeasement. This was no inconsiderable legacy for Eisenhower's successor, whose opportunities for negotiations with the Soviet Union were greater, but whose base of support, both at home and overseas, was considerably more precarious than the universally popular "Ike's" had been.

But the U-2 incident of May 1960 and the cancellation of the Paris summit that followed it suggest that Eisenhower was no more inclined at the end of his term than he had been at the beginning to give negotiations priority over other approaches to containment. The President knew that an overflight so close to the summit could be dangerous—he later acknowledged that he had anticipated the consequences of a failure, but "had not felt he could oppose the combined opinion of all his associates. He added that the action that was taken was probably the right action, and what he would have done anyhow even if his advisers had correctly assessed the potential reaction." Once the plane was shot down, Khrushchev offered Eisenhower ample opportunity to disavow responsibility for having dispatched it, but the President refused, whether for reasons of personal honesty or from a desire to avoid giving credence to Democratic charges

---

* Eisenhower had intended to make Khrushchev's invitation to the United States contingent on progress at a forthcoming Geneva foreign ministers' conference on Berlin, but through a misunderstanding this qualification was not conveyed to the Soviet leader, who accepted with alacrity. (Goodpaster notes, Eisenhower conversation with Dillon and Murphy, July 22, 1959, Eisenhower Papers, Whitman File: DDE Diary, Box 27, "Staff Notes—July 59 (2).")

of not being in control of his own administration. The whole U-2 affair had been a "stupid . . . mess" that had ruined all his efforts to end the Cold War, Eisenhower commented bitterly later that summer.[91] But if ending the Cold War had in fact been his first priority, then the ease with which he allowed other considerations to distract him from the pursuit of negotiations did not fit well with that objective.

V

Contrary to the claims of "revisionist" historians, then, Eisenhower was something less than a "genius." He achieved his goal of greater deterrence at less cost, but only by narrowing the means of deterrence to nuclear weapons and little else, by confusing what, in the "third world," he was trying to deter, by failing to follow through on his own commitment to negotiations, and, it must be added, by benefiting from a considerable amount of good luck. Still, his strategy was coherent, bearing signs of his influence at every level, careful, for the most part, in its relation of ends to means, and, on the whole, more consistent with than detrimental to the national interest. It is a modest claim, but nonetheless a more favorable one than one can reasonably make about either the strategy that preceded, or the one that followed, the "New Look."

Kennedy, Johnson, and Flexible Response

John F. Kennedy attached even greater importance than usual to the task of putting "distance" between himself and his predecessor. His campaign critique of the previous administration had been no hasty accommodation to the requirements of winning a nomination, as Eisenhower's had been in 1952. The Massachusetts senator had articulated the basic elements of his position well before the Los Angeles convention in July 1960.[1] Nor were his criticisms aimed at gaining the support of a particular wing of the Democratic party, as Eisenhower had sought to do with the Republicans eight years earlier. Most Democrats shared Kennedy's reservations about the existing administration's conduct of foreign and national security affairs, as did a fair number of prominent Republicans.[2] Mixed with this uneasiness over past policies was a "generational" imperative, symbolized vividly in the transfer of power from the oldest elected president to the youngest: there was somehow the feeling that the promise—indeed the legitimacy—of a new generation of national leadership would be called into question if its programs were not made to differ visibly and substantially from what had gone before.

This preoccupation with creating a distinct identity manifested itself in the rhetoric of Kennedy's inaugural address ("the torch has been passed to a new generation of Americans, born in this century, tempered by war, disciplined by a hard and bitter peace"), in the emphasis on youth and vigor reflected in many of his early appointments, in an impatience with established bureaucratic structures, in the premium placed on working long hours and reaching quick decisions, in the preference for action over inaction, even in so small a thing as the new President's reluctance to be photographed playing golf, for fear this might suggest comparison with his more leisurely predecessor. "The United States needs a Grand Objective," one new Kennedy appointee wrote in a memorandum that caught precisely the spirit of the new administration. "[W]e behave as if . . . our real objective is to sit by our pools contemplating the spare tires around our middles. . . . The key consideration is not that the Grand Objective be exactly right, it is that we have one and that we start moving toward it."[3]

One element in this new identity was to be a more efficient formulation of national strategy. Kennedy believed that the National Security Council under Eisenhower had become bloated and unwieldy: so much of its time was spent producing policy papers on every conceivable subject, clearing them through the appropriate bureaucracies, and then discussing them in lengthy formal meetings with the President that the whole apparatus had become a barrier rather than the impetus to coordinated action it was supposed to have been. Actual decisions on critical issues, Kennedy correctly noted, had been made independently by Eisenhower and a few key advisers in the privacy of the Oval Office. The new Chief Executive resolved to cut back the National Security Council staff, to downgrade that organization from its previous position as the main national security decision-making body, and to rely more on direct contacts with individual departments or on *ad hoc* task forces for recommendations. The new system might sacrifice something in orderliness of procedure, but Kennedy thought that the advantages in terms of responsiveness and flexibility would be worth it.[4]

There emerged, then, no single dominant voice comparable to that of Dulles during most of the Eisenhower years; instead Kennedy deliberately cultivated a variety of advisers. He had intended the State Department to have primary responsibility for coordinating foreign and national security policy, but his Secretary of State, the self-effacing and modest Dean Rusk, proved either unwilling or unable to perform that role. As a consequence, influence gravitated to Kennedy's own White House staff, notably McGeorge Bundy, Assistant to the President for National Security Affairs, to the Department of Defense, where Robert S. McNamara was imposing the kind of vigorous leadership State lacked, to General Maxwell D. Taylor, at first a personal adviser to Kennedy on military affairs, then chairman of the Joint Chiefs of Staff, and to selected State Department officials whose views Kennedy found congenial, especially Charles E. Bohlen and Llewellyn Thompson on Soviet affairs, George

Ball on NATO and Western European matters, Roger Hilsman on East Asia and counter-insurgency, Richard Goodwin on Latin America, and Averell Harriman on everything.[5] The man most successful in articulating an overall strategic concept for the administration, though, was Walt Whitman Rostow, during 1961 an aide to Bundy on the National Security Council staff, and from December of that year the occupant of Kennan's old position as Chairman of the Policy Planning Council at State.*

Rostow had formidable skills as a rapid synthesizer of complex information (critics would say he was too masterful in this area, to the point of oversimplification): "Walt can write faster than I can read," Kennedy once joked. These qualities made him seem the ideal long-range planner, however. "Over here in the White House . . . we are pretty much restricted to what comes out of the bureaucracy," Kennedy told him. "I want you to go over there [State] and catch hold of the process where it counts."[6]

Within four months of his arrival Rostow had completed a 285-page draft statement of "Basic National Security Policy" comparable in purpose to, but much broader in scope than, the studies Eisenhower's National Security Council had regularly produced.† Kennedy never formally approved Rostow's "BNSP" draft, partly because of unresolved questions relating to the use of tactical nuclear weapons, partly for fear that an official endorsement might tie the President's hands.[7] The document was widely circulated within the government, though, and in retrospect it stands, along with Kennedy's public pronouncements, as the most comprehensive guide to what the administration thought it was trying to do in world affairs.

The basic assumptions of the Kennedy strategy remained in place after Lyndon B. Johnson became President, despite the new chief executive's dramatically different personal style. The very manner in which he assumed the office placed a premium on continuity; moreover Johnson himself had few disagreements with the approach Kennedy had sought to follow. Johnson retained most of the slain President's top advisers—notably Rusk, McNamara, Taylor, and Bundy—and when Bundy finally resigned as presidential national security adviser early in 1966, Johnson turned to the most energetic exponent of the Kennedy strategy, Rostow,

---

*The name of this organization and the title of its chief have varied slightly over the years from the original "Director of the Policy Planning Staff."

† Rostow's predecessor, George McGhee, had initiated the draft, but Rostow supervised its completion and the final version bears unmistakable and pervasive signs of his influence.

as his successor. It is impossible, of course, to know whether Kennedy would have handled events of the 1963–1969 period as Johnson did. What is not in doubt, though, is that the intellectual framework through which both men viewed the world was much the same.

I

John F. Kennedy's vision of the kind of world in which American institutions could survive and prosper differed from that of his predecessors only in the greater clarity and candor with which he expressed it. "[T]he interest of the United States of America," he proclaimed two months before his death, "is best served by preserving and protecting a world of diversity in which no one power or no one combination of powers can threaten the security of the United States." It had been the collapse of German and Japanese power at the end of World War II that had propelled the United States permanently into the international arena; the idea ever since had been that if "neither Russia nor China could control Europe and Asia . . . then our security was assured." There was, thus, "one simple central theme of American foreign policy . . . and that is to support the independence of nations so that one bloc cannot gain sufficient power to finally overcome us."[8]

Split infinitive notwithstanding, this was the most precise public explanation by an American president of what all postwar chief executives had believed, but rarely stated: that the American interest was not to remake the world, but to balance power within it; that nationalism, so long as it reflected the principle of self-determination, posed no threat to American institutions; that the United States therefore could more easily accommodate itself to a diverse world than could its more autocratic adversaries. As Kennan had insisted in 1948, the goal was to be particularism, not universalism. Kennedy's famous revision of Woodrow Wilson—"if we cannot now end our differences, at least we can help to make the world safe for diversity"—reflected no new insight, then: it was merely a public acknowledgment of an assumption upon which his administration, and the two that preceded it, had operated all along.[9]

But Kennedy and his advisers, like John Foster Dulles and the drafters of NSC-68, differed from Kennan in their conviction that the balance of power was fragile. Power, they believed, was as much a function of perceptions as of hardware, position, or will: minute shifts in its distribution—

or even the appearance of such shifts—could cause chain reactions of panic to sweep the world, with potentially devastating consequences. "[I]f you don't pay attention to the periphery," Rusk warned, "the periphery changes. And the first thing you know the periphery is the center. . . . [W]hat happens in one place cannot help but affect what happens in another."[10] The United States had an obligation to act, therefore, to prevent changes on the world scene that might restrict diversity by concentrating power in hostile hands.

The great problem was how to strike a balance. Actions taken to restore stability could impede diversity, giving the United States the appearance of a reactionary gendarme propping up unpopular but ideologically reliable regimes against indigenous—and inevitable—revolutions. Alternatively, excessive restraint in such matters could leave the way open for adversaries to exploit opportunities, with the United States wringing its hands ineffectually on the sidelines. The new administration regarded its predecessor as having committed both errors: the objection was not to Eisenhower's interventions in the internal affairs of other countries, but to his reluctance to provide the means of doing so without risking escalation or inaction, and to the fact that where he had acted, he had usually done so for the purpose of sustaining the status quo. What Kennedy hoped to do was to align American interests to a greater extent with the processes of irreversible change, while at the same time lowering the dangers of either humiliation or nuclear war.

The new strategy went well beyond Dulles's sporadic efforts to identify change in international relations—and the heightened sense of nationalism that almost always accompanied it—as consistent with U.S. interests. Pre-inaugural task force reports on Africa and Latin America stressed the need to support "progressive" elements in those parts of the world, without being too particular as to whether they took forms initially sympathetic to private enterprise, democratic institutions, or the American position in the Cold War. These were familiar forces, Rusk argued in an early speech:

> To state them simply, they are a quest for freedom—national and individual—a groping for a rule of law, and a yearning for economic and social improvement. So identified, our relation to them becomes clear. They are congenial forces, rooted in ideas upon which we have built our own nation, a striving which has been part of our own struggle, aspirations which we share with human beings in all parts of the world.

Rostow, the administration's chief theorist on problems of modernization, put the issue more candidly in his March 1962 "BNSP" draft: "On balance, our interests are likely to be better served by accepting the risks of leaning forward towards more modern groups than the risks of clinging to familiar friends rooted in the past." Washington needed the ability to develop rapport and understanding "with the next government while dealing effectively with the current government."[11]

Rostow saw no contradiction between this apparent call for intervention in the internal affairs of other countries and the administration's commitment to autonomy and self-determination. The United States would be most secure, he argued, in a world in which nations had the maximum opportunity to determine their own future; this did not mean that the United States needed societies abroad framed in its own image. Nor did it require "that all societies at all times accept democratic values as their aspiration and that they move uninterruptedly toward its achievement." But,

> major losses of territory or of resources would make it harder for the U.S. to create the kind of world environment it desires, might generate defeatism among governments and peoples in the non-Communist world, or give rise to frustrations at home (thereby increasing the danger that the U.S. might rashly initiate war); and it could make more difficult the maintenance of a balance of military power between East and West.

It would be difficult, in an era of modern technology and communications, "to envisage the survival of democratic American society as a beleaguered island in a totalitarian sea." It was, therefore, "in the American interest that the societies of Eurasia, Africa, and Latin America develop along lines broadly consistent with our own concepts of individual liberty and government based on consent."[12] Intervention might be necessary, to be sure, but it would be intervention on behalf of diversity, not in opposition to it.

If it was in the American interest to welcome but to guide change, so too, Kennedy and his advisers thought, was it necessary to expand the means available to deter undesirable shifts in the balance of power. Eisenhower, they believed, had relied too heavily on the threatened use of nuclear weapons to achieve that goal: his attachment to solvency as an interest co-equal with security not only reflected outdated economics, it also ran needless risks by leaving the nation few options for action below the nuclear level. Kennedy regarded it as a major priority of his administration to expand this range of available options: "We intend to have a wider choice," he told the nation in July 1961, "than humiliation or all-out nuclear war."[13]

Eisenhower's assumption had been that because means were inelastic, interests had to compete with one another: resources allocated to defense could only come at the expense of other priorities whose neglect might defeat the purposes of defense in the first place. But in the "new economics" of the Kennedy administration domestic and foreign interests were assumed to be complementary: the economy could withstand, even benefit from, increases in spending for both national defense and domestic reform. Military expenditures ought not to be kept below the level needed for security "because of the mistaken notion that the economy is unable to bear any extra burdens," Paul A. Samuelson, one of Kennedy's key economic advisers, wrote in a pre-inaugural task force report. "[A]ny stepping up of these programs that is deemed desirable for its own sake can only help rather than hinder the health of our economy in the period immediately ahead." Far from being a constraint, the economy, in this expansionist perspective, could provide means of sustaining more activist policies both at home and abroad. As Walter Heller, another of Kennedy's top advisers, later put it, "prosperity and rapid growth . . . put at [the President's] disposal, as nothing else can, the resources needed to achieve great societies at home and grand designs abroad."[14]

That there were echoes of NSC-68 in these arguments was no accident: several convergent lines of inheritance connected Kennedy's views on these matters to those that had been dominant during the last years of the Truman administration. One was political tradition. Democrats had generally been more tolerant of expensive domestic and national security programs than had more fiscally cautious Republicans.[15] Then, too, Kennedy's economic advisers, like Keyserling under Truman, were Keynesian expansionists, committed to full employment and economic growth, less concerned than their Republican counterparts about budget deficits and inflation.[16] Finally, several of the key architects of NSC-68—notably Dean Acheson, Dean Rusk, and Paul Nitze—were influential in the councils of the Kennedy administration, Acheson as a consultant and outspoken advocate of toughness during the 1961 Berlin crisis, Rusk as a Secretary of State fully attuned to the uses of military power, Nitze as chairman of Kennedy's pre-inaugural task force report on national security policy and as Assistant Secretary of Defense for International Security Affairs.[17]

The change in emphasis was not long in coming. For reasons more political than economic, Kennedy paid tribute to the virtues of a balanced budget during his first year in office, but he made it clear that such considerations would not inhibit him from increasing defense spending. "Our arms must be adequate to meet our commitments and ensure our security, without being bound by arbitrary budget ceilings," he told the Congress in

March 1961; "we must not shrink from additional costs where they are necessary."[18] Later that year, at the urging of his economic advisers, he rejected the idea of a tax increase to finance the Berlin crisis defense buildup; by 1962 he was explaining publicly that surpluses acquired at the expense of economic growth did not necessarily prevent inflation, but that deficits incurred in the process of stimulating such activity might.[19] It was left to Kennedy's more voluble successor to set out the implications of this line of reasoning in more comprehensible terms: "We are the richest nation in the history of the world," Lyndon B. Johnson proclaimed in July 1964. "We can afford to spend whatever is needed to keep this country safe and to keep our freedom secure. And we shall do just that."[20]

It had been an assumption of all postwar administrations that the disproportionate economic and military strength of the United States gave it unique responsibilities in maintaining the world balance of power. "[W]e are the key, the archstone, the basic element in the strength of the entire free world," Kennedy noted in 1963,[21] and it is doubtful that either of his immediate predecessors would have disagreed with him. But perceptions of means had shaped both the nature and the extent of that commitment: Truman prior to 1950, and Eisenhower throughout his term, had assumed that limited resources necessarily restricted the range of actions the United States could take in defense of global equilibrium. Kennedy's more expansive perception of means paved the way for a more activist foreign policy, as NSC-68 had done eleven years earlier. The new president did not take literally the rhetoric of his inaugural address—"we shall pay any price, bear any burden, meet any hardship, support any friend, oppose any foe to assure the survival and success of liberty." He warned repeatedly that the United States could not act alone, that it could not defend those incapable of defending themselves, and that it would not unnecessarily run the risk of nuclear war.[22] But the mood of his administration, as of his successor's, was to favor action over inaction all else being equal, to pay greater attention to controlling risks than costs, and to harness what it regarded as virtually unlimited capabilities in the task of defending American interests.

II

If the Kennedy administration was reasonably clear about interests, it was less so about potential threats to them. One of the major ambiguities of the Eisenhower-Dulles years—the tendency to portray international communism as an implacable and efficient monolith while acknowledging its frailties and vulnerabilities—grew more noticeable under Kennedy. Contributing further to the confusion was the Soviet Union's own inconsistency: at no point during the Cold War did its behavior oscillate more between extremes of belligerence and conciliation than during Kennedy's years in office. Then too, there was an increasing conviction on the part of administration officials that the United States could threaten itself by appearing weak and irresolute. The result was a perception of danger but of elusiveness as well, making it difficult to know how, or to what, to respond.

The Kennedy administration moved quickly, on the basis on new analytical techniques, to lower its estimates of the Soviet threat in two key areas: strategic missiles and conventional forces in Europe. Access to U-2 intelligence convinced the new President and his advisers that Eisenhower had been right in denying that there had ever been a "missile gap" of any consequence. The phrase had had a "useful shorthand effect of calling attention to . . . our basic military posture," McGeorge Bundy noted in March 1961, "but no one has ever supposed that a naked count of missiles was in and of itself a sufficient basis for national security." By the fall of that year, new satellite reconnaissance capabilities had confirmed that even in strict numerical terms, the United States was well ahead of the Russians in operational ICBMs.[23]* After some thought, Kennedy authorized Deputy Secretary of Defense Roswell Gilpatric to make that fact public in late October; the following month the President himself pointedly observed that "in terms of total military strength, the United States would not trade places with any nation on earth."[24]

A similar but less conspicuous reassessment of Soviet capabilities was taking place with regard to the military balance in central Europe. Traditionally that balance had been measured in army divisions: by that scale, which gave Warsaw Pact forces approximately 175 as compared to NATO's 25, the defense problem looked hopeless short of using nuclear weapons.

---

* Paul Nitze noted in 1963 that "even before that [intelligence] break-through, three things markedly reduced the vulnerability to be expected of our retaliatory forces to attack by the estimated Soviet strategic forces—and hence reduced the real significance of the so-called gap. First, there had been modest but significant downward revision in our intelligence estimates of the Soviet ICBM program. Second, a cumulative series of defense improvements, including early warning, had begun to make themselves felt, and the first three Polaris submarines went on station in 1961. Third, although President Kennedy's own defense program would have its major impact in succeeding years, the increase in SAC's fifteen-minute ground alert from one-third to one-half of its aircraft added immediately to SAC survivability." (Nitze to Bundy, June 17, 1963, Kennedy Papers, National Security File, Box 298, "Missile Gap.")

But the application of systems analysis techniques (one of McNamara's innovations at the Pentagon) created a wholly different picture. Defense planners calculated that if the Russians were in fact equipping 175 divisions at roughly U.S. standards, then they would have to be spending eight times what Washington was for the purpose. Even allowing for more spartan standards, the cost of such a force would have been far beyond what the Soviet economy could reasonably support, given its relatively low gross national product and even lower agricultural productivity. At the same time, intelligence estimates were placing Soviet military manpower at only about twice that of the United States (2,000,000 versus 960,000), and NATO manpower actually ahead of the Warsaw Pact (6,000,000 versus 4,500,000). The explanation turned out to be surprisingly simple: Soviet divisions were only about one-third the size of U.S. and NATO divisions, and hence presumably only about one-third as effective.[25] The result of these recalculations of Soviet missile and manpower capabilities was to give the West, for the first time since 1945, a sense of overall military parity with the Soviet Union, possibly even superiority.

But this reassurance did not eliminate, and may even have contributed to, a greater danger of war by miscalculation as Khrushchev sought to redress what he perceived to be a deteriorating military situation by threatening West Berlin, resuming nuclear testing in the atmosphere, and, ultimately, placing medium- and intermediate-range ballistic missiles in Cuba. In retrospect, these maneuvers appear to have had as their objective a display of power sufficient to frighten the U.S. and its allies into accepting a relaxation of tensions, while at the same time placating the increasingly critical Chinese and protecting the only communist regime in the Western hemisphere.[26] The risk, though, Rostow was warning seven months before Soviet missiles were discovered in Cuba, was that Kremlin leaders "might underestimate the importance attached by the U.S. to particular interests or areas, and initiate action in the belief that the U.S. will not respond."[27] To its credit, the Kennedy administration saw Khrushchev's provocations more as acts of desperation than of imminent war: its firm but restrained response, reflecting a self-confidence in the adequacy of its own deterrence that the Soviet leader obviously lacked, appears to have convinced him, after the confrontation of October 1962, to seek détente by more straightforward means.

The dangers of nuclear war had receded by 1963, therefore, but the threat from more limited forms of aggression had not. Kennedy and his advisers had taken with the utmost seriousness Khrushchev's January 1961 speech offering support to "wars of national liberation": it was, they thought, evidence of a new communist campaign to seize control of anti-colonial and other revolutionary movements in the "third world." "[W]e are opposed around the world by a monolithic and ruthless conspiracy that relies primarily on covert means for expanding its sphere of influence," Kennedy warned later that year. The struggle might have been switched from Europe to Asia, Africa, and Latin America, from nuclear and conventional weaponry to irregular warfare, insurrection, and subversion, but it was no less real for that. The fact that "men are knifed in their homes and not shot in the fields of battle" did not alter the need to protect them from such assaults, for if those methods were successful in countries like Laos and South Vietnam, then "the gates will be opened wide."[28]

Once again, it was Rostow who supplied the key assumptions behind this perception of threat. As a prominent member of the so-called Charles River school of development economists, centered at Harvard and M.I.T. in the 1950's, Rostow had become convinced that the future struggle between communism and capitalism would take the form of contests to demonstrate the relevance of each ideology to the development process in the "third world." Communists believed

> that the techniques of political centralization under dictatorial control—and the projected image of Soviet and Chinese Communist economic progress— will persuade hesitant men, faced by great transitional problems, that the Communist model should be adopted for modernization, even at the cost of surrendering human liberty.

Rostow liked to describe communists unflatteringly as "scavengers of the modernization process": the unavoidable traumas of that process made developing countries susceptible to this "disease of the transition to modernization." If the "third world" was not to succumb to these evils, with all the implications that would pose for the world balance of power, then the United States and other "developed" countries would have to demonstrate that economic progress could take place within a democratic framework: "the emerging less developed nations must be persuaded that their human and national aspirations will be better fulfilled within the compass of [the free] community than without."[29]

But Rostow's view implied common action, if not common direction, on the part of international communism, and this was difficult to reconcile with the centrifugal tendencies he and others saw at work within that movement. Nationalism, he maintained, had proven to be the most durable of the postwar ideologies: both Washington and Moscow had suffered and could expect to suffer more defections from their respective camps as the "diffusion of power" away from the bipolar world of the late 1940's progressed. The Sino-Soviet split was real and likely to get worse: "It could give rise to increased factionalism in national Communist parties, weaken the overall thrust of world Communism, and facilitate the emergence of more independent and nationalistic Communist states, especially in Eastern Europe."[30] And yet, Rostow seemed to expect all communists to act alike when tempted by opportunities to exploit modernization stresses in the "third world." Communists might quarrel with one another but, so far as global stability was concerned, their interests collectively were fundamentally hostile to those of the West.

The problem with this view was that the whole idea of maintaining a balance of power had been to prevent concentrations of hostile force; adversaries fragmented among themselves presumably balanced themselves, without the need for outside countervailing pressure. One implication of living with diversity, after all, had been that the United States could tolerate varying degrees of enmity in the world so long as it was neither consolidated nor coordinated. To question this premise would be to arrive at universalism by the back door: the United States really would need a world resembling it in order to be secure. Rostow never worked out this contradiction, which had the United States attempting to counter-balance a mythical monolith. His own confusion on this point reflected that of the administration as a whole.

Kennedy's government was less prone than Eisenhower's to perceive threats to the balance of power in ideological terms. It was too easy, the new President told the nation in June 1961, "to dismiss as Communist-inspired every anti-government or anti-American riot, every overthrow of a corrupt regime, or every mass protest against misery and despair." Khrushchev had been right in claiming that "there are many disorders throughout the world, and he should not be blamed for them all." Nor were American allies all paragons of democracy. The overused term "free world," Arthur Schlesinger, Jr., privately pointed out, included Paraguay, Nicaragua, and Franco's Spain—"Whom are we fooling?" Kennedy was more sympathetic to neutralism than Eisenhower and Dulles had been; less worried that nationalism would not be able to sustain itself against communist threats. He was even prepared to accept the idea that communists might come to power from time to time by democratic means. "What we find objectionable, and a threat to the peace," he told Soviet journalist

Alexei Adzhubei, "is when a system is imposed by a small militant group by subversion, infiltration, and all the rest."[31]

Moreover, the administration shared Rostow's view that the Sino-Soviet split was serious. Despite cautious public statements by Kennedy and other officials, and despite reluctance on the part of the State Department to abandon familiar references to the "Sino-Soviet bloc,"[32] evidence of growing differences between Moscow and Beijing impressed American observers. Llewellyn Thompson, the United States ambassador to the Soviet Union, raised the possibility as early as February 1961 that given their differences with the Chinese, the Russians might well have come to realize that "even [an] all-Communist world would leave them beset with enormous problems." The Central Intelligence Agency noted in April that ideology had become a divisive rather than a unifying force in the communist world; two years later it concluded that "the U.S.S.R. and China are now two separate powers whose interests conflict on almost every issue." The year 1963 brought indications, most conspicuously in the form of the Limited Nuclear Test Ban Treaty, that Khrushchev was willing to incur Mao Zedong's wrath to move toward détente with the West. By 1964 the Johnson administration, worried about China's imminent nuclear capability, was even considering the possibility of cooperation with the Soviet Union against that country, up to and including "preventive military action."[33]*

That such a maneuver could even be discussed—no action was taken—suggests the extent to which perceptions of threat had shifted since Eisenhower's day. Eisenhower and Dulles had been willing to risk at least

---

*"(1) We are not in favor of unprovoked unilateral U.S. military action against Chinese nuclear installations at this time. We would prefer to have a Chinese test take place than to initiate such action now. If for other reasons we should find ourselves in military hostilities at any level with the Chinese Communists, we would expect to give very close attention to the possibility of an appropriate military action against Chinese nuclear facilities.

"(2) We believe that there are many possibilities for joint action with the Soviet Government if that Government is interested. Such possibilities include a warning to the Chinese against tests, a possible undertaking to give up underground testing and to hold the Chinese accountable if they test in any way, and even a possible agreement to cooperate for preventive military action. We therefore agree that it would be most desirable for the Secretary of State to explore this matter very privately with Ambassador Dobrynin, as soon as possible." (Bundy memorandum of Johnson conversation with Rusk, McNamara, and John McCone, September 15, 1964, *FRUS: 1964–68*, XXX, document 49. For the background of this document, see Gordon H. Chang, "JFK, China, and the Bomb," *Journal of American History*, LXXIV [March, 1988], 1287–1310; also Craig deLaurier, "The Ultimate Enemy: Kennedy, Johnson and the Chinese Nuclear Threat, 1961–1964," Senior Essay, Department of History, Yale University, April, 2000.)

limited nuclear war to deter minimal gains by communist powers. Johnson was now contemplating working with one communist power to prevent the acquisition of a nuclear capability by another. This was striking evidence of a newfound willingness to distinguish between threats: "different dangers require different policies and different actions," Johnson commented on the day before the first Chinese nuclear test.[34] It also suggested that nuclear war had come to be seen in Washington as a threat in itself, greater in magnitude than most provocations that could conceivably have justified resort to it.

But, curiously, this altered perception of threat produced no change in official perceptions of undifferentiated interests. Both Kennedy and Johnson retained the same "zero-sum game" view of the world that had characterized the Eisenhower administration—the idea that victories for communism anywhere represented losses for the United States. "I know full well," Kennedy commented two months before his death, "that every time a country, regardless of how far away it may be from our own borders . . . passes behind the Iron Curtain the security of the United States is thereby endangered." Johnson added the following year that "surrender anywhere threatens defeat everywhere."[35] Statements like these left more questions than answers: If communism was no longer a monolith, who then was the enemy? If threats to the world balance of power were no longer cohesive, why should every alteration in that balance imperil the United States? If it was really in Washington's interest to accept a world of diversity, why did it react with such alarm to changes in the status quo?

One answer might be found in Rostow's assumption that, whatever their differences, all communists had in common interests hostile to those of the "free world," and that sooner or later they could be expected to act on that basis, whether in a coordinated manner or not. "Caesar and Pompey and Antony and Octavius and the others did not fall out until they were successful," Kennedy reminded a press conference in 1961. "We cannot afford the luxury of permitting [that] kind of success." But that argument was hard to sustain in the face of indications that the communist world was fragmenting *prior* to achieving its objectives, and that some parts of it— notably the Soviet Union after the Cuban missile crisis—seemed prepared to work with the capitalist world against other parts of it. "[L]ong-range interests of geography and nationalism play a part even behind the Iron Curtain," Kennedy acknowledged, also shortly before his assassination. The CIA predicted in 1964 that "communism in the future will come to possess still less doctrinal uniformity than it now has. Indeed, the national and doctrinal antagonisms which exist may occasionally lead to armed conflict;

the communist world may come to be as diverse and undisciplined as the non-Communist world."[36]

Another explanation might have been that the Chinese had now replaced the Russians as the major threat to global equilibrium. There was, to be sure, no hint of détente in Beijing's rhetoric, whether directed at Moscow or Washington; nor were there indications that the Chinese shared the fear of nuclear war that had grown so strong in those two capitals. China had the world's largest land army, already tested in battle against the United States; it was also on the verge of developing nuclear weapons. But China lacked the industrial base necessary to sustain war at a sophisticated level; its primitive air force and navy would not be able to deliver nuclear weapons; and it had the additional disadvantage of sharing a 5,000-mile border with an increasingly hostile Soviet Union. Moreover, as the CIA noted in the summer of 1963, Chinese actions, as opposed to rhetoric, had been cautious: "we do not believe that they will act recklessly or run very great risks. . . . The Chinese have thus far shown a marked respect for U.S. power, and we do not expect them to change this basic attitude."[37] As a threat worthy in itself of a worldwide response, then, China was not very credible.

What the Kennedy and Johnson administrations came to fear most, one gathers, was not so much communism, which was too fragmented, or the Soviet Union, which was too committed to détente, or even China, which was too impotent, but rather the threat of embarrassment, of humiliation, of appearing to be weak. Both presidents could accept the argument that Eisenhower and Dulles had overextended the United States; the problem, however, was that these commitments could not be abandoned without appearing to call into question more vital obligations elsewhere. The United States was overcommitted in Southeast Asia, Kennedy told Walter Lippmann in March 1961, but it was necessary to deal with facts as they were. A genuine neutralization of Laos would be acceptable—unilateral intervention, as Eisenhower had recommended, would not work. But "[w]e cannot and will not accept any visible humiliation over Laos." Johnson made the same point after his trip to Southeast Asia as Vice President the following May: the alternative to aiding the countries of that region was to "throw in the towel . . . and pull our defenses back to San Francisco. . . . [W]e would say to the world . . . that we don't live up to treaties and don't stand by our friends."[38]

Kennedy explained the problem candidly in an interview given shortly after the Cuban missile crisis. The danger had not been that the Russians would actually fire missiles from Cuba, he noted; had they intended to start a nuclear war, their own home-based weapons would have been adequate for the purpose. But a successful deployment, publicly revealed, "would have politically changed the balance of power. It would have appeared to, and appearances contribute to reality."[39] This, in a nutshell, was the threat: that having committed itself to maintaining the existing distribution of power in the world, the United States could not allow challenges to that distribution even to *appear* to succeed against its will, because perceptions of power could be as important as the real thing. Like Rostow, an administration committed to diversity, aware of the divisions among its adversaries, had nonetheless worked itself into a universal obligation to maintain a status quo which, if it did not precisely resemble the United States, was at least one that familiarity had made comfortable.

All of which suggests that while expanding perceptions of threat can broaden interests and enlarge means, the reverse is not necessarily the case. The narrowed perception of threat that followed Khrushchev's moves toward détente and confirmation of the Sino-Soviet split produced no corresponding reduction of interests; instead these remained much as they had been during the Eisenhower administration. This, in turn, suggests that interests may be as much functions of means as of threats, for while both threats and means expanded in 1950, what happened during the Kennedy administration was a contraction of threats combined with a proliferation of means over and above what the previous incumbent had been willing to supply. The result was a containment strategy reminiscent of NSC-68 in its commitment to flexible but appropriate response regardless of costs; different from that earlier document, though, in its vagueness regarding just what was to be contained.

III

Strategies of containment, to this point, had alternated between concepts of symmetrical and asymmetrical response. Both Kennan and Dulles had called for asymmetry—countering challenges to the balance of power not necessarily at the levels at which they had occurred, but rather on terrain and with instruments best calculated to apply American strengths against adversary weaknesses. For Kennan, the favored instrument had been economic aid; for Dulles, the nuclear deterrent. Both the authors of NSC-68 and the later Democratic critics of the "New Look" had questioned asymmetry on the grounds that it provided insufficient means to respond to varieties of challenge. With this in mind, the Kennedy administration, in formulating a strategy appropriate to its perception of interests and threats, now moved back to symmetry as the desired approach. As usual, it was left to Rostow to state the problem most succinctly:

> It should be noted that we have generally been at a disadvantage in crises, since the Communists command a more flexible set of tools for imposing strain on the Free World—and a greater freedom to use them—than we normally command. We are often caught in circumstances where our only available riposte is so disproportionate to the immediate provocation that its use risks unwanted escalation or serious political costs to the free community. This asymmetry makes it attractive for Communists to apply limited debilitating pressures upon us in situations where we find it difficult to impose on them an equivalent price for their intrusions. We must seek, therefore, to expand our arsenal of limited overt and covert countermeasures if we are in fact to make crisis-mongering, deeply built into Communist ideology and working habits, an unprofitable occupation.[40]

This symmetrical approach came to be known publicly, borrowing from Maxwell Taylor's book *The Uncertain Trumpet*, as the strategy of "flexible response."

Kennedy set out its objectives in his first message to Congress on defense, in March 1961: "to deter all wars, general or limited, nuclear or conventional, large or small—to convince all potential aggressors that any attack would be futile—to provide backing for the diplomatic settlement of disputes—to insure the adequacy of our bargaining power for an end to the arms race." Eisenhower and Dulles had sought similar goals, of course, but at minimal cost: as a consequence, they had been prepared to run the risks either of not acting at all, or of responding at levels beyond the original provocation. Kennedy, possessed of an economic rationale for disregarding costs, placed his emphasis on minimizing risks by giving the United States sufficient flexibility to respond without either escalation or humiliation. This would require a capacity to act at all levels, ranging from diplomacy through covert action, guerrilla operations, conventional and nuclear war. Equally important, though, it would require careful control: "We believe in maintaining effective deterrent strength," the new President stressed, "but we also believe in making it do what we wish, neither more nor less."[41]*

---

*McGeorge Bundy warned Kennedy shortly after his inauguration that existing war plans placed "a debatable emphasis (1) on strategic as against limited-war forces, (2) on 'strike-first', or 'counter-force' strategic planning, as against a 'deterrent' or 'second strike' posture, and (3) on decisions-in-advance, as against decisions in the light of all the circumstances. These three

The administration placed great emphasis, hence, on calibration, or "fine tuning"—ensuring that actions taken were appropriate to the situation—and on integration—applying to the tasks at hand all available instruments, in a coordinated and purposeful manner. These tendencies can be seen in six major areas, all of them central to Kennedy's strategy: (1) the bolstering of conventional and unconventional military capabilities; (2) the strategic missile buildup, which proceeded even after the myth of the "missile gap" had been exposed; (3) renewed efforts to solidify alliances; (4) a new emphasis on the non-military instruments of containment; (5) attempts to manage more effectively domestic resources vital to defense; and (6) an expansion of Eisenhower's earlier efforts to open up areas for possible negotiations with the Russians.

Top priority went to decreasing the reliance on nuclear weapons to deter limited aggression that had been so prominent a feature of the Eisenhower administration's strategy: "We attach the greatest importance," a State Department analysis noted in February 1961, "to 'raising the threshold' beyond which the President might have to decide to initiate the use of nuclear weapons." Non-nuclear conflict had posed the "most active and constant threat to Free World security," Kennedy told the Congress the following month, yet "such conflicts do not justify and must not lead to a general nuclear attack." The United States, accordingly, had to "increase our ability to confine our response to non-nuclear weapons, and to lessen the incentive for any limited aggression by making clear what our response will accomplish." Local forces of resistance could handle many of these situations, but the United States also had to be prepared "to make a substantial contribution in the form of strong, highly mobile forces trained in this type of warfare." Such a capability would do two things, a Policy Planning Council study pointed out later that year. It would eliminate the tendency to confuse nuclear power with usable power: "In conditions of nuclear stalemate, initiating a recourse to nuclear weapons is irrational. The threat to do so is only convincing if it comes from an opponent who has been driven to desperation." But it would also provide a credible means of matching non-nuclear escalation: "The threat of using non-

forces in combination have created a situation today in which a subordinate commander faced with a substantial Russian military action could start the thermonuclear holocaust on his own initiative if he could not reach you (by failure of communication at either end of the line.)" (Bundy to Kennedy, January 30, 1961, *FRUS: 1961–63*, VIII, Document 7.)

nuclear force against an opponent who can far out-escalate us without having recourse to nuclear weapons is not a threat which inspires respect."[42]

McNamara initially thought that additional conventional forces would not be necessary: energies rather should be devoted, he argued, toward developing unconventional forces capable of countering "indirect aggression." But the 1961 Berlin crisis convinced him that additional regular troops were in fact needed, both as a sign of resolve and as a way of increasing the number of escalatory steps that could be taken prior to resorting to nuclear weapons. Kennedy handled the immediate problem by calling up reserves; the longer-range solution was to boost combat-ready Army divisions from 11 to 16, a force estimated to be capable of coping simultaneously with major wars in Europe and Asia and a "minor" crisis elsewhere.[43] The outcome of the Cuban missile crisis appeared to confirm the wisdom of that approach: the presence of usable conventional forces, Kennedy believed, had left Khrushchev no choice but to withdraw his missiles or risk nuclear war. Had a comparable situation occurred in 1961, McNamara later admitted, the United States could not have mustered a credible invasion force without first bringing home troops stationed overseas. Kennedy drew the appropriate conclusions: "a line of destroyers in a quarantine, or a division of well-equipped men on a border, may be more useful to our real security than the multiplication of awesome weapons beyond all rational need."[44]

The administration placed special emphasis on bolstering NATO's conventional capabilities. Eisenhower and Dulles had persuaded the allies that nuclear deterrence was the most credible and least costly way of discouraging a Soviet conventional attack. They had dispatched both tactical nuclear weapons and intermediate-range ballistic missiles to Europe—the idea had been that any Soviet invasion would be met, whether immediately or after a brief "pause" for the Russians to reconsider, by a nuclear retaliatory response. A variety of concerns caused the Kennedy administration to question this strategy: its desire to increase the range of available options prior to resort to nuclear war; its estimates of the damage a war fought even with tactical nuclear weapons would cause; its recent downgrading of Soviet conventional force levels in Europe; its belief that the United States and its allies could afford to do more in that area; and its fear that continued reliance on nuclear weapons might lead to their further proliferation. The new approach was not popular with the Europeans, who took the view that an emphasis on conventional forces could only imply lack of confidence in nuclear deterrence. But McNamara insisted that deterrence would work more reliably with multiple options than with just one: "We must be in a position to confront [the U.S.S.R.] at any level of provocation with an appropriate military response."[45]

Conventional forces alone could not be of much help, though, in countering the support Khrushchev had promised for "wars of national liberation." What was needed here, the administration insisted, was a vastly increased capability for counter-insurgency warfare, based on the proposition that the only way to fight guerrillas was to employ their tactics on their terrain. This further manifestation of symmetrical response took the form of intensified training for "special forces" versed in the techniques of political, social, and economic "action" as well as irregular warfare; obligatory courses on counter-insurgency at the war colleges and in the Foreign Service; and avid discussions within the highest circles of the administration of the writings of Mao Zedong, Vo Nguyen Giap, and Che Guevara. It was to be "a dynamic national strategy," a determinedly enthusiastic Pentagon report concluded in July 1962: "an action program designed to defeat the Communist without recourse to the hazard or the terror of nuclear war; one designed to defeat subversion where it had already erupted, and, even more important, to prevent its taking initial root. Put otherwise—it was a strategy of both therapy and of prophylaxis."[46]

The influence of Rostow was unmistakable in all of this—his commitment to economic development not as a traditionally liberal end in itself, but as a means of stabilizing the world balance of power (a "Chester Bowles with machine guns," one colleague called him); his assumption that the balance of power was so delicate that even slight shifts might upset it; his conviction that victories for communism anywhere (even though communism was itself fragmenting) would bring about such shifts. Rostow did not, to be sure, favor intervention against all communist-led insurgencies: the primary responsibility for countering them, he insisted, remained with "local forces," motivated presumably by a sense of their own nationalism. But where that motive did not exist, or where the insurgency threatened to overwhelm it, Washington had to be prepared to act at the appropriate level: "the U.S. cannot accept in principle an asymmetry which allows Communist probes into the free community without possibility of riposte."[47]

The administration's desire to reduce its dependence on nuclear weapons did not, however, imply any corresponding determination to cut back on either their number or variety. "Nuclear and non-nuclear power complement each other," McNamara insisted in 1962, "just as together they complement the non-military instruments of policy."[48] Eisenhower's critics had complained both about his reliance on such weapons and his failure to provide enough of them. Despite their quick confirmation that the "missile gap" did not exist, Kennedy and his advisers remained determined to upgrade American strategic capabilities beyond what Eisenhower had contemplated. The result, by mid-1964, was an increase of 150 percent in the number of nuclear weapons available, a 200 percent boost in deliverable megatonnage, the construction of ten additional Polaris submarines (for a total of 29) and of 400 additional Minuteman missiles (for a total of 800) above what the previous administration had scheduled.[49]

The motives behind this strategic buildup were mixed. Certainly there was a reluctance initially to admit that Democratic charges of a "missile gap" had been ill-founded. Bureaucratic considerations played a role also: it was easier to avoid the kind of inter-service squabbling that had embarrassed the Eisenhower administration by erring on the side of a generous rather than a parsimonious defense budget. Additional numbers of weapons helped as well to increase both invulnerability and reliability; they also provided more options for the use of such weapons if that should become necessary. But the principal motive behind the buildup was simply to hold on to that position of strategic superiority so dramatically revealed by the final discrediting of the "missile gap" myth. As Assistant Secretary of Defense Paul Nitze told the International Institute for Strategic Studies in December 1961, "we believe that this force, including the U.K. nuclear forces and the NATO forces deployed on the Continent, gives the West a definite nuclear superiority. We further believe that this superiority can be maintained into the future. . . . Furthermore, we believe this superiority, particularly when viewed from the Soviet side, to be strategically important in the equations of deterrence and strategy."[50]

Not everyone in the administration agreed that the drive for strategic superiority was wise. Maxwell Taylor worried about the resulting competition for funds with conventional forces: "we are not moving rapidly enough in our efforts to raise the threshold at which it is necessary for us to initiate the use of nuclear weapons." Budget Director David Bell warned that the strategic buildup might provoke a response in kind from the Russians. Carl Kaysen, a member of Bundy's staff, agreed:

> They are perfectly capable of such a response. At present, the most sensible interpretation of their own missile development is that it rests on the concept of finite deterrence. It is certainly to our advantage to have it do so. The

Air Force has in the past equated national security with an ever increasing strategic striking force, and this position has wide popular support. The view is filled with dangers; to the extent that the best evidence indicates that it lacks justification, it is important to move our military planning away from it as soon as possible.

Revised estimates of actual Soviet missile strength had not been taken into account in setting U.S. strategic goals, Kaysen reminded Kennedy; "any error on the side of generosity has the undesirable consequence of stepping up the arms race. In a world of missiles and thermonuclear warheads more arms do not in any simple way add more security." Kennedy acknowledged the validity of the reasoning, but failed to endorse the conclusion. "[I]t's a deadly business, this competition," he told a press conference early in 1962. "And I don't say that much security comes out of it. But less security would certainly come out of it if we permitted them to make a decisive breakthrough in an area like an ICBM."[51]

There was, accordingly, no cutback in the missile program, but McNamara did undertake an ambitious effort to achieve some measure of control over how a future nuclear war might be fought. Existing arrangements provided little or no leeway in such matters. "In essence," Bundy had told Kennedy in the summer of 1961, "the current plan calls for shooting off everything we have in one shot, and it is so constructed as to make any more flexible course very difficult." McNamara hoped to increase the range of alternatives open to the President in a nuclear war, while at the same time minimizing as much as possible both the damage should such an event occur, and the likelihood of its occurring. With this in mind, he initially advocated targeting opposing forces, not cities, as a means of giving adversaries "the strongest imaginable incentive to refrain from striking our own cities." In time, though, McNamara came to regard deterring an attack as more important than limiting damage should one take place: that seemed to rule out "counterforce" strikes, since for deterrence to work both sides had to have confidence in their forces' ability to survive a surprise attack and still be capable of retaliation.[52] By the end of the Kennedy administration, then, the peculiar logic of "mutual assured destruction" was beginning to emerge—the idea that one's population could best be protected by leaving it vulnerable, so long as the other side faced comparable vulnerabilities.

The administration's preoccupation with finding alternatives to the use of nuclear weapons would appear to have made it sympathetic to Kennan's 1949 suggestion that the United States adopt a policy of "no first use."

And, indeed, Kennedy did in his initial public statement on defense strategy pledge that "our arms will never be used to strike the first blow in any attack." The emphasis on beefing up NATO conventional forces seemed consistent with this approach, as did the effort put into ensuring the survival of the nation's strategic forces against any Soviet "first strike." Still, the administration was never willing wholly to abandon the option of preemption, partly because it believed, unlike Kennan, that nuclear weapons could be made a rational instrument of policy, partly because of the deterrent potential of such a posture. "We should try to convey a reasonably subtle message to the Communists," Rostow wrote in 1962. "We wish to assure them that we do not intend to strike them first if they do not transgress the frontiers of the free community, but that we might well strike first under certain circumstances if they do."

> In short, we should not so preclude the possibility of launching the first nuclear blow as to deny ourselves the deterrent advantage of Soviet uncertainty on this point; nor should we so commit ourselves to this concept as to maximize its destabilizing effect in periods of tension, or to create an unbalanced resource allocation which would render U.S. and allied forces vulnerable to non-nuclear attack and require a nuclear riposte contrary to our allied interests, if such an attack were to be countered.[53]

John Foster Dulles had been right, then, about the virtues of unpredictability as a deterrent. Where Kennedy and his advisers differed was on the need to combine it with the flexibility to act across the entire spectrum of conceivable responses.

A third area of emphasis for the Kennedy administration involved rationalizing, and thereby strengthening, overseas alliances. Not surprisingly, it was NATO that presented the most formidable difficulties. Despite efforts to bolster the alliance's conventional capabilities, neither the United States nor the Europeans were willing to dispense wholly with nuclear weapons as a deterrent to Soviet aggression. This had been an additional reason for Kennedy's unwillingness to rule out an American "first strike"; his administration actually increased the number of tactical nuclear weapons stationed in Europe by some 60 percent despite deep reservations as to how they could be used in such heavily populated areas.* But given the frequent shifts that had taken place in Washington's

---

* Not only did tactical nuclear weapons contaminate the surrounding battlefield, Maxwell Taylor reminded Kennedy in May 1962, they also left craters, set forest fires, and blew down trees. But the Russians were deploying them heavily, and this suggested the need to increase

strategic thinking in recent years, and given the impossibility of proving ahead of time that the United States would actually risk its own cities to defend those of its allies, the Europeans found reliance on the American deterrent increasingly unsettling, even humiliating. Nor was the Kennedy administration unsympathetic: it genuinely supported the concept of a self-reliant, independent, preferably unified Europe, capable simultaneously of resisting the Soviet Union, submerging what was left of German nationalism, and relieving Washington of some of its global responsibilities.[54] The problem was to reconcile the attributes of sovereignty implied in those aspirations with their all-too-obvious absence in the field of nuclear defense.

One way, of course, would have been for the NATO countries to develop their own nuclear weapons, as by 1961 both Britain and France had done. But the Kennedy administration emphatically discouraged this alternative, for several reasons. Small national nuclear forces, McNamara insisted, would be neither numerous nor accurate enough to constitute an effective deterrent; they would, however, make their home countries targets for Soviet attack. Nor, without a unified command structure, could such weapons be used in the coordinated manner prescribed by the strategy of "flexible response"; possibilities for miscalculations, even accidents, would accordingly be great. There was also the danger that if other NATO countries developed nuclear weapons the West Germans would want them too, a prospect that would not only provoke the Russians but might so upset Germany's neighbors as to break up the alliance. "We do not believe in a series of national deterrents," Kennedy noted in May 1962. "We believe that the NATO deterrent, to which the United States has committed itself so heavily, provides very adequate protection."[55]

Another approach would have been to make available American nuclear weapons and means of delivery, but with arrangements for shared control. The Eisenhower administration had done just that in 1957 when it placed intermediate-range ballistic missiles (IRBMs) in Britain, Italy, and Turkey, under restrictions that provided for U.S. custody of the actual warheads, but granted the host countries a veto on their use. This move had been made more to compensate for what was then perceived to be an insufficiency of ICBMs than from any attempt to reconcile sovereignty and security within NATO, though. By 1961 Washington's ICBM superi-

American capabilities in that area. (Taylor to Kennedy, May 25, 1962, Kennedy Papers, NSC Files, Box 274, "Department of Defense.")

ority had been firmly established, the IRBMs in Europe were obsolete, and, lacking hardened silos, increasingly vulnerable to Soviet attack. Kennedy had them quietly removed in 1963,* proposing as a substitute a "multilateral nuclear force" of some 25 surface ships equipped with 2,500-mile-range Polaris missiles and manned by mixed crews, all under the authority of the NATO supreme commander. The idea here was to kill several birds with one stone: the MLF would provide a secure mobile base for the European deterrent away from populated areas; mixed manning would prevent the withdrawal of units for extraneous purposes; and, by making decisions to fire missiles contingent upon the agreement of all NATO members, the MLF would afford each of them, nuclear and non-nuclear power alike, a sense of involvement in its own defense.[56] It seemed, at first glance, to be the only way to combine an alliance's need for unified command with the *amour propre* of its respective constituents.

But the MLF never left port. Neither the British nor the French were willing to give up their own independent deterrents to join in the scheme; France indeed refused to participate in any form. Only the West Germans, who saw in the MLF their only chance to gain access to nuclear weapons, supported it, and that fact alone was enough to make the plan suspect in the eyes of many other Europeans. Critics pointed out rightly that the MLF placed no restrictions whatever on the American deterrent, but at the same time gave Washington the freedom to veto operations of the MLF. And no one was certain that ships with mixed crews and command structures based on the unanimity of thirteen separate nations would work well in times of crisis. The MLF had always been the brainchild of "Atlanticists" within the State and Defense departments; neither Kennedy nor Johnson was ever sufficiently committed to it to press it upon the reluctant Europeans. When, by 1965, it had become apparent that the practical difficulties were substantial and that the Europeans' support for the plan was lukewarm, Johnson quietly allowed it to die.[57] NATO had to continue to live, then, with its anomalies: national nuclear forces, unverifiable but indispensable American security guarantees, the irony of an independence that required dependence in order to be secure.

---

* The presence of Jupiter missiles in Turkey became a public issue in October 1962 when Khrushchev made their withdrawal a condition for removing Soviet missiles from Cuba. Kennedy agreed, but only on the condition that the deal be kept secret—as it was for another three decades. (See Philip Nash, *The Other Missiles of October: Eisenhower, Kennedy, and the Jupiters, 1957–1963* [Chapel Hill: 1997], pp. 116–75.)

The Kennedy administration viewed its alliance commitments outside NATO somewhat differently from its predecessor. Skeptical of Dulles's strategy of forming alliances for deterrent as well as war-fighting purposes, it tended to differentiate between what Rostow called the "hard core"—the "developed" countries of Western Europe, Canada, Japan, Australia, and New Zealand—and their "softer" counterparts along the periphery of Asia from Korea to Iran. These latter alliances, Rostow noted in 1962, had "not worked out too well": neither SEATO nor CENTO could match the forces arrayed against them, hence their members tended to call upon the United States for support, even against indigenous insurrections. To be sure, Washington could not abandon these alliances, whatever the original wisdom of making them. But it should "seek to promote other, more broadly-based, and less defense-oriented regional links," while at the same time working "to reorient the military efforts of the Asian participants toward coping with Communist supported *coups de main* and guerrilla operations."[58]

There was, in this proposed shift of emphasis, a realization that the non-military instruments of containment had become at least as important as their military counterparts: using these instruments became the fourth major element in Kennedy's strategy. Central to it was Rostow's idea of "immunizing" "third world" countries against the "disease" of communism. This meant accepting the inevitability, even the desirability, of change, but also the necessity of guiding it in non-communist directions. It could be done, the President and his advisers thought, not by opposing communism directly, as Dulles's alliances had seemed to do, but rather by reverting to the approach of the Marshall Plan a decade and a half earlier—employing American resources to mitigate or remove conditions that made communism attractive in the first place.[59] Rostow defined the task with characteristic amplitude: "Within the framework of power designed to protect the frontiers of freedom and to induce processes of peaceful change, . . . to assure an environment of sustained progress towards higher standards of economic welfare, social justice, individual liberties, and popularly based governments throughout the free community."[60]

Military assistance of course could contribute to this goal, but so too could "diplomacy . . . , information activities, exchange programs of all kinds, help in educational and cultural advancement, people-to-people activities, assistance in economic programming, technical assistance, the provision of capital, the use of surpluses, policy towards trade and commodity price stabilization, and a variety of other actions capable of affecting the orientation of men and institutions within these societies towards their problems."* With such a range of means available there was, Rostow noted, an obvious need for careful planning, coordination, and measurement of effects. It was also important to recognize that the process would be delicate and uneven. It might at times be in the American interest to encourage radical change—"it would have been in Batista's Cuba." At other times, it might be better to seek to move the modernization process forward within a traditionalist framework, as in Iran or South Vietnam. Certainly the United States did not require "that all societies at all times accept democratic values as their aspiration and that they move uninterruptedly toward its achievement." But it was vital that "third world" countries develop "along lines broadly consistent with our own concepts of individual liberty and government based on consent."[61]

The Kennedy administration evolved a variety of mechanisms with which to pursue those objectives. One of the most ambitious was the Alliance for Progress, a plan to provide some $20 billion in U.S. aid to Latin America over a ten-year period, contingent upon proportional commitments from the governments of that region and their willingness to undertake internal reforms, particularly with respect to land tenure and tax structure. The assumption, Kennedy's task force on Latin America noted, was that the United States "cannot stabilize the dying reactionary situation. It must, therefore, seek to bring about stability at a tolerable level of social organization without leaving the transformation to be organized by Communists." Arthur Schlesinger, Jr., put it more dramatically: if the "middle-class revolution" failed, he warned, then the "workers-and-peasants' revolution" would become inevitable.[62] Similar in intent, though simpler in organization, was the Peace Corps, which sent thousands of American volunteers to "third world" countries to organize small-scale health, educational, and agricultural projects; a Food for Peace program, designed to facilitate the disposal of American agricultural surpluses in such areas; and a new Agency for International Development, charged

---

* Rostow predictably viewed economic development as the major priority: "it should be possible," he wrote Kennedy in March 1961, "if we all work hard, for Argentina, Brazil, Colombia, Venezuela, India, the Philippines, Taiwan, Turkey, Greece—and possibly Egypt, Pakistan, Iran, and Iraq—to have attained self-sustaining growth by 1970 and to be drawing from special international sources either no capital or much diminished volumes of capital. In population these nations would include more than 80% of Latin America and well over half of the other underdeveloped portions of the Free World." (Rostow to Kennedy, March 2, 1961, Kennedy Papers, NSC Files, Box 212, "Latin America.")

with shifting the emphasis in foreign aid from military to economic assistance. There was also a strong element of "nation-building" in the administration's approach to counter-insurgency: "our central task in the underdeveloped areas," Rostow told the Army Special Warfare School in June 1961, "is to protect the independence of the revolutionary process now going forward."[63]

What these initiatives had in common was nothing less than a determination to alter the internal structures of foreign societies to enable them to withstand unavoidable pressures for revolutionary change without resorting to communist solutions. Economic development, combined with social and political reform, would accomplish that objective; American money, American technology, and the force of the American example would provide the impetus. The goal would be a world of diverse sovereign states, with power predominant in none of them. "The independence of nations is a bar to the Communists' 'grand design,'" Kennedy noted in 1962; "it is the basis of our own."[64]

Paralleling this belief in its ability to "manage" foreign societies was a high degree of confidence on the administration's part that it could employ domestic resources vital to defense more efficiently than before: this was the fifth distinctive element in its strategy. The idea manifested itself most clearly in McNamara's Pentagon, where the new Secretary of Defense ostentatiously installed new management techniques, based on systems analysis, designed to make possible a closer correspondence between overall strategy and the military instruments provided to implement it. Eisenhower had restricted the military tightly in terms of total budget allocations, but had left the individual services free for the most part to work out how they would use what they got. The result was an emphasis on prestigious but often redundant or ineffective weapons systems, cutbacks in less glamorous but necessary support facilities, and open inter-service disputes over roles and missions that the White House was never able to stop. Kennedy's approach was to abolish arbitrary budget ceilings, but to insist on a closer and more detailed scrutiny of how each service spent its appropriation.[65]

McNamara sought to accomplish this by evolving a "Planning-Programming-Budgeting System," or PPBS, a series of procedures designed to identify requirements for defense in the light of national strategy, and then to ensure that actual forces reflected those needs, and were not simply the product of inter- or intra-service compromises. PPBS assumed: (1) that forces should be structured by tasks, not organizational interests; (2) that costs ("inputs" in Pentagon jargon) should be measured in relation to benefits ("outputs"); (3) that alternative methods of accomplishing objectives should be capable of evaluation; (4) that short-term planning should reflect long-term goals; and (5) that the Secretary of Defense should have the capacity (and the staff) to make such judgments independently of the individual services. McNamara applied PPBS to a variety of problems, ranging from deciding what "mix" of missiles and bombers would project the most credible deterrent or weighing the lives various civil defense programs would save against their costs to choosing between plastic and stainless-steel turbine wheels in generators (at a not inconsiderable difference of $2 versus $175 each) or the standardization of belt buckles and underwear for military personnel.[66]

How much money McNamara actually saved is difficult to determine. Defense expenditures increased from $49.6 billion in fiscal 1961 to $54.8 billion in fiscal 1964. But much of that increase grew out of the administration's determination to build a symmetrical response capability: presumably without PPBS it would have been greater. Certainly PPBS did not represent *carte blanche* for the military—the three services' original request in fiscal 1964, for example, had totaled $67 billion. And because the gross domestic product increased by 4 percent annually during this period, the percentage of it devoted to defense actually declined slightly, from 9.4 percent in fiscal 1961 to 8.5 percent in fiscal 1964.[67] What is clear is that PPBS and associated techniques reflected the administration's confidence in its ability to manage the defense establishment without resorting to arbitrary budget ceilings. They also reflected as well, though, the equally strong conviction that the national economy itself could be manipulated to provide the resources necessary to sustain that establishment at whatever level Washington considered desirable.

The Kennedy administration had from the beginning considered a high rate of economic growth essential if the nation was to maintain its international position. Such a growth rate would provide the means of allocating increasing resources to defense without lowering the high standard of living that made the United States a model for much of the rest of the world, and, in turn, made world responsibilities tolerable to the American public. It would also allow the United States to absorb industrial and raw-material exports from other friendly countries, thereby sustaining their economic health, without weakening the value of the dollar.[68] Eisenhower's failure to maintain a high growth rate, Kennedy's advisers argued, had produced three recessions during his term in office, most of the restrictions imposed on military spending during those years, and, by the time the new administration took office, a serious balance of payments problem. The difficulty, they suggested, had been outdated economics: Eisenhower's refusal to apply Keynesian techniques for managing the economy to produce the all-important high growth rate.[69]

Walter Heller, Chairman of the Council of Economic Advisers, soon convinced Kennedy that Eisenhower's persistent efforts to balance the budget had in fact acted as a "fiscal drag" on the economy, with high taxes soaking up purchasing power, constraining growth, and producing recurrent recessions. The better approach, Heller suggested, would be to make expansion, not solvency, the chief priority: if the former occurred, the latter would take care of itself. Heller's prescription was a deliberate unbalancing of the budget in the form of a tax cut designed to stimulate the economy, thereby generating in time the revenues necessary to produce a moderate surplus without restricting growth. Inflation was of course a danger, as Eisenhower had warned, but it could be dealt with as necessary by reversing the procedure, increasing taxes, and thus dampening down excessive expansion. The nation could not afford to leave the economy to stabilize itself, Heller insisted: the federal government had an obligation to use the fiscal tools available to it to produce sustained but prudent growth. Kennedy's acceptance of this argument—implied in his call for a tax cut in 1963—represented for Heller "the completion of the Keynesian revolution": henceforth there would of necessity be a place for "the political economist at the President's elbow."[70]

The "McNamara revolution" in the Pentagon and the "Keynesian revolution" in economics both implied a rejection of Eisenhower's administrative style, which had concentrated on setting guidelines at the top without getting involved in detailed day-to-day management of either the defense establishment or the national economy. This approach had been, in a way, a rough analog to the "New Look" strategy, with its assumption that maintaining the capacity to act at the highest level of violence would preclude the need to act anywhere else. "Flexible response," on the other hand, assumed both the necessity and the competency to be able to act at all levels, to use the full range of available means, but to do so in a manner carefully calibrated to overall ends. In this sense it may be said to have had its domestic analog in the supremely confident management techniques of Robert McNamara and Walter Heller.

An Eisenhower legacy Kennedy did not reject was that of seeking negotiations with the Soviet Union to relax tensions: the new administration's continuation and expansion of this approach constituted the sixth and final element in its strategy of containment. "Let us never negotiate out of fear," Kennedy had proclaimed, in the appositive rhetoric of his inaugural address, "but let us never fear to negotiate."[71] In fact, the impeccably anti-communist Eisenhower had removed many of the risks from such contacts with the "enemy" by showing that they could be engaged in without appeasement. Kennedy as a consequence found it easier than it otherwise might have been to incorporate the patient skills of the diplomat into his arsenal of "flexible responses."

"[W]e should try to work over the longer run toward tacit understandings with the U.S.S.R. as to the ground rules covering our competitions," Rostow wrote in his March 1962 BNSP draft. "If they are convinced of our capacity and will to deal with their efforts to extend power into the free community, it may become increasingly possible to make them feel that we share a common interest in the exercise of restraint." Cessation of conflict with the Soviet Union was out of the question for the foreseeable future, "nevertheless, there may be (and it is in our interest that there should be) agreements on specific issues and perhaps periods of relative tranquility." The fact that the Soviet Union was a communist state was not, in itself, cause for war; rather, the United States should acknowledge the U.S.S.R.'s position as a great power and hold out to it the prospect of "constructive participation" in world affairs. "This will not change the basic policy of Soviet leaders now in power, but it may have some moderating effects on their conduct, or that of their successors."[72]

Implementing this strategy, though, was no simple matter. Khrushchev was still punctuating his own calls for "peaceful coexistence" with provocations like the "wars of national liberation" speech, a new ultimatum on Berlin, the resumption of nuclear tests, and the decision to place missiles in Cuba, none of which seemed calculated to relax tensions (although the Soviet leader, in his peculiar logic, apparently intended those maneuvers to produce just that result). Nonetheless, Kennedy did carefully seek out and try to exploit opportunities for negotiations in each of these crises. The initial test of the "national liberation" strategy came with the upsurge of fighting in Laos in 1961: here the new President rejected recommendations to retaliate by bombing North Vietnam, or to send U.S. ground troops, or to use nuclear weapons, in favor of seeking a tenuous agreement with the U.S.S.R. to neutralize that remote country, thereby removing it from the arena of Cold War crises.[73] Similarly, on Berlin, Kennedy repudiated hardline advice from Dean Acheson and others, choosing instead a flexible negotiating posture that abridged no Western rights but at the same time tacitly acknowledged Khrushchev's interest in stabilizing his shaky position in East Germany.[74] And on nuclear weapons, the administration resumed its own tests in 1962 with reluctance and only after long delay, while simultaneously pressing Moscow to agree to ban such tests in the future.[75]

Kennedy's commitment to negotiations came through most clearly in the wake of the Cuban missile crisis, an event critics once cited, paradoxically, to demonstrate his reluctance to use the instruments of diplomacy.[76] It is true that the President refused to negotiate on the presence of missiles in Cuba: the inescapable delays of such a process, he feared, would allow the Russians to complete their installations on the island, thus gaining the objective negotiations were supposed to prevent.* But the administration was quick to see that Khrushchev's capitulation had discredited once and for all his strategy of seeking détente through intimidation; accordingly, it was prepared to move vigorously on the negotiating front once the crisis had been resolved. "In these circumstances," a State Department analysis concluded, 'it is vitally important that the US take the initiative in offering to negotiate on major issues between East and West."[77] Kennedy, struck by the extent to which mutual misperceptions had brought on the crisis, aware of how similar situations had produced war in 1914, 1939, and 1950, needed little urging. "There appear to be no differences between your views and mine regarding the need for eliminating war in this nuclear age," he wrote Khrushchev early in 1963. "Perhaps only those who have the responsibility for controlling these weapons fully realize the awful destruction their use would bring."[78]

The year 1963 brought the first tangible fruits of negotiations in the form of a treaty banning all but underground nuclear tests, establishment of the Moscow-Washington "hot line," joint support for a United Nations resolution opposing the placement of nuclear weapons in outer space, and the sale of some $250 million worth of surplus American wheat to the U.S.S.R. It is important to note, though, that these accomplishments stemmed more from shifts in Soviet than American policy. Kennedy's ap-

---

* There also existed within the administration a certain degree of confidence that, given American strength, negotiations would not be necessary to get the missiles out of Cuba. "We have the strategic advantage in our general war capabilities; we have the tactical advantages of moral rightness, of boldness, of strength, of initiative, and of control of this situation," Maxwell Taylor wrote McNamara on October 26, 1962. "This is no time to run scared." (Kennedy Papers, NSC Files, Box 36, "Cuba—General.")

proach all along had been to try to make competition less dangerous by identifying and isolating from the struggle areas of congruent interest.* As he noted in his famous American University address in June 1963, "even the most hostile nations can be relied upon to accept and keep those treaty obligations, and only those treaty obligations, which are in their own interests."[79] It takes two to negotiate, though, and it was not until Khrushchev himself came to see the advantages of that procedure that even limited progress toward détente became possible.

The People's Republic of China showed no comparable interest in negotiations during the Kennedy years, nor is it all that clear that the United States would have responded had it done so. Kennedy himself had no patience with the fiction that Taiwan represented all of China, but he was unwilling to assume the domestic political liabilities that would have been involved in shifting diplomatic recognition, or even allowing Beijing's admission to the United Nations. There was also within the administration the view that the Sino-Soviet split could best be perpetuated by seeking détente with the Russians while maintaining pressure on the Chinese. Rostow summarized the argument in his "BNSP" draft:

> Although there is little that the U.S. can do to promote that split, we should at least avoid measures which might have the effect of healing it; thus we should not so openly favor Khrushchev's point of view as to make it difficult for him to justify it within the Communist camp. More importantly, we should not make it look as though Khrushchev's preference for negotiation and peaceful settlements over fighting is vain, when, indeed, Khrushchev acts in terms of that enunciated preference. And we should make it clear that the contrary Chinese view, if put to the test, is likely to entail swift disaster.

There would be, Rostow added, no ultimate impediment to an improvement in relations with China when that state was prepared "to modify its aggressive stance and behavior and recognize de facto the existence of an independent Taiwan." And, indeed, late in 1963 Kennedy authorized his Assistant Secretary of State for Far Eastern Affairs, Roger Hilsman, to pre-

---

* Rostow had reservations about seeking a test ban agreement with the Russians until they had agreed to withdraw their troops from Cuba and to honor the 1962 Geneva agreement on Laos. Kennedy rejected this early "linkage" strategy, though, and conducted the test ban talks without setting preconditions for Soviet behavior on other issues. (Rostow memorandum, July 5, 1963, Kennedy Papers, NSC Files, Box 265, "ACDA—Disarmament Harriman Trip II.") For an earlier Rostow attempt to "link" negotiations with Soviet restraint on arms shipments, see Rostow to Bundy, January 21, 1961, *ibid.*, Box 176, "U.S.S.R.—General."

pare a major speech on China looking forward to the day when "the Chinese Communist regime will eventually forsake its venomous hatreds . . . and . . . accept again a world of diversity." The speech was made more with the idea of demonstrating American reasonableness in the face of Chinese intransigence than from any immediate desire to change policy, though; reciprocal conciliatory gestures from Beijing were neither expected nor forthcoming.[80]

Kennedy's record on negotiations with the only communist state in the Western Hemisphere is similarly mixed. The administration did arrange with Fidel Castro a release of prisoners from the Bay of Pigs landings in return for medicine and agricultural equipment; during 1963 there were hints from both sides of a willingness to discuss other issues. Kennedy claimed to have no objection to the Cuban revolution itself; it was the danger of Soviet control, he repeatedly emphasized, that provided grounds for concern. The only thing dividing the United States and Cuba, he noted in a speech four days before he died, was the attempt to make the island "a weapon in an effort dictated by external powers to subvert the other American republics. . . . As long as this is true, nothing is possible. Without it, everything is possible." At the time of his death, Kennedy had at least two secret contacts under way to explore opportunities for improved relations with Castro. But the Central Intelligence Agency was also secretly organizing, at this time, plans to sabotage the Cuban economy, to conduct hit and run raids along the coast, and repeated but unsuccessful attempts to assassinate Castro.[81] How much of this Kennedy knew of and had specifically authorized is still unclear; what is obvious, though, is that these exercises served to undermine whatever possibilities existed of normalizing relations.

But whatever the frustrations of dealing with Cuba after the missile crisis, the administration regarded its handling of that affair as a textbook demonstration of "flexible response" in action, and, hence, as a model to be followed elsewhere. A draft National Security Action Memorandum of February 1963 emphasized the probable need in the future to be able to employ this "controlled and graduated application of integrated political, military, and diplomatic power." That would involve as well the ability to "increase by increments the overall pressures on the opponent," to "control the nature and pace of escalation," and to concert "political, economic, diplomatic, psychological, and military actions . . . with a view to their combined effect upon progress toward our overall objective."[82] But as the missile crisis had shown, none of this lay beyond the capacity of a "flexible response" strategy now validated, it seemed, by the harsh test of practical experience.

IV

In presenting the strategy of "flexible response" to the public, Kennedy and his advisers were continually torn between urges to arouse and to educate. There was, on the one hand, the belief that Eisenhower had not made the nation face up to the threats confronting it; that the new administration had a duty, accordingly, to awaken the country—shock it if necessary—out of its complacency. On the other hand, there was a comparable sense of obligation to persuade the public to take a calmer and more rational view of the Cold War, to abandon the passions and oversimplifications characteristic of the early years of that conflict. These conflicting impulses colored Kennedy's public explanation of his strategy throughout his term in office.

Certainly Kennedy made no effort to minimize the perils facing the country. "If you are awaiting a finding of 'clear and present danger,'" he told a group of newspaper publishers shortly after the Bay of Pigs incident, "then I can only say that the danger has never been more clear and its presence has never been more imminent." He liked to use an exhortation delivered by George William Curtis over a century earlier at the time of the Kansas-Nebraska Act:

> Would you have counted him a friend of ancient Greece who quietly discussed the theory of patriotism on that hot summer day through whose hopeless and immortal hours Leonidas and the three hundred stood at Thermopylae for liberty? Was John Milton to conjugate Greek verbs in his library when the liberty of Englishmen was imperiled?

It was the duty of the educated man, Kennedy insisted, "to give his objective sense, his sense of liberty to the maintenance of our society at a critical time." There was no attempt to gloss over differences with Khrushchev following the Vienna summit in June 1961: "We have wholly different views of right and wrong, of what is an internal affair and what is aggression, and, above all . . . of where the world is and where it is going." Nor did Kennedy seek to muffle the ultimate threat at the moment of ultimate peril, in October 1962: "We will not prematurely or unnecessarily risk the costs of worldwide nuclear war in which even the fruits of victory would be ashes in our mouth—but neither will we shrink from that risk at any time it must be faced."[83]

There was also great concern with demonstrating resolve and determination—perhaps an understandable trait in an administration that feared humiliation above all else. This showed in a tendency to turn crises first into public tests of strength, and only then to pursue negotiations;[84] the pattern was the same on Laos, Berlin, nuclear testing, and Soviet missiles in Cuba. At times, Kennedy even seemed to seek stiff challenges, as in his commitment, made shortly after the embarrassing Bay of Pigs affair, to place an American on the moon by the end of the decade. "But why, some say, the moon?" he asked students at Rice University the following year. "[W]hy climb the highest mountain? Why, 35 years ago, fly the Atlantic? Why does Rice play Texas?" The United States was going to the moon not because it was easy but because it was hard, "because that goal will serve to organize and measure the best of our energies and abilities."[85] It was as if Kennedy had accepted Dulles's old argument that challenges were desirable, even necessary, to bring out the best in the American people.

With one exception, though, there is little evidence that the administration deliberately conveyed to the public a sense of urgency greater than what it actually felt itself. This was, after all, the high point of Soviet unpredictability in the Cold War. It would be surprising, under these circumstances, if a tendency to invest local events with global significance had not existed. The one area where greater danger was implied than the administration knew to be the case was strategic arms: public admissions that the "missile gap" did not exist never equaled in frequency or intensity Kennedy's earlier assertions that it did. This aside, the strident official rhetoric of Kennedy and his advisers can be taken as a fairly reliable reflection of their private concerns.

But alongside this rhetoric there existed within the administration a growing impatience with what Kennedy called "the stale and sterile dogmas of the cold war." The classic Cold War mentality, Bundy's aide Carl Kaysen noted in 1961, had become an end in itself: it failed "to contribute to the main positive goals of our foreign policy." Moreover, it ran the risk of reviving McCarthyism:

> McCarthyism was not unconnected with the fact that we were literally at war with the Soviet Union in Korea. Both our history, and the great success in political and economic terms of our society make it appropriate for us to be much more conservative in moving away from simple Lockean concepts of property and liberty than are other societies. . . . A highly military stance

abroad makes us increasingly intolerant of this difference, and [causes] a corresponding increase in the political weight of those radical right wing elements which see in the difference a threat to the American way of life. Further, when we take a strongly military stance, we face a dearth of suitable objects of action. This aggravates the internal political consequences of such a stance, and we seek enemies within when we cannot come to grips with the enemies without.

Another problem was the sheer inappropriateness of simplistic Cold War thinking to the complexities of international affairs. "It is a dangerous illusion," Kennedy warned, in what may have been an indirect jab at Dulles, "to believe that the policies of the United States, stretching as they do worldwide, under varying and different conditions, can be encompassed in one slogan or one adjective, hard or soft or otherwise." Such thinking also contributed to stereotypes on both sides that made it difficult to adjust to change. "Countries change. Situations change. And we have to be realistic enough to see where the real danger lies."[86]

Kennedy did make an effort, during the last year of his life, to bridge the gap between popular perceptions of the Cold War as a struggle between good and evil and the complexities of the world as it was. "[W]e are not engaged in a debate, seeking to pile up debating points," he reminded his audience at American University in June 1963. "We are not here distributing blame or pointing the finger of judgment. . . . No government or social system is so evil that its people must be considered as lacking in virtue":

> World peace, like community peace, does not require that each man love his neighbor—it requires only that they live together in mutual tolerance, submitting their disputes to a just and peaceful settlement. And history teaches us that enmities between nations, as between individuals, do not last forever.

Both Moscow and Washington had an interest in avoiding "those confrontations which bring an adversary to a choice of either a humiliating retreat or a nuclear war": that "would be evidence only of a bankruptcy of our policy—or of a collective death-wish for the world." Under these circumstances, it was not inconsistent to sign an atmospheric nuclear test ban treaty while continuing underground tests, to sell the Russians wheat while denying them strategic goods, to investigate possibilities for joint space ventures while vigorously pursuing a unilateral American space program, to explore opportunities for disarmament while maintaining a stockpile of arms. The goal was the same in each case: to convince Kremlin leaders "that it is dangerous for them to engage in direct or indirect aggression, futile for them to attempt to impose their will and their system on other unwilling people, and beneficial to them, as well as to the world, to join in the achievement of a genuine and enforceable peace."[87]

Implied in these statements was the toleration of diversity, the reliance on balancing rather than projecting power to achieve it, that was basic to Kennedy's view of American interests. But the President continued until the day of his death to mix these calls for reason and calm with impassioned exhortations to defend "frontiers of freedom" everywhere. "You must wonder when it is all going to end and when we can come back home," he told a Montana audience in September 1963. "Well, it isn't going to end . . . because what happens in Europe or Latin America or Africa directly affects the security of the people who live in this city, and particularly those who are coming after." And again, two months later:

> Without the United States, South Viet-Nam would collapse overnight. Without the United States, the SEATO alliance would collapse overnight. Without the United States the CENTO alliance would collapse overnight. Without the United States there would be no NATO. And gradually Europe would drift into neutralism and indifference. Without the efforts of the United States in the Alliance for Progress, the Communist advance onto the mainland of South America would long ago have taken place.

"We are still the keystone in the arch of freedom," Kennedy added, in these remarks delivered on the morning of November 22, 1963, "and I think we will continue to do as we have done in the past, and the people of Texas will be in the lead."[88]

What all of this suggests, then, is that Kennedy's public rhetoric accurately reflected his own private ambivalences regarding interests and threats. The United States could, in principle, live comfortably in a diverse world organized along balance of power lines, but at the same time it could not even appear to withdraw from what were admittedly overextended positions without setting off a crisis of confidence that would undermine American interests everywhere. Self-confidence, not interests, was indivisible; it was in this clash of abstract ideas with the imperatives of the real world that the central—and unresolved—strategic dilemma of "flexible response" lay.

Implementing Flexible Response:
Vietnam as a Test Case

In order to discuss the implementation of "flexible response," it is necessary to make a choice. One can examine in overview a series of events in
which that strategy manifested itself: the Bay of Pigs, Laos, Berlin, the
Cuban missile crisis, the Dominican Republic. Or, one can focus in detail
on the event that because of its duration, divisiveness, and cost, overshadowed them all: the war in Vietnam. There are two good reasons for
choosing the second approach. First, American policy in Southeast Asia
reflected in practice virtually all of the elements of "flexible response."
Second, Kennedy, Johnson, and their advisers regarded Vietnam as a fair
test of that strategy. It had been Eisenhower's inability to deal with comparable problems that had produced the "flexible response" critique in the
first place. If the strategy could not be made to work in Vietnam, then
there would be serious grounds upon which to question its applicability
elsewhere. American leaders took on this test fully aware of the potential
difficulties, but at the same time fully confident of their ability to sur-
mount them.

To say that their confidence was misplaced is to understate: rarely have
accomplishments turned out so totally at variance with intended objectives. The war did not save South Vietnam, it did not deter future aggression, it did not enhance the credibility of United States commitments elsewhere in the world, it did not prevent recriminations at home. It is too
easy to blame these disparities on deficiencies in the postwar national security decision-making structure, substantial though those may have been.
There has been, as we have seen, no single approach to containment; to

indict all manifestations of that strategy is only to be vague. Nor is it helpful to ascribe the failure in Vietnam to the shift in leadership at the White House after November 22, 1963, however strikingly the personalities of Kennedy and Johnson may have differed. For Johnson followed the strategy of "flexible response" faithfully in Vietnam, perhaps more so than Kennedy himself would have done.

The American defeat there grew out of assumptions derived quite logically from that strategy: that the defense of Southeast Asia was crucial to the maintenance of world order; that force could be applied in Vietnam with precision and discrimination; that the means existed to evaluate performance accurately; and that success would enhance American power, prestige, and credibility in the world. These assumptions in turn reflected a curiously myopic preoccupation with process—a disproportionate fascination with means at the expense of ends—so that a strategy designed to produce a precise correspondence between intentions and accomplishments in fact produced just the opposite.

I

Officials of the Kennedy and Johnson administrations liked to insist that their policies in Vietnam were consistent with the overall direction of American foreign policy since 1947: the military effort there, they maintained, was but another in a long series of steps taken to demonstrate that aggression did not pay. "The challenge that we face today in Southeast Asia," Johnson argued, "is the same challenge that we have faced with courage and that we have met with strength in Greece and Turkey, in Berlin and Korea, in Lebanon and in Cuba." The "great lesson of this generation" was that "wherever we have stood firm, aggression has ultimately been halted."[1] To question the need for a similar commitment to South Vietnam, these statements implied, was to dispute the very assumptions that had sustained the strategy of containment from its beginnings.

In fact, though, those assumptions had shifted over the years. Kennan had stressed distinctions between vital and peripheral interests, between varieties of threats to them, and between levels of feasible response given available means; the Kennedy and Johnson administrations made no such distinctions. Kennan had sought to maintain the global balance of power by applying a combination of political, economic, military, and psychological leverage in carefully selected pivotal areas; Johnson by 1965 was relying almost exclusively on the use of military force in a theater chosen by adversaries. Kennan had hoped to harness forces of nationalism, even where communist, to contain the expanding power and influence of the Soviet Union; Johnson sought to oppose communism, even where nationalist, for the purpose of preserving American credibility in the world. And, in a final ironic twist, Johnson and later Nixon came to rely with plaintive consistency on the assistance of the Soviet Union, the original target of containment, to extricate the United States from the tangle in which its own strategy had ensnared it.

One might explain these mutations as the result of obtuseness, short-sightedness, or even absent-mindedness, but there is no evidence these qualities played any more prominent role during the Kennedy-Johnson years than is normally the case. What was distinctive about those two administrations, however, was their commitment to symmetrical response, and it is here that one must look to account for an evolution of strategic thinking all the more striking for the fact that those carrying it off seemed unaware that it had occurred.

It had been, of course, NSC-68 that had shifted perceptions of threat from the Soviet Union to the international communist movement as a whole. That document had also provided a rationale for expanding means and, as a consequence, interests. Eisenhower had rejected the analysis of means set forward in NSC-68, but not its assessment of threats or interests; for this reason he had been willing to extend an ambiguous commitment to the defense of South Vietnam through the SEATO treaty,* an initiative consistent with his administration's concern to achieve maximum deterrence at minimum cost. Expense was of less concern to Kennedy, who, confronted with an upsurge of Viet Cong insurgency, reverted to NSC-68's concept of expandable means but coupled it with a determination to honor Eisenhower's commitment, even though it had been extended largely as a substitute for means. At the same time, Kennedy was

---

* The SEATO treaty, signed September 8, 1954, provided that in case of "armed attack" against any of its signatories or against states or territories which the signatories "by unanimous agreement may hereafter designate," they would "in that event act to meet the common danger in accordance with [their] constitutional processes." In the event of a threat "other than by armed attack" or "by any fact or situation which might endanger the peace of the area," the signatories would "consult immediately in order to agree on the measures which should be taken for the common defense." South Vietnam was not a signatory to the treaty, but a protocol attached to it did extend its provisions to cover "the states of Cambodia and Laos and the free territory under the jurisdiction of the State of Vietnam." (*American Foreign Policy, 1950–1955: Basic Documents* [Washington: 1957], pp. 913–14, 916.)

determined to lower the risks of escalation or humiliation that earlier strategy had run. This resolve led, in time, to the deployment of American ground forces, first as "advisers" to the South Vietnamese, then, under Johnson, as full-fledged combatants.

But what, precisely, was the United States' interest in Vietnam? Why was the balance of power at stake there? Walt Rostow had warned in his 1962 "BNSP" draft that "major losses of territory or of resources would make it harder for the U.S. to create the kind of world environment it desires, . . . generate defeatism among governments and peoples in the non-Communist world, or give rise to frustrations at home." But when pressed to explain why the "loss" of such a small and distant country would produce these drastic consequences, Washington officials generally cited the SEATO treaty obligation, which, if not honored, would raise doubts about American commitments elsewhere in the world. "The integrity of the U.S. commitment is the principal pillar of peace throughout the world," Rusk wrote in 1965. "If that commitment becomes unreliable, the communist world would draw conclusions that would lead to our ruin and almost certainly to a catastrophic war."[2]

This was curious reasoning. It required justifying the American commitment to South Vietnam as essential to the maintenance of global stability, but then portraying that stability as endangered by the very vulnerability of Washington's commitment. It involved both deterring aggression and being held hostage to the prospect of aggression. The confusion, it would appear, stemmed from the failure of both the Kennedy and Johnson administrations to articulate independently derived conceptions of interest in Southeast Asia. Instead, they viewed the American stake there as determined exclusively by threats and obligations: the security of the United States, indeed of the entire non-communist world, was imperiled *wherever* communist challenges came up against American guarantees. Vietnam might be insignificant in itself, but as a point of intersection between threat and commitment, it was everything.

Nothing in this argument required the threat to be centrally directed, or even coordinated with communist activities elsewhere. There were, to be sure, frequent references early in the war to the Sino-Soviet plan for "world domination,"[3] but these became less common as evidence of the Moscow-Beijing split became irrefutable. Rationales then shifted to the containment of China, but only briefly; by early 1965 the predominant concern, as Under-Secretary of Defense John McNaughton put it, was simply "to avoid a humiliating US defeat (to our reputation as a guarantor)."[4] Communism need not pose a coordinated threat to the world balance of power, then, but because victories for communism at the expense of the United States, even if uncoordinated, could result in humiliation, the challenge to global stability was no less real. The only difference was that it was now Washington's fear of retreat that linked these threats, not the internal discipline and control of international communism itself.

Nor did the American commitment in question need to have been prudent. There was a definite sense within the Kennedy administration that Eisenhower had overextended the United States in Southeast Asia. Rostow, as has been seen, would have preferred a less formal alliance structure based on offshore strongpoints;[5] Robert Komer, one of his assistants, privately described SEATO in 1961 as a "millstone" directed against non-existent dangers of overt aggression. Nonetheless, Rostow wrote Kennedy later that year: "Surely we are hooked in Viet-Nam; surely we shall honor our . . . SEATO commitment." The problem, simply, was that the dangers of disengagement seemed at each stage to outweigh the costs of pressing on. "The reasons why we went into Vietnam . . . are now largely academic," McNaughton wrote in 1966. "At each decision point we have gambled; at each point, to avoid the damage to our effectiveness of defaulting on our commitment, we have upped the ante. We have not defaulted, and the ante (and commitment) is now very high."[6]

There was a distinct self-reinforcing tendency in all of this. The more the administration defended its Vietnam polices in terms of safeguarding credibility, the more American credibility seemed to depend upon the success of those policies. "To leave Viet-Nam to its fate would shake . . . confidence . . . in the value of an American commitment and in the value of America's word," Johnson proclaimed in April 1965. And again, in May: "There are a hundred other little nations . . . watching what happens. . . . If South Viet-Nam can be gobbled up, the same thing can happen to them." And still again, in July: "If we are driven from the field in Viet-Nam, then no nation can ever again have the same confidence in . . . American protection."[7] Perceptions in international relations are only in part the product of what people believe; they arise as well from what nations claim. Given the frequency and intensity of these and other comparable pronouncements, it is hardly surprising that they were taken seriously, both at home and abroad. And yet the irony is that the administration made them to stave off pressures for withdrawal that could lead to humiliation; their effect, though, was to widen the very gap between promise and performance from which humiliation springs.

But why this extreme fear of humiliation in the first place? Partly, one suspects, because it might suggest weakness to adversaries: "lessons" of Munich, after all, were still very much alive. Vietnam had also become something of a matter of personal pride: "we have not lost a single nation to communism since 1959," Johnson liked to boast.[8] But a deeper concern, oddly enough, may have been not so much what the world might think as what the United States might do. There was, within both the Kennedy and Johnson administrations, a strange dread of American irrationality—of the unpredictable reactions that might ensue if the United States was perceived to have "lost" Vietnam. Rusk and McNamara had warned as early as 1961 that such a development "would stimulate bitter domestic controversies in the United States and would be seized upon by extreme elements to divide the country and harass the Administration." Rostow's "BNSP" draft even raised the possibility that "the U.S. might rashly initiate war" if confronted by a major defeat.[9] Johnson may well have entertained the strongest fears of all: "I knew that if we let Communist aggression succeed in taking over South Vietnam," he later recalled,

> there would follow in this country an endless national debate—a mean and destructive debate—that would shatter my Presidency, kill my administration, and damage our democracy. I knew that Harry Truman and Dean Acheson had lost their effectiveness from the day that the Communists took over in China. I believed that the loss of China had played a large role in the rise of Joe McCarthy. And I knew that all these problems, taken together, were chickenshit compared with what might happen if we lost Vietnam.[10]

The ultimate danger, then, was what the United States might do to itself if it failed to meet obligations it itself had established.

Shortly after the Johnson administration left office, William Whitworth, a writer for the *New Yorker*, sought to interview several of the former President's advisers on the underlying geopolitical rationale for the Vietnam War. The only one who would see him was Eugene V. Rostow, Walt Rostow's older brother, who had served as Under-Secretary of State for Political Affairs from 1966 to 1969. The ensuing discussion took on a revealing circularity. Asked why American security depended upon the defense of Southeast Asia, Rostow emphasized the need to maintain a "balance of power" in the world. But when queried as to why it had been necessary to do that, Rostow fell back upon a classic "flexible response" argument: the need to be able to handle, without resort to nuclear weapons, problems such as Vietnam. Whitworth found this puzzling: "We have the balance in order to deal with the problem, and we have to deal with the problem in order to preserve the balance. The theory is eating its own tail." "Well, in a sense, you're right," Rostow replied. "All I can say is that it has always been very dangerous for people when a potentially hostile power establishes hegemony. I can't particularize how that potential hegemony would be exercised, but I would prefer, even at considerable cost, to prevent the risk."[11]

This spectacle of theories eating tails was no rare thing in Vietnam: the expansion of means to honor a commitment made as a substitute for means; the justification of that commitment in terms of a balance of power made shaky by the commitment's existence; the defense, in the interests of credibility, of policies destructive of credibility; the search, ultimately, for domestic consensus by means that destroyed that consensus—all of these reflect the failure of the "flexible response" strategy to proceed in an orderly manner through the stages of identifying interests, perceiving threats, and selecting appropriate responses. Instead, threats and responses became interests in themselves, with the result that the United States either ignored or forgot what it had set out to do in Vietnam at just the moment it was resolving, with unprecedented determination, to do it.

II

A second prominent feature of "flexible response" as applied in Vietnam was the belief in "calibration," or "fine tuning"—that by being able to move up or down a range of precisely calculated actions, the United States could deter aggression without either extreme escalation or humiliation. "Our military forces must be . . . used in a measured, limited, controlled and deliberate way, as an instrument to carry out our foreign policy," one of McNamara's assistants wrote in late 1964. "Never must military operations become an end in themselves." Johnson made the same point some months later: he would not heed, he insisted, "those who urge us to use our great power in a reckless or casual manner. . . . We will do what must be done. And we will do only what must be done."[12] And yet, since this strategy in the end produced *both* escalation *and* humiliation, it would appear to have contained, as did official thinking on the balance of power, certain deficiencies.

Deterrence, ideally, should involve expressing determination without having to exhibit it. John Foster Dulles had attempted this delicate maneuver by threatening to use nuclear weapons to discourage aggression at all levels—an approach that at least had the merit of separating the pro-jection of resolve from its actual demonstration, so long as skill, or luck, held out. Lacking the previous administration's self-confidence in such matters, convinced as well of the ineffectiveness of that strategy in limited war situations, Kennedy and his advisers had ruled out nuclear threats in areas like Southeast Asia, but not the need to manifest American firmness there. "We must produce quickly a course of action which convinces the other side we are dead serious," Rostow had warned Kennedy in August 1961. "What the U.S. does or fails to do," Maxwell Taylor added a few months later, "will be decisive to the end result."[13] The difficulty was that, short of embracing Dulles's strategy, all conceivable projections of resolve seemed to require, in one form or another, demonstrations of it.

This did not bother the Joint Chiefs of Staff, who, as early as May 1961, had recommended the dispatch of United States troops to South Vietnam "to provide a visible deterrent to potential North Vietnamese and/or Chi-nese Communist action," and to "indicate the firmness of our intent to all Asian nations." An old Vietnam hand, Brigadier General Edward Lans-dale, explained the rationale as follows:

> US *combat* forces, even in relatively small units, are the symbol of our na-tional power. If an enemy engages one of our combat units, he is fully aware that he automatically has engaged the entire power of the US. This symbol of real national strength, employed wisely in Germany, Greece, and the For-mosa Straits in a manner not unlike that contemplated for Thailand and Vietnam, has "kept the peace." When the mission of such US force is prop-erly announced and followed immediately by a firm action, recent history teaches that the effect is just the reverse of "escalation" and that our action obtains world support outside the [Sino-Soviet] Bloc.

"[T]he point of installing token US forces before the event," Robert Komer added, "is to signal our intentions to the other fellow, and thus hopefully avoid having to face up to the commitment of substantial US forces after a fracas has developed." It was true that the United States might "end up with something approaching another Korea, but I think the best way of avoiding this is to move fast now before the war spreads to the extent that a Korean type commitment is required."[14]* This theory that immediate small-scale involvement could make massive long-term in-

---

* "I'm no happier than anyone about getting involved in another squalid, secondary theatre in Asia. But we'll end up doing so sooner or later anyway because we won't be willing to accept another defeat. If so, the real question is not whether but how soon and how much!" (Komer to Bundy, October 31, 1961, Kennedy Papers, NSC Files, Box 231, "Southeast Asia—General.")

volvement unnecessary formed the basis of recommendations by Maxwell Taylor and Walt Rostow for the introduction of some 8,000 U.S. combat troops into South Vietnam in November 1961. "In our view," Taylor wrote the President, "nothing is more calculated to sober the enemy and to discourage escalation . . . than the knowledge that the United States has prepared itself soundly to deal with aggression at any level."[15]

But Kennedy had long been skeptical about the wisdom of sending American forces to fight in Southeast Asia. He had reminded his advisers the previous July of "the reluctance of the American people and of many distinguished military leaders to see any direct involvement of U.S. troops in that part of the world. . . . [N]othing would be worse than an unsuccessful intervention in this area." State Department assessments reinforced this view:

> We do not think the presence of US troops would serve to deter infiltrations short of overt armed intervention. There is not much reason for supposing the Communists would think our troops would be much more successful against guerrilla operations in South Viet-Nam than French troops were in North Viet-Nam. Counter-guerrilla operations require highly selective application of force; selection requires discrimination, and alien troops simply lack the bases for discriminating between friend and foe, except by the direction in which they shoot.

If the South Vietnamese themselves were not willing to make a "serious national effort," Dean Rusk warned in November, then it was "difficult to see how [a] handful [of] American troops can have [a] decisive influence." Persuaded by these arguments, concerned as well about priorities elsewhere (notably Berlin) and the risk of upsetting negotiations then in progress on Laos, Kennedy deferred implementing the Taylor-Rostow recommendation for combat troops. It would have been "like taking a drink," he explained to Arthur Schlesinger. "The effect wears off, and you have to take another."[16]

It is important to note, though, that Kennedy's decision against sending combat troops to Vietnam was not a rejection of "calibration"—just the opposite. The full Taylor-Rostow recommendations, he thought, would have constituted too abrupt an escalation of pressure; he preferred, instead, a more gradual approach, involving an increase of American economic and military aid to Saigon, together with the introduction of U.S. "advisers." Nothing in this procedure precluded the dispatch of ground troops at a later date if that should become necessary. Nor were there illusions as to the impact of these decisions on American credibility: "We are fully cognizant," the State Department cabled its embassy in Saigon, "of [the] extent to which [these] decisions if implemented . . . will sharply increase the commitment of our prestige struggle to save SVN."[17] Kennedy's actions reflected doubts only about the appropriate level of response necessary to demonstrate American resolve, not about the importance of making that demonstration in the first place.

"Calibration" during the next two years took the form primarily of efforts to transform South Vietnam into a sufficiently self-reliant anticommunist bastion so that no direct commitment of United States forces would be necessary. The goal, according to Roger Hilsman, was to devise "an integrated and systematic military-political-economic strategic counterinsurgency concept," to orient Saigon's military and security forces "increasingly toward counter-guerrilla or unconventional warfare tactics," to "broaden the effective participation of Vietnamese Government officials in the formulation and execution of government policy," and to "identify the populace with the Vietnamese Government's struggle against the Viet Cong."[18] All of this required several delicate balancing acts: moderating President Ngo Dinh Diem's autocratic control enough to win popular support for his government without at the same time weakening it to the point that it could not resist Viet Cong pressures; providing the assistance necessary for Diem to survive without discrediting him as an American puppet; taking care, simultaneously, to see that Washington's interest in Diem's survival did not allow him to make a puppet out of the United States. In the end, the line proved too fine to walk. Frustrated by Diem's repression of Buddhist critics, fearful of a secret deal between his government and North Vietnam, Kennedy in August 1963 authorized a carefully orchestrated effort—in itself an example of "calibration"—to overthrow him.[19] As it happened, though, Washington was able to control neither the timing nor the manner of Diem's removal, nor had it given much thought to what would replace him. The effect was that the very instability Kennedy had feared would dominate politics in Saigon did so for years to come.

The resulting Viet Cong gains led the Johnson administration by the end of 1964 to approve what Kennedy had rejected—a combat role for the United States in Vietnam, Even so, though, the principle of "calibration" would still apply; there would be no sharp, all-out application of force. Rather, the plan, in Johnson's words, was for military pressures against North Vietnam "progressively mounting in scope and intensity for the purpose of convincing the leaders of the DRV that it is to their interest to cease to aid the Viet Cong and to respect the independence and security of South Vietnam." This "slow squeeze" strategy contemplated action strong enough to end the existing deteriorating situation, but not so violent as to knit the North Vietnamese people more closely together, provoke Chinese Communist intervention, arouse world opinion, or preclude opportunities for an eventual negotiated settlement. The objective, Bundy noted on the eve of the first air strikes against the North in February 1965, was "to keep before Hanoi the carrot of our desisting as well as the stick of continued pressure. . . . Once such a policy is put into force, we shall be able to speak in Vietnam on many topics and in many ways, with growing force and effectiveness."[20]*

The bombing campaign against North Vietnam was intended to be the most carefully calibrated military operation in recent history. Great significance was attached to not crossing certain geographic "thresholds" for fear of bringing in the Chinese, as had happened in Korea, to avoiding civilian casualties that might intensify opposition to the war within the United States and elsewhere, and to combining the bombing with various inducements, especially periodic bombing pauses and offers of economic aid, to bring Hanoi to the conference table. Target selection was done in Washington, often in the White House itself, with the President at times personally monitoring the outcome of particular missions. Extraordinary precision was demanded of pilots—one 1966 order specified that piers at Haiphong could be hit only if no tankers were berthed at them, that vessels firing on American planes could be struck only if they were "clearly North Vietnamese," and that no attacks were to be launched on Sunday.[21] Even with such restrictions, though, the scale and intensity of the bombing progressively mounted, from 25,000 sorties† and 63,000 tons of bombs dropped in 1965 to 108,000 sorties and 226,000 tons in 1967, from missions directed initially at military bases in the southern "panhandle" of North Vietnam to infiltration routes, transportation facilities, and petroleum storage areas throughout the country, ultimately to factories and power plants in the Hanoi-Haiphong complex itself.[22] None of it produced discernible progress toward what it was supposed to accomplish: a

---

* Eugene Rostow argued that Johnson's "bold but prudent action in Vietnam had posed two things: that we would risk bombs over New York in order to protect Saigon, and that Moscow would not bomb New York to protect Hanoi. This was an event and a demonstration of capital importance, which should greatly fortify our system of alliances, and weaken that of our enemies." Rostow memorandum, April 10, 1965, enclosed to Bill Moyers to Bundy, April 13, 1965, Johnson Papers, NSF Country Files: Vietnam, Box 16, "Memos—Vol. XXXII.")
† A sortie is one flight by one plane.

tapering off of infiltration into South Vietnam, and movement toward negotiations.

Meanwhile, pressures had been building for the introduction of ground troops. Bundy had recommended this option as early as May 1964: the idea, he wrote Johnson, would be one of "marrying Americans to Vietnamese at every level, both civilian and military . . . to provide what [Saigon] has repeatedly asked for: the tall American at every point of stress and strain." "I do not at all think it is a repetition of Korea," he added in August. "It seems to me at least possible that a couple of brigade-size units put in to do specific jobs . . . might be good medicine everywhere." Rostow agreed, pointing out that such troops could usefully serve as bargaining chips in any future negotiations. By February 1965 Rusk too had endorsed the idea, along with the bombing, as a way to send "a signal to Hanoi and Peiping that they themselves cannot hope to succeed without a substantial escalation on their part, with all the risks they would have to face."[23]

The decisive argument in the end, though, proved to be General William Westmoreland's assertion that troops were needed to guard the air base at Da Nang from which some of the strikes against the north were being launched, a claim almost certainly advanced with a view to securing presidential authorization of a combat mission whose scope could then be widened far beyond the limited purposes for which it was made.[24] This "entering wedge" worked, and by early April 1965 Johnson had approved a combat role for United States forces in Vietnam. The pattern of escalation quickly went beyond Bundy's two brigades: from an initial deployment of 3,500 Marines at Da Nang, U.S. troop strength rose to 184,000 by the end of 1965, 385,000 by the end of 1966, and 486,000 by the end of 1967.[25] Nor, as the Tet offensive of early 1968 seemed to show,* was there convincing evidence that those troops had come any closer to accomplishing their mission than had the bombing campaign.

What strikes one in retrospect about the strategy of calibrated escalation is the extent to which, as so often happened in Vietnam, the effects produced were precisely opposite from those intended. The objective of applying incremental pressures beginning in 1961 had been to avoid a

* The Tet offensive was in fact a major military defeat for the North Vietnamese and their Viet Cong allies, but this would not become apparent for some years to come. The immediate psychological impact in the United States, however, was devastating. (Lewis Sorley, *A Better War: The Unexamined Victories and Final Tragedy of America's Last Years in Vietnam* [New York: 1999], pp. 12–15.)

massive American military involvement: token commitments, it was thought, would demonstrate resolve, thereby obviating the necessity for larger commitments later. The theory was that of vaccination, in that exposure to minimum risk was to provide immunities against more serious dangers. Another analogy, used at the time, was that of a plate-glass window, insufficiently strong in itself to keep out a thief, but capable of producing such conspicuous consequences if shattered as to discourage theft from being attempted in the first place. Getting involved, in short, was the best way to avoid getting involved: "I deeply believe," Rostow had written in August of that year, "that the way to save Southeast Asia and to minimize the chance of deep U.S. military involvement there is for the President to make a bold decision very soon."[26]

Bold decisions were made (admittedly not in as bold a manner as Rostow had wanted), but the effect was hardly to minimize American involvement. United States manpower, resources, and prestige were far more deeply committed by 1968 than even "worst case" scenarios seven years earlier had indicated. McNamara had estimated in November 1961 that in the unlikely event that both North Vietnam and China overtly intervened in the war, Washington might have to send six divisions, or 205,000 men. Beijing did not intervene, Hanoi kept its own participation below the level of overt acknowledgment, but still the United States had more than doubled McNamara's prediction as to "the ultimate possible extent of our military commitment."[27] Calibrated pressures as a deterrent obviously had not worked.

One reason was a persistent lack of clarity as to who, or what, was being deterred. Impressed by Khrushchev's "wars of national liberation" speech, the Kennedy administration had at first located the roots of Viet Cong insurgency in Moscow: Rostow in 1961 had even advocated an early form of "linkage," making it clear to the Kremlin that no progress toward détente could take place while guerrilla activity continued in Southeast Asia.[28]* By 1964, though, Beijing, not Moscow, had come to be seen as the culprit: the

* Rostow wanted Kennedy to warn Khrushchev at Vienna that if the United States were "drawn deeper and more directly on to the Southeast Asian mainland," this would require a major increase in military spending and difficulties in relations with Moscow because "it is difficult for a democracy simultaneously to gear itself for possible military conflict and also to take the steps necessary to ease tensions and to expand the area of U.S.-Soviet collaboration." (Rostow to Kennedy, May 11, 1961, Kennedy Papers, NSC Files, Box 231, "Southeast Asia— General.") There is no evidence that Kennedy actually raised this point with Khrushchev at Vienna—perhaps he realized that the Soviet leader might welcome rather than regret an American distraction in Southeast Asia.

objectives of American policy, National Security Council staff member Michael Forrestal argued late that year, should be to "delay China's swallowing up Southeast Asia until (a) she develops better table manners and (b) the food is somewhat more indigestible." The absence of official relations precluded opportunities for diplomatic "linkage" with Beijing, however, and Johnson's advisers, remembering miscalculations during the Korean War, were extremely cautious about applying military pressure in any form. "China is there on the border with 700 million men," Johnson noted; "we could get tied down in a land war in Asia very quickly if we sought to throw our weight around."[29]

The alternative, it would appear, was direct pressure against Hanoi, but things were not quite that simple. John McNaughton in September 1964 identified at least four separate "audiences" aside from Moscow and Beijing that the United States would have to influence: "the Communists (who must feel strong pressures), the South Vietnamese (whose morale must be buoyed), our allies (who must trust us as 'underwriters'), and the US public (which must support our risk-taking with US lives and prestige)." The difficulty, of course, was that actions directed at one "audience" might affect others in undesirable ways. Too sharp an escalation aimed at Hanoi risked alienating public opinion in the United States and elsewhere in the world, not to mention the danger of Chinese intervention. Moreover, such action would accomplish little as long as instability continued to reign in Saigon, as it had since the overthrow of Diem late in 1963. On the other hand, though, further restraint could only accelerate deterioration of the military situation in the South. It also conveyed the appearance of weakness and indecisiveness, not only in Hanoi and among American allies in Asia, but in Saigon itself, where the resulting low morale produced still more instability. The need, McNaughton argued, was for action taken "with special care—signaling to the DRV that initiatives are being taken, to the GVN that we are behaving energetically . . . and to the US public that we are behaving with good purpose and restraint."[30] But "calibration" implies a single target: where several exist, in a constantly shifting but interrelated pattern, the attainment of a precise correspondence between intentions and consequences becomes no easy matter.*

---

* McNamara succinctly summarized the problem of impressing multiple "audiences" in a July 1965 memorandum to Johnson: "Our object in Vietnam is to create conditions for a favorable outcome by demonstrating to the VC/DRV that the odds are against their winning. We want to create these conditions, if possible, without causing the war to expand into one with China or the Soviet Union and in a way which preserves support of the American people and, hopefully,

A second problem flowed directly from the first. By eschewing anything other than gradual escalation, matched carefully to the level of enemy provocation, the Johnson administration was in effect relinquishing the initiative to the other side. This was, of course, a standard military criticism of White House policy: the argument was that if only restraints on air and ground action could be lifted, the war could be ended rapidly.[31]* Given the subsequently demonstrated ability of the North Vietnamese and Viet Cong to hold out for years under much heavier pressures, the claim, in retrospect, seems unconvincing. Still, there was one valid element in the military's argument. Theorists of international relations have suggested that deterrence is more likely to work when a potential aggressor is unsure of his ability to control the risks involved in the action he is contemplating. If that confidence exists, deterrence will probably be ineffective.[32] This idea of cultivating uncertainty in the minds of adversaries had been central to Dulles's strategy of "retaliation"—with what effects it is impossible to say, given the difficulty of trying to prove what deterrence deterred. But uncertainty did not carry over into the strategy of "calibration." To proclaim that one intends to do only what is necessary to counter aggression and no more is, after all, to yield control over one's actions to those undertaking the aggression. Washington officials may have had the illusion that they were making decisions on Vietnam force deployments during the Johnson years, but in fact those choices were being made, as a consequence of the administration's own strategy, in Hanoi.[33]

The alternative was some kind of negotiated settlement with North Vietnam, an option the administration was careful never to rule out. "[W]e should strike to hurt but not to destroy," Bundy noted in May 1964, "for the purpose of changing the North Vietnamese decision on intervention in the South." Taylor seconded the point some months later: "it is well to remind ourselves that 'too much' in this matter of coercing Hanoi may be as bad as 'too little.' At some point, we will need a relatively cooperative

---

of our allies and friends." (McNamara to Johnson, July 20, 1965, *FRUS: 1964–68*, III, document 67.)

* Perhaps the most pungent expression of this idea came from General Thomas S. Power, Strategic Air Force Commander, who told a Pentagon audience in 1964 that "the task of the military in war was to kill human beings and destroy man-made objects," and to do it "in the quickest way possible." It had been "the moralists who don't want to kill" that had given "Hitler his start and got us into the mess in Cuba and Viet-Nam." The "computer types who were making defense policy don't know their ass from a hole in the ground." (Summary, Power briefing, April 28, 1964, Johnson Papers, NSF Agency File, Box 11–12, "Defense Dept. Vol. I.")

leadership in Hanoi willing to wind up the VC insurgency on terms satisfactory to us and our SVN allies."[34] But Johnson and his advisers were
wary of a "neutralist" solution for South Vietnam along the lines of the
shaky 1962 truce in Laos—perhaps with good reason, given the speed
with which Hanoi violated the agreements eventually reached at Paris
1973. Their preferred option was to achieve success on the battlefield, and
then approach North Vietnam: "After, *but only after,* we have established
[a] clear pattern [of] pressure hurting DRV and leaving no doubts in
South Vietnam of our own resolve, we could . . . accept [a] conference
broadened to include [the] Vietnam issue," the State Department cabled
Saigon in August 1964. Such negotiations, if they did occur, would have to
bring "Hanoi (and Peiping) eventually [to] accept idea of getting out."[35]
This familiar but elusive position of "negotiation from strength" had two
difficulties: it contained no safeguards against attempts by Hanoi to bolster its own negotiating position, or against the progressively deeper
American involvement the strategy of "calibration" was supposed to
prevent.

Finally, the strategy of "calibration" broke down because it failed to ensure that force, once applied, would be used as a precise and discriminat-
ing instrument of policy. It did nothing to prevent the subordination of
strategic interests to those of the organizations implementing the strategy.
Large bureaucracies all too often develop their own institutional momentum: "standard operating procedures" can make an organization impervi-
ous either to instructions from above or to feedback from below.[36] One
strength of McNamara's reforms in the Pentagon had been the extent to
which he had overcome this problem in dealing with the military on nuclear and budgetary matters. No such successes, however, occurred in
Vietnam. Instead, once American forces were committed, Washington
seemed to lose control, leaving the military with a degree of autonomy surprising in an administration that had prided itself on having reduced military authority over the conduct of national security affairs.[37]

This generalization may seem out of place when applied to a war whose
soldiers complained regularly about civilian-imposed constraints, but the
military's grievances in this regard should be treated with skepticism. It is
true that during the early period of American involvement, there were significant restrictions on the nature and scope of U.S. military activity, but as
time went on without the desired enemy response, these gradually
dropped away. By August of 1967, for example, the White House had authorized for bombing some 95 percent of the North Vietnamese targets
requested by the Joint Chiefs of Staff. Moreover, the Air Force's institu-

tional interests were allowed to influence the conduct of the air war in important ways. Despite an obvious (and widely appreciated) inapplicability to guerrilla warfare, the Air Force insisted successfully on a campaign of strategic bombing in North Vietnam, and even on the use of B-52s, designed originally to deliver nuclear weapons against Soviet targets, to hit suspected Viet Cong emplacements in the south. Similarly, it relied heavily on high-performance jet aircraft for other bombing missions, despite studies indicating that slower propeller-driven models would have been three times as accurate, from five to thirteen times less costly, but with roughly the same loss ratio.[38] It was, in retrospect, an adaptation of ends to fit preferred means, rather than the other way around.

The tendency was even more obvious with regard to the ground war. Like most of his Army colleagues, General Westmoreland had little sympathy for or understanding of the irregular warfare concepts that had been popular during the early Kennedy administration: the function of infantry, he insisted, was to seek out, pursue, and destroy enemy forces. As a consequence, he never seriously considered the strategy of holding and securing territory recommended by most counter-insurgency theorists, and implemented with considerable success by the Marines in the area around Da Nang in 1965 and 1966.[39] Instead he chose to emphasize large-scale "search and destroy" operations, designed to wear the enemy down through sheer attrition. These not only disrupted efforts at pacification and provided the enemy with sufficient advance warning to escape; they also frequently forced the Americans to destroy villages in order to reach Viet Cong troops and arms caches located deliberately within those villages. Random "harassment and interdiction" fire against "suspected" but unobserved enemy targets did little to convince inhabitants of the regions affected that their security would be enhanced by supporting Saigon. The Westmoreland strategy even involved, in some instances, the deliberate creation of refugees as a means of securing the countryside, as complete a reversal as can be imagined from the original objectives the American commitment in South Vietnam had been intended to serve.[40]

It was left to the Navy, though, to come up with the most striking example of weapons ill-suited to tasks by retrieving from mothballs the U.S.S. *New Jersey*, the world's last functioning battleship, for the purpose of shelling the jungle in a manner reminiscent of nothing so much as an incident in Joseph Conrad's *Heart of Darkness*:

> Once, I remember, we came upon a man-of-war anchored off the coast. There wasn't even a shed there, and she was shelling the bush. It appears the French had one of their wars going on thereabouts. . . . In the empty

immensity of earth, sky, and water, there she was, incomprehensible, firing into a continent. Pop, would go one of the six-inch guns; a small flame would dart and vanish, a little white smoke would disappear, a tiny projectile would give a feeble screech—and nothing happened. Nothing could happen. There was a touch of insanity in the proceeding, a sense of lugubrious drollery in the sight; and it was not dissipated by somebody on board assuring me earnestly there was a camp of natives—he called them enemies—hidden out of sight somewhere.[41]

It was all a remarkable departure from the injunctions to do just enough, but no more than was necessary, with which the United States had entered the conflict in Vietnam.

"[T]he central object of U.S. military policy is to create an environment of stability in a nuclear age," Rostow wrote in 1966; "this requires as never before that military policy be the servant of political purposes and be woven intimately into civil policy." To be sure, this had been the objective all along of the "calibration" strategy. It reflected the confidence in the ability to "manage" crises and control bureaucracies that was characteristic of "flexible response," the concern to integrate force and rationality, to find some middle ground between the insanity of nuclear war and the humiliation of appeasement. But it was also a curiously self-centered strategy, vague as to the objects to be deterred, heedless of the extent to which adversaries determined its nature and pace, parochial in its assumption that those adversaries shared its own preoccupations and priorities, blind to the extent to which the indiscriminate use of force had come to replace the measured precision of the original concept. "Despite its violence and difficulties, our commitment to see it through in Vietnam is essentially a stabilizing factor in the world," Rostow had insisted, no doubt with complete sincerity and the best of intentions.[42] But when sincerity and good intentions come to depend upon myopic self-absorption, then the price can be high indeed.

III

One of the curious things about the breakdown of "calibration" was official Washington's inability to detect the fact that it had occurred. Gaps between objectives sought and results produced widened with only infrequent attempts to call attention to what was happening: those warnings that were advanced produced few discernible responses. This pattern suggests yet another deficiency in "flexible response" theory as applied in

Vietnam: a persistent inability to monitor performance, an absence of mechanisms for ensuring that correspondence between the intent of one's actions and their actual consequences that is essential for an effective strategy.

That such lapses should have occurred is puzzling, given the great emphasis both Kennedy and Johnson placed on management techniques designed to achieve precise adaptations of resources to objectives. Exponents of "systems analysis" have explained that their ideas were not applied in Vietnam until it was too late to avoid involvement, but that, once put to use, they quickly revealed the futility of the existing strategy.[43] This view is correct, but narrow. It is true that the Systems Analysis Office in the Pentagon did not begin making independent evaluations of the war until 1966. But, in a larger sense, the Kennedy-Johnson management techniques had been present all along, in the form of both administrations' confidence that they could control bureaucracies with precision, use force with discrimination, weigh costs against benefits, and relate short-term tactics to long-term objectives. The failure to achieve these standards suggests difficulties in applying the new methods, but not their absence.

One reason "systems analysis" broke down in Vietnam was its heavy reliance on easily manipulated statistical indices as measurements of "progress" in the war. Here the primary responsibility rests with McNamara, who insisted on applying to that complex situation the same emphasis on quantification that had served him well in the more familiar worlds of big business and the Pentagon.[44]* The difficulty, of course, was that the voluminous calculations McNamara insisted on were no better than the accuracy of the statistics that went into them in the first place: there were few if any safeguards against distortion. "*Ah, les statistiques!*" Roger Hilsman reports one South Vietnamese general as having exclaimed. "Your Secretary of Defense loves statistics. We Vietnamese can give him all he wants. If you want them to go up, they will go up. If you want them to go down, they will go down."[45] Or, in the succinct parlance of a later generation of computer specialists, "garbage in, garbage out."

The problem manifested itself first with regard to South Vietnamese performance following the introduction of United States advisers in 1961.

---

* McNamara "has been trying to think of ways of dealing with this problem [Vietnam] for so long that he has gone a little stale," Bundy wrote to Johnson in June 1964. "Also, in a curious way, he has rather mechanized the problem so that he misses some of its real political flavor." (Bundy to Johnson, June 6, 1964, *FRUS: 1964–68*, I, document 204.)

The very presence of the Americans, it had been thought, would make possible more accurate monitoring of the situation,[46] but in fact the opposite occurred. The advisers depended on information furnished them by Diem's officers, many of whom combined a desire to please their powerful ally with a reluctance to risk their own necks in battle. The result was a deliberate inflation of statistical indices, the extent of which became clear only after the fall of Diem in November 1963. Of some 8,600 "strategic hamlets" Diem claimed to have constructed, it turned out that only about 20 percent existed in completed form. A high percentage of military operations initiated by Saigon—possibly as many as one-third— were launched in areas where the Viet Cong were known *not* to be. One district chief had listed all twenty-four hamlets in his district as secure when in fact he controlled only three. "[T]he situation has been deteriorating . . . to a far greater extent than we had realized," McNamara acknowledged ruefully, "because of our undue dependence on distorted Vietnamese reporting."[47]*

Not all such misrepresentations came from the South Vietnamese, though. Anxious to meet Washington's expectations of success, General Paul D. Harkins, commander of U.S. advisers in Vietnam, systematically ignored or suppressed reports from his own subordinates questioning Saigon's optimistic assessments of the war. As a result, Taylor and McNamara could report with conviction as late as October 1963 that "the tactics and techniques employed by the Vietnamese under U.S. monitorship are sound and give promise of ultimate victory."[48] Evidence that the situation was not in fact that rosy did occasionally surface, whether from the rare official visitor who managed to evade Harkins's packaged briefings and carefully guided tours, or from the more frequent published reporting of skeptical American correspondents in Saigon, especially Neil Sheehan and David Halberstam. But although Kennedy worried about these discrepancies, he at no point gave up primary reliance on official channels as a means of monitoring progress in the war. Johnson, if anything, depended on them more heavily.[49] It has been suggested that the accuracy of information tends to decline as the level of its classification rises, if for no other

---

* The difficulties did not end in 1963. The number of "Viet Cong" turned in under the Third Party Inducement Program, which provided monetary rewards for identifying "defectors" willing to rally to Saigon's cause, rose from 17,836 in 1968 to 47,088 in 1969, at which point it was discovered that many of the alleged "defectors" were not Viet Cong at all, but South Vietnamese who had made a deal with friends to report them, and then split the reward. (Guenter Lewy, *American in Vietnam* [New York: 1978], pp. 91–92.)

reason than that opportunities for independent verification are diminished thereby.[50] The proposition may not be universally applicable, but that the White House would have been better off reading Halberstam than Harkins seems beyond dispute.

These problems did not disappear with the onset of active American military involvement in Vietnam. The most notorious example was the use of enemy "body counts" as the chief indicator of "progress" in the ground war. The argument has been made that in such a conflict, where conventional indices—territory taken, distances covered, cities occupied—meant little, emphasis on these kinds of macabre statistics was unavoidable.[51] That may be, but what seems odd is the importance accorded them, given their widely acknowledged inaccuracy. Contemporary evaluations identified a margin of error of from 30 to 100 percent in these statistics, partly as the result of double or triple counting, partly because of the difficulty of distinguishing combatants from non-combatants, partly because of pressure from field commanders for higher and higher levels of "performance."[52] A more reliable index of success in the war was available—the number of North Vietnamese-Viet Cong weapons captured—but it was never given the significance of the body counts, probably because the figures were much less impressive. "It is possible that our attrition estimates substantially overstate actual VC/NVA losses," McNamara admitted in 1966. "For example, the VC/NVA apparently lose only about one-sixth as many weapons as people, suggesting the possibility that many of the killed are unarmed porters or bystanders."[53]

Similar statistical inflation occurred in the air war as well. Despite its acknowledged unreliability in an age of high-performance jet aircraft, pilot instead of photographic reconnaissance was generally used to measure the effectiveness of bombing in the North, presumably because damage claims tended to be higher. Photographic confirmation, when requested, was often not for the purpose of verifying pilot reports but to boost "sortie rates." Allocations of fuel and ordnance depended on these rates; they inevitably became an object of competition between the Air Force and the Navy, both of which shared the task of bombing North Vietnam. The results were predictable: a preference for aircraft with small bomb-load capacities which necessitated more frequent missions; the expenditure of bombs on marginal or already destroyed targets; even, during periods of munitions shortages, the flying of sorties without bombs. As one Air Force colonel put it: "bombs or no bombs, you've got to have more Air Force over the target than Navy."[54]

A second reason for the failure to monitor performance was a persistent tendency to disregard discouraging intelligence. It is a myth that the United States stumbled blindly into the Vietnam War. At every stage in the long process of escalation informed estimates were available which accurately (and pessimistically) predicted the outcome.* As early as November 1961, for example, the CIA was forecasting that North Vietnam would be able to match, through increased infiltration, any U.S. troop commitment to South Vietnam, and that bombing the North would not significantly impede that process. Two-and-a half years later, a series of war games in which several key officials of the Johnson administration took part produced precisely the same conclusion.[55] Despite his own enthusiasm for this alternative in 1961 and 1964, Maxwell Taylor by 1965 was strongly opposing the introduction of combat forces on the grounds that a "white-faced soldier armed, equipped and trained as he is [is] not [a] suitable guerrilla fighter for Asian forests and jungles." Clark Clifford, Johnson's long-time personal friend and future Defense Secretary, was warning in May 1965 that Vietnam "could be a quagmire. It could turn into an open end commitment on our part that would take more and more ground troops, without a realistic hope of ultimate victory." George Ball, in a series of eloquent dissents from official policy, stressed that "a deep commitment of United States forces in a land war in South Viet-Nam would be a catastrophic error. If there ever was an occasion for a tactical withdrawal, this is it." Even William P. Bundy, one of the original architects of "calibration," had concluded by June of 1965 that any level of commitment beyond 70,000 to 100,000 troops would pass "a point of sharply diminishing returns and adverse consequences."[56]

"There are no signs that we have throttled the inflow of supplies for the VC," McNamara acknowledged after five months of bombing. "Nor have our air attacks on North Vietnam produced tangible evidence of willingness on the part of Hanoi to come to the conference table in a reasonable mood." And even if military successes on the ground could be achieved, there was no guarantee that these would not simply "drive the VC back into the trees" from which they could launch attacks at some future date. "[I]t is not obvious," the Secretary of Defense admitted, "how we will be able to disengage our forces from Vietnam." And yet, despite this gloomy

---

* "The information I received [on Vietnam] was more complete and balanced than anyone outside the mainstream of official reporting could possibly realize." (Lyndon B. Johnson, *The Vantage Point: Perspectives of the Presidency, 1963–1969* [New York: 1971], p. 64.)

appraisal, McNamara recommended a continuation of the bombing and an increase in troop strength from 75,000 to 175,000—200,000. Early in 1966, on the basis of no more encouraging signs of progress in ground or air operations, he endorsed a new troop ceiling of 400,000, acknowledging at the same time that the North Vietnamese and Viet Cong could probably match those increases. It might be possible, he thought, eventually to contain the enemy with 600,000 men, but that would risk bringing in the Chinese Communists. "It follows, therefore, that the odds are about even that, even with the recommended deployments, we will be faced in early 1967 with a military stand-off at a much higher level, with pacification hardly underway and with the requirement for the deployment of still more U.S. forces."[57]

McNamara's perseverance in the face of pessimism was not atypical—indeed, the Defense Secretary allowed the second sentiment to overwhelm the first sooner than most officials did. Westmoreland, in December 1965, for example, admitted that "notwithstanding the heavy pressures on their transportation system in the past 9 months, they [the North Vietnamese] have demonstrated an ability to deploy forces into South Vietnam at a greater rate than we are deploying U.S. forces." Nevertheless, "our only hope of major impact on the ability of the DRV to support the war in Vietnam is continuous air attack . . . from the Chinese border to South Vietnam." The CIA, whose assessments of the consequences of escalation had been especially discouraging, acknowledged in March 1966 that the bombing so far had been ineffective, but then recommended more of it, with fewer restraints. Later that year, in a comment characteristic of the resolute optimism of Johnson administration officials, Robert Komer argued that "by themselves, none of our Vietnam programs offer high confidence of a successful outcome. . . . Cumulatively, however, they *can* produce enough of a *bandwagon psychology* among the southerners to lead to such results by end-1967 or sometime in 1968. At any rate, do we have a better alternative?"[58]

The problem, as Komer suggested, was that however unpromising the prospects of continued escalation, the alternatives seemed even worse. Withdrawal would constitute humiliation, with all that implied for the maintenance of world order. Negotiations prior to establishing a "position of strength" could only lead to appeasement. Continuation of the status quo would not work because the status quo was too delicate. Public opinion remained solidly behind escalation until 1968; indeed, Johnson saw himself as applying the brake, not the accelerator.[59] As a result, there developed a curious mixture of gloom and optimism: things were bad, they were likely to get worse before they got better, but since the alternatives to the existing strategy appeared even more forbidding, there seemed to be little choice but to "press on."

What has not been satisfactorily explained, though, is how the Johnson administration came to define its options so narrowly. In retrospect, quite a lot—negotiations on Hanoi's terms, a gradual relinquishment of responsibility for the war to the South Vietnamese, even a phased withdrawal in the anticipation of an eventual North Vietnamese-Viet Cong victory—would have been preferable to the strategy actually followed, which produced those same results but at vastly greater costs than if they had been sought in the mid-1960's. As George Kennan reminded the Senate Foreign Relations Committee in 1966, "there is more respect to be won in the opinion of this world by a resolute and courageous liquidation of unsound positions than by the most stubborn pursuit of extravagant and unpromising objectives."[60] But Johnson and his advisers could never bring themselves to consider "heretical" options, despite abundant evidence that their strategy was not working. Their hesitancy suggests still another reason for the failure to monitor performance in Vietnam: an absence of mechanisms for forcing the consideration of unpalatable but necessary alternatives.

Several explanations have been advanced to account for this lapse. It has been argued that there was a premium on "toughness" during the Kennedy-Johnson years; that advocates of a compromise settlement bore a far heavier burden of proof than did supporters of escalation.[61] But this view fails to explain Johnson's tenacious search for a negotiated settlement with Hanoi, carried on not just for the purpose of defusing opposition to the war at home but also in the genuine hope of finding a way out consistent with American credibility.[62] It has been pointed out that Johnson's circle of advisers narrowed as critics of the war proliferated, and that this limited the Chief Executive's exposure to dissenting points of view.[63] But the President did keep on and listen to "house heretics" like George Ball; more significantly, he paid close attention to McNamara's growing doubts about the war in 1966 and 1967, but still refused to change the strategy.[64] It has been suggested that the whole national security decision-making system was at fault: the system "worked" in that it produced the results it had been "programmed" to produce, given prevailing assumptions about containment and the balance of power since 1945; the error was in the "programming."[65] But this argument oversimplifies variations in perceptions of interests and threats over the years. While it is true that all postwar administrations committed themselves to the general objective of containment, they differed significantly over what was to be contained and over the means available to do it.

It is this problem of perceived means that best explains the Johnson administration's inability to come up with alternatives in Vietnam. The mechanism that most often forced the consideration of unpalatable options in the postwar years was budgetary: when one knows one has only limited resources to work with, distinctions between the vital and the peripheral, between the feasible and the unfeasible, come more easily, if not less painfully. The Eisenhower administration found this out in 1954, when it decided that the "unacceptable" prospect of a communist North Vietnam was in fact preferable to the more costly alternative of direct U.S. military involvement. But budgetary concerns carried little weight during the Kennedy and Johnson administrations. The theory of "flexible response" implied unlimited means and, hence, little incentive to make hard choices among distasteful alternatives.

Kennedy did from time to time emphasize the existence of limits beyond which Washington could not go in aiding other countries. "[T]he United States is neither omnipotent or omniscient," he pointed out in 1961: "we are only 6 percent of the world's population . . . we cannot right every wrong or reverse each adversary." The abortive 1963 plan for a phased withdrawal of American advisers from South Vietnam may have reflected Kennedy's sense that the limits of feasible involvement in that country were approaching.[66] But there is no conclusive evidence that Kennedy, on fiscal grounds, was considering a diminished American role there; certainly Johnson did not do so. The new President dutifully stressed the need for economy during his first months in office, but more for the purpose of enhancing his reputation with the business community than from any great concern about the limits of American power in the world scene.[67] And, as the Vietnam crisis intensified, so too did the conviction of Johnson and his advisers that the United States could afford whatever it would take to prevail there.

"[L]et no one doubt for a moment," Johnson proclaimed in August 1964, "that we have the resources and we have the will to follow this course as long as it may take." In a White House meeting the following month, Rusk pointed out that it had cost $50,000 per guerrilla to suppress the insurgency in Greece in the later 1940's; in Vietnam "it would be worth any amount to win." Johnson agreed, emphasizing the need for all to understand "that it was not necessary to spare the horses." "Our assets, as I see them, are sufficient to see this thing through if we enter the exercise with adequate determination to succeed," Rostow wrote in November 1964; "at this stage in history we are the greatest power in the world—if we behave like it." Five months later, as direct American military involvement in Vietnam was beginning, McNamara informed the Joint Chiefs of Staff and the service secretaries that "there is an unlimited appropriation available for the financing of aid to Vietnam. Under no circumstances is a lack of money to stand in the way of aid to that nation." There were always costs in meeting "commitments of honor," Rusk commented in August of that year. "But I would suggest, if we look at the history of the last 30 to 40 years, that the costs of *not* meeting your obligations are far greater than those of meeting your obligations."[68]

"The world's most affluent society can surely afford to spend whatever must be spent for its freedom and security," Johnson told the Congress early in 1965. This assumption of virtually unlimited resources goes far toward explaining the persistence of what was acknowledged to be a costly and inefficient strategy. The idea was that if the United States could simply stay the course, regardless of the expense, it would prevail. "I see no choice," the President added, later that year, "but to continue the course we are on, filled as it is with peril and uncertainty and cost in both money and lives." It might take "months or years or decades," but whatever troops General Westmoreland required would be sent "as requested." "Wastefully, expensively, but nonetheless indisputably, we are winning the war in the South," Robert Komer concluded late in 1966. "Few of our programs—civil or military—are very efficient, but we are grinding the enemy down by sheer weight and mass." Westmoreland agreed. "We'll just go on bleeding them until Hanoi wakes up to the fact that they have bled their country to the point of national disaster for generations. Then they will have to reassess their position."[69]

But McNamara's "systems analysis" specialists had reached the conclusion, by 1966, that it might take generations to bring the North Vietnamese to that point. Their studies showed, for example, that although enemy attacks tended to produce significant enemy casualties, operations launched by U.S. and South Vietnamese forces produced few if any. This suggested that despite the massive American military presence in the south, the North Vietnamese and Viet Cong still retained the initiative, and hence could control their losses. Other studies indicated that while the number of bombing raids against North Vietnam had quadrupled between 1965 and 1968, they had not significantly impaired Hanoi's ability to supply its forces in the south: enemy attacks there had increased by a factor of five, and in places by as much as eight, during the same period. The bombing was estimated to have done some $600 million worth of damage in the north, but at a cost in lost aircraft alone of $6 billion. Sixty-five percent of the bombs and artillery rounds expended in Vietnam were being used against unobserved targets, at a cost of around $2 billion a year. Such strikes, the analysts concluded, probably killed about 100 North Vietnamese or Viet Cong in 1966, but in the process provided 27,000 tons of dud bombs and shells which the enemy could use to make booby traps, which that same year accounted for 1,000 American deaths. But most devastating of all, the systems analysts demonstrated in 1968 that despite the presence of 500,000 American troops, despite the expenditure of more bomb tonnage than the United States had dropped in all of World War II, despite estimated enemy casualties of up to 140,000 in 1967, the North Vietnamese could continue to funnel at least 200,000 troops a year into South Vietnam indefinitely. As one analyst wrote, "the notion that we can 'win' this war by driving the VC/NVA from the country or by inflicting an unacceptable rate of casualties on them is false."[70]

Only the last of these studies had any noticeable impact outside the Office of the Secretary of Defense: persuasive though they were, there was little incentive, in an administration confident that it could sustain the costs of the war indefinitely, to pay much attention to them.[71] It was not until Johnson personally became convinced that the costs of further escalation would outweigh the conceivable benefits that the discipline of stringency could begin to take hold. That did not happen until after the Tet offensive of February 1968, when the President received Westmoreland's request for an additional 206,000 troops, a figure that could not have been met without calling up the Reserves and without major domestic and international economic dislocations.* Johnson had always regarded these as limits beyond which he would not go, not on the basis of rigorous statistical analysis, but rather from the gut political instinct that if he passed those points, public support for the war would quickly deteriorate.[72] In the end, then, the Johnson administration based its ultimate calculation of costs and benefits on criteria no more sophisticated than those employed by

---

* Curiously, Westmoreland's request was apparently prompted by the Chairman of the Joint Chiefs of Staff, General Earle G. Wheeler, as a means of forcing the reluctant Johnson to call up the Reserves. (Herbert Y. Schandler, *The Unmaking of a President: Lyndon Johnson and Vietnam* [Princeton: 1977], pp. 116, 138.)

Eisenhower prior to 1961, or by Truman prior to 1950. The techniques of systems analysis, which had been designed to avoid the need for such arbitrary judgments, in fact only deferred them.

Several circumstances discouraged the objective evaluation of performance in Vietnam. The military's relative autonomy gave it a large degree of control over the statistical indices used to measure "progress" in the war; this, combined with the organizationally driven compulsion to demonstrate success and the traditional reluctance of civilians in wartime to challenge military authority, made it difficult to verify charges of ineffectiveness.[73] Such accurate intelligence as did get through tended to be disregarded because alternative courses of action seemed worse than the option of "pressing on." And the perception of unlimited means made perseverance even in the face of unpromising signals seem feasible: far from widening alternatives, the abundance of means, and the consequent lack of incentives to make hard decisions, actually narrowed them. As a result, the postwar administration most sensitive to the need to monitor its own performance found itself ensnared inextricably in a war it did not understand, could not win, but would not leave.

IV

Effectiveness in strategy requires not only the ability to identify interests and threats, calibrate responses, and monitor implementation, however; it also demands a sense of proportion, an awareness of how commitments in one sphere compare with, and can distract attention as well as resources away from, obligations elsewhere. Johnson and his subordinates thought they had this large perspective: Vietnam, they repeatedly insisted, was important not just in itself, but as a symbol of American resolve throughout the world.* The line between a symbol and a fixation is a fine one, though; once it is crossed, perspectives narrow, often unconsciously, with the result that means employed can become inappropriate to, even destructive of,

---

* "The idea that we are here simply because the Vietnamese want us to be here . . . ; that we have no national interest in being here ourselves; and that if some of them don't want us to stay, we ought to get out is to me fallacious," Ambassador Henry Cabot Lodge cabled from Saigon in 1966. "In fact, I doubt whether we would have the moral right to make the commitment we have made here solely as a matter of charity towards the Vietnamese and without the existence of a strong United States interest. . . . Some day we may have to decide how much it is worth to us to deny Viet-Nam to Hanoi and Peking—regardless of what the Vietnamese may think." (Lodge to State Department, May 23, 1966, *Pentagon Papers*, IV, 99–100.)

ends envisaged. This narrowing of perspective, this loss of proportion, this failure to detect the extent to which short-term means can corrupt long-term ends, was the fourth and most lasting deficiency of "flexible response" as applied in Vietnam.

The tendency appeared clearly in South Vietnam itself, where the administration failed to anticipate the sheer strain several hundred thousand U.S. troops would place on the social and economic structure of that country. Despite American efforts to keep it down, the cost of living in the cities rose by at least 170 percent between 1965 and 1967, just as Westmoreland's "search and destroy" operations were swelling their populations with refugees. Corruption, of course, had always been present in Vietnam, but the proliferation of television sets, motorcycles, watches, refrigerators, and loose cash that accompanied the Americans greatly intensified it. "[T]he vast influx of American dollars," one observer recalls, "had almost as much influence . . . as the bombing had on the country-side":

> It turned the society of Saigon inside out. . . . In the new economy a prostitute earned more than a GVN minister, a secretary working for USAID more than a full colonel, a taxi owner who spoke a few words of English more than a university professor. . . . The old rich of Saigon had opposed the Communists as a threat to their position in society; they found that the Americans took away that position in a much quicker and more decisive fashion—and with it, what was left of the underpinning of Vietnamese values.

A similar phenomenon spread to rural areas as well: "Around the American bases from An Khe to Nha Trang, Cu Chi, and Chu Lai, there had grown up entire towns made of packing cases and waste tin . . . entire towns advertising Schlitz, Coca-Cola, or Pepsi Cola . . . towns with exactly three kinds of industry—the taking in of American laundry, the selling of American cold drinks to American soldiers, and prostitution for the benefit of the Americans."[74]

The effect of this overbearing presence was to erode South Vietnam's capacity for self-reliance, the very quality the Americans had sought to strengthen in the first place. To be sure, Washington never succeeded in controlling its clients in all respects: the very profligacy of the U.S. investment in South Vietnam made occasional threats to cut it off less than credible. "The harsh truth is," one report noted early in 1968, "that given a showdown situation or an intolerable divergence between GVN and US methods, the US advisor will lose." But recalcitrance is not the same thing as independence. The same report noted that "[t]he Vietnamese in the street is firmly convinced that the US totally dominates the GVN and dictates exactly what course shall be followed."[75] And Vietnamese at the military or governmental level, while certainly not puppets, while clearly resentful at the extent to which the Americans had come to dominate their culture, were at the same time terrified at the prospect that the Americans might one day leave.[76] The result was an ambiguous but deep dependency, the extent of which became clear only after the United States did at last withdraw from the war, in 1973.

It is hard to say, in retrospect, what the cross-over point would have been between the level of outside aid necessary to sustain South Vietnam against its enemies and the amount beyond which self-reliance would have been impaired. Perhaps there was no such point; perhaps South Vietnam never had the capacity to stand on its own. What is clear, though, is that Washington made few efforts to find out. The American buildup took place almost totally without regard to the destructive impact it was having on the society it was supposed to defend. "It became necessary to destroy the town, to save it," an Air Force major explained, following the bombing of a Mekong delta village occupied by Viet Cong after the Tet offensive in 1968.[77] The comment could be applied to the whole American experience in Vietnam, and to the dilemma of disproportionate means which the strategy of "flexible response," despite its original emphasis on matching response to offense, never seemed able to resolve.

Securing South Vietnam's independence had not been the only reason for the American presence in that country, though: there had also been a determination to show potential aggressors elsewhere that aggression would not pay. "To withdraw from one battlefield means only to prepare for the next," Johnson argued. "We must say in southeast Asia—as we did in Europe . . . 'Hitherto shalt thou come, but no futher.' "[78] Interestingly, administration officials did not consider success in South Vietnam as necessarily a requirement in communicating that message. However things turned out there, John McNaughton reflected in 1964, it was "essential . . . that [the] US emerge as a 'good doctor.' We must have kept promises, been tough, taken risks, gotten bloodied, and hurt the enemy very badly." Sustained reprisals against the north might not work, McGeorge Bundy acknowledged early in 1965—the chances of success, he thought, were between 25 and 75 percent. But "even if it fails, the policy will be worth it. At a minimum it will damp down the charge that we did not do all we could. . . . Beyond that, a reprisal policy . . . will set a higher price for the future upon all adventures of guerrilla warfare."[79] The important thing, in projecting resolve, was to make a commitment; failure, while both possible and undesirable, would not be as bad as not having acted in the first place.

And yet, the signal actually communicated was very different. The inability of the steadily growing American commitment to halt North Vietnamese infiltration or Viet Cong attacks—a pattern made painfully evident by the 1968 Tet offensive—seemed only to demonstrate the irrelevancy of the kind of power the United States could bring to bear in such situations: technology, in this respect, may well have been more of a hindrance than a help in Vietnam.[80] The war also confirmed Mao Zedong's theory that relatively primitive forces could prevail against more sophisticated adversaries if they had both patience and will, qualities Ho Chi Minh perceived more accurately than Johnson to be lacking in the American attitude toward Vietnam.[81] Finally, Washington's commitment in that country had grown to the point, by 1968, that the United States would have been hard-pressed to respond anywhere else in the world had a comparable crisis developed.[82] What was demonstrated in Vietnam, then, was not so much the costs of committing aggression as of resisting it, a somewhat different message from what the administration had sought to convey.

The disproportionate commitment in Vietnam contributed to an erosion in overall U.S. military capabilities as well. Following its humiliation in the Cuban missile crisis, the Soviet Union embarked on a steady, long-term program of bolstering its strength in strategic weapons. The Johnson administration decided not to respond with a corresponding American buildup, partly because it underestimated the extent of what the Russians were doing,[83] partly because McNamara had become convinced that the point of diminishing returns in American strategic programs had been reached, but partly also because the mushrooming costs of the Vietnam War made the administration reluctant to go to Congress with requests for expensive new systems to counter Soviet increases.[84] The whole "flexible response" strategy had been based on the continued maintenance of strategic superiority over the Russians: "I have not become President to give away this advantage," Johnson had announced, two weeks after Kennedy's death.[85] And yet, by the time Johnson left office in 1969, Moscow was on the verge of parity with the United States in land-based ICBMs, and had building programs under way that would secure numerical superiority in this and several other categories of strategic weapons systems by the mid-1970's.

One can argue at length about the wisdom of the decision not to match the Soviet military buildup. The acceptance of parity did make possible negotiations on limiting strategic arms, which the Russians agreed to in 1968, but at the same time there was no guarantee that those discussions would succeed, or that Moscow would exhibit unilateral restraint in areas not covered by them. Such considerations played little role in the Johnson administration's thinking, though. It was budgetary pressures and anti-military sentiment generated by Vietnam that made it unfeasible even to suggest major increases in U.S. strategic capabilities in the late 1960's (with the exception of multiple warheads for ICBMs, which were relatively inexpensive, and a rudimentary anti-ballistic missile system, which the Congress forced on a reluctant administration). As Henry Kissinger, who would later have to live with the consequences of these decisions, recalled: "at the precise moment that our national debate should have concentrated on the implications of this new situation, *all* our defense programs were coming under increasing attack."[86] It was a startling demonstration of the short-sightedness Washington's fixation on Vietnam was capable of inducing.

American escalation in Vietnam probably did not impair, on any lasting basis, prospects for détente with the Soviet Union. That process coincided with the coming to power of Leonid Brezhnev and Alexei Kosygin, who, unlike Khrushchev, preferred to delay efforts to improve relations with the United States until the U.S.S.R. had reached rough strategic parity. The new Kremlin leaders did not welcome the American escalation in Vietnam, but they did little to discourage Hanoi's counter-escalation or to help arrange negotiations. At one point, in 1966, a Soviet official even advised the Johnson administration to *increase* American troop strength in South Vietnam.[87] Nor is it clear that United States involvement there did anything to heal the Sino-Soviet split, as critics of the war feared it might. Instead, the deepening American commitment set off a rancorous competition between Moscow and Beijing to aid Hanoi, with the result that the two communist giants' relations with each other worsened rather than improved.[88] Vietnam did interfere with one other American initiative toward the communist world, though: this was Johnson's campaign, initiated in 1964, to "build bridges" to the nations of Eastern Europe by increasing economic ties with them. This not-so-subtle attempt to weaken Moscow's control over its satellites foundered when Congress, angry over Soviet and East European assistance to North Vietnam, refused to relax discriminatory tariff barriers on trade with communist countries.[89]

What strikes one about these developments is how little effort the Johnson administration made to gauge Vietnam's impact on them.* It was as if escalation there was taking place in a geopolitical vacuum—although, in contrast, the consequences of *not* escalating were thought to have global significance. In retrospect, it can be argued that all of these initiatives—progress toward détente with the Russians, exploitation of the Sino-Soviet split, the improvement of ties with Eastern Europe—reflected interests more vital than those at stake in Vietnam. But Washington did not see it that way at the time; the fact that the war damaged only the last of these can be chalked up to good luck, but not to foresight or careful planning.

Vietnam distracted attention from other problems as well. General Charles De Gaulle's intransigence and the continuing debate over nuclear strategy placed NATO under serious strains during the mid-1960's, but the Johnson administration, following the demise of the multilateral nuclear force concept, had few suggestions to make toward relieving them. Relations with Latin America, which Kennedy had emphasized, were for the most part neglected under Johnson; the exception was the 1965 crisis in the Dominican Republic, when the President abruptly sent in the Marines, thus violating a long-standing U.S. policy of avoiding overt intervention in that part of the world. The Middle East became the focus of attention only during the June 1967 Arab-Israeli War: the administration did little to try to head off that conflict, or to resolve the resulting difficulties created by the Israeli occupation of Arab territory and by Moscow's growing influence in the region. The 1968 Soviet invasion of Czechoslovakia also caught the administration off guard, able to do little in response but to postpone (and then only briefly) talks on strategic arms limitation. What all of these episodes had in common is that they were forced on the consciousness of Washington officials, who had to take time away from Vietnam to deal with them. As a consequence, they tended to be handled on an *ad hoc*, crisis-management basis, with little attention to the context in which they had occurred, and only minimal reflection upon their long-term implications.[90]

* Administration officials did, in 1964, consider the anticipated deterioration of Sino-Soviet relations as one reason for delaying escalation, on the theory that as the split became more severe a response by either side would become more difficult. (See Johnson to Lodge, March 20, 1964, *Pentagon Papers*, III, 511; Bundy memorandum, Johnson meeting with advisers, September 9, 1964, *FRUS: 1964–68*, I, document 343; also Johnson, *The Vantage Point*, p. 67.) But the available record contains no evidence that the consequences of escalation on Sino-Soviet relations were seriously considered.

But the greatest distractions of all came in domestic affairs, which Johnson himself had regarded as his highest priority. "I do not want to be the President who built empires, or sought grandeur, or extended dominion," he told the Congress in March 1965:

> I want to be the President who educated young children to the wonders of their world. I want to be the President who helped to feed the hungry and to prepare them to be taxpayers instead of taxeaters.
>
> I want to be the President who helped the poor to find their own way and who protected the right of every citizen to vote in every election.
>
> I want to be the President who helped to end hatred among his fellow men and who promoted love among the people of all races and all religions and all parties.
>
> I want to be the President who helped to end war among the brothers of this earth.[91]

And, indeed, Johnson's domestic legislative accomplishments had, by that time, surpassed those of any president since Franklin D. Roosevelt. Johnson claimed, in retrospect, to have anticipated the corrosive effect the war would have on those programs: "I knew from the start that I was bound to be crucified either way I moved. If I left the woman I really loved—the Great Society—in order to get involved with that bitch of a war on the other side of the world, then I would lose everything at home. . . . But if I left that war and let the Communists take over South Vietnam, then I would be seen as a coward and my nation would be seen as an appeaser and we would both find it impossible to accomplish anything for anybody anywhere on the entire globe."[92]

At the time, Johnson thought that he could avoid having to make that choice. "I was determined to be a leader of war *and* a leader of peace," he recalled. "I refused to let my critics push me into choosing one or the other. I wanted both, I believed in both, and I believed America had the resources to provide for both."[93] Providing for both, though, involved concealing the nature and cost of the war as long as possible. Hence, Johnson publicly discounted the prospect of a direct American role in Vietnam prior to the 1964 election, despite the fact that his advisers expected it and were even exchanging ideas on how to provoke it.* Even after the elec-

---

* "The concept of the course of action described above in essence is: by doing legitimate things to provoke a DRV response and to be in a good position to seize on that response, or upon an unprovoked DRV action, to commence a crescendo of GVN-US military actions against the DRV." (John McNaughton draft, "Plan of Action for South Vietnam," September 3, 1964, *Pentagon Papers*, III, 558–59.) "The main further question is the extent to which we should add elements to the above actions that would tend deliberately to provoke a DRV reaction, and consequent retaliation by us." (McGeorge Bundy draft, consensus reached in dis-

tion, when plans for reprisals against North Vietnam had been approved in principle, Johnson insisted that it was "a matter of the highest importance that the substance of this position should not become public except as I specifically direct." And in April 1965, after authorizing a ground combat mission for U.S. forces in Vietnam, he directed that those actions should be taken "in ways that should minimize any appearance of sudden changes in policy. . . . These movements and changes should be understood as being gradual and wholly consistent with existing policy." It was not until June that the public found out about the assigned tasks of American troops in Vietnam, and then only through an inadvertently candid State Department press briefing.[94]

Once the nature of U.S. involvement in the war had become clear, the President sought to conceal the costs, lest they provide an excuse for cutting back on Great Society programs. He told McNamara in July 1965 to plan on implementing the new and more active combat role with an immediate additional appropriation of only $330-400 million. Bundy suggested that $2 billion was the more realistic figure through the end of the year: "Bob is afraid we simply cannot get away with the idea that a call-up of the planned magnitude can be paid for anything so small as another few hundred million." By October 1966, McNamara was reporting actual war costs over and above those of the peacetime defense establishment at $9.4 billion for fiscal 1966, an estimated $19.7 billion for fiscal 1967, and a projected annual rate of $22.4 billion by the end of that period. "As we look a year or two ahead," William P. Bundy had warned in the spring of 1966, "with a military program that would require major further budget costs—with all their implications for taxes and domestic programs—and with steady or probably rising casualties, the war could well become an albatross around the Administration's neck, at least equal to what Korea was for President Truman in 1952."[95]

Johnson was fully sensitive to this danger, and with it in mind refused throughout 1966 to seek an increase in taxes sufficient to counter the inflationary pressures this expansion in military spending was generating. Not until early 1967 did he ask for an income tax surcharge to finance the war; Congress, in turn, delayed approving it until June 1968, and then only at the price of cutting back Johnson's domestic programs.[96] The "new economics," upon which the budgetary assumptions of "flexible response" had been grounded, assumed not only timely tax cuts to stimulate a stagnant

cussions with Taylor, Rusk, McNamara and Wheeler, for review by the President, September 8, 1964, *ibid.*, p. 562.) For Johnson's public disclaimers, see *JPP: 1963–64*, pp. 1126–27, 1164.

economy, but equally timely tax increases to cool down an overheated one. But, as Johnson later acknowledged, the difficulties of obtaining the latter far outweighed those of securing the former. The problem had not been just the Congress's reluctance to pass a tax increase, though; it had also been the President's reluctance to fight for one at a time when his political prestige was higher, and his party's strength on Capitol Hill stronger, than it was at the beginning of 1967.[97]*

It was Johnson's perception of virtually unlimited means—the belief that the nation could afford both "guns" and "butter" at the same time—that led him into this unprecedented attempt to fight a costly war and sustain a costly reform program at the same time. The effort, in the end, proved futile: the Great Society ultimately had to be sacrificed to pay for the war. But the long struggle to avoid making that choice had its own, even more lasting, consequences. The President's determination to conceal the costs and nature of the war produced an erosion of official credibility that would persist for years afterward. Even more costly, in the long run, was the inflationary spiral set in motion by Johnson's decision to finance the war on a deferred basis; the effects would remain for over a decade following his departure from the White House.†

"We must not destroy what we are attempting to defend." So Dwight Eisenhower summarized the most consistent single element in his thinking on national security policy: the processes of defense, he repeatedly argued, should never be allowed to overshadow the purposes of defense. This sensitivity to the need to keep ends and means in balance was precisely what was lacking in the Kennedy and Johnson administrations. There was instead a preoccupation with process at the expense of objectives, a fascination so great with *how* things were to be done that it tended to obscure what *was* being done. It is ironic that this should have occurred under administrations that prided themselves on their ability to match means to ends in the most appropriate manner; one cannot help but conclude that the very abundance of means which seemed to be available dur-

---

*The Democrats had lost forty-seven seats in the House of Representatives in the 1966 elections.

† Rostow did not see Vietnam war spending as having had this decisive an effect. "For reasons quite independent of war expenditures, productivity decelerated and the decline in basic commodity prices (whose reduction from 1951 on damped inflation) bottomed out. . . . The deceleration of productivity and leveling off and then slow rise down to the explosion of 1972–1973 of basic commodity prices was . . . common to the whole advanced industrial world." (Letter to the author, September 22, 1980.)

ing those years contributed to the problem. The bracing discipline of stringency, after all, provides more powerful incentives toward efficiency than even the most sophisticated management techniques.

Strategy is the calculated relationship of ends and means, but that implies equal attention to all four components in the definition: calculations *and* relationships, ends *and* means. Where that does not exist—where calculations become more important than relationships being calculated, where means attract greater attention than ends—then what one has is not so much bad strategy as no strategy at all. This, then, was the unexpected legacy of "flexible response": not "fine tuning" but clumsy overreaction, not coordination but disproportion, not strategic precision, but, in the end, a strategic vacuum.

Nixon, Kissinger, and Détente

The 1968 presidential campaign was unusual in that, unlike those of 1952 and 1960, it provided little indication of the direction in which the new administration would move once in office. Richard Nixon had made an issue of Johnson's inability to end the Vietnam War and had promised that he would do so, although without saying how or when. He had also implied, with references to an era of confrontation giving way to one of negotiation, a continuation of the previous administration's efforts to arrange a relaxation of tensions with the Soviet Union. There had even been hints, in a *Foreign Affairs* article the previous year and in occasional campaign speeches, of a willingness to consider a new relationship with the People's Republic of China.[1] But, in general, voters going to the polls on election day, 1968, had no idea that they were ushering in the most sweeping changes in United States foreign policy since the idea of containment had first emerged two decades earlier.

The world confronting the new administration in January 1969 was ripe with possibilities for new approaches. Johnson had already made the decision to put a ceiling on U.S. troop commitments in Southeast Asia and to begin the process of "Vietnamization" that, he hoped, would eventually permit an American withdrawal. China, emerging from the self-imposed isolation of the Great Cultural Revolution, was on the verge of a military confrontation with the Russians along its Manchurian border. The Soviet Union was about to achieve numerical parity in strategic missiles, but confronted increasing economic difficulties at home that appeared likely to make it more rather than less dependent on the West.

This "objective" situation, then, probably would have produced major changes in American diplomacy, whoever entered the White House on January 20, 1969.

The fact that the new occupant was Richard Nixon, and that he chose as his national security adviser Dr. Henry Kissinger, brought two new elements into the equation. One was Nixon's unique combination of ideological rigidity with political pragmatism: the first, in a curious way, had contributed to the second. Nixon had been so staunch an anti-communist over the years that flexibility now took on the aura of statesmanship rather than softness, thus according him greater freedom of action than his more liberal rivals for the presidency could have expected. The other new element was Kissinger's conceptual approach to the making of national security policy. As a student more of the history than of the "science" of politics, he held in contempt the fascination with process that had characterized the Kennedy and Johnson administrations. "Crisis management, the academic focus of the Sixties, was no longer enough," he later wrote. "Crises were symptoms of deeper problems which if allowed to fester would prove increasingly unmanageable. . . . It was my conviction that a concept of our fundamental national interests would provide a ballast of restraint and an assurance of continuity." "The combination was unlikely," Nixon recalled, "the grocer's son from Whittier and the refugee from Hitler's Germany, the politician and the academic. But our differences helped make the partnership work."[2]

What this odd alliance of Nixon and Kissinger sought was a strategy that would combine the tactical flexibility of the Kennedy-Johnson system with the structure and coherence of Eisenhower's, while avoiding the shortsighted fixations that had led to Vietnam or the ideological rigidities of a John Foster Dulles.[3] To a remarkable extent, they succeeded, but only by concentrating power in the White House to a degree unprecedented since the wartime administration of Franklin D. Roosevelt. The price was an uninformed, sullen, and at times sabotage-minded bureaucracy, a Congress determined to reassert its eroded constitutional authority without any sense of how far that authority could feasibly extend, and, ultimately, the resignation of a president certain otherwise to have been impeached and convicted for abusing the overwhelming power his own system had given him. It is a tribute to the logic of the Nixon-Kissinger strategy that its fundamental elements survived these upheavals, with Kissinger, as Secretary of State after 1973, remaining in charge of foreign policy through the end of the Ford administration four years later.

It is also significant that the Nixon-Kissinger strategy returned, in its underlying assumptions, to many of the ideas upon which George Kennan had based his original strategy of containment more than two decades before. Containment, it seemed, was coming back to concerns and concepts that had animated it during the earliest days of the Cold War—and those ideas were being used, as Kennan had hoped to use them, to try to end the Cold War.

I

All previous postwar administrations had associated American interests in one way or another with a world of diversity. Universalism—attempting to transform the world to make it resemble the United States—had at no point been seen as consistent with either national capabilities or national ideals. There had thus been an implied commitment, however rarely acknowledged, to preserving an international equilibrium in order that diversity might flourish. But the view had also prevailed, after 1950, that only the United States could ensure that diversity: the threats confronting it were too overwhelming, the balance of power was too delicate, for Washington to act only when its immediate interests were endangered. In the continuing postwar emergency, all interests were vital, all threats were deadly, all commitments had to be credible. The effect had been to push the United States into universalism by the back door: the defense of diversity in what seemed to be a dangerous world had produced most of the costs, strains, and self-defeating consequences of indiscriminate globalism.

This had happened, Kissinger believed, because successive administrations had lost sight of the kind of international order they should have been seeking in the first place. Conceptual coherence had broken down. There had been too many *ad hoc* decisions made without reference to larger objectives, too much reliance by excessively pragmatic leaders upon excessively self-centered bureaucracies:

> Problems are segmented into constituent elements, each of which is dealt with by experts in the special difficulty it involves. There is little emphasis or concern for their inter-relationship. Technical issues enjoy more careful attention, and receive more sophisticated treatment, than political ones. . . . Things are done because one knows how to do them and not because one ought to do them.

This fascination with process had obscured the relationship between intentions and consequences: an obsession with means had led to the neglect, and even the corruption, of ends. What was needed, Kissinger insisted in 1968, was a "philosophical deepening" in American foreign policy: "we will never be able to contribute to building a stable and creative world order until we first form some conception of it."[4]

The first requirement for such a "deepening" was to recognize the multidimensional nature of power in the world: there was no single index by which the influence of states could be measured. Nuclear weapons, given the constraints on their use in an approaching era of parity, were of decreasing practical utility. Kissinger liked to point out that in no crisis since 1962 had the strategic balance determined the outcome. Vietnam had amply demonstrated the limits of conventional military force applied under constraints imposed by public opinion and the dangers of escalation. Ideology was proving to be a feeble force when arrayed against the compulsions of nationalism; territory bore little relationship to political influence; economic strength seemed at times to have little to do with any of these. And, underlying all of these complexities, there was the increasing importance of psychology: the perception of power had become as important as power itself.[5]

It was too simplistic, therefore, to continue thinking of the balance of power as a "zero sum game," in which "gains" for one side invariably meant "losses" for the other.[6] What might appear as a loss in one area—the stalemate in Vietnam, for example, or the Soviet attainment of strategic parity—could be compensated for by gains in others—an opening to China, or a negotiated settlement on arms control. It was the overall calculus of power that was important, not the defeats or victories that might take place in isolated theaters of competition. The Kennedy and Johnson administrations had erred by making Vietnam a symbol of American power and commitment throughout the world. The Nixon administration, taking advantage of its more ecumenical definition of power, would seek to reduce Vietnam to its proper perspective—"a small peninsula on a major continent," as Kissinger put it[7]—and to concentrate on global relationships.

The United States could move, then, from a fixed to a flexible perception of interests in the world, so long as an overall balance of power was maintained. This did not mean a withdrawal from existing obligations: in their determination to honor prior commitments, in their fear of what would happen to American credibility if they failed, Nixon and Kissinger differed little from their predecessors. But their approach did imply an unwillingness henceforth to assume the sole responsibility for securing global equilibrium. The changing nature of power had made the international balance more stable than in the past. In an age in which economic measures could counterbalance military strength, in which nationalism could neutralize ideology, there was less need than there once might have been for the United States to act alone to preserve world order.[8]

A second requirement for a more precise conceptualization of interests was to purge foreign policy of certain illusions about the nature of the international order. Despite the acceptance of diversity as an inevitable condition in world affairs, despite the recognition that it was not inconsistent with American security requirements, there lingered in the United States, Kissinger believed, a reluctance to accept the fact that conflict and disharmony were and would continue to be inescapable characteristics of international life. There was still the belief that somehow the United States might transcend the international order, instead of simply having to operate within it. These unrealistic hopes, and the corrosive effects of reality upon them, had produced oscillations between isolationism and overextension in the American approach to the world. Foreign policy had ranged too widely "between poles of suspicion and euphoria." What was needed, Kissinger thought, was the realism to accept the world as it was, together with the ingenuity to make the best of it.[9]

This meant giving up efforts, as a matter of vital national interest, to change the internal nature of other societies. There had been too much of a tendency in other administrations to confuse reform with geopolitics. The new administration did not accept the view, so firmly held by its immediate predecessors, that economic development, or the evolution of democratic procedures, would, in themselves, enhance American security throughout the world. It all depended on the geopolitical context. Economic change and political reform could produce as much instability as they prevented. Kissinger was well aware of Alexis de Tocqueville's observation that existing orders are most threatened when conditions improve, rather than the other way around. Nor were there guarantees that states that were economically advanced, or that had democratic governments, would always support American interests. All else being equal, the United States would of course prefer institutions abroad compatible with its own at home. But not at the expense of the balance of power: to subordinate the requirements of international equilibrium to those of internal reform was, Kissinger believed, to risk precisely those fluctuations between hyperactivity and petulant withdrawal that had prevented, in the past, a clear view of where American interests lay.[10]

Maturity also demanded recognition that the geopolitical interests of ideologically disparate states could, in certain areas, be congruent. Once diplomacy was purged of its sentimental and emotional components, it should be possible to identify and build upon those common interests held even by previously irreconcilable antagonists: survival, security, a congenial international environment. The key to such an accomplishment, Kissinger believed, was mutual restraint. Differences could not be expected to evaporate overnight; there would have to be a willingness to tolerate not only incompatible internal systems but also conflicting international interests in certain parts of the world. If this could be achieved, then there might well emerge a level "of shared geopolitical interest transcending philosophies and history" upon which, as Kissinger would later write of Nixon and the Chinese Communists, "even the former Red-baiter and the crusaders for world revolution [could find] each other."[11]

A third prerequisite for conceptual coherence in foreign policy was a recognition of limits. Kissinger had never held the view, fashionable among defense intellectuals in the 1960's, that maintaining the balance of power required indefinitely expandable means: such profligacy, he thought, was more likely in the end to destabilize rather than stabilize the international order. "No country," he wrote in 1968, "can act wisely simultaneously in every part of the globe at every moment of time." The difficulty was that objectives tended to expand as means did, thereby producing not only eventual exhaustion but also increasing resistance from other nations who would see in a quest for absolute security absolute insecurity for themselves. The beginning of wisdom in human as well as international affairs was knowing when to stop: it was significant that the three statesmen Kissinger had chosen to write about in his career as a historian—Metternich, Castlereagh, and especially Bismarck—had all had this quality, so conspicuously lacking in recent American diplomacy.[12]

It was hardly surprising, then, that one of Kissinger's earliest priorities had been to shift the emphasis in official thinking on defense policy from "superiority" to "sufficiency."[13] The terminology itself referred to the strategic weapons balance, but the underlying assumptions had wider ramifications: that efforts to surpass the Russians in the past had only provoked comparable efforts on their part; that the interests of both sides might now better be served by exhibiting mutual restraint. Economic necessity had already to an extent forced this position on the Johnson administration—especially in the area of strategic weapons—but it was Nixon and Kissinger who elevated it to the status of doctrine. "Sufficiency," it is important to note, never meant unilateral restraint: Kissinger was convinced that Moscow would regard that as a weakness, and would only seek to exploit it.[14] It did, though, mean a recognition that quests for "superiority" were likely to be both costly and self-defeating, and that a combination of pressures and inducements aimed at convincing the Russians that "sufficiency" was in their own best interests would, simultaneously, best serve those of the United States.

But what would be the specific elements of a strategy that recognized the new dimensions of power, integrated them into the international system as it was, and did so without exhausting American resources? Kissinger never answered this question directly, but Nixon provided a revealing hint, in the curiously offhand manner he at times reserved for significant pronouncements, when he briefed a group of news media executives in Kansas City in July 1971. There were, he told them, five great economic powers in the world: the United States, the Soviet Union, Western Europe, Japan, and China. "[T]hese are the five that will determine the economic future and, because economic power will be the key to other kinds of power, the future of the world in other ways in the last third of this century." It had been an extemporaneous speech, the President later told a keenly interested Zhou Enlai, but it reflected a "well-considered conviction."[15]* Early in 1972, in an interview with *Time* magazine, Nixon made his concept more explicit. "[T]he only time in the history of the world that we have had any extended period of peace," he noted, echoing the thesis of Kissinger's book *A World Restored*, "is when there has been a balance of power. It is when one nation becomes infinitely more powerful in relation to its potential competitor that the danger of war arises. . . . I think it will be a safer world and a better world if we have a stronger, healthy United States, Europe, Soviet Union, China, Japan, each balancing the other, not playing one against the other, an even balance."[16]

Implied here, whether Nixon realized it or not, was a return to Kennan's 1948 concept of five centers of industrial-military power, and to the need to keep any one of them from dominating the others.† Kissinger

---

* The pronouncement was unusual in that it had not been cleared with Kissinger, who was on a secret trip to China at the time and who learned of it from Zhou Enlai. (Henry Kissinger, *White House Years* [Boston: 1979], pp. 748–49.)

† One difference was that Kennan had considered Great Britain and the Rhine valley as separate power centers, and had not included China.

never explicitly associated himself with this geopolitical formulation, perhaps because it suggested simplistic analogies drawn from his own historical writings (something he always cautioned against),[17] perhaps because of
the potential for misunderstanding involved in publicly designating some
parts of the world as more "vital" than others (as Dean Acheson had discovered after his "defensive perimeter" speech in 1950), perhaps because
of the criticisms Nixon's statement immediately encountered from the academic and strategic studies communities (Japan and Western Europe,
while indisputably major economic powers, would not for years have the
capacity to defend themselves without the help of the United States;
China was neither a military nor an economic superpower).[18] But, if analyzed
in a broad context, Nixon's vision of a pentagonal world operating on balance
of power principles does appear consistent with what Kissinger—and Kennan some quarter of a century earlier—had been trying to accomplish.

Kissinger had long argued that the emerging shift from a bipolar to a
multipolar world was in the best interests of the United States. Bipolarity,
he wrote in 1968, encouraged rigidity:

> A bipolar world loses the perspective for nuance; a gain for one side appears
> as an absolute loss for the other. Every issue seems to involve a question of
> survival. The smaller countries are torn between a desire for protection and
> a wish to escape big-power dominance. Each of the superpowers is beset by
> the desire to maintain its preeminence among its allies, to increase its influ-
> ence among the uncommitted, and to enhance its security vis-à-vis its
> opponent.

Multipolarity would not, in itself, guarantee stability, Kissinger was careful
to point out. In the absence of a sense of common danger, coordinated action would be more difficult to achieve: "Rigidity is diminished, but so is
manageability." But a multipolar system would provide greater opportunities for working out a shared concept of international order; it also had
built into it a degree of "natural" or "organic" balance not present in a
bipolar system with, accordingly, less need for individual elements in the
balance to bear the primary burden of maintaining it. "A more pluralistic
world," Kissinger concluded, "is profoundly in our long-term interests."[19]

In specific terms, Kissinger favored a united but *independent* Western
Europe: unlike most "Atlanticists" in the Kennedy and Johnson administrations, he had sympathized with De Gaulle's insistence on achieving
unity by reconciling the sovereign interests of European states, rather
than by subordinating them to an integrationist "grand design" devised in
Washington.[20] After an initial period of acknowledged neglect, Kissinger

was quick, in 1973, to embrace a central principle of what had come to be known as "trilateralism": that Japan was a major center of world power in its own right, and had to be given attention in the future comparable to that accorded Western Europe.[21] Both Nixon and Kissinger had, by 1969, independently reached the conclusion that China should be brought out of the isolation imposed partially by American policy, partially by itself: "no stable and enduring international order is conceivable," the President's first foreign policy report concluded, "without the contribution of this nation of more than 700 million people."[22] And, with regard to the Soviet Union, the Kissinger strategy was not to try to deny legitimate security interests, but to persuade the Kremlin leadership to define those interests within the framework of a multipolar world order.[23]

Critics notwithstanding, this pentagonal concept did not depend upon every element within the structure having the same kind of power. "It is wrong to speak of only one balance of power," Kissinger observed in 1973, "for there are several which have to be related to each other."

> In the military sphere, there are two superpowers. In economic terms, there are at least five major groupings. Politically, many more centers of influence have emerged. . . . When we refer to five or six or seven major centers of power, the point being made is not that others are excluded but that a few short years ago everyone agreed that there were only two.[24]

By stressing their economic strength, Japan and Western Europe could play a role in the world out of proportion to their military power. China's importance, for the moment, lay primarily in the ideological field—in the challenge it posed to Soviet control over the international communist movement. Only the United States and the U.S.S.R. had the qualifications to be superpowers in every sense of the word, but the increasingly fragmented nature of power had confronted them, in many areas, with sufficient competition from the rest of the world to create the conditions for multipolarity.

It was possible to have multipolar equilibrium, therefore, even with gross disproportions in the varieties of power available to the nations constituting it. The American interest was to preserve that balance, applying leverage selectively where necessary, but with the realization that the balance itself was now more stable than in the days of the bipolar Cold War. At the same time, it was necessary to try to move beyond the balance of power toward a new world order in which stability would result, not from the clash of competing interests, but from the evolution of "habits of mutual restraint, coexistence, and, ultimately, cooperation." This, Kissinger insisted, was what was meant by "détente."[25]

Kissinger's "philosophical deepening," then, constituted a major change in official perceptions of American interests in the world, but it was not an unprecedented innovation. The overall concept, not just the occasional references to a pentagonal world, was strikingly similar to what Kennan had put forward between 1947 and 1949. Like Kissinger, Kennan had based his definition of interests on a multidimensional assessment of power: military strength had by no means been the only decisive element in world affairs. Like Kissinger, Kennan had favored stability over reform: to change the world to make it resemble the United States, he had argued, would be both costly and self-defeating. Like Kissinger, Kennan had been fully aware of the limits of American power, and of the need to align it as much as possible with existing trends, rather than trying to fight them. Like Kissinger, Kennan had identified American interests with maintaining a balance of power in a multipolar world. And like Kissinger, Kennan had evolved a conception of interests capable of standing on its own, independent, as intervening strategies had not been, of both threats and commitments. It was with good reason that Kennan could say, a year after Kissinger's appointment as Secretary of State, that "Henry understands my views better than anyone at State ever has."[26]

II

Just as interests were perceived more flexibly during the Nixon administration, so, too, threats came to be perceived more narrowly. The prevailing pattern since the Korean War had been to rely primarily on ideology as a means with which to predict adversaries' behavior. Considerations based on history, economics, ethnicity, or geography might, from time to time, cause disputes among communist states, but in the end common ideological priorities would govern. Victories for communism, whether coordinated or not, would either threaten or appear to threaten the balance of power in the world, and therefore had to be resisted. There had been no effort to "roll back" communism from positions it had gained at the end of World War II: indeed, the United States had even been willing to work with some communists—Tito's Yugoslavia, for example, or, if Johnson had had his way, other states in Eastern Europe—to oppose the hegemonic aspirations of others. But further changes in the status quo beneficial to communism could not be tolerated; those that had occurred since 1945—in China, Cuba, or North Vietnam—could not be publicly sanctioned. Threats to the balance of power in general, and to United States security in particular, were still defined, as late as 1969, in terms of the existence of an ideology that was, by definition, hostile.

Nixon and Kissinger set out quite deliberately to eliminate ideology as the chief criterion by which to identify threats. "[W]e have no permanent enemies," Kissinger announced in December 1969; "we will judge other countries, including Communist countries, . . . on the basis of their actions and not on the basis of their domestic ideology." Ideological differences were deeply rooted and would not disappear overnight. But in an age of shared nuclear peril, even the most ideologically antagonistic states could find interests in common. "We have broken out of the old pattern," Nixon told Zhou Enlai in Beijing in February 1972:

> We look at each country in terms of its own conduct rather than lumping them all together and saying that because they have this kind of philosophy they are all in utter darkness. I would say in honesty . . . that my views, because I was in the Eisenhower administration, were similar to those of Mr. Dulles at that time. But the world has changed since then. . . . As the Prime Minister [Zhou] has said in a meeting with Dr. Kissinger, the helmsman must ride with the waves or he will be submerged with the tide.

"What brings us together," the President reminded an approving Mao Zedong, "is a recognition of a new situation in the world and a recognition on our part that what is important is not a nation's internal political philosophy. What is important is its policy toward the rest of the world and toward us."[27]

Much had changed since the day, only four-and-a-half years earlier, when Dean Rusk had invoked, as a major justification for the continuing American escalation in Vietnam, the threat of "a billion Chinese . . . armed with nuclear weapons," spurred on by Beijing's "militant doctrine of world revolution."[28] What made Nixon's de-emphasis on ideology possible, of course, was the now irrefutable evidence of Sino-Soviet antagonism: "international Communist unity has been shattered," his first annual foreign policy report noted bluntly.[29] Another contributing factor was Nixon's ideological flexibility, the product of an earlier inflexibility so consistent in its anti-communism that critics could now hardly accuse him of "softness" or "naivete." "Those on the right can do what those on the left only talk about," he explained to Mao in 1972. "I like rightists," the aging revolutionary cheerfully acknowledged.[30]

It had been the Nixon-Kissinger redefinition of interests, though, that had chiefly made possible this altered perception of threat. Since 1950 American administrations had been in the habit of defining interests, not according to some independently derived standard of what was necessary to make the United States secure in the world, but in terms of threats that seemed to exist to it. "Containing communism" had become an interest in and of itself, without regard to the precise way in which communism as a unified force might endanger American security. Threats had been allowed to determine interests, rather than the other way around. What Nixon and Kissinger did with their concept of a multipolar world order was to arrive at a conception of interests independent of threats, and then define threats in terms of interests. Since those interests required equilibrium but not ideological consistency, since American means of achieving equilibrium alone were limited, it followed that the United States could feasibly work with states of differing, even antipathetic, social systems as long as they shared the American interest in maintaining global stability. "The leaders of China were beyond ideology in their dealings with us," Kissinger recalled. "Their peril had established the absolute primacy of geopolitics."[31]

But if communism itself was no longer a threat, what was? Here the Nixon administration returned to the perception that had shaped the original Kennan approach to containment: the combination of hostility and capability that existed in the foreign policy of the Soviet Union. The U.S.S.R., Kissinger believed, sought constantly, for a combination of historical and ideological reasons, to expand its power in the world. Security for Russia had always meant insecurity for Russia's neighbors. All Leninism had done had been to give "the expansionist instinct a theoretical formulation that applied universally around the globe. It salved Russian consciences; it compounded the problem for all other peoples." But that expansionism proceeded according to no fixed timetable: the Kremlin would exploit opportunities presented to it, but it would also retreat in the face of resistance. "To foreclose Soviet opportunities is the essence of the West's responsibility," Kissinger concluded: "It is up to us to define the limits of Soviet aims."[32]

What made the situation different from Kennan's day, though, were the vast gains in industrial, technological, and military power the Russians had made relative to the United States and its allies during the 1960's. For the first two decades following the end of World War II, there could have been no question in the minds of Soviet leaders that they were operating from a position of weakness vis-à-vis the West (although they did often succeed in concealing this fact from their Western counterparts). But by the time the Nixon administration took office, the Soviet Union was approaching parity with the United States in long-range missile capability,* and was for the first time developing the means to project conventional power far beyond its borders. Soviet aspirations, Kissinger had to acknowledge, were "now rooted in real power, rather than a rhetorical manifestation of a universalist doctrine, which in fact has very little validity or appeal."[33]

To be sure, the Soviet system still had its weaknesses. It lacked mechanisms for the orderly succession of leaders. It was developing a sluggish bureaucracy whose priorities did not always coincide with those of the Communist party. Its domestic economy was grossly inefficient, especially in the key areas of agriculture and computer technology. Its foreign policy was often clumsy and inept. Its officials operated with a lack of poise and self-confidence that was striking in comparison to the subtle and sophisticated Chinese.[34] Nonetheless, the Soviet Union alone combined both the ability and the motive to challenge the balance of power upon which Nixon and Kissinger had based the vital interests of the United States. As a consequence, relations with Moscow became, as they had been for Kennan, the central preoccupation of their diplomacy.

One problem with Kennan's strategy, though, had always been how to distinguish between real and apparent shifts in the balance of power. Because perceptions rivaled reality in shaping world events, even the appearance of changes in the existing order could, in their effects, approximate real ones. Kennan had never solved this problem, which had led him into supporting the defense of Greece, Turkey, and South Korea, even though none of those countries could remotely have been considered to be among his five vital centers of industrial-military power.[35] The problem had been less noticeable in succeeding administrations, which had tended to see all interests as equally vital, and therefore all threats as equally significant. But Nixon and Kissinger had reverted to a differentiated conception of interests: this raised the question, once again, of differentiating between varieties of threat. The administration found it difficult to do this, in practice, in a manner consistent with the de-emphasis on ideology it had advocated in principle.

---

* The Russians in mid-1965 had had 224 ICBMs and 107 SLBMs, as compared to 934 and 464 for the United States. By the end of 1970, the Russians were expected to have 1,290 ICBMs and 300 SLBMs, as compared to 1,054 and 656 for the United States. (Annual foreign policy report, February 18, 1970, *NPP: 1970*, p. 173.)

By all logic, an administration concerned primarily about the dangers of Soviet expansionism, determined to downplay the importance of ideology in world affairs, should have taken a relatively tolerant attitude toward independent Marxism, not just in China but wherever it appeared. In certain areas, it did do this: Nixon and Kissinger continued long-standing ties to Tito's Yugoslavia and, through presidential visits to that country, Romania, and Poland, sought to revive in a more muted form Johnson's idea of "building bridges" to Eastern Europe.[36] But there was, in the Nixon administration, a strong intolerance of Marxism elsewhere: in Vietnam, where Nixon continued for four years the costly American effort to deny Hanoi a victory; in Chile, where the United States sought covertly to "destabilize" the freely elected government of Salvador Allende; in Western Europe, where Kissinger viewed with obvious alarm the growth of "Eurocommunism"; and in Angola, where the Ford administration's hostility left the Marxist independence movement there little choice but to align itself with Moscow. There is no evidence in retrospect that any of these movements had been instigated by the Kremlin, or that Soviet leaders could have counted on controlling them, had they all been successful.[37] Still, the Nixon and Ford administrations worked with great zeal to oppose them, as if the success of any one of them could be decisive in altering the balance of power.

Why the willingness to tolerate ideological differences in dealing with so conspicuously communist a country as China, but not with indigenous Marxism elsewhere? It has been suggested that a "perceptual lag" was operating here: that Nixon and Kissinger responded to these situations with the outdated reflexes of the Cold War, not realizing the extent to which their own policies had made that view of the world obsolete. Kissinger's own account of the Chilean affair seems to confirm this: "[E]ven the most apparently 'independent' Communist parties of Western Europe and Latin America follow the Soviet lead in foreign policy without significant exceptions," he insisted. "Nor is the problem simply a matter of Communist parties. Radical politics in today's world encompasses a network of sympathetic organizations and groups that cover the globe, carrying out terrorist outrages or financing them, transferring weapons, infiltrating media, seeking to sway political processes." But Kissinger's own strategy had assumed, and often proclaimed, the breakup of communism as a monolith; nor was it easy, as he himself admitted, to establish connections between communist parties and the far more numerous—and more active—radical organizations that increasingly manifested their presence around the world.[38]

The more likely explanation is that each of these movements, if allowed to proceed unopposed, would have produced changes in the status quo that might have *appeared* to shift the balance of power.* The administration's willingness to deal with communist regimes in China and Eastern Europe constituted recognition of an existing status quo, but not the creation of a new one; the consequences, hence, were more predictable. Like Kennedy, Johnson, and their advisers, Nixon and Kissinger feared developments capable of embarrassing or humiliating the United States, even if they proceeded from no central or coordinated design. As Nixon explained at the time of the Cambodian invasion in April 1970: "If, when the chips are down, the world's most powerful nation, the United States of America, acts like a pitiful, helpless giant, the forces of totalitarianism and anarchy will threaten free nations and free institutions throughout the world." Great nations had to preserve their dignity, even while cutting their losses. "We could not simply walk away from [Vietnam] as if we were switching a television channel," Kissinger later wrote. "It seemed to me important for America not to be humiliated, not to be shattered, but to leave Vietnam in a manner that even the protesters might later see as reflecting an American choice made with dignity and self-respect."[39]

Nixon and Kissinger did not entirely succeed, then, in eliminating ideology from their calculations of threat. Ideological differences with existing communist powers would not be allowed to stand in the way of alignments dictated by balance of power considerations, but the administration was not prepared to tolerate further victories for communism, even when it took indigenous, and independent, forms. The dangers of humiliation, of conveying the appearance of weakness to real adversaries, were too great to permit acquiescence in the triumph even of hypothetical adversaries.

III

What grew out of this perception of interests and threats was a strategy that came to be known, all too loosely, as "détente." The term did not originate with either Nixon or Kissinger—Kennedy had used it to describe the process of relaxing tensions with the Soviet Union as early as 1963.[40] Nor

* In discussing the strategic arms race in 1974, Kissinger noted that "[w]hile a decisive advantage is hard to calculate, the appearance of inferiority—whatever its actual significance—can have serious political consequences." (Statement to Senate Foreign Relations Committee, September 19, 1974, in Henry A. Kissinger, *American Foreign Policy*, third edition [New York: 1977], p. 160.)

did the word convey the same meaning in all quarters—it was French, critics liked to point out, and had no precise equivalent in either English or Russian.* Nixon and Kissinger were clear about the meaning they attached to "détente," though: they viewed it as yet another in a long series of attempts to "contain" the power and influence of the U.S.S.R., but one based on a new combination of pressures and inducements that would, if successful, convince Kremlin leaders that it was in their country's interest to be "contained." The goal, as had been the case with Kennan two decades earlier, was nothing less than to change the Soviet Union's conception of international relations, to integrate it as a stable element into the existing world order, and to build on the resulting equilibrium a "structure of peace" that would end once and for all that persistent abnormality known as the "Cold War."

The first requirement for implementing the strategy of détente was to engage the Soviet Union in serious negotiations on substantive issues. Negotiations had always been held out as the *ultimate* objective of containment: the idea since 1950 had been that once the West reached a "situation of strength" with respect to the Russians, they would be willing to talk and the crisis that had produced the Cold War would have come to an end. But Kissinger thought this reasoning specious for several reasons. First, he had long insisted that no nation could be expected to accommodate itself willingly to an international order that left it in a permanent position of inferiority. The Russians had no business demanding absolute security for themselves at the price of absolute insecurity for everyone else, but the West had no right to do that either: "stability depends on the relative satisfaction and therefore also the relative dissatisfaction of the various states."[41]† Second, the West in fact had never been more powerful

---

* "Détente" in French means "calm, relaxation, easing," but it can also mean the trigger of a gun. The closest Russian equivalent is "razriadka," which means a "lessening," or "reduction," or "relaxation," but also "discharging" or "unloading."

† "Could a power achieve all its wishes," Kissinger had written in 1957, "it would strive for absolute security, a world-order free from the consciousness of foreign danger and where all problems have the manageability of domestic issues. But since absolute security for one power means absolute insecurity for all others, it is never obtainable as a part of a 'legitimate' settlement, and can be achieved only through conquest.

"For this reason an international settlement which is accepted and not imposed will always appear *somewhat* unjust to any one of its components. Paradoxically, the generality of this dissatisfaction is a condition of stability, because were any one power *totally* satisfied, all others would have to be *totally* dissatisfied and a revolutionary situation would ensue. The foundation of a stable order is the *relative* security—and therefore the *relative* insecurity—of its members." (Henry A. Kissinger, *A World Restored* [New York: 1957], pp. 144–45.)

vis-à-vis the Soviet Union than in the early days of the Cold War. Postponing negotiations until some mythical position of "strength" had been reached had only allowed Moscow the opportunity to build actual strength—as it had now done. Finally, negotiations were not, in themselves, a sign of weakness. Properly managed, with a view to the identification of common interests as well as the frank recognition of irreconcilable antagonisms, they could become the primary means of building a stable world order, not simply a luxury to be enjoyed once stability had been achieved.[42]

These negotiations should be conducted, Kissinger insisted, without illusions. "We will deal with the Communist countries on the basis of a precise understanding of what they are about in the world, and then of what we can reasonably expect of them and ourselves." Ideological differences should not be obscured for the purpose of reaching superficial agreements, but neither should negotiations be dictated by the pressures for "success" that had so often, in the past, raised and then dashed Western expectations regarding "summitry." Careful and deliberate preparation was vital: "we will not become psychologically dependent on rapid or extravagant progress." Above all, negotiations, and the agreements they produced, would have to offer solid mutual benefits if they were to have lasting effects: "We must be mature enough to recognize that to be stable a relationship must provide advantages to both sides, and that the most constructive international relationships are those in which both parties perceive an element of gain. . . . The balance cannot be struck on each issue every day, but only over the whole range of relations and over a period of time."[43]

What prospect was there that the Soviet Union would be willing to negotiate on this basis? That country, Kissinger argued, had reached a crucial turning point in its own affairs: there were "ambiguous tendencies" that could lead Moscow into either cooperation or further confrontation with the West. These included: (1) rivalries within the international communist movement that intensified pressures to compete for the "mantle of militancy" in Asia, but at the same time relaxed inhibitions about dealing with the United States and forced the U.S.S.R. to reassess its own security concerns; (2) the achievement of Soviet strategic parity, which doubtless tempted Kremlin leaders to press on for superiority but at the same time freed them from their fear of inferiority and thus made possible, for the first time, serious negotiations on arms control; (3) the expansion of Soviet military and economic power into the "third world," which meant a growth of Moscow's influence but at the same time a new interest in controlling crises there; and (4) the emergence, inside the U.S.S.R., of a mature industrial economy, which could serve as the base for a major arms buildup but at the same time might make feasible a consumer-oriented society, integrated with and to an extent dependent on the industrialized West. American objectives in these circumstances were simple, Kissinger argued: to try to reinforce those "tendencies" inclined in the direction of accommodation, and to discourage those that were not.[44]

Kissinger's approach here resembled, as did so many other aspects of his strategy, what Kennan had been trying to do in the late 1940's. Kennan, it will be recalled, had compared Soviet power to a growing tree: it was possible to channel its energies in certain directions, but only by a combination of external pressures and inducements, steadily but selectively applied. Abrupt or extreme constraints would not work. The idea had been to convince the Russians that their own best interests lay in exhibiting restraint: "If . . . situations can be created in which it is clearly not to the advantage of their power to emphasize the elements of conflict in their relations with the outside world, then their actions, and even the tenor of their propaganda to their own people, can be modified."[45] Kissinger's technique of identifying "ambiguous tendencies" within the Soviet system, and then attempting to strengthen those that were positive and deter those that were not, was very much in the same tradition: it was, like Kennan's, an exercise in behavior modification, based on the application of appropriate punishments and rewards, designed, simultaneously, to prod and cajole a heretofore "revolutionary" state into accepting the "legitimacy" of the existing international order.*

Success in this endeavor did not, any more for Kissinger than for Kennan, require changing the internal nature of the Soviet regime. Encrustations of history and ideology were too deep: "we cannot demand," Kissinger argued, "that the Soviet Union, in effect, suddenly reverse five decades of Soviet, and centuries of Russian, history." Efforts should go,

---

* "'Legitimacy' as here used should not be confused with justice. It means no more than an international agreement about the nature of workable arrangements and about the permissible aims and methods of foreign policy. It implies the acceptance of the framework of the international order by all major powers, at least to the extent that no state is so dissatisfied that, like Germany after the Treaty of Versailles, it expresses its dissatisfaction in a revolutionary foreign policy. . . . [T]he distinguishing feature of a revolutionary power is not that it feels threatened—such a feeling is inherent in the nature of international relations based on sovereign states—*but that nothing can reassure it*. Only absolute security—the neutralization of the opponent—is considered a sufficient guarantee, and thus the desire of one power for absolute security means absolute insecurity for all the others." (Kissinger, *A World Restored*, pp. 1–2.)

rather, toward changing Moscow's approach to the outside world, toward convincing Soviet leaders that it was in their own interest to stress cooperation over confrontation in their dealings with the West. At the same time, though, the U.S.S.R. was not immune to internal pressures for change: "Changes in Soviet society have already occurred, and more will come." Such trends would be more likely to develop, Kissinger pointed out, in an atmosphere of détente: "A renewal of the Cold War will hardly encourage the Soviet Union to . . . adopt a more benevolent attitude toward dissent."[46] Internal change, then, should not be made a condition for negotiations, but it was itself a condition that might well evolve from them.

A second and related element in the strategy of détente was the concept of "linkage." Attempts to modify Soviet behavior would not succeed, Kissinger believed, if negotiations were allowed to proceed in separate compartments, with progress in one unaffected by difficulties in another. "I am convinced that the great issues are fundamentally inter-related," he wrote, in a letter prepared for Nixon's signature in February 1969:

> I recognize that the previous Administration took the view that when we perceive a mutual interest on an issue with the U.S.S.R., we should pursue agreement and attempt to insulate it as much as possible from the ups and downs of conflicts elsewhere. This may well be sound on numerous bilateral and practical matters such as cultural or scientific exchanges. But, on the crucial issues of our day, I believe we must seek to advance on a front at least broad enough to make clear that we see some relationship between political and military issues. I believe that the Soviet leaders should be brought to understand that they cannot expect to reap the benefits of cooperation in one area while seeking to take advantage of tension or confrontation elsewhere.

The Russians themselves saw "ambiguous tendencies" in American policy, Kissinger reminded Nixon. They were unsure whether "reasonable" or "adventurous" forces would prevail within the new administration, and were seeking to use the prospect of negotiations to encourage the former and discourage the latter. What the United States had to do was to "utilize this Soviet interest, stemming as I think it does from anxiety, to induce them to come to grips with the real sources of tension, notably in the Middle East, but also in Vietnam." The basic issue, as Kissinger later put it, was "whether we will use them or they will use us."[47]

The trick was to seize the initiative, and this Nixon and Kissinger quickly sought to do. They began with an estimate of Moscow's priorities: a strategic arms agreement that would freeze Western but not Soviet weapons systems at existing levels; a relaxation of trade barriers that would permit badly needed imports of Western food and technology, together with the credits to pay for them; the stability, even respectability, that would come from Western recognition, once and for all, of post-World War II boundaries in Eastern Europe; and opportunities to advance Soviet interests in the "third world" without risking war. Against these, they balanced American priorities: a negotiated settlement of the Vietnam War that would not result in humiliation; an acknowledgment by the Russians of permanent Western rights in Berlin; a strategic arms agreement that would limit the continuing Soviet military buildup; and some means of managing "third world" crises so that they would neither get out of hand nor further Moscow's designs. Nixon and Kissinger then made it clear that negotiations were interlocked: progress toward satisfying Soviet priorities could not come without equivalent progress, across the board, in satisfying those set by the United States.[48]

The Russians did not take easily to this procedure. Their preferred approach was compartmentalization: issues should be treated as discrete units, with cooperation on one taking place independently of such competition as might exist on others.[49] To get them to accept the concept of linkage, Nixon and Kissinger had to feign relative disinterest in reaching agreements: they sought constantly to convince Kremlin leaders that they needed negotiations more than the United States did. Nixon thus delayed, for several months, beginning strategic arms talks the Johnson administration had already agreed to in principle. There was, again in contrast to Johnson, no rush to the summit; instead Nixon and Kissinger insisted on detailed and deliberate preparation, with virtual guarantees of success assured in advance. Nor were they above holding the summit "hostage" to the satisfaction of other priorities. In December 1971, for example, Kissinger openly threatened to cancel it unless the Russians prevailed on their ally, India, not to invade West Pakistan. And in May 1972, two weeks before he was to meet with Brezhnev for the first time, Nixon in response to a North Vietnamese offensive ordered the mining of Haiphong harbor, despite the incorrect expectation of most of his advisers, Kissinger included, that such a move would kill the summit.[50]

Linkage could work in several ways. It could be used as a tool of crisis management, as in the India-Pakistan War, or during the hectic month of September 1970, when the administration headed off both a Soviet attempt to build a submarine base in Cuba and a Syrian invasion of Jordan by warning Moscow that such actions could torpedo détente. It could be used to create bargaining chips in direct talks with the Russians: there would be no strategic arms agreement or recognition of boundaries in Eastern Europe, Kissinger made it clear, without a permanent settlement of the Berlin issue. It could be used to induce third parties to negotiate: a major function of linkage was to secure Soviet cooperation in ending the Vietnam War by holding back on SALT and the relaxation of trade barriers until Moscow had put pressure on Hanoi to moderate its requirements for a cease-fire. It could even be used, more subtly, to make the U.S.S.R. economically dependent on the West: "Over time," Kissinger suggested, "trade and investment may leaven the autarkic tendencies of the Soviet system, invite gradual association of the Soviet economy with the world economy, and foster a degree of interdependence that adds an element of stability to the political equation."[51]

All of this tied in with Kissinger's "behavior modification" strategy: linkage provided the means by which both positive and negative reinforcement would take place. But linkage was, for Kissinger, more than just a negotiating instrument. It reflected as well the reality that, however diffuse and multidimensional power had become in the more relaxed international environment of the 1970's, its elements still affected one another. Interests and threats, however capable of differentiation or specification, still did not exist in discrete vacuums.

> Displays of American impotence in one part of the world . . . would inevitably erode our credibility in other parts of the world. . . . Our posture in arms control negotiations could not be separated from the resulting military balance, nor from our responsibilities as the major military power of a global system of alliances. By the same token, arms limitation could almost certainly not survive in a period of growing international tensions. We saw linkage, in short, as synonymous with an overall strategic and geopolitical view.

There was little recognition of this within the bureaucracy which, compartmentalized itself, tended to look at the world in compartmentalized terms. Linkage served, then, as a means of imposing conceptual order on American policy as well as a device for moving Soviet policy in desirable directions. It was, Kissinger recalled, "another of the attempts of the new Administration to free our foreign policy from oscillations between overextension and isolation and to ground it in a firm conception of the national interest."[52]

Yet another form of linkage—one important enough to merit consideration as a third distinctive element in the Nixon-Kissinger strategy—was the effort to establish relations between the United States and the Soviet Union's chief rival in the communist world, the People's Republic of

China, as a means of putting further pressure on Moscow. The idea was not new: Kennan had advocated exploiting fissures within the communist bloc as early as 1948, and Washington's policy toward Yugoslavia had had that objective ever since. But the principal conflict within the communist world, between the Soviet Union and China, had been going on openly for more than a decade without any significant American attempt to take advantage of it. The problem had been that relations with Beijing were, if anything, worse than those with Moscow: bitterness over China's role in the Korean War still rankled, as did Beijing's sympathy for, and aid to, North Vietnam. Considerations of domestic politics made any thought of withdrawing support from Nationalist China imprudent, if not unthinkable; furthermore, Communist China during the mid-1960's seemed determined to cut itself off from the rest of the world as a by-product of Mao Zedong's quixotic quest for an institutionalized revolution. Accordingly, little had been done to exploit the Sino-Soviet split at the time the Nixon administration took office.

During the late 1960's, both Nixon and Kissinger had reached the conclusion that it would not be wise to continue to try to isolate mainland China. "Taking the long view," Nixon had written in 1967, "we simply cannot afford to leave China forever outside the family of nations, there to nurture its fantasies, cherish its hates and threaten its neighbors." But before the United States could change its attitude toward China, that country would have to change its attitude toward the world: China could be pulled back into the international community only "as a great and progressing nation, not as the epicenter of world revolution." Kissinger, writing a year earlier, had argued that such a change might in fact be possible: despite China's ostentatious ideological militancy, its leaders had not yet become dependent upon their own bureaucracies, and hence might have greater flexibility in changing their policies than their counterparts in the Soviet Union.[53] In a speech written for Nelson Rockefeller during the 1968 campaign, Kissinger had advocated learning "to deal imaginatively with several competing centers of Communist power. . . . In a subtle triangle of relations between Washington, Peking, and Moscow, we improve the possibilities of accommodations with each as we increase our options with both." Still, the Nixon administration did not have, upon taking power, any specific plan for reconciliation with China, or any indication that such an initiative, if offered, would be reciprocated.[54]*

* Nixon did authorize Kissinger, on February 1, 1969, to "plant" the idea with East European sources that the United States was "exploring" a rapprochement with China. "The maneuver,"

What focused attention on the problem was the outbreak of fighting between Soviet and Chinese forces along the Ussuri River in March 1969, followed by discreet inquiries from Moscow as to what the American response would be if the Kremlin should authorize a pre-emptive attack against Chinese nuclear facilities.[55] Only five years before, on the eve of China's first nuclear test, the Johnson administration had considered the possibility of joint Soviet-American military action against that country,[56] but now the Nixon administration took a wholly different tack. Acting in line with Kissinger's theory that it was better in a triangular relationship to side with the weaker instead of the stronger antagonist, Nixon told an incredulous cabinet on August 14 that the United States could not allow China to be defeated in a Sino-Soviet war. "The worst thing that could happen for us would be for the Soviet Union to gobble up Red China," he explained several days later. "We can't let it happen. . . . We're not doing this because we love the Chinese. We just have to see to it that the U.S. plays both sides."[57]

This was a remarkable position to take, well before diplomatic contacts of consequence had begun with the Chinese, well before Washington knew how Beijing would react. It reflected the assumption, consistent with the Nixon administration's revised assessment of interests and threats, that American security required maintenance of a global balance of power, that China was a crucial element in that balance, and that therefore the United States had a stake in China's survival, regardless of what kind of regime was in charge there. The point was as much to make Moscow *think* that a Sino-American rapprochement was under way as to achieve one: as Kissinger wrote Nixon after a conversation with a worried Soviet Ambassador Anatoly Dobrynin, "there is no advantage in giving the Soviets excessive reassurance."[58]

In fact, though, the Chinese—themselves adept at triangular politics—did respond, and two-and-a-half years later, Nixon found himself reciting Mao Zedong's poetry in the Great Hall of the People in Beijing. Kissinger repeatedly insisted that the new Sino-American relationship was in no way directed against Moscow: this, he later acknowledged, was "the conventional pacifier of diplomacy by which the target of a maneuver is given a formal reassurance intended to unnerve as much as to calm, and which would defeat its purpose if it were actually believed." At the same time,

Kissinger recalls, "was intended to disquiet the Soviets, and almost certainly—given Nixon's preoccupations—to provide an incentive for them to help us end the war in Vietnam." (*White House Years*, p. 169.)

though, he stressed with equal fervor the need to avoid giving the Chinese a veto over American relations with the Soviet Union: "we were not willing to foreclose the option of a genuine easing of tensions with Moscow if that in time could be achieved." The idea was to walk a fine line: to refrain from tempting either side into retaliation or blackmail by giving it the impression that the United States was "using" it against the other. "The hostility between China and the Soviet Union served our purposes best if we maintained closer relations with each side than they did with each other. The rest could be left to the dynamic of events."[59]

It is difficult to think of anything the Nixon administration could have done that would have produced a more dramatic shift in world power relationships of greater benefit to the United States at less cost. For the first time since the Korean War, it was Russians, and not Americans, who faced rivals more determined to contain them than to contain each other. As a consequence, Nixon and Kissinger had been able, even before formally consummating the new Sino-American relationship, to abandon the old "two-and-a-half war" standard used since the Kennedy administration to calculate conventional force requirements.* "I believe that a simultaneous Warsaw Pact attack in Europe and a Chinese conventional attack in Asia is unlikely," Kissinger had written to Nixon as early as October 1969. "In any event, I do not believe such a simultaneous attack could or should be met with ground forces." Accordingly, he recommended, and Nixon accepted, reliance henceforth on a "one-and-a-half war" standard—conventional forces capable of meeting major aggression in Europe or Asia, but not in both at the same time.[60] Triangular politics had made possible progress toward John Foster Dulles's old goal of maximum deterrence at minimum cost—not by threatening escalation, though, but through the simple approach, made feasible by the triumph of geopolitics over ideology, of reducing the number of adversaries to be deterred.

This reduction in adversaries, in turn, made possible a fourth key element in the Nixon-Kissinger strategy: a phasing down of American commitments in the world, formally expressed in what came to be known as the Nixon Doctrine.† Delivered first to an informal press briefing on

---

* Public announcement of the "one-and-a-half war" standard apparently played a major role, in turn, in convincing Beijing that the Nixon administration was serious about wanting an improvement in relations with China. (See Kissinger, *White House Years*, pp. 221–22.)

† The press initially labeled Nixon's pronouncement the "Guam doctrine," much to the discomfort of its author, who, as Kissinger later wrote, thought that the phrase should commemorate "the person rather than the place." (Kissinger, *White House Years*, p. 224.)

Guam in July 1969, and as later refined by the White House, it consisted of three propositions:

> First, the United States will keep all of its treaty commitments.
>
> Second, we shall provide a shield if a nuclear power threatens the freedom of a nation allied with us or a nation whose survival we consider vital to our security.
>
> Third, in cases involving other types of aggression, we shall furnish military and economic assistance when requested in accordance with our treaty commitments. But we shall look to the nation directly threatened to assume the primary responsibility of providing the manpower for its defense.

Kissinger later further generalized the doctrine into an assertion "that the United States will participate in the defense and development of allies and friends, but that America cannot—and will not—conceive *all* the plans, design *all* the programs, execute *all* the decisions and undertake *all* the defense of the free nations of the world." The United States would give first priority to its own interests: "Our interests must shape our commitments, rather than the other way around."[61]

Since it provided for honoring existing obligations, the Nixon Doctrine changed little immediately with respect to Asia, the part of the world to which the President had originally applied it. But as an indication of shifts in long-term global strategy, it was significant. It constituted the first official acknowledgment of what Johnson had tacitly recognized early in 1968 when he turned down Westmoreland's request for an additional 206,000 troops to be sent to Vietnam—that the United States could not afford indefinitely to proliferate foreign commitments, and then undertake to honor them on a timetable and in a manner set by its adversaries.[62] Resources—economic and human—were not inexhaustible: like Eisenhower and Dulles after the Korean War, Nixon and Kissinger were now, in the wake of Vietnam, proclaiming their own "New Look" in the form of a determination to regain the initiative by shifting the arena of competition onto terrain more favorable to the United States.

The most obvious manifestation of the Nixon Doctrine was, of course, the gradual withdrawal of American troops from South Vietnam. With a steadiness that surprised (but did not gratify) its critics, the administration, from mid-1969 until the signing of the Paris peace agreements in January 1973, removed U.S. troops at a rate roughly comparable to that with which they had been introduced between 1965 and 1968. This withdrawal proceeded, for the most part, unaffected by the pressures of anti-war demonstrations at home, North Vietnamese offensives, progress in "Vietnamization," or prospects for peace. It was very much influenced, though, by calculations as to how much longer Congress would tolerate an American military presence in South Vietnam without acting on its own to terminate it.[63]

Paradoxically, this process of gradual withdrawal actually expanded Nixon's flexibility with regard to Vietnam, at least in a tactical sense. Proclamations implying an *intention* to disengage from the war could buy time against immediate pressures to do just that. They could also spur Saigon into assuming greater responsibility for its own defense, something it was unlikely to do as long as Americans remained to run things. Most important, though, the withdrawal of troops made it possible for the administration to fight the war on more favorable terms than before. Johnson and his advisers had often considered invading Cambodia, striking at the Ho Chi Minh trail in Laos, mining Haiphong harbor, and bombing Hanoi, but they had always held back for fear of provoking Chinese intervention.[64] Now, with China on the verge of a new and friendlier relationship with the United States, Zhou Enlai discreetly let it be known that such tactical escalations in support of a strategic withdrawal could proceed with impunity.[65] Nixon was thus able to do more in Vietnam with 50,000 troops than Johnson had felt able to do with 500,000: it was a revealing commentary on the not always obvious relationship between levels of force and freedom of action.

But how could the United States reduce its commitments in the world without at the same time conveying the appearance of weakness, and thus risking humiliation that Nixon and Kissinger, like their immediate predecessors, so strongly feared? Their answer—and this was the fifth major element of their strategy—can be found in this technique of covering strategic withdrawals with tactical escalations: the idea was to show that the United States could act if it chose to, and thereby to create questions in the minds of adversaries as to whether it would or not. Uncertainty itself became a deterrent, much as it had been in Dulles's "retaliation" strategy a decade and a half earlier. The administration deliberately set out to show itself capable of taking unpredictable, unpopular, even apparently irrational actions in order to keep its power credible.

Nixon hardly needed to be reminded of the virtues of cultivating unpredictability. He had noted with approval, as early as 1953, advice to this effect from South Korean President Syngman Rhee (who managed to be unpredictable in dealing with everybody): "The more I traveled and the more I learned in the years that followed, the more I appreciated how wise the old man had been." He had long admired, and after 1969 sought to emulate, Charles De Gaulle's insight that the leader, to conserve his power, must project an aura of mystery, even myth, to those around him. Nixon prided himself extravagantly on having had the will to act in Vietnam in ways that Johnson had not: "What distinguishes me from Johnson," he wrote Kissinger, "is that I have the *will* in spades." And in March 1973, he gleefully recorded in his diary the comment of a recently released prisoner-of-war about the bombing of Hanoi three months earlier: "the North Vietnamese really thought that the President was off his rocker. . . . [I]t was absolutely essential for them to think that."[66]

Kissinger, too, saw advantages in projecting uncertainty, but from a more theoretical point of view. His famous 1957 book, *Nuclear Weapons and Foreign Policy*, had argued eloquently for a strategy based on ambiguous threats; a decade later, he had noted that for the purposes of deterrence, "a bluff taken seriously is more useful than a serious threat taken as a bluff." He had suggested to Nixon early in 1969 that uncertainty as to American intentions might make the Russians more willing to negotiate. Some years later he observed that, in dealing with Moscow, "[s]ilence was the best middle ground between reassurance, which would be self-defeating, and intransigence, which might turn out to be provocative." He retrospectively defended the decision to send a carrier task force into the Bay of Bengal during the 1971 India-Pakistan War as having conveyed the risk of irrational action: it "committed us to no final act, but it created precisely the margin of uncertainty needed to force a decision [not to invade West Pakistan] by New Delhi and Moscow." And, again, with reference to North Vietnam: "Confrontations end when the opponent decides that the risks are not worth the objective, and for this the risks must be kept high and incalculable."[67]

It was in Vietnam, of course, that the administration most often used unpredictability to enhance credibility. Both Nixon and Kissinger were convinced that Johnson had overcommitted the United States in Vietnam, but once there, they thought, it could not afford to appear to have been pushed out. "We think . . . that it is important for the health of the society and the stability of the international system that we get out with some dignity," Kissinger told a group of university presidents in 1972. His concern, he later noted in his memoirs, was to "end the war in a manner that gave some meaning to the sacrifices that had been made: as an exercise of our own will rather than through the exhaustion of endless discord."[68] To this end, the administration refused to accept North Vietnam's demand that it arrange for the deposition of South Vietnamese President Nguyen Van Thieu prior to the conclusion of a final settlement. But the means available to apply pressure on Hanoi were steadily diminishing, what with troop withdrawals proceeding at a pace just ahead of Congress's growing determination to end the war on its own terms. Consequently, Nixon and Kissinger resorted to the mining of Haiphong and, later, the B-52 bombing of Hanoi, as ways to create enough uncertainty about American intentions in the minds of North Vietnamese leaders to make them accept Washington's position.

As had been the case in the Johnson and Kennedy administrations, though, the audience for this demonstration of resolve was seen as including more than just North Vietnam. If the United States allowed itself to be humiliated in Southeast Asia, Nixon and Kissinger believed, then not only the credibility of its commitments elsewhere but its own self-confidence would suffer irreparable harm. Prestige was a tangible but volatile commodity: "we had to remember," Kissinger later insisted, "that scores of countries and millions of people relied for their security on our willingness to stand by allies, indeed on our confidence in ourselves. . . . [M]y appointment to high office entailed a responsibility to help end the war in a way compatible with American self-respect and the stake that all men and women of goodwill had in America's strength and purpose."[69] Unpredictability, then, was the instrument by which "dignity" and "honor" would be salvaged from the debacle of overcommitment that was the war in Vietnam.

Obviously a complex, subtle, and closely interwoven strategy like that of Nixon and Kissinger required, for its implementation, precise coordination and control. "Fine tuning" was of no less importance than it had been in the Kennedy and Johnson administrations, but unlike their predecessors, Nixon and Kissinger doubted the possibility of achieving it through established mechanisms of government. Instead they resolved—and this was the last distinctive element of their approach to détente—to isolate the bureaucracy from the policy-making process almost entirely, centralizing decisions to an unprecedented degree in their own hands.

Wariness regarding bureaucracies was nothing new for either man. Nixon came into office with all the suspicions of a chronic outsider: the State Department, he was convinced, was untrustworthy, the CIA was infested with "Ivy League liberals," the government as a whole was filled with East Coast establishment Democrats who would, as he told his new cabinet, "either sabotage us from within, or they'll just bring back their old bosses." Kissinger's attitude was less visceral, but no less skeptical. He had for years laced his writings with sallies against bureaucracies: "The motivation of a bureaucracy is its quest for safety," he had written in 1957; "it measures success by errors avoided rather than by goals achieved; it prides itself on objectivity which is a denial of the necessity of great conception." Or, again in 1966:

> bureaucracy absorbs the energies of top executives in reconciling what is expected with what happens; the analysis of where one is overwhelms the consideration of where one should be going. Serving the machine becomes a more absorbing occupation than defining its purpose. . . . Attention tends to be diverted from the act of choice—which is the ultimate test of statesmanship—to the accumulation of facts. . . . Certainty is purchased at the cost of creativity.

"It seemed to me no accident," Kissinger noted in his memoirs, "that most great statesmen had been locked in permanent struggle with the experts in their foreign offices, for the scope of the statesman's conception challenges the inclination of the expert toward minimum risk."[70]

The Nixon-Kissinger experience was no exception. "Linkage" was central to the new administration's strategy, but achieving it required the ability to evaluate separate issues in relation to each other, a sense of timing and priority, and the discipline to enforce decisions with firmness. The bureaucracy possessed none of these qualities. Organized methodically into regional and functional units, it had an irresistible tendency to compartmentalize, to view problems as discrete entities without reference either to the context in which they appeared or to their implications for overall policy. Hence, the State Department sought to propel the administration into talks with the Russians on arms control, trade, and the Middle East before Nixon and Kissinger had had a chance to apply the pressures they thought necessary to ensure the success of those negotiations. The department's Soviet specialists initially opposed the "opening" to China for fear it would worsen relations with Moscow when the whole idea had been to use it to give the Russians a motive for moving in the opposite direction. Later, the department tried to delay implementing the "China card" because of the sheer difficulty of explaining it to allies, neutrals, the Russians, and the press. The Pentagon pushed inexorably for Vietnam troop withdrawals in an effort to reduce costs in the face of declining Congressional appropriations, but with little sense of how declining American power in the field would affect the course of peace negotiations. And, as always, there was the risk of leaks: the more agencies and individuals who knew of a decision, the greater the danger of finding it on the front page of the *New York Times* or the *Washington Post* the following morning.[71]

Reinforcing these tendencies was the distinctive personality and, hence, operating style, of Richard M. Nixon. There was, in him, a curious dependence upon personal isolation from all but a tiny circle of advisers, partly to allow time for reflection and self-control, partly to avoid unpleasant confrontations with subordinates (which Nixon seemed to fear more than any president since Franklin Roosevelt), partly as a safeguard against his own impulsive outbursts which, if taken literally, could have produced embarrassing results.* It was not Nixon's staff who isolated him, Kissinger later recalled: "Nixon insisted on isolating himself." The effect was to tempt him "into an endless guerrilla war to circumvent his own subordinates whom he never considered as his own."[72]

The instrument chosen to satisfy both Nixon's and Kissinger's determination to segregate policy-making from the bureaucracy was the famous (or infamous) "backchannel" system: parallel sets of negotiations on the same issue, one conducted more or less in the public eye by subordinates and their foreign counterparts, the second proceeding independently and on a top-secret basis between Kissinger himself, or his immediate aides, and those close to the top on the other side. The Vietnam peace negotiations, the SALT talks, diplomacy regarding Berlin, the Middle East, and, of course, China all proceeded in this manner, with those engaged in public discussions more often than not unaware of the private negotiations going on behind their backs. The system could, at times, produce odd effects: the President and Soviet Foreign Minister Andrei Gromyko conspiring over how to keep sensitive information from Nixon's first (and now little-remembered) Secretary of State, William P. Rogers; reliance on personal couriers, even handwritten documents, to avoid the risks of transmitting information through conventional channels; the discovery, at one point, of a "spy" on Kissinger's staff, recruited by no less august a body than the Joint Chiefs of Staff. It was not, Kissinger admitted, a system that could stand institutionalization. But, given the stakes involved, the personalities, and the problems, reliance on "backchannels" seemed appropriate at the time. Nixon's "administrative approach was weird and its human cost unattractive, yet history must also record the fundamental fact that major successes were achieved that had proved unattainable by conventional procedures."[73]

* Such as his proposal in 1971 to send Thomas E. Dewey on a secret mission to Beijing after that statesman had been dead for several months. (Kissinger, *White House Years*, p. 715.)

The Nixon-Kissinger strategy was, in several ways, a return to the concept of asymmetrical response. Vietnam had demonstrated both the costs and the futility of trying to counter aggression on terrain selected by adversaries; it is significant that, in attempting to end the war, the Nixon administration widened it in ways difficult for Hanoi to match. But the Nixon-Kissinger commitment to asymmetry went well beyond Vietnam. The Nixon Doctrine reflected a determination to apply strengths against weaknesses while leaving to allies forms of military activity uncongenial to the United States. Linkage was asymmetry extended to the diplomatic field: it was based on the assumption that inducements and constraints applied in one area could affect developments in wholly different ones. The administration's emphasis on negotiations as a means of reconstituting a power balance threatened by Soviet military might was also a form of asymmetry: no corresponding American military buildup took place.

There was, then, a continuity in concept, if not in tactics or circumstances, between the strategies of the Nixon administration, those of Truman prior to 1950, and Eisenhower's throughout his term. All of them shared a perception of limited means, and of the need, as a consequence, to shift the location and character of the nation's response away from the other side's provocations, lest that side gain the initiative and thereby deplete limited American resources. It was only when means were perceived as expandable—as in the Truman administration after NSC-68, or in the Kennedy and Johnson administrations—that symmetrical response became feasible: in both cases, though, the practical costs of implementing what had seemed to be a theoretically defensible strategy in the end undermined that strategy, with results that led, in time, to asymmetry again.

IV

Symmetrical or asymmetrical, strategies if they are to succeed must be capable of winning public and Congressional support. Nixon and Kissinger went about this task in a strangely ambivalent way. On the one hand, they set forth the broad outlines of their strategy with a candor and clarity unmatched by any other postwar administration. They coupled this, though, with an equally unprecedented reliance on secrecy—at times even outright deception—at the tactical level. The assumption seems to have been that while the public and its representatives had a right to know in what general direction the nation was heading, judgments as to appropriate measures for getting there were best left to those at the top, with minimal interference from below.[74] It was an approach better calculated to facilitate innovation than to elicit enthusiasm on the part of those necessarily left in the dark as to how such accomplishments had been brought about.

Kissinger had proposed, during the early days of the administration, issuing in the President's name an annual report on foreign policy, roughly comparable to the Defense Department "posture statements" that McNamara had originated during the early 1960's. The report was to serve, Kissinger recalled, "as a conceptual outline of the President's foreign policy, as a status report, and as an agenda for action. It could simultaneously guide our bureaucracy and inform foreign governments about our thinking."[75] Drafted largely by Kissinger and his staff, the four reports issued between 1970 and 1973—each around 200 pages in length—constituted a serious and frank effort to explain the basic geopolitical assumptions behind the administration's approach to the world. The first report set the tone by stating candidly that "our objective, in the first instance, is to support our *interests* over the long run with a sound foreign policy." There followed a detailed discussion, often at a philosophical level, that set forward with surprising explicitness most of the fundamental elements of the Nixon strategy—the use of negotiations to integrate the Soviet Union into the existing international order, the idea of "linkage," the possibility of a new relationship with China, the Nixon Doctrine—often before events had taken place that made possible their implementation.[76]

Kissinger later admitted that the annual foreign policy reports had probably failed in getting across to the public the conceptual basis of the administration's strategy. The problem was the media, which "would cover only the section on Vietnam, probing for hot news or credibility gaps, ignoring the remainder as not newsworthy."[77] After becoming Secretary of State in September 1973, he dropped the reports, relying instead on a series of carefully crafted and, on the whole, no less candid public speeches to convey a sense of his strategy—with not much better results, as far as press coverage was concerned.[78] Still, Kissinger must be credited with having made a more sustained and more serious effort than any of his predecessors to explain openly the general outlines of what the administration of which he was a part was trying to do.

This candor emphatically did not extend, though, to the level of tactics. The administration secretly bombed North Vietnamese sanctuaries in Cambodia from March 1969, despite public assurances that it would respect that country's neutrality. Similar deception occurred with regard to the Allende regime in Chile: "the government's legitimacy is not in question," Kissinger wrote in the second annual foreign policy report; "we will not be the ones to upset traditional relations."[79] Again, during the India-Pakistan War, the administration followed a secret pro-Pakistani policy at a time when public opinion was almost unanimously condemning that government's atrocities in what was to become Bangladesh; in this case, Nixon and Kissinger suffered the indignity of having their cover "blown" when columnist Jack Anderson published leaked versions of their internal deliberations.[80] Negotiations by the "backchannel" system were yet another example of administration secrecy at the tactical level. On such issues as Berlin, Vietnam, and China, potential adversaries often knew more about what was going on than did American allies, or the American public.

Kissinger and Nixon justified this resort to secrecy on the grounds of necessity: their considerable achievements, they argued, could never have been carried out if subjected throughout to the full glare of publicity. One reason was inherent in the very nature of diplomacy itself: "Any successful negotiation must be based on a balance of mutual concessions," Kissinger noted. "The sequence in which concessions are made becomes crucial; it can be aborted if each move has to be defended individually rather than as a part of a mosaic before the reciprocal move is clear." Speed could also be important at critical moments: to allow the process of bureaucratic clearances to determine the pace of negotiations could be to wreck them. Another problem involved allies: even the best intentioned of them could torpedo delicate discussions by demanding to be consulted—and reassured—ahead of time. "Secrecy unquestionably exacts a high price in the form of a less free and creative interchange of ideas within the government," Nixon later admitted. "But I can say unequivocally that without secrecy there would have been no opening to China, no SALT agreement with the Soviet Union, and no peace agreement ending the Vietnam war." Kissinger put it more bluntly: "To maintain our control over the presentation of the event was synonymous with maintaining control over our policy and its consequences."[81]

But what of the constitutionally sanctioned right of Congress to monitor foreign policy? Nixon's belief in the unlimited foreign policy powers of the president became clear during the Watergate crisis. Kissinger, retrospectively, took a more subtle view. "That the Congress should play a major role in the conduct of foreign policy was beyond argument," he wrote. But "our system cannot function . . . when the Congress attempts to prescribe day-to-day tactical decisions."

> The Congress can and ought to scrutinize the consequences of diplomacy. It cannot carry it out. . . . The prime function of Congress is to pass laws with a claim to permanence: It deals in the predictable. Diplomacy requires constant adjustment to changing circumstance; it must leave a margin for the unexpected; the unpredictable is what always happens in foreign affairs. Nuance, flexibility, and sometimes ambiguity are the tools of diplomacy. In law, they are vices; certainty and clarity are the requirements there. . . . Legislation often emerges from the compromise of conflicting interests; random coalitions form and fade. . . . Foreign policy requires a consistent view of the national interest. The legislator practices the art of reconciling pressure groups on a single issue; the foreign-policymaker deals with the same international actors over and over again, rarely concluding an issue or terminating a relationship.[82]*

Finding the proper balance between administrative flexibility and Congressional responsibility was no easy task, though; more than anything else this problem would bedevil, during the last four years of Kissinger's incumbency as chief diplomat, implementation of the strategy he and Nixon had originated.

V

Whether one looks at definitions of interest, perceptions of threat, formulations of responses, or their justification, there were striking similarities in the approaches to containment advocated by George Kennan in the late 1940's and by Henry Kissinger in the early 1970's. Both adhered to a multidimensional conception of power in the world. Both insisted that means were limited, and that distinctions had to be made, accordingly, between vital and peripheral interests. Both saw the Soviet Union, and not international communism, as the major threat to those interests. Both sought to contain that threat by responding asymmetrically: by relying on diversity to maintain the balance of power, by exploiting fissures within the international communist movement, by combining pressures and inducements to try to bring about long-term changes in the Soviet concept of international relations. Both believed in leaving the conduct of foreign policy in the hands of a professional elite, with only the broad outlines of policy cleared

* For a similar argument by Kennan, see his *Memoirs: 1925–1950*, pp. 323–24.

in advance with Congress and the public. There were, to be sure, also differences. Kennan's authority in the Truman administration never approximated Kissinger's under Nixon. Kissinger centralized both the policy-making and policy-implementing processes more than Kennan would have done. Certainly Kennan lacked Kissinger's remarkable instinct for bureaucratic survival. But these differences were primarily personal, procedural, and circumstantial: on the substance of policy, on the underlying assumptions that informed the American approach to the world, the congruence in viewpoint was impressive.

There is no evidence that Kissinger consciously drew on Kennan's ideas in planning policy during the Nixon administration, although the two men did know each other and doubtless followed each other's writings. Rather, their congruent approaches seem to have grown out of a shared commitment to the "realist" tradition in American foreign policy,[83] an intellectual orientation solidly grounded in the study of European diplomatic history, a degree of detachment from the academic and policy-making elites of the 1950's and 1960's, and, above all, a sense of strategy—an insistence on the importance of establishing coherent relationships between ends and means. It was on this last point, more than anything else, that the Kennan-Kissinger connection primarily rested: both men understood the existence of a strategic "logic" transcending time and circumstance; a way of thinking that can make ideas formulated in one context relevant to very different ones; that can make it possible for thoughtful individuals, separated in their periods of public responsibility by a quarter of a century, to apply with some success similar strategies to vastly dissimilar situations.

Implementing Détente

The extent to which Kissinger's strategy succeeded had become the subject of sharp debate, though, by the time the Ford administration left office. Critics in the intellectual-academic community, never quite prepared to forgive Kissinger's association with the distasteful Nixon, charged him with conceptual inconsistency, a proclivity for show over substance, and a tendency to view the world from a "Sovietocentric" perspective.[1] Leading Democrats, eager to find an issue with which to regain the White House, accused Kissinger of having allowed American military strength to decline, on the one hand, and of insensitivity to human rights on the other.[2] Rightwing Republicans echoed the same complaints, and even managed to incorporate them into their 1976 platform, over the objections of their narrowly selected nominee, Gerald Ford.[3] Détente was very much on the defensive, therefore, when Kissinger relinquished the direction of American foreign policy early in 1977. As had so often been the case in the past, criticisms developed during the campaign would become, in large part, the basis upon which the new administration of Jimmy Carter would define its approach to the world in the years that followed.

These charges boiled down to four major points, although not all critics gave equal weight to each of them: (1) that linkage had not produced the results the administration had promised; (2) that the global military balance had been allowed to shift in favor of the Soviet Union; (3) that excessive concentration on relations with the U.S.S.R. and China had led to the neglect or distortion of other pressing issues; and (4) that no attempt had been made to maintain the foundation of moral principle upon which

United States foreign policy had to rest if it was to command support at home and abroad. Each of these criticisms needs to be examined in turn to assess its validity, but in doing so certain guidelines should be kept in mind. One must distinguish between situations Nixon and Kissinger inherited, and those they created. One must differentiate between events within and beyond their capacity to control. One must consider alternatives to courses of action actually followed. One must in particular avoid *ex post facto* judgments: the fairer procedure is to evaluate the strategy according to the goals its architects set for it, not by some external frame of reference they themselves did not impose. Finally, one must pay due regard to the complexities of personality: to the fact that morality and amorality, idealism and cynicism, candor and deception, even, in Nixon's case, geopolitical wisdom and criminal corruption, can coexist in the same person, and even form interrelated elements of the same strategy.

I

Any retrospective assessment of the Nixon-Kissinger approach to containment must begin with its centerpiece: the assumption that the Soviet Union could be brought, over time, to accept the constraints of a stable world order through that sophisticated combination of pressures and inducements known as linkage. As one slightly patronizing critic later described the strategy: "The bear would be treated like one of B.F. Skinner's pigeons: There would be incentives for good behavior, rewards if such behavior occurred, and punishments if not."[4] There is no doubt that both Nixon and Kissinger originally conceived of détente in much this way: the idea, Nixon wrote, had been "to involve Soviet interests in ways that would increase their stake in international stability and the status quo. There was no thought that such commercial, technical, and scientific relationships could by themselves prevent confrontations or wars, but at least they would have to be counted in a balance sheet of gains and losses whenever the Soviets were tempted to indulge in international adventurism." "We seek," Kissinger told the Senate Foreign Relations Committee in 1974, "regardless of Soviet intentions, to serve peace through a systematic resistance to pressure and conciliatory responses to moderate behavior."[5]

But by the time Ford and Kissinger left office three years later, there was reason to question how much Soviet behavior had actually changed.

The Russians had, by then: (1) tolerated without warning Washington an Egyptian surprise attack on Israel in 1973; (2) furnished aid and encouragement to communists in Portugal following that country's revolution in 1974; (3) done nothing to keep North Vietnam from overrunning South Vietnam in 1975; (4) used Cuban troops to install a Marxist government in Angola that same year; and (5) tightened controls on Jews and dissidents at home. Within the next three years, they would, in addition: (1) virtually wipe out, by arrest or forced exile, the remaining Soviet dissident community; (2) actively support Marxist regimes first in Somalia, then in Ethiopia; (3) exploit Marxist coups in South Yemen and Afghanistan; and (4) when their clients in that latter country seemed to be losing control late in 1979, simply invade it. Throughout all of this, Moscow was steadily building up its military forces, while simultaneously (and piously) calling for mutual adherence to the principles of "peaceful coexistence." It was hardly, on the face of things, the pattern of restraint one would have expected had the Nixon-Kissinger strategy of behavior modification worked as planned.

In fairness to the designers of that strategy, it should be pointed out that they did not expect it to eliminate all aspects of Soviet-American competition overnight. As Kissinger cautiously put it in 1974: "Détente encourages an environment in which competitors can regulate and restrain their differences and *ultimately* move from competition to cooperation."[6] Still, though, it is clear that Nixon and Kissinger, through their strategy of behavior modification, did hope to accomplish at least two things: to secure the Soviet Union's aid in "managing" crises in the "third world"; and to enmesh the U.S.S.R. in a network of economic relationships that would make it difficult, if not impossible, for the Russians to take actions in the future detrimental to Western interests. In both of these areas, the administration failed to achieve its goals. The reasons why say much about the limitations of linkage.

The first problem with linkage was its assumption that the Soviet Union could, or would, help the United States maintain stability in the "third world." Like many comparable ideas in the history of American foreign policy, this one was based on narrow experience and wishful thinking. The experience was a series of events between 1970 and 1972 that seemed to show how linkage could be used to induce Soviet restraint: Moscow's agreement, in September 1970, not to build a submarine base in Cuba after Washington had objected; Syria's withdrawal from Jordan that same month after Kissinger had put pressure on the Russians; India's decision not to invade West Pakistan in December 1971, after he had threatened to break off plans for the Moscow summit the following year; and, most convincingly, the fact that the major breakthrough in the protracted Vietnam peace negotiations had come after Nixon had made it clear to Brezhnev, at the summit, that future progress toward détente would be contingent on just such a development.[7] The wishful thinking was that these had not been isolated events; that, rather, they indicated a willingness on Moscow's part to sacrifice opportunities for gains at the expense of the United States in the "third world" in favor of the benefits to be derived from economic contacts, arms control, and the overall relaxation of tensions that would come with détente.

In fact, though, there was no way to prove that this application of forceful but asymmetrical pressures had worked: as with Eisenhower's deterrence strategy two decades earlier, it was difficult to establish the relationship between cause and effect. It may be that the Soviet Union had never intended in the first place to challenge the 1962 Kennedy-Khrushchev "understanding" prohibiting the introduction of strategic weapons into Cuba. It is not at all clear now that Moscow controlled Syrian or Indian behavior. Certainly Kissinger in time came to believe that the Russians had been telling the truth when they claimed that their influence in Hanoi was limited.[8] It is curious that an administration so impressed by evidence of fragmentation within the international communist movement should have relied, to the extent that it did, on Moscow's ability to dictate the behavior of clients elsewhere in the world. The whole theory of Soviet-American cooperation to "manage" "third world" crises depended upon the continued primacy of the superpowers when in fact their authority—on both sides—was rapidly waning.

The question also arises: why *should* Kremlin leaders have cooperated to "manage" such crises, even if they could have? They made no secret of their view that détente did not mean an end to Soviet-American competition in the "third world," only an agreement that such rivalries would not be allowed to escalate to dangerous levels. As Brezhnev put it in 1972:

> The CPSU [Communist Party of the Soviet Union] has always held, and now holds, that the class struggle between the two systems—the capitalist and the socialist—in the economic and political, and also, of course, the ideological domains, will continue. That is to be expected since the world outlook and the class aims of socialism and capitalism are opposite and irreconcilable. But we shall strive to shift this historically inevitable struggle onto a path free from the perils of war, of dangerous conflicts, and an uncontrolled arms race.[9]

Moreover, and apart from any ideological motivation, the U.S.S.R. could hardly be expected to work too hard to extricate the United States from situations its own short-sightedness had gotten it into. "[T]he only gainer in having the [Vietnam] war continue is the Soviet Union," Nixon admitted to Zhou Enlai in 1972. "They want us tied down."[10] Still, the administration persisted in seeking Moscow's help to prevent not only escalation but also exhaustion and embarrassment. Brezhnev, as Nixon had shrewdly guessed, was not prepared to go that far.

There remained the option of either ignoring "third world" crises detrimental to American interests, or of escalating them to the point that would give the Russians sufficient incentive to exercise restraint. The administration preferred the latter alternative,* as its actions in Cuba, Jordan, and the India-Pakistan War showed—even more obvious examples were the mining of Haiphong harbor just prior to the 1972 Moscow summit, and Kissinger's authorization of a global military alert to deter Brezhnev from acting unilaterally to enforce a cease-fire during the 1973 Arab-Israeli War.[11] Successful though they may have been in the short run, such tactics posed the same dilemma that had bedeviled Eisenhower's application of asymmetrical response two decades earlier: one resorted to escalation to prevent escalation, and so ran the risk, if the other side did not back down, of bringing about precisely what one had sought to avoid.

A second problem with linkage as an instrument of behavior modification was that it assumed tight control over the array of pressures and inducements to be applied. Despite the unprecedented centralization Nixon and Kissinger managed to impose on the Executive Branch, such control did not come easily. Bureaucracies still generated their own momentum, in directions not always consistent with White House policy. Even more serious difficulties arose in Congress, where legislators insisted on setting their own price for economic concessions beyond the point Nixon and Kissinger thought appropriate for linkage, while at the same time narrowing the President's authority to use military means to compel adversaries to show restraint. By 1974, the Watergate crisis—the product, ironically enough, of single-minded determination to preserve presidential power[12]—had still

---

* "During the period of crisis the elements from which policy is shaped suddenly become fluid. In the resulting upheaval the statesman must act under constant pressure. Paradoxically, this confers an unusual capacity for creative action; everything suddenly depends on the ability to dominate and impose coherence on confused and seemingly random occurrences. Ideally this should occur without the use of force; however, sometimes one can avoid the use of force only by threatening it." (Kissinger, *White House Years*, p. 597.)

further eroded the position of the White House, so that the "imperial presidency" under which linkage had been conceived was no longer in existence to sustain implementation.

One reason why the Russians had moved toward détente in the first place had been a desire to bolster their notoriously inefficient economy with imports of food and technology from the West. Fully aware of the importance Moscow attached to this goal, Nixon and Kissinger sought to extract two benefits from it: to integrate the Soviet economy with that of the West to such an extent that the Russians would have few motives for upsetting the international status quo, and, somewhat contradictorily, to induce Soviet political cooperation by extending economic concessions only as a reward for good behavior. They resolved, accordingly, to make possible grain sales, the extension of "most-favored nation" treatment (MFN), and Export-Import Bank credits, but only in return for a successful outcome of the May 1972 summit. As Kissinger later put it, the White House was determined "to have trade follow political progress and not precede it."[13]

This strategy ran into difficulties almost immediately. The Commerce Department, reflecting the business community's single-minded preoccupation with exports to the U.S.S.R., resisted attaching any conditions to trade, which it tended to regard as an end in itself. The Agriculture Department allowed the Russians quietly to buy massive quantities of American wheat at bargain prices during the summer of 1972, thereby pleasing farmers but undercutting any possibility of linking such sales to political concessions. Linkage thus required tighter coordination within the bureaucracy than even the highly centralized Nixon administration was able to achieve. But the gravest problems developed with Congress, where Senator Henry Jackson in October of that year took oblique aim at the Soviet Union by proposing an amendment to the Trade Reform Act denying MFN and Eximbank credits to countries with "non-market economies" that restricted or taxed the emigration of their own citizens.[14]

The Jackson amendment was a clumsy attempt, by a coalition of conservatives worried about aiding the Soviet Union in any form and liberals determined to make an issue of Moscow's treatment of Jews and dissidents, to impose their own form of linkage, quite without regard to how this would affect the larger pattern of Soviet-American relations. It had been proposed, Kissinger complained, after talks with the Russians had been completed, a fact sure to raise questions in Moscow about American reliability. It seemed to make "domestic compatibility" a condition for progress toward détente when in fact that process had been aimed at building an international framework tolerant of domestic differences. "[T]he issue is not whether we condone what the U.S.S.R. does internally," Kissinger commented in 1974:

> it is whether and to what extent we can risk other objectives—and especially the building of a structure for peace—for those domestic changes. I believe that we cannot, and that to do so would obscure, and in the long run defeat, what must remain our overriding objective—the prevention of nuclear war.[15]

Despite strong protests from the White House, Congress finally passed a modified version of the Jackson amendment, whereupon the Russians early in 1975 abruptly rejected the whole package of economic arrangements worked out three years earlier on the grounds that the amended trade bill constituted an unacceptable intrusion into their domestic affairs.

This abortive Congressional attempt at linkage undermined the Nixon-Kissinger strategy in several ways. It overloaded the linkage mechanism by demanding concessions that outweighed, from the perspective of the other side, the value of what was being offered in return. It made it impossible to test Kissinger's theory that economic interdependence would encourage the Russians to exercise political restraint. It gave Moscow an excuse to avoid strict compliance with other joint agreements, since, it could argue, Washington had not lived up to this one. And Jewish emigration from the Soviet Union actually went down after 1973; by 1975, the number of emigrants had been cut in half.* In short, the Jackson amendment failed, in the end, to serve either the cause of détente, or trade, or human rights.

Nixon and Kissinger found it as difficult to insulate military "sticks" from Congressional interference as they did economic "carrots." An inadvertent by-product of their decision to stretch out troop withdrawals from Vietnam had been a growing determination on Capitol Hill to restrict the President's war-making authority. The administration had managed at each stage of the de-escalation process to stay one step ahead of efforts to legislate withdrawal, but in the summer of 1973, six months after the Vietnam cease-fire but while the United States was still bombing Cambodia, Congress finally imposed over Nixon's veto an end to all American combat

---

* Exit visas for Israel issued to Soviet citizens peaked at approximately 33,500 in 1973, but declined to 20,000 in 1974, 13,000 in 1975, and increased only slightly to 14,000 in 1976. (State Department press release, July 1977.)

involvement in Indochina. Later that year, again over a presidential veto, it generalized this restriction in the form of the War Powers Act, which placed a 60-day limit on future military deployments overseas without Congressional consent.[16] The implications were considerable for a strategy that depended upon credible threats to use force as a means of inducing Soviet restraint in "third world" areas.

These implications appeared first in Vietnam itself, where Nixon had unilaterally promised the Saigon government that he would guarantee the cease-fire, if necessary by military action. Congressional restrictions now made that impossible, and the North Vietnamese quickly began taking advantage of the situation. The United States would not forget "who put us in this uncomfortable position," Kissinger warned Soviet Ambassador Dobrynin. "In that case," the Russian diplomat replied with unusual pointedness, "you should go after Senator Fulbright."[17] In the spring of 1975, with Congressional restraints still in place, the Ford administration was obliged to watch with impotent frustration as North Vietnam at last over-ran South Vietnam. Similar constraints arose with respect to Angola that same year, when the Congress blocked efforts to send clandestine aid to anti-Marxist forces in that country after Soviet-backed Cuban troops had appeared on the scene. "[O]ur legislatively imposed failure even to send financial help to Africans who sought to resist," a deeply disturbed Kissinger predicted, "will lead to further Soviet and Cuban pressures on the mistaken assumption that America has lost the will to counter adventurism or even to help others do so."[18]

Soviet "adventurism" in Africa and the Middle East did continue, and there is some reason to think that the erosion of presidential authority in the United States encouraged it.[19] But the Russians had never ruled out such "adventurism" in the first place, only its escalation to the point that might threaten a direct Soviet-American confrontation. There were limits to how far even Kissinger would have gone to bring that about: at no point was he willing to send U.S. troops back into Southeast Asia or into Africa; and there is no convincing evidence that the kind of limited military and economic aid he was contemplating would have been sufficient to reverse the outcomes there. By early 1976, he had decided that progress on arms control was too important to be made contingent on Soviet restraint in such areas.[20]* Economic coercion might have been applied, but not with-

---

* Kissinger did warn, though, that events like Angola could, in the long run, create an environment unfavorable to the future of arms control.

out alienating the farmers and businessmen who had now become enthusiastic boosters of détente. There would have been little to bargain with in these situations, even if Congress had allowed the White House a free hand.

The decline of presidential authority did certainly throw into disarray the coordinated application of pressures and inducements that were supposed to bring about modifications in Soviet behavior. Linkage had always implied central direction: the goal had been to find the right combination of "sticks" and "carrots" to produce desired results, and that was not likely to happen unless the same authority controlled both of them. In fact, as Kissinger later noted,

> the collapse of our executive authority as a result of Watergate, the erosion of the leadership structure even in the Congress, the isolationism born of the frustrations of Vietnam, and an emerging pattern of geopolitical abdication conspired to prevent the establishment of the balance of incentives and penalties that might have preempted several crises and in the long run given us a genuine period of restraint. Instead, we ended up achieving the worst of all results: constant pinpricks of the Soviet bear (denial of MFN status, for example), but not coupled with a readiness on our part to run the risks that alone could produce Soviet caution (in Angola, for example).[21]

In this sense, then, linkage never got a fair trial—in large part because it required a degree of political centralization Congress found unacceptable in the wake of Vietnam and Watergate. But the consequences, as Kissinger suggested, were equally unfortunate: the United States wound up in the awkward position of provoking, but not deterring, its major antagonist.

A third difficulty with linkage was that the White House led Congress and the public to expect too much from it. Kissinger later denied that the administration had "oversold" détente, pointing out that its official statements had been careful to stress "the limits, the ambiguities, the competition inherent in the relationship, the requirement of vigilance, as well as the very real progress that had been made." Strictly speaking, this was correct. As Nixon had emphasized in his 1972 annual foreign policy report: "We do not, of course, expect the Soviet Union to give up its pursuit of its own interests. We do not expect to give up pursuing our own. . . . For a long period of time, competition is likely to be the hallmark of our relationship with the Soviet Union."[22] But not all such pronouncements were given equal weight; some of the more conspicuous ones did raise expectations beyond the point prudence might have dictated.

The most notable example was the famous statement of "Basic Principles" governing Soviet-American relations, ostentatiously signed by Nixon and Brezhnev at the May 1972 Moscow summit. This agreement, suggested originally by the Russians but drafted by the Americans, obliged both sides to "do their utmost to avoid military confrontations," to "exercise restraint" in their mutual relations, and to "recognize that efforts to obtain unilateral advantage at the expense of the other, directly or indirectly, are inconsistent with these objectives." Nixon later dignified it further by insisting that "These are serious obligations. . . . The leaders of the Soviet Union are serious men. Their willingness to commit themselves to certain principles for the future must be taken as a solemn obligation."[23]

It is hard to know why the administration went out on this particular limb, the shakiness of which should have been evident to anyone familiar with the history of comparably vague joint pronouncements in Soviet-American relations, and especially to an administration whose whole strategy had assumed continuing competition. Kissinger, somewhat defensively, later explained the statement as an attempt to humor Moscow's propensity for "ritual solemn declarations," and as an unavoidable nod to diplomatic niceties. "Of course, these principles were not a legal contract. They were intended to establish a standard of conduct by which to judge whether real progress was being made and in the name of which we could resist their violation. . . . If we fulfilled our responsibility to block Soviet encroachments, coexistence could be reliable and the principles of détente could be seen to have marked the path to a more hopeful future."[24]

But the "Basic Principles" statement had two unforeseen effects. It conveyed the false impression that détente meant a cessation of Soviet-American competition everywhere, and so made the measures necessary to counter Moscow's initiatives in those fields where competition was continuing appear both provocative and unnecessary. At the same time, it established a conspicuous standard of behavior which the Russians, with their view of détente as compartmentalized competition, were sure not to meet. It was not just Congress that put the United States in the awkward position of annoying but not deterring the Kremlin, then. White House rhetoric, in this instance at least, produced much the same result.

Similar consequences grew out of the Helsinki agreement of August 1975 in which, in exchange for Western recognition of the "non-violability" of postwar boundaries in Europe, the Soviet Union committed itself to a broad package of obligations designed to promote the cause of human rights within its territory and those of its satellites.[25] Kissinger's original instinct had been not to try to link détente to changes in the internal structure of the Soviet state: the goal, rather, had been to modify Moscow's external behavior. But domestic pressures, of which the Jackson amendment had been the most obvious, made that position difficult to sustain, and after becoming Secretary of State in 1973 Kissinger shifted to the argument that the relaxation of international tensions that would accompany détente might bring about a relaxation of internal controls within the Soviet bloc as well.[26] When the Russians continued to push, with curious persistence, for a formal acknowledgment of the World War II territorial settlement, Kissinger saw the opportunity to placate domestic critics by securing in return Moscow's promise to allow its citizens greater opportunities for travel, emigration, and exchanges of ideas with the West.[27]

But written obligations to respect human rights at home constrained the Russians no more than the "Basic Principles" had forced them to exhibit restraint abroad: despite Helsinki, controls on dissidents tightened in the years that followed. Whatever the administration's hopes, Kremlin leaders did not see détente as inconsistent with repression. Kissinger probably never expected literal compliance with either Helsinki or the "Basic Principles." He was too sensitive to the importance of power and interests to think that either could be circumscribed by ink. But by sanctioning those agreements without the means of securing compliance, he not only created unwarranted expectations among less sophisticated observers, he also inadvertently strengthened the view that the Soviet Union could not be relied upon to honor any agreements with the United States, whether based on mutual interests or not. That attitude would not be conducive to winning domestic support for the "structure of peace" he and Nixon so often talked about.

There was, in fact, something patronizing about the idea that one could "train" the U.S.S.R., like some laboratory animal, to respond in predictable ways to a succession of positive and negative stimuli. It assumed, to an extent that seems ill-founded in retrospect, Moscow's ability (and desire) to control its own clients, as well as the President's capacity to coordinate American foreign policy. It left little room for recalcitrance—for resistance to being "managed"—on the part of either people or things. It gave rise to false hopes and, as a consequence, to growing disillusionment. Finally, it contained no safeguards against what one might call "reverse linkage": against the possibility that the Russians, all along, might have viewed détente as their own instrument for inducing complacency in the West while they finished assembling the ultimate means of applying pressure—their emergence as a full-scale military rival of the United States.

II

One of the ironies of the Nixon administration is the extent to which it came under attack, while in office, for excessive reliance on the military components of power. From a remarkably wide circle of opinion—antiwar militants, academic defense specialists, Congressional critics, former officials of the Johnson administration—there came the charge that Nixon and Kissinger were seeking to perpetuate the high levels of military spending generated by the Vietnam War—and thus to deny the nation the "peace dividend" a phasing down of military operations was supposed to bring. It was symptomatic of the times that the Senate in 1971 almost passed an amendment proposed by its respected majority leader, Mike Mansfield, that would have reduced the American commitment to NATO by half—all that prevented approval of this drastic measure was a last-minute offer by Brezhnev to begin talks on mutual troop reductions in Europe. The Brookings Institution, reflecting views of the administration's critics, regularly proposed "alternative" budgets in the early 1970's that would have lowered defense appropriations by an annual average of 15 percent. During the 1972 campaign, Nixon's opponent, Senator George McGovern, went even further, promising cuts that would have reduced military spending 35 percent by fiscal 1975.[28]

In fact, though, the Nixon-Ford years saw the most substantial reductions in American military capabilities relative to those of the Soviet Union in the entire postwar era. Washington deployed only two new strategic weapons systems during that period—the Minuteman III MIRVed ICBM, and the Poseidon SLBM—while the Russians made operational eight new or updated ICBMs, two new SLBMs, and the Backfire bomber, capable, by some estimates, of reaching American targets. United States deployable ground forces were cut by 207,000 men between 1970 and 1977; Soviet manpower, already almost twice that of the United States, grew during the same period by an additional 262,000 men. The Soviet Navy, although still far behind its American counterpart in aircraft carriers, was by 1977 approaching parity in other categories of surface combatants and had maintained a long-standing lead in attack submarines. Defense expenditures as a percentage of gross domestic product shrank, in the United States, from 8.1 percent in fiscal 1970 to 4.9 percent in fiscal 1977; comparable figures for the Soviet Union are estimated to have run between 11 and 13 percent during the same period. Adjusting for inflation, American defense outlays actually declined at an annual rate of 4.5 percent between 1970 and 1975; corresponding estimates for the Soviet Union show an annual increase of around 3 percent.[29]

Militarism, then, was hardly the problem. Future historians are more likely to be impressed by criticisms that became common during the middle and late 1970's: that Nixon, Ford, and Kissinger presided over the dismantling rather than the aggrandizement of the American military machine; that they acquiesced in the emergence, for the first time since World War II, of a serious rival to the United States in virtually all categories of military competition. "Under Kissinger and Ford," Ronald Reagan proclaimed during the 1976 campaign, "this nation has become Number Two in a world where it is dangerous—if not fatal—to be second best. All I can see is what other nations the world over see: collapse of the American will and the retreat of American power."[30]

There was a sense of resigned acceptance about Kissinger's pronouncements on the growth of Soviet military strength. "[A]n inescapable reality of the 1970's," he wrote, in Nixon's first annual foreign policy report, "is the Soviet Union's possession of powerful and sophisticated strategic forces approaching, and in some categories, exceeding our own in numbers and capability." This situation, he emphasized, was one the Nixon administration had inherited: it was the product of decisions made in the 1960's by the Russians, who in the wake of the Cuban missile crisis resolved never again to be caught with only rhetorical weapons to fall back on, and by the Johnson administration, which decided that to try to match or surpass the Soviet buildup would be neither desirable nor feasible, given the constraints of the Vietnam War. "No policy or decision on our part brought this about," Kissinger stressed in 1976. "Nothing we could have done would have prevented it. Nothing we can do now will make it disappear."[31]

Compounding the difficulty were strong anti-military attitudes in Congress, which though largely a product of Johnson's involvement in Vietnam, nonetheless peaked during the Nixon years. Between 1950 and 1969, Congressional cuts in defense budget requests had averaged only $1.7 billion annually, as compared to $9.2 billion for non-defense items. During the next six years the balance was reversed, with defense requests suffering average annual cuts of $6.0 billion, while the non-defense budget was increased by an average of $4.7 billion. There took place, as a result, a dramatic decrease in defense spending as a percentage of total government expenditures—from 41.8 percent in fiscal 1970 to 23.8 percent in fiscal 1977, the lowest figure since before World War II. Redressing the military equilibrium by symmetrical means—by attempting to match the Soviets weapon for weapon—would have been a clear impossibility in this political climate. "In the anti-military orgy spawned by Vietnam," Kissinger recalled, "to have challenged the overwhelming Congressional sentiment for 'domestic priorities' [would have been] almost certainly an exercise in futility."[32]

Instead, the administration chose not to confront Congress directly, but to embark upon a two-phase "damage limitation" operation, designed to preserve the fundamental elements of American military strength through what it knew would be the lean years immediately ahead, while at the same time preparing the way for the long-term expansion in military capabilities that would be necessary to counter-balance the Russians. This program consisted of (1) the appeasement of Congress, with a view to defusing as much as possible growing anti-military sentiment there, and (2) negotiations with the Soviet Union aimed at restricting as much as possible its own military buildup, without constraining in any significant way comparable measures the United States might choose to take once the furor over Vietnam had died down.

The principal architect of the Congressional appeasement strategy was Secretary of Defense Melvin Laird, himself an ex-Congressman and the one member of Nixon's cabinet with national security responsibilities who managed to evade tight White House control. Laird, whose skill at bureaucratic gamesmanship would later elicit tributes from an impressed Kissinger,* saw as his chief mission forcing the American military to adapt to a harsher, post-Vietnam environment without significant loss of either morale or capabilities. Congressional budget cuts, he believed, were inevitable; nothing was to be gained by fighting them. The trick, rather, was to anticipate likely reductions, where possible pre-empt them by cutting

---

* "Laird's maneuvers were often as Byzantine in their complexity or indirection as those of Nixon, [but] he accomplished with verve and surprising goodwill what Nixon performed with grim-determination and inward resentment. . . . There was about him a buoyancy and a rascally good humor that made working with him as satisfying as it could on occasion be maddening." (Kissinger, *White House Years*, p. 32.)

defense requests before they went to Congress, where necessary even co-operate with Congressional leaders in making further cuts where they would do the least harm. To a remarkable degree, Laird managed to maintain professional military support in this painful process and to minimize Congressional hostility. "He preserved the sinews of our strength," Kissinger later acknowledged, "and laid the basis for expansion when the public mood changed later. . . . This was a major achievement."[33]

Laird's maneuvers made possible planning for several new strategic weapons systems—the B-1 bomber, the Trident submarine, the cruise missile—but only at the price of a substantial reduction in conventional forces, which accounted for the bulk of "controllable" defense spending. Air Force squadrons had declined from 169 in fiscal 1968 to 110 by fiscal 1974; Army and Marine divisions from 23 to 16 during the same period; Navy ships (including submarines) from 976 to 495.[34] Simple numerical indices can be misleading, and it is no doubt true that qualitative improvements compensated, in part, for these sharp quantitative cutbacks. It is also true that some such reductions would have occurred in any event in the wake of Vietnam and with the transition from the "two and a half" to the "one and a half" war standard.* Still, the scope and extent of the cuts were striking: there can be no question that they restricted severely the capacity of the United States to project conventional military power elsewhere in the world at a time when Soviet capabilities were growing.

Kissinger wondered, in retrospect, whether the policy of appeasing Congress had been wise: "Accommodation failed to placate the critics and may have demoralized supporters of a strong defense; . . . it seemed to grant the precepts of the critics with which the Administration in fact disagreed and cause the debate to turn on the implementation of agreed assumptions." Moreover, measures taken to facilitate that policy—defense budget cuts, as well as troop withdrawals from Vietnam and the phasing out of the draft—were generally irreversible once initiated, and hence difficult to coordinate with Kissinger's efforts to reassure allies or negotiate acceptable settlements with adversaries. Still, as he noted, "ringing Presidential speeches on the importance of defense . . . were met with derision and indignation in the media and the Congress. . . . Supporters of defense . . . did not rush to the barricades."[35] It may well have been that the only way to deal with post-Vietnam anti-militarism was for the administration to take on some of the aspects of anti-militarism itself.

* See p. 295.

The second element in the administration's post-Vietnam "damage limitation" strategy was to seek arms control agreements with the Soviet Union that would constrain its military buildup, without significantly restricting measures the United States might feasibly take in the future to upgrade its own capabilities. Through a remarkable combination of feigned disinterest, linkage, bargaining, and sheer bluff, Nixon and Kissinger had managed, by 1972, to negotiate a strategic arms agreement that did just that. The SALT Interim Agreement placed numerical limits on ICBM and SLBM "launchers"—a category of weaponry the Soviets had been expanding in recent years, but in which United States capabilities had remained stable since the mid-1960's. SALT I imposed no limitation on long-range bombers, where the United States was overwhelmingly dominant, on fighter-bombers stationed in Europe and capable of hitting Soviet targets with nuclear weapons, or on the development of new and more accurate strategic missiles, a technology in which the Americans could be expected to excel. The one disadvantage from Washington's point of view was that the Interim Agreement froze Soviet missile strength at a point considerably higher than that of the United States (1330 vs. 1054 ICBMs, 950 vs. 656 SLBMs), but that asymmetry was justified by the fact that American missiles were more accurate, and in large part MIRVed.[36] On balance, given trends in strategic weapons development over the previous decade, SALT I was clearly to the advantage of the United States.

One thing SALT could not do, though, was to ensure that the nation used the opportunities thereby provided to maintain strategic parity with the Soviet Union. Confronted with SALT's quantitative limits, the Russians quickly shifted their emphasis to qualitative improvements, including the deployment of their own MIRVs. They also took advantage of ambiguities in the Interim Agreement to build a new generation of "heavy" ICBMs, whose destructive power appeared usable only for the purpose of knocking out American land-based missiles, now left vulnerable by the ban on ABMs.[37] To be sure, nothing in SALT I prohibited the United States from further qualitative improvements in its own strategic systems, and Kissinger, for one, was determined to move in this direction. "The way to use this freeze is for us to catch up," he told Laird, shortly after the 1972 Moscow summit. "If we don't do this we don't deserve to be in office." Laird agreed, and with characteristic audacity made the Pentagon's endorsement of SALT I contingent on prior Congressional approval of the B-1 bomber and the Trident submarine. Within the next year, the administration also added plans for a mobile, land-based ICBM, and sub-sonic, terrain-hugging cruise missiles. "We were determined," Kissinger later recalled, "to avoid ever again being in a situation where only the Soviets had strategic programs under way."[38]

But by the same time the SALT I Interim Agreement had expired in October 1977, none of these systems was in place, or even near deployment. The problem was in part the inevitable delays that accompany development of any new weapons system, but both Congress and the Executive Branch must bear some responsibility for it as well. Nixon and Kissinger had failed to foresee the extent to which the Russians would stretch the limits of SALT. Instead they pictured that agreement as part of a larger process by which both sides had committed themselves to show restraint in their dealings with each other.[39] This made it difficult to put across the idea that SALT I should be taken as an opportunity to catch up with the Russians: if restraint was to be the pattern of the future, the argument ran, why endanger it by increasing defense spending? But if the administration miscalculated, so too did Congress. After years of trying to stop the Vietnam War, after the more recent trauma of Watergate, there were many on Capitol Hill whose concern about "imperial" presidencies and foreign policies left little room for the possibility that threats might still come from without as well as from within. As late as 1975, Congress could still cut the military budget by $7 billion, long after trends in Soviet military spending had become too obvious to ignore.[40]*

Because of the administration's failure consistently to portray détente as the Russians understood it—as a continuing competitive relationship— and because of Congress's preoccupation with past abuses at the expense of future dangers, the United States did not take full advantage of the opportunities SALT I allowed to rebuild its military capabilities. In a narrow sense, SALT did what Kissinger had intended: it constrained areas of recent Soviet weapons development without unduly restricting those into which the United States might reasonably choose to move in the near future.[41] But that, alone, could not ensure continued strategic stability. To reach that goal the United States, like the U.S.S.R., would actually have to

---

* In a series of articles published in 1974, Albert Wohlstetter had demonstrated not only that Soviet military spending had exceeded that of the United States on strategic weapons for the past decade, but that U.S. projections had consistently underestimated the scale of the Soviet buildup. (Albert Wohlstetter, "Is There a Strategic Arms Race?" *Foreign Policy*, #15 [Summer 1974], 3–20; "Rivals but No Race," *ibid*., #16 [Fall 1974], 48–81.)

build the systems SALT permitted. It was the delay in doing this, not the provisions of SALT I itself, that gave the Russians the strategic edge they had gained by the end of the Ford administration.

The SALT I agreement resulted from a rare conjunction of technological and political trends, the continuation of which could not be guaranteed in the future. In a technological sense, the agreement was unusual in that deployments of the systems the two superpowers most wanted to limit—ICBMs and ABMs—could easily be monitored by satellite and other forms of reconnaissance. The qualitative improvements both sides moved into after SALT I—the development of compact but highly accurate cruise missiles by the United States, the MIRVing of its "heavy" ICBMs and deployment of the Backfire bomber by the Soviet Union—did not lend themselves as readily to verification by the non-intrusive remote sensors upon which SALT I depended. That fact would complicate the task of extending the agreement to other categories of weapons systems.[42]

Similarly, the political base upon which SALT rested in the United States was a shaky one, despite SALT I's overwhelming approval by the Congress in 1972.* SALT had involved tolerating asymmetries—an American qualitative lead in ICBMs and SLBMs in return for a Soviet quantitative lead. But asymmetries, however justifiable, tend to set off insecurities, and the SALT I asymmetry was no exception. Soon after Congress approved SALT I, it also passed a resolution by Senator Henry Jackson specifying that in future SALT negotiations the principle of numerical parity with the Russians would be maintained. Jackson's concern was that the American qualitative lead would prove transitory, and that the nation needed the added insurance quantitative parity would give it. The U.S. technological lead did indeed prove fragile—in part because of the parsimony of Jackson's Congressional colleagues—but the requirement to seek numerical parity turned out to be a crude way of dealing with the problem. The Russians were not prepared to accord parity in all areas, claiming, with some justification, that Soviet and American defense missions were themselves asymmetrical. And the Pentagon itself did not want parity in all areas—it had deliberately chosen not to match the Soviet Union's de-

---

* SALT I took the form of a treaty limiting both sides to no more than two ABM emplacements each, approved by the Senate in August 1972, and a five-year interim agreement placing ceilings on ICBM and SLBM launcher construction, approved by Congressional joint resolution in September 1972.

ployment of large, liquid-fueled "heavy" missiles, insisting that lighter, more accurate, solid-fueled missiles would do just as well.[43] Added to the difficulties of verification, these political complications made the task of extending the SALT process into new areas an arduous one.

The SALT I ABM treaty was amended by mutual consent in 1974 to allow each side only one, instead of the original two, ABM emplacements initially agreed upon. Later that year, at the Ford-Brezhnev summit at Vladivostok, the two sides agreed further on a mutual limitation of 2,400 strategic delivery systems, including ICBMs, SLBMs, and heavy bombers, and to a sub-ceiling of 1,320 on ICBMs and SLBMs equipped with MIRVs. This represented a step in the direction of numerical parity, but only in *aggregate* terms, not in individual categories of weapons systems. For the next two years, negotiations revolved around the question of whether the American cruise missile and the Soviet Backfire bomber would be included in SALT II and, if so, how limits on them would be verified. No agreement had been reached by the time the Ford administration left office early in 1977.[44]

SALT clearly, then, did not live up to the hopes of its sponsors. It is worth asking, though, whether the United States would have been better off without it. In the absence of SALT, there would have been nothing to induce the Russians to cut back their ICBMs, SLBMs, and ABMs to the extent that they did, nor is it likely that Congress would have funded increases in comparable American programs. SALT hardly left the United States defenseless: the strategic imbalance was never close to the point at which the Russians could have launched pre-emptive strikes against American missile installations without suffering devastating retaliation. Certainly the monitoring of Soviet strategic capabilities would have been more difficult without SALT. The unprecedented and extended Soviet-American dialogue on these highly sensitive issues gave the United States valuable information about Soviet strategic systems that would have been hard to come by in any other way. Finally, but not least in importance, the overall goal of lowering the dangers of nuclear war was important enough to justify accepting reasonable risks in order to progress toward it.

SALT was criticized because it coincided in time with the emergence of the Soviet Union as a full-fledged strategic rival to the United States. It did not, however, bring that event about. SALT was intended neither to maintain nor to regain American dominance: as Kissinger commented in 1976, "no reasonable leader should encourage the illusion that America can ever again recapture the strategic superiority of the early post-war period."[45]

SALT was, rather, like Laird's budget cuts, a "damage-limitation" operation, designed to make the transition from superiority to parity as safe and painless as possible for the United States. It was an accommodation to reality, carried out with some skill from an unfavorable position in less than congenial circumstances.

Any administration would have found it difficult to maintain the military balance of power in the situation that confronted Nixon and Kissinger in 1969: the coincidence of unprecedented Soviet military expansion with unprecedented domestic anti-military sentiment was no easy problem to overcome. It is to their credit that they grasped from the start the disturbing implications of these intersecting trends, and tried, through means that were both realistic and imaginative, to counter them. That they did not fully succeed was a function, not of limited vision, but of limited power, a curious difficulty in an administration to which the adjective "imperial" was frequently applied. In fact, though, the Nixon administration never dominated Congress on defense matters; it was, rather, the other way around, and became more so as the President's authority eroded in the wake of the Watergate affair.

It is with Congress that the primary responsibility rests for the relative decline in American military power that took place during the 1970's. The difficulty was a simple inability (or unwillingness) to differentiate between real and imagined threats to national security. By the time Nixon took office, legislators on Capitol Hill had been deceived so many times about the conduct of the war in Southeast Asia that they treated with justifiable skepticism warnings emanating from the Executive Branch as to what might happen if they failed to fund defense budget requests at the desired level. Nixon's own credibility was never high with the Congressional Democratic majority in the first place, and it got lower, again justifiably, as time went on. But in its analysis of the Soviet military buildup, the administration if anything understated the danger: still the Congress tended to dismiss these warnings as just one more cry of "wolf." Not until after 1975 did a majority of legislators begin to take seriously the implications of the Soviet buildup; even then the only response was to reverse the steady decline in the defense budget, but not significantly to increase it.[46]

In the long run, it made little difference. Kissinger would have been the first to admit that power, in the modern world, has many components, of which the military is only one. The whole basis of his strategy had been to tolerate asymmetries on the assumption that deficiencies in one area could be compensated for in others. But that strategy also depended on letting no single asymmetry get too far out of line, and this is what he thought Congress, with its post-Vietnam hostility toward the military, had done. By the time the Ford administration left office the position of overall military superiority the United States had enjoyed since 1945—and of which it had been aware since 1961—had passed from the scene. It would be left to Ronald Reagan to regain it.

III

Relations with the Soviet Union were hardly the only problem confronting United States foreign policy during the Nixon-Ford years. Events in much of the rest of the world were proceeding more or less independently of what was happening in Washington or Moscow, and yet with important implications for American interests and global stability. A third major criticism of Kissinger's diplomacy was that he neglected these problems: that in his fascination with great power politics he lost sight of the fact that the great powers no longer had the capacity to shape the entire international order. "In the end," one observer noted, "the most telling criticism of the Kissinger achievement will [be] . . . that it was too largely irrelevant."[47] There is a certain irony in this charge, since Kissinger as a student of international politics had himself called attention to and had even welcomed the diffusion of superpower authority.[48] Yet there is also accuracy in it, for by 1977 one could point to a long series of what can only be called blunders in dealing with the world apart from Russia and China. These reflected a short-sightedness surprising in administrations that had prided themselves, with some justification, on taking a long-range view.

In southern Africa, for example, the Nixon administration embarked early in 1970 on a quiet but deliberate policy of relaxing pressures against the white minority regimes there, on the assumption, as a National Security Council memorandum put it, that

> The whites are here to stay and the only way that constructive change can come about is through them. There is no hope for the blacks to gain the political rights they seek through violence, which will lead only to chaos and increased opportunities for the Communists. We can, by selective relaxation of our stance toward the white regimes, encourage some modification of their current racial and colonial policies and through more substantial economic assistance to the black states . . . help to draw the two groups together and exert some influence on both for peaceful change.[49]

It was a policy reflecting all the prescience of a Marie Antoinette in 1789, for within five years, Portuguese authority in Angola and Mozambique had collapsed, the white-ruled governments of Rhodesia and South Africa were coming under increasing pressure, and blacks were in fact showing every sign of attaining political control—although with little help from, or reason for gratitude toward, the United States.

A similar myopia seemed to shape official attitudes toward Pakistan during that country's bloody civil conflict and subsequent war with India in 1971. The crisis had arisen over West Pakistan's refusal to grant autonomy to the citizens of East Pakistan, separated by some 1,000 miles of Indian territory. Officially sanctioned repression of the ensuing revolt there had grown to the stage, by March of that year, that State Department reports were speaking of "selective genocide"; later estimates would suggest that well over a million Bengalis had been killed. But the Nixon administration, intent on using Pakistan as an intermediary in its "opening" to Beijing, carefully refrained from criticizing the government in Islamabad and delayed cutting off arms shipments to it as long as possible. When India intervened to set up the independent state of Bangladesh in what had been East Pakistan, Nixon secretly ordered Kissinger to "tilt" American policy in favor of the Pakistanis, for fear of offending the Chinese. The effect, though, was to alienate India, now clearly the dominant power in the region, and, through Washington's apparent indifference to Pakistani atrocities, much of world opinion as well.[50]

The Nixon administration associated itself with another losing cause in 1972 when it approved a secret program of virtually unlimited conventional arms sales to the Shah of Iran, on the assumption that his government would be a reliable long-term ally in an unstable part of the world. This generosity did not keep the Shah from seeking large oil price increases the following year. Nor did Washington anticipate the extent to which the Shah's own modernization program—carried out, as Kissinger later ruefully admitted, in strict accordance with American theories that economic development produced political stability—would within seven years bring about his downfall, leaving Iran's vast store of American-supplied arms in the hands of forces bitterly hostile to the United States.[51]

In the Middle East, in 1973, the administration not only failed to anticipate the Arab-Israeli War—in part, it has been argued, because American and Israeli intelligence relied too much on each other—but, more significantly, the capacity of the Arab oil-producing states to impose first an embargo and then unprecedented price increases on their principal export.

This happened despite the fact that declining reserves and growing imports had made Western vulnerability in this respect obvious for some time. As a consequence, Nixon and Kissinger found themselves surprised by one of the most fundamental but at the same time the most predictable changes in world power relationships in recent years.[52]

In Cyprus, in 1974, the United States failed, despite forewarning, to stop the right-wing government in Greece, which it had been supporting with arms sales in return for military base privileges, from toppling the regime of Archbishop Makarios, who had hitherto managed skillfully to keep the island independent of either Greek or Turkish domination. This event brought about both the collapse of the Greek government and a Turkish invasion of the island; the latter development, in turn, set off a rebellion in Congress, where a vociferous Greek-American lobby managed to impose an arms embargo on the Turks, over Kissinger's opposition. The United States wound up, as a result, having alienated both sides, with unfortunate consequences for NATO and the whole American position in the Eastern Mediterranean.[53]

In Angola in 1975, the Ford administration again supported the losing side when it decided to furnish covert assistance to anti-Marxist factions in a three-way struggle for control of that country. It did this despite the fact that one of those groups was closely tied to Zaire, the other to South Africa, neither of them particularly popular causes in Angola; despite indications that a diplomatic resolution of the crisis might still be possible; despite State Department warnings that covert aid could not be kept secret and might in fact induce the Soviet Union to undertake the same thing. Arguments over whether Moscow or Washington provoked each other into intervening in Angola are complex and perhaps unresolvable—not least because of Fidel Castro's decision, made on his own, to send military assistance to the Angolan Marxists. What is clear is that by the end of 1975 the U.S.S.R. was openly supporting its clients in Angola (including the Cuban troops fighting on their behalf), while Congress had learned of American covert involvement there and had voted to cut it off. "It is obvious," a frustrated State Department official commented, "that the United States made mistakes."[54]

Meanwhile, relations with the NATO countries and Japan had been allowed to deteriorate, more from inattention than from deliberate design. The Nixon administration in 1971 inadvertently delivered two sharp blows to Japan by failing to warn Tokyo in advance, first of the Kissinger trip to Beijing in July, and then of the decision the following month to impose an import surcharge and suspend the dollar's convertibility into gold. Requirements of secrecy accounted in part for these discourtesies, but so too did a self-centered policy-making process in Washington, oblivious, for the most part, to the impact its actions would have on allies. Two years later, conscious of the extent to which he had neglected NATO in his preoccupation with the Soviet Union, China, and Vietnam, Kissinger proclaimed 1973 to be the "year of Europe," and suggested a series of economic and defense measures designed to link the NATO countries and Japan more closely with the United States. The allies' response, though, was decidedly tepid—one suspects they found it patronizing to be assigned a "year," all the more so when such other pressures as Watergate and the Middle East kept Kissinger from in fact devoting much time to their affairs.[55]

NATO again became the object of Kissinger's concern in 1974 and 1975, but only because of his fears that communists in France, Italy, and Portugal might enter coalition governments in those countries by constitutional means. The crisis in Portugal had arisen as a consequence of the April 1974 revolution, which, in addition to dislodging the Portuguese empire in southern Africa, had produced a socialist government at home with some communist participation. "You are allowing excessive Communist Party influence in the government," Kissinger bluntly told Foreign Minister Mario Soares the following October: "You are a Kerensky."* For the next several months, Kissinger talked of isolating Portugal economically and excluding it from NATO, as if the country had already been "lost" to communism. When, in 1975, the French and Italian communist parties committed themselves publicly to democratic procedures and to independence from Moscow, Kissinger was openly skeptical. Communists could not be trusted to keep their promises, he warned; once in power they would never voluntarily give it up. It was an odd position for someone who had built a strategy of dividing adversaries, downplaying ideology, and relying on agreements with communist states to build a new international order. As it turned out, Kissinger exaggerated both the dangers and prospects of "Eurocommunism": communist parties did not come to power in Western Europe; NATO did not have to be protected against subversion from within. This happened more in spite of than because of

---

* "I certainly don't want to be a Kerensky," Soares replied. Kissinger: "Neither did Kerensky." (Tad Szulc, "Lisbon & Washington: Behind the Portuguese Revolution," *Foreign Policy*, #21 [Winter, 1975–76], 3.) It was, Kissinger later acknowledged, a "not-so-tactful comment." (Henry Kissinger, *Years of Renewal* [New York: 1999], p. 630).

Kissinger's warnings, however. The effect of his alarms was to place the United States in opposition, once again, to something it could not (by avowable means, at least) have prevented.[56]

What all of these events had in common was the tendency of the Nixon and Ford administrations to deal with them in global rather than regional terms.[57] When Kissinger spoke of the need for a "philosophical deepening" in the United States approach to world affairs, he had in mind ending the fascination with "crisis management" that had led previous administrations to preoccupy themselves with regional issues—like Vietnam—at the expense of global strategy. Kissinger had resolved to reverse the procedure: to concentrate on building a stable international order among the superpowers, and then to handle such crises as developed elsewhere according to how they might facilitate, or interfere with, that grand design. Only in this way, he thought, could the sense of direction and proportion that had been missing from recent American foreign policy be restored.

But attaining perspective requires sacrificing detail: oversimplification is the price one pays for a larger view. The Nixon-Kissinger strategy tended to impose categories of thought derived from the global superpower competition upon regional events, with results that deadened sensitivity to the distinctive contexts within which they had developed.* Neither Nixon nor Kissinger could accept, for example, the possibility that Marxism might be an indigenous, popular, and quite independent force in certain parts of the world; instead they insisted that the coming to power of such governments anywhere could only erode American credibility everywhere. Similarly, there was a tendency to let anticipated reactions in Moscow or Beijing govern Washington's response to events taking place in other parts of the world. "I admit it's not a brilliant position," Kissinger

---

*An extreme example of this tendency occurred in May 1975, when Cambodian gunboats seized the American freighter *Mayaguez* and its crew in the Gulf of Thailand. Determined not to tolerate another *Pueblo* incident (the North Korean seizure of an American intelligence vessel in 1968), eager to make the point that the United States could still act forcefully despite the fall of Saigon two weeks earlier, Kissinger persuaded Ford to order air strikes against the port of Kompong Som and an amphibious assault on the island of Koh Tang (at a cost of eighteen Americans killed in combat and another twenty-three in a helicopter crash) without waiting to see whether diplomatic measures could secure release of the crew—in fact, the crew was being released as the air strikes and landings were taking place. It was left to the White House photographer, David Kennerly, to suggest to the assembled members of the National Security Council that the Cambodians might have been acting on their own, and not as part of a larger plot to humiliate the United States. (See Gerald Ford, *A Time to Heal* [New York: 1979], pp. 275–84; Kissinger, *Years of Renewal*, pp. 547–75; and Christopher Jon Lamb, *Belief Systems and Decision Making in the Mayaguez Crisis* [Gainesville: 1989]).

told Nixon late in 1971, commenting on American support for Pakistan, "but if we collapse now the Soviets won't respect us for it; the Chinese will despise us and the other countries will draw their own conclusions."[58] This concern with what others might think obscured the causes of regional instability; it also ran the risks of overcommitment and loss of initiative that had plagued the nation during the Vietnam War. In this sense, it is hard to see how Kissinger's "philosophical deepening" advanced things very far.

A related difficulty was that the Nixon-Kissinger strategy relied on tightly centralized control to ensure conceptual coherence—control purchased by cutting the bureaucracy almost entirely out of the decision-making process. This meant that regional expertise, of the kind necessary to avoid the distortions inherent in applying global perspectives to local problems, was too often neglected. In the India-Pakistan crisis, in Portugal, and in Angola, there were specialists who warned of the dangers inherent in this approach, but their advice was not heeded; in the case of Iran, such advice apparently was not even sought. Similarly, in the Arab-Israeli War, the OPEC oil embargo, and the Cyprus crisis, closer attention to what experts on those subjects were saying could have helped Washington avoid being surprised to the extent that it was.[59] Bureaucracy, Kissinger liked to complain, stifled innovation, and certainly there was much truth in that. But bureaucracy, properly used, can monitor disparate and complex events without oversimplification, warn ahead of time of approaching dangers, and thus reduce the chances of being caught off guard. A major liability of the Nixon-Kissinger administrative style was that it virtually precluded using the bureaucracy in that way.

Finally, there was always the danger, in such a highly centralized strategy, that issues would come to be seen in terms of personalities as well as interests. It was not without significance that Nixon and Kissinger got along well with Zhou Enlai, the Shah of Iran, and President Yahya Khan of Pakistan, but less so with the Japanese, and emphatically not with Prime Minister Indira Gandhi of India.[60] In systems that concentrate authority at the top, personal relationships make a difference: they can lead to blindness regarding the shortcomings and vulnerabilities of friends, and to deep suspicions of those who would, for whatever reasons, seek to exploit them. The distinction between policy and petulance in such circumstances becomes thin.*

---

*There is also the danger that wholly extraneous factors can affect decision-making. It has been argued, for example, that Nixon's frustration over the Senate's rejection of two Supreme Court appointments, together with his exhilaration over having seen the movie "Patton" several times, contributed to the decision to invade Cambodia in 1970. (See William Shawcross,

In fairness to Kissinger, it should be noted that he had the capacity, at times, to learn from mistakes, and to move quickly to correct them. Hence, despite having been surprised by the 1973 Arab-Israeli War, he responded to that crisis with creativity and skill, shifting American policy from its earlier pro-Israeli stance to one of relative impartiality. He thereby gained the United States new support in the Arab world (and brought about a corresponding decline of Soviet influence) without permanently alienating the Israelis, or their powerful allies inside the United States.[61] Similarly, after the Angola fiasco, Kissinger persuaded President Ford that the United States should now align itself with rather than against black liberation movements in southern Africa. In an act of political courage given his difficult fight for renomination, Ford in April 1976 authorized Kissinger to proclaim "unrelenting opposition" to the white minority regime in Rhodesia, and to insist on an end to "institutionalized inequality" in South Africa.[62] Neither of these initiatives promised rapid or permanent solutions to the problems they addressed, but they did mark an ability to profit by experience that had not always been present in recent American foreign policy.

Nevertheless, there was always something extemporaneous about Kissinger's handling of events outside the immediate Washington-Moscow-Beijing axis. Too often the United States found itself confronting predictable crises with frantic improvisations, long-term problems with short-term palliatives, irreversible trends with grudging but half-hearted resistance. It is curious that this should have been so, given Kissinger's insistence on conceptual coherence in the conduct of foreign policy. But it was, in a way, that very search for coherence that produced the problem. Kissinger's grand geopolitical vision required oversimplification, centralization, even personalization, if it was to prevail against fragmenting and inertial tendencies present within the bureaucracy. The price, though, was inattention to problems beyond the domain of the great powers, and then, when they became too serious to ignore any longer, a tendency to try to impose great power solutions on them. However much Kissinger had done to invigorate and rationalize the concept of containment, it was, in his mind, still that—a strategy for limiting the expanding influence of the Soviet Union. As such, it provided a less than adequate intellectual focus for dealing with the growing number of issues that lay beyond that sphere.

Sideshow: Kissinger, Nixon and the Destruction of Cambodia [New York: 1979], pp. 134–35; also H. R. Haldeman, *The Haldeman Diaries: Inside the Nixon White House* [New York: 1994], p. 147.)

IV

Centralization had another unfortunate effect as well in the eyes of Kissinger's critics: it eroded the foundation of moral principle upon which American foreign policy had to rest if it was to reflect the nation's most fundamental aspirations. As presidential candidate Jimmy Carter put it during the 1976 campaign:

> Our foreign policy is being evolved in secret, and in its full details and nuances, it is probably known to one man only. . . . Because we have let our foreign policy be made for us, we have lost something crucial in the way we talk and the way we act toward other peoples of the world. . . . [I]t must be the responsibility of the President to restore the moral authority of this country in its conduct of foreign policy.

For too long, Carter charged, foreign policy had consisted "almost entirely of maneuver and manipulation, based on the assumption that the world is a jungle of competing national antagonisms, where military supremacy and economic muscle are the only things that work and where rival powers are balanced against each other to keep the peace." That approach might have been appropriate in 1815, or even 1945, but not in the 1970's. Kissinger's "Lone Ranger" foreign policy "inherently has had to be closely guarded and amoral, and we have had to forego openness, consultation and a constant adherence to fundamental principles and high moral standards."[63]

Whatever one thinks of Carter's assumption that democratic decision-making produces moral diplomacy, there was a widespread sense, by the end of the Ford administration, that Kissinger and the presidents he served had neglected the proper alignment between policy and principle that any nation must have in order to maintain legitimacy while wielding power. At its most extreme, this argument led to charges of complicity in nothing less than genocide. Thus, it was suggested, Nixon and Kissinger carefully looked the other way while Nigeria in 1969–1970 starved out the Biafran rebels. They insisted on supporting Pakistan in 1971, despite that government's slaughter of its own citizens in its rebellious eastern provinces. They only temporarily suspended aid to Burundi, despite evidence between 1972 and 1974 of officially sanctioned mass murders carried out against the numerically dominant but politically powerless Hutu population there. And, through their casual expansion of the Vietnam War into Cambodia, they set in motion the chain of events that would lead after 1975 to the depredations of Pol Pot and the Khmer Rouge, and to the near-extermination of an entire people. "Cambodia," one critic has asserted, "was not a mistake; it was a crime."[64]

The assumption here is that statesmen must be judged by the conse-quences of their actions, whatever their intent.[65] That standard would be fair enough if it could be demonstrated that a direct relationship exists be-tween actions taken and effects produced, but that demonstration is diffi-cult to make in the four cases cited. The extent of Nigerian and Pakistani atrocities was not at first clearly understood in Washington, nor is there ev-idence that even if it had been, it would have been within the administra-tion's power to stop them. The same was true of Burundi, which rated so low in the White House scale of priorities that Kissinger took the unaccus-tomed step of delegating key decisions regarding that country to subordi-nates.[66] In the case of Cambodia, it was North Vietnamese forces, not Americans, who first violated neutrality there; the advent of Pol Pot was less a function of the 1970 U.S. military "incursion" than of Hanoi's final victory over South Vietnam in 1975. To blame Washington for the horrors that occurred in these situations is not only to give undue weight to single elements in complex causal chains; the argument suggests as well a certain backhanded chauvinism, assuming as it seems to that violence and terror have no independent existence in the world, and that they appear only as the result of action (or inaction) by the United States.

A more convincing version of the "amorality" critique is that Nixon and Kissinger too often allowed ends to justify means: that in their haste to ac-complish specific objectives, they at times employed methods inappropri-ate to, and even destructive of, the larger goals they were trying to achieve. To be sure, it would be difficult to find anyone who has ever wielded power of whom the same, to one degree or another, could not be said. As the theologian Reinhold Niebuhr once pointed out, "the egoistic corrup-tion of universal ideals is a much more persistent fact in human conduct than any moralistic creed is inclined to admit."[67] What was distinctive about Nixon and Kissinger, however, is the extent to which the corruption of ends by means became visible while they were still in power. It did so with particular clarity in two situations where the relationship between ac-tions taken and effects produced could hardly be denied: the administra-tion's efforts to remove the democratically elected Marxist government of Salvadore Allende in Chile, and its attempts to salvage American credibil-ity while seeking to end the Vietnam War.

Throughout the Cold War, the United States had claimed to oppose communism, not because it was revolutionary, but because it denied free-dom of choice. Should a people ever freely elect a government of that per-suasion, the argument ran, Washington would respect that judgment. Thus, Nixon acknowledged early in 1971 that although Allende's election was "not something that we welcomed, . . . that was the decision of the people of Chile, and . . . therefore we accepted that decision. . . . [F]or the United States to have intervened—intervened in a free election and to have turned it around, I think, would have had repercussions all over Latin America that would have been far worse than what has happened in Chile." Later that year, in a section of the administration's annual foreign policy report headed "A Community of Diversity," Kissinger noted: "We hope that governments will evolve toward constitutional procedures. But it is not our mission to try to provide—except by example—the answers to such questions for other sovereign states. . . . [W]e are prepared to have the kind of relationship with the Chilean government that it is prepared to have with us."[68]

And yet, long before the 1970 elections had taken place, the White House had authorized covert action designed to swing them to Allende's opponents. It sought—by means that included consideration of a military coup—to keep him from taking power. Once he was in office, it applied economic and political pressure aimed at "destabilizing" his regime. It did all this on the basis of vague fears that Chile under Allende would become a communist dictatorship, along the lines of Castro's Cuba. "I don't see why we have to let a country go Marxist just because its people are irresponsible," Kissinger is said to have commented, in an Orwellian remark that seemed to suggest a willingness to subvert democracy in order to preserve democracy. Whether Allende would in fact have gone the way of Castro is impossible to know: he was overthrown and died—whether by assassination or suicide has never been clear—in September 1973, to the unconcealed glee (although apparently without the direct involvement) of the Nixon administration. It soon became obvious, first, that Nixon and Kissinger had lied about American covert operations in Chile; second, that their actions confirmed the view of Marxism's more militant exponents that that ideology could succeed in Latin American only by violent means and only over the opposition of the United States; and third, that the administration had failed its own test of tolerating distasteful but democratic regimes.[69]

Kissinger's position on Chile, as on Eurocommunism in Western Europe, was that the United States could accept only a certain range of political outcomes, even if produced by democratic means. The American commitment to diversity did not extend to the acceptance of governments that might in some way upset the balance of power. As Kissinger acknowledged to his staff at one point: "We set the limits of diversity."[70] But the costs of limiting diversity could be high, as Kissinger found out when information on the Chilean affair became public late in 1974, setting off a protracted (and highly public) Congressional investigation into this and other covert activities.[71] Moreover, the dangers that had justified this departure from principle could never be proven, since the actions involved had been intended to prevent hypothetical threats from becoming real ones. Nixon may well have been more prophetic than he knew when he said, for public consumption in 1971, that the repercussions of intervention in Chile would be worse than the provocations that might cause it in the first place.

A similar resort to means inconsistent with ends shaped the Nixon administration's de-escalation of the war in Vietnam. The chief rationale for remaining in that country until an acceptable peace settlement had been achieved had been to preserve self-confidence at home and respect abroad. "A nation cannot remain great if it betrays its allies and lets down its friends," Nixon told the nation in his first major address on Vietnam in late 1969. "Our defeat and humiliation in South Vietnam without question would promote recklessness in the councils of those great powers who have not yet abandoned their goals of world conquest." Kissinger made the same point in emotional terms in his memoirs, a decade later:

> I believed in the moral significance of my adopted country. America, alone of the free countries, was strong enough to assure global security against the forces of tyranny. Only America had both the power and the decency to inspire other peoples who struggled for identity, for progress and dignity. . . . There was no one now to come to America's rescue if we abandoned our international responsibilities or if we succumbed to self-hatred.

The prerequisites for an acceptable settlement were simple: the return of American prisoners-of-war, and the survival of South Vietnam as an independent state. Within these narrow limits, the administration was successful. Hanoi after four years came around to Washington's position on the prisoners and the continuation of the Thieu regime in Saigon, so that, by its own standards, the White House could claim upon conclusion of the Paris peace agreements in January 1973 to have achieved "an honorable ending to a long and costly effort."[72]

But were the means chosen appropriate to the ends sought—self-assurance at home and respect abroad? Measurements of such intangibles will always be imprecise; still there is reason to question whether the methods Nixon and Kissinger used to ward off defeat and humiliation in Vietnam did not bring about some of the very consequences they had sought to prevent. Despite evidence of the obviously corrosive effect it had had on official credibility during the Johnson years, they continued to resort to, and even expanded, the use of deception to increase freedom of action. Hence, Nixon could publicly claim, in March 1970, that "we respect Cambodia's neutrality," when in fact he had a year earlier ordered the secret bombing of that country, and the falsification of military records to cover up the fact.[73] Later that year, he dispatched American ground troops into Cambodia to demonstrate, as he put it, that the United States was not a "pitiful helpless giant," but in the process set off not only unprecedented domestic disorders but also the first serious Congressional efforts to limit the President's war-making authority. Concern over the resulting challenge to presidential power provoked Nixon into sanctioning the wire-taps and break-ins that led to Watergate;* that event in turn produced an erosion of presidential power that not only made it difficult to implement linkage or to rearm in the face of the Soviet military buildup, but also made it impossible for the Ford administration to honor Nixon's pledge to save South Vietnam if the cease-fire broke down, as it did in 1975.

One might well wonder whether all of this—along with the additional 20,553 American and unknown number of Vietnamese lives lost between 1969 and 1973[74]—was worth it to defend a concept of American "honor" thought to require the survival of a government in Saigon incapable of standing on its own, even after years of support. To be sure, that government's collapse in 1975 set off surprisingly little recrimination within the United States; there was no replay of the "who lost China" debates of a quarter century earlier, or alarm among American allies. This fact has been taken as a retrospective justification for the strategy of protracted withdrawal.[75] Still, one has the impression that those Nixon and Kissinger were trying to impress by remaining in Vietnam—the American public, allies overseas, certainly the Chinese, possibly even the Russians—would

---

* "In hindsight I can see that, once I realized the Vietnam war could not be ended quickly or easily and that I was going to be up against an anti-war movement that was able to dominate the media with its attitudes and values, I was sometimes drawn into the very frame of mind I so despised in the leaders of that movement. They increasingly came to justify almost anything in the name of forcing an immediate end to a war they considered unjustified and immoral. I was similarly driven to preserve the government's ability to conduct foreign policy and to conduct it in the way that I felt would best bring peace. I believed that national security was involved. I still believe it today, and in the same circumstances, I would act now as I did then. History will make the final judgment on the actions, reactions, and excesses of both sides; it is a judgment I do not fear." (*RN: The Memoirs of Richard Nixon* [New York: 1978], pp. 514–15.)

have reacted more with relief than chagrin had the official perception of "honor" permitted withdrawal at an earlier date, and at less expense. For "honor" must also be tempered, at least in the affairs of nations, by common sense: that quality is rarely enhanced, even in the eyes of sympathetic observers, by the passionate pursuit of untenable objectives at exorbitant costs.

Yet another aspect of the "amorality" argument was the charge that Nixon and Kissinger attached greater importance to stability and order in international relations than to the cause of "human rights." Curiously, this position found support on both the right and left wings of the American political spectrum.[76] Liberals could criticize the administration's close ties with authoritarian regimes in South Korea, the Philippines, Pakistan, Iran, Greece, Portugal, and, after 1973, Chile: it had acquiesced in the suppression of democratic procedures in those countries, the argument ran, because the United States needed their help to maintain the world balance of power against communism. Conservatives, conversely, could complain about the administration's reluctance to protest violations of human rights in the Soviet Union, Eastern Europe, and China: the cause of dissent in those countries, they claimed, had been sacrificed on the altar of détente.

There were elements of truth in both of these arguments. The Nixon administration—like all of its postwar predecessors—was clearly more tolerant of authoritarianism on the right than on the left. Such regimes ran no risks of becoming Soviet satellites; moreover, there persisted in Washington the belief that right-wing dictatorships were more likely to be reversible than those on the left.[77] As a consequence, the White House tended not to make an issue of the suppression of human rights in countries otherwise on the "correct" side in the Cold War. Nor was there an inclination to hold détente hostage to improvements in Moscow's treatment of its own people or its satellites, as was apparent in Kissinger's hostility to the Jackson amendment, Ford's decision, supported by Kissinger, not to receive the exiled Aleksandr Solzhenitsyn at the White House on the eve of the 1975 Helsinki Conference, and Kissinger's support—through the inadvertently publicized "Sonnenfeldt doctrine"*—of a more "organic"

* So called for Helmut Sonnenfeldt, counselor to the State Department and a close Kissinger adviser, who told a group of American ambassadors on what he thought was an off-the-record basis in London in December 1975 that "it must be our policy to strive for an evolution that makes the relationship between the Eastern Europeans and the Soviet Union an organic one. . . . [O]ur policy must be a policy of responding to the clearly visible aspirations in Eastern Europe for a more autonomous existence within the context of a strong Soviet geopolitical influence." (Summary of remarks, *New York Times*, April 6, 1976.)

relationship between Eastern Europe and the Soviet Union.[78] These were positions consistent with the administration's determination to stress interests over ideology in its diplomacy: "Our objective," Kissinger later recalled, "was to purge our foreign policy of all sentimentality."[79]

But an unsentimental foreign policy did not, in Kissinger's mind, necessarily imply an amoral one. There was in his thinking a surprisingly strong concern with the moral dimensions of world politics: his speeches on the subject as Secretary of State may well represent the most sustained official attempt since Woodrow Wilson to reconcile the competing claims of power and ideals.[80] Kissinger resolved the dilemma in a classic Niebuhrian sense (much as Kennan also had done years earlier): balance of power politics, he argued, were not inconsistent with moral principles, because ideals could hardly flourish under conditions of perpetual war or anarchy. Some minimal standard of order, achieved by manipulating power, was necessary before justice could be attained. "The true task of statesmanship," he suggested in 1975, "is to draw from the balance of power a more positive capacity to better the human condition—to turn stability into creativity, to transform the relaxation of tensions into a strengthening of freedom, to turn man's preoccupations from self-defense to human progress." Or, as he put it in his memoirs: "If history teaches anything it is that there can be no peace without equilibrium and no justice without restraint. But I believed equally that no nation could face or even define its choices without a moral compass that set a course through the ambiguities of reality and thus made sacrifices meaningful."[81]

There has been a perennial and probably unresolvable debate over the extent to which foreign policy should reflect moral principles. On the one hand, it has been argued, it is important for a nation to "stand" for something: an ideology based on shared aspirations can generate self-confidence, a sense of momentum, the conviction that "history" is on one's side. But ideologies, as Kissinger liked to warn, can also be dangerous: excessive preoccupation with them can lead to misperceptions of one's own or an adversary's power; it can also preclude agreements that might otherwise be in the mutual interests of both. There is little reason to doubt that the Nixon-Kissinger effort to "purge" foreign policy of "sentimentality" was carried out in the sincere belief that only on such a basis could agreements be reached that would reduce Cold War tensions. The issue, though—and the point upon which the "amorality" of Kissinger's diplomacy hinges—is this: did he carry that process so far as to undermine the ideological foundation necessary for the conduct of a self-confident and popularly supported foreign policy?

The very fact that the "amorality" issue had raised such widespread concern by 1976 would suggest that the answer was yes, regardless of whether that concern was based on logical analysis, political expediency, or emotional impulse. Despite conscientious efforts, Kissinger never succeeded in building the public consensus necessary to sustain his strategy of approaching "justice" by way of "order," of integrating human rights with the requirements of geopolitical stability. Kissinger himself had foreseen the difficulty in 1968: "equilibrium is not a purpose with which we can respond to the travail of our world."[82] Still, the claims of "justice" had not figured prominently in the priorities of previous postwar administrations that had had to cope with less "orderly" international environments. It is, in a way, a tribute to Kissinger, and to the presidents he served, that they succeeded, however briefly, in imparting enough "order" to world affairs that the American people could indulge in the unaccustomed luxury of applying to them the standards of "justice."

V

Henry Kissinger largely succeeded in his goal of imparting intellectual coherence to the conduct of American foreign policy. As a result, the United States moved, during the first years of the Nixon administration, from self-destructive entanglement in an interminable war to emergence as the pivot in the triangular balance of power that, for the most part, shaped the course of world affairs at that time. Rarely has a nation executed a more impressive or rapid shift from defeat to dominance. The achievement proved impossible to sustain, though, because it required insulating the policy-making process from those who by law, tradition, or operational necessity had come to have influence over it. Aware of the problem, Kissinger made a valiant effort to convince Congress, the bureaucracy, and the public of the rationale behind his policy, but he never entirely succeeded. In the end, the system he created, like those of Metternich, Castlereagh, and Bismarck that he had written about—and like Kennan's as well—depended upon the unlikely coincidence of strategic vision with decisive authority. History, as Kissinger would have been the first to acknowledge, does not tolerate such coincidences for very long.

Reagan, Gorbachev, and the Completion of Containment

By the time Henry Kissinger stepped down as Secretary of State with the departure of the Ford administration from office in January 1977, the limits of both symmetrical and asymmetrical containment had become clear.

Symmetry offered protection against incremental threats, against the danger that peripheral challenges to the balance of power might become major ones, if not in fact, then psychologically, which amounted to the same thing. It made available multiple levels of response, affording policymakers choices wider than those of escalation or humiliation. But it also involved letting adversaries select the nature and location of competition, and that, for the nation on the defensive, required virtually unlimited resources. Despite expansionist economic theory, the United States never generated either the capabilities or the will that would have been necessary to support symmetrical containment over an extended period of time. Attempts to do so, as in Korea and Vietnam, had only led to frustration, disillusionment, and exhaustion. One might, in such situations, win battles—even that was not always assured—but one could as well, in doing so, lose the war.

Asymmetry recognized the reality of limited resources, stressing the need to pick and choose the manner of one's response, lest wars in fact be lost while winning battles. It concentrated less on a multiplicity of options than on a variety of means, emphasizing the need to act in circumstances, at times, and in ways that would apply one's strengths against adversary weaknesses. It retained, thereby, the initiative, but often at the price of yielding positions not easily defended, or of expanding the confrontation to exploit new positions that could be. It required, as a result, steady nerves: one had to distinguish rationally, even cold-bloodedly, between peripheral and vital interests, tolerable and intolerable threats, feasible and unfeasible responses. There was little protection against the emergence of psychological insecurities or the invocation of moral principles, neither of which could be disregarded in a democracy. It was difficult enough to maintain one's balance when walking a tightrope, as Kennan had once suggested;[1] all the more so when critics, whatever their reasons, had chosen to shake it at both ends.

The obvious solution would have been to devise some new strategy of containment, neither symmetrical nor asymmetrical in character, drawing upon the strengths of each approach while rejecting their weaknesses. Jimmy Carter, Ford's successor as president, sought to do just this and failed. Ronald Reagan, Carter's successor, attempted the same feat, and succeeded beyond all expectations. As a result, Reagan's successor, George H. W. Bush, inherited a world in which the threat containment was meant to contain no longer existed. By the time he left office, neither did the country that had posed that threat through over four decades of Cold War.

I

Jimmy Carter entered the White House in 1977 determined to reverse the preoccupation with containment that had dominated American foreign policy for so many years. The time had come, he insisted, to move beyond the belief "that Soviet expansion was almost inevitable but that it must be contained," beyond "that inordinate fear of communism which once led us to embrace any dictator who joined us in that fear," beyond the tendency "to adopt the flawed and erroneous principles and tactics of our adversaries, sometimes abandoning our own values for theirs," beyond the "crisis of confidence" produced by Vietnam and "made even more grave by the covert pessimism of some of our leaders." "It is a new world," Carter argued, "but America should not fear it. It is a new world, and we should help to shape it. It is a new world that calls for a new American foreign policy—a policy based on constant decency in its values and on optimism in our historical vision."[2]

And yet, less than three years later, Carter was describing the state of Soviet-American relations as "the most critical factor in determining whether the world will live in peace or be engulfed in global conflict," praising past efforts at containment, calling for steps toward reconstituting the military draft and lifting "unwarranted restraints" on intelligence collection capabilities, increasing defense spending by 5 percent annually, expressing a determination to make the Russians "pay a concrete price for their aggression," and even proclaiming his own "Carter doctrine": that "any attempt by any outside force to gain control of the Persian Gulf region will be regarded as an assault on the vital interests of the United States of America, and such an assault will be repelled by any means necessary, including military force."[3] Reports of containment's demise, it appeared, had been somewhat premature.

Much can happen in three years: it would not be the first time an administration had been forced, within so brief a period, to rethink its most fundamental geopolitical assumptions. But when the Truman administration did this in 1950, it was moving from an asymmetrical approach to containment—Kennan's—to a symmetrical one—NSC-68. The Carter administration, in contrast, had difficulty aligning itself with either tradition, or indeed with any coherent conception of American interests in the world, potential threats to them, or feasible responses. The reasons included disagreements among Carter's advisers, growing out of an unusual interaction of domestic politics, clashing personalities, and external circumstances, together with the President's inability to resolve them. But there was also increasing evidence that neither symmetry nor asymmetry provided a satisfactory method of containment any longer, and that that strategy, if it was to survive, was at last going to have to evolve into something new.

All incoming administrations try to distinguish themselves from their predecessors, but Carter's determination to do so was particularly striking. Whether one looks at his emphasis on human rights and morality, on openness and de-centralization, on solidifying relations with allies and neutrals, on giving up linkage as a means of modifying Soviet behavior, or on removing the U.S.S.R. from the privileged position it had long occupied as the central obsession of American foreign policy, one senses an almost desperate effort to establish a distinctive identity, to escape the lengthy and intimidating shadow of Henry Kissinger.[4]

One explanation, curiously, was that Carter had so few differences of substance with Kissinger's policies. There was no effort to revive the last Democratic administration's commitment to symmetrical response—to return to the view that all interests were vital, all threats were dangerous, and all means were available to counter them. Instead, Carter retained the Republicans' asymmetrical approach of differentiating between vital and peripheral interests, of distinguishing between levels of threat, and of keeping responses commensurate with means. He continued Kissinger's practice of working with some communists to contain others. Nor did the new administration question the importance of negotiations with the Russians, especially on the control of strategic arms. Even its ostentatious abandonment of linkage[5] was less of a departure from past practice than it initially seemed: Kissinger himself had concluded, early in 1976, that SALT was too important to be used as a bargaining chip.[6] In terms of methods, then, the continuities were considerable.

Appearances, however, were quite another matter. Carter and his advisers developed no new strategy, but they did graft onto the basic premises of the old one certain highly visible initiatives designed to make it *seem* as though the American approach to the world had changed. Some of this was simple one-upmanship; some of it was also an effort to build domestic support for détente, which Kissinger had never managed to do. The resulting fusion of surface innovation with subsurface continuity gave rise to such confusion, however, that the image the Carter administration in fact conveyed, at least in its dealings with the Soviet Union, was that of having no strategy at all.

The most obvious example came with regard to human rights, the issue Carter had focused on during the campaign as a way of distinguishing his own policies from those of Nixon, Ford, and Kissinger. The President's personal commitment to this cause was not in doubt;[7] still, there were compelling political reasons for making it a priority, providing as it did a way to win the support of critics on the Right who had objected to Kissinger's "appeasement" of the Soviet Union, and those on the Left who had worried about his "amorality." Carter chose to do this, however, at just the moment his negotiators were trying to persuade the Russians to make deep cuts in the SALT II limits on strategic weapons—cuts that would have benefited the United States disproportionately.[8] Kremlin leaders could hardly have been expected to accept such a deal without the sense that they could trust the new administration in Washington. "Whether Carter meant it or not," the long-time Soviet ambassador to the United States Anatoly Dobrynin later recalled, "his policy was based on linking détente to the domestic situation in the Soviet Union. This represented an abrupt departure from the policy followed by preceding administrations, inevitably making his relations with Moscow tense."[9]

Carter's simultaneous pursuit of contradictory policies had to do, in part, with who he was: he prided himself on being both a moralist and an engineer, a combination conducive to self-confidence, to be sure, but also to a certain fascination with technical and ultimate questions that left little room for the realm of strategy that lay in between.[10] As a result, the new President failed to align his moral and domestic political commitment to human rights with his geopolitical and (given the alternative) humane determination to achieve arms control. He thought he could embrace the cause of dissidents in the Soviet Union, with all that implied in terms of interfering in the internal affairs of that country, and still continue "business as usual" on other issues. It did no good to abandon linkage publicly in an effort to rationalize this approach, because Moscow was certainly prepared to link the issues of arms control and human rights, even if Washington was not.

Nor were Carter's advisers helpful in clarifying priorities. His national security adviser, Zbigniew Brzezinski, had an academic background similar to Kissinger's; conceptually, though, the two could hardly have been more different. Kissinger had articulated a consistent view of international affairs: one could read *A World Restored* (published in 1957) and find in it a generally reliable guide to the policies he would seek to implement a decade and a half later. Brzezinski's writings showed no such depth. There was instead, as one critic put it, an "enduring penchant for fashionable issues and concepts that are adopted or discarded in the light of changing circumstances, . . . an unbecoming reliance on the intellectual cliché of the moment."[11] Once installed as national security adviser, Brzezinski by his own account sought inconsistent objectives: to put the Soviet Union "ideologically on the defensive" with respect to human rights, to "promote a more comprehensive and more reciprocal détente," and to "move away from what I considered our excessive preoccupation with the U.S.-Soviet relationship."[12] The premise seemed to be that one could reform, negotiate with, and ignore the U.S.S.R., all at the same time.

Carter's Secretary of State, Cyrus Vance, sought a more straightforward approach. A New York lawyer with extensive Washington experience during the Kennedy and Johnson administrations, Vance saw his chief task as one of negotiating with the Russians to lower the risks of nuclear war, to avoid the distractions and dangers of "third world" conflicts, and to build a stable long-term superpower relationship. He distrusted the "globalist" perspective that saw all interests and threats as interconnected; he disliked linking progress in one set of negotiations to what was happening in others; and while sympathetic to the cause of human rights, he was disinclined to make it the predominant standard by which relations between Washington and Moscow were to be conducted.[13]

It did not take long for Vance and Brzezinski to get at odds with one another, or for the tension between them to be reflected in the administration's public pronouncements on Soviet-American relations. The clearest example came on June 7, 1978, in a speech that Carter largely wrote himself for delivery at the U.S. Naval Academy. It was, as one historian has put it, "so disjunctive in its combined reaffirmation of détente and articulation of a confrontational strategy that the general reaction was perplexity."[14] Jokes abounded that the President had simply stapled together drafts by Brzezinski and Vance. For Dobrynin, the absence of any "solid and consistent direction" in Carter's policy evoked an image from Russian literature: Ivan Krylov's fable about a cart ineffectively pulled by "a swan, a pike, and a crayfish."[15]

The problem with trying to sustain Kissinger's strategy while placating his critics was that the former Secretary of State and his adversaries had held mutually exclusive views of the U.S.S.R. Kissinger had seen it as a state with which reasonable accommodations could be worked out, given firmness and patience on the American side, while his critics regarded it as an aggressive and immoral power with which the United States could not deal on any basis other than resistance. One could not embrace one position without rejecting the other; and yet, this was precisely the choice Carter hoped to avoid making. As a result, he never developed a sense of priorities—a clear idea of what to do first, what to postpone, and what not to attempt at all. "At least for me," he later acknowledged, "it was natural to move on many fronts at once."[16] Policy-makers must almost always choose between praiseworthy but incompatible objectives. The Carter administration was singularly ill-equipped to do so.

Internal disarray, however, was not the only difficulty the Carter administration faced. It had the misfortune to come into office as the Soviet Union was launching a new series of challenges to the global balance of power, but also at a time when the United States faced unusual constraints in trying to counter them. Solving these problems would have taxed the skills of even the best organized and most consistent of administrations. Carter did not handle these challenges particularly well; still, given their complexity and intractability, one wonders how well others might have done.

There had long been speculation as to whether the Soviet Union's emergence as a full-fledged military rival of the United States would make it easier or more difficult to deal with.[17] One school of thought had held that parity would induce self-assurance, a sense of restraint, and a willingness to negotiate on the part of Kremlin leaders. Another had insisted that parity would bring arrogance, aggressiveness, contempt for Western weakness, and a determination to exploit this condition where it could be done without the risk of war. Carter saw both theories proven at least partially right during his term in office. Despite his human rights campaign, the Russians continued serious talks on limiting strategic arms, making in the course of them a surprising number of concessions to the Americans.[18] But they also chose, during these years, to deploy a new generation of SS-20 intermediate-range missiles in Europe, to provide military assistance to Marxist regimes in Angola and Ethiopia, and most disturbingly, in December 1979, to invade Afghanistan.

It is clear now that these were the terminal excesses of a declining empire, but they did not seem so at the time. The Brezhnev regime, it appeared, had taken the American defeat in Vietnam as a signal to seek opportunities elsewhere in the "third world"—an accurate enough assessment, Soviet sources now confirm.[19] Quite independently, the United States had suffered major setbacks with the overthrow of its long-time client, the Shah of Iran, in January 1979, the coming to power of the Sandinista government in Nicaragua in July, and the seizure of American hostages in Tehran in November. The Soviet invasion of Afghanistan, therefore, was only the most dramatic of a series of humiliations for the United States that were raising questions about whether any form of containment—symmetrical or asymmetrical—could reverse a tide of history that seemed to be flowing in a decidedly unfavorable direction.

Compounding these difficulties were constraints unprecedented in the postwar era on the American ability to act in world affairs. These included the effects of a post-Vietnam conviction on the part of much of the foreign policy "establishment" that there were few if any occasions upon which the United States might legitimately use force.[20] Another problem was the debilitating impact of inflation, a continuing and corrosive legacy of the Vietnam War, exacerbated by a growing dependence on Middle East oil that further limited the nation's capacity to act.

It is not surprising, then, that divided counsels should have existed inside the Carter administration, with Brzezinski and the National Security Council staff favoring a hard line toward the Russians even if it meant delaying SALT II, but with Vance, the State Department, and the arms control community emphasizing continued negotiations, on the theory that the Russians would eventually overextend and defeat themselves in the "third world." Afghanistan settled this debate: that first use of Red Army troops outside the Soviet Union and Eastern Europe since the end of World War II left the administration little choice but to withdraw the

SALT II treaty from the Senate, and to call a halt, for the time being, to any further steps in the direction of détente.

Those who listened to the President's forceful "Carter doctrine" speech on January 23, 1980, might well have concluded that Afghanistan had shocked his administration into embracing the undifferentiated view of interests and threats that was characteristic of symmetrical response. But Carter gave no hint of how the nation could generate the means necessary to sustain such a strategy in an era of energy dependency and double-digit inflation. The difficulties the White House had in rallying support for its new tough line, what with widespread opposition to draft registration, grain and technology embargoes, and even its boycott of the Moscow Olympics, reflected not only a crisis of leadership at the top but a resistance to being led from below that, even in a more disciplined administration than Carter's, would not have boded well for a coherent grand strategy, much less an effective one.

II

Because the Carter strategy—such as it was—failed to fit within the Cold War categories of symmetrical or asymmetrical containment, it is difficult to claim that the outcome of the 1980 election was an endorsement or a repudiation of either approach. What it did confirm was a growing sense of alarm: the Soviet Union, it seemed, was on a roll; the United States appeared to be in retreat, if not actual decline. Dissatisfaction with existing policy was at least as strong as it had been in 1952, 1960, 1968, and 1976, which meant that Ronald Reagan's decisive victory was a mandate to reverse course and reassert American strength. What that implied for the strategy of containment, however, was not at all clear.

The greatest uncertainty had to do with the man who took office on January 20, 1981. Reagan was the first major American politician—though not the last—to have begun his career as a film and television star. He had gained political prominence as a Barry Goldwater conservative, as governor of California from 1967 to 1975, and as a presidential contender during the 1968 and 1976 campaigns. He had been as critical of Republican as of Democratic approaches to containment, having almost derailed Ford's nomination in 1976 by condemning the alleged amorality of Kissinger's policies, but having also accused Carter, in 1980, of allowing moral concerns to inhibit the use of American power. Only one thing seemed obvious at the time of Reagan's inaugural: détente was dead, buried, and in the new administration at least not mourned. As the new President himself had admitted to a radio audience three years earlier, "I didn't exactly tear my hair and go into a panic at the possibility of losing détente."[21]

For years intellectuals, journalists, and political opponents derided Reagan as a telegenic lightweight, too simple-minded to know what containment had been about, much less to have had constructive ideas about how to ensure its success. It is true that Reagan relied more on instincts than on systematic study in shaping his positions: in this, he differed conspicuously from Carter. Derived from his Midwestern upbringing, his experiences in Hollywood, and an occasional tendency to conflate movies with reality, those instincts included an unshakable belief in democracy and capitalism, an abhorrence of communism, an impatience with compromise in what he regarded as a contest between good and evil, and—very significantly—a deep fear that the Cold War might end in a nuclear holocaust, thereby confirming the Biblical prophecy of Armageddon.[22] This was, to say the least, an unorthodox preparation for the presidency. When combined with the fact that Reagan took office as the oldest elected chief executive—he turned seventy shortly after his inauguration—it seemed reasonable to expect an amiable geriatric who would for the most part follow the lead of his own advisers.

That expectation turned out to be wrong on several counts. First, it overlooked the skill with which Reagan had managed his pre-presidential career: it was no small matter to have shifted the Republican Party to the right while centrist Republican presidents—Nixon and Ford—were occupying the White House.[23] Second, it failed to take into account Reagan's artful artlessness: his habit of *appearing* to know less than his critics did, of *seeming* to be adrift even as he proceeded quietly toward destinations he himself had chosen.[24] Third, it neglected what Reagan himself had said in hundreds of radio scripts and speech drafts prepared between 1975 and 1980: these almost daily commentaries, composed in longhand on legal pads without the assistance of speechwriters, provided a more voluminous record of positions taken on national and international issues than had been available for any other modern presidential aspirant.[25] They put forward no comprehensive strategy for ending the Cold War. That would emerge only gradually, in response to what happened after Reagan entered the White House. These broadcasts and speeches did, however, contain most of the ideas that lay behind that strategy—and they establish that the ideas largely came from Reagan himself.

The one most obvious at the time was optimism: faith in the ability of the United States to compete successfully within the international system. One would have to go back to Roosevelt in 1933 to find a president who entered office with comparable self-confidence in the face of bleak prospects. Like F.D.R., Reagan believed that the nation was stronger than it realized, that time was on its side, and that these facts could be conveyed, through rhetoric, style, and bearing, to the American people. "[I]t is important every once and a while to remind ourselves of our accomplishments . . . *lest* we let someone talk us into throwing out the baby with the bathwater," he told his radio audience in 1976. "[T]he system has never let us down—we've let the system down now & then because we're only human."[26]

It followed from this that the Soviet Union was weaker than it appeared to be, and that time was not on its side: Reagan had insisted as early as 1975 that communism was "a temporary aberration which will one day disappear from the earth because it is contrary to human nature."[27] This too was an unusual posture for an incoming president. The fundamental premise of containment had always been that the United States was acting *defensively* against an adversary that was on the offensive, and was likely to continue on that path for the foreseeable future. Now, just at the moment when the U.S.S.R. seemed to be pushing for superiority in strategic weaponry as well as influence on a global scale, Reagan rejected that premise, raising the prospect of regaining and indefinitely sustaining American preeminence.

He did so by assuming expandable resources on the part of the United States, a view consistent with NSC-68, which Reagan read and discussed on the air shortly after it was declassified in 1975. He concluded, as he later recalled, that "capitalism had given us a powerful weapon in our battle against Communism—*money*. The Russians could never win the arms race; we could outspend them forever."[28] Meanwhile, the Soviet Union was denying its people "all kinds of consumer products" in its quest for military supremacy. "We could have an unexpected ally," he noted in 1977, "if citizen Ivan is becoming discontented enough to start talking back."[29] After becoming president, Reagan quickly became convinced, on the basis of intelligence reports, that the Soviet economy "was a basket case, partly because of massive spending on armaments. . . . I wondered how we as a nation could use these cracks in the Soviet system to accelerate the process of collapse."[30]

The Soviet Union was also vulnerable, Reagan insisted, within the realm of ideas. Despite his support for the Committee on the Present Danger, founded by Paul Nitze in 1976 to warn of the Soviet military buildup,* Reagan had never accepted the assumption that armaments alone could make the U.S.S.R. an effective competitor with the United States. Moscow's failure to respect human rights, he maintained, was a serious weakness, even in a military superpower. Although Reagan had opposed the Helsinki Conference, which he regarded—shortsightedly—as having ratified Soviet control over Eastern Europe, by 1979 he was acknowledging that "something [is] going on behind the Iron Curtain that we've been ignoring and [that offers] hope for all mankind. . . . [A] little less détente . . . and more encouragement to the dissidents might be worth a lot of armored divisions."[31]

Mutual Assured Destruction, however, had to go. Unlike all previous presidents dating back to Kennedy, Reagan refused to accept the proposition that a nuclear balance of terror could ever lead to a stable international system: it was "the craziest thing I ever heard of."[32] The SALT process, geared as it was toward reinforcing MAD, was flawed because it did nothing to reverse reliance on nuclear weapons or to diminish the risks that their continued existence in such vast numbers entailed. "I have repeatedly stated that I would be willing to negotiate an honest, verifiable reduction in nuclear weapons . . . to the point that neither of us represented a threat to the other," Reagan wrote in a 1980 speech draft. "I cannot, however, agree to a treaty—specifically the Salt II treaty, which, in effect, legitimizes a nuclear arms buildup."[33]

The problem with détente was not that it had encouraged negotiations with the U.S.S.R., but rather that it had done so without enlisting American strengths: the idea had been to "seek agreements just for the sake of having an agreement." The Russians had to understand that "we are . . . building up our defense capability pending an agreement by both sides to limit various kinds of weapons." But "if we have the will & the determination to build a deterrent capability . . . we can have real peace. . . . [T]he men in the Kremlin could in the face of such determination decide that true arms limitation makes sense."[34] In Reagan's view, then, *rejecting* détente was the way to reduce the danger of nuclear war and move toward a negotiated settlement of Cold War differences.

Such a settlement would require, however, a fundamental change in the

---

*The Committee on the Present Danger took its name from an earlier organization that had been formed in 1950 to lobby for the implementation of NSC-68. See Paul H. Nitze, with Ann M. Smith and Steven L. Rearden, *From Hiroshima to Glasnost: At the Center of Decision: A Memoir* (New York: 1989), pp. 353–54; also Jerry W. Sanders, *Peddlers of Crisis: The Committee on the Present Danger and the Politics of Containment* (Boston: 1983).

nature of the Soviet Union itself. This had been the long-term objective of containment since Kennan first articulated that strategy; but as the nuclear danger had grown, the American interest in encouraging reform within the U.S.S.R. had receded—until the Carter administration made the promotion of human rights there one of its chief priorities.[35] Carter, however, had sought to do this while preserving détente, a futile endeavor because one could hardly challenge a state's internal makeup while simultaneously soliciting its cooperation within the international arena. For Reagan, reforming the Soviet Union required abandoning détente. "Our foreign policy should be to show by example the greatness of our system and the strength of American ideals," he wrote in August 1980. "[W]e would like nothing better than to see the Russian people living in freedom & dignity instead of being trapped in a backwash of history *as they are.*"[36]

Reagan was, then, no lightweight. He came into office with a clear set of ideas, developed for the most part on his own, on how to salvage the strategy of containment by returning to the objective Kennan had set for it in 1947: "to increase enormously the strains under which Soviet policy must operate, to force upon the Kremlin a far greater degree of moderation and circumspection than it has had to observe in recent years, and in this way to promote tendencies which must eventually find their outlet in either the break-up or the gradual mellowing of Soviet power."[37] Reagan would do this, not by acknowledging the current Soviet regime's legitimacy but by challenging it; not by seeking parity in the arms race but by regaining superiority; not by compromising on the issue of human rights but by capitalizing on it as a weapon more powerful than anything that existed in the military arsenals of either side. "The Reagan I observed may have been no master of detail," Soviet Ambassador Dobrynin later observed, "but he had a clear sense of what he wanted."[38]

III

Like earlier strategies of containment, Reagan's was not fully formed when he entered the White House. He was determined to distance himself, as several of his predecessors had sought to do, from what he regarded as the discredited policies of a defeated incumbent. He was unusual, however, in that he rejected the legacies of earlier administrations as well, including those of his fellow Republicans Nixon and Ford. The new President also departed from precedent by relying on no principal adviser to help shape and articulate his strategy. Despite the presence of heavyweights like

Alexander Haig and George Shultz in the State Department, Caspar Weinberger in the Defense Department, and William Casey in the Central Intelligence Agency, no one in Reagan's administration wielded the influence that Kennan, Nitze, Dulles, Rostow, Kissinger, and Brzezinski had had within the administrations they served: Shultz would come closest, but only in Reagan's second term. The fact that Reagan went through *six* national security advisers—Richard Allen, William Clark, Robert McFarlane, John Poindexter, Frank Carlucci, and Colin Powell—suggests the extent to which he was, in the end, his own chief strategist. It was obvious, Dobrynin concluded after his first long conversation with the President, "that Reagan was the real boss."[39]

Reagan's objective was straightforward, if daunting: to prepare the way for a new kind of Soviet leader by pushing the old Soviet system to the breaking point. Kennan, Nitze, and other early strategists of containment had always held out the possibility that Moscow might someday acknowledge the failures of Marxism-Leninism and the futility of Russian imperialism—the two foundations upon which the Soviet state had been constructed.[40] But neither symmetrical nor asymmetrical containment had produced anything like that result, and by the time Reagan took office early in 1981 the apparent strength and actual behavior of the U.S.S.R. made the prospect seem very distant indeed. It was not at all clear then that the Soviet economy was approaching bankruptcy, that Afghanistan would become Moscow's Vietnam, that the appearance of a Polish labor union called Solidarity portended the end of communism in Eastern Europe, or that the U.S.S.R. itself would disappear in just over a decade.

The strategy Reagan developed over the next several years did not cause these things to happen. They resulted from structural tensions that had been building within the Soviet Union and its satellites for many years. Even if Carter had been re-elected in 1980, they would at some point have produced a crisis. Whether it would have come as quickly or with such decisive results, though, is another matter. For however Carter's policies may have appeared from Moscow's perspective, no administration prior to Reagan's had deliberately sought to exploit those tensions with a view to destabilizing the Kremlin leadership and accelerating the decline of the regime it ran.

All previous shifts between symmetrical and asymmetrical containment had taken place in response to what presidents and their advisers thought the *American* system could stand. Thus, Truman was moving even before Korea toward a reorientation of strategy on the basis of claims that the economy could tolerate large increases in the defense budget without setting off inflation. Eisenhower's rejection of those arguments, together with his concerns about the political costs of limited wars, drove his administration back to asymmetry in the form of the New Look. Kennedy and Johnson embraced an expansionist economic philosophy without which their return to symmetrical response would not have been possible. Nixon, Ford, and Kissinger, recoiling from the excesses of Vietnam, reverted to asymmetry again. And one of the reasons Carter continued the substance, though not the appearance, of Kissinger's strategy was that the inflationary spiral set off by the last application of symmetrical response still persisted, ruling out further experimentation with that approach.

None of these shifts, however, had had much to do with what the *Soviet* system could stand. Even the Carter administration, which did challenge Moscow on the issue of human rights, refrained from any systematic effort to take advantage of internal weaknesses within the U.S.S.R. Its first presidential directive on national strategy, prepared in 1977, called attention to American technological, economic, and political strengths, while noting that "the Soviet Union continues to face major internal economic and national difficulties." It failed to build on this insight, though, recommending instead efforts to secure Moscow's cooperation in managing regional conflicts and achieving arms control agreements, as well as "involv[ing] the Soviet Union constructively in global activities, such as economic and social developments and peaceful non-strategic trade." Despite all that had happened by 1981, that strategy of seeking a partnership with the Brezhnev regime was still in place when Carter left office.[41]

The first Reagan directive on national strategy, in contrast, called explicitly, in May 1982, for efforts to force "the U.S.S.R. to bear the brunt of its economic shortcomings, and to encourage long-term liberalizing and nationalist tendencies within the Soviet Union and allied countries."[42] Three weeks later, in a speech to the members of the British Parliament, Reagan elaborated on what he had in mind. Karl Marx had been right, he pointed out, in predicting "a great revolutionary crisis . . . where the demands of the economic order are conflicting directly with those of the political order." This was happening, though, not in the capitalist world but in the Soviet Union, a country that "runs against the tide of history by denying human freedom and human dignity to its citizens." Nuclear superpower status provided no immunity from this great trend, for "[a]ny system is inherently unstable that has no peaceful means to legitimize its leaders." The West, therefore, should insist "that freedom is not the sole prerogative of a lucky few, but the inalienable and universal right of all human beings." What was needed was "a plan and a hope for the long term—the march of freedom and democracy that will leave Marxism-Leninism on the ash-heap of history."[43]*

No American president had ever before talked like this, and the effects were profoundly unsettling in Moscow. It had been difficult, Dobrynin later recalled, to imagine that anyone could be worse than Carter, "but it soon became clear that in ideology and propaganda Reagan [was] . . . far more threatening."[44] The new administration sought, in the words of National Security Decision Directive 75, completed in January 1983, "[t]o contain and over time reverse Soviet expansionism by competing effectively on a sustained basis with the Soviet Union in all international arenas."[45] The contest would range from buildups in nuclear and conventional weaponry through new and openly discussed war-fighting strategies, economic sanctions, the aggressive promotion of human rights, and overt and covert support for anti-Soviet resistance movements in Eastern Europe and Afghanistan as well as for opponents of Marxist regimes in Angola, Ethiopia, and Nicaragua. As Reagan's British Parliament speech made clear, the strategy would also include the vigorous employment of rhetoric as an instrument of psychological warfare, a trend which culminated in the President's March 1983 claim that the Soviet Union was "the focus of evil in the modern world."[46]

All of this came at a time when the domestic strains that had long been building within the U.S.S.R. had converged to produce a stagnant economy, environmental degradation, the beginnings of social unrest, and—remarkably for an advanced industrial society—declining life expectancy. Soviet military expenditures, meanwhile, were now consuming between 15 and 20 percent of gross domestic product; the comparable figure for the United States, through the last half of the 1970's, had averaged slightly under 5 percent.[47] The aging Kremlin leadership, burdened by both ideological and biological senescence, could only respond autistically to these developments, a trend that continued even after Brezhnev's death in November 1982, when the Politburo appointed successors, Yuri Andropov and Konstantin Chernenko, who were themselves approaching their deathbeds.[48] Reagan had, in this sense, picked a good time to push.

Pushing, however, still carried risks. Reagan could hardly dismantle détente and exploit Soviet vulnerabilities without reviving fears of nuclear

---

*The historian Richard Pipes, then serving on the National Security Council staff, played a significant role in shaping the drafting of these documents. (Richard Pipes, Vixi: Memoirs of a Non-Belonger [New Haven: 2003], pp. 197–200.)

war. This is indeed what happened during the first two years of his administration, a period that seemed at the time—and still seems—the most
dangerous one in Soviet-American relations since the Cuban missile crisis.
Some of these fears resulted from the collapse of arms control negotiations, despite Reagan's willingness to abide by the numerical limits of the
unratified SALT II treaty. Some arose from rhetorical excesses on the part
of Reagan's subordinates, notably the official who immortalized himself by
extending the assurance that with "enough shovels" to build backyard
bomb shelters, it should be possible to survive a nuclear attack. Some grew
out of protests in Europe against the forthcoming installation there of Pershing II and cruise missiles, NATO's response to the Soviet SS-20 deployment of the late 1970's. All of these fears were reflected in the campaign,
within the United States, for a "freeze" on the production, testing, and deployment of Soviet and American nuclear weapons, in Jonathan Schell's
best-selling 1982 book, *The Fate of the Earth*, a graphic account of the
physical and biological consequences of nuclear war, and in the equally explicit ABC television production, *The Day After*, which riveted a national
audience in the fall of 1983 with its portrayal of a nuclear attack on the
United States.[49]

What hardly anyone realized at the time was that Reagan also feared a
nuclear apocalypse—perhaps more deeply than most of his critics did. He
had warned, as early as 1976, of "horrible missiles of destruction that can,
in a matter of minutes, . . . destroy virtually the civilized world we live
in."[50] His rejection of Mutual Assured Destruction, and hence of the
SALT process, stemmed from a long-standing conviction that relying on
nuclear weapons to keep the peace was certain sooner or later to bring on
a nuclear war. Détente itself, he believed, had frozen the nuclear danger
in place, rather than doing anything to alleviate it. Soon after entering the
White House, he began promoting initiatives to reduce that threat: these
involved shifting SALT to START—from "strategic arms limitation talks"
to "strategic arms reduction talks"—as well as endorsing the then radical
idea of seeking an agreement with Moscow to phase out all intermediate-
range nuclear missiles in Europe. But because the very concept of arms
control as it had evolved over the past two decades had assumed that arms
reduction was impossible, these Reagan proposals were widely regarded
as efforts to kill rather than to advance progress toward eliminating the nuclear peril.[51] Then Reagan really shook up the arms control community,
the anti-nuclear protesters, the Russians, and most of his own advisers as
well.

The Strategic Defense Initiative, which the President announced on March 23, 1983, shattered orthodoxies on all sides. By endorsing a program to defend the United States against long-range nuclear missile attacks, Reagan called into question the 1972 Soviet-American treaty banning strategic defenses, a fundamental pillar of the SALT I agreements. In doing so, he denied the basic premise of Mutual Assured Destruction, which was that vulnerability could produce safety. He thereby reversed an American position on arms control dating back to the Kennedy administration. He raised the prospect of extending the arms race into outer space, a region hitherto off limits to it. He exploited an overwhelming American superiority in computer technology, precisely the field in which the Soviet Union would find it most difficult to keep up. But he also linked SDI to the goal of *lowering* the nuclear danger: missile defense, he insisted, could in time make nuclear weapons "impotent and obsolete."[52]

Reagan did not invent the idea of strategic missile defense. The United States and the Soviet Union had made efforts to develop such systems prior to the SALT I agreements, and the Anti-Ballistic Missile Treaty had even allowed limited deployments.[53] Technical problems caused the Pentagon to abandon these, however, so that only the concept remained alive through the end of the 1970's, especially at the Lawrence Livermore Nuclear Laboratory, where Edward Teller, the father of the American H-bomb, had strongly endorsed it. But it was nowhere near the mainstream of policy until Reagan placed it there—very much to the consternation of aides and allies. "I was completely taken by surprise," Paul Nitze, the chief White House arms control negotiator, later acknowledged. "I had no idea," Secretary of State Shultz recalled, "that anything regarding strategic defense was on the president's agenda." Secretary of Defense Weinberger immediately scrambled "to ensure that the announcement did not fall on totally astonished NATO ears."[54]

From an operational perspective, SDI was as remote from reality in 1983 as Khrushchev's claims of strategic missile superiority had been in the 1950's. Reagan's interest in the concept had grown more out of incredulity that the United States lacked the means of defending itself against a Soviet attack—and perhaps also out of movies and science fiction—than from an informed assessment of what might be technologically feasible.[55] Two decades later a workable system seems almost as far away as it did then. As grand strategy, though, SDI was a striking demonstration of killing multiple birds with a single stone: in one speech Reagan managed simultaneously to pre-empt the nuclear freeze movement, to raise the prospect of not just reducing but eliminating the need for nuclear weapons, to reassert American technological preeminence, and, by challenging the Soviet Union in an arena in which it had no hope of being able to compete, to create the strongest possible incentive for Soviet leaders to reconsider the reasons for competition in the first place. To reinforce that argument, he later proposed—in a gesture so unorthodox that virtually no one apart from himself took it seriously—to *share* the technology of SDI with the nation against whose weapons it was to be developed.[56]

Reagan had never ruled out the possibility of negotiations with Moscow, as long as they could be geared toward ending, not perpetuating, the Cold War. He had written to Brezhnev as early as April 1981—while recovering from a nearly fatal assassination attempt—to express his hope for a "meaningful and constructive dialogue which will assist us in fulfilling our joint obligation to find lasting peace."[57] His May 1982 national strategy directive had predicted that although the next few years "will likely pose the greatest challenge to our survival and well-being since World War II, . . . our response could result in a fundamentally different East-West relationship by the end of the decade."[58] He made it clear, in a quiet meeting with Secretary of State Shultz in February 1983—*before* the "evil empire" and SDI speeches—that he wanted to begin talking to the Russians, despite the reservations of his own staff.[59]* "Probably, people in the Soviet Union regard me as a crazy warmonger," he acknowledged shortly thereafter to Ambassador Dobrynin. "But I don't want a war between us, because I know it would bring countless disasters. We should make a fresh start."[60] He proposed, as a test of the possibilities, that the Soviet government facilitate the emigration, with no publicity, of a group of Pentecostals who had taken refuge in the American embassy in Moscow five years earlier and had not been allowed to leave. The release did occur, with minimal publicity, in July.[61]

None of this, however, reassured the new—but already mortally ill—Soviet leader, Yuri Andropov. He bitterly denounced SDI, claiming that the Americans were "devising one option after another in their search for best ways of unleashing nuclear war in the hope of winning it."[62] When the

---

* NSDD-75, which Reagan approved in January 1983, set out as a major objective of American strategy "[t]o engage the Soviet Union in negotiations to attempt to reach agreements which protect and enhance U.S. interests and which are consistent with the principle of strict reciprocity and mutual interest. This is important when the Soviet Union is in the midst of a process of political succession." (NSDD-75, "U.S. Relations with the U.S.S.R.," January 17, 1983, p. 1.)

Soviet air force shot down a civilian South Korean airliner over Sakhalin on September 1, having mistaken it for an American reconnaissance plane, he insisted that the incident had been a "sophisticated provocation, organized by the US special services."[63] And after the West German Bundestag voted, in November, to go ahead with the deployment of Pershing II and cruise missiles, Andropov ordered his negotiators to break off arms control talks altogether, leaving Soviet-American relations at their lowest point in years.

These public positions were not nearly as ominous, though, as the conviction that had taken hold within Andropov's mind that the Reagan administration was planning a nuclear first-strike against the U.S.S.R. While still KGB chief in 1981, Andropov had instructed Soviet intelligence agencies to undertake a world-wide effort aimed at detecting evidence of such planning. When none was found, they fabricated it rather than question the assumption that had led to the order in the first place.[64] That operation was still under way in November 1983, as the United States and its NATO allies began a major military exercise known as "Able-Archer 83." Such maneuvers had taken place in the past, but these had a higher level of participation by top officials and new communications procedures, all carefully monitored in Moscow. Primed by Andropov to assume the worst, Soviet intelligence concluded that Able-Archer might be a ruse to cloak preparations for an actual attack—in which case Soviet war plans called for launching a pre-emptive nuclear strike against the United States.[65]

Fortunately, the Able-Archer crisis ended peacefully, but it badly shook Reagan, who had the nuclear danger very much on his mind in the fall of 1983. He had previewed *The Day After*, and shortly thereafter—having postponed it several times—he received his first full Pentagon briefing on American nuclear war plans: "[T]here were still some people at the Pentagon who claimed a nuclear war was 'winnable,'" he later wrote. "I thought they were crazy. Worse, it appeared there were also Soviet generals who thought in terms of winning a nuclear war."[66] After a British spy in Moscow, Oleg Gordievsky, confirmed how close to war the Able-Archer crisis had come, Reagan resolved to take a new approach. He chose, once again, to make a speech, on January 16, 1984, this time not for the purpose of rattling the Kremlin leadership, but rather to reassure it. The most important passage was unmistakably his own:

> Just suppose with me for a moment that an Ivan and an Anya could find themselves, say, in a waiting room, or sharing a shelter from the rain or a storm with a Jim and Sally, and that there was no language barrier to keep

them from getting acquainted. Would they then deliberate the differences between their respective governments? Or would they find themselves comparing notes about their children and what each other did for a living? Before they parted company they would probably have touched on ambitions and hobbies and what they wanted for their children and the problems of making ends meet. And as they went their separate ways, maybe Anya would say to Ivan, "wasn't she nice, she also teaches music." Maybe Jim would be telling Sally what Ivan did or didn't like about his boss. They might even have decided that they were all going to get together for dinner some evening soon. Above all, they would have proven that people don't make wars.[67]

Within three weeks of this speech Andropov was dead. His feeble successor, Chernenko, maintained a hard line initially, but Reagan interpreted this as weakness: "maybe they are scared of us, and think we are a threat."[68]

In an effort to alleviate these anxieties, the President made a point, in September 1984, of inviting Soviet Foreign Minister Andrei Gromyko to a carefully prepared meeting at the White House. Three hours of arguments with "this frosty old Stalinist" convinced Reagan that he had achieved little: "If I scored any points, Gromyko didn't admit it to me. He was as hard as granite."[69] The President stuck to his strategy, though: his national security adviser, Robert McFarlane, assured Dobrynin in December that Reagan "believed that he had fulfilled the basic task of his presidency, which was to restore the potential of the American armed forces." Now it was time "to improve relations with the Soviet Union gradually and reach agreements on reducing nuclear arms."[70] When it became apparent that Weinberger and Casey were trying to get Shultz fired for seeking to reopen talks with the Russians, Reagan came down firmly on the Secretary of State's side: "George is carrying out my policy," he noted in his diary. "I'm going to meet with Cap and Bill and lay it out to them. Won't be fun, but it has to be done."[71]

Shultz's policy—following Reagan's lead—had one additional dimension, which was to wait for the Grim Reaper to complete his work in Moscow. "Sooner or later," he told the President in the summer of 1984, "the Soviets would have to face the hurdle of a generational turnover when the senior members of the Politburo retired or died and would be replaced by younger men who might have a significantly different outlook." These would be "post-World War II people. I suspect that ideology will be less of a living force for them, that they will believe more in technology and will look for policies that are genuinely effective. . . . It will pay dividends to treat them with civility, whatever our differences might be and to recognize the importance of their country."[72] Reagan needed no prompting to see the benefits of fresh leadership in the Kremlin. "How am I supposed to get anyplace with the Russians," he asked his wife, Nancy, after the news came of Chernenko's death on March 10, 1985, "if they keep dying on me?"[73]

IV

But they did not. The circumstances that produced Mikhail Gorbachev's appointment as General Secretary of the Communist Party of the Soviet Union on March 11 are, even now, not completely clear. What was apparent at the time, though, was that an important turning point had been reached. Gorbachev himself recalls telling his wife, Raisa, on the eve of his elevation, that "We can't go on living like this." He later acknowledged, as if to echo Reagan and Shultz: "The very system was dying away; its sluggish senile blood no longer contained any vital juices."[74] The Secretary of State, who attended Chernenko's funeral, saw the new leader's potential immediately: "Gorbachev," he told the press, "is totally different from any Soviet leader I've ever met."[75] Shultz's assessment still holds despite all that has happened since: Gorbachev was indeed the Kremlin leader for whom Reagan—and strategists of containment as far back as Kennan—had been waiting.

There were, in retrospect, three Soviet Unions during the era of détente. The one most visible from the outside was an ambitiously self-confident superpower whose global influence seemed to be growing at a time when that of the United States definitely was not. Since its invasion of Czechoslovakia in 1968, the U.S.S.R. had claimed the right, in what came to be known as the Brezhnev Doctrine, to intervene whenever "external and internal forces hostile to socialism try to turn the development of a given socialist country in the direction of the restoration of the capitalist system."[76] From within, however, the Soviet Union was a very different place. Socialism had burdened it with sclerotic leadership, a bloated and corrupt bureaucracy, an economy that diminished expectations, a dangerously unhealthy environment, and a political system that appeared to leave little if any room for dissent, fresh thinking, or prescriptions for change. Except that it did: there was a third and, at the time, almost invisible Soviet Union—but, for the history of containment, it turned out to be the most significant one.

It existed within the minds of a new generation of scientists, engineers, technicians, administrators, diplomats, intelligence analysts, lawyers, and teachers, all of whom had benefited from the heavy investment the Kremlin had made, during the 1950's and 1960's, in mass higher education. The purpose had been to strengthen the Soviet system in its competition with capitalism: Khrushchev had promised, after all, to overtake the West, not just in military capabilities but in the quality of everyday life, by 1980.[77] It is difficult to educate, however, without provoking curiosity. That quality, in turn, produces questioning, which leads to criticism, which if unanswered invites dissatisfaction with the status quo. In the United States and Western Europe, where the postwar era also saw a vast expansion of university education, the result was an open assault by youthful rebels on "establishments" of all kinds. In the U.S.S.R. the challenge was, necessarily, more discreet. It took place quietly within seminar rooms, walks in parks, kitchen table conversations that extended far into the night—and, most importantly, in the thinking of an emerging Soviet elite who had come to see, thanks to the education the system had provided them, that the system itself could not, in its existing form, survive.[78]

Gorbachev was the first member of that generation to reach the top in the Kremlin hierarchy. His presence there did not immediately improve Soviet-American relations: "Gorbachev will be as tough as any of their leaders," Reagan predicted in April 1985. "If he wasn't a confirmed ideologue, he never would have been chosen by the Politburo."[79] Soviet sources confirm, in turn, that Gorbachev was then, and remained for months to come, suspicious of Reagan.[80] But the new Kremlin leader—unlike his recent predecessors—was not so locked into ideology that he allowed it to close his eyes, ears, or mind. Exchanging messages with Brezhnev, Andropov, and Chernenko had been like conversing with robots, a frustrating experience for a president like Reagan who prided himself on his communications skills. Gorbachev, in contrast, was as unrobotic as it was possible to imagine, and Reagan was quick to sense the opportunity thereby provided. He had always intended for his strategy of confrontation to prepare the way for one of persuasion:* now the moment had come.

---

* NSDD-75 had concluded that "the U.S. must demonstrate credibly that its policy is not a blueprint for an open-ended, sterile confrontation with Moscow, but a serious search for a stable and constructive long-term basis for U.S.-Soviet relations." (NSDD-75, January 17, 1983, p. 9.)

The points of which he hoped to convince the skeptical but attentive Gorbachev boiled down to three:

First, *that the United States was sincere in seeking to lower the danger of nuclear war.* Reagan had long believed that "if I could ever get in a room alone with one of the top Soviet leaders, there was a chance the two of us could make some progress. . . . I have always placed a lot of faith in the simple power of human contact in solving problems."[81] It sounded naive, but when this finally happened—when Reagan actually did sit down across from Gorbachev, with only their interpreters present, at their first summit conference in Geneva on November 19, 1985—several interesting things occurred. One was that the meeting ran well beyond the time scheduled for it. Another was that an unscheduled meeting followed later in the day, at which the two leaders agreed to hold future summits in Washington and in Moscow. But the really big story, as Shultz recalled, was "that they had hit it off as human beings."[82] Despite vigorous disagreements on responsibility for the Cold War, human rights, regional conflicts, and especially SDI, Reagan found "something likeable about Gorbachev. There was warmth in his face and his style, not the coldness bordering on hatred I'd seen in most other senior Soviet leaders I'd met until then."[83] Gorbachev caught the mood as well: "something important happened to each of us on that day. . . . We both sensed that we must maintain contact and try to avoid a break."[84]

At one point during these conversations, Reagan suggested to Gorbachev that if there were no nuclear missiles, then there would be no need for defenses against them.[85] The President's desire to rid the world of all nuclear weapons—not just missiles—was nothing new: he had been talking about this for years, to the puzzlement of his aides, few of whom took him literally. Gorbachev did, though. In January 1986, no doubt with Reagan's Geneva comment in mind, he publicly proposed phasing out nuclear weapons and ballistic missiles by the year 2000. Most of Reagan's advisers dismissed this as a publicity stunt, and perhaps it was. But as one of Gorbachev's top aides noted at the time, the Soviet leader was "taking this 'risk' because, as he understands, it's no risk at all—because nobody would attack us even if we disarmed completely."[86] That was a big change from the fears that had beset Andropov and Chernenko: Reagan's reassurances at last were working. The President himself liked the Gorbachev proposal and wanted to go further: "Why wait until the end of the century for a world without nuclear weapons?" he asked Shultz. It was a good question, and it led the Secretary of State to conclude that, "utopian though his dream might be, the shared view of Reagan and Gorbachev on the desirability of eliminating nuclear weapons could move us toward the massive reductions in medium-range and strategic ballistic missiles that Reagan had proposed back in 1981 and 1982."[87]

The months that followed saw a top-level Soviet-American consensus begin to emerge in support of a proposition that, only a few years earlier, would have seemed improbable if not ludicrous: that it might indeed be possible to move, not just from the limitation to the reduction of strategic arms, but toward their *drastic* reduction, perhaps even *elimination*. It was Reagan who, by challenging the conventional wisdom of détente, the SALT process, and the concept of MAD that lay behind it, brought the United States around to this position. It was also he who persuaded Gorbachev—face-to-face in Geneva in front of a fireplace—that he meant what he said. And when Gorbachev claimed to share that vision, it was Reagan who reciprocated by assuming sincerity on the part of the Soviet leader, despite evidence to the contrary. Chance then intervened to reinforce this meeting of minds: the Chernobyl nuclear disaster of April 26, 1986, which contaminated large portions of Ukraine and Byelorussia, could hardly have been more effective in dramatizing a common nuclear danger. Reagan, by this time, did not need to be convinced. Gorbachev, however, was severely shaken by what had happened: what may have been opportunistic anti-nuclearism on his part now became much more serious.[88]

The next superpower summit, held at Reykjavik, Iceland, in October 1986, was the most astonishing one of the postwar era.[89] It had been hastily arranged to resolve a stalemate in negotiations on intermediate range missiles in Europe. To the surprise of Reagan and his advisers, though, Gorbachev arrived with far more sweeping proposals. Not only would he now accept Reagan's long-standing proposal to phase out such missiles altogether, he would also agree to a 50 percent cut in Soviet and American strategic weapons across the board, without insisting that British and French weapons be included in the count. This went well beyond any possibility of a publicity stunt, and the Americans responded quickly by offering to phase out all ballistic missiles within a decade in return for the right to deploy defenses against cruise missiles and bombers. Gorbachev countered by advancing his proposal for the abolition of all nuclear weapons to the year 1996. Reagan immediately jumped at this, and for a moment it appeared as though the leaders of the United States and the Soviet Union had agreed on a position that went beyond everyone's wildest dreams.*

It did not happen, though, because Gorbachev made his offer contingent upon banning the further development of SDI. Reagan, who saw SDI as necessary to ensure a safe transition to a non-nuclear world, refused to relinquish it. The summit broke up with angry words and anguished faces—but Gorbachev, collecting his wits prior to the inevitable press conference, resolved to "cool off and think it all over thoroughly. . . . [T]he merciless, often cynical and cheeky journalists. . . standing in front of me seemed to represent mankind waiting for its fate to be decided. At this moment I realized the true meaning of Reykjavik and knew what further course we had to follow." The summit, he announced, "[i]n spite of all its drama . . . is not a failure—it is a breakthrough, which allowed us for the first time to look over the horizon."[90] It was at Reykjavik, Dobrynin recalled, that "Gorbachev put away passion and decided that he could and would work with Reagan," that he was "a person capable of taking great decisions."[91] Reagan, who later admitted that "I was mad and showed it," also had second thoughts: "Despite a perception by some that the Reykjavik summit was a failure, I think history will show it was a major turning point in the quest for a safer and secure world."[92]

An agreement to phase out all nuclear weapons, had one been reached at Reykjavik, probably would not have held up. No one had thought through the implications for NATO strategy, which still relied upon nuclear "first-use" to counter Soviet conventional force superiority in Europe: "I felt as if there had been an earthquake beneath my feet," British Prime Minister Margaret Thatcher remembered.[93] Nor was it clear how such an agreement would affect the nuclear capabilities of France, China, India, or Israel, none of whose leaders were any more likely than Thatcher to accept, even as an aspiration, the idea of nuclear abolition. Still, the fact that the leaders of the United States and the Soviet Union had briefly done so was important. It paved the way for the Intermediate Nuclear Forces

---

*The American record of the Reykjavik conference quotes Reagan as follows: "The President [said that] ten years from now he would be a very old man. He and Gorbachev would come to Iceland, and each of them would bring the last nuclear missile from each country with them. Then they would give a tremendous party for the whole world. . . . The President . . . would be very old by then and Gorbachev would not recognize him. The President would say, 'Hello, Mikhail.' And Gorbachev would say, 'Ron, is it you?' And then they would destroy the last missile." (Tom Simons notes, Reagan-Gorbachev meeting, October 12, 1986, Executive Secretariat, NSC: Records, File 869075, Ronald Reagan Library. I am indebted to Matthew Ferraro for this document.)

Treaty, signed at the third Reagan-Gorbachev summit in Washington in December 1987, which did bring about the dismantling and destruction of an entire category of weapons, under the watchful eyes of witnesses from both sides. It created the basis for deep cuts in ICBMs, SLBMs, and bombers that would, by the end of the century, significantly reduce the number of nuclear weapons Russians and Americans had targeted at one another.* And it led Gorbachev, on his return to Moscow, to report to the Politburo in words that acknowledged Reagan's persuasiveness:

> In Washington, probably for the first time we clearly realized how much the human factor means in international politics. Before . . . we treated such personal contacts as simply meetings between representatives of opposed and irreconcilable systems. Reagan for us was merely the spokesman of the most conservative part of American capitalism and its military-industrial complex. But it turns out that politicians, including leaders of government if they are really responsible people, represent purely human concerns, interests, and the hopes of ordinary people—people who vote for them in elections and who associate their leaders' names and personal abilities with the country's image and patriotism. . . . In our age, it turns out, this has the biggest impact on political decisions. . . . And it was in Washington that we saw it so clearly for the first time.[94]

Gorbachev made a similar point when, on this visit, he met Kennan: "We in our country believe that a man may be the friend of another country and remain, at the same time, a loyal and devoted citizen of his own," the Soviet leader told the original strategist of containment. "[T]hat is the way we view you."[95]

The second point of which Reagan hoped to persuade Gorbachev was *that a command economy, when coupled with authoritarian politics, was a prescription for obsolescence in the modern world.* Reagan had argued this often in the past, most colorfully in May 1981, when he predicted that "[t]he West won't contain communism, it will transcend communism. It won't bother to . . . denounce it, it will dismiss it as some bizarre chapter in human history whose last pages are even now being written."[96] But he left it to Shultz—who had taught economics at Stanford—to put the case to the new Kremlin leader. The Secretary of State was eager to do so, convinced that the generational shift in Moscow had opened the way for fresh

---

*In 1985, the Soviet Union was estimated to have over 40,000 nuclear weapons, and the United States approximately 24,000. By 2002, these numbers were down to approximately 11,000 each for Russia and the United States. (National Resources Defense Council, "US-U.S.S.R./Russian Nuclear Stockpile, 1945–2002," at http://www.nrdc.org/nuclear/nudb/dafig 11.asp.)

thinking. What Gorbachev needed, he thought, was a tutorial on trends that "were already transforming the worlds of finance, manufacturing, politics, scientific research, diplomacy, indeed, everything." The conclusion would be that "[t]he Soviet Union would fall hopelessly and permanently behind the rest of the world in this new era unless it changed its economic and political system."[97]

Shultz began the seminar in Moscow in November 1985, just before the first Geneva summit. "Society is beginning to reorganize itself in profound ways," he told Gorbachev. "Closed and compartmented societies cannot take advantage of the information age. People must be free to express themselves, move around, emigrate and travel if they want to, challenge accepted ways without fear. . . . The Soviet economy will have to be radically changed to adapt to the new era." Gorbachev responded surprisingly well to this, joking that Shultz should take over the Soviet planning ministry "because you have more ideas than they have." Shultz's observations on economics had attracted his interest, Gorbachev told Dobrynin afterward. "On that subject, he would willingly talk with Shultz in the future."[98]

What Shultz was arguing, in effect, was that Soviet power was becoming monodimensional in an increasingly multidimensional world. "The Soviet Union is a superpower only because it is a nuclear and ballistic missile superpower," he told his own advisers early in 1986.[99] It made sense, then, to reduce Soviet and American capabilities in that particular area—as both Reagan and Gorbachev seemed to want to do—because the United States and its allies were so far ahead of the Soviet Union in all other areas. It was also important, though, to be certain that Gorbachev understood the failures of the Soviet system in these other areas, together with the need to correct them. The only way he would be able to do that, Shultz believed, would be to "change the Soviet system. So we need to keep trying to influence Gorbachev in that direction."[100]

Shultz's seminar resumed on his next trip to Moscow, in April 1987. This time he had pie charts ready estimating the global distribution of gross domestic product and international trade through the year 2000, projections not at all to the advantage of the U.S.S.R. "What drives this growth?" he asked, professorially. "Science and technology," Gorbachev responded. "Yes," Shultz acknowledged, "but hitched to an incentive-based, market-oriented economic system. . . . There was a time when a government could control its scientific establishment and be basically successful. No longer." Shultz went on to point out that Marxism had always stressed the distinction between capital and labor. "But that dichotomy is becoming obsolete because we have entered a world in which the truly important capital is human capital, what people know, how freely they exchange information and knowledge, and the intellectually creative product that emerges." "We should have more of this kind of talk," Gorbachev acknowledged.[101]

It would be too much to claim that Shultz's tutorials planted the idea of *perestroika* in Gorbachev's mind: the Soviet economy faced such severe problems by the mid-1980's that there was no real alternative to fundamental restructuring. What Shultz did do was to explain why this was the case, and to point the way toward possible solutions. The Soviet leader himself was soon acknowledging the need "to get rid of the force of habit in our thinking" while recognizing "a world of fundamental social shifts, of an all-embracing scientific and technological revolution, . . . of radical changes in information technology."[102] He admitted to Shultz, in April 1988, that he had thought a lot about "the charts you brought on what the world would look like in a few years," and had "consulted experts." If the trends projected in them continued, "our two countries have a lot of reason to cooperate."[103] A month later Reagan himself, with Gorbachev's approval, was standing beneath a huge bust of Lenin at Moscow State University, lecturing students on "a very different revolution that is taking place right now, quietly sweeping the globe without bloodshed or conflict. . . . It's been called the technological or information revolution, and as its emblem, one might take the tiny silicon chip, no bigger than a fingerprint."[104]

So just as Reagan had established common ground with Gorbachev on the dangers posed by nuclear weapons, Shultz managed something similar with respect to economic and technological issues. The idea, in both instances, was to bring the new Soviet leader around to the American way of thinking—and by doing so, to change the nature of the regime he led.

The Reagan administration's third objective was to persuade Gorbachev *that the Soviet Union had itself become, over the years, what it had originally sought to overthrow—an oppressive empire.* The principal instrument of persuasion here was the Reagan Doctrine: a plan to turn the forces of nationalism against the gains the Soviet Union had made in recent years in the "third world," and eventually against its sphere of influence in Eastern Europe itself. The idea echoed Kennan's predictions, from as early as 1947, that Stalin's determination to control communist parties beyond the boundaries of the U.S.S.R. might come across, in those regions, as a new form of imperialism which would, in time, generate local resistance.[105] Yugoslavia's defection from the Soviet bloc in 1948 and the rise of Sino-Soviet antagonism during the 1950's had proven him right; in the early 1970's Nixon and Kissinger capitalized on that latter development by playing the world's most populous communist state off against its most powerful communist state. They had remained pessimistic, however, about the possibility that nationalism might trump Marxism in Latin America, Africa, and Southeast Asia. They were slow to detect evidence, in the emergence of "Eurocommunism," that this had already begun to happen within the communist parties of Western Europe. And they saw few if any signs that resistance to Soviet authority in Eastern Europe might develop anytime soon: Kissinger himself went along reluctantly with the Helsinki Conference, and on balance preferred to stabilize rather than to try to upset the status quo in that part of the world. Political problems and economic stagnation would eventually bring about the collapse of the Soviet empire, he believed, but the way to hasten that process would be to delay a confrontation with the West, not to encourage one.[106]

By the end of the Carter administration the situation had changed. The expanding Soviet presence in southern and eastern Africa, the emergence of a Marxist regime in Nicaragua, the rise of Solidarity in Poland, and especially the invasion of Afghanistan suggested that the possibility might now exist to turn the tables on the Russians and begin portraying *them* as the new imperialists. Carter had created the basis for such an effort by authorizing overt and covert aid to anti-Soviet resistance movements in all of these regions; but since he had never given up the hope of reviving détente, he was wary of publicizing what he was doing.[107] The Reagan administration, which had fewer such inhibitions, expanded this assistance, and by early 1983 the shape of a strategy was beginning to emerge. There were, NSDD-75 pointed out, "a number of important weaknesses and vulnerabilities within the Soviet empire which the U.S. should exploit," by seeking "wherever possible to encourage Soviet allies to distance themselves from Moscow in foreign policy and to move toward democratization domestically."[108]

Reagan's use of the term "evil empire," in March 1983, was the first public hint of this strategy: he had chosen the phrase, he admitted, "with malice aforethought; I wanted to remind the Soviets [that] we knew what they were up to."[109] In October of that year he authorized an American occupation of Grenada, a small Caribbean republic in which the Cubans and the Russians had been seeking to establish a sympathetic government.[110]

By January 1985, Reagan was openly promising support to those "who are risking their lives—on every continent, from Afghanistan to Nicaragua—to defy Soviet-supported aggression and secure rights which have been ours from birth."[111] A month later Shultz elaborated publicly on what the Reagan Doctrine meant. "For many years," he noted, "we saw our adversaries act without restraint to back insurgencies around the world to spread communist dictatorships." In line with the "infamous" Brezhnev Doctrine, "any victory of communism was held to be irreversible." But in recent years, "Soviet activities and pretensions have run head-on into the democratic revolution. People are insisting on their right to independence, on their right to choose their government free of outside control." The United States had not created this phenomenon of "popular insurgencies *against* communist control." What was happening in Poland, Afghanistan, Cambodia, Nicaragua, Ethiopia, Angola, and even inside the Soviet Union itself was no different from what was taking place in South Africa, South Korea, the Philippines, and Chile: the citizens of those countries were simply seeking to determine their own futures. "The nature and extent of our support—whether moral support or something more—necessarily varies from case to case. But there should be no doubt about where our sympathies lie."[112]

The Reagan Doctrine was firmly in place, therefore, before Gorbachev took power. Once he had done so, Reagan and Shultz set out to convince him of its logic: that just as the tides of history were running against command economies, so they were also running against latter-day empires. The issue was an entirely pragmatic one, the President wrote to Gorbachev in February 1986: the war in Afghanistan "is unlikely to bring any benefit to the Soviet Union, so why is it continued?" Resistance there did not flow from the actions of the United States. "Even if we wished we do not have the power to induce thousands of people to take up arms against a well trained foreign army equipped with the most modern weapons." At the same time, though, "who can tell the people of another country they should not fight for their motherland, for their independence and for their national dignity?"[113]

Gorbachev, on Afghanistan, needed little convincing. He admitted to Reagan, at Geneva, that he had known nothing about the 1979 invasion until it had been announced on the radio. The President viewed this as confirmation that "it was a war he had no responsibility—and little enthusiasm—for."[114] The United States continued nevertheless to supply military assistance to the Afghan *mujahadeen*, including Stinger anti-aircraft missiles, which proved lethally effective against Soviet air operations. By September 1987, Gorbachev's new foreign minister, Eduard Shevardnadze, was assuring Shultz privately that the U.S.S.R. would soon leave Afghanistan, and that it would welcome American assistance in facilitating that process.[115] Shultz concluded from this that "the Brezhnev Doctrine was dead; the Reagan Doctrine was driving spikes into that coffin. The Soviets wanted to get out of Afghanistan, and I felt they were fading in other regional hot spots. I was hearing more and more about the possibility of change in at least some of the Warsaw Pact countries. I felt that a profound, historic shift was under way."[116]

And so it was—except that the shift had begun long before Shultz or anyone else in the Reagan administration had suspected. Recent research in Soviet archives suggests that the Brezhnev Doctrine from the beginning had been little more than a bluff. Brezhnev and his advisers had quietly concluded, after the invasion of Czechoslovakia in 1968, that the U.S.S.R. could never again use force to reassert its authority against an Eastern European satellite that was seeking either to reform or reject socialism. Moscow did succeed in convincing General Wojciech Jaruzelski to declare martial law in Poland in December 1981, thereby—for the moment at least—suppressing Solidarity. Had he refused to do so, however, the Soviet Union would almost certainly not have intervened, and its sphere of influence in Eastern Europe might have begun to unravel almost a decade earlier than it actually did.[117] Gorbachev himself attempted to signal an end to the Brezhnev Doctrine at his first meeting with Warsaw Pact leaders in September 1985, only to meet with incredulity: "I had the feeling that they were not taking [what I said] altogether seriously. . . . they probably thought that they would just wait and see."[118] When Reagan publicly challenged Moscow's control over East Germany, in a dramatic speech in West Berlin in June 1987—"Mr. Gorbachev, tear down this wall!"—the Kremlin's response was surprisingly restrained. Reagan, for his part, "never dreamed that in less than three years the wall would come down and a six-thousand-pound section of it would be sent to me for my presidential library."[119]

The final acknowledgment that the Brezhnev Doctrine was dead—and that the Reagan Doctrine had driven spikes into its coffin—came shortly after Reagan left office, when the year 1989 saw one Eastern European country after another throw out their Soviet-installed governments with no apparent objections, and certainly no resistance, from Moscow. It was a sign of how far things had come when Gorbachev's press spokesman, Gennadi Gerasimov, announced—with a degree of whimsy unprecedented for a Soviet official—that the Brezhnev Doctrine had been replaced with the Sinatra Doctrine: the Eastern Europeans were now "doing it their way."[120] Throughout these months of toppling dominoes, Gorbachev recalls, "not once did we contemplate the possibility of going back on the fundamental principles of the new political thinking—freedom of choice and noninterference in other countries' domestic affairs."[121] The irony is that Brezhnev himself, had he still been in power, would have had little choice but to do the same.

V

George F. Kennan had warned, as the Cold War was beginning, against the illusion that American leaders might influence their Soviet counterparts "by reasoning with them, by arguing with them, by going to them and saying: 'Look here, this is the way things are.'" They were not about to turn around and say: "'By George, I never thought of that before. We will go right back and change our policies.'. . . They aren't that kind of people."[122] That was true enough of Stalin, Khrushchev, Brezhnev, Andropov, and Chernenko: certainly Reagan's own efforts to get through to these last three Soviet leaders, upon whom death in rapid succession imposed its own term limits, brought minimal results. Gorbachev, however, was different. Neither the Soviet Union nor the Russian empire that preceded it had ever before produced a leader who combined openness to the outside world with an unwillingness to employ brutality.* He *was* prepared, therefore, to listen to an American administration that said: "Look here, this is the way things are." And he *did* change Soviet policies, more fundamentally than he or anyone else could possibly have expected.

One of the best explanations for why Gorbachev chose this path has come from Reagan himself. "When I met him for the first time in the fall of [1985]," the former President wrote in his memoirs, "he made it plain that he believed wholeheartedly in the Communist system of government. I inferred from his remarks that he thought Communism had been managed poorly and it was his intention to change its management." At some

---

* A fact that distinguished him from such earlier "reformist" rulers as Peter the Great, Catherine II, Alexander I, Alexander II, and Nikita Khrushchev.

point, however, "he ultimately decided to abandon many of the fundamental tenets of Communism along with the empire that Joe Stalin had
seized in Eastern Europe after World War II."

One reason, Reagan speculated, may have been that "the metamorpho-
sis started when he was still a young man, working his way up the inefficient and corrupt Communist bureaucracy and witnessing the brutality of
the Stalin regime." But it could also have resulted from "discovering that
the three percent of Soviet agricultural land cultivated by private profit-
making farmers produced forty percent of the meat in his country." Or
possibly "the robust recovery of the American and Western European
economies following the recession of the early eighties—while the Communist economies went nowhere—convinced him that central planning
and bureaucratic control . . . sapped the people's incentive to produce and
excel." Whatever the case, Gorbachev must have realized that the Soviet
Union

> could no longer support or control Stalin's totalitarian empire; the survival of
> the Soviet Union was more important to him. He must have looked at the
> economic disaster his country was facing and concluded that it couldn't con-
> tinue spending so much of its wealth on weapons and an arms race that—as
> I told him at Geneva—we would never let his country win. I'm convinced
> that the tragedy at Chernobyl . . . also affected him and made him try harder
> to resolve Soviet differences with the West. And I think in our meetings I
> might have helped him understand why we considered the Soviet Union
> and its policy of expansionism a threat to us. I might have helped him see
> that the Soviet Union had less to fear from the West than he thought, and
> that the Soviet empire in Eastern Europe wasn't needed for the security of
> the Soviet Union.

In the end, Reagan concluded, "Gorbachev had the intelligence to admit
Communism was not working, the courage to battle for change, and, ultimately, the wisdom to introduce the beginnings of democracy, individual
freedom, and free enterprise."[123]

There is less triumphalism in this account than in those put forward by
many of Reagan's advisers and acolytes.[124] Indeed there is little in it to
which Gorbachev himself could take exception. It places the Soviet leader
in the center of the picture, thereby reflecting the conviction of Kennan
and the other early architects of containment that the Soviet system would
change only when it produced a leader who was willing to make it happen.
It emphasizes the structural deficiencies within that system that had
brought it to the point of crisis. It stresses the contrast that had developed,

as a result, between the respective accomplishments of capitalism and communism. It acknowledges the role of accident. In the end, Reagan claimed credit only for having explained a few things: that the U.S.S.R. could not hope to win an arms race with the United States, that Soviet expansionism—past and present—had created more vulnerabilities than strengths, and that common interests could outweigh long-standing differences. Gorbachev has provided no comparably succinct account of his political and ideological trajectory in his own voluminously unreflective memoir. But he has made a point of insisting that "the 40th President of the United States will go down in history for his rare perception."[125]

It seems reasonable, then, to follow Reagan's lead, and seek no single explanation for what happened in the Soviet Union under Gorbachev: internal developments were surely more important than external pressures and inducements, although in just what proportion may not be clear for decades. What one can say now is that Reagan saw Soviet weaknesses sooner than most of his contemporaries did; that he understood the extent to which détente was perpetuating the Cold War rather than hastening its end; that his hard line strained the Soviet system at the moment of its maximum weakness; that his shift toward conciliation preceded Gorbachev; that he combined reassurance, persuasion, and pressure in dealing with the new Soviet leader; and that he maintained the support of the American people and of American allies. Quite apart from whatever results this strategy produced, it was an impressive accomplishment simply to have devised and sustained it: Reagan's role here was critical.

What one can also say is that Reagan—and Shultz—had a clearer vision than Gorbachev, in 1985, of the changes the Soviet Union would have to make in order to survive. Gorbachev knew only that his country could not continue along the path that it had followed under his predecessors. The next six-and-a-half years would see his initial efforts to redeem Marxism-Leninism while remaining a superpower dissolve into an increasingly desperate series of improvisations that ultimately led to the complete collapse of Soviet authority, at first abroad, and then at home.[126] Reagan, to be sure, shed no tears over the demise of the U.S.S.R. But it was Gorbachev's actions, not his, that brought about that outcome. So who had a strategy and who did not? That question, at least, is easy to answer.

The more difficult question is where the Reagan strategy fits within the traditions of symmetrical and asymmetrical containment. For in his assumption of unlimited resources—his belief that "we could outspend them forever"[127]—he was squarely within the symmetrical containment camp. In contrast to the authors of NSC-68 and the strategists of the Kennedy and Johnson administrations, however, Reagan made this calculation on the basis of what the Soviet economy, not his own, could withstand. He thereby exploited the multidimensional nature of American power at a time when Soviet power was becoming increasingly monodimensional. This allowed retaining the initiative while shifting the competition onto terrain that favored the United States, an approach consistent with the legacy of asymmetrical containment.[128] Reagan thereby avoided the costs, risks, and frustrations of competing on terms set by the other side—the symmetrical response dilemma that had undermined domestic support for the wars in Korea and Vietnam. But he also yielded no gains to the U.S.S.R., whether by acknowledging its spheres of influence or by overlooking the mistreatment of those who lived under its rule: in this way, he insulated his administration from the fears of falling dominoes and the moral qualms that had beset practitioners of asymmetrical containment.

To a greater degree than any of his Cold War predecessors, therefore, Reagan drew on the strengths of both symmetry and asymmetry, while avoiding their weaknesses. He did so, not because he knew these terms, but because he understood the paradox they were meant to illustrate: that competing at times and in places chosen by adversaries minimizes risks but drives up costs, while competing at times and in places of one's own choosing minimizes costs but drives up risks. And so, without ever putting it in quite this way, Reagan devised a remedy: a strategy of high risks and costs that sought, by *changing rather than containing* an adversary, to make possible a world of much lower risks and costs.[129] In doing so, he resolved a contradiction that had bedeviled strategists of containment from the earliest days of the Cold War.

"Reagan's was an astonishing performance," Henry Kissinger has written, "and, to academic observers, nearly incomprehensible. . . . When all was said and done, a president with the shallowest academic background was to develop a foreign policy of extraordinary consistency and relevance."[130] Reagan did this by drawing upon a few simple habits: a focus on outcomes rather than on details; a willingness to choose among priorities rather than to be pulled apart by them; an understanding that priorities can shift as policies achieve their purposes; a refusal to be intimidated by orthodoxies; a realization that power resides as much in ideas as in material capabilities; an ability to combine conviction with the capacity to express it; a belief that no strategy can sustain itself if it fails to advance the principles upon which the society it seeks to defend is based. Reagan's foibles—of which there were many—were also, in a way, a source of strength, because they encouraged others so easily to underestimate him. And he always counter-balanced these quirks with healthy reserves of good humor and common sense.* It was these qualities, together with the reforms Gorbachev brought about within the Soviet Union, that allowed *both* leaders to achieve the result Kennan had hoped for from the strategy of containment when, four decades earlier, he first proposed it.[131]

Kennan had been no admirer of Reagan during his presidency. But when I asked him in 1996 who or what had ended the Cold War, his answer reflected significant reassessment. "I think the historical forces were a greater factor in overcoming the Cold War than were the actions of any individuals," he replied. "But if you have to find two individuals who contributed greatly to this, I would put first of all Gorbachev . . . but also Ronald Reagan, who in his own inimitable way, probably not even being quite aware of what he was really doing, did what few other people would have been able to do in breaking this log jam."[132] Of course, it is also possible that Reagan really *did* know, all along, what he was doing.

VI

By the time Reagan left office in January 1989, the strategy of containment had largely achieved its purposes: a Soviet leader had indeed acknowledged the failures of Marxism-Leninism and the futility of Russian imperialism. The incoming administration of George H. W. Bush found it difficult to believe what had happened. "I was suspicious of Gorbachev's motives and skeptical of his prospects," Bush's new national security adviser Brent Scowcroft remembered. "He was trying to kill us with kindness. . . . My fear was that Gorbachev could talk us into disarming . . . and that, in a decade or so, we could face a more serious threat than ever before."[133] Bush himself, who had known Gorbachev since their first meeting at Chernenko's funeral in 1985, was less distrustful; nevertheless, "I certainly did not want to make a foolish or short-sighted move."[134] The result

---

* Most of the time. Reagan's most glaring departure from common sense came with the Iran-Contra affair, a complicated scheme he had authorized to secure the release of American hostages in the Middle East by selling arms to the Iranians, then using the profits to support the anti-Sandinista resistance in Nicaragua. The resulting investigations preoccupied the administration for months in the aftermath of the 1986 Reykjavik summit, and may well have contributed to its failure to follow up the progress that was made there toward phasing out reliance on nuclear weapons. (Peter Kornbluh and Malcolm Byrne, eds., *The Iran-Contra Scandal: The Declassified History* [New York: 1993], provides the basic documentation.)

was an extended review of Soviet-American relations that took months to determine what had been obvious to Reagan and Shultz: that the Soviet Union under Gorbachev was a very different country from what it had been throughout most of the Cold War.

Gorbachev, for his part, appeared to have anticipated Scowcroft by seeking to remove all sources of conflict with Washington. It was as if he had taken literally the strategy the Kremlin's long-time American expert, Georgii Arbatov, had been jokingly recommending, which was to "contain" the United States by depriving it of an enemy.[135] Gorbachev had announced, at the United Nations, in December 1988, a *unilateral* withdrawal of 500,000 Soviet troops from eastern and central Europe. He did nothing to halt the collapse of Moscow's authority in Poland and Hungary during the summer of 1989. He told the East Germans, at their fortieth anniversary celebrations in October, that they would have to reform themselves: when they did not and the Berlin Wall came down the following month, he let it be known that he approved of what had happened. He made no effort to preserve the remaining Soviet satellite governments in Czechoslovakia, Bulgaria, and Romania, all of which were gone by the end of the year. And at Gorbachev's first summit with President Bush, held at Malta in December, he made a point of acknowledging the legitimacy of an American role in Europe, while failing to specify what the Soviet role there should be.[136]

By then it was becoming clear, though, that if Gorbachev had any strategy of containment, it was not one aimed at the United States. Rather, its purpose was to contain the consequences, for his own country, of a set of events that no one in either Moscow or Washington could now control. For once Gorbachev let it be known that the Soviet Union would not forcibly resist demands for self-determination, there was no stopping them. He had no choice but to accept the dismantling, almost overnight, of the sphere of influence Stalin had constructed so long ago in Eastern Europe. He had no means of resisting pressures—from within Germany and from the Bush administration—for the reunification of that country. He had no way to prevent the newly unified German state from being incorporated into NATO: a geopolitical outcome, conventional wisdom had always insisted, that the Soviet Union would never accept. And, of course, in the end he also lacked the means to deny self-determination to the non-Russian republics of the U.S.S.R., or for that matter to the Russian republic as well, now headed by his freely elected rival, Boris Yeltsin.

Not the least of the ironies associated with Gorbachev is the fact that, despite having made self-determination possible throughout the Soviet Union and Eastern Europe, he never subjected himself to a democratic election.[137] As a result, his domestic base of support diminished even as his international reputation grew: that left him vulnerable to the coup that almost removed him from power in August 1991, and to the irrelevance that finally did end his rule on Christmas Day of that year, when the Soviet Union itself at last ceased to exist.

"During these last few months," President Bush told the nation that evening, "you and I have witnessed one of the greatest dramas of the 20th century, the historic and revolutionary transformation of a totalitarian dictatorship, the Soviet Union, and the liberation of its peoples." The United States for over four decades had led the struggle "against communism and the threat it posed to our most precious values. . . . That confrontation is now over." It was a hastily composed speech that seemed almost to shrink from the significance of what it was saying: Bush lacked Reagan's skill in connecting language with history. The history itself, though, was right. The United States had indeed avoided the alternatives of war and appeasement that seemed to be the only ones open to the West when Kennan composed his "long telegram"—also hastily—forty-five years earlier. "Our enemies," Bush concluded succinctly, "have become our partners."[138]

CHAPTER TWELVE

Epilogue: Containment After the Cold War

Great grand strategies are bounded by time and space, but they also transcend time and space. They all arise, as containment did, within particular periods, places, and sets of circumstances. They cannot be divorced, in this sense, from the historical contexts in which they originated. And yet, the adjective "great" implies relevance beyond context. It suggests that the strategy in question can serve as a guide in periods, places, and circumstances yet to come.

When George F. Kennan returned to Washington in the spring of 1946, having riveted the attention of the United States government with the longest telegram ever sent from its embassy in Moscow, his first job was to design a course on strategy and policy at the National War College. "We found ourselves thrown back," he recalled, "on the European thinkers of other ages and generations: on Machiavelli, Clausewitz, Gallieni—even Lawrence of Arabia." Total war in a nuclear age would be "suicidal" or at least "out of accord with every principle of humanity," and yet there was no American tradition of limited war. It was necessary, then, to explore other traditions: for example, Talleyrand's view that "nations ought to do one another in peace the most good, in war—the least possible evil," or Gibbon's claim that the "temperate and indecisive conflicts" of the eighteenth century had been a strength rather than a weakness of that era.[1] Kennan was relying here upon the principle of *transferability*: that grand strategies from the past could suggest what to emulate and what to avoid in shaping grand strategies for the future.

It seems fair enough, therefore, to apply this standard to the strategy

Kennan himself devised after moving to the State Department early in 1947. To what extent might containment work in other periods, places, and sets of circumstances? Not at all, he seemed to suggest during the Vietnam War: "I emphatically deny the paternity of any efforts to invoke that doctrine today in situations to which it has, and can have, no proper relevance."[2] The possibility that there could be *strategies* of containment— that his own strategy could spawn mutations of which he disapproved—left Kennan frustrated, apologetic, and often angry. The sensation, he recalled, was that of having "inadvertently loosened a large boulder from the top of a cliff and now helplessly witness[ing] its path of destruction in the valley below, shuddering and wincing at each successive glimpse of disaster."[3]

Disasters did occur, and Vietnam was the worst of them. But by the end of the Cold War, the successes of containment had clearly outweighed its failures. There was no war with the Soviet Union, as there had been twice with Germany and once with Japan between 1914 and 1945. There was no appeasement either, as there had been in the years between the two world wars. Whatever the oscillations between symmetry and asymmetry, whatever the miscalculations, whatever the costs, the United States and its allies sustained a strategy that was far more consistent, effective, and morally justifiable than anything their adversaries were able to manage. Indeed it is difficult to think of *any* peacetime grand strategy in which the results produced in the end corresponded more closely with the objectives specified at the beginning.

Students of strategy will be studying containment, hence, for decades, even centuries to come. Leaders will be applying its lessons in periods, places, and circumstances that nobody can now foresee. Transferability, however much Kennan might resist the notion, is unavoidable. But because the context can never again be that of the Cold War, not all aspects of that strategy are likely to transfer equally well.

I

Kennan suggested one that might not as early as 1947: it was the requirement that the adversary to be contained *share one's own sense of risk*. Containment probably would not have succeeded against Napoleon or Hitler, he pointed out, because both had set deadlines—determined presumably by their own mortality—for achieving their goals. Sticking to timetables was more important to them than avoiding war. They lacked the caution that Marxism-Leninism had instilled in Soviet leaders: "the Kremlin is under no ideological compulsion to accomplish its purposes in a hurry," Kennan noted in the "X" article. "Like the Church, it is dealing in ideological concepts which are of long-term validity. . . . It has no right to risk the existing achievements of the revolution for the sake of vain baubles of the future."[4] Convinced that history was on their side, Stalin and his successors were prepared to be patient: that bought the time needed for containment to demonstrate that they were wrong.

Nor is it clear that containment would have worked against states whose leaders believed, as Sir Michael Howard has put it, "in the inevitability of, and the social necessity for, armed conflict in the development of mankind."[5] Such views were common in the late nineteenth and early twentieth centuries, a fact that helps to explain how so many great powers could have blundered so easily, in 1914, into a Great War. But that global conflict and the one that followed in 1939 profoundly shook "bellicist" assumptions; the use of atomic bombs in 1945 shattered them. Quite apart from the presence of a cautious adversary, therefore, there was in the postwar era a far more favorable psychological climate than had previously existed for developing "measures short of war," such as containment.[6]

That sense of shared risk persisted throughout the Cold War, which is why the adjective remained attached to the noun. It did not matter whether Democrats or Republicans occupied the White House, or whether reformers or reactionaries inhabited the Kremlin: all feared a third world war. All had societies to defend, and hence a state to preserve. Total war had ceased to be a means by which that could be done, even if limited wars were still possible.[7] It is hardly surprising, then, that Kennan and his war college students read Clausewitz, for it was his great principle that the use of force must never become an end in itself: "The political object is the goal, war is the means of reaching it, and means can never be considered in isolation from their purpose."[8] No major leader during the Cold War would have disagreed.[9]

That fact suggests a second limitation on containment's applicability beyond a Cold War context, which is that it was a *state-based strategy*. It depended not only on the fear of all-out war, but also upon the existence of identifiable regimes that could manage the running of risks short of war. This too was consistent with Clausewitz: where else could the capacity to constrain force come from if not the state, the entity created, at the dawn of the modern era, to monopolize the means of violence?[10] To imagine Clausewitz apart from the state is to imagine a boat without water. Might the same be said, then, of containment? Can that strategy function in an environment in which states are no longer the principal threats to be contained?

The attacks of September 11, 2001, posed that question for the United States in the starkest possible terms. On that day, nineteen members of a terrorist gang killed more Americans on their own soil than had the Imperial Japanese Navy six decades earlier at Pearl Harbor. The George W. Bush administration was quick to conclude, in response, that Cold War strategies—containment and the deterrence that accompanied it—would not have worked against al-Qaeda. How does one contain someone who, before striking, is invisible? How does one deter someone who, in the act of striking, is prepared to commit suicide? These problems led Bush, in the fall of 2002, to announce a new grand strategy of *pre-emption*:* that the United States would henceforth act multilaterally where possible, but unilaterally where necessary, to take out terrorists before they could hit their intended targets.[11] The purpose was to defend states against stateless enemies.

Bush's strategy was less of an innovation than it at first seemed to be. Pre-emption had never been ruled out during the Cold War: no American president, in a nuclear age, would have knowingly risked another Pearl Harbor. The doctrine was simply not publicized to the extent that Bush chose to do.[12] Nor was al-Qaeda an entirely stateless enemy. Osama bin Laden ran it from Taliban-controlled Afghanistan, against which the Bush administration had swiftly and successfully retaliated in the fall of 2001. Its first clear act of pre-emption also took place against a state, Iraq, in March 2003. The justifications cited included claims that Saddam Hussein had supported al-Qaeda while accumulating weapons of mass destruction, neither of which held up under subsequent scrutiny. A justification not cited—but undoubtedly present—was that deposing the Iraqi despot would frighten the leaders of any other states who might be harboring terrorists or thinking about doing so: that, however, was deterrence, with a view to countering an anticipated danger. Pre-emption by

---

* In doing so, Bush broadened the Cold War definition of "pre-emption"—action taken against a state that was about to launch an attack—to include the Cold War meaning of "prevention"—action taken against a state that might, at some point in the future, have that capability. He did so because the distinction makes little sense when one is dealing with invisible and potentially suicidal terrorist gangs. (For more on this, see John Lewis Gaddis, "Grand Strategy in the Second Term," *Foreign Affairs*, LXXIV [January/February 2005], 3.)

the Bush administration's logic, then, led back to containment. It did not replace containment.[13]

There is, however, another way of understanding September 11 that, if confirmed, might indeed make containment obsolete. It comes from claims that the attacks could only have happened because the international state system had become weaker than it once was. The simultaneous advance of economic integration and political fragmentation had diminished the capacity of *all* states to control what went on within their territories and across their borders.[14] If September 11 initiated a new age of insecurity in which the actions of only a few individuals could endanger entire societies, then strategies of containment as traditionally conceived would be of little use. Containment presumed threats from states seeking to survive. It was never meant for movements seeking martyrdom. Preemption in situations like this, the argument runs, may be the only feasible option.

A third limitation on containment's relevance beyond a Cold War context has to do with the persistence, throughout that conflict, of *something worse than American hegemony.** It is clear in retrospect that the United States retained a preponderance of power—in all of the categories that constitute power—throughout the last half of the twentieth century.[15] As the Norwegian historian Geir Lundestad has pointed out, however, it did so more often by invitation than imposition.[16] For as long as the Soviet Union was the alternative, there was always something worse, in the eyes of most of the rest of the world, than the prospect of American domination. That minimized the "friction"—to use Clausewitz's term—that hegemony might otherwise have generated.

With the end of the Cold War, the unintended advantage the Soviet Union had given the United States disappeared—as did the urgency of cultivating allies and neutrals who, if neglected, might defect to the other side, or at least threaten to do so. Multilateral consultation diminished steadily throughout the administrations of George H. W. Bush and Bill Clinton, not because the principle was objectionable, but because the practice seemed less necessary than it had during the Cold War. The George W. Bush administration inherited what was coming to be called American unilateralism. It did not invent it.[17]

---

* I owe this "something worse" principle to Kennan, who got it from Hilaire Belloc's poem, in his *Cautionary Tales*, about the unfortunate Jim, who was eaten by a lion: "And always keep a-hold of Nurse / For fear of finding something worse."

It did, however, intensify unilateralism in several ways: through tactless diplomacy with respect to the Kyoto Protocol on global climate change, the International Criminal Court, and the Anti-Ballistic Missile Treaty; through the casualness with which it brushed aside offers of help from NATO allies in invading Afghanistan; through its single-minded determination to overthrow Saddam Hussein despite widespread opposition within the international community; and through its reluctance to acknowledge, having conquered Iraq, that it had no clear idea what to do there. All of this led to an unprecedented loss of support throughout the rest of the world for the United States and its foreign policy objectives. The view seemed to be emerging that there could be *nothing worse* than American hegemony if it was to be used in this way.[18]

If this trend continues, then the basis for American power will indeed have shifted from invitation to imposition, a very different context from the one in which containment arose during the Cold War. When Kennan wrote in 1947 that "the United States need only measure up to its own best traditions,"[19] he assumed that those traditions would have greater appeal beyond its borders than would those of the Soviet Union and the international communist movement. He was right about that: the existence of such rivals provided an eminently realistic reason for Americans to respect their own ideals and to try to reflect them, for the most part successfully, in their actions. But if in the absence of useful adversaries the United States ceases to do that—if it creates a new tradition of imposed rather than invited power—then it should hardly be surprised to find little that might transfer from the strategy of containment that produced its own preeminence.

II

Containment cannot to be expected to succeed, therefore, in circumstances that differ significantly from those that gave rise to it, sustained it, and within which it eventually prevailed. Kennan's objection to invoking it "in situations to which it has, and can have, no proper relevance," in this sense, makes sense. He never claimed that the pre-containment strategies he studied at the National War College could be wrenched from their historical contexts and applied uncritically in the early Cold War. And yet, he obviously did believe in *selective* transferability: otherwise there would have been no point in teaching the grand strategists of the past to his war college students. It is worth considering then, from this perspective, what aspects of containment might remain relevant in a post-Cold War, post-September 11 world.

One has to do with a kind of intellectual geography: the fact that Kennan's strategy of containment *mapped out a path between dangerous— even deadly—alternatives.* Despite the persistence of a multipolar international system, the dominant trend in thinking about strategy through the end of World War II was one of bipolar extremes: war *or* peace, victory *or* defeat, appeasement *or* annihilation. The idea that there could be something in between—neither war *nor* peace, neither victory *nor* defeat, neither appeasement *nor* annihilation—had never been clearly articulated. It had been implicit, as Kennan noted, in the strategies of earlier eras; but it had disappeared with the advent of mass mobilizations, lethal technologies, and the total wars they made possible. Imagination itself had failed, making the first half of the twentieth century a period of unprecedented violence among the great powers: there seemed to be no middle ground.

The second half of the twentieth century turned out to be very different. Despite the emergence of a bipolar international system, the dominant trend in thinking about strategy was one of avoiding extremes. Nuclear weapons had something to do with this, to be sure, but so too did the idea of containment—which preceded the Soviet-American nuclear stalemate by almost a decade. When seen in this context, then, containment was a feat of imagination, made all the more impressive by the bleak circumstances in which it originated. The transferable lesson here is a psychological one: that any strategy in which the only choices available are deadly, dangerous, or otherwise undesirable requires rethinking. That is how Nixon and Kissinger responded when they inherited the Vietnam War, the product of an inability to rethink. In doing so, they were following Kennan's precedent.

A second transferable principle follows: it is that a desirable alternative in strategy is for *enemies to defeat themselves.* The idea goes back at least as far as Sun Tzu. It pervades Clausewitz. It is what Marx and Lenin expected would happen to capitalism, the internal contradictions of which were to supposed bring about its collapse.[20] Both Kennan in the late 1940's and Reagan in the early 1980's reversed this logic, insisting that it was Marxism-Leninism, not capitalism, that carried within itself the seeds of its own destruction. The United States could, through its actions, increase the strains under which the Soviet Union and its allies operated: in the end, though, the inefficiencies of command economies, the absence of political accountability, and the improbability that an internationalist ideology could indefinitely suppress nationalist instincts would cause communism's demise. Americans and their allies needed only to be firm and remain patient while this happened.

The idea also makes sense in a post-September 11 era, for the interests of terrorists and the states that support them—or at least tolerate them—are not in all instances the same. Terrorists have no economic program; states in an increasingly interdependent world must have one. Terrorists substitute intimidation for representation, a bargain that has not proven sustainable in a democratizing age. Finally, states seek to survive even if terrorists do not: even rogue states have an interest in preserving the international state system, because they have no way of knowing what might replace it. These contradictions are at least as striking as the ones within the communist world that the Cold War practitioners of containment successfully exploited.

How does one know, though, when such opportunities exist? Answering this question brings up a third transferable principle from the strategy of containment, which is that *history is a better guide than theory in shaping it.* Kennan's insights during the early Cold War went well beyond the conventional wisdom of the time: that Stalin was not another Hitler; that an authoritarian state need not be impermeable to external influences; that an ideology based upon a deterministic view of the past could miscalculate the future; that international communism would not remain monolithic; that war and appeasement were not the only choices open to the United States and its allies in dealing with the dangers that confronted them.

It is not at all clear what *theories* might have yielded such conclusions. They came instead from Kennan's reading of Gibbon on the Roman Empire, from his knowledge of the history and culture of Russia, from his own crash course on the great grand strategists while at the National War College—and even from works of imagination, as when Kennan used Thomas Mann's novel *Buddenbrooks* to make the point, about the Soviet Union, that "human institutions often show the greatest outward brilliance at a moment when inner decay is . . . farthest advanced."[21] Formal theory, in seeking universal validity, too often disconnects itself from the flow of time. It pays insufficient attention to how things became what they are, which usually offers the best clue as to what they will become. History, in contrast—but also literature—distills past experience in such a way as to *prepare* one for future uncertainties, rather in the way that athletic training builds stamina and accumulates experience, but does not in itself determine the outcome of future games.[22]

The process is intuitive, even impressionistic, involving the ability to see that a current situation is "like" one or more that have existed in the past, and that it is worth knowing how they were handled. It requires the self-confidence to be selective, the self-discipline to be clear, and a certain amount of self-dramatization when needed to get one's point across: what else could an 8,000-word telegram be? It benefits greatly from insights into human nature, which theory rarely provides. It is ironic that Kennan is remembered today as one of the founders of "realism" within the field of international relations, for he never considered himself to be a theorist at all.[23] He was, however, by temperament, training, and later in life by choice, a historian. And he would have liked to have been a novelist.

A fourth aspect of containment that might well transfer to other contexts is the extent to which, as implemented, it combined *coherence with accountability*. Here Kennan was less than prescient: he worried that the volatilities of domestic politics would make it difficult, if not impossible, for a democracy to sustain a consistent grand strategy.* In one sense, he was right: there were repeated oscillations between symmetrical and asymmetrical containment, with each new administration appearing to have to learn their virtues and deficiencies. When one looks at the American record throughout the Cold War, though, one cannot help but be struck by the extent to which the larger objectives of containment—avoiding the extremes of war and appeasement while waiting for the Soviet Union to change itself—remained the same, regardless of which party occupied the White House and which approach to containment each chose to embrace.

From that perspective, then, the shifts that took place can be seen as course corrections imposed by the obligation of accountability inherent in democratic procedures. The requirement to hold an election every four

---

* "I sometimes wonder whether . . . a democracy is not uncomfortably similar to one of those prehistoric monsters with a body as long as this room and a brain the size of a pin: he lies there in his comfortable primeval mud and pays little attention to his environment; he is slow to wrath—in fact, you practically have to whack his tail off to make him aware that his interests are being disturbed; but, once he grasps this, he lays about him with such blind determination that he not only destroys his adversary but largely wrecks his native habitat." (*American Diplomacy: 1900–1950* [Chicago: 1951], p. 66.)

years may have made it difficult to maintain consistency, but it was a safe-guard against complacency, against the tendency to persist in counterpro-ductive strategies in the face of evidence suggesting that they were just that. To see the value of such accountability, consider the performance of the Soviet Union, China, and the satellite regimes of Eastern Europe, where the only way to replace ineffective strategies was to wait for their ar-chitects to die or to be overthrown. This did, of course, happen, but not frequently enough to provide protection against the dangers of authoritar-ian autism—the tendency to persist in error which the absence of ac-countability encourages.

Nor did alternations between symmetry and asymmetry impede an-other kind of accountability, which was the need to combine *leadership with consent*. It is striking that after four and a half decades of the Cold War, the alliances with which the United States began that contest were largely intact, while the Soviet Union had hardly any allies left. The prospect of something worse than American hegemony helps in part to ex-plain this outcome. It is also the case, though, that the strategists of con-tainment, whether of the symmetrical or asymmetrical persuasion, never underestimated the importance of allies. They worked hard to maintain multilateral consent for United States leadership in waging the Cold War, without at the same time allowing the need for consultation to paralyze the alliance. Containment in that respect also sets a standard to which future grand strategists—perhaps even current ones—might aspire.

A final lesson from the past that will be usable in the future comes chiefly from Eisenhower—although Kennan agreed with it: it was that containment *must not destroy what it was attempting to defend*. Eisen-hower's concern was that, in the effort to contain an authoritarian adver-sary, the United States itself might become authoritarian, whether through the imposition of a command economy or through the abridg-ment of democratic procedures. That never happened. Despite the military-industrial complex the nation maintained its markets; despite Mc-Carthyism it sustained and ultimately strengthened civil liberties; despite the excesses of Vietnam and Watergate the strategy of containment never came close to corrupting fundamental American values. They remained, at the end of the Cold War, what they had been at its beginning. The same can hardly be said of fundamental Marxist-Leninist values. So in this sense too, containment was consistent with Clausewitz: it was an extension of war, diplomacy, and values by other means.

III

George F. Kennan celebrated his 100th birthday on February 16, 2004. Born thirteen years before the Soviet Union, he had now survived, by thirteen years, its demise. Physically frail but still mentally alert, the old statesman held court, in the upstairs bedroom of his Princeton home, for a stream of visitors including family, friends, his biographer, and even the Secretary of State of the United States, Colin Powell.

Fifty-eight years earlier, almost to the day, sick in another bedroom from the rigors of a Moscow winter and irritated as usual at the Department of State, Kennan had summoned his secretary, Dorothy Hessman, and dictated an unusually long telegram. That document has a better claim than any other to having laid out the path by which the international system found its way from the trajectory of self-destruction it was on during the first half of the twentieth century to one that had, by the end of the second half, removed the danger of great power war, revived democracy and capitalism, and thereby enhanced the prospects for human liberty beyond what they had ever been before.*

An extravagant claim? Perhaps—but would anyone on February 22, 1946, have regarded the world as safe from the scourge of great power war? How could it be, when in contrast to the aftermath of World War I, it had not even been possible after World War II to convene a comprehensive peace conference? As safe from the dangers of authoritarianism? How could it be, when the Western democracies had had to rely upon one authoritarian state to defeat the others? As safe from a recurrence of economic collapse? How could it be, since there was no assurance that another global depression would not return? As safe from abuses of human rights? How could it be, when one of the most advanced nations in Europe had just committed the crime of genocide on an unprecedented scale? As safe from the fear that in any future war no one would be safe? How could the world be that either, with atomic weapons now having been developed, with little prospect that they would remain under exclusive American control?

What Kennan opened up, on that bleak day in Moscow in 1946, was a

---

* The "long telegram" was on display, on this centennial occasion, in an appropriately long display case in Firestone Library at Princeton University.

way out: a grand strategy that rejected both the appeasement and the isolationism that had led to World War II, on the one hand, and on the other the alternative of a third world war, the devastation from which, in a nuclear age, could be unimaginable. Fifty-eight years later there was more than just a 100th birthday to celebrate.*

---

*George F. Kennan died peacefully, surrounded by family, in the upstairs bedroom of his Princeton home on the evening of March 17, 2005, at the age of 101.

Appendix: National Defense Expenditures as a Percentage of Total Government Expenditures and Gross Domestic Product: 1945–1992†

Fiscal year	Total government expenditures (billions $)	National security expenditures (billions $)	Percentage of total expenditures allocated to defense (billions $)	Percentage of gross domestic product allocated to defense (billions $)
1945	92.7	83.0	89.5	37.5
1946	55.3	42.7	77.3	19.2
1947	34.5	12.8	37.1	5.5
1948	29.8	9.1	30.6	3.5
1949	38.8	13.1	33.9	4.8
1950	42.6	13.7	32.2	5.0
1951	45.5	23.6	51.8	7.4
1952	67.7	46.1	68.1	13.2
1953	76.1	52.8	69.4	14.2
1954	70.9	49.3	69.5	13.1
1955	68.4	42.7	62.4	10.8
1956	70.6	42.5	60.2	10.0
1957	76.6	45.4	59.3	10.1
1958	82.4	46.8	56.8	10.2
1959	92.1	49.0	53.2	10.0
1960	92.2	48.1	52.2	9.3
1961	97.7	49.6	50.8	9.4
1962	106.8	52.3	49.0	9.2
1963	111.3	53.4	48.0	8.9
1964	118.5	54.8	46.2	8.5
1965	118.2	50.6	42.8	7.4
1966	134.5	58.1	43.2	7.7
1967	157.5	71.4	45.4	8.8
1968	178.2	81.9	46.0	9.4
1969	183.6	82.5	44.9	8.7
1970	195.6	81.7	41.8	8.1
1971	210.2	78.8	37.5	7.3
1972	230.7	79.1	34.3	6.7
1973	245.7	76.7	31.2	5.8
1974	269.4	79.3	29.5	5.5
1975	332.3	86.5	26.0	5.5
1976	371.8	89.6	24.1	5.2
TQ*	96.0	22.3	23.2	4.8
1977	409.2	97.2	23.8	4.9
1978	458.7	104.5	22.8	4.7
1979	504.0	116.3	23.1	4.6
1980	590.9	134.0	22.7	4.9
1981	678.2	157.5	23.2	5.1
1982	745.7	185.3	24.8	5.7
1983	808.4	209.9	26.0	6.1
1984	851.9	227.4	26.7	5.9

(continued)

Fiscal year	Total government expenditures (billions $)	National security expenditures (billions $)	Percentage of total expenditures allocated to defense (billions $)	Percentage of gross domestic product allocated to defense (billions $)
1985	946.4	252.7	26.7	6.1
1986	990.4	273.4	27.6	6.2
1987	1,004.1	282.0	28.1	6.1
1988	1,064.5	290.4	27.3	5.8
1989	1,143.6	303.6	26.5	5.6
1990	1,253.2	299.3	23.9	5.2
1991	1,324.4	273.3	20.6	4.6
1992	1,381.6	298.4	21.6	4.8

*Transitional quarter, to allow for shifting the beginning of the fiscal year from July 1 to October 1.
†Source: U.S. Office of Management and Budget, *The Budget for Fiscal Year 2005, Historical Series* (Washington: 2004), pp. 45–50.

Notes

Preface

1. J.H. Hexter, *On Historians* (Cambridge, Mass.: 1979), pp. 241–43.
2. Alexander L. George, "The 'Operational Code': A Neglected Approach to the Study of Political Decision-Making," *International Studies Quarterly*, XII (June 1969), 190–222.
3. Henry A. Kissinger, *White House Years* (Boston: 1979), p. 54.
4. Alexander L. George, "Case Studies and Theory Development: The Method of Structured, Focused Comparison," in Paul Gordon Lauren, ed., *Diplomacy: New Approaches in History, Theory, and Policy* (New York: 1979), pp. 43–68.

Preface—Revised and Expanded

1. John Lewis Gaddis, *Strategies of Containment: A Critical Appraisal of Postwar American National Security Policy* (New York: Oxford University Press, 1982), p. 353.

ONE. *Prologue*

1. Roosevelt to Churchill, November 19, 1942, in Francis L. Loewenheim, Harold D. Langley, and Manfred Jonas, eds., *Roosevelt and Churchill: Their Secret Wartime Correspondence* (New York: 1975), p. 282. George C. Herring credits Representative Clifford Woodrum of Virginia with the proverb. See his *Aid to Russia: Strategy, Diplomacy, the Origins of the Cold War* (New York: 1973), p. 22.
2. Quoted in Keith David Eagles, "Ambassador Joseph E. Davies and American-Soviet Relations, 1937–1941" (Ph.D. Dissertation, University of Washington, 1966), p. 328.
3. "X," "The Sources of Soviet Conduct," *Foreign Affairs*, XXV (July 1947), 575.
4. *New York Times*, June 24, 1941.
5. *Life*, XXV (August 30 and September 6, 1948), 83–97, 86–103.
6. Bullitt to Roosevelt, January 29 and August 10, 1943, Franklin D. Roosevelt Papers, PSF

"Bullitt," Franklin D. Roosevelt Library, Hyde Park, New York. See also Bullitt to Roosevelt, May 12, 1943, *ibid.* Slightly abridged versions of these memoranda are published in Orville H. Bullitt, ed., *For the President: Personal and Secret: Correspondence Between Franklin D. Roosevelt and William C. Bullitt* (Boston: 1972), pp. 575–79.

7. See, on this point, Robert Dallek, *Franklin D. Roosevelt and American Foreign Policy: 1932–1945* (New York: 1979), pp. 410–11, 414–15, 430, 432, 469.

8. Minutes of the Combined Chiefs of Staff meeting with Roosevelt and Churchill, Quebec, August 23, 1943, U. S. Department of State, *Foreign Relations of the United States* [hereafter *FRUS:*] *The Conferences at Washington and Quebec, 1943* (Washington: 1970), p. 942; and Joint Chiefs of Staff minutes, meeting with Roosevelt, en route to Teheran, November 19, 1943, *FRUS: The Conferences at Cairo and Tehran, 1943* (Washington: 1961), p. 255. See also Warren F. Kimball, *Swords or Ploughshares? The Morgenthau Plan for Defeated Nazi Germany, 1943–1946* (Philadelphia: 1976), pp. 13–15; and Mark A. Stoler, *Allies and Adversaries: The Joint Chiefs of Staff, the Grand Alliance, and U.S. Strategy in World War II* (Chapel Hill: University of North Carolina Press, 2000), pp. 133, 136.

9. Roosevelt to Churchill, April 6, 1945, in Loewenheim *et al.*, eds., *Roosevelt and Churchill*, p. 705.

10. Maxim Litvinov to the Soviet foreign ministry, November 8 and 17, 1933, Ministerstvo innostrannykh del SSSR, *Dokumenty vneshnei politiki, SSSR* (Moscow: 1967–), XVI, 609, 658–59. See also Thomas R. Maddux, *Years of Estrangement: American Relations with the Soviet Union, 1933–1941* (Tallahassee: 1980), pp. 14–15; and, for an overdrawn Soviet account of Roosevelt's preoccupation with "balance of power" politics, Nikolai V. Sivachev and Nikolai N. Yakovlev, *Russia and the United States*, translated by Olga Adler Titelbaum (Chicago: 1979), pp. 124, 137, 150.

11. See John Lewis Gaddis, *Russia, the Soviet Union, and the United States: An Interpretive History*, second edition (New York: 1990), pp. 136–43.

12. The standard account has long been Raymond H. Dawson, *The Decision to Aid Russia, 1941: Foreign Policy and Domestic Politics* (Chapel Hill: 1959); but see also Maddux, *Years of Estrangement*, pp. 147–56.

13. For evidence on the likelihood of a Soviet "separate peace" during World War II, see Vojtech Mastny, *Russia's Road to the Cold War: Diplomacy, Warfare, and the Politics of Communism, 1941–1945* (New York: 1979), pp. 73–85. On Japan, see Ernest R. May, "The United States, the Soviet Union, and the Far Eastern War, 1941–1945," *Pacific Historical Quarterly*, XXIV (May, 1955), 153–74; and Louis Morton, "Soviet Intervention in the War with Japan," *Foreign Affairs*, XL (July, 1962), 653–62.

14. Richard M. Leighton, "The American Arsenal Policy in World War II: A Retrospective View," in Daniel R. Beaver, ed., *Some Pathways in Twentieth Century History: Essays in Honor of Charles Reginald McCrane* (Detroit: 1969), pp. 221–52. See also Kent Roberts Greenfield, *American Strategy in World War II: A Reconsideration* (Baltimore: 1963), p. 74.

15. Maurice Matloff, "The 90-Division Gamble," in Kent Roberts Greenfield, ed., *Command Decisions* (Washington: 1960), pp. 365–81. See also Forrest C. Pogue, *George C. Marshall: Organizer of Victory* (New York: 1973), pp. 357–58, 361, 492–94.

16. W. Averell Harriman and Elie Abel, *Special Envoy to Churchill and Stalin, 1941–1946* (New York: 1975), p. 74. See also Stoler, *Allies and Adversaries*, p. 56.

17. *Ibid.*, pp. 111–12; Greenfield, *American Strategy in World War II*, pp. 71–73.

18. See, on this point, James MacGregor Burns, *Roosevelt: The Soldier of Freedom* (New York: 1970), p. 546.

19. Sivachev and Yakovlev, *Russia and the United States*, p. 163. For Stalin's suspicions of

Roosevelt, see John Lewis Gaddis, *We Now Know: Rethinking Cold War History* (New York: 1997), pp. 21–23.

20. Roosevelt informal remarks to the Advertising War Council Conference, March 8, 1944, Samuel I. Rosenman, ed., *The Public Papers and Addresses of Franklin D. Roosevelt*, 13 vols. (New York: 1938–1950), XIII, 99.

21. See, on this point, Martin Weil, *A Pretty Good Club: The Founding Fathers of the U.S. Foreign Service* (New York: 1978), pp. 67–69.

22. Roosevelt to Pope Pius XII, September 3, 1941, Elliott Roosevelt, ed., *F. D. R., His Personal Letters: 1928–1945*, 2 vols. (New York: 1950), II, 1204–5.

23. Daniel Yergin, *Shattered Peace: The Origins of the Cold War and the National Security State* (Boston: 1977), pp. 10, 44.

24. Dallek, *Roosevelt and American Foreign Policy*, pp. 102–3; Maddux, *Years of Estrangement*, pp. 92–99.

25. Memorandum, Roosevelt-Molotov conversation, May 29, 1942, *FRUS: 1942*, II, 568–69. See also the Wallace diary, November 30, 1942, in John Morton Blum, ed., *The Price of Vision: The Diary of Henry A. Wallace, 1942–1946* (Boston: 1973), p. 138; Roosevelt to George Norris, September 21, 1943, Roosevelt Papers, PPF 880; and Charles Bohlen's notes, Roosevelt-Stalin conversation, November 29, 1943, *FRUS: Cairo and Tehran*, pp. 530–32.

26. Wallace diary, December 16, 1942, Blum, ed., *The Price of Vision*, p. 146. See also Bohlen notes, Roosevelt-Stalin meeting, Teheran, November 28, 1943, *FRUS: Cairo and Tehran*, pp. 485–86; and Christopher Thorne, *Allies of a Kind: The United States, Great Britain, and the War Against Japan, 1941–1945* (New York: 1979), pp. 419–20.

27. Michael Schaller, *The U.S. Crusade in China, 1938–1945* (New York: 1979), pp. 98–99; also Dallek, *Roosevelt and American Foreign Policy*, pp. 390–91; and Thorne, *Allies of a Kind*, pp. 307–8.

28. See George F. Kennan, *The Decline of Bismarck's European Order: Franco-Russian Relations, 1875–1890* (Princeton: 1979), especially pp. 421–22.

29. Wm. Roger Louis, *Imperialism at Bay: The United States and the Decolonization of the British Empire, 1941–1945* (New York: 1978). See also the appropriate chapters in Thorne, *Allies of a Kind*.

30. Herring, *Aid to Russia*, pp. 38, 47–48, 86.

31. *Ibid.*, pp. 144–78; John Lewis Gaddis, *The United States and the Origins of the Cold War, 1941–1947* (New York: 1972), pp. 128–29, 197.

32. Martin J. Sherwin, *A World Destroyed: The Atomic Bomb and the Grand Alliance* (New York: 1975), pp. 67–140. See also Stoler, *Allies and Adversaries*, p. 133; and two articles by Barton J. Bernstein, "The Quest for Security: American Foreign Policy and International Control of Atomic Energy, 1942–1946," *Journal of American History*, LX (March, 1974), 1003–44; and "Roosevelt, Truman, and the Atomic Bomb, 1941–1945: A Reinterpretation," *Political Science Quarterly*, XC (Spring, 1975), 23–69.

33. See, for example, Gaddis Smith, *American Diplomacy During the Second World War, 1941–1945* (New York: 1965), pp. 11, 14–16.

34. This point is well made in Arthur Schlesinger, Jr., "Origins of the Cold War," *Foreign Affairs*, XLVI (October, 1967), 48–49.

35. Vladimir O. Pechatnov and C. Carl Edmondson, "The Russian Perspective," in Ralph B. Levering, Vladimir O. Pechatnov, Verena Botzenhart-Viehe, and C. Carl Edmondson, *Debating the Origins of the Cold War: American and Russian Perspectives* (New York: 2002), p. 93.

36. Mastny, *Russia's Road to the Cold War*, pp. 270–71. See also Bradley F. Smith and Elena Agarossi, *Operation Sunrise: The Secret Surrender* (New York: 1979).

37. Wallace diary, November 30, 1942, Blum, ed., *The Price of Vision*, p. 138.

38. Gaddis, *The United States and the Origins of the Cold War*, pp. 23–31, 149–71.

39. Herring, *Aid to Russia*, pp. 80–142; Stoler, *Allies and Adversaries*, pp. 132–33.

40. Lynn Etheridge Davis, *The Cold War Begins: Soviet-American Conflict over Eastern Europe* (Princeton: 1974), pp. 62–171. See also Weil, *A Pretty Good Club*, pp. 105–8; Hugh DeSantis, *The Diplomacy of Silence: The American Foreign Service, the Soviet Union, and the Cold War, 1933–1947* (Chicago: 1980), pp. 106–30; and Charles E. Bohlen, *Witness to History, 1929–1969* (New York: 1973), pp. 121–26.

41. Harriman to Harry Hopkins, September 10, 1944, *FRUS: 1944*, IV, 989; Deane to George C. Marshall, December 2, 1944, *FRUS: 1944*, IV, 992–98; Harriman and Abel, *Special Envoy*, pp. 335–49; and John R. Deane, *The Strange Alliance: The Story of Our Efforts at Wartime Cooperation with Russia* (New York: 1947).

42. George F. Kennan, *Memoirs: 1925–1950* (Boston: 1967), pp. 204, 220–23, 250, 253, 256.

43. Harriman to Hopkins, September 10, 1944, *FRUS: 1944*, IV, 989–90; see also Harriman and Abel, *Special Envoy*, pp. 414–15; and Bohlen, *Witness to History*, pp. 164, 175–76.

44. Gaddis, *The United States and the Origins of the Cold War*, pp. 200–6, 217–20, 230–33. See also Yergin, *Shattered Peace*, pp. 69–86; and Alonzo L. Hamby, *Man of the People: A Life of Harry S. Truman* (New York: 1995), pp. 315–18.

45. John Lewis Gaddis, "Harry S. Truman and the Origins of Containment," in Frank J. Merli and Theodore A. Wilson, eds., *Makers of American Diplomacy* (New York: 1974), pp. 503–6.

46. Quoted in Patricia Dawson Ward, *The Threat of Peace: James F. Byrnes and the Council of Foreign Ministers, 1945–1946* (Kent, Ohio: 1979), p. 22.

47. Gaddis, *The United States and the Origins of the Cold War*, pp. 215–24, 240–41; Herring, *Aid to Russia*, pp. 180–236; Thomas G. Paterson, *Soviet-American Confrontation: Postwar Reconstruction and the Origins of the Cold War* (Baltimore: 1973), pp. 33–46.

48. Ward, *The Threat of Peace*, pp. 31, 34; Davis, *The Cold War Begins*, pp. 288–334; Geir Lundestad, *The American Non-Policy Towards Eastern Europe, 1943–1947* (Oslo: 1978), pp. 235–48, 271–78.

49. Minutes, meeting of the secretaries of State, War, and Navy, October 10, 1945, *FRUS: 1945*, II, 56. See also the Stettinius diary, September 28, 1945, in Thomas M. Campbell and George C. Herring, Jr., eds., *The Diaries of Edward R. Stettinius, Jr., 1943–1946* (New York: 1946), pp. 427–28.

50. Gaddis, *The United States and the Origins of the Cold War*, p. 260. See also OSS R & A 2060, "Russian Reconstruction and Postwar Foreign Trade Developments," September 9, 1944, Office of Intelligence Research Files, Department of State Records, Record Group 59, National Archives.

51. Memorandum, Byrnes-Stalin meeting, December 23, 1945, *FRUS: 1945*, II, 752–53. For the Ethridge report, see Davis, *The Cold War Begins*, pp. 322–26.

52. Ward, *The Threat of Peace*, pp. 48–49; Gaddis, *The United States and the Origins of the Cold War*, pp. 268–73.

53. Yergin, *Shattered Peace*, pp. 147–62; Ward, *The Threat of Peace*, pp. 50–77; Gaddis, *The United States and the Origins of the Cold War*, pp. 273–96.

54. Kennan to the State Department, February 22 and March 20, 1946, *FRUS: 1946*, VI, 699–700, 721–22. The full "long telegram" is in *ibid.*, pp. 699–709.

55. Kennan to the State Department, March 20, 1946, *ibid.*, p. 723.

56. Kennan, *Memoirs: 1925–1950*, pp. 294–95. For the reception of Kennan's analyses in Washington, see Bruce R. Kuniholm, *The Origins of Cold War in the Near East: Great Power Conflict and Diplomacy in Iran, Turkey, and Greece* (Princeton: 1980), pp. 310–13; David Mayers, *George F. Kennan and the Dilemmas of US Foreign Policy* (New York: 1998), pp. 99–102; and Wilson D. Miscamble, C.S.C., *George F. Kennan and*

the Making of American Foreign Policy, 1947–1950 (Princeton: 1992), pp. 25–28. For contemporary reactions, see Walter Millis, ed., *The Forrestal Diaries* (New York: 1951), pp. 135–40; *The Journals of David E. Lilienthal: The Atomic Energy Years, 1945–1950* (New York: 1964), p. 26; and an H. Freeman Matthew memorandum, "Political Estimate of Soviet Policy for Use in Connection with Military Studies," April 1, 1946, *FRUS: 1946*, I, 1167.

57. Kennan to the State Department, February 22, 1946, *ibid.*, VI, 708–9.

58. Byrnes radio address, May 20, 1946, *Department of State Bulletin* [hereafter *DSB*], XIV (June 2, 1946), 950.

59. These postulates are drawn from the following sources: Byrnes speech to the Overseas Press Club, New York, February 28, 1946, *DSB*, XIV (March 10, 1946), 355–58; Byrnes speech to the Society of the Friendly Sons of St. Patrick, New York, March 16, 1946, *ibid.*, XIV (March 24, 1946), 481–86; Memorandum prepared by Admiral Forrest P. Sherman, March 17, 1946 [misdated 1945], James V. Forrestal Papers, Box 71, "Miscellaneous Folder, 1946," Princeton University Library; SWNCC 202/2, "Policy Concerning Provision of United States Government Military Supplies for Post-War Armed Forces of Foreign Nations," March 21, 1946, *FRUS: 1946*, I, 1145–60; SWN-4096, "Foreign Policy of the United States," March 29, 1946, *ibid.*, pp. 1165–66; Matthews memorandum, April 1, 1946, *ibid.*, pp. 1167–71; Truman Army Day speech, April 6, 1946, *DSB*, XIV (April 21, 1946), 622–24; James C. Dunn to Byrnes, April 18, 1946, *FRUS: 1946*, II, 72; Clark M. Clifford to Truman, "American Relations with the Soviet Union," September 24, 1946, published in Arthur Krock, *Memoirs: Sixty Years on the Firing Line* (New York: 1968), pp. 419–82.

60. *Ibid.*, p. 482.

61. SWN-4096, March 29, 1946, *FRUS: 1946*, I, 1165.

62. Kuniholm, *The Origins of the Cold War in the Near East*, pp. 303–410.

63. Herbert Feis, *Contest over Japan* (New York: 1967), pp. 127–51; John Lewis Gaddis, "Korea in American Politics, Strategy, and Diplomacy, 1945–50," in Yonosuke Nagai and Akira Iriye, eds., *The Origins of the Cold War in Asia* (New York: 1977), pp. 280–81.

64. Bruce Kuklick, *American Policy and the Division of Germany: The Clash with Russia over Reparations* (Ithaca: 1972), pp. 205–25; John H. Backer, *The Decision to Divide Germany: American Foreign Policy in Transition* (Durham: 1978), pp. 141–44.

65. Ward, *The Threat of Peace*, pp. 78–171.

66. See, on this point, Kuniholm, *The Origins of the Cold War in the Near East*, pp. 381–82.

67. For an elaboration of this argument, see John Lewis Gaddis, "Was the Truman Doctrine a Real Turning Point?" *Foreign Affairs*, LII (January, 1974), 386–402.

68. James F. Schnabel, *The Joint Chiefs of Staff and National Policy, 1945–1947* (Wilmington, Del.: 1979), p. 238. See also the general account of demobilization, *ibid.*, pp. 195–238.

69. See Appendix.

70. Gaddis, *The United States and the Origins of the Cold War*, pp. 341–46.

TWO. *Kennan and Containment*

1. Kennan, *Memoirs: 1925–1950*, p. 294.

2. *Ibid.*, pp. 307–9, 327. See also Miscamble, *Kennan and the Making of American Foreign Policy*, pp. 3–40.

3. "The Sources of Soviet Conduct," *Foreign Affairs*, XXV (July, 1947), 566–82. For the circumstances surrounding publication of this article, see Kennan, *Memoirs: 1925–1950*, pp. 354–57.

4. Walter Lippmann, *The Cold War: A Study in U.S. Foreign Policy* (New York: 1947).

5. Kennan, *Memoirs: 1925–1950*, pp. 357–63. See also John Lewis Gaddis, "Containment: A Reassessment," *Foreign Affairs*, LV (July, 1977), 873–87.

6. See, for example, Charles Gati, "What Containment Meant," *Foreign Policy*, #7(Summer, 1972), 22–40; Eduard M. Mark, "What Kind of Containment?" in Thomas G. Paterson, ed., *Containment and the Cold War* (Reading, Mass: 1973), pp. 96–109; C. Ben Wright, "Mr. 'X' and Containment," *Slavic Review*, XXXV (March, 1976), 1–31; Gaddis, "Containment: A Reassessment," pp. 873–87; Eduard Mark, "The Question of Containment: A Reply to John Lewis Gaddis," *Foreign Affairs*, LVI (January, 1978), 430–40; John W. Coogan and Michael H. Hunt, "Kennan and Containment: A Comment," Society for Historians of American Foreign Relations *Newsletter*, IX (March, 1978), 23–25; Frank Costigliola, " 'Unceasing Pressure for Penetration,': Gender, Pathology, and Emotion in George Kennan's Formation of the Cold War," *Journal of American History*, LXXXIII (March, 1997), 1309–39; as well as the more general accounts of Kennan's thinking contained in Mayers, *George Kennan*, Miscamble, *Kennan and the Making of American Foreign Policy*, Walter L. Hixson, *George F. Kennan: Cold War Iconoclast* (New York: 1989), and Anders Stephanson, *Kennan and the Art of Foreign Policy* (Cambridge, Mass.: 1989).

7. Kissinger, *White House Years*, p. 135.

8. Draft paper, "Comments on the General Trend of U.S. Foreign Policy," August 20, 1948, George F. Kennan Papers, Princeton University.

9. PPS/23, "Review of Current Trends: U.S. Foreign Policy," February 24, 1948, *FRUS: 1948*, I, 526–27. See also George F. Kennan, *Realities of American Foreign Policy* (Princeton: 1954), pp. 3–30; and Jonathan Knight, "George Frost Kennan and the Study of American Foreign Policy: Some Critical Comments," *Western Political Quarterly*, XX (March, 1967), 150–51.

10. National War College lecture [hereafter NWC], "What Is Policy?" December 18, 1947, in Giles D. Harlow and George C. Maerz, *Measures Short of War: The George F. Kennan Lectures at the National War College, 1946–47* (Washington: 1991), p. 298; NWC lecture, "Where Are We Today?" December 21, 1948, Kennan Papers, Box 17.

11. *Ibid.*; NWC lecture, "Planning of Foreign Policy," June 18, 1947, in Harlow and Maerz, eds., *Measures Short of War*, pp. 213–14.

12. PPS/23, February 24, 1948, *FRUS: 1948*, I, 527; Kennan to Dean Acheson, November 14, 1949, *FRUS: 1949*, II, 19.

13. NWC lecture, December 21, 1948, Kennan Papers, Box 17.

14. "Comments on the General Trend of U.S. Foreign Policy," August 20, 1948, *ibid.*, Box 23.

15. NWC lecture, "Contemporary Problems of Foreign Policy," September 17, 1948, *ibid.*, Box 17. See also Kennan's lecture at the Naval War College, "U.S. Foreign Policy, October 11, 1948, *ibid.*; Kennan's briefing at the State Department China Round Table discussion, October 6, 1949, copy in Harry S. Truman Papers, PSF, Box 174, Subject File: "Foreign Affairs: China: Record of Round Table Discussion," Harry S. Truman Library; Kennan, *Realities of American Foreign Policy*, pp. 63–65; Kennan, *Memoirs: 1925–1950*, p. 359.

16. Address to the Academy of Political Science, New York, November 10, 1949, Kennan Papers, Box 1.

17. PPS 39/1, "U.S. Policy Toward China," November 23, 1948, *FRUS: 1948*, VIII, 208.

18. NWC lecture, September 17, 1948, Kennan Papers, Box 17; Report on "International Control of Atomic Energy," January 20, 1950, *FRUS: 1950*, I, 44. See also Kennan's NWC lecture, "Where Do We Stand?" December 21, 1949, Kennan Papers, Box 17.

19. Naval Academy address, May 9, 1947, *ibid.* See also "Comments on the General Trend of U.S. Foreign Policy," August 20, 1948, *ibid.*, Box 23.

20. NWC lecture, September 17, 1948, Kennan Papers, Box 17. See also PPS/13, "Resume of World Situation," November 6, 1947, *FRUS: 1947*, I, 772; and Kennan, *Memoirs: 1925–1950*, pp. 365–66.

21. Unpublished paper, "The Soviet Way of Thought and Its Effect on Foreign Policy," January 24, 1947, Kennan Papers, Box 16. See also "The Sources of Soviet Conduct," pp. 566–71; and NWC lecture, "The World Position and Problems of the United States," August 30, 1949, Kennan Papers, Box 17.

22. Kennan to the State Department, February 22, 1946, *FRUS: 1946*, VI, 700–1; "The Sources of Soviet Conduct," pp. 571–73; NSC 20/1, "U.S. Objectives with Respect to Russia," August 18, 1948, in Thomas H. Etzold and John Lewis Gaddis, eds., *Containment: Documents on American Policy and Strategy, 1945–1950* (New York: 1978), pp. 185–86; Kennan to Robert G. Hooker, October 17, 1949, *FRUS: 1949*, I, 403–4.

23. "The Soviet Way of Thought and Its Effect on Foreign Policy," January 24, 1947, Kennan Papers, Box 16; "The Sources of Soviet Conduct," p. 573.

24. NSC 20/2(PPS 33), "Factors Affecting the Nature of U.S. Defense Arrangements in the Light of Soviet Policies," August 25, 1948, *FRUS: 1948*, I, 619; NWC lecture, September 17, 1948, Kennan Papers, Box 17. Kennan repeatedly emphasized the unlikelihood of the Soviet Union starting a war. See his lecture to Foreign Service and State Department personnel, September 17, 1946, *ibid.*, Box 16; comments at the Air War College, April 10, 1947, *ibid.*, Box 17; address at the Naval Academy, May 9, 1947, *ibid.*; PPS/13, November 6, 1947, *FRUS: 1947*, I, 770–71; talk to the Secretary of the Navy's Council, December 3, 1947, Kennan Papers, Box 17; statement to a meeting of the Armed Services Committee, January 8, 1948, *ibid.*, unsent letter to Walter Lippmann, April 1, 1948, quoted in *Memoirs: 1925–1950*, p. 361; NWC lecture, August 30, 1948, Kennan Papers, Box 17; and briefing to the State Department China Round Table discussion, October 6, 1948, Truman Papers, PSF Box 174: "China: Record of Round Table Discussion."

25. NWC lecture, June 18, 1947, quoted in Kennan, *Memoirs: 1925–1950*, p. 351. See also the NWC lecture of March 28, 1947, quoted in *ibid.*, p. 318; and a lecture to the Foreign Service Institute, "Basic Objectives of United States Foreign Policy," January 19, 1949, Kennan Papers, Box 17.

26. NWC lecture, March 28, 1947, quoted in Kennan, *Memoirs: 1925–1950*, p. 319; Foreign Service Institute lecture, January 19, 1949, Kennan Papers, Box 17; Academy of Political Science address, November 10, 1949, *ibid.*, Box 1.

27. "The Sources of Soviet Conduct," p. 582; NWC lecture, December 21, 1949, Kennan Papers, Box 17. See also Kennan to Hooker, October 17, 1949, *FRUS: 1949*, I, 404–5.

28. This is a distillation of Kennan's thinking based on his writings and lectures between 1947 and 1949, and on an interview with him at Princeton, New Jersey, on February 2, 1977. See, in particular, NSC 20/1, August 18, 1948, in Etzold and Gaddis, eds., *Containment*, pp. 176–89; NWC lecture, September 17, 1948, Kennan Papers, Box 17; Naval War College lecture, October 11, 1949, *ibid.*; notes prepared for a seminar at Princeton, January 23–26, 1949, and for a presentation to the House Armed Services Committee, January 25, 1949, *ibid.*; and NWC lecture, August 30, 1949, *ibid.*

29. PPS/13, November 6, 1947, *FRUS: 1947*, I, 771; talk on "Russian-American Relations" to the Board of Governors of the Federal Reserve System, December 1, 1947, and to the Secretary of the Navy's Council, December 3, 1947, Kennan Papers, Box 17; PPS/1, "Policy with Respect to American Aid to Western Europe," May 23, 1947, *FRUS: 1947*, III, 225.

30. See, on this point, Hadley Arkes, *Bureaucracy, the Marshall Plan, and the National Interest* (Princeton: 1972), p. 51.

31. PPS/1, May 23, 1947, *FRUS: 1947*, III, 227. See also Kennan's notes for a conversation with Marshall, July 21, 1947, *ibid.*, p. 335; and PPS/4, "Certain Aspects of the European

Recovery Program from the United States Standpoint (Preliminary Report), July 23, 1947, in Etzold and Gaddis, eds., *Containment*, p. 110.

32. PPS/23, February 24, 1948, *FRUS: 1948*, I, 515–18. See also PPS/13, November 6, 1947, *FRUS: 1947*, I, 774–75.

33. NWC lecture, December 21, 1948, Kennan Papers, Box 17. See also PPS/10, "Results of Planning Staff Study of Questions Involved in the Japanese Peace Settlement," October 14, 1947, *FRUS: 1947*, VI, 537–43; Kennan comments at a meeting of the Secretary of the Navy's Council, January 14, 1948, Kennan Papers, Box 17; PPS/28, "Recommendations with Respect to U.S. Policy Toward Japan," March 25, 1948, *FRUS: 1948*, VI, 694; Kennan briefing at State Department China Round Table discussion, October 6, 1949, Truman Papers, PSF Box 174, "China: Record of Round Table Discussion"; Kennan talk to CIA conference, October 14, 1949, Kennan Papers, Box 17. See also Takeshi Igarashi, "George F. Kennan and the Redirection of American Occupation Policy for Japan: The Formulation of National Security Council Paper 13/2," unpublished paper prepared for the Amherst College Conference on the Occupation of Japan, Amherst, Massachusetts, August 20–23, 1980.

34. Kennan post-lecture comment, NWC lecture, "Measures Short of War (Diplomatic)," September 16, 1946, Kennan Papers, Box 16; "Comments on the General Trend of U.S. Foreign Policy," August 20, 1948, *ibid.*, Box 23; NSC 20/2 (PPS/33), "Factors Affecting the Nature of the U.S. Defense Arrangements in the Light of Soviet Policies," August 25, 1948, *FRUS: 1948*, I, 621–22.

35. "Comments on the General Trend of U.S. Foreign Policy," August 20, 1948, Kennan Papers, Box 23; NWC lecture, "Soviet Diplomacy," October 6, 1947, in Harlow and Maerz, eds., *Measures Short of War*, p. 260.

36. See, on this point, Kennan to Marshall, January 20, 1948, *FRUS: 1948*, III, 7–8.

37. Leighton, "The American Arsenal Policy in World War II," pp. 221–52.

38. Talk given to the Board of Governors of the Federal Reserve System, December 1, 1947, and to the Secretary of the Navy's Council, December 3, 1947, Kennan Papers, Box 17.

39. Kennan notes for a State Department seminar, October 6, 1949, Kennan Papers, Box 23; NWC lecture, December 18, 1947, in Harlow and Maerz, eds., *Measures Short of War*, p. 304; NWC lecture, May 6, 1947 (question and answer period), *ibid.*, p. 198. For Kennan's views on Greece and Turkey, see the preceding note. His ideas on the "defensive perimeter" can be found in the minutes of the Secretary of the Navy's Council meeting of January 14, 1948, Kennan Papers, Box 17; PPS/23, February 23, 1948, *FRUS: 1948*, I, 525; Kennan to Marshall, March 14, 1948, *ibid.*, pp. 533–34; and Naval War College lecture, October 11, 1948, Kennan Papers, Box 17.

40. NWC lecture, December 18, 1947, in Harlow and Maerz, eds., *Measures Short of War*, p. 302; Kennan to MacArthur, March 5, 1948, enclosed in PPS/28, March 25, 1948, *FRUS: 1948*, VI, 699. See also Kennan's comments during the fifth Washington Explanatory Talks on Security, July 9, 1948, *ibid.*, III, 177; PPS/37, "Policy Questions Concerning a Possible German Settlement," August 12, 1948, *ibid.*, II, 1290, 1295–96; and PPS/43, "Considerations Affecting the Conclusion of a North American Security Pact," November 23, 1948, *ibid.*, III, 287.

41. NSC 20/1, August 18, 1948, in Etzold and Gaddis, eds., *Containment*, pp. 176–78. See also the minutes of the Policy Planning Staff meeting of March 1, 1949, *FRUS: 1949*, V, 9–10; and Kennan's NWC lecture, August 30, 1949, Kennan Papers, Box 17.

42. NSC 20/1, August 18, 1948, in Etzold and Gaddis, eds., *Containment*, pp. 186–87.

43. *Ibid.*, p. 192; NSC 58/2 (PPS/59), December 8, 1949, "United States Policy Toward the Soviet Satellite States in Eastern Europe," *FRUS: 1949*, V, 48–49.

44. PPS/13, November 6, 1947, *FRUS: 1947*, I, 773–74. See also NWC lecture, "The Background of Current Russian Diplomatic Moves," December 10, 1946, Kennan Papers, Box

16; University of Virginia lecture, "Russian-American Relations," February 20, 1947, *ibid.*; extemporaneous talk to selected industrial leaders, January 14, 1948, *ibid.*, Box 17; and PPS/35, "The Attitude of This Government Toward Events in Yugoslavia," June 30, 1948, *FRUS: 1948*, IV, 1079–81.

45. Naval War College lecture, October 11, 1948, Kennan Papers, Box 17; University of Virginia lecture, February 20, 1947, *ibid.*, Box 16. Kennan's remark about a Chinese Communist victory threatening the Soviet Union occurs in the minutes of a meeting of the Secretary of the Navy's Council, January 4, 1948, *ibid.*, Box 17. See also the transcript of a question and answer session with Kennan at the NWC, May 6, 1947, in Harlow and Maerz, eds., *Measures Short of War*, p. 199; PPS/13, November 6, 1947, *FRUS: 1947*, I, 775–76; Kennan handwritten notes on China, February, 1948, Kennan Papers, Box 23; NWC lecture, September 17, 1948, *ibid.*, Box 17; PPS/39, "United States Policy Toward China," September 7, 1948, *FRUS: 1948*, VIII, 17; PPS 39/1, November 23, 1948, *ibid.*, pp. 208–9; Kennan briefing to State Department China Round Table discussion, October 6, 1949, Truman Papers, PSF Box 174, "China: Record of Round Table Discussion"; and Kennan, *Memoirs: 1925–1950*, pp. 373–74.

46. NWC lecture, May 6, 1947, in Harlow and Maerz, eds., *Measures Short of War*, p. 191; University of Virginia lecture, February 20, 1947, *ibid.*, Box 16.

47. *Ibid.* See also PPS/1, May 23, 1947, *FRUS: 1947*, III, 224–25, 229–30; talk to Board of Governors, Federal Reserve System, December 1, 1947, and to the Secretary of the Navy's Council, December 3, 1947, Kennan Papers, Box 17; NWC lecture, December 18, 1947, in Harlow and Maerz, eds., *Measures Short of War*, p. 306.

48. Lecture at Joint Orientation Conference, Pentagon, November 8, 1948, Kennan Papers, Box 17. See also Kennan's Air War College lecture, April 10, 1947, *ibid.*; and NSC 20/2, August 25, 1948, *FRUS: 1948*, I, 619.

49. PPS/23, February 24, 1948, *FRUS: 1948*, I, 519. See also Kennan talk to selected industrial leaders, January 14, 1948, Kennan Papers, Box 17.

50. NWC lecture, September 17, 1948, *ibid.*; NSC 58/2, December 8, 1949, *FRUS: 1949*, V, 54. See also notes taken by Robert Joyce at a Policy Planning Staff meeting on April 1, 1949, *ibid.*, p. 12; and Kennan's comments at a meeting of the American members of the Combined Policy Committee, September 13, 1949, *ibid.*, I, 521.

51. Kennan memorandum, January 10, 1949, *FRUS: 1949*, VIII, 26–27; minutes, Policy Planning Staff meeting of October 11, 1949, *ibid.*, I, 400; draft memorandum to Acheson, February 17, 1950, *FRUS: 1950*, I, 161. See also Kennan's lecture at the Joint Orientation Conference, Pentagon, September 19, 1949, Kennan Papers, Box 17.

52. Joint Orientation Conference lecture, November 8, 1948, *ibid.*

53. Kennan, *Memoirs: 1925–1950*, pp. 129–30; Joint Orientation Conference lecture, September 19, 1949, Kennan Papers, Box 17; NSC 58/2, December 8, 1949, *FRUS: 1949*, V, 51. See also Kennan's lecture to Foreign Service and State Department personnel, September 17, 1946, Kennan Papers, Box 16.

54. See NSC 20/1, August 18, 1948, in Etzold and Gaddis, eds., *Containment*, pp. 178–81; and Kennan, *Memoirs: 1925–1950*, p. 365.

55. "International Control of Atomic Energy," January 20, 1950, *FRUS: 1950*, I, 37; NWC lecture, December 21, 1949, Kennan Papers, Box 17. See also Kennan's lecture to Foreign Service and State Department personnel, September 17, 1946, *ibid.*, Box 16; and NSC 20/1, August 18, 1948, in Etzold and Gaddis, eds., *Containment*, pp. 174–75, 191–93.

56. Lecture to Foreign Service and State Department personnel, September 17, 1946, quoted in Kennan, *Memoirs: 1925–1950*, p. 302; PPS/23, February 24, 1948, *FRUS: 1948*, I, 522–23; Kennan unsent letter to Lippmann, April 6, 1948, Kennan Papers, Box 17. See also George Urban, "A Conversation with George F. Kennan," *Encounter*, XLVII (September, 1976), 31.

57. University of Virginia lecture, February 20, 1947, Kennan Papers, Box 16; NWC lecture, October 6, 1947, in Harlow and Maerz, eds., *Measures Short of War*, p. 258; NSC 20/1, August 18, 1948, in Etzold and Gaddis, eds., *Containment*, p. 187. See also Kennan, *Memoirs: 1925–1950*, p. 303; and Kennan's unpublished paper, "The Soviet Way of Thought and Its Effect on Foreign Policy," January 24, 1947, Kennan Papers, Box 16.

58. *Ibid.*; University of Virginia lecture, February 20, 1947, *ibid.*; Naval Academy address, May 9, 1947, *ibid.*, Box 17. For Kennan's interest in early American diplomacy, see his address to the Academy of Political Science, November 10, 1949, *ibid.*, Box 1; and Kennan, *Realities of American Foreign Policy*, pp. 6–14.

59. NWC lecture, August 30, 1949, Kennan Papers, Box 17. See also Kennan, *Memoirs: 1925–1950*, p. 405n.

60. PPS/23, February 24, 1948, *FRUS: 1948*, I, 513; draft memorandum for Acheson, February 17, 1950, *FRUS: 1950*, I, 166–67.

61. Kennan to Dean Rusk, September 7, 1949, *FRUS: 1949*, I, 381; Kennan diary entry, November 19, 1949, quoted in *Memoirs: 1925–1950*, p. 467; talk to CIA conference, October 14, 1949, Kennan Papers, Box 17. See also Kennan to Robert A. Lovett, August 5, 1948, *FRUS: 1948*, I, 599; Kennan to Acheson and James E. Webb, April 14, 1949, *FRUS: 1949*, I, 282; and Paul Hammond, "NSC-68: Prologue to Rearmament," in Warner R. Schilling, Paul Y. Hammond, and Glenn H. Snyder, *Strategy, Policy, and Defense Budgets* (New York: 1962), pp. 315–18.

62. Kennan post-lecture comment, NWC lecture, September 16, 1946, Kennan Papers, Box 16; Kennan personal memorandum, January 23, 1948, quoted in *Memoirs: 1925–1950*, p. 405n. For Kennan's views on the Truman Doctrine, see *ibid.*, pp. 54, 322–23; and PPS/1, May 23, 1947, *FRUS: 1947*, III, 229–30.

63. Kennan to Acheson, November 14, 1949, *FRUS: 1949*, II, 18; NWC lecture, December 21, 1949, Kennan Papers, Box 17.

THREE. *Implementing Containment*

1. Kennan, *Memoirs: 1925–1950*, p. 403.

2. See, for example, Wright, "Mr. 'X' and Containment," pp. 1–36; Mark, "What Kind of Containment?," pp. 96–109; also Louis Halle, *The Cold War as History* (New York: 1967), pp. 106–8.

3. Coogan and Hunt, "Kennan and Containment," p. 25.

4. Kennan, *Memoirs: 1925–1950*, pp. 343, 393.

5. See, especially, the succinct summary of Kennan's three stages of containment included in NSC 52/3, "Governmental Programs in National Security and International Affairs for the Fiscal Year 1951," approved by the National Security Council on September 29, 1949, *FRUS: 1949*, I, 386–87.

6. Gaddis, *The United States and the Origins of the Cold War*, pp. 1–31. See also Dean Acheson, *Present at the Creation: My Years in the State Department* (New York: 1969), pp. 726–27.

7. JCS 1769/1, "United States Assistance to Other Countries from the Standpoint of National Security," April 29, 1947, *FRUS: 1947*, I, 748; Bohlen memorandum, August 30, 1947, *ibid.*, p. 763; Forrestal Diary, November 7, 1947, Millis, ed., *The Forrestal Diaries*, p. 341. (Marshall's statement is in Forrestal's paraphrase.) The Kennan memorandum read by Marshall was a summary of PPS 13, "Resume of World Situation," November 6, 1947, *FRUS: 1947*, I, 770n–71n. See also a memorandum by the Executive Committee on the Regulation of Armaments, "Applying the Truman Doctrine to the United Nations,"

July 30, 1947, *ibid.*, pp. 579–80; and Millis, ed., *The Forrestal Diaries*, pp. 307, 349–51, 366–67.

8. See, on this point, Alan K. Henrikson, "America's Changing Place in the World: From 'Periphery' to 'Centre'?" in Jean Gottmann, ed., *Centre and Periphery: Spatial Variation in Politics* (Beverly Hills, Cal., 1980), especially pp. 83–86. For an early example of Mackinder's influence on American geopolitical thinking, see Nicholas John Spykman, *America's Strategy in World Politics: The United States and the Balance of Power* (New York: 1942), especially pp. 194–99; also Charles Kruszewski, "The Pivot of History," *Foreign Affairs*, XXXII (April, 1954), 388–401; and G. Etzel Pearcy, "Geopolitics and Foreign Relations," *DSB*, L (March 2, 1964), 318–30. On Mackinder himself, see Brian W. Blouet, *Halford Mackinder: A Biography* (College Station, Tx.: 1987).

9. NSC 7, "The Position of the United States with Respect to Soviet-Directed World Communism," March 30, 1948, *FRUS: 1948*, I, 546; NSC 20/4, "U.S. Objectives with Respect to the U.S.S.R. to Counter Soviet Threats to National Security," November 23, 1948, *ibid.*, p. 667. See also JCS 1769/1, April 29, 1947, *FRUS: 1947*, I, 739; and CIA 1, "Review of the World Situation as It Relates to the Security of the United States," September 28, 1947, Truman Papers, PSF Box 255, "Central Intelligence Report– ORE 1948."

10. "The Sources of Soviet Conduct," p. 581. My distinction between "perimeter" and "strongpoint" defense owes much to Edward N. Luttwak, *The Grand Strategy of the Roman Empire* (Baltimore: 1976), pp. 19, 130–31, 137.

11. Marshall to Lovett, April 23, 1948, *FRUS: 1948*, III, 103. See also Warner R. Schilling, "The Politics of National Defense: Fiscal 1950," in Schilling, *et al.*, *Strategy, Politics, and Defense Budgets*, especially pp. 98–114. For a broader perspective on concerns about national solvency, as well as the possibility of a garrison state, see Michael J. Hogan, *A Cross of Iron: Harry S. Truman and the Origins of the National Security State, 1945–1954* (New York: 1998); and Aaron L. Friedberg, *In the Shadow of the Garrison State: America's Anti-Statism and Its Cold War Strategy* (Princeton: 2000).

12. See, on this point, U. S. Congress, House of Representatives, Committee on Foreign Affairs [hereafter HFAC], *Assistance to Greece and Turkey* (Washington: 1947), pp. 14–15; U. S. Congress, Senate, Committee on Foreign Relations [hereafter SFRC], *Assistance to Greece and Turkey* (Washington: 1947), p. 13; and executive session testimony in SFRC, *Legislative Origins of the Truman Doctrine* (Washington: 1973), pp. 17, 22. See also *DSB*, XVI (May 4, 1947), 849, 870, 879–90, 882; and an interim State-War-Navy Coordinating Committee report, "Policies and Principles for Extension of U.S. Aid to Foreign Nations," April 21, 1947, *FRUS: 1947*, III, 208–9.

13. Truman speech to Inter-American Conference, Rio de Janeiro, September 2, 1947, *Public Papers of the Presidents: Harry S. Truman, 1947* [hereafter *TPP*], p. 430; Lovett memorandum of conversation with the Turkish Ambassador, July 21, 1948, *FRUS: 1948*, III, 197. See also Robert P. Patterson to Dean Acheson, April 4, 1947, *FRUS: 1947*, VI, 626–27; JCS 1769/1, April 29, 1947, *ibid.*, I, 739; and Lovett's comments at the first meeting of the Washington Exploratory Talks on Security, July 6, 1948, *FRUS: 1948*, III, 150.

14. See, for example, JCS 1769/1, April 29, 1947, *FRUS: 1947*, I, 738–46; JCS 1725/1, "Strategic Guidance for Industrial Mobilization Planning," May 1, 1947, in Etzold and Gaddis, eds., *Containment*, pp. 302–11; CIA 1, September 26, 1947, Truman Papers, PSF Box 255; JCS 1844/13, "Brief of Short Range Emergency War Plan (HALFMOON), July 21, 1948, in Etzold and Gaddis, eds., *Containment*, pp. 315–23; JCS 1844/46, "Joint Outline Emergency War Plan 'OFFTACKLE,'" December 8, 1949, Joint Chiefs of Staff Records, 381 U.S.S.R. (3–2–46), Sec. 40, Record Group 218, National Archives. See also the summary of war plans in Forrestal to Truman, January 6, 1948, Truman Papers, PSF Box 156, "Subject File: Cabinet: Defense, Secy. of– reports."

15. JWPC 476/2, "The Soviet Threat in the Far East and the Means Required to Oppose It: Short Title: MOONRISE," Joint Chiefs of Staff Records, 381 U.S.S.R. (3–2–46), sec. 6, Record Group 218, National Archives; CIA ORE 17–49, "The Strategic Importance of the Far East to the U.S. and the U.S.S.R.," May 4, 1949, Truman Papers, PSF Box 256, "Central Intelligence Reports: ORE 1949"; Acheson executive session testimony before the Senate Foreign Relations Committee, October 12, 1949, and May 1, 1950, SFRC hearings, *Reviews of the World Situation: 1949–1950* (Washington: 1974), pp. 87, 291–92; and Charlton Ogburn, Jr., memorandum, "Decisions Reached by Consensus at the Meetings with the Secretary and the Consultants on the Far East," November 2, 1949, *FRUS: 1949*, IX, 160–61. For more on the "defensive perimeter" concept, see John Lewis Gaddis, *The Long Peace: Inquiries into the History of the Cold War* (New York: 1987), pp. 72–103.

16. PPS 23, February 24, 1948, *FRUS: 1948*, I, 525; Kennan to Marshall, March 14, 1948, *ibid.*, p. 531–38. See also General MacArthur's interview in the *New York Times*, March 2, 1949; and Acheson's speech to the National Press Club, January 12, 1950, *DSB*, XXII (January 23, 1950), 111–18.

17. William Appleman Williams, *The Tragedy of American Diplomacy* (New York: 1962), p. 49; N. Gordon Levin, *Woodrow Wilson and World Politics: America's Response to War and Revolution* (New York: 1968), pp. 16–28; Leighton, "The American Arsenal Policy in World War II," pp. 221–52.

18. Forrestal to Chan Gurney, December 8, 1947, Millis, ed., *The Forrestal Diaries*, p. 350; Truman state of the union address, January 7, 1948, *TPP: 1948*, p. 8. See also Truman's address to the American Society of Newspaper Editors, April 17, 1948, *ibid.*, p. 222; Marshall to Lovett and Forrestal, November 8, 1948, *FRUS: 1948*, I, 654–55; and Schilling, "Fiscal 1950," pp. 31–32, 183–98.

19. Forrestal to Gurney, December 8, 1947, Millis, ed., *The Forrestal Diaries*, pp. 350–51. See also Melvyn P. Leffler, *A Preponderance of Power: National Security, the Truman Administration, and the Cold War* (Stanford: 1992), pp. 148–51. Some representative intelligence estimates on the Soviet willingness to risk war are J.I.C. 308/2, "Estimate of the Intentions and Capabilities of the U.S.S.R. Against the Continental United States and the Approaches Thereto, 1948–1957," February 16, 1948, Army Staff Records, ABC 381 U.S.S.R. 2 Mar 46, Sec. 5-B, National Archives; reports on "Soviet Intentions" prepared by the Joint Intelligence Committee, U.S. Embassy, Moscow, April 1, 1948, and April 5, 1948, *FRUS: 1948*, I, 551–52 and *FRUS: 1949*, V, 604–9; CIA ORE 22–48, "Possibility of Direct Soviet Military Action During 1948," April 2, 1948, Truman Papers, PSF Box 255, "Central Intelligence Reports: ORE 1948"; CIA ORE 46–49, "The Possibility of Direct Soviet Military Action During 1949," May 3, 1949, *ibid.*, Box 256, "Central Intelligence Reports, ORE 1949"; JCS 1924/6, "Current Estimate of the International Situation," September 3, 1949, Army Staff Records, G-3 144–150 092 TS Sec. III-A, Case 44.

20. Undated Truman memorandum, probably early 1949, Truman Papers, PSF Box 150, Subject File: "Bureau of Budget: Budget-misc. 1945–53."

21. Forrestal to the National Security Council, April 19, 1948, *FRUS: 1948*, I, 565. For documentation regarding the Italian and Greek situations, see *ibid.*, III, 724–93, and IV, 1–101.

22. Acheson executive session testimony, April 21, 1949, SFRC Hearings, *The Vandenberg Resolution and NATO* (Washington: 1973), p. 232. See also FACC D-3, "Basic Policies of the Military Assistance Program," February 8, 1949, *FRUS: 1949*, I, 254–55.

23. David Alan Rosenberg, "American Atomic Strategy and the Hydrogen Bomb Decision," *Journal of American History*, LXVI (June, 1979), 62–87. See also Gaddis, *The Long Peace*, pp. 106–15.

24. See, on this point, the Forrestal Diary, May 7, 1948, Millis, ed., *The Forrestal Diaries*, pp. 431–31.

25. NSC 10/2, "Directive on Office of Special Projects," June 18, 1948, in Etzold and Gaddis, eds., *Containment*, pp. 125–28. See also George F. Kennan, *Memoirs: 1950–1963* (Boston: 1972), pp. 202–3; Anne Karalekas, "History of the Central Intelligence Agency," in U.S. Congress, Senate, Select Committee to Study Government Operations with Respect to Intelligence Activities, *Final Report: Supplementary Detailed Staff Reports on Foreign and Military Intelligence: Book IV* (Washington: 1976), p. 31; and Michael Warner, ed., *CIA Cold War Records: The CIA under Harry Truman* (Washington: 1994). Vojtech Mastny, *The Cold War and Soviet Insecurity: The Stalin Years* (New York: 1996), pp. 80–85, 116–21, 128–33, provides one of the few specific accounts of CIA operations in Eastern Europe and their possible consequences.

26. John D. Hickerson memorandum of conversation with Lord Inverchapel, January 21, 1948, *FRUS: 1948*, III, 11. See also Lovett to William L. Clayton and Jefferson Caffery, August 26, 1947, *FRUS: 1947*, III, 383; Marshall's speech to the Chicago Chamber of Commerce, November 18, 1947, *DSB*, XVII (November 23, 1947), 1026; and his testimony before the Senate Foreign Relations Committee, January 8, 1948, SFRC Hearings, *European Recovery Program* (Washington: 1948), p. 13.

27. See, on this point, NSC 1/2, "The Position of the United States with Respect to Italy," February 10, 1948, *FRUS: 1948*, III, 765–69; NSC 1/3, "Position of the United States with Respect to Italy in the Light of the Possibility of Communist Participation in the Government by Legal Means," March 8, 1948, *ibid.*, pp. 775–79; and Marshall's speech at the University of California, Berkeley, March 19, 1948, *DSB*, XVIII (March 28, 1948), 424.

28. Thorp to Marshall, April 7, 1948, *FRUS: 1948*, I, 558; "State Department Comments on NSC 49," September 30, 1949, enclosed in NSC 49/1, October 4, 1949, *FRUS: 1949*, VII, 872–73. See also Geir Lundestad, *America, Scandinavia, and the Cold War, 1945–1949* (New York: 1980), pp. 109–66.

29. SWNCC-FPI 30, "Informational Objectives and Main Themes," March 3, 1947, *FRUS: 1947*, V, 77–78. The last sentence was taken verbatim from a speech Secretary of State James F. Byrnes had made to the Overseas Press Club in New York on February 28, 1946 (*DSB*, XIV [March 10, 1946], 357); in slightly altered form it was included in Truman's March 12, 1947, speech to Congress [*TPP: 1947*, p. 179]. See also Byrnes's speech to the Cleveland Council on World Affairs, January 11, 1947, *DSB*, XVI (January 19, 1947), 88–89.

30. *TPP: 1947*, p. 178.

31. *Ibid.*, pp. 177–78; Truman extemporaneous comments to the Association of Radio News Analysts, May 13, 1947, *ibid.*, p. 238; Truman speech at Charlottesville, Virginia, July 4, 1947, *ibid.*, p. 324. See also Marshall's address to the United Nations General Assembly, Paris, September 23, 1948, *DSB*, XIX (October 3, 1948), 432.

32. Acheson testimony, March 24, 1947, SFRC Hearings, *Aid to Greece and Turkey*, p. 30; Ayres Diary, May 22–23, 1947, Eban A. Ayres Papers, Box 26, Harry S. Truman Library; Joseph M. Jones to Acheson, May 20, 1947, *FRUS: 1947*, III, 233n. See also the colloquy between Acheson and Senator Claude Pepper in the SFRC hearings cited above, p. 42; Acheson's testimony before the House Foreign Affairs Committee, March 21, 1947, HFAC Hearings, *Aid to Greece and Turkey*, pp. 32–33; and Margaret Truman, *Harry S. Truman* (New York: 1973), p. 344.

33. Memorandum of comments by Under Secretary of State Clayton at a meeting of State Department heads of offices, May 28, 1947, *FRUS: 1947*, III, 235. See also Bohlen, *Witness to History*, pp. 264–65; Kennan, *Memoirs: 1925–1950*, pp. 341–42; and Arkes, *Bureaucracy, the Marshall Plan, and the National Interest*, pp. 52–55.

34. NSC 1/1, "The Position of the United States with Respect to Italy," November 14, 1947, *FRUS: 1948*, III, 724–26; NSC 5, "The Position of the United States with Respect to

Greece," January 6, 1948, *ibid.*, IV, 2–7; NSC 1/2, February 10, 1948, *ibid.*, III, 765–69; NSC 5/2, "The Position of the United States with Respect to Greece," February 12, 1948, *ibid.*, IV, 46–51; NSC 1/3, March 8, 1948, *ibid.*, III, 775–79.

35. Truman off-the-record press conference with editors of business and trade papers, April 23, 1948, *TPP: 1948*, p. 232; PPS 35, June 30, 1948, *FRUS: 1948*, IV, 1079–81. The National Security Council approved PPS 35 as NSC 18 on September 2, 1948 (*ibid.*, p. 1079n).

36. Acheson to U.S. Embassy, Belgrade, February 25, 1949, *FRUS: 1949*, V, 873; Truman press conference, December 22, 1949, *TPP: 1949*, pp. 585–86. For the blooming mill controversy, see *FRUS: 1949*, V, 896–921; also Lorraine M. Lees, *Keeping Tito Afloat: The United States, Yugoslavia, and the Cold War* (University Park, Pa.: 1997), pp. 43–79.

37. Moscow Embassy Joint Intelligence Committee report, "Soviet Intentions," April 5, 1949, *FRUS: 1949*, V, 605; NSC 58/2, "United States Policy Toward the Soviet Satellite States in Eastern Europe," *ibid.*, pp. 50–51; Foy Kohler to Acheson, April 12, 1949, *ibid.*, 13–16; State Department policy statement, "Yugoslavia," September 1, 1949, *ibid.*, pp. 941–44; "Conclusions and Recommendations," London Conference of Eastern European Chiefs of Mission, October 26, 1949, *ibid.*, pp. 28–35; George W. Perkins to Acheson, November 7, 1949, *ibid.*, pp. 36–38. The Policy Planning Staff paper that provided the basis for NSC 58/2 was PPS 59, August 25, 1949, *ibid.*, pp. 21–26.

38. Kirk to Acheson, October 7, 1949, *FRUS: 1949*, IX, 107–8. See also a State Department circular instruction, "Basic Factors in Soviet Far Eastern Policy," October 13, 1948, *FRUS: 1948*, I, 642–43; NSC 34/2, "U.S. Policy Toward China," February 28, 1949, *FRUS: 1949*, IX, 491–95; Kohler to Acheson, May 20, 1949, *ibid.*, V, 892; and Kirk to Acheson, August 13, 1949, *ibid.*, p. 923.

39. See, for example, John Carter Vincent to Marshall, June 20, 1947, *FRUS: 1947*, VII, 849; O. Edmund Clubb to Marshall, August 28, 1947, *ibid.*, pp. 264–65; W. Walton Butterworth executive session testimony, March 20, 1948, SFRC Hearings, *Foreign Relief Assistance Act of 1948* (Washington: 1973), p. 438; State Department circular instruction, "Pattern of Soviet Policy in Far East and Southeast Asia," October 13, 1948, *FRUS: 1948*, I, 639; Acheson and Butterworth executive session testimony, March 18, 1949, SFRC Hearings, *Economic Assistance to China and Korea* (Washington: 1974), pp. 30–36; Philip C. Jessup executive session testimony, October 12, 1949, SFRC Hearings, *Reviews of the World Situation*, p. 99.

40. NSC 41, draft report on "United States Policy Regarding Trade with China," February 28, 1949, *FRUS: 1949*, IX, 826–34; Acheson statement at National Security Council meeting, March 1, 1949, *ibid.*, pp. 295–96; Acheson executive session testimony, October 12, 1949, SFRC Hearings, *Reviews of the World Situation*, pp. 97–98; Acheson memorandum of conversation with the Joint Chiefs of Staff, December 29, 1949, *FRUS: 1949*, IX, 465–67.

41. Acheson memorandum of conversation with Truman, November 17, 1949, Dean Acheson Papers, Box 64, "Memoranda of Conversations, October–November, 1949," Harry S. Truman Library; NSC 48/2, "The Position of the United States with Respect to Asia," December 30, 1949, *FRUS: 1949*, VII, 1219. For the conclusions of the State Department's "consultants" see a memorandum by Charlton Ogburn, Jr., "Decisions Reached by Consensus at the Meetings with the Secretary and the Consultants on the Far East," November 2, 1949, *FRUS: 1949*, IX, 160–62; and "Outline of Far Eastern and Asian Policy for Review with the President," enclosed in Jessup to Acheson, November 16, 1949, *ibid.*, VII, 1213. For more on the recognition debate, see Nancy Bernkopf Tucker, *Patterns in the Dust: Chinese-American Relations and the Recognition Controversy, 1949–1950* (New York: 1983).

42. See, for example, Acheson to the Consulate General, Hanoi, May 20, 1949, *FRUS: 1949*, VII, 29; and Acheson's press conference statement, February 1, 1950, *DSB*, XXII (February 13, 1950), 244.

43. PPS 53, July 6, 1949, *FRUS: 1949*, IX, 356–59. See also Kennan, *Memoirs: 1950–1963*, p. 54.

44. An example of this trend is the article "Stalin on Revolution," published in *Foreign Affairs*, XXVII (January 1949), 175–214, under the pseudonym "Historicus" but written by George Allen Morgan, First Secretary of the U.S. Embassy in Moscow. For examples of administration anti-communist rhetoric, see Truman's inaugural address, January 20, 1949, *TPP: 1949*, pp. 112–13; Jessup's speech at Miami, Florida, August 24, 1949, *DSB*, XXI (September 5, 1949), 346; and John E. Peurifoy's speech at Walterboro, South Carolina, October 24, 1949, *ibid.*, XXI (October 31, 1949), 673.

45. Smith comment at Policy Planning Staff meeting, March 1, 1949, *FRUS: 1949*, V, 10; Cavendish W. Cannon to Acheson, April 25, 1949, *ibid.*, p. 889 (this dispatch, sent to U.S. missions in London, Paris, Rome, Athens, Moscow, Warsaw, Prague, Sofia, Budapest, Bucharest, and to U.S. posts in China, was actually written by William K. K. Leonhart, second secretary of the embassy in Belgrade); "Conclusions and Recommendations," London conference of East European chiefs of mission, October 26, 1949, *ibid.*, p. 31.

46. Cannon to Acheson, April 25, 1949, *FRUS: 1949*, V, 889. For more on this strategy of seeking to divide the international communist movement, see Gaddis, *The Long Peace*, pp. 147–94.

47. NSC 20/4, November 23, 1948, *FRUS: 1948*, I, 668. This statement came from an earlier Policy Planning Staff study, PPS 38, August 18, 1948, the conclusions of which can be found in *ibid.*, pp. 609–11.

48. See, for example, Truman's speech at Miami, Florida, October 18, 1948, *TPP: 1948*, pp. 816–17; Acheson statement to the press, May 19, 1949, *DSB*, XX (May 19, 1949), 675–76; Acheson speech at Berkeley, California, March 16, 1950, *ibid.*, XXII (March 27, 1950), 473–78.

49. JCS 1725/1, May 1, 1947, in Etzold and Gaddis, eds., *Containment*, p. 303; CIA 1, September 26, 1947, Truman Papers, PSF Box 255; Joint Intelligence Committee report, April 1, 1948, *FRUS: 1948*, I, 552. Estimates of Soviet and Western military strength in Europe are from Thomas W. Wolfe, *Soviet Power and Europe, 1945–1970* (Baltimore: 1970).

50. "Washington Exploratory Conversations on Security," September 9, 1948, *FRUS: 1948*, III, 237–48. See also Daryl J. Hudson, "Vandenberg Reconsidered: Senate Resolution 239 and American Foreign Policy," *Diplomatic History*, I (Winter, 1977), 46–63.

51. PPS 43, "Considerations Affecting the Conclusion of a North Atlantic Security Pact," November 23, 1948, *FRUS: 1948*, III, 285–87. See also Kennan to Lippmann, April 6, 1948, Kennan Papers, Box 17; Kennan to Lovett, April 29, 1948, *FRUS: 1948*, III, 108–9; Kennan comments at the fifth meeting of the Washington Exploratory Conversations on Security, July 9, 1948, *ibid.*, p. 177; and Kennan's lectures at the National War College, September 17, 1948, the Naval War College, October 11, 1948, and the Joint Orientation Conference at the Pentagon, November 8, 1948, all in the Kennan Papers, Box 17. Miscamble, *Kennan and the Making of American Foreign Policy*, pp. 113–40, provides a thorough account of Kennan's reservations about NATO.

52. See Willard Thorp to Marshall, April 7, 1948, *FRUS: 1948*, I, 560; Lovett to Harriman, December 3, 1948, *ibid.*, III, 305; FACC D-3, "Basic Policies of the Military Assistance Program," February 7, 1949, *FRUS: 1949*, I, 255; and Acheson's executive session testimony, February 18 and April 21, 1949, SFRC Hearings, *Vandenberg Resolution and NATO*, pp. 99, 215, 232.

53. George H. Butler memorandum, March 19, 1948, *FRUS: 1948*, III, 58; Hickerson comments, second meeting, US-UK-Canada Security Conversations, March 23, 1948, *ibid.*, p. 65; Marshall to Lovett, April 23, 1948, *ibid.*, p. 103; Joseph C. Satterthwaite to Lovett, October 26, 1948, *ibid.*, IV, 173–75. For documentation on proposals for a "Pacific Pact," see *FRUS: 1949*, VII, 901–2, 1115–92.

54. Bohlen to Marshall S. Carter, November 7, 1948, *FRUS: 1948*, I, 654n; Marshall to Forrestal, November 8, 1948, *ibid.*, p. 655; executive session testimony of Acheson, Harriman, and Louis Johnson, April 21, 1949, SFRC Hearings, *Vandenberg Resolution and NATO*, pp. 216–16, 221, 235; Foreign Assistance Correlation Committee paper, "Military Rights Question," May 20, 1949, *FRUS: 1949*, I, 312; Acheson executive session testimony, August 2, 1949, SFRC Hearings, *Military Assistance Program, 1949* p. 30.

55. Kennan Naval War College lecture, October 11, 1948, Kennan Papers, Box 17; Kennan lecture to the Joint Orientation Conference, Pentagon, November 8, 1948, *ibid.*; Kennan NWC lecture, September 17, 1948, *ibid.*

56. London Conference communiqué, June 7, 1948, *FRUS: 1948*, II, 316; Marshall to the U.S. Embassy in London, February 20, 1948, *ibid.*, p. 72; Department of State policy statement, "Germany," August 26, 1948, *ibid.*, 1319.

57. See Kennan to James F. Byrnes, March 6, 1946, *FRUS: 1946*, V, 516–20, and Carmel Offie, May 10, 1946, *ibid.*, pp. 555–56; also Kennan, *Memoirs: 1925–1950*, pp. 257–58.

58. PPS 37, "Policy Questions Concerning a Possible German Settlement," August 12, 1948, *FRUS: 1948*, II, 1287–97. See also PPS/23, February 24, 1948, *ibid.*, I, 515–18.

59. PPS 37/1, "Position To Be Taken by the U.S. at a CFM Meeting," November 15, 1948, *FRUS: 1948*, II, 1320–38. "Program A," entitled "A Program for Germany," was dated November 12, 1948, and included as a subannex to PPS 37/1.

60. Murphy to Jacob D. Beam, December 7, 1948, *FRUS: 1948*, II, 1320n; Murphy memorandum, "U.S. Policy Respecting Germany," *FRUS: 1949*, III, 125; Kohler to Acheson, May 6, 1949, *ibid.*, pp. 866–67; Johnson to Acheson, May 14, 1949, *ibid.*, p. 876. See also Kennan, *Memoirs: 1925–1950*, pp. 444–45; and Miscamble, *Kennan and the Making of American Foreign Policy*, pp. 141–77.

61. Murphy memorandum, conversation with Acheson, March 9, 1949, *FRUS: 1949*, III, 103; Jessup to Acheson, April 19, 1949, *ibid.*, pp. 859–62; Acheson memorandum, "An Approach to the CFM," enclosed in Acheson to Lewis Douglas, May 11, 1949, *ibid.*, p. 873; Kennan to Acheson, May 29, 1949, *ibid.*, p. 889.

62. NSC 13/2, "Recommendations with Respect to United States Policy Toward Japan," approved by Truman on October 9, 1948, *FRUS: 1948*, VI, 858–62. For Kennan's views, see PPS 28, March 25, 1948, *ibid.*, pp. 691–719; and his *Memoirs: 1925–1950*, pp. 391–93.

63. For documentation on these decisions, see *FRUS: 1949*, VII, 850–939; and *FRUS: 1950*, VI, 1109–61.

64. Acheson to Sir Oliver Franks, December 24, 1949, *FRUS: 1949*, VII, 927.

65. Kennan to Acheson, August 21, 1950, *FRUS: 1950*, VII, 627. See also Kennan, *Memoirs: 1950–1963*, pp. 40–41; and Acheson, *Present at the Creation*, pp. 445–46.

66. William J. Sebald to Acheson, August 15, 1949, *FRUS: 1949*, VII, 831. For other examples of MacArthur's support for neutralization, see *ibid.*, pp. 657, 685, 806, 862, and 891; also Kennan, *Memoirs: 1950–1963*, pp. 50–51.

67. Acheson memorandum of conversation with Ernest Bevin and Robert Schuman, September 17, 1949, *FRUS: 1949*, VII, 861; Acheson to Franks, December 24, 1949, *ibid.*, p. 928.

68. Kennan, *Memoirs: 1925–1950*, pp. 427–28, 447–48; *Memoirs: 1950–1963*, p. 53.

69. Kennan, *Memoirs: 1925–1950*, p. 472.

70. Kennan memorandum, "The International Control of Atomic Energy," January 20, 1950, *FRUS: 1950*, I, 39.

71. *Ibid.*, pp. 29–30; Kennan draft memorandum to Acheson (not sent but discussed with Acheson), *ibid.*, pp. 161–62, 165.
72. General Advisory Committee Statement, enclosed in J. Robert Oppenheimer to David E. Lilienthal, October 30, 1949, *FRUS: 1949*, I, 571; Lilienthal to Truman, November 9, 1949, *ibid.*, p. 580; minutes, Policy Planning Staff meeting of November 3, 1949, *ibid.*, p. 576; and Acheson memorandum of December 20, 1949, *ibid.*, p. 613.
73. McMahon to Truman, November 21, 1949, *FRUS: 1949*, I, 593; Bradley to Johnson, November 23, 1949, *ibid.*, pp. 595–96; Strauss to Truman, November 25, 1949, *ibid.*, p. 597; report by the Special Committee of the National Security Council to the President, "Development of Thermonuclear Weapons," January 31, 1950, *FRUS: 1950*, I, 515. See also Bradley to Johnson, January 13, 1950, *ibid.*, pp. 503–11.
74. Truman to Acheson and Johnson, January 31, 1950, *ibid.*, pp. 141–42.
75. Ayres Diary, February 4, 1950, Ayres Papers, Box 27.
76. See, on this point, the report by the Special Committee of the National Security Council to the President, January 31, 1950, *FRUS: 1950*, I, 522.
77. Kennan, *Memoirs: 1925–1950*, pp. 474–75.
78. NSC 68, "United States Objectives and Programs for National Security," April 14, 1950, *FRUS: 1950*, I, 264. This document is fully discussed in Chapter Four. See also Paul Y. Hammond, "NSC-68: Prologue to Rearmament," in Schilling, Hammond, and Snyder, *Strategy, Politics, and Defense Budgets*, p. 312.
79. See, for example, Acheson's remarks to a meeting of the Advertising Council at the White House, February 16, 1950, *DSB*, XXII (March 20, 1950), 427–29. See also Coral Bell, *Negotiation from Strength: A Study in the Politics of Power* (New York: 1963), pp. 3–30.
80. Kennan, *Memoirs: 1925–1950*, p. 305.
81. See, on this point, Arkes, *Bureaucracy, the Marshall Plan, and the National Interest*, p. 182.
82. Kennan diary, November 22, 1949, quoted in Kennan, *Memoirs: 1925–1950*, p. 468.
83. Nitze comment at meeting of the State-Defense Departments Policy Review Group, March 2, 1950, *FRUS: 1950*, I, 177.
84. Kennan diary, July 12, 1950, quoted in Kennan, *Memoirs: 1925–1950*, p. 499.
85. Hammond, "NSC-68," p. 309.
86. Kennan, *Memoirs: 1925–1950*, pp. 407–8.
87. See *FRUS: 1949*, III, 694–751; also Philip C. Jessup, "The Berlin Blockade and the Use of the United Nations," *Foreign Affairs*, L (October 1971), 163–73.
88. For a contemporary appraisal along these lines, see a memorandum by Charles Yost, director of the State Department's Office of European Affairs, "Basic Negotiations with the Soviet Union," February 15, 1950, *FRUS: 1950*, I, 153–59.
89. Kennan, *Memoirs: 1925–1950*, pp. 465–66. See also Kennan to Marshall and Lovett, August 5, 1948, *FRUS: 1948*, I, 599; and Kennan to Dean Rusk, September 7, 1949, *FRUS: 1949*, I, 381.
90. Hammond, "NSC-68," pp. 317–18.
91. Acheson, *Present at the Creation*, pp. 347–48.
92. Extemporaneous remarks to the National Council of Negro Women, November 17, 1950, *DSB*, 23 (November 27, 1950), 839.

FOUR. *NSC-68 and the Korean War*

1. Kennan, *Memoirs: 1925–1950*, p. 408.
2. On the origins of NSC-68, see Paul Y. Hammond's classic account, in Schilling, Hammond, and Snyder, *Strategy, Politics, and Defense Budgets*, pp. 267–330; also Samuel F.

Wells, Jr., "Sounding the Tocsin: NSC 68 and the Soviet Threat," *International Security*, IV (Fall, 1979), 116–38; and Fred M. Kaplan, "Our Cold-War Policy, Circa '50," *New York Times Magazine*, May 18, 1980, pp. 34ff. Ernest R. May, ed., *American Cold War Strategy: Interpreting NSC 68* (Boston: 1993), provides a useful set of commentaries on NSC-68 by historians as well as those involved in its drafting.

3. NSC-68, April 4, 1950, *FRUS: 1950*, I, 237–39.

4. *Ibid.*, pp. 238, 240.

5. Nitze memorandum, "Recent Soviet Moves," February 8, 1950, *ibid.*, p. 145; NSC-68, April 14, 1950, *ibid.*, pp. 263–64.

6. Bradley statement before House Armed Services Committee, [hereafter HASC], October 19, 1949, HASC Hearings: *Unification and Strategy* (Washington: 1949), p. 518. See also Truman to Sidney Souers, July 1, 1949, enclosed in NSC 52, "Governmental Programs in National Security and International Affairs for the Fiscal Year 1951," July 5, 1949, *FRUS: 1949*, I, 349–51.

7. NSC-68, April 14, 1950; *FRUS: 1950*, I, 256–58, 286. See also pp. 246, 249. The President's economic report is in *TPP: 1950*, pp. 18–31.

8. Alonzo L. Hamby, *Beyond the New Deal: Harry S. Truman and American Liberalism* (New York: 1973), pp. 297–303; Edward S. Flash, Jr., *Economic Advice and Presidential Leadership: The Council of Economic Advisers* (New York: 1965), pp. 21–39. See also Friedberg, *In the Shadow of the Garrison State*, pp. 106–7.

9. Hamilton Q. Dearborn memorandum, approved by Keyserling, May 8, 1950, *FRUS: 1950*, I, 311.

10. Records, meeting of the Policy Review Group, March 16, 1950, *ibid.*, p. 199.

11. NSC-68, April 14, 1950, *FRUS: 1950*, I, 243–44.

12. *Ibid.*, pp. 238, 240, 245.

13. *Ibid.*, p. 280. See also pp. 247–48.

14. *Ibid.*, 251, 267. See also a memorandum by the National Security Resources Board, "Comments on NSC/68 Programs," May 29, 1950, *ibid.*, pp. 316–21.

15. Kennan to Acheson, January 6, 1950, *FRUS: 1950*, I, 132. See also Kennan to Bohlen, March 15, 1949; *FRUS: 1949*, V, 593–94.

16. NSC-68, April 14, 1950, *FRUS: 1950*, I, 264, 290. See also Nitze, "Recent Soviet Moves," February 8, 1950, *ibid.*, pp. 145–46.

17. NSC-68, April 14, 1950, *FRUS: 1950*, I, 249, 261, 264.

18. See Kennan, *Memoirs: 1925–1950*, pp. 311–12.

19. NSC-68, April 14, 1950, *FRUS: 1950*, I, 252–53.

20. *Ibid.*, pp. 253, 283.

21. Acheson, *Present at the Creation*, p. 374. See also Friedberg, *In the Shadow of the Garrison State*, pp. 109–11.

22. Acheson, *Present at the Creation*, p. 377; Hammond, "NSC-68," pp. 318–19, 344.

23. NSC-68, April 14, 1950, *FRUS: 1950*, I, 281–82. See also memoranda of discussions in the 4th meeting of the NSC-68 ad hoc committee, May 12, 1950, *ibid.*, pp. 312–13, and in the Under-Secretary of State's Advisory Committee, June 6, 1950, *ibid.*, p. 324.

24. NSC-68, April 14, 1950, *FRUS: 1950*, I, 244. See also p. 267.

25. *Ibid.*, pp. 264, 267–69.

26. *Ibid.*, pp. 247, 255. See also p. 285.

27. *Ibid.*, p. 260.

28. Joint Chiefs of Staff to the Secretary of Defense, "Military Objectives in Military Aid Programs," January 26, 1950, U.S. Department of Defense, *United States-Vietnam Relations, 1945–1967* (Washington: 1971), VIII, 274; Acheson executive session testimony, March 29, 1950, SFRC Hearings: *Reviews of the World Situation*, p. 273; Raymond A. Hare to James E. Webb, April 5, 1950, *FRUS: 1950*, I, 220. For more on the Truman administra-

tion strategy of promoting divisions within the communist world, see Gaddis, *The Long Peace*, pp. 147–73.

29. NSC-68, April 14, 1950, *FRUS: 1950*, I, 263–64.
30. Dulles memorandum, May 18, 1950, *ibid.*, p. 314.
31. See, on this point, the documents in *ibid.*, VI, 346–51; also Gaddis, *The Long Peace*, pp. 84–86.
32. NSC-68, April 14, 1950, *FRUS: 1950*, I, 241–42.
33. *Ibid.*, pp. 273, 276.
34. *Ibid.*, pp. 273–74. See also Bell, *Negotiation From Strength*, pp. 3–30.
35. William F. Schaub to James S. Lay, May 8, 1950, *FRUS: 1950*, I, 301.
36. NSC-68, April 14, 1950, *ibid.*, p. 248. See also Willard Thorp to Acheson, April 5, 1950, *ibid.*, pp. 218–20.
37. *Ibid.*, p. 273.
38. NSC-68, April 1950, *FRUS: 1950*, I, 239–40. See also Bohlen to Nitze, April 5, 1950, *ibid.*, pp. 223–24.
39. Hammond, "NSC-68," pp. 298–326.
40. Record of meeting, Policy Review Group, March 16, 1950, *FRUS: 1950*, I, 197–98; Barrett to Acheson, April 6, 1950, *ibid.*, p. 226.
41. Acheson, *Present at the Creation*, p. 375. See also Bohlen to Nitze, April 5, 1950, *FRUS: 1950*, I, 222.
42. Speech to the American Society of Newspaper Editors, April 22, 1950, *DSB*, XXII (May 1, 1950), 675. See also Acheson's speeches at Dallas, Texas, June 13, 1950, and Harvard University, June 22, 1950, *ibid.*, XXII (June 26, 1950) 1037–41, 1056, and XXIII (July 3, 1950), 14–17, 38; and his executive session testimony before the Senate Foreign Relations Committee, SFRC *Hearings: Reviews of the World Situation*, especially pp. 287, 310.
43. NSC-68, April 14, 1950, *FRUS: 1950*, I, 240.
44. Record of meeting, Policy Review Group, March 2, 1950, *ibid.*, pp. 177–79. See also Schaub to Lay, May 8, 1950, *ibid.*, p. 301.
45. See, on this point, Gaddis, *We Now Know*, pp. 70–75; William Stueck, *The Korean War: An International History* (Princeton: 1995), pp. 31–41, and *Rethinking the Korean War: A New Diplomatic and Strategic History* (Princeton: 2002), pp. 69–77.
46. I.F. Stone, *The Hidden History of the Korean War* (New York: 1952), pp. 1–66; D.F. Fleming, *The Cold War and Its Origins, 1917–1960* (Garden City, N.Y.: 1961), pp. 592–608; Stephen E. Ambrose, *Rise to Globalism: American Foreign Policy, 1938–1970* (Baltimore: 1971), pp. 192–97; Joyce and Gabriel Kolko, *The Limits of Power: The World and United States Foreign Policy, 1945–1954* (New York: 1972), pp. 565–85; and Bruce Cumings, *The Origins of the Korean War: The Roaring of the Cataract, 1947–1950* (Princeton: 1990), especially pp. 410–13.
47. Dulles and John M. Allison to Acheson and Rusk, June 25, 1950, *FRUS: 1950*, VII, 140; Kennan unsent memorandum to Acheson, June 26, 1950, Kennan Papers, Box 24; Truman radio-television address, September 1, 1950, *TPP: 1950*, p. 610. See also John D. Hickerson's address in New York, September 17, 1950, *DSB*, XXIII (October 2, 1950), 544; and Ernest R. May, *"Lessons" of the Past: The Use and Misuse of History in American Foreign Policy* (New York: 1973), pp. 52–86.
48. Acheson report to Cabinet meeting, July 14, 1950, *FRUS: 1950*, I, 345 (this report was based on a memorandum by Charles E. Bohlen). See also "Korea (Preliminary Version)," an intelligence estimate prepared by the State Department's Office of Intelligence Research, June 25, 1950, *ibid.*, VII, 148–54; Kirk to Acheson, June 27, 1950, *ibid.*, p. 199; Caspar D. Green memorandum, Acheson conversation with Wilhelm Munthe de Morgenstierne, June 30, 1950, Acheson Papers, Box 65, "Memoranda of Conversations, May–June, 1950"; Kennan draft memorandum, "Estimate: Possible Further Danger

Points in Light of Korean Situation," June 30, 1950, Kennan Papers, Box 24; NSC 73, "The Position and Actions of the United States with Respect to Possible Further Soviet Moves in the Light of the Korean Situation," July 1, 1950, *FRUS: 1950*, I, 331–38.

49. Acheson report to Cabinet meeting, July 14, 1950, *ibid.*, I, 345; Acheson executive session testimony before the Senate Foreign Relations Committee, July 24, 1950, SFRC Hearings, *Reviews of the World Situation*, p. 323; Acheson handwritten memorandum to "Jim" [Webb?], August, 1950, Acheson Papers, Box 65, "Memoranda of conversations, August, 1950." On Korea as favorable terrain on which to fight, see also NSC 73, July 1, 1950, *FRUS: 1950*, I, 332, and Pace, Matthews, and Finletter to Johnson, August 1, 1950, *ibid.*, pp. 354–55.

50. See Carlton Savage to Nitze, August 3, 1950; *ibid.*, 359; Jessup to Matthews, August 17, 1950, *ibid.*, pp. 370–71; and *ibid.*, VII, 187n.

51. Joint Chiefs of Staff to Johnson, July 10, 1950, *ibid.*, p. 346.

52. Allison to Nitze, July 24, 1950, *ibid.*, VII, 460–61. See also Allison to Rusk, July 1 and 15, 1950, *ibid.*, pp. 272, 393–95.

53. Kennan diary notes, July 21 and 31, 1950, quoted in Kennan, *Memoirs: 1925–1950*, pp. 488–89; Kennan to Acheson, August 8, 1950, *FRUS: 1950*, I, 363; transcript, Kennan background press conference, August 22, 1950, Kennan Papers, Box 18.

54. NSC 81/1, "United States Courses of Action with Respect to Korea," approved by Truman September 11, 1950, *FRUS: 1950*, VII, 712–21. For the possibility of exacerbating Sino-Soviet tensions, see preliminary drafts of this document from the Defense Department, July 31 and August 7, 1950, and from Allison, August 12, 1950, *ibid.*, pp. 506–7, 532, 569–70. See also Stueck, *The Korean War*, pp. 88–91; and James I. Matray, "Truman's Plan for Victory: National Self-Determination and the Thirty-Eight Parallel Decision in Korea," *Journal of American History*, LXVI (September 1979), 314–33.

55. Allison memorandum, Acheson conversation with Kenneth Younger, October 4, 1950, *FRUS: 1950*, VII, 868.

56. See, on this point, Acheson, *Present at the Creation*, pp. 513–15; and James F. Schnabel, *Policy and Direction: The First Year* (Washington: 1972), pp. 306–26.

57. Jessup notes, Acheson meeting with Marshall and the Joint Chiefs of Staff, December 3, 1950, *FRUS: 1950*, VII, 1324; Joint Chiefs of Staff to MacArthur, December 29, 1950, *ibid.*, p. 1625.

58. This decision is documented in detail in *ibid.*, pp. 1237–1634.

59. Acheson, *Present at the Creation*, p. 513.

60. *Ibid.*, pp. 529–33; Kennan, *Memoirs: 1950–1963*, pp. 35–37.

61. Press conference of May 4, 1950, *TPP: 1950*, p. 286.

62. Barbara Evans notes, Acheson report on Cabinet meeting, July 14, 1950, *FRUS: 1950*, I, 345. See also Stuart Symington (chairman, National Security Resources Board) to the National Security Council, July 6, 1950, *ibid.*, pp. 340–41.

63. Hammond, "NSC-68," pp. 351–59; *FRUS: 1950*, I, 352–53, 420–21.

64. Keyserling memorandum, "The Economic Implications of the Proposed Programs: Required Fiscal, Budgetary and Other Economic Policies," enclosed in NSC 68/3, "United States Objectives and Programs for National Security," December 8, 1950, *ibid.*, pp. 428–30.

65. Pace, Matthews, and Finletter to Johnson, August 1, 1950, *FRUS: 1950*, I, 355; Acheson executive session testimony, July 24, 1950, SFRC Hearings: *Reviews of the World Situation*, p. 327; NSC 73/4, "The Position and Actions of the United States with Respect to Possible Further Soviet Moves in the Light of the Korean Situation," August 25, 1950, *FRUS: 1950*, I, 385.

66. Acheson executive session testimony, May 1, 1950, SFRC Hearings: *Reviews of the World Situation*, p. 292.

67. NSC 82, "United States Position Regarding Strengthening the Defense of Europe and the Nature of Germany's Contribution Thereto," approved by Truman on September 11, 1950, published in the form of a communication from Johnson and Acheson to Truman, September 8, 1950, *FRUS: 1950*, III, 273–78.

68. Acheson remarks to Bevin and Schuman, New York, September 15, 1950, enclosed in Acheson to Webb, September 17, 1950, *ibid*., p. 316.

69. See Pace, Matthews, and Finletter to Johnson, August 1, 1950, *ibid*., I, 353.

70. Acheson, *Present at the Creation*, 437–45.

71. Acheson memorandum, conversation with Senator Bourke Hickenlooper, December 27, 1950, *FRUS: 1950*, I, 488–89. See also Acheson's CBS television interview, September 10, 1950, *DSB*, XXIII (September 18, 1950), 464.

72. Acheson extemporaneous remarks at a State Department National Conference on Foreign Policy, November 15, 1950, *DSB*, XXIII (November 27, 1950), 855. See also Acheson to Loy Henderson, September 1, 1950, *FRUS: 1950*, VI, 479–80; Acheson circular telegram, November 5, 1950, *ibid*., VII, 1049; Clubb to Rusk, November 10, 1959, *ibid*., pp. 1123–24; Rusk memorandum of conversation with the Swedish ambassador, November 13, 1950, *ibid*., pp. 1141–42.

73. Livingston Merchant to Rusk, November 27, 1950, *ibid*., VI, 581. See also Truman radio-television address, September 1, 1950, *TPP: 1950*, p. 613; Acheson television interview, September 10, 1950, *DSB*, XXIII (September 18, 1950), 463; and Philip C. Jessup's speech to the Philadelphia World Affairs Council, November 24, 1950, *ibid*., XXIII (December 4, 1950), 886.

74. Truman public statement on Taiwan policy, August 27, 1950, *TPP: 1950*, pp. 599–600; Truman radio-television address, September 1, 1950, *ibid*., p. 613; Acheson CBS television interview, September 10, 1950, *DSB*, XXIII (September 18, 1950), 463, Acheson executive session testimony, Senate Foreign Relations Committee, September 11, 1950, SFRC Hearings, *Reviews of the World Situation*, p. 354. For Chinese Communist resentment over the Taiwan decision, see Loy Henderson to Acheson, August 24, 1950; *FRUS: 1950*, VI, 447, transmitting a report from K. M. Pannikar, the Indian ambassador in Beijing.

75. Kirk to Acheson, July 21, 1950, *ibid*., VII, 443–44; Jessup to Matthews, August 17, 1950, *ibid*., I, 370–71.

76. On this point, see Gaddis, *The Long Peace*, p. 86.

77. Kennan to Acheson, August 21, 1950, *FRUS: 1950*, VII, 624.

78. Jessup notes, National Security Council meeting, November 28, 1950, *FRUS: 1950*, VII, 1246.

79. Minutes, Truman-Attlee meetings of December 4 and 5, 1950, *ibid*., pp. 1368–69, 1397–1403. See also Acheson's memorandum of a conversation with Winston Churchill and Anthony Eden, January 6, 1952, Acheson Papers, Box 66, "Memoranda of conversations, January, 1952."

80. MacArthur to Carlos P. Romulo, December 26, 1950, Douglas MacArthur Papers, Record Group 5, Box 1A, File 5, MacArthur Memorial, Norfolk, Virginia; and to Robert C. Richardson, March 20, 1951, *ibid*., Box 49. See also MacArthur to the Joint Chiefs of Staff, November 7, 29, December 3 and 30, 1950, *FRUS: 1950*, VII, 1077n, 1253n, 1320–22, 1630–33; and J. Lawton Collins to the Joint Chiefs of Staff, December 7, 1950, summarized in *ibid*., p. 1469n.

81. U.S. Congress, Senate, Committees on Armed Services and Foreign Relations, *Military Situation in the Far East* (Washington: 1951), pp. 144–45, 732, 1764.

82. Hoover nationwide radio broadcast, December 20, 1950, in Herbert Hoover, *Addresses upon the American Road: 1950–1955* (Stanford: 1955), pp. 3–10. See also Hoover's radio address of February 9, 1951, and his statement before the Senate Armed Services and Foreign Relations Committees, February 27, 1951, in *ibid*., pp. 11–31.

83. Robert A. Taft, *A Foreign Policy for Americans* (Garden City, N.Y.: 1951), pp. 68–70, 78, 101. See also James T. Patterson, *Mr. Republican: A Biography of Robert A. Taft* (Boston: 1972), pp. 474–96.

84. John Foster Dulles, "A Policy of Boldness," *Life*, XXXII (May 19, 1952), 146–60.

85. Truman radio-television address, March 6, 1952, *TPP: 1952*, pp. 194–95; Truman speech at AMVETS headquarters, Washington, April 18, 1952, *ibid.*, pp. 279–80. For other similar statements by the President, see *ibid.*, pp. 42–43, 56–57, 222, and 407.

86. Acheson to Nitze, July 12, 1950, Acheson Papers, Box 65, "Memoranda of conversations, July 1950"; Nitze to Acheson, November 22, 1950, *FRUS: 1950*, I, 420; Harry S. Truman, *Memoirs: Years of Trial and Hope, 1946–1952* (Garden City, N.Y.: 1956), p. 388; Philip C. Jessup memorandum, Acheson meeting with Marshall and the Joint Chiefs of Staff, December 3, 1950, *FRUS: 1950*, VII, 1326. See also Ambassador Alan Kirk's memorandum of a conversation with Truman on December 19, 1950, *ibid.*, I, 482.

87. NSC 48/5, "United States Objectives, Policies, and Courses of Action in Asia," May 17, 1951, *FRUS: 1951*, VI, 37; Acheson memorandum, conversation with Churchill and Anthony Eden, Washington, January 6, 1952, Acheson Papers, Box 66, "Memoranda of conversations, January, 1952."

88. Acheson memorandum, meeting with Truman, Churchill and Eden, January 5, 1952, Acheson Papers, Box 66, "Memoranda of conversations, January, 1952." See also McLellan, *Dean Acheson*, pp. 349–56.

89. NSC 135/3, "Reappraisal of United States Objectives and Strategy for National Security," September 25, 1952, Modern Military Records Division, National Archives.

90. NSC 141, "Reexamination of United States Programs for National Security," January 19, 1953, Modern Military Records Division, National Archives.

91. McLellan, *Dean Acheson*, p. 398. The quotation from Acheson is on p. 282.

92. John Paton Davies memorandum, September 22, 1950, *FRUS: 1950*, VII, 754; Acheson National War College address, August 27, 1951, Acheson Papers, Box 69, "Classified Off the Record Speeches, 1947–52."

93. *Ibid.*; Acheson speech to Army War College group, Washington, October 2, 1952, Acheson Papers, Box 69, "Classified Off the Record Speeches, 1947–52."

FIVE. *The New Look*

1. Eisenhower's motives in running for president can best be sampled in C. L. Sulzberger's diary entries, published in Sulzberger, *A Long Row of Candles* (New York: 1969), especially pp. 617, 646, 672, 683–86, 699–705, but see also Herbert S. Parmet, *Eisenhower and the American Crusades* (New York: 1972), pp. 45–47; Peter Lyon, *Eisenhower: Portrait of the Hero* (Boston: 1974), pp. 425–33; Stephen E. Ambrose, *Eisenhower: Soldier, General of the Army, President-Elect, 1890–1952* (New York: 1983), pp. 500–1, 527–28; and Dwight D. Eisenhower, *The White House Years: Mandate for Change, 1953–1956* (Garden City, N.Y.: 1963), pp. 13–22.

2. Eisenhower to Dulles, June 20, 1952, John Foster Dulles Papers, Box 60, "Eisenhower" folder, Princeton University; Eisenhower to T. J. Davis, April 17, 1952, Dwight D. Eisenhower Papers, 1916–52, Box 31, Dwight D. Eisenhower Library. For Eisenhower's concern over the economy, see Eisenhower to Louis Johnson, August 26, 1949, *ibid.*, Box 56; and his statement before the House Armed Services Committee, October 20, 1949, HASC Hearings, *Unification and Strategy* (Washington: 1949), p. 565.

3. Eisenhower to Dulles, April 15, 1952, Eisenhower Papers, 1916–52, Box 33; Dulles to Eisenhower, April 25, 1952, *ibid.*; Eisenhower to Dulles, June 20, 1952, Dulles Papers,

Box 60, "Eisenhower" folder; Sulzberger diary, July 6–10, 1952, in Sulzberger, *A Long Row of Candles*, pp. 767–71.

4. Robert A. Divine, *Foreign Policy and U. S. Presidential Elections: 1952–1960* (New York: 1974), pp. 34–36, 53–56; Robert R. Bowie and Richard H. Immerman, *Waging Peace: How Eisenhower Shaped an Enduring Cold War Strategy* (New York: 1998), pp. 73–75. The foreign policy plank of the 1952 Republican platform is in *Documents on American Foreign Relations: 1952* (New York: 1953), pp. 80–85.

5. See, on this point, Richard H. Immerman, "Eisenhower and Dulles: Who Made the Decisions?" *Political Psychology*, I (Autumn, 1979), 3–20.

6. Eisenhower inaugural address, January 20, 1953, *Public Papers of the Presidents: Dwight D. Eisenhower* [hereafter *EPP*], *1953*, p. 6; Eisenhower speech at Minneapolis, June 10, 1953, *ibid.*, p. 389.

7. Dulles speech to Rotary International, Seattle, June 10, 1954, *DSB*, XXX (June 21, 1954), 939; Eisenhower handwritten note, week of February 7, 1954, Eisenhower Papers, Whitman File: DDE Diary, Box 3, "Jan.–Nov. 54"; Eisenhower press conference, August 4, 1954, *EPP: 1954*, p. 684; Eisenhower conversation with C. D. Jackson, August 11, 1954, Eisenhower Papers, Whitman File: Diary Series, Box 3, "Aug 54 (3)."

8. Dulles speech to French National Political Science Institute, Paris, May 4, 1952, *Vital Speeches*, XVIII (June 1, 1952), 495; James Hagerty diary, April 26, 1954, Hagerty Papers, Box 1, Eisenhower Library; Eisenhower to Churchill, March 29, 1955, Eisenhower Papers, Whitman File: DDE Diary, Box 6, "Mar. 55 (1)." Eisenhower's domino theory" statement is in *EPP: 1954*, p. 383.

9. Dulles speech to the American Association for the United Nations, New York, December 29, 1950, *DSB*, XV (January 15, 1951), 88; Dulles to Kennan, October 29, 1952, Dulles Papers, Box 61, "Kennan" folder; Dulles National War College address, June 16, 1953, *DSB*, XXVIII (June 29, 1953), 895. See also Dulles speeches of April 11 and October 10, 1955, *ibid.*, XXXII (April 25, 1955), 675, and XXXIII (October 24, 1955), 640–41.

10. Eisenhower press conference, June 17, 1953, *EPP: 1953*, p. 440; Eisenhower to Dulles, June 20, 1952, Dulles Papers, Box 60, "Eisenhower" folder. See also Eisenhower to T. J. Davis, April 17, 1952, Eisenhower Papers, 1916–52, Box 31; Eisenhower speech to the National Junior Chamber of Commerce, Minneapolis, June 6, 1953, *EPP: 1953*, pp. 389–90; Eisenhower press conference statement, April 7, 1954, *EPP: 1954*, p. 383; Eisenhower address at Transylvania College, April 23, 1954, *ibid.*, pp. 419–20.

11. Eisenhower to Mrs. Robert Patterson, June 15, 1953 (unsent), Eisenhower Papers, Whitman File: DDE Diary, Box 2, "Dec. 52–July 53 (2)"; Eisenhower speech to National Education Association dinner, Washington, June 22, 1954, *EPP: 1954*, p. 586. See also Eisenhower to Dulles, March 26, 1958, Eisenhower Papers, Whitman File: DDE Diary, Box 19, "DDE Dictation Mar. 58."

12. Dulles speech to National Alumni Luncheon, Princeton University, February 22, 1952, *Vital Speeches*, XVIII (March 15, 1952), 333; Eisenhower speech to American Society of Newspaper Editors, April 16, 1953, *EPP: 1953*, p. 182; Eisenhower to Joseph Dodge, November 5, 1953, Eisenhower Papers, Whitman File: DDE Diary, Box 2, "Nov. 53 (2)"; Eisenhower remarks to Association of Land-Grant Colleges and Universities, November 16, 1954, *EPP: 1954*, p. 1055.

13. Eisenhower press conferences, April 23 and 30, 1953, *EPP: 1953*, pp. 209, 239; Dulles statement to Senate Foreign Relations and House Foreign Affairs Committees, May 5, 1953, *DSB*, XXVIII (May 25, 1953), 737. See also Eisenhower to Alfred M. Gruenther, May 4, 1953, and Benjamin F. Caffey, July 27, 1953, Eisenhower Papers, Whitman File: DDE Diary, Box 2, "Dec. 52–July 53."

14. NSC 162/2, "Basic National Security Policy," October 30, 1953, *FRUS: 1952–54*, II, 589; Eisenhower press conference, March 2, 1955, *EPP: 1955*, p. 310.

15. Emmet John Hughes, *The Ordeal of Power: A Political Memoir of the Eisenhower Years* (New York: 1963), p. 72. Short's comment is in the notes of the legislative leadership meeting of April 30, 1953, Eisenhower Papers, Whitman File: DDE Diary, Box 2, "Staff Notes, Jan.–Dec. 53." For Eisenhower's ties to the business community, see Lyon, *Eisenhower*, pp. 373–76, 395–97, 405–10.

16. *Ibid.*, pp. 56–58. See also Bowie and Immerman, *Waging Peace*, pp. 48, 63; and Christopher Bassford, *Clausewitz in English: The Reception of Clausewitz in Britain and America, 1815–1945* (New York: 1994), pp. 157–62.

17. Eisenhower remarks to USIA staff, November 10, 1953, *EPP: 1953*, p. 754: Eisenhower press conference, January 12, 1955, *EPP: 1955*, p. 57. See also Eisenhower to T. J. Davis, April 17, 1952, Eisenhower Papers: 1916–52, Box 31; and Eisenhower press conferences, March 7 and May 23, 1956, *EPP: 1956*, pp. 292–93, 525. Compare with Carl von Clausewitz, *On War*, edited and translated by Michael Howard and Peter Paret (Princeton: 1976), pp. 87, 101, 112, 142–43, 179, 230.

18. Eisenhower press conference, November 11, 1953, *EPP: 1953*, p. 760; Eisenhower to Frank Altschul, October 25, 1957, Eisenhower Papers, Whitman File: DDE Diary, Box 16, "Oct. 57"; NSC 5707/8, "Basic National Security Policy," June 3, 1957, *FRUS: 1955–57*, XIX, 509. (Emphasis added.)

19. See, for example, James David Barber, *The Presidential Character: Predicting Performance in the White House* (Englewood Cliffs, N.J.: 1972), pp. 156–72. For a contrasting viewpoint, see Fred I. Greenstein, "Eisenhower as an Activist President: A New Look at the Evidence," *Political Science Quarterly*, XCIV (Winter, 1979–80), 575–99; also more generally Greenstein, *The Hidden-Hand Presidency: Eisenhower as Leader* (New York: 1982).

20. See John Michael Guhin, *John Foster Dulles: A Statesman and His Times* (New York: 1972), pp. 116–28; also Ronald W. Pruessen, *John Foster Dulles: The Road to Power* (New York: 1982), pp. 254–58.

21. *Ibid.*, pp. 286–87, 306–7. See also Hughes, *Ordeal of Power*, pp. 109–10, 204–8; and Townsend Hoopes, *The Devil and John Foster Dulles* (Boston: 1973), pp. 358, 488.

22. Dulles radio-television address, January 27, 1953, *DSB*, XXVIII (February 9, 1953), 212–13; Dulles statement to Senate Foreign Relations and House Foreign Affairs Committees, May 5, 1953, *ibid.*, XXVIII (May 25, 1953), 736–37.

23. Dulles speech at Colgate University, July 7, 1950, *DSB*, XXIV (July 17, 1950), 88; Dulles speech at National War College, June 16, 1953, *ibid.*, XXVIII (June 29, 1953), 895. See also John Foster Dulles, *War or Peace* (New York: 1950), pp. 7–16.

24. Dulles speech to the Congress of Industrial Organizations, Cleveland, November 18, 1953, *DSB*, XXIX (November 30, 1953), 741; Dulles speech at Williamsburg, Virginia, May 15, 1954, *ibid.*, XXX (May 24, 1954), 779.

25. Dulles's speech at Caracas, Venezuela, March 4, 1954, *ibid.*, XXX (March 15, 1954), 379; Dulles press conference, April 3, 1956, *ibid.*, XXXIV (April 16, 1956), 642.

26. Dulles speech at Geneva Conference on Korea, April 28, 1954, *DSB*, XXX (May 10, 1954), 706; Dulles press conference, April 3, 1956, *ibid.*, XXIV (April 16, 1956), 642; Andrew H. Berding, *Dulles on Diplomacy* (Princeton: 1965), pp. 7–8, 30–31.

27. Sulzberger diary, December 13, 1951, in Sulzberger, *A Long Row of Candles*, pp. 706–7. See also Lyon, *Eisenhower*, pp. 365–66.

28. Eisenhower press conferences, June 17 and November 11, 1953, *EPP: 1953*, pp. 431–32, 760; Eisenhower speech at Des Moines, Iowa, August 30, 1954, *EPP: 1954*, p. 788.

29. See, on this point, Glenn H. Snyder, "The 'New Look' of 1953," in Schilling, Hammond, and Snyder, *Strategy, Politics, and Defense Budgets*, pp. 400–2.

30. Dulles speech to the French National Political Science Institute, Paris, May 5, 1952, *Vital Speeches*, XVIII (June 1, 1952), 493; Eisenhower radio address, May 19, 1953, *EPP: 1953*,

p. 307. Other estimates questioning the likelihood of war can be found in NSC 162/2, October 30, 1953, *FRUS: 1952–54*, II, 582; and NSC 5501, January 7, 1955, *FRUS: 1955–57*, XIX, 28–29. See also Hoopes, *Dulles*, pp. 192–93; and Berding, *Dulles on Diplomacy*, pp. 136–37.

31. Dulles speech to American Society of International Law, April 27, 1950, *DSB*, XXII (May 8, 1950), 717; Robertson speech to Louisville Chamber of Commerce, October 14, 1953, *ibid.*, XXIX (November 2, 1953), 594; Eisenhower speech to American Legion Convention, August 30, 1954, *EPP: 1954*, p. 780; Eisenhower to John S. D. Eisenhower, June 16, 1953, Eisenhower Papers, Whitman File: DDE Diary, Box 2, "Dec 52–July 53 (2)." See also Dulles's speech to the French National Political Science Institute, Paris, May 5, 1952, *Vital Speeches*, XVIII (June 1, 1952), 493; and his radio-television address, January 27, 1953, *DSB*, XXVIII (February 9, 1953), 213.

32. Eisenhower press conference, December 2, 1954, *EPP: 1954*, pp. 1074–75; Eisenhower to Frank Altschul, October 25, 1957, Eisenhower Papers, Whitman File: DDE Diary, Box 16, "Oct 57."

33. Dulles remarks to New York State Republican dinner, May 7, 1953, *DSB*, XXVIII (May 18, 1953), 707; Dulles speech at Caracas, Venezuela, March 4, 1954, *ibid.*, XXX (March 15, 1954), 379; Dulles speech to the Foreign Policy Association, February 16, 1955, *ibid.*, XXXII (February 28, 1955), 329; Dulles speech to American Legion convention, Miami, October 10, 1955 *ibid.*, XXXIII (October 24, 1955), 639; Allen Dulles speech to the International Association of Chiefs of Police, Philadelphia, October 3, 1955, *ibid.*, XXXIII (October 17, 1955), 603.

34. Dulles speech at Geneva Conference on Korea, April 28, 1954, *DSB*, XXX (May 10, 1954), 706; Smith CBS television interview, August 1, 1954, *ibid.*, XXX (August 9, 1954), 191; Robertson speech to Greater Philadelphia Chamber of Commerce, January 13, 1955, *ibid.*, XXXII (January 24, 1955), 131; Allen Dulles speech to International Association of Chiefs of Police, October 3, 1955, *ibid.*, XXXIII (October 17, 1955), 600.

35. NSC 5501, January 7, 1955, *FRUS: 1955–57*, XIX, 28; Eisenhower to Bernard Montgomery, May 2, 1956, Eisenhower Papers, Whitman File: DDE Diary, Box 9, "May 56 Misc (5)."

36. Dulles untitled memorandum, June 16, 1949, Dulles Papers, Box 40, "Council of Foreign Ministers" folder; "Notes on Foreign Policy," enclosed in Dulles to Homer Ferguson, June 28, 1949, *ibid.*, Box 41, "Ferguson" folder; Dulles to Eisenhower, June 25, 1952, *ibid.*, Box 57, "Bebler" folder; NSC 166/1, "U.S. Policy Toward Communist China," November 6, 1953, *FRUS: 1952–54*, XIV, 296 ; Minutes, Eisenhower-Churchill-Bidault meeting, December 7, 1953, *FRUS: 1952–54*, III, 711; Berding, *Dulles on Diplomacy*, p. 33. See also a Department of State Office of Intelligence Research Report, #7070, "Sino-Soviet Relations: A Reappraisal," November 4, 1955, Department of State Records, Research and Analysis Reports, Diplomatic Branch, National Archives.

37. Minutes, Eisenhower-Churchill-Bidault meeting, December 7, 1953; Dulles to Chester Bowles, March 25, 1952, Dulles Papers, Box 58, "Bowles" folder; NSC 148, "United States Policies in the Far East" (draft), April 6, 1953, Eisenhower Papers, White House Office Files: Office of the Special Assistant for National Security Affairs, Box 24; NSC 166/1, November 6, 1953, *FRUS: 1952–54*, XIV, 297–98; Dulles press conferences, April 26, 1955, and April 24, 1956, *DSB*, XXXII (May 9, 1955), 756, and XXXIV (May 7, 1956), 752.

38. For more on the Dulles strategy of seeking to exploit potential Sino-Soviet differences, see Gaddis, *The Long Peace*, pp. 174–82, and *The United States and the End of the Cold War: Implications, Provocations, Reconsiderations* (New York: 1992), pp. 73–79.

39. Murphy speech to Zionist Organization of America, New York City, June 24, 1954, *DSB*, XXXI (July 5, 1954), 3; Dulles remarks at Advertising Club of New York, March 21, 1955,

ibid., XXXII (April 4, 1955), 551–52. See also Dulles's remarks to the Associated Church Press, Washington, April 13, 1955, *ibid.*, XXXII (April 25, 1955), 676; and NSC 166/1, November 6, 1953, *FRUS; 1952–54*, XIV, 294.

40. Eisenhower to Churchill, March 29, 1955, Eisenhower Papers, Whitman File: DDE Diary, Box 6, "Mar 55 (1)"; Berding, *Dulles on Diplomacy*, p. 63.

41. *Ibid.*, p. 24; Dulles speech to the Associated Press, New York, April 23, 1956, *DSB*, XXXIV (April 30, 1954), 708.

42. Dulles, *War or Peace*, p. 242.

43. Bowie and Immerman, *Waging Peace*, pp. 123–38.

44. Kennan, *Memoirs: 1950–1963*, p. 182. See also Snyder, "The New Look," p. 409.

45. Eisenhower speech to New York State Republican Committee, May 7, 1953, *EPP: 1953*, p. 265; Notes, Eisenhower meeting with bipartisan legislative leaders, January 5, 1954, Eisenhower Papers, Whitman File: DDE Diary, Box 3, "Staff Notes, Jan–Nov, 54"; Notes, Eisenhower meeting with Republican legislative leaders, April 30, 1953, *ibid.*, Box 2, "Staff Notes, Jan–Dec 53"; Dulles speech to the Council on Foreign Relations, January 12, 1954, *DSB*, XXX (January 25, 1954), 108.

46. *Ibid.* See also John Foster Dulles, "Policy for Security and Peace," *Foreign Affairs*, XXXII (April 1954), 357–59.

47. See, on this point, a report by Lieutenant General H. R. Harmon, USAF, "Evaluation of Effect on Soviet War Effort Resulting from the Strategic Air Offensive," May 11, 1949, in Etzold and Gaddis, eds., *Containment*, pp. 360–64; also Rosenberg, "American Atomic Strategy and the Hydrogen Bomb Decision," pp. 72–73; and Gaddis, *We Now Know*, p. 89.

48. Eisenhower speech to the United Nations, December 8, 1953, *EPP: 1953*, p. 815; Dulles, "Policy for Security and Peace," p. 358.

49. Hagerty Diary, January 5, 1954, Hagerty Papers, Box 1; Dulles to Eisenhower, September 6, 1953, Eisenhower Papers, Whitman File: International Series, Box 33, "Dulles/Korea/Security Policy"; Eisenhower memorandum, November 11, 1953, *ibid.*, Whitman File: DDE Diary, Box 2, "Nov. 53 (2)." See also Eisenhower to Gruenther, October 27, 1953, *ibid.*, "Oct. 53 (2)."

50. Dulles memorandum, June 23, 1953, Dulles Papers, Box 57, "Baldwin" folder; Eisenhower United Nations speech, December 8, 1953, *EPP: 1953*, p. 815; Gruenther speech to National Security Industrial Association, New York, September 29, 1954, *DSB*, XXXI (October 18, 1954), 564; Dulles press conference remarks, December 21, 1954, *ibid.*, XXXII (January 3, 1955), 14; Eisenhower press conference, March 16, 1955, *EPP: 1955*, p. 332.

51. NSC 162/2, October 30, 1953, *FRUS: 1952–54*, II, 593; Hagerty diary, December 13, 1954, Hagerty Papers, Box 1; NSC 5501, January 7, 1955, *FRUS: 1955–57*, XIX, 32. See also the notes of an Eisenhower meeting with bipartisan legislative leaders, January 5, 1954, Eisenhower Papers, Whitman File: DDE Diary, Box 3, "Staff Notes, Jan–Dec. 54." For more on Eisenhower's thinking about the use of nuclear weapons, see Gaddis, *We Now Know*, pp. 226–34; also Campbell Craig, *Destroying the Village: Eisenhower and Thermonuclear War* (New York: Columbia University Press, 1998).

52. Eisenhower press conferences of February 3 and March 17, 1954, *EPP: 1954*, pp. 229, 325; notes, Eisenhower-Dulles conversation, July 20, 1954, Eisenhower Papers, Whitman File: Diary Series, Box 2, "July 54 (3)." For Eisenhower's approval of the Dulles speech, see the Hagerty diary, January 12, 1954, Hagerty Papers, Box 1.

53. Dulles, "Policy for Security and Peace," pp. 356, 358; Dulles speech to National 4-H Clubs Congress, Chicago, November 29, 1954, *DSB*, XXXI (December 13, 1954), 892. See also Dulles's House Foreign Affairs Committee testimony, April 5, 1954, *ibid.*, XXX (April 19, 1954), 579.

54. NSC 5501, January 7, 1955, *FRUS: 1955–57*, XIX, 32. The same statement was repeated in NSC 5602/1, March 15, 1956, *ibid.*, pp. 246–47, and NSC 5707/8, June 3, 1957, *ibid.*, pp. 511–12.

55. James Shepley, "How Dulles Averted War," *Life*, XL (January 16, 1956), 78.

56. NSC 162/2, October 30, 1953, *FRUS: 1952–54*, II, 583; Dulles, "Policy for Security and Peace," pp. 355–57.

57. See, on this point, Hoopes, *Dulles*, pp. 162–66.

58. Dulles memorandum of June 23, 1952, Dulles Papers, Box 57, "Baldwin" folder; see also his press conference comment of December 1, 1954, *DSB*, XXXI (December 13, 1954), 897.

59. Goodpaster memorandum, Eisenhower conference with science advisers, March 29, 1957, Eisenhower Papers, Whitman File: DDE Diary, Box 13, "Mar 57 Diary Staff Memos (1)"; Memorandum of Eisenhower telephone conversation with Carl Hayden, August 29, 1957, *ibid.*, Box 15, "Aug 57 Telephone." See also Eisenhower's press conference, January 12, 1955, *EPP: 1955*, p. 57.

60. Dulles speech to the American Legion convention, Miami, October 10, 1955, *DSB*, XXXIII (October 24, 1955), 642; Dulles speech at Iowa State College, June 9, 1956, *ibid.*, XXXIV (June 18, 1956), 999–1000. See also Guhin, *John Foster Dulles*, pp. 252–64; and H. W. Brands, *The Specter of Neutralism: The United States and the Emergence of the Third World, 1947–1960* (New York: 1989), pp. 305–7.

61. Eisenhower to Edgar Eisenhower, February 27, 1956, Eisenhower Papers, Whitman File: DDE Diary, Box 7, "Feb 56 Misc (1)." (Emphasis in original.) See also Eisenhower's press conference, June 6, 1956, *EPP: 1956*, p. 555.

62. Eisenhower to Dulles, October 24, 1953, Eisenhower Papers, Whitman File: DDE Diary, Box 2, "Oct. 53 (2)."

63. NSC 162/2, October 30, 1953, *FRUS: 1952–54*, II, 580; Dulles radio-television address, January 27, 1953, *DSB*, XXVIII (February 9, 1953), 216; Dulles press conference statement, June 30, 1953, *ibid.*, XXIX (July 13, 1953), 40; Dulles speech to Congress of Industrial Organizations, Cleveland, November 18, 1953, *ibid.*, XXIX (November 30, 1953), 741, 744.

64. Dulles executive session testimony, Senate Foreign Relations Committee, February 26, 1953, SFRC Hearings: *83rd Congress, 1st Session*, pp. 172, 180.

65. Dulles speech at Williamsburg, Virginia, May 15, 1954, *DSB*, XXX (May 24, 1954), 781; Dulles press conference statement, June 27, 1956, *ibid.*, XXXV (July 9, 1956), 47; Dulles speech to Dallas Council on World Affairs, October 27, 1956, *ibid.*, XXXV (November 5, 1956), 697; Dulles press conference statement, July 16, 1957, *ibid.*, XXXVII (August 5, 1957), 228.

66. See above, p. 140; Dulles comments at bipartisan legislative leadership meeting, January 1, 1957, Eisenhower Papers, Whitman File: DDE Diary, Box 12, "Jan 57 Misc (4)"; and Eisenhower press conferences, April 3 and August 21, 1957, *EPP: 1957*, pp. 247, 625. For a contemporary critique of "liberation" by Kennan, see his *Realities of American Foreign Policy*, pp. 76–81.

67. NSC 162/2. October 30, 1953, *FRUS: 1952–54*, II, 580; Dulles briefing for Eisenhower, Churchill, and Bidault, Bermuda, December 7, 1953, Eisenhower Papers, Whitman File: International Meetings Series, Box 1, "Bermuda-State Dept. Report"; Dulles press conference, June 28, 1955, *DSB*, XXXIII (July 11, 1955), 51; Dulles comments to Boys' Nation, Washington, July 27, 1953, *ibid.*, XXIX (August 10, 1953), 176. See also, on the political asylum principle, Walter Robertson's speech to the Virginia Society of Baltimore, January 22, 1954, *ibid.*, XXX (February 1, 1954), 151.

68. Nixon radio-television address, December 23, 1953, *DSB*, XXX (January 4, 1954), 11. For the MIG offer, see Hughes, *Ordeal of Power*, pp. 101–2.

69. For these episodes, see William Taubman, *Khrushchev: The Man and His Era* (New York: 2003), pp. 417–18, 428–35.

70. NSC 5412, "Covert Operations," March 15, 1954, Eisenhower Papers, White House Office Files: Office of the Special Assistant for National Security Affairs, Box 7; Karalekas, "History of the Central intelligence Agency," pp. 31, 41.

71. NSC 5412, March 15, 1954. This summary of CIA operations is based on U.S. Congress, Senate (94th Cong., 2nd Sess.) Select Committee To Study Governmental Operations with Respect to Intelligence Activities, *Alleged Assassination Plots Involving Foreign Leaders* (Washington: 1975); *ibid., Foreign and Military Intelligence, Book 1, Final Report* (Washington: 1976); and on William R. Corson, *The Armies of Ignorance: The Rise of the American Intelligence Empire* (New York: 1977), pp. 331–80; Thomas Powers, *The Man Who Kept the Secrets: Richard Helms and the CIA* (New York: 1979), pp. 39–44, 85–92, 106–18; John Ranelagh, *The Agency: The Rise and Decline of the CIA* (New York: 1986), pp. 229–348. Several official histories of Eisenhower administration covert operations have now also been published, among them: Nicholas Cullather, *Operation PBSUCCESS: The United States and Guatemala, 1952–1954* (Washington: 1994); Kevin C. Ruffner, ed., *CORONA: America's First Satellite Program* (Washington: 1995); and R. Cargill Hall and Clayton D. Laurie, eds., *Early Cold War Overflights, 1950–1956*, 2 volumes (Washington: 2003).

72. *Alleged Assassination Plots*, pp. 260–69; Corson, *Armies of Ignorance*, pp. 23, 346–47.

73. See, for example, public statements by Dulles on Iran, September 24, 1953, *DSB*, XXIX (October 5, 1953), 443–44; Dulles and Eisenhower on Guatemala, June 30 and August 30, 1954, *ibid.*, XXXI (July 12, 1954), 43–44 and *EPP: 1954*, p. 789; and Eisenhower on Indonesia, April 30, 1958, *EPP: 1958*, p. 789.

74. Eisenhower to Lewis Douglas, March 29, 1955, Eisenhower Papers, Whitman File: DDE Diary, Box 6, "Mar. 55 (1)." Emphases in original.

75. Eisenhower press conferences, March 19 and April 2, 1953, *EPP: 1953*, pp. 106, 147; December 2, 1954, *EPP: 1954*, p. 1076; February 2, 1955, *EPP: 1955*, p. 235; and January 30, 1957, *EPP: 1957*, p. 98.

76. Hughes, *Ordeal of Power*, p. 105; Eisenhower to Dulles, September 8, 1953, Eisenhower Papers, Whitman File: International Series, Box 33, "Dulles/Korea/Security Policy"; Eisenhower dictated note, January 24, 1958, *ibid.*, DDE Diary, Box 17, "Jan 58."

77. See Dulles's speech at Williamsburg, Virginia, May 15, 1954, *DSB*, XXX (May 24, 1954), 780; also Gaddis, *The United States and the End of the Cold War*, pp. 79–84.

78. NSC 162/2, October 30, 1953, *FRUS: 1952–54*, II, 584; NSC 5501, January 7, 1955, *FRUS: 1955–57*, XIX, 36; NSC 5707/8, June 3, 1957, *ibid.*, p. 518.

79. Nikita Khrushchev, *Khrushchev Remembers: The Last Testament*, translated and edited by Strobe Talbott (Boston: 1974), p. 363.

80. This analysis is based on Hoopes, *Dulles*, especially pp. 6, 124–25, 244, 252, 350, 358, 488.

81. Eisenhower to E. E. Hazlett, October 23, 1954, Eisenhower Papers, Whitman File: DDE Diary, Box 5, "Oct. 54 (1)"; Eisenhower Diary, January 10, 1956, in Robert H. Ferrell, ed., *The Eisenhower Diaries* (New York: 1981), p. 306.

82. See, on this point, Hughes, *The Ordeal of Power*, pp. 346–50.

SIX. *Implementing the New Look*

1. See Appendix.

2. For preliminary assessments, however, see Zubok and Pleshakov, *Inside the Kremlin's Cold War*; Chen, *Mao's China and the Cold War*; Gaddis, *We Now Know*; and Taubman, *Khrushchev*.

3. Early expressions of this view include Vincent P. DeSantis, "Eisenhower Revisionism," *Review of Politics*, XXXVIII (April 1976), 190–207; Gary W. Reichard, "Eisenhower as President: The Changing View," *South Atlantic Quarterly*, LXXVII (Summer 1978), 265–81; George H. Quester, "Was Eisenhower a Genius?" *International Security*, IV (Fall 1979), 159–79. For later and fuller assessments, see Greenstein, *The Hidden-Hand Presidency*; Bowie and Immerman, *Waging Peace*; Stephen E. Ambrose, *Eisenhower: The President* (New York: 1984); as well as Chester J. Pach, Jr., and Elmo Richardson, *The Presidency of Dwight D. Eisenhower*, revised edition (Lawrence, Kansas: 1991). For reconsiderations of Eisenhower "revisionism," see Richard H. Immerman, "Confessions of an Eisenhower Revisionist: An Agonizing Reappraisal," *Diplomatic History* XIV (Summer, 1990), 319–42; and Stephen G. Rabe, "Eisenhower Revisionism: A Decade of Scholarship," *ibid.*, XVII (Winter, 1993), 97–115.

4. Henry A. Kissinger, *Nuclear Weapons and Foreign Policy* (New York: 1957), p. 172; Louis J. Halle, *Civilization and Foreign Policy: An Inquiry for Americans* (New York: 1955), p. 215. The most influential single critique of the massive retaliation strategy was Maxwell D. Taylor, *The Uncertain Trumpet* (New York: 1959).

5. Eisenhower state of the union address, January 6, 1955, *EPP: 1955*, p. 12; Dulles speech to the Dallas Council on World Affairs, October 27, 1956, *DSB*, XXXV (November 5, 1956), 695. See also Eisenhower's press conference of January 12, 1955, *EPP: 1955*, pp. 58–59; Dulles's speech to the Associated Press, New York City, April 22, 1957, *DSB*, XXVI (May 6, 1957).

6. Notes, legislative leadership meeting, December 13, 1954, Eisenhower Papers, Whitman File: DDE Diary, Box 3, "Staff Notes, Jan–Dec. 54." See also Eisenhower, *Mandate for Change*, p. 452.

7. Goodpaster memorandum, Eisenhower-Radford conversation, May 14, 1956, Eisenhower Papers, Whitman File: DDE Diary, Box 8, "May 56 Goodpaster." See also the Hagerty Diary, January 3 and 4, 1955, Hagerty Papers, Box 1; and Eisenhower-Radford telephone conversation, February 1, 1955, Eisenhower Papers, Whitman File: DDE Diary, Box 5, "Phone Calls, Jan–July, 55 (2)."

8. Goodpaster memorandum, Eisenhower conversation with Maxwell Taylor, May 24, 1956, Eisenhower Papers, Whitman File: DDE Diary, Box 8, "May 56 Goodpaster"; Eisenhower to Christian A. Herter, July 31, 1957, ibid., Box 14, "July 57 DDE Dictation." See also Kissinger, *Nuclear Weapons and Foreign Policy* pp. 183–89.

9. NSC 162/2, October 30, 1953, *FRUS:1952–54*, II, 585; Gruenther quotation in Richard P. Stebbins, *The United States in World Affairs: 1956* (New York: 1957), pp. 370–71. See also Gruenther's speech to the National Security Industrial Association, New York, September 29, 1954, *DSB*, XXXI (October 18, 1954), 564; and George H. Quester, *Nuclear Diplomacy: The First Twenty-Five Years*, second edition (New York: 1973), p. 111.

10. Eisenhower, *The White House Years: Waging Peace, 1956–1961* (Garden City, N.Y.: 1965), p. 336n.

11. See above, pp. 120–21.

12. NSC 147, "Analysis of Possible Courses of Action in Korea," April 2, 1953, *FRUS: 1952–54*, XV, 844.

13. Dulles briefing for Eisenhower, Churchill, and Bidault, Bermuda, December 7, 1953, Eisenhower Papers, Whitman File: International Meetings Series, Box 1, "Bermuda—State Dept. Report."

14. Hagerty Diary, January 5, 1954, Hagerty Papers, Box 1. See also Dulles speech to American Legion Convention, St. Louis, September 2, 1953, *DSB*, XXIX (September 14, 1953), 339; and Eisenhower, *Mandate for Change*, p. 181.

15. NSC Action #1074-a, April 5, 1954, *The Pentagon Papers (Senator Gravel Edition): The Department of Defense History of United States Decision-Making on Vietnam*, 4 vols.

(Boston: 1971), I, 466–70. See also Radford to Wilson, May 26, 1954, *ibid.*, pp. 512–14; and SNIE 10-4-54, "Communist Reactions to Certain U.S. Courses of Action with Respect to Indochina," June 15, 1954, *ibid.*, pp. 525–31.

16. On this point, see "Army Position on NSC Action No. 1074-A," undated, *Pentagon Papers*, I, 471–72.

17. Dulles to Eisenhower, September 4, 1958, *FRUS: 1958–60*, XIX, 133.

18. Eisenhower, *Mandate for Change*, pp. 476–77; Dulles to Eisenhower, September 4, 1958, *FRUS: 1958–60*, XIX, 133.

19. See, on this point, Alexander L. George and Richard Smoke, *Deterrence in American Foreign Policy: Theory and Practice* (New York: 1974), p. 370; also Gaddis, *We Now Know*, pp. 105, 250–52.

20. Dulles press conference statement, September 30, 1958, *DSB*, XXXIX (October 20, 1958), 602. The Acheson quotation is in Richard P. Stebbins, *The United States in World Affairs: 1958* (New York: 1959), p. 320. See also Hoopes, *Dulles*, pp. 449–52.

21. See, on this point, George and Smoke, *Deterrence in American Foreign Policy*, pp. 516–17.

22. Snyder, "The 'New Look' of 1953," pp. 384, 394, 396, 457; Eisenhower, *Mandate for Change*, p. 452n; *Statistical History of the United States*, pp. 718, 742E. See also Friedberg, *In the Shadow of the Garrison State*, pp. 127–33.

23. On this point, see George and Smoke, *Deterrence in American Foreign Policy*, p. 370.

24. Kissinger, *Nuclear Weapons and Foreign Policy*, p. 185.

25. Hagerty Diary, December 2, 1954, Hagerty Papers, Box 1.

26. Eisenhower press conference, March 17, 1954, *EPP: 1954*, p. 325; Eisenhower remarks at the National Defense Executive Reserve Conference, Washington, November 14, 1957, *EPP: 1957*, p. 818. See also Eisenhower's press conference of March 25, 1955, *EPP: 1955*, p. 358.

27. Hagerty Diary, July 27, 1954, Hagerty Papers, Box 1; Eisenhower Diary, January 23, 1956, in Ferrell, ed., *The Eisenhower Diaries*, pp. 311–12. See also Eisenhower's press conferences of February 9, 1955, *EPP: 1955*, pp. 255–56, March 7, 1956, *EPP: 1956*, pp. 297–98, and June 26, 1957, *EPP: 1957*, p. 504–5; also Eisenhower to Bernard Montgomery, May 2, 1956, Eisenhower Papers, Whitman File: DDE Diary, Box 9, "May 56 Misc (5)"; and Eisenhower telephone conversation with Styles Bridges, May 21, 1957, *ibid.*, Box 13, "May 57 Misc (2)."

28. "Basic National Security Policy (Suggestions of the Secretary of State)," November 15, 1954, *ibid.*, II, 772–75. See also minutes, National Security Council meetings of August 5 and 12, 1954, *FRUS: 1952–54*, XV, 706–7, 1485.

29. For more on this, see Gaddis, *The United States and the End of the Cold War*, pp. 66–73; also Campbell Craig, *Destroying the Village: Eisenhower and Thermonuclear War* (New York: 1998), pp. 50–52.

30. See, on this point, Friedberg, *In the Shadow of the Garrison State*, pp. 137–39.

31. I have borrowed, in the paragraphs that follow, from the argument in Gaddis, *We Now Know*, pp. 233–34.

32. Memorandum, NSC meeting, February 7, 1957, *FRUS: 1955–57*, XIX, 416. See also Eisenhower's comments at the NSC meetings of December 20, 1956, and April 11, 1957, *ibid.*, pp. 381, 473. For a particularly insightful discussion of Eisenhower's thinking and the probable influence of Clausewitz on it, see Peter J. Roman, *Eisenhower and the Missile Gap* (Ithaca: 1995), pp. 65, 83–84, 111.

33. See Marc Trachtenberg, *History and Strategy* (Princeton: 1991), pp. 40–42.

34. Craig, *Destroying the Village*, pp. 55, 106–7; Roman, *Eisenhower and the Missile Gap*, pp. 86–7.

35. Memorandum, NSC meeting, February 27, 1956, *FRUS: 1955–57*, XIX, 211. See also Eisenhower's comments on a Net Evaluation Subcommittee briefing, January 23, 1956, *ibid.*, pp. 190–91.

36. Memorandum, Eisenhower conversation with Arthur Radford and Maxwell Taylor, May 24, 1956, *ibid.*, p. 313. See also William Burr, "Avoiding the Slippery Slope: The Eisenhower Administration and the Berlin Crisis, November 1958–January 1959," *Diplomatic History*, XVIII (Spring, 1994), 182.

37. Eisenhower phone conversation with George Humphrey, December 7, 1956, Eisenhower Papers, Whitman File: DDE Diary, Box 11, "Dec. 56 Phone Calls." See also, on this point, Douglas Kinnard, *President Eisenhower and Strategy Management: A Study in Defense Politics* (Lexington: 1977), especially pp. 123–36.

38. John F. Kennedy, *The Strategy of Peace*, edited by Allan Nevins (New York: 1960), p. 6; Notes, Cabinet meeting of November 6, 1959, Eisenhower Papers, Whitman File: DDE Diary, Box 29, "Staff Notes-Nov. 59 (3)."

39. Dulles CIO speech, Cleveland, November 18, 1953, *DSB*, XXIX (November 30, 1953), 742. See also Walter Robertson's talk at the Johns Hopkins School of Advanced International Studies, Washington, August 8, 1955, *ibid.*, XXXIII (August 22, 1955), 296.

40. Berding, *Dulles on Diplomacy*, pp. 130–32; Eisenhower to Alfred Gruenther, November 30, 1954, Eisenhower Papers, Whitman File: DDE Diary, Box 5, "Nov. 54 (1)"; NSC 5602, "Basic National Security Policy" (draft), February 8, 1956, Modern Military Records Division, National Archives. See also Dulles's radio-television address, March 23, 1956, *DSB*, XXIV (April 2, 1956), 540; his press conference, October 2, 1956, *ibid.*, XXXV (October 15, 1956), 577; and Stebbins, *The United States in World Affairs: 1956*, p. 5.

41. See, on this point, Herbert S. Dinerstein, *The Making of a Missile Crisis: October, 1962* (Baltimore: 1976), pp. 19–20.

42. Eisenhower to George Humphrey, July 22, 1958, Eisenhower Papers, Whitman File: DDE Diary, Box 21, "DDE Dictation-July 58." See also a Goodpaster memorandum of a conversation between Eisenhower, Secretary of State Herter, and other advisers, December 29, 1959, *ibid.*, Box 30, "Staff Notes-Dec. 59."

43. Eisenhower to Winston Churchill, January 25, 1955, Eisenhower Papers, Whitman File: DDE Diary, Box 5, "Jan. 55 (1)."

44. See, on these points, Stebbins, *The United States in World Affairs: 1956*, pp. 116–17; Hoopes, *Dulles*, p. 313; Taylor, *The Uncertain Trumpet*, pp. 9–10.

45. "RC" memorandum, "NSC 177 and Special Annex (Dec. 30–31/53)," January 6, 1954, Eisenhower Papers, White House Office Files: Office of the Special Assistant for National Security Affairs, Box 6; Hagerty Diary, April 26, 1954, Hagerty Papers, Box 1.

46. Eisenhower to Gruenther, June 8, 1954, Eisenhower Papers, Whitman File: DDE Diary, Box 4, "Diary June 54 (2)"; Goodpaster memorandum, Eisenhower conversation with Arthur Flemming, October 30, 1956, *ibid.*, Box 11, "Oct. 56 Diary—Staff Memos"; Dulles radio-television address, March 23, 1956, *DSB*, XXXIV (April 2, 1956), 540.

47. Eisenhower to Gruenther, April 26, 1954, Eisenhower Papers, Whitman File: DDE Diary, Box 3, "Diary Jan–Nov 54 (2)."

48. *DSB*, XXXVI (January 21, 1957), 86. For more on the Eisenhower Doctrine, see Salim Yaqub, *Containing Arab Nationalism: The Eisenhower Doctrine and the Middle East* (Chapel Hill: 2004).

49. See, on this general argument, George and Smoke, *Deterrence in American Foreign Policy*, pp. 6–7, 506, 547–48.

50. Eisenhower to George Humphrey, March 27, 1957, Eisenhower Papers, Whitman File: DDE Diary, Box 13, "Mar 57 Misc (1)"; Dulles speech to Associated Press, New York, April 22, 1957, *DSB*, XXVI (May 6, 1957), 719.

51. Eisenhower press conference, August 20, 1958, *EPP: 1958*, pp. 630–31.

52. For more on Khrushchev's strategy, see Gaddis, *We Now Know*, pp. 234–44, as well as a still useful older account, Arnold Horelick and Myron Rush, *Strategic Power and Soviet Foreign Policy* (Chicago: 1966).

53. Taylor, *The Uncertain Trumpet*, p. 131. See also Roman, *Eisenhower and the Missile Gap*, pp. 30–62.

54. Eisenhower radio-television address, November 7, 1957, *EPP: 1957*, p. 793.

55. NSC 5602, February 8, 1956 (draft), annex, p. 32.

56. Eisenhower comments to Republican legislative leaders, January 8, 1958, Eisenhower Papers, Whitman File: DDE Diary, Box 18, "Staff Notes, Jan. 58."

57. NSC 5724, "Deterrence and Survival in the Nuclear Age," November 7, 1957, *FRUS: 1955–57*, XIX, 648.

58. Aliano, *American Defense Policy from Eisenhower to Kennedy*, pp. 109–15, 191–94. See also Roman, *Eisenhower and the Missile Gap*, pp. 118–21; and Eisenhower, *Waging Peace*, p. 221.

59. *Ibid.*, pp. 221–23; NSC 5724/1, "Comments and Recommendations on Report to the President by the Security Resources Panel of the ODM Science Advisory Committee," December 16, 1957, Eisenhower Papers, White House Office Files: Office of the Special Assistant for National Security Affairs, Box 75. See also Friedberg, *In the Shadow of the Garrison State*, pp. 137–39.

60. See Appendix.

61. NIE 11/8/1–61, "Strength and Deployment of Soviet Long Range Ballistic Missile Forces," September 21, 1961, in Ruffner, ed., *CORONA*, P. 130. See also Horelick and Rush, *Strategic Power and Soviet Foreign Policy*, pp. 35–36; John Prados, *The Soviet Estimate: U.S. Intelligence Analysis and Russian Military Strength* (New York: 1982), pp. 117–18; and Fred Kaplan, *The Wizards of Armageddon* (New York: 1983), pp. 286–90.

62. Notes, Cabinet meeting, October 18, 1957, Eisenhower Papers, Whitman File: DDE Diary, Box 16, "Oct. 57 Staff Notes (1)"; Goodpaster notes, Eisenhower-McElroy conversation, October 31, 1957, *ibid.*; Goodpaster notes, Eisenhower conversation with T. Keith Glennan, November 17, 1959, *ibid.*, Box 29, "Staff Notes-Nov. 59 (2)." See also Eisenhower, *Waging Peace*, pp. 127–38, 144–47.

63. Goodpaster memorandum of conversation between Eisenhower, Donald A. Quarles, and others, October 8, 1957, Eisenhower Papers, Whitman File: DDE Diary, Box 16, "Oct. 57 Staff Notes (2)"; Goodpaster notes, Eisenhower conference with scientific advisers, March 4, 1959, *ibid.*, Box 25, "Staff Notes, Mar. 1–15, 59 (1)"; Kistiakowsky Diary, January 7 and July 8, 1960, in George B. Kistiakowsky, *A Scientist in the White House* (Cambridge, Massachusetts: 1976), pp. 219, 367. See also *ibid.*, p. 312; Eisenhower, *Waging Peace*, p. 547n; Powers, *The Man Who Kept the Secrets*, pp. 95–98; and, for the history of the U-2 program, Michael R. Beschloss, *Mayday: Eisenhower, Khrushchev, and the U-2 Affair* (New York: 1986), pp. 67–161.

64. Eisenhower press conference, March 2, 1955, *EPP: 1955*, p. 303; Persons memorandum, Eisenhower conversation with Senators Duff and Saltonstall, April 4, 1956, Eisenhower Papers, Whitman File: DDE Diary, Box 8, "Apr 56 Misc (5)"; Eisenhower press conference, June 6, 1956, *EPP: 1956*, p. 554; Notes, Eisenhower meeting with Republican legislative leaders, June 24, 1958, Eisenhower Papers, Whitman File: DDE Diary, Box 20, "June 58 Staff Notes (2)"; Kistiakowsky Diary, April 1, 1960, in Kistiakowsky, *A Scientist in the White House*, p. 293. See also Charles C. Alexander, *Holding the Line: The Eisenhower Era, 1952–1961* (Bloomington: 1975), pp. 226–27.

65. Goodpaster notes, Eisenhower meeting with Killian, Kistiakowsky, and York, February 4, 1958, Eisenhower Papers, Whitman File: DDE Diary, Box 18, "Staff Memos, Feb. 58";

Goodpaster memorandum, Eisenhower-Allen Dulles conversation, June 17, 1958, *ibid.*, Box 20, "June 58 Staff Notes (3)"; Kistiakowsky Diary, November 16, 1959, in Kistiakowsky, *A Scientist in the White House*, pp. 160, 162.

66. Cabinet notes, June 3, 1960, Eisenhower Papers, Whitman File: DDE Diary, Box 33, "Staff Notes, June 60 (2)."

67. See above, pp. 157–59.

68. Hughes, *Ordeal of Power*, p. 342. See also Hoopes, *Dulles*, pp. 222, 295.

69. *Ibid.*, p. 489.

70. See Gaddis, *We Now Know*, pp. 234–53.

71. Dulles to Eisenhower, September 6, 1953, *FRUS: 1952–54*, II, 457–60; Eisenhower to Dulles, September 8, 1953, *ibid.*, p. 460.

72. Dulles to Eisenhower, September 6, 1953, *FRUS: 1952–54*, II, 458.

73. Notes, Cabinet meeting of July 10, 1953, quoted in Hughes, *Ordeal of Power*, p. 137; Eisenhower-Dulles telephone conversation, December 2, 1953, Eisenhower Papers, Whitman File: Diary Series, Box 1, "Nov–Dec 53 (2)."

74. Speech to the American Society of Newspaper Editors, April 16, 1953, *EPP: 1953*, pp. 179–88. On the background of this speech, see Hughes, *Ordeal of Power*, pp. 100–15.

75. Hagerty Diary, February 8, 1955, Hagerty Papers, Box 1. See also Eisenhower, *Mandate for Change*, pp. 504–6; and Hoopes, *Dulles*, pp. 287–95.

76. See Bell, *Negotiation from Strength*, pp. 3–136.

77. Eisenhower memorandum, December 10, 1953, Eisenhower Papers, Whitman File: DDE Diary, Box 2, "Oct–Dec 53." See also Eisenhower to Milton Eisenhower, December 11, 1953, *ibid.*, Box 2, "Dec (2)"; and Eisenhower, *Mandate for Change*, p. 254.

78. Eisenhower to Richard L. Simon, April 4, 1956, Eisenhower Papers, Whitman File: DDE Diary, Box 8, "Apr. 56 Misc (5)"; Goodpaster memorandum, Eisenhower-Dulles-Joint Chiefs of Staff conversation, March 1, 1956, *ibid.*, Box 7, "Mar. 56 Goodpaster"; John S.D. Eisenhower memorandum, Eisenhower conversation with Lewis Strauss, August 9, 1957, *ibid.*, Box 15, "Aug. 57 Memo on Appointments (2)"; Eisenhower-Dulles telephone conversation, April 7, 1959, *ibid.*, Box 25, "Telephone Calls, Apr. 59"; Goodpaster memorandum, Eisenhower conversation with Douglas Dillon, June 15, 1959, ibid., Box 26, "Staff Notes, June 1–15, 59 (2)"; Goodpaster memorandum, Eisenhower conversation with Llewellyn Thompson, October 16, 1959, ibid., Box 29, "Staff Memos, Oct. 59 (2)."

79. For a succinct summary of these negotiations, see Alexander, *Holding the Line*, pp. 94–98, 201–10. See also Eisenhower, *Waging Peace*, pp. 466–84; on the issue of nuclear testing, Robert A. Divine, *Blowing on the Wind: The Nuclear Test Ban Debate, 1954–1960* (New York: 1978); and on the surprise attack conference, Jeremi Suri, "America's Search for a Technological Solution to the Arms Race: The Surprise Attack Conference of 1958 and a Challenge to Eisenhower Revisionists," *Diplomatic History*, XXI (Summer, 1997), 417–51.

80. See Chen, *Mao's China and the Cold War*, pp. 170–71.

81. Dulles San Francisco speech, June 28, 1957, *DSB*, XXVIII (July 15, 1957), 91–95. See also John Gittings, *The World and China, 1922–1972* (New York: 1974), pp. 201–5.

82. See, for example, Ulam, *The Rivals*, pp. 212–13; and Gaddis, *Russia, the Soviet Union, and the United States* (1978 edition), pp. 222–23.

83. Minutes, Dulles briefing for Eisenhower, Churchill, and Bidault, Bermuda, December 7, 1953, Eisenhower Papers, Whitman File: International Meetings Series, Box 1, "Bermuda—State Dept. Report." See also NSC 148, "United States Policies in the Far East," April 6, 1953, *ibid.*, White House Office Files: Office of the Special Assistant for National Security Affairs, Box 24; NSC166/1, November 6, 1953, *FRUS: 1952–54*, XIV, 278–306.

84. For more on this, see Gaddis, *The Long Peace*, pp. 174–87.

85. Eisenhower to Alfred Gruenther, February 1, 1955, Eisenhower Papers, Whitman File: DDE Diary, Box 6, "Feb. 55(2)"; Hagerty Diary, February 3 and April 4, 1955, Hagerty Papers, Box 1.

86. State Department press release, August 11, 1958, *DSB*, XXXIX (September 8, 1958), 389; Gordon Gray memorandum of conversation with Eisenhower, November 5, 1958, Eisenhower Papers, Whitman File: DDE Diary, Box 23, "Staff Notes—Nov. 58."

87. See, for example, Gittings, *The World and China 1922–1972*, pp. 196–201, 217–20; Donald S. Zagoria, *The Sino-Soviet Conflict, 1956–1961* (Princeton: 1962), pp. 200–217; William E. Griffith, *The Sino-Soviet Rift* (Cambridge, Mass.: 1964), p. 21.

88. Ridgway memorandum, enclosed in Twining to Wilson, August 11, 1954, Eisenhower Papers, White House Office Files, Office of the Special Assistant for National Security Affairs, Box 10, "NSC 5429/5 (1)"; Eisenhower to Wallace, June 8, 1957, *ibid.*, Whitman File: DDE Diary, Box 14, "June 57 Misc (2)"; John S.D. Eisenhower memorandum, Eisenhower conversation with the Nigerian prime minister, October 8, 1960, *ibid.*, Box 34, "Staff Notes, Oct. 60 (1)."

89. See, on this point, George and Smoke, *Deterrence in American Foreign Policy*, pp. 407–11; and the more detailed analysis in Jack M. Schick, *The Berlin Crisis, 1958–1962* (Philadelphia: 1971), pp. 29–68; and Marc Trachtenberg, *A Constructed Peace: The Making of the European Settlement, 1945–1963* (Princeton: 1999), pp. 251–83.

90. Goodpaster notes, Eisenhower conversation with Herter, Dillon, Murphy, *et al.*, September 24, 1959, Eisenhower Papers, Whitman File: DDE Diary, Box 28, "Staff Notes—Sept. 59 (1)."

91. Goodpaster memorandum, Eisenhower conversation with Herter, *et al.*, July 11, 1960, Eisenhower Papers, Whitman File: DDE Diary, Box 33, "Staff Notes—July 60"; Kistiakowsky, *A Scientist at the White House*, p. 375. Beschloss, *Mayday*, provides the best account of the crisis itself.

SEVEN. *Flexible Response*

1. See the collection of excerpts from Kennedy's 1954–1960 speeches in Kennedy, *The Strategy of Peace*.

2. Divine, *Foreign Policy and U.S. Presidential Elections, 1952–1960*, pp. 221–27; Aliano, *American Defense Policy from Eisenhower to Kennedy*, pp. 214–16, 237–45; Lawrence Freedman, *Kennedy's Wars: Berlin, Cuba, Laos, and Vietnam* (New York: Oxford University Press, 2000), pp. 3–35.

3. Kennedy inaugural address, January 20, 1961, *Public Papers of the Presidents: John F. Kennedy* [hereafter *KPP*]: *1961*, p. 1; John McNaughton to McGeorge Bundy, September 28, 1961, John F. Kennedy Papers, NSC File, Box 273, "Department of Defense," John F. Kennedy Library. See also David Halberstam, *The Best and the Brightest* (New York: 1972), p. 39.

4. McGeorge Bundy to Henry M. Jackson, September 4, 1961, Kennedy Papers, NSC File, Box 283, "NSC General." See also Arthur M. Schlesinger, Jr., *A Thousand Days: John F. Kennedy in the White House* (Boston: 1965), pp. 420–21; Theodore C. Sorensen, *Kennedy* (New York: 1965), pp. 281–85.

5. Schlesinger, *A Thousand Days*, pp. 406–37; Sorensen, Kennedy, pp. 269–71, 287–90; Freedman, *Kennedy's Wars*, pp. 35–41.

6. Halberstam, *The Best and the Brightest*, p. 158; Schlesinger, *A Thousand Days*, p. 445. My understanding of Rostow was considerably enhanced by an "operational code" analysis

done by Allan Carlson, "Walt Rostow's World View," a 1974 Ohio University seminar paper.

7. Rostow draft, "Basic National Security Policy," March 26, 1962, Department of State S/P Files: Lot 69, D 121, BNSP Draft 3/26/62, Record Group 59, National Archives. The draft is summarized in *FRUS: 1961–63*, VIII, document 70, as is the immediate response of Kennedy and his advisers. See also W. W. Rostow, *The Diffusion of Power: An Essay in Recent History* (New York: 1972), pp. 174–76.

8. Kennedy Salt Lake City address, September 26, 1963, *KPP: 1963*, p. 736. For the background of this address, see Schlesinger, *A Thousand Days*, pp. 979–80.

9. Kennedy American University address, June 10, 1963, *KPP: 1963*, p. 462. See also Kennedy's state of the union address, January 11, 1962, *KPP: 1962*, p. 10, and his address at the Free University of Berlin, June 26, 1963, *KPP: 1963*, p. 527; also Dean Rusk's statement before the Senate Foreign Relations Committee, May 31, 1961, *DSB*, XLIV (June 19, 1961), 948; and Rostow's draft "Basic National Security Policy," March 26, 1962, pp. 12–13, 20–21, 30–31.

10. Rusk press conference, May 4, 1961, *DSB*, XLIV (May 22, 1961), 763. The intellectual roots of this idea are persuasively laid out in Frank Ninkovich, *Modernity and Power: A History of the Domino Theory in the Twentieth Century* (Chicago: 1994).

11. Rusk speech at the University of California, Berkeley, March 20, 1961, *DSB*, XLIV (June 19, 1961), 516; Rostow draft, "Basic National Security Policy," March 26, 1962, p. 112. See also "Africa Task Force Report," December 31, 1960, Kennedy Papers, Pre-Presidential File, Box 1073; and "Report to the President-Elect of the Task Force on Immediate Latin American Problems," *ibid.*, Box 1074; also Arthur M. Schlesinger, Jr., to Kennedy, March 10, 1961, *FRUS: 1961–63*, XII, document 7; and Schlesinger, *A Thousand Days*, p. 558.

12. Rostow draft, "Basic National Security Policy," March 26, 1962, pp. 8–11.

13. Kennedy radio-television address, July 25, 1961, *KPP: 1961*, p. 535. See also Kennedy's message to Congress, March 28, 1961, *ibid.*, p. 230; Kennedy's remarks to the Military Committee of NATO, April 10, 1961, *ibid.*, p. 255; Kennedy American University address, June 10, 1963, *KPP: 1963*, p. 462.

14. Samuelson report, "Prospects and Policies for the 1961 American Economy," January 6, 1961, Kennedy Papers, Pre-Presidential File, Box 1071, "Economy-Samuelson Report"; Walter W. Heller, *New Dimensions of Political Economy* (Cambridge, Mass.: 1966), p. 11.

15. See, on this point, Samuel P. Huntington, *The Common Defense: Strategic Programs in National Politics* (New York: 1961), pp. 264–67; and Seymour E. Harris, *The Economics of the Political Parties* (New York: 1962), especially pp. 3–19, 341–49.

16. Herbert Stein, *The Fiscal Revolution in America* (Chicago: 1969), pp. 379–84; Schlesinger, *A Thousand Days*, p. 630.

17. *Ibid.*, pp. 153, 155–57, 299–300, 381–84.

18. Kennedy message to Congress, March 28, 1961, *KPP: 1961*, pp. 230–31.

19. Heller, *New Dimensions of Political Economy*, pp. 32–33; Schlesinger, *A Thousand Days*, pp. 630, 645–48; Friedberg, *In the Shadow of the Garrison State*, pp. 145–46. See also Kennedy's speech at Yale University, June 11, 1962, *KPP: 1962*, pp. 470–75.

20. Johnson remarks at the Pentagon, July 21, 1964, *Public Papers of the Presidents: Lyndon B. Johnson* [hereafter *JPP*]: *1964*, p. 875.

21. Kennedy remarks to American embassy staff, Bad Godesburg, West Germany, June 23, 1963, *KPP: 1963*, p. 501.

22. Kennedy inaugural address, January 22, 1961, *KPP: 1961*, p. 1. See also *ibid.*, pp. 340, 359, 535, 725–26; *KPP: 1963*, pp. 659–60, 735.

23. See, for example, a CIA National Intelligence Estimate 11-8/1-61 (August 1961), "Strength and Deployment of Soviet Long Range Ballistic Missile Forces," in Donald P.

Steury, *Intentions and Capabilities: Estimates on Soviet Strategic Forces, 1950–1983* (Washington: 1996), pp. 121–38. Ruffner, ed., *CORONA*, documents the early history of American reconnaissance satellites.

24. Bundy to Theodore C. Sorensen, March 13, 1961, *FRUS: 1961–63*, VIII, Document 21; Kennedy press release, November 2, 1961, *KPP: 1961*, p. 693. See also Kennedy's press conference, November 8, 1961, *ibid.*, p. 702. Gilpatric's speech is reported in the *New York Times*, October 22, 1961; for background on it, see Freedman, *Kennedy's Wars*, pp. 82–85; Bundy, *Danger and Survival*, pp. 381–3; and Roger Hilsman, *To Move a Nation: The Politics of Foreign Policy in the Administration of John F. Kennedy* (New York: 1967), pp. 163–64.

25. Alain C. Enthoven and K. Wayne Smith, *How Much Is Enough? Shaping the Defense Program, 1961–1969* (New York: 1971), pp. 132–42. See also Freedman, *Kennedy's Wars*, pp. 107–8; and William W. Kaufman, *The McNamara Strategy* (New York: 1964), pp. 83–87.

26. Gaddis, *We Now Know*, pp. 248–66.

27. Rostow draft, "Basic National Security Policy," March 26, 1962, pp. 8, 40.

28. Kennedy speech to American Newspaper Publishers' Association, New York, April 27, 1961, *KPP: 1961*, p. 336; Kennedy address to the United Nations General Assembly, September 25, 1961, *ibid.*, p. 624. See also Kennedy's press conference, June 2, 1961, *ibid.*, p. 431.

29. Rostow speech to the U.S. Army Special Warfare School, Fort Bragg, North Carolina, June 28, 1961, *DSB*, XLV (August 7, 1961), p. 235; Rostow draft, "Basic National Security Policy," March 26, 1962, pp. 25–26. See also Schlesinger, *A Thousand Days*, pp. 587–89; and W. W. Rostow, *The Stages of Economic Growth: A Non-Communist Manifesto* (New York: 1960).

30. Rostow draft, "Basic National Security Policy," March 26, 1962, pp. 118, 174–75, 198.

31. Kennedy radio-television address, June 6, 1961, *KPP: 1961*, p. 445; Schlesinger to McGeorge Bundy, May 27, 1961, Kennedy Papers, National Security Files, Box 36, "Cuba-General"; Kennedy-Adzhubei interview, November 25, 1961, *KPP: 1961*, p. 743. See also *ibid.*, pp. 1, 10–11, 742; *KPP: 1962*, p. 12; *KPP: 1963*, pp. 509, 527.

32. Schlesinger, *A Thousand Days*, p. 415. For representative public statements by Kennedy, see *KPP: 1961*, pp. 140, 436–37, 705; *KPP: 1962*, pp. 3, 66–67, 265, 827; *KPP: 1963*, pp. 17–18, 611, 725.

33. Thompson to State Department (seen by Kennedy), February 1, 1961, *FRUS: 1961–63*, V, document 20; CIA study, "The Sino-Soviet Dispute and Its Significance," April 1, 1961, Kennedy Papers, National Security Files, Box 176, "U.S.S.R.-General"; Ray S. Cline memorandum, "Sino-Soviet Relations," January 14, 1963, *ibid.*, Box 180, "U.S.S.R.-General"; Bundy memorandum, Johnson conversation with Rusk, McNamara, and McCone, September 15, 1964, *FRUS: 1964–68*, XXX, document 49.

34. Johnson remarks at Al Smith memorial dinner, New York, October 14, 1964, *JPP: 1963–64*, p. 1329.

35. Kennedy remarks at Great Falls, Montana, September 26, 1963, *KPP: 1963*, p. 727; Johnson remarks at Associated Press luncheon, New York, April 20, 1964, *JPP: 1963–64*, p. 494.

36. Kennedy press conference, Paris, June 2, 1961, *KPP: 1961*, pp. 436–37; Kennedy remarks at Billings, Montana, September 25, 1963, *KPP: 1963*, p. 725; CIA Office of National Estimates, "Trends in the World Situation," June 9, 1964, Johnson Papers, National Security Files: Agency-CIA, Box 5–10.

37. CIA SNIE 13-4-63, "Possibilities of Greater Militancy by the Chinese Communists," July 31, 1963, Kennedy Papers, NSC Files, Box 314, Folder 10, "NSC Meetings, #516, 7/31/63."

38. Kennedy-Lippmann conversation, March 20, 1961, quoted in Schlesinger, *A Thousand Days*, pp. 331–32; Johnson to Kennedy, May 23, 1961, *Pentagon Papers*, II, 58–59.

39. Kennedy radio-television interview, December 17, 1962, *KPP: 1962*, p. 898.

40. Rostow draft, "Basic National Security Policy," March 26, 1962, pp. 173–74. See also pp. 67–68.

41. Kennedy message to Congress, March 28, 1961, *KPP: 1961*, p. 230; Kennedy remarks to the Military Committee of NATO, April 10, 1961, *ibid.*, p. 255. See also Kennedy radio-television address, July 25, 1961, *ibid.*, p. 535; and his address at the University of North Carolina, October 12, 1961, *ibid.*, p. 668.

42. "Foreign Policy Considerations Bearing on the US Defense Posture," enclosed in Rusk to David Bell, February 4, 1961, *FRUS: 1961–63*, document 10; Kennedy message to Congress, March 28, 1961, *KPP: 1961*, p. 232; Policy Planning Council memorandum, "Security in Southeast Asia," July 27, 1961, enclosed in McGhee to Rostow, July 28, 1961, Kennedy Papers, NSC Files, Box 231, "Southeast Asia-General."

43. McNamara to Kennedy, May 10, 1961, *FRUS: 1961–63*, VIII, document 27. See also Kaufman, *The McNamara Strategy*, pp. 66–68, 79–80; and Enthoven and Smith, *How Much Is Enough*, p. 214.

44. Kennedy state of the union address, January 14, 1963, *KPP: 1963*, p. 18. See also Kennedy's remarks at the Economic Club of New York, December 14, 1962, *KPP: 1962*, pp. 885–87; and McNamara to Kennedy, April 17, 1963, Kennedy Papers, NSC Files, Box 274, "Department of Defense."

45. Quoted in Kaufman, *The McNamara Strategy*, p. 128. See also *ibid.*, pp. 102–34.

46. "Summary Report, Military Counterinsurgency Accomplishments Since January, 1961," enclosed in Lemnitzer to Bundy, July 21, 1962, Kennedy Papers, NSC Files, Box 319, "Special Group (CI)." See also Hilsman, *To Move a Nation*, pp. 424–25; and Arthur M. Schlesinger, Jr., *Robert Kennedy and His Times* (Boston: 1978), pp. 459–67.

47. Rostow draft, "Basic National Security Policy," March 26, 1962, pp. 41, 56–58, 65–66, 72–73. See also Schlesinger, *A Thousand Days*, p. 422.

48. McNamara speech to Fellows, American Bar Foundation, Chicago, February 17, 1962, *Vital Speeches*, XXVIII (March 1, 1962), 298.

49. Undated memorandum, "Strategic Retaliatory Forces," Johnson Papers, NSF-Agency Files, Boxes 11–12, "Defense Department, Volume I." See also Jerome H. Kahan, *Security in the Nuclear Age: Developing U.S. Strategic Arms Policy* (Washington: 1975), p. 85.

50. Nitze speech to the International Institute of Strategic Studies, London, December 11, 1961, copy in Kennedy Papers, NSC Files, Box 273, "Department of Defense." See also "Foreign Policy Considerations Bearing on the US Defense Posture," enclosed in Rusk to David Bell, February 4, 1961, *FRUS: 1961–63*, document 10; Kennedy message to Congress, March 28, 1961, KPP: 1961, p. 234; Kennedy budget message, January 18, 1962, *KPP: 1962*, pp. 43–44. See also Kahan, *Security in the Nuclear Age*, pp. 88–90, and Harland B. Moulton, *From Superiority to Parity: The United States and the Strategic Arms Race, 1961–1971* (Westport, Conn.: 1973), pp. 79, 122–23.

51. Taylor to Bell, November 13, 1961, Kennedy Papers, NSC Files, Box 275, "Department of Defense FY 63 Budget"; Bell to Kennedy, November 13, 1961, *ibid.*; Kaysen to Bundy, November 13, 1961, *ibid.*; Taylor to Bell, November 21, 1961, *ibid.*; Kaysen to Kennedy, November 22 and December 9, 1961, *ibid.*; Kennedy press conference, February 7, 1962, *KPP: 1962*, p. 127.

52. Bundy to Kennedy, July 7, 1961, Kennedy Papers, NSC Files, Box 81, "Germany-Berlin: General"; McNamara address at Ann Arbor, Michigan, June 16, 1962, *Vital Speeches*, XXVIII (August 1, 1962), 626–29. See also Kaufman, *The McNamara Strategy*, pp. 113–17, 148–49; Moulton, *From Superiority to Parity*, pp. 82–93, 100–102; and Bundy, *Danger and Survival*, pp. 545–48..

53. Kennedy message to Congress, March 28, 1961, *KPP: 1961*, p. 230; Rostow draft, "Basic National Security Policy," March 26, 1962, pp. 47–49. See also Kennedy press conference, March 29, 1962, *KPP: 1962*, p. 276.

54. Rostow draft, "Basic National Security Policy," March 26, 1962, pp. 121–23. See also Schlesinger, *A Thousand Days*, pp. 855–56; Kaufman, *The McNamara Strategy*, p. 124; and Henry A. Kissinger, *The Troubled Partnership: A Re-appraisal of the Atlantic Alliance* (New York: 1965), pp. 106–17.

55. Kennedy press conference, May 17, 1962, KPP: 1962, p. 402. See also McNamara's address at Ann Arbor, Michigan, June 16, 1962, *Vital Speeches*, XXVIII (August 1, 1962), 626–29; Kaufman, *The McNamara Strategy*, p. 116–18; Kissinger, *The Troubled Partnership*, p. 143; and Trachtenberg, *A Constructed Peace*, pp. 284–85, 304–5.

56. Philip Nash, *The Other Missiles of October: Eisenhower, Kennedy, and the Jupiters, 1957–1963* (Chapel Hill: 1997), provides the best analysis of the decisions to deploy and to withdraw IRBMs from Europe. For the origins of the MLF, see Bundy, *Danger and Survival*, pp. 488–89.

57. *Ibid.*, pp. 494–98, 503–5. See also Rostow, *The Diffusion of Power*, pp. 391–94; and Schlesinger, *A Thousand Days*, pp. 853–56.

58. Rostow draft, "Basic National Security Policy," March 26, 1962, p. 25, 121, 141–44.

59. See, on these points, the report of Kennedy's Latin American task force, January 4, 1961, Kennedy Papers, Pre-Presidential File, Box 1074, "Latin America"; Kennedy inaugural address, January 20, 1961, *KPP: 1961*, p. 1; Schlesinger to Kennedy, March 10, 1961, *FRUS: 1961–63*, XII, document 7; Kennedy message to Congress, March 22, 1961, *KPP: 1961*, p. 205; Rostow to Bundy, May 13, 1961, Kennedy Papers, NSC Files, Box 2, "Africa"; Kennedy remarks at National Conference on International Economic and Social Development, June 16, 1961, *KPP: 1961*, p. 463; State Department guidelines on Africa, enclosed in McGhee to Rostow, September 22, 1961, Kennedy Papers, NSC Files, Box 2, "Africa."

60. Rostow draft, "Basic National Security Policy," March 26, 1962, p. 25.

61. *Ibid.*, pp. 10, 95–97, 110–11.

62. Latin American task force report, January 4, 1961, Kennedy Papers, Pre-Presidential File, Box 1074, "Latin America"; Schlesinger to Kennedy, March 10, 1961, *FRUS: 1961–63*, XII, document 7.

63. Rostow speech at Fort Bragg, North Carolina, June 28, 1961, *DSB*, XLV (August 7, 1961), 235. See also Schlesinger, *A Thousand Days*, pp. 593–94, 604–9.

64. Kennedy state of the union address, January 11, 1962, *KPP: 1962*, p. 12.

65. Enthoven and Smith, *How Much Is Enough*, pp. 8–30, 36; Kaufman, *The McNamara Strategy*, p. 48.

66. Enthoven and Smith, *How Much Is Enough*, pp. 33–47; Kaufman, *The McNamara Strategy*, pp. 172–99.

67. Kaufman, *The McNamara Strategy*, p. 179. See also Appendix.

68. Heller, *New Dimensions of Political Economy*, p. 11; Rostow draft, "Basic National Security Policy," March 26, 1962, pp. 209–210. See also Harris, *The Economics of the Political Parties*, pp. 212–13.

69. *Ibid.*, pp. 223–28. See also Paul A. Samuelson's task force report on the economy, January 6, 1961, Kennedy Papers, Pre-Presidential File, Box 1071, "Economy-Samuelson Report." For the balance of payments problem, see Francis J. Gavin, *Gold, Dollars, and Power: The Politics of International Monetary Relations, 1958–1971* (Chapel Hill: 2004), pp. 33–57.

70. Heller, *New Dimensions of Political Economy*, pp. 2, 29–36, 65. See also Stein, *The Fiscal Revolution in America*, pp. 372–453.

71. *KPP: 1961*, p. 2.

72. Rostow draft, "Basic National Security Policy," March 26, 1962, pp. 171–72, 176–78, 180–81.

73. See, on the Laos crisis, Freedman, *Kennedy's Wars*, pp. 293–304.

74. Kennedy to Rusk, August 21, 1961, *FRUS: 1961–63*, XIV, document 122; Kennedy-Adzhubei interview, November 25, 1961, *KPP: 1961*, pp. 750–51. See also Schlesinger to Bundy, July 18, 1961, Kennedy Papers, NSC Files, Box 81, "Germany-Berlin: General"; Bundy to Kennedy, July 19 and August 11, 1961, *ibid.*; Kaysen to Bundy, August 22, 1961, *ibid.*; Box 82, "Germany-Berlin: General"; Harriman to Kennedy, September 1, 1961, *ibid.*; also Schlesinger, *A Thousand Days*, pp. 383–400; and Freedman, *Kennedy's Wars*, pp. 66–91.

75. *Ibid.*, pp. 458–97.

76. See, for example, Richard J. Walton, *Cold War and Counterrevolution: The Foreign Policy of John F. Kennedy* (New York: 1972), pp. 103–42; Louise FitzSimons, *The Kennedy Doctrine* (New York: 1972), pp. 126–72; Bruce Miroff, *Pragmatic Illusions: The Presidential Politics of John F. Kennedy* (New York: 1976), pp. 82–100.

77. "G/PM" memorandum, "Significance of the Soviet Backdown for Future US Policy," October 29, 1962, Kennedy Papers, NSC Files, Box 36, "Cuba-General." See also Schlesinger to Bundy, October 26, 1962, *ibid.*; Harriman to George Ball, October 26, 1962, *ibid.*; Rostow memorandum, October 27, 1962, enclosed in William H. Brubeck to Bundy, October 28, 1962, *ibid.*; Rostow to Bundy, October 31, 1962, *ibid.*; Box 37, "Cuba-General."

78. Kennedy to Khrushchev, January 20, 1963, *KPP: 1963*, p. 53. See also Kennedy's radio-television interview, December 17, 1962, *KPP: 1962*, p. 898. For more on Kennedy's willingness to seek a negotiated solution, see Gaddis, *We Now Know*, pp. 269–72.

79. Kennedy American University address, June 10, 1963, *KPP: 1963*, p. 462.

80. Rostow draft, "Basic National Security Policy," March 26, 1962, pp. 198–200; Hilsman speech at San Francisco, December 13, 1963, *DSB*, L (January 6, 1974), 11–17. See also Schlesinger, *A Thousand Days*, pp. 479–80; Hilsman, *To Move a Nation*, pp. 346–57.

81. Kennedy speech at Miami, November 18, 1963, *KPP: 1963*, p. 876. See also Schlesinger, *Robert Kennedy and His Times*, pp. 533–58.

82. L.J. Legere to Bundy, with enclosure, February 18, 1963, Kennedy Papers, NSC Files, Box 37, "Cuba-General."

83. Kennedy speech to American Newspaper Publishers' Association, New York, April 27, 1961, *KPP: 1961*, p. 336; speech at George Washington University, May 3, 1961, *ibid.*, p. 347; radio-television address, June 6, 1961, *ibid.*, p. 443; radio-television address, October 22, 1962, *KPP: 1962*, p. 807.

84. See, on this point, Miroff, *Pragmatic Illusions*, pp. 66–67, 81–82.

85. Kennedy address at Rice University, September 12, 1962, *KPP: 1962*, p. 669.

86. Kennedy speech at Berkeley, March 23, 1962, *KPP: 1962*, p. 264; Kaysen to Bundy, August 22, 1961, Kennedy Papers, NSC Files, Box 82, "Germany-Berlin: General"; Kennedy address at the University of North Carolina, October 12, 1961, *KPP: 1961*, p. 668; Kennedy interview with Alexei Adzhubei, November 25, 1961, *ibid.*, p. 752.

87. Kennedy American University address, June 10, 1963, *KPP: 1963*, pp. 461–62; Kennedy address at the University of Maine, October 19, 1963, *ibid.*, p. 796.

88. Kennedy remarks, Great Falls, Montana, September 26, 1963, *KPP: 1963*, p. 727; Kennedy remarks to Fort Worth Chamber of Commerce, November 22, 1963, *ibid.*, p. 889.

EIGHT. *Implementing Flexible Response*

1. Johnson remarks at Syracuse University, August 5, 1964, *JPP: 1963–4*, p. 930; Johnson remarks to members of Congressional Committees, May 4, 1965, *JPP: 1965*, p. 487. See also Rostow to Kennedy, August 17, 1961, Kennedy Papers, NSC File, Box 231, "Southeast Asia-General"; McNamara statement, "United States Policy in Vietnam," March 26, 1964, *DSB*, XX (April 13, 1964), p. 566; Johnson address at Johns Hopkins University, April 7, 1965, *JPP: 1965*, p. 395; Johnson remarks to National Rural Electric Cooperative Association, July 14, 1965, *ibid.*, p. 751; Johnson press conference statement, July 28, 1965, *ibid.*, pp. 794–95.

2. Rostow draft, "Basic National Security Policy," March 26, 1962, p. 9; Rusk memorandum, July 1, 1965, *Pentagon Papers*, IV, 23. See also Rusk and McNamara to Kennedy, November 11, 1961, *ibid.*, II, 111; Johnson remarks to members of Congressional Committees, May 4, 1965, *JPP: 1965*, p. 486; and Rostow to McNamara, May 2, 1966, Johnson Papers, NSF Agency File, Boxes 11–12, "Defense Department Vol. III."

3. See, for example, the Joint Chiefs of Staff to McNamara, January 13, 1962, *Pentagon Papers*, II, 664; Roger Hilsman address, Tampa, Florida, June 14, 1963, *DSB*, XIX (July 8, 1963), 44; Johnson remarks at the National Cathedral School, Washington, June 1, 1965, *JPP: 1965*, p. 600.

4. McNaughton memorandum, "Proposed Course, of Action re Vietnam," March 24, 1965, *Pentagon Papers*, III, 695. See also Michael Forrestal to William P. Bundy, November 4, 1964, *ibid.*, p. 592. For further official perceptions of lack of coordination in the international communist movement, see Thomas L. Hughes to Hilsman, April 20, 1963, Kennedy Papers, NSC Files, Box 314, Folder 6; Hilsman to Rusk, July 31, 1963, *ibid.*, Folder 10; Johnson to Lodge, March 20, 1964, *Pentagon Papers*, III, 511; Bundy to Johnson, October 21, 1964, Johnson Papers, National Security Files—NSC Staff, Box 2, "Memos for the President, vol. 7"; Rostow to Rusk, December 16, 1964, *ibid.*, NSF Country Files—Vietnam, Box 11, "Memos, Vol. XXIII."

5. See above, p. 222.

6. Komer memorandum, "A Doctrine of Deterrence for SEA—The Conceptual Framework," May 9, 1961, Kennedy Papers, NSC File, Box 231, "Southeast Asia-General"; Rostow to Kennedy, August 17, 1961, *ibid.*, McNaughton memorandum, January 18, 1966, *Pentagon Papers*, IV, 47. See also Rostow's draft, "Basic National Security Policy," March 26, 1962, pp. 141–44, and Arthur Schlesinger's account of Kennedy's conversation with Khrushchev at Vienna in June 1961, in *A Thousand Days*, p. 368.

7. Johnson, Johns Hopkins address, April 7, 1965, *JPP: 1965*, p. 395; Johnson remarks to members of Congressional committees, May 4, 1965, *ibid.*, p. 491; Johnson press conference statement, July 28, 1965, *ibid.*, pp. 794.

8. Johnson remarks in Hartford, Connecticut, September 18, 1964, *JPP: 1964*, p. 1148. See also Johnson's remarks in Detroit, Michigan, September 7, 1964, *ibid.*, p. 1050; May, *"Lessons" of the Past*, especially pp. 112–14; and, for a more comprehensive analysis, Yuen Foong Khong, *Analogies at War: Korea, Munich, and the Vietnam Decisions of 1965* (Princeton: 1992).

9. Rusk and McNamara to Kennedy, November 11, 1961, *Pentagon Papers*, II, 111; Rostow draft, "Basic National Security Policy," March 26, 1962, p. 9. See also William P. Bundy to McNaughton, November 26, 1964, *Pentagon Papers*, III, 658.

10. Quoted in Doris Kearns, *Lyndon Johnson and the American Dream* (New York: 1976), pp. 253–53. See also Lyndon B. Johnson, *The Vantage Point: Perspectives of the Presidency, 1963–1969* (New York: 1971), pp. 151–52.

11. William Whitworth, *Naive Questions About War and Peace* (New York: 1970), pp. 105–6, 124.

12. Joseph Califano draft presidential statement, December 2, 1964, enclosed in Califano to Bundy, December 3, 1964, Johnson Papers, NSF—Agency Files, Boxes 11–12, "Defense Department Volume I"; Johnson message to Congress on Vietnam appropriations, May 4, 1965, *JPP: 1965*, p. 497. See also *JPP: 1963–64*, pp. 372, 1174, *JPP: 1965*, p. 489.

13. Rostow to Kennedy, August 17, 1961, Kennedy Papers, NSC File, Box 231, "Southeast Asia-General"; Taylor to Kennedy, October 24, 1961, *Pentagon Papers*, II, 88.

14. Joint Chiefs of Staff to Gilpatric, May 10, 1961, *Pentagon Papers*, II, 49; Lansdale to Gilpatric, May 10, 1961, Kennedy Papers, NSC File, Box 231, "Southeast Asia-General"; Komer to Rostow, August 2, 1961, *ibid.*; Komer to Bundy, October 31, 1961, *ibid.* See also Komer memorandum, "A Doctrine of Deterrence for SEA—The Conceptual Framework," May 9, 1961, *ibid.*

15. Taylor to Kennedy, November 3, 1961, *Pentagon Papers*, II, 654. See also, on the Taylor-Rostow report, *ibid.*, II, 73–120; Rostow, *The Diffusion of Power*, pp. 270–71, 274–79; and Maxwell Taylor, *Swords and Ploughshares* (New York: 1972), pp. 225–48.

16. Bundy memorandum, Kennedy meeting with advisers, July 28, 1961, *FRUS: 1961–63*, I, document 109; Policy Planning Council memorandum, "Security in Southeast Asia," July 27, 1961, enclosed in McGhee to Rostow, July 28, 1961, Kennedy Papers, NSC Files, Box 231, "Southeast Asia—General"; Rusk to State Department, November 1, 1961, *Pentagon Papers*, II, 105; Schlesinger, *A Thousand Days*, p. 547. See also Freedman, *Kennedy's Wars*, pp. 330–34.

17. Rusk to Nolting, November 14, 1961, *Pentagon Papers*, II, 119.

18. Hilsman to Harriman, June 18, 1962, *Pentagon Papers*, II, 673.

19. See, for example, Hilsman's elaborate "Action Plan" for South Vietnam, undated, Kennedy Papers, NSC File, Box 317, "Meetings on Vietnam"; also the *Pentagon Papers*, II, 201–76; and Freedman, *Kennedy's Wars*, pp. 367–97.

20. Johnson to Taylor, December 3, 1964, *FRUS: 1964–68*, I, document 435; Bundy memorandum, "A Policy of Sustained Reprisal," February 7, 1965, *Pentagon Papers*, III, 690; Bundy to Johnson, February 7, 1965, *ibid.*, p. 311. See also Kearns, *Johnson and the American Dream*, pp. 264–65. For the evolution of the "slow squeeze" option, see the *Pentagon Papers*, III, 206–51, 587–683.

21. JCS to CINCPAC, June 22, 1966, *Pentagon Papers*, IV, 105–6.

22. George C. Herring, *America's Longest War: The United States and Vietnam, 1950–1975*, second edition (New York: 1986), pp. 146–47.

23. Bundy to Johnson, May 22 and August 31, 1964, *FRUS: 1964–68*, I, documents 167 and 335; Rostow to McNamara, November 16, 1964, *Pentagon Papers*, III, 632; Rusk memorandum, "Viet-Nam," February 23, 1965, *FRUS: 1964–68*, II, document 157.

24. See, on this point, Guenter Lewy, *America in Vietnam* (New York: 1978), pp. 42–46; Robert L. Gallucci, *Neither Peace Nor Honor: The Politics of the American Military in Viet-Nam* (Baltimore: 1976), pp. 111–12; and the analysis in the *Pentagon Papers*, III, 429–33.

25. Figures on troop strength are from Herbert Y. Schandler, *The Unmaking of a President: Lyndon Johnson and Vietnam* (Princeton: 1977), p. 352.

26. Rostow to Robert F. Kennedy, August 18, 1961, Kennedy Papers, NSC File, Box 231, "Southeast Asia-General." See also Komer, "A Doctrine of Deterrence for SEA—The Conceptual Framework," May 9, 1961, *ibid.*

27. McNamara to Kennedy, November 8, 1961, *Pentagon Papers*, II, 108.

28. Rostow to Kennedy, May 11, 1961, Kennedy Papers, NSC File, Box 231, "Southeast Asia-General."

29. Forrestal to William P. Bundy, November 23, 1964, *Pentagon Papers*, III, 644; Johnson remarks at the University of Akron, October 21, 1964, *JPP: 1964*, p. 1391. See also *ibid.*, pp. 1164–65.

30. McNaughton draft, "Plan of Action for South Vietnam," September 3, 1964, *Pentagon Papers*, III, 559. See also Taylor to Rusk, August 18, 1964, *ibid.*, pp. 545–48; Bundy memorandum, meeting with Johnson, September 9, 1964, *FRUS: 1964–68*, I, document 343; William H. Sullivan to William P. Bundy, November 6, 1964, *Pentagon Papers*, III, 594; Rostow to Rusk, November 23, 1964, *ibid.*, pp. 654–46; Taylor briefing of November 27, 1964, *ibid.*, pp. 671–72; William P. Bundy memorandum, November 28, 1964, *ibid.*, p. 676; Bundy memorandum, December 28, 1964, *FRUS: 1964–68*, I, document 474; Bundy to Johnson, January 27, 1965, *ibid*, II, document 42. See also Leslie H. Gelb and Richard Betts, *The Irony of Vietnam: The System Worked* (Washington, D.C.: 1979), pp. 12–13.

31. See, for example, the Joint Chiefs of Staff to McNamara, January 22, 1964, *Pentagon Papers*, III, 497–98; also Gallucci, *Neither Peace Nor Honor*, pp. 38–39.

32. George and Smoke, *Deterrence in American Foreign Policy*, p. 529.

33. See, on this point, Alain Enthoven to Clark Clifford, March 20, 1968, in Enthoven and Smith, *How Much Is Enough*, pp. 298–99; and Schandler, *The Unmaking of a President*, pp. 31–32, 46.

34. Bundy to Johnson, May 22, 1964, *FRUS: 1964–68*, I, document 167; Taylor to State Department, November 3, 1964, *Pentagon Papers*, III, 591. See also Taylor to State Department, August 18, 1964, *ibid.*, pp. 546–47.

35. Rusk to Lodge, August 14, 1964, *ibid.*, II, 330. See also William P. Bundy's first draft of this cable, *ibid.*, III, 526; and, for the administration's resistance to neutralization, Fredrik Logevall, *Choosing War: The Lost Chance for Peace and the Escalation of War in Vietnam* (Berkeley: 1999).

36. See, on this point, Graham T. Allison, *Essence of Decision: Explaining the Cuban Missile Crisis* (Boston: 1971), pp. 83, 89.

37. Gelb and Betts, *The Irony of Vietnam*, pp. 239–40; Lewy, *America in Vietnam*, pp. 114–16.

38. Gallucci, *Neither Peace Nor Honor*, pp. 73–80; Lewy, *America in Vietnam*, p. 98.

39. Gallucci, *Neither Peace Nor Honor*, pp. 114–15, 119–20; Lewy, *America in Vietnam*, pp. 43, 51, 117.

40. *Ibid.*, pp. 52, 65, 99–101, 106, 108–14, 118–19; Frances FitzGerald, *Fire in the Lake: The Vietnamese and the Americans in Vietnam* (Boston: 1972), pp. 344–45.

41. Joseph Conrad, *Heart of Darkness*, edited by Robert Kimbrough (New York: 1971), p. 14.

42. Rostow to McNamara, May 2, 1966, Johnson Papers, NSF Agency File, Boxes 11–12, "Defense Department Vol. III." See also Rostow's 1962 draft "Basic National Security Policy," p. 38.

43. Enthoven and Smith, *How Much Is Enough*, pp. 270–71.

44. See David Halberstam's evocative portrait of McNamara in *The Best and the Brightest*, pp. 215–50. McNamara describes his own enthusiasm for quantification in his memoir, *In Retrospect: The Tragedy and Lessons of Vietnam* (New York: 1995), p. 6.

45. Hilsman, *To Move a Nation*, p. 523.

46. See, on this point, the *Pentagon Papers*, II, 410–11.

47. McNamara to Johnson, December 21, 1963, *ibid.*, III, 494. See also John McCone to McNamara, December 21, 1963, *ibid.*, p. 32; and Johnson, *The Vantage Point*, p. 63. The examples of distorted South Vietnamese reporting are from Hilsman, *To Move a Nation*, pp. 522–23.

48. Taylor and McNamara to Kennedy, October 2, 1963, *Pentagon Papers*, II, 187. See also Halberstam, *The Best and the Brightest*, pp. 200–205.

49. Bundy memorandum, Kennedy meeting with Taylor and McNamara, *FRUS: 1961–63*, IV, document 143. See also Hilsman, *To Move a Nation*, pp. 446–67, 502–4.

50. Gallucci, *Neither Peace Nor Honor*, pp. 132–35; Gelb and Betts, *The Irony of Vietnam*, pp. 304–5. See also Roberta Wohlstetter, *Pearl Harbor: Warning and Decision* (Stanford: 1962), pp. 122–24.

51. Dave Richard Palmer, *Summons of the Trumpet: U.S.-Vietnam in Perspective* (San Rafael, Cal.: 1978), pp. 119–20.

52. Lewy, *America in Vietnam*, pp. 78–82; Enthoven and Smith, *How Much Is Enough*, pp. 295–96.

53. McNamara to Johnson, November 17, 1966, *Pentagon Papers*, IV, 371.

54. Quoted in Gallucci, *Neither Peace Nor Honor*, p. 84. See also *ibid.*, pp. 80–85; Gelb and Betts, *The Irony of Vietnam*, pp. 309–10.

55. Special National Intelligence Estimate 10-4-61, November 5, 1961, *Pentagon Papers*, II, 107; Robert H. Johnson to William P. Bundy, March 31, 1965, Johnson Papers, NSF Country Files—Vietnam, Box 16, "Memos, Vol. XXXII." See also Gelb and Betts, *The Irony of Vietnam*, pp. 25–26; Halberstam, *The Best and the Brightest*, pp. 460–62; and Johnson, *The Vantage Point*, pp. 147–49.

56. Taylor to State Department, February 22, 1965, *Pentagon Papers*, III, 419; Clifford to Johnson, May 17, 1965, *FRUS: 1964–68*, II, document 307; Ball memorandum, "Cutting Our Losses in South Viet-Nam," June 28, 1965, *ibid.*, III, document 26; William P. Bundy memorandum, "Holding On in South Vietnam," June 20, 1965, Johnson Papers, NSF Country Files: Vietnam, Box 74, "1965 Troop Decision." See also David L. DiLeo, *George Ball, Vietnam, and the Rethinking of Containment* (Chapel Hill: 1991).

57. McNamara to Johnson, July 20, 1965, *FRUS: 1964–68*, III, document 67; McNamara to Johnson, January 24, 1966, *Pentagon Papers*, IV, 49–51.

58. Westmoreland cable, December 27, 1965, *Pentagon Papers*, IV, 39. The CIA and Komer reports are discussed in *ibid.*, pp. 71–74, 389–91. (Emphases in original.)

59. Gelb and Betts, *The Irony of Vietnam*, pp. 159–60. See also Johnson, *The Vantage Point*, p. 147; and Kearns, *Lyndon Johnson and the American Dream*, p. 282.

60. Senate Committee on Foreign Relations, Hearings, *Supplemental Foreign Assistance Fiscal Year 1966—Vietnam* (Washington: 1966), pp. 335–36.

61. Richard J. Barnet, *Roots of War* (Baltimore: 1972), pp. 109–15.

62. See the list of American peace initiatives and Hanoi's responses in Appendix A to Johnson, *The Vantage Point*, pp. 579–89.

63. Gallucci, *Neither Peace Nor Honor*, pp. 132–34.

64. See Johnson's personally drafted memorandum on McNamara's recommendations, December 18, 1967, *FRUS: 1964–68*, V, document 441; also McNamara, *In Retrospect*, pp. 305–14.

65. Gelb and Betts, *The Irony of Vietnam*, pp. 2–3.

66. Kennedy address at the University of Washington, November 16, 1961, *KPP: 1961*, p. 726. See also *ibid.*, pp. 340–41, 359, *KPP: 1963*, pp. 659–60, 735; and the *Pentagon Papers*, II, 161.

67. *JPP: 1963–64*, pp. 44, 89, 122, 150.

68. Johnson remarks to American Bar Association meeting, New York, August 12, 1964, *ibid.*, p. 953; Bundy memorandum, Johnson conference with advisers, September 9, 1964, *FRUS: 1964–68*, I, document 343; Rostow to Rusk, November 23, 1964, *Pentagon Papers*, III, 647; McNamara to the Joint Chiefs of Staff and service secretaries, March 1, 1965, *ibid.*, p. 94; Rusk CBS-TV interview, August 9, 1965, *DSB*, LIII (August 30, 1965), 344. (Emphasis in original.)

69. Johnson report to Congress on national defense, January 18, 1965, *JPP: 1965*, p. 69; Johnson remarks to members of Congressional delegations, May 4, 1965, *ibid.*, p. 487; Johnson press conference, July 28, 1965, *ibid.*, pp. 795, 799; Komer memorandum, date not given,

Pentagon Papers, II, 575; Westmoreland statement to press, April 14, 1967, quoted in Lewy, *America in Vietnam*, p. 73.

70. Enthoven and Smith, *How Much Is Enough*, pp. 290–306.

71. *Ibid.*, pp. 292–93.

72. Schandler, *The Unmaking of a President*, pp. 39, 56, 100–102, 228–29, 290–92. See also Johnson, *The Vantage Point*, pp. 149, 317–19, 406–7.

73. See, on this point, Gallucci, *Neither Peace Nor Honor*, pp. 128–30.

74. FitzGerald, *Fire in the Lake*, pp. 315–16, 349, 352–53.

75. MACCORDS report on Bien Hoa province for period ending December 31, 1967, *Pentagon Papers*, II, 406.

76. FitzGerald, *Fire in the Lake*, p. 357.

77. Quoted in Alexander Kendrick, *The Wound Within: America in the Vietnam Years, 1945–1974* (Boston: 1974), p. 251.

78. Johnson address at Johns Hopkins University, April 7, 1965, *JPP: 1965*, p. 395.

79. McNaughton draft memorandum, "Aims and Options in Southeast Asia," October 13, 1964, *Pentagon Papers*, III, 582; Bundy memorandum, "A Policy of Sustained Reprisal," February 7, 1965, *ibid.*, p. 314.

80. See, on this point, Lewy, *America in Vietnam*, pp. 60, 96, 175, 181–82, 207, 306, 437–38.

81. See especially "On Protracted War," in the *Selected Military Writings of Mao Tse-tung* (Peking: 1967), pp. 210–19.

82. Johnson, *The Vantage Point*, p. 389. See also Schandler, *The Unmaking of a President*, pp. 109, 171.

83. See, on this point, Albert Wohlstetter, "Is There a Strategic Arms Race?" *Foreign Policy*, #15 (Summer, 1974), 3–20; "Rivals but No Race," *ibid.*, #16 (Fall, 1974), 48–81.

84. Moulton, *From Superiority to Parity*, pp. 283–92. See also Ernest J. Yanarella, *The Missile Defense Controversy: Strategy, Technology, and Politics, 1955–1972* (Lexington, Ky.: 1977), pp. 114–15, 151.

85. Johnson remarks to State Department employees, December 5, 1963, *JPP: 1963–64*, p. 28.

86. Kissinger, *White House Years*, p. 196.

87. Arthur Barber memorandum of conversation with Soviet official Pavlichenko, July 28, 1966, Johnson Papers, NSF Agency File: Department of Defense, Boxes 11–12, "Vol. IV." See also Johnson, *The Vantage Point*, pp. 475–76; Rostow, *The Diffusion of Power*, pp. 376–77; and for the overall Soviet response, Ilya V. Gaiduk, *The Soviet Union and the Vietnam War* (Chicago: 1996).

88. See, on this point, Qiang Zhai, *China and the Vietnam Wars, 1950–1975* (Chapel Hill: 2000), pp. 164–68.

89. Johnson, *The Vantage Point*, pp. 471–73.

90. See the critique of Johnson administration's policies in Roger Morris, *Uncertain Greatness: Henry Kissinger and American Foreign Policy* (New York: 1977), pp. 11–22.

91. Johnson speech to Congress, March 15, 1965, *JPP: 1965*, pp. 286–87.

92. Quoted in Kearns, *Lyndon Johnson and the American Dream*, pp. 251–52.

93. *Ibid.*, p. 283.

94. Johnson to Rusk, McNamara, and McCone, December 7, 1964, *FRUS: 1964–68*, I, document 440; NSAM 328, April 6, 1965, *Pentagon Papers*, III, 703. See also *ibid.*, pp. 447, 460.

95. McGeorge Bundy to Johnson, July 21, 1965, Johnson Papers, NSF Country Files: Vietnam, Box 74, "1965 Troop Decision"; McNamara to Johnson, October 26, 1966, *FRUS: 1964–68*, IV, document 285; William P. Bundy memorandum, "Basic Choices in Vietnam," April 16, 1966, *Pentagon Papers*, IV, 88.

96. Johnson, *The Vantage Point*, pp. 438–60; Rostow, *The Diffusion of Power*, pp. 316–18.

97. Johnson, *The Vantage Point*, p. 440. See also Kearns, *Lyndon Johnson and the American Dream*, pp. 300–2.

NINE. *Nixon, Kissinger, and Détente*

1. See, for the major themes of Nixon's campaign speeches, his acceptance address to the Republican National Convention, *New York Times*, August 9, 1968. See also Richard M. Nixon, "Asia After Vietnam," *Foreign Affairs*, XLVI (October 1967), 121–23.

2. Kissinger, *White House Years*, p. 65; *RN: The Memoirs of Richard Nixon* (New York: 1978), p. 562.

3. See, on this point, Kissinger, *White House Years*, pp. 41–43.

4. Henry A. Kissinger, *American Foreign Policy*, third edition (New York: 1977), pp. 29, 79, 97, reprinting material originally published as Kissinger, "Domestic Structures and Foreign Policy," *Daedalus*, XCV (Spring, 1966), 503–29; and Kissinger, "Central Issues in American Foreign Policy," in Kermit Gordon, ed., *Agenda for the Nation* (Washington: 1968), pp. 585–614. See also Kissinger, *White House Years*, pp. 11, 39, 41–43, 65.

5. Kissinger, "Central Issues," in *American Foreign Policy*, pp. 59–64. See also Kissinger's address at San Francisco, February 3, 1976, *ibid.*, p. 310; and Kissinger, *White House Years*, pp. 66–67.

6. Kissinger, "Central Issues," in *American Foreign Policy*, p. 56.

7. Kissinger, *White House Years*, p. 1049.

8. See, on the transition from bipolarity to multipolarity, Kissinger, "Central Issues," in *American Foreign Policy*, pp. 56–57, 74; also Peter W. Dickson, *Kissinger and the Meaning of History* (New York: 1978), p. 89.

9. Kissinger statement to Senate Foreign Relations Committee, September 19, 1974, speech to Cincinnati Chamber of Commerce, September 16, 1975, and speech at San Francisco, February 3, 1976, all in Kissinger, *American Foreign Policy*, pp. 146–47, 281, 302.

10. Kissinger, *White House Years*, pp. 69, 662–64, 914–15, 1088–89, 1260. See also Kissinger, *American Foreign Policy*, pp. 40, 82, 124–26, 172–73, 209–10, 282.

11. Kissinger, *White House Years*, p 1089. See also Nixon's annual foreign policy reports, February 18, 1970, *Public Papers of the Presidents: Richard M. Nixon* [hereafter *NPP*]: *1970*, pp. 178–79, and February 24, 1971, *NPP: 1971*, p. 304; also Dickson, *Kissinger and the Meaning of History*, pp. 90–92.

12. Kissinger, "Central Issues," *American Foreign Policy*, p. 74. See also Dickson, *Kissinger and the Meaning of History*, pp. 92–94, 100–102. Kissinger treated Metternich and Castlereagh in his doctoral dissertation, *A World Restored* (New York: 1957), and Bismarck in "The White Revolutionary: Reflections on Bismarck," *Daedalus*, XCVII (Summer, 1968), 888–924.

13. See Nixon's press conference, January 27, 1969, *NPP: 1969*, p. 19; also Nixon, *RN*, p. 415.

14. Kissinger, *White House Years*, p. 535.

15. Kansas City speech, July 6, 1971, *NPP: 1971*, p. 806; Kissinger, *White House Years*, p. 1072.

16. *Time*, XCIX (January 3, 1972), 15.

17. See Kissinger's address to the *Pacem in Terris* III conference, Washington, October 8, 1973, in *American Foreign Policy*, pp. 128–29.

18. Representative critiques included: Stanley Hoffmann, "Weighing the Balance of Power," *Foreign Affairs*, L (July 1972), 618–43; Alastair Buchan, "A World Restored?" *ibid.*, pp. 644–59; Zbigniew Brzezinski, "The Balance of Power Delusion," *Foreign Policy*, #7

(Summer, 1972), 54–59; and James Chace, "The Five-Power World of Richard Nixon," *New York Times Magazine*, February 20, 1972, pp. 14ff.

19. Kissinger, "Central Issues," in *American Foreign Policy*, pp. 56–57, 74. See also Kissinger, *White House Years*, pp. 68–69.

20. See, on this point, Henry A. Kissinger, *The Troubled Partnership: A Re-Appraisal of the Atlantic Alliance* (New York: 1965), especially pp. 41–64; also Kissinger, *White House Years*, pp. 68–69.

21. See Kissinger's "Year of Europe" speech, delivered to the Associated Press Annual Luncheon, New York, April 23, 1973, in Kissinger, *American Foreign Policy*, p. 102; also Dickson, *Kissinger and the Meaning of History*, pp. 135–36.

22. Annual foreign policy report, February 18, 1970, *NPP: 1970*, p. 181. See also Nixon, "Asia After Vietnam," pp. 121–23; Kissinger, *White House Years*, pp. 163–65; and Kissinger, *American Foreign Policy*, pp. 38–39.

23. Annual foreign policy report, February 9, 1972, *NPP: 1972*, pp. 204–5.

24. Kissinger address to the *Pacem in Terris* III conference, Washington, October 8, 1973, in *American Foreign Policy*, pp. 128–29.

25. Kissinger address at San Francisco, February 3, 1976, in *American Foreign Policy*, p. 305.

26. Interview with the author, October 31, 1974.

27. Kissinger, *White House Years*, p. 192; Nixon, *RN*, pp. 562, 565. See also Nixon's annual foreign policy report, February 18, 1970, *NPP: 1970*, pp. 116–17, 178–79.

28. Rusk press conference, October 12, 1967, *DSB*, LVII (October 30, 1967), 563.

29. Annual foreign policy report, February 18, 1970, *NPP: 1970*, p. 116.

30. Nixon, *RN*, p. 562. See also Kissinger, *White House Years*, p. 1061.

31. Kissinger, *White House Years*, p. 1063.

32. *Ibid*, pp. 116–19 (emphasis in original.)

33. Kissinger San Francisco speech, February 3, 1976, in *American Foreign Policy*, p. 304.

34. Kissinger, *White House Years*, pp. 119–20, 526–27, 542, 545, 554–57, 711, 1055–56, 1138–39, 1292–93.

35. See, on this point, Chapters Two and Three.

36. Kissinger, *White House Years*, pp. 156–58, 927–30, 1265–68.

37. See, for Vietnam, Gaiduk, *The Soviet Union and the Vietnam War*, pp. 194–245; for Chile, Peter Kornbluh, ed., *The Pinochet File: A Declassified Dossier on Atrocity and Accountability* (New York: 2003); for Eurocommunism, Raymond L. Garthoff, *Détente and Confrontation: American-Soviet Relations from Nixon to Reagan*, revised edition (Washington: 1994), pp. 537–55; and for Angola, Piero Gleijeses, *Conflicting Missions: Havana, Washington, and Africa, 1959–1976* (Chapel Hill: 2002), pp. 230–72.

38. Kissinger, *White House Years*, p. 659. See also Morris, *Uncertain Greatness*, pp. 232–33.

39. Nixon radio-television address, April 30, 1970, *NPP: 1970*, p. 409; Kissinger, *White House Years*, pp. 227–29. See also John G. Stoessinger, *Henry Kissinger: The Anguish of Power* (New York: 1976), p. 216; Coral Bell, *The Diplomacy of Détente: The Kissinger Era* (New York: 1977), p. 227; and Tad Szulc, *The Illusion of Peace: Foreign Policy in the Nixon Years* (New York: 1978), pp. 352–53.

40. Kennedy speech at the University of Maine, October 19, 1963, *KPP: 1963*, p. 795.

41. Kissinger address to the *Pacem in Terris* III conference, Washington, October 8, 1973, in *American Foreign Policy*, p. 121. See also *ibid.*, p. 35; and Nixon's annual foreign policy report, February 18, 1970, *NPP: 1970*, p. 122.

42. Kissinger, *White House Years*, pp. 61–62, 1302.

43. Annual foreign policy report, February 18, 1970, *NPP: 1970*, pp. 178–79; Kissinger state-

ment to the Senate Foreign Relations Committee, September 19, 1974, in *American Foreign Policy*, p. 145.

44. Annual foreign policy report, February 9, 1972, *NPP: 1972*, pp. 206–7. See also Kissinger's statement to the Senate Foreign Relations Committee, September 19, 1974, in *American Foreign Policy*, pp. 88, 148–49; and Kissinger, *White House Years*, p. 128.

45. NSC 20/1, August 18, 1948, in Etzold and Gaddis, eds., *Containment*, p. 187.

46. Kissinger statement to the Senate Foreign Relations Committee, September 19, 1974, in *American Foreign Policy*, pp. 172–73. See also *ibid.*, pp. 124–26, 145, and 157; also Nixon's annual foreign policy report, February 18, 1970, *NPP: 1970*, p. 178.

47. Nixon to Rogers, Laird, and Helms (drafted by Kissinger), February 4, 1969, quoted in Kissinger, *White House Years*, p. 136; Kissinger to Nixon, February 18, 1969, *ibid.*, pp. 143–44. See also *ibid.*, p. 1134.

48. Kissinger, *White House Years*, pp. 127–30, 265–69; Nixon, *RN*, p. 346.

49. Edmonds, *Soviet Foreign Policy, 1962–1973*, p. 3; Garthoff, *Détente and Confrontation*, p. 52.

50. Kissinger, *White House Years*, pp. 130–38, 903–18, 1174–94.

51. Kissinger statement to the Senate Foreign Relations Committee, September 19, 1974, in *American Foreign Policy*, pp. 158–59. See also Kissinger, *White House Years*, pp. 127–30, 265–69, 619, 627–31, 639–52.

52. *Ibid.*, pp. 129–30.

53. Nixon, "Asia After Vietnam," pp. 121–23; Kissinger, "Domestic Structures," *American Foreign Policy*, pp. 38–39.

54. Kissinger, *White House Years*, pp. 165–70.

55. *Ibid.*, pp. 183–85. See also p. 548.

56. See above, pp. 209–10.

57. Quoted in William Safire, *Before the Fall: An Inside View of the Pre-Watergate White House* (New York: 1975), p. 370. See also Kissinger, *White House Years*, pp. 178–82, 185–86.

58. Kissinger, *White House Years*, p. 187. See also *ibid.*, pp. 764–65; and, for Dobrynin's perspective, Anatoly Dobrynin, *In Confidence: Moscow's Ambassador to Six Cold War Presidents (1962–1986)* (New York: 1995), p. 202.

59. Kissinger, *White House Years,* pp. 712, 836–37, 1076.

60. *Ibid.*, pp. 220–21.

61. Nixon radio-television address, November 3, 1969, *NPP: 1969*, pp. 905–6; annual foreign policy report, February 18, 1970, *NPP: 1970*, pp. 118–19. For Nixon's initial informal enunciation of the Nixon Doctrine, see his press briefing on Guam, July 25, 1969, *NPP: 1969*, pp. 544–55.

62. See, on this point, Kissinger, *White House Years*, p. 232.

63. *Ibid.*, pp. 260–61, 271–77, 475–82, 984–86, 1329.

64. Johnson, *The Vantage Point*, pp. 368–69.

65. Kissinger, *White House Years*, p. 1304.

66. Nixon, *RN*, pp. 129, 864; Kissinger, *White House Years*, p. 1199. See also Safire, *Before the Fall*, p. 691; and H.R. Haldeman, *The Ends of Power* (New York: 1978), p. 122.

67. Kissinger, "Central Issues," in *American Foreign Policy*, p. 61; Kissinger, *White House Years*, pp. 617, 912, 1117. See also Stephen Graubard, *Kissinger: Portrait of a Mind* (New York: 1973), p. 66.

68. Kissinger, *White House Years*, pp. 1199, 1349.

69. *Ibid.*, pp. 228–29.

70. Nixon, *RN*, p. 352; Kissinger, *A World Restored*, p. 210; Kissinger, "Domestic Structures,"

American Foreign Policy, p. 18; Kissinger, White House Years, p. 39. See also ibid., pp. 11, 14–15; and Graubard, Kissinger, pp. 50–51, 101–2, 229–32.

71. Kissinger, White House Years, pp. 130, 136–38, 189–90, 477–83, 688, 984–85.

72. Ibid., pp. 48, 822. See also pp. 495, 564, 606, 674.

73. Ibid, p. 841. See also pp. 722–26, 837, 917; and Stoessinger, Kissinger, pp. 209–11.

74. See Jonathan Schell, The Time of Illusion (New York: 1976), pp. 6–7.

75. Kissinger, White House Years, pp. 158–59.

76. NPP: 1970, p. 119. The four annual foreign policy reports, dated February 18, 1970, February 25, 1971, February 9, 1972, and May 3, 1973, can be most conveniently located in the appropriate volumes of the Nixon Public Papers.

77. Kissinger, White House Years, p. 159. See also ibid., p. 1053.

78. The most important of these speeches are in Kissinger, American Foreign Policy, pp. 116–429.

79. Annual foreign policy report, February 25, 1971, NPP: 1971, p. 246. See also Nixon's press conference, March 21, 1970, NPP: 1970, p. 292.

80. Kissinger, White House Years, pp. 917–18.

81. Ibid., pp. 762, 803; Nixon, RN, p. 390.

82. Kissinger, White House Years, p. 940.

83. See, on this point, Dickson, Kissinger and the Meaning of History, pp. 155–57.

TEN. *Implementing Détente*

1. See, for example, Stanley Hoffmann, "Choices," Foreign Policy, #12 (Fall, 1973), 3–42; Zbigniew Brzezinski, "The Deceptive Structure of Peace," ibid., #14 (Spring, 1974), 35–56; Hoffmann, "Weighing the Balance of Power," pp. 618–48.

2. See Carter's comments in the second televised debate with Ford, October 6, 1976, in U.S. Congress, House of Representatives, Committee on House Administration, The Presidential Campaign, 1976 (Washington: 1979), III, 93–118; also Bell, The Diplomacy of Détente, pp. 50, 52–53, 216–17.

3. Gerald R. Ford, A Time to Heal (New York: 1979), p. 398; Elizabeth Drew, American Journal: The Events of 1976 (New York: 1977), pp. 391–92.

4. Stanley Hoffmann, Primacy or World Order: American Foreign Policy Since the Cold War (New York: 1978), p. 46.

5. Nixon, RN, p. 618; Kissinger statement to Senate Foreign Relations committee, September 19, 1974, in American Foreign Policy, p. 145.

6. Ibid., p. 147. (Emphasis added.)

7. See on these episodes, Nixon, RN, pp. 483–89, 525–31, 613–14; Kissinger, White House Years, pp. 619, 627–31, 639–52, 903–18, 1302, 1341–59; also Szulc, The Illusion of Peace, p. 331.

8. Kissinger, White House Years, pp. 265–69, 1022, 1135, 1151–52. For a retrospective assessment of the Cuban, Syrian, and India-Pakistan crises, see Garthoff, Détente and Confrontation, pp. 87–95, 98–99, and 296–314.

9. Leonid Brezhnev, On the Policy of the Soviet Union and the International Situation (Garden City, N.Y.: 1973), p. 231.

10. Nixon, RN, p. 568.

11. See, on these episodes, Nixon, RN, pp. 599–608, 938–41; Kissinger, White House Years, pp. 1164–85; and Henry Kissinger, Years of Upheaval (Boston: 1982), pp. 575–91.

12. Nixon, *RN*, p. 515. See also Keith W. Olson, *Watergate: The Presidential Scandal That Shook America* (Lawrence, Kansas: 2003).

13. Kissinger, *White House Years*, p. 1134. See also Peter G. Peterson, *U.S.-Soviet Commercial Relations in a New Era* (Washington: 1972), pp. 3–4; and Kissinger's statement to Senate Foreign Relations Committee, September 19, 1974, in *American Foreign Policy*, p. 158–59.

14. Kissinger, *White House Years*, pp. 1269–72. For the Jackson amendment, see the *Congressional Record*, October 4, 1972, pp. 33658–59.

15. Kissinger statement to Senate Finance Committee, March 7, 1974, *DSB*, LXX (April 1, 1974), 323–25. See also Kissinger's speech to the *Pacem in Terris* III conference, Washington, October 8, 1973, and his statement to the Senate Foreign Relations Committee, September 19, 1974, in *American Foreign Policy*, pp. 125, 172–73; also Nixon's speech at the U.S. Naval Academy, June 5, 1974, *NPP: 1974*, pp. 471–72.

16. Herring, *America's Longest War*, p. 261–62.

17. Nixon, *RN*, p. 889. See also p. 718.

18. Kissinger speech at Dallas, Texas, March 22, 1976, *American Foreign Policy*, p. 360. See also Henry Kissinger, *Years of Renewal* (New York: 1999), pp. 520–46, 791–833.

19. See Odd Arne Westad, "The Fall of Détente and the Turning Tides of History," in Westad, ed., *The Fall of Détente: Soviet-American Relations during the Carter Years* (Oslo: 1997), pp. 1–12.

20. Kissinger press conference, January 14, 1976, *DSB*, LXXIV (February 2, 1976), 125–26.

21. Kissinger, *White House Years*, p. 1143.

22. *Ibid.*, p. 1255; Annual foreign policy report, February 9, 1972, *NPP: 1972*, p. 211. See also Kissinger's press conference, November 21, 1973, *DSB*, LXIX (December 10, 1973), 706–7.

23. Annual foreign policy report, May 3, 1973, *NPP: 1973*, p. 375. The "Basic Principles" agreement is in *DSB*, LXVI (June 26, 1972), 898–99.

24. Kissinger, *White House Years*, pp. 1132, 1250 (emphasis in the original).

25. The "Final Act" of the Conference on Security and Cooperation in Europe, signed at Helsinki on August 1, 1975, is in *DSB*, LXXIII (September 1, 1975), 323–50.

26. See Kissinger's speech to the *Pacem in Terris* III conference, Washington, October 8, 1973, *American Foreign Policy*, p. 125; Kissinger statement to the Senate Foreign Relations Committee, September 19, 1974, *ibid.*, pp. 172–73; Kissinger speech at Minneapolis, July 15, 1975, *ibid.*, pp. 208–9.

27. Kissinger, *Years of Upheaval*, pp. 635–48.

28. Lawrence J. Korb, *The Fall and Rise of the Pentagon: American Defense Policies in the 1970s* (Westport, Conn.: 1979), pp. 69–73. See also Kissinger, *White House Years*, pp. 199–202, 938–49; and Don Oberdorfer, *Senator Mansfield: The Extraordinary Life of a Great American Statesman and Diplomat* (Washington: 2003), pp. 387–91.

29. John M. Collins, *American and Soviet Military Trends Since the Cuban Missile Crisis* (Washington: 1978), pp. 44–45, 93, 101, 107, 184, 260, 265–67, 274. See also Korb, *The Fall and Rise of the Pentagon*, pp. 155–57; and Appendix.

30. Quoted in Ford, *A Time to Heal*, p. 373.

31. Annual foreign policy report, February 18, 1970, *NPP: 1970*, p. 172. Kissinger speech, Dallas, Texas, March 22, 1976, *American Foreign Policy*, p. 350. See also Kissinger's speech at San Francisco, February 3, 1976, *ibid.*, pp. 301–4, 311–12; and Kissinger, *White House Years*, pp. 196–98.

32. Korb, *The Fall and Rise of the Pentagon*, pp. 51–52; Kissinger, *White House Years*, p. 215. See also Appendix.

33. Kissinger, *White House Years*, pp. 32–33. See also Korb, *The Fall and Rise of the Pentagon*, pp. 84–96.
34. *Ibid.*, p. 42; Kissinger, *White House Years*, pp. 214–15.
35. *Ibid.*, p. 215.
36. For a well-informed account of the SALT I negotiations, see John Newhouse, *Cold Dawn: The Story of SALT* (New York: 1973).
37. Strobe Talbott, *Endgame: The Inside Story of SALT II* (New York: 1979), pp. 24–27.
38. Kissinger, *White House Years*, pp. 1245–46. See also Kissinger's statement to the Senate Foreign Relations Committee, September 19, 1974, *American Foreign Policy*, p. 166; and Korb, *The Fall and Rise of the Pentagon*, p. 94.
39. Annual foreign policy report, May 3, 1973, *NPP: 1973*, p. 374. See also Kissinger statement to the Senate Foreign Relations Committee, September 19, 1974, *American Foreign Policy*, p. 164.
40. Korb, *The Fall and Rise of the Pentagon*, p. 104, 150.
41. See, on this point, Kissinger, *White House Years*, pp. 1244–45; also Kissinger's statement to the Senate Foreign Relations Committee, September 19, 1974, *American Foreign Policy*, p. 164; and Kissinger's speech, Dallas, Texas, March 22, 1976, *ibid.*, pp. 357–58.
42. See, on this point, Jerome H. Kahan, *Security in the Nuclear Age: Developing U.S. Strategic Arms Policy* (Washington: 1975), pp. 286–88.
43. Talbott, *Endgame*, p. 24–26, 220.
44. *Ibid.*, pp. 31–37.
45. Kissinger speech, Dallas, March 22, 1976, *American Foreign Policy*, p. 354.
46. Korb, *The Fall and Rise of the Pentagon*, pp. 151–60.
47. Morris, *Uncertain Greatness*, p. 298.
48. Kissinger, "Central Issues" in *American Foreign Policy*, p. 74.
49. Mohammed A. El-Khawas and Barry Cohen, eds., *The Kissinger Study of Southern Africa: National Security Study Memorandum 39* (Westport, Conn.: 1976), pp. 105–6. See also Morris, *Uncertain Greatness*, pp. 107–20; Szulc, *The Illusion of Peace*, pp. 219–25; Anthony Lake, *The "Tar Baby" Option: American Policy Toward Southern Rhodesia* (New York: 1976), pp. 123–57; and John A. Marcum, "Lessons of Angola," *Foreign Affairs*, LIV (April 1976), 407–8. For Kissinger's own brief comment on this memorandum, see *Years of Renewal*, p. 903.
50. Morris, *Uncertain Greatness*, pp. 212–30; Szulc, *The Illusion of Peace*, pp. 405–6, 441–44; Garthoff, *Détente and Confrontation*, pp. 295–322; Jussi Hanhimäki, *The Flawed Architect: Henry Kissinger and American Foreign Policy* (New York: 2003), pp. 172–84. The figure for Bengali casualties comes from http://www.genocidewatch.org/genocidetable 2003.htm. Kissinger's defense of his policy is in *White House Years*, pp. 842–928; see also Nixon, *RN*, pp. 525–31.
51. Kissinger's acknowledgment is in *White House Years*, pp. 1259–60. See also Gary Sick, *All Fall Down: America's Tragic Encounter with Iran* (New York: 1985); and James A. Bill, *The Eagle and the Lion: The Tragedy of American-Iranian Relations* (New Haven: 1988).
52. Szulc, *The Illusion of Peace*, pp. 437–39, 749–52. See also, for a pre-October 1973 appraisal, James E. Akins, "The Oil Crisis: This Time the Wolf Is Here," *Foreign Affairs*, LI (April 1973), 462–90. For Kissinger's account, see *Years of Upheaval*, pp. 450–544, 854–95; as well as Henry Kissinger, *Crisis: The Anatomy of Two Major Foreign Policy Crises* (New York: 2003).
53. Lawrence Stern, "Bitter Lessons: How We Failed in Cyprus," *Foreign Policy*, #19 (Summer, 1975), 34–78; see also Bell, *The Diplomacy of Détente*, pp. 138–55; Kissinger, *Years of Renewal*, pp. 192–239; and Monteagle Stearns, *Entangled Allies: U.S. Policy Toward Greece, Turkey, and Cyprus* (New York: 1992).

54. Davis, "The Angola Decision of 1975," pp. 109–24; Marcum, "Lessons of Angola," pp. 407–25. See also Kissinger, *Years of Renewal*, pp. 791–833; and Gleijeses, *Conflicting Missions*, pp. 246–372.

55. Kissinger, *White House Years*, pp. 761–62, 955, and *Years of Upheaval*, pp. 128–94; Szulc, *The Illusion of Peace*, pp. 416–17, 457–58, 689–92; Brown, *The Crises of Power*, pp. 114–18. The "year of Europe" speech, delivered in New York on April 23, 1973, is in Kissinger, *American Foreign Policy*, pp. 99–113.

56. Tad Szulc, "Lisbon & Washington: Behind the Portuguese Revolution," *Foreign Policy*, #21 (Winter, 1975–76), 3–62; Peter Lange, "What Is To Be Done—About Italian Communism," *ibid.*, pp. 224–40. See also Stoessinger, *Kissinger*, pp. 145–53; Bell, *The Diplomacy of Détente*, pp. 229–30; and Kissinger, *Years of Renewal*, pp. 626–34.

57. My distinction between "global" and "regional" perspectives follows Marcum, "Lessons of Angola," p. 418; and Gerald J. Bender, "Angola, the Cubans, and American Anxieties," *Foreign Policy*, #31 (Summer, 1978), 3–30.

58. Kissinger, *White House Years*, p. 898.

59. See, on this point, Morris, *Uncertain Greatness*, pp. 216–23, 252–53, 272–73; Szulc, *The Illusion of Peace*, pp. 438–39, 450–52, 585; and Davis, "The Angola Decision of 1975," pp. 113–17.

60. Kissinger, *White House Years*, pp. 743–47, 848–49, 1258–65; Bell, *The Diplomacy of Détente*, p. 130.

61. *Ibid.*, pp. 92–97; Brown, *The Crises of Power*, pp. 101–5. See also Edward R.F. Sheehan, *The Arabs, Israelis, and Kissinger: A Secret History of American Diplomacy in the Middle East* (New York: 1976), *passim*; and William B. Quandt, *Decade of Decisions: American Policy Toward the Arab-Israeli Conflict, 1967–1976* (Berkeley: 1977), pp. 207–87.

62. Kissinger speech at Lusaka, Zambia, April 27, 1976, in *American Foreign Policy*, pp. 372, 376. See also Ford, *A Time to Heal*, pp. 380–81; Bell, *The Diplomacy of Détente*, pp. 177–83; Kissinger, *Years of Renewal*, pp. 958–1016; and John Osborne, *White House Watch: The Ford Years* (Washington: 1977), pp. 324–30.

63. Carter speech to the Chicago Council on Foreign Relations, March 15, 1976, and to the Foreign Policy Association, New York, June 23, 1976; *The Presidential Campaign, 1976*, volume 1, part 1, pp. 110–13, 266.

64. William Shawcross, *Sideshow: Kissinger, Nixon, and the Destruction of Cambodia* (New York: 1979), p. 396. See also Morris, *Uncertain Greatness*, pp. 120–30, 213–30, 265–68; and Christopher Hitchens, *The Trial of Henry Kissinger* (New York: 2001).

65. Shawcross, *Sideshow*, p. 396.

66. Morris, *Uncertain Greatness*, p. 268.

67. Reinhold Niebuhr, "The Children of Light and the Children of Darkness," in Robert McAfee Brown, ed., *The Essential Reinhold Niebuhr* (New Haven: 1986), p. 171.

68. Nixon radio-television interview, January 4, 1971, *NPP: 1971*, p. 12; Annual foreign policy report, February 25, 1971, *NPP: 1971*, pp. 246–47.

69. Morris, *Uncertain Greatness*, pp. 240–41; Szulc, *The Illusion of Peace*, pp. 720–25. Kissinger's defense of his Chilean policy is in *White House Years*, pp. 653–83; *Years of Upheaval*, pp. 374–413; and *Years of Renewal*, pp. 749–60. See also U.S. Congress, Senate, Select Committee To Study Government Operations with Respect to Intelligence Activities, *Covert Action in Chile, 1963–1973* (Washington: 1975); and Peter Kornbluh, ed., *The Pinochet File: A Declassified Dossier on Atrocity and Accountability* (New York: 2003).

70. Quoted in Morris, *Uncertain Greatness*, p. 241.

71. Kissinger, *Years of Renewal*, pp. 310–43.

72. Nixon radio-television address, November 3, 1969, *NPP: 1969*, pp. 903; Kissinger, *White*

House Years, p. 229; Annual foreign policy report, May 3, 1973, *NPP: 1973*, p. 376. See also Nixon, *RN*, p. 348.

73. Nixon press conference, March 21, 1970, *NPP: 1970*, p. 292. See also Hanhimäki, *The Flawed Architect*, pp. 43–46.

74. Herring, *America's Longest War*, p. 256.

75. Bell, *The Diplomacy of Détente*, pp. 127–29, 224; Brown, *The Crises of Power*, p. 52.

76. Elizabeth Drew, "A Reporter at Large: Human Rights," *New Yorker*, LIII (July 18, 1977), 36; Bell, *The Diplomacy of Détente*, pp. 31–32.

77. See, on this point, Richard H. Ullman, "Washington, Wilson, and the Democrat's Dilemma," *Foreign Policy*, #21 (Winter, 1975–76), 108–9; and Stoessinger, *Kissinger*, p. 218. Jeane Kirkpatrick would later popularize this argument in her influential article, "Dictatorships and Double Standards," *Commentary*, LXVIII (November, 1979), 34–45.

78. Ford, *A Time to Heal*, pp. 297–98; Kissinger, *Years of Renewal*, pp. 648–52, 861–67.

79. Kissinger, *White House Years*, p. 191.

80. See, especially, Kissinger's speeches at Minneapolis, July 15, 1975, and Montreal, August 11, 1975, also his 1968 essay, "Central Issues in Foreign Policy," all printed in Kissinger, *American Foreign Policy*, pp. 91–97, 195–236. For the background of Kissinger's "heartland" speeches, see Walter Isaacson, *Kissinger: A Biography* (New York: 1992), pp. 658–59. My understanding of Kissinger's position on morality and foreign policy has been enhanced by reading Schuyler Schouten, "Kissinger's Realist Ethics: Morality and Pragmatism in American Foreign Policy," senior essay, Department of History, Yale University, April, 2003.

81. *Ibid.*, pp. 218–19; Kissinger, *White House Years*, p. 55.

82. Kissinger, "Central Issues," *American Foreign Policy*, p. 94.

ELEVEN. *The Completion of Containment*

1. See above, p. 72.

2. Speech at the University of Notre Dame, May 22, 1977, *Public Papers of the Presidents: Jimmy Carter:* [hereafter *CPP*] *1977*, pp. 956–57.

3. Carter state of the union address, January 23, 1980, *CPP: 1980*, pp. 196–98.

4. Talbott, *Endgame*, pp. 48–50; Dan Caldwell, "US Domestic Politics and the Demise of Détente," in Odd Arne Westad, ed., *The Fall of Détente: Soviet-American Relations during the Carter Years* (Oslo:1997), pp. 105–6.

5. Cyrus Vance interview, February 3, 1977, *DSB*, LXXVI (February 21, 1977), 148. See also Zbigniew Brzezinski, *Power and Principle: Memoirs of the National Security Adviser, 1977–1981* (New York: 1983), pp. 185–86.

6. See above, p. 314.

7. Carter discusses the origins of his commitment to human rights in *Keeping Faith: Memoirs of a President* (New York: 1982), pp. 141–44. See also Tony Smith, *America's Mission: The United States and the Worldwide Struggle for Democracy in the Twentieth Century* (Princeton: 1994), pp. 239–65.

8. Talbott, *Endgame*, pp. 60–61.

9. Dobrynin, *In Confidence,* p. 388.

10. See, on this point, Stanley Hoffmann, "The Hell of Good Intentions," *Foreign Policy*, #29 (Winter, 1977–78), pp. 12–13; also Hugh Sidey, "Assessing a Presidency," *Time*, CXVI (August 18, 1980), 10–15, and Brzezinski, *Power and Principle*, pp. 14, 49, 71.

11. Simon Serfaty, "Brzezinski: Play It Again, Zbig," *Foreign Policy*, #32 (Fall, 1978), pp. 6–7.

12. Brzezinski, *Power and Principle*, pp. 148–49.

13. Gaddis Smith, *Morality, Reason, and Power: American Diplomacy in the Carter Years* (New York: 1986), pp. 40–42. See also Vance's memoir, *Hard Choices: Critical Years in America's Foreign Policy* (New York: 1983).

14. Garthoff, *Détente and Confrontation*, p. 666. The speech is in *CPP: 1978*, pp. 1052–58.

15. Dobrynin, *In Confidence*, p. 387. See also Dobrynin's report to Moscow, "Soviet-American Relations in the Contemporary Era," July 11, 1978, in Westad, ed., *The Fall of Détente*, pp. 213–20. Brzezinski's account of the drafting of the June 7 Carter speech is in *Power and Principle*, p. 320.

16. Carter, *Keeping Faith*, p. 66. See also Brzezinski, *Power and Principle*, p. 145.

17. See, for example, Wolfe, *Soviet Power and Europe, 1945–1970*, pp. 501–6.

18. Talbott, *Endgame*, pp. 134–35, 181–83.

19. Dobrynin, *In Confidence*, pp. 402–7. See also Westad, "The Fall of Détente and the Turning Tides of History," pp. 11–12.

20. Smith, *Morality, Reason, and Power*, pp. 242–45. See also, for a contemporary assessment, Carl Gershman, "The Rise & Fall of the New Foreign Policy Establishment," *Commentary*, LXX (July, 1980), 13–24.

21. Reagan radio script, March 23, 1977, in Kiron K. Skinner, Annelise Anderson, and Martin Anderson, eds., *Reagan In His Own Hand* (New York: 2001), p. 118.

22. Lou Cannon, *President Reagan: The Role of a Lifetime* (New York: 1991), pp. 280–96, summarizes Reagan's instinct-based orthodoxies, their origins, and the extent to which they departed from established information-based Cold War orthodoxies.

23. See, on this point, Lee Edwards, *The Conservative Revolution: The Movement That Remade America* (New York: 1999), especially pp. 201–5.

24. For another president who operated in this way, see Greenstein, *The Hidden-Hand Presidency: Eisenhower as Leader*, especially pp. 34–35, 53.

25. Skinner, ed., *Reagan In His Own Hand*, reprints several hundred hand-written commentaries on a wide range of domestic and foreign policy issues that Reagan prepared for his nationally syndicated radio program between 1975 and 1979. See also, on his speechwriting habits, Ronald Reagan, *An American Life* (New York: 1990), p. 246.

26. Radio script, December 22, 1976, in *ibid.*, p. 12. See also scripts for May 25, 1977, October 10, 1978, November 28, 1978, and June 29, 1979, *ibid.*, pp. 85–86, 94–95, 146–47, 149–50. For the Roosevelt-Reagan analogy, see Cannon, *President Reagan*, pp. 109–11.

27. Radio script, May, 1975, in Skinner, ed., *Reagan In His Own Hand*, p. 12. For evidence of even earlier Reagan thinking along these lines, see Paul Lettow, *Ronald Reagan and His Quest to Abolish Nuclear Weapons* (New York: 2005), pp. 16, 27.

28. Reagan, *An American Life*, p. 267. For Reagan's commentaries on NSC-68, see his radio scripts of May 4, 1977, in Skinner, ed., *Reagan In His Own Hand*, pp. 109–13.

29. Radio script, May 25, 1977, in Skinner, ed., *Reagan In His Own Hand*, p. 147.

30. Reagan, *An American Life*, p. 238.

31. Radio script, June 29, 1979, in Skinner, ed., *Reagan In His Own Hand*, pp. 149–50. See also *ibid.*, pp. 129–34, 150–56.

32. Reagan, *An American Life*, p. 13. See also Lettow, *Ronald Reagan*, pp. 22–23.

33. Reagan's handwritten draft of a speech to the Veterans of Foreign Wars, Chicago, August 18, 1980, in Skinner, ed., *Reagan In His Own Hand*, especially p. 484; also Reagan, *An American Life*, pp. 257–58; Reagan's radio broadcast of December 12, 1978, in Skinner, ed., *Reagan In His Own Hand*, pp. 86–87; and Cannon, *President Reagan*, pp. 292–93, 305, 320, 751. I have benefited, as well, from reading Matthew Ferraro, "Going M.A.D.: Morality, Strategy, and Mutual Assured Destruction, 1957 to 1986," a senior essay prepared in the Yale University Department of History, 2004.

34. Reagan speech draft of August 18, 1980, in Skinner, ed., *Reagan In His Own Hand*, pp. 484–85.
35. For more on this point, see Gaddis, *The United States and the End of the Cold War*, pp. 39–45.
36. Reagan speech draft of August 18, 1980, in Skinner, ed., *Reagan In His Own Hand*, p. 485. I have edited this passage slightly for clarity.
37. Kennan, "The Sources of Soviet Conduct," p. 582.
38. Dobrynin, *In Confidence*, p. 477.
39. *Ibid.*, p. 521. See also Fareed Zakaria, "The Reagan Strategy of Containment," *Political Science Quarterly*, CV (Autumn, 1990), 373–74.
40. Gaddis, *The United States and the End of the Cold War*, pp. 27–29.
41. PD/NCS-18, "U.S. National Strategy," August 24, 1977, http://www.jimmycarter library.org/ documents/pddirectives/pd18.pdf; PD/NSC-62, "Modifications in U.S. National Strategy, January 15, 1981, http://www.jimmycarterlibrary.org/documents/pd directives/pd62.pdf.
42. NSDD 32, "U.S. National Security Strategy," May 20, 1982, http://www.fas.org/irp/off docs/ nsdd/nsdd-032.htm. See also, for background on this document, Lettow, *Ronald Reagan*, pp. 65–72.
43. Reagan address to members of the British Parliament, London, June 8, 1982, *Public Papers of the Presidents: 1982* [hereafter *RPP*] (Washington: 1983), pp. 744–47. See also Reagan's speech at Notre Dame University, May 17, 1981, *RPP: 1981*, especially p. 434.
44. Dobrynin, *In Confidence*, p. 484.
45. NSDD 75, "U.S. Relations with the Soviet Union," January 17, 1983, http://www.fas.org/ irp/offdocs/nsdd/nsdd-075.htm. For more on this document, see Richard Pipes, *Vixi: Memoirs of a Non-Belonger* (New Haven: 2003), pp. 188–202; and Lettow, *Ronald Reagan*, pp. 77–82.
46. Speech to the National Association of Evangelicals, Orlando, Florida, March 8, 1983, *RPP: 1983*, p. 364. For more on Reagan's rhetoric, see William K. Muir, Jr., "Ronald Reagan: The Primacy of Rhetoric," in Fred I. Greenstein, ed., *Leadership in the Modern Presidency* (Cambridge, Mass.: 1988), pp. 260–95.
47. Stephen Kotkin, *Armageddon Averted: The Soviet Collapse, 1970–2000* (New York: 2001), especially pp. 10–30, provides a good overview of the problems confronting the Soviet Union during this period; but see also Ronald Grigor Suny, *The Soviet Experiment: Russia, the U.S.S.R., and the Successor States* (New York: 1998), pp. 436–42. The figures on Soviet military spending come from Aaron Friedberg, *In the Shadow of the Garrison State: America's Anti-Statism and Its Cold War Grand Strategy* (Princeton: 2000), pp. 82–83. See also William E. Odom, *The Collapse of the Soviet Military* (New Haven: 1998), especially pp. 49–64. For the American figures, see Appendix.
48. Soviet leadership autism is well described in Dobrynin, *In Confidence*, pp. 472–76; and at considerably greater length in Georgi Arbatov, *The System: An Insider's Life in Soviet Politics* (New York: 1992), pp. 190–294.
49. See Spencer R. Weart, *Nuclear Fear: A History of Images* (Cambridge, Mass.: 1988), pp. 375–88; Beth A. Fischer, *The Reagan Reversal: Foreign Policy and the End of the Cold War* (Columbia, Mo.: 1997), pp. 115–20; and, for the administration's rhetorical excesses, Robert Scheer, *With Enough Shovels: Reagan, Bush, and Nuclear War* (New York: 1983).
50. Speech to the 1976 Republican National Convention, quoted in Cannon, *President Reagan*, p. 295. Cannon provides a brief account of Reagan's anti-nuclear views in *ibid.*, pp. 287–95. For a more recent and comprehensive treatment, see Lettow, *Ronald Reagan*, pp. 3–82.
51. Talbott, *Deadly Gambits*, pp. 80–81.
52. Radio-television address, March 23, 1983, *RPP: 1983*, pp. 442–43.

53. See above, p. 324n.

54. Nitze, *From Hiroshima to Glasnost*, p. 401; George P. Shultz, *Turmoil and Triumph: My Years as Secretary of State* (New York: 1993), p. 249; Caspar W. Weinberger, *Fighting for Peace: Seven Critical Years in the Pentagon* (New York: 1990), p. 306.

55. For the origins of Reagan's interest in SDI, see Cannon, *President Reagan*, pp. 292–93, 319; Lettow, *Ronald Reagan*, pp. 19–42; and Martin Anderson, *Revolution: The Reagan Legacy*, expanded and updated edition (Stanford: 1990), pp. 80–99.

56. Lettow, *Ronald Reagan*, pp. 120–21, 214–15; Mira Duric, *The Strategic Defense Initiative: US Policy and the Soviet Union* (Aldershot, England: 2003), pp. 24–25.

57. Reagan to Brezhnev, April 24, 1981, quoted in Reagan, *An American Life*, p. 273. See also, for Dobrynin's impression of Reagan's letter and Brezhnev's response, *In Confidence*, pp. 492–93.

58. NSDD 32, May 20, 1982, p. 3.

59. Shultz, *Turmoil and Triumph*, pp. 163–67. See also Don Oberdorfer, *From the Cold War to a New Era: The United States and the Soviet Union, 1983–1991*, updated edition (Baltimore: 1998), pp. 15–21.

60. Dobrynin, *In Confidence*, pp. 517–18.

61. *Ibid.*, pp. 518–21, 529–30; Shultz, *Turmoil and Triumph*, pp. 165–71.

62. Quoted in Duric, *The Strategic Defense Initiative*, p. 41.

63. Andropov statement, September 28, 1983, *Current Digest of the Soviet Press*, XXXV (October 26, 1983), 1.

64. Dobrynin, *In Confidence*, pp. 522–24; Christopher Andrew and Oleg Gordievsky, *KGB: The Inside Story of Its Foreign Operations from Lenin to Gorbachev* (New York: 1990), pp. 583–99.

65. For the Able-Archer crisis, see *ibid.*, pp. 599–601; also Fischer, *The Reagan Reversal*, pp. 122–31; Oberdorfer, *From the Cold War to a New Era*, pp. 65–68; and Robert M. Gates, *From the Shadows: The Ultimate Insider's Story of Five Presidents and How They Won the Cold War* (New York: 1996), pp. 266–73.

66. Reagan, *An American Life*, p. 586. See also pp. 588–89.

67. Reagan television address, January 16, 1984, *RPP: 1984*, p. 45. See also, on the preparation of this speech, Jack F. Matlock, Jr., *Autopsy on an Empire: The American Ambassador's Account of the Collapse of the Soviet Union* (New York: 1995), pp. 83–86.

68. Reagan, *An American Life*, p. 602.

69. *Ibid.*, p. 605.

70. Dobrynin, *In Confidence*, p. 563. See also, on this point, Barbara Farnham, "Reagan and the Gorbachev Revolution: Perceiving the End of Threat," *Political Science Quarterly*, CXVI (Summer, 2001), p. 233.

71. Reagan, *An American Life*, pp. 602–5.

72. Shultz, *Turmoil and Triumph*, p. 478.

73. Reagan, *An American Life*, p. 611.

74. Mikhail Gorbachev, *Memoirs* (New York: 1995), pp. 165, 168. See also, on Gorbachev's appointment, Kotkin, *Armageddon Averted*, pp. 54–57.

75. Shultz, *Turmoil and Triumph*, pp. 532–33.

76. Brezhnev speech to the 5th Congress of the Polish United Workers Party, November 12, 1968, quoted in Matthew J. Ouimet, *The Rise and Fall of the Brezhnev Doctrine in Soviet Foreign Policy* (Chapel Hill, North Carolina: 2003), p. 67.

77. William Taubman, *Khrushchev: The Man and His Era* (New York: 2003), pp. 507–11. For the Soviet educational investment, see Suny, *The Soviet Experiment*, p. 440.

78. The best book on the relationship between higher education and social protest in the 1960's is Jeremi Suri, *Power and Protest: Global Revolution and the Rise of Détente* (Cambridge, Mass.: 2003). For the rise of the new Soviet intelligentsia, see Robert D.

English, *Russia and the Idea of the West: Gorbachev, Intellectuals, and the End of the Cold War* (New York: 2000).

79. Reagan, *An American Life*, p. 615.

80. William D. Jackson, "Soviet Reassessment of Ronald Reagan, 1985–1988," *Political Science Quarterly*, CXIII (Winter, 1998–99), 621–22; Vladislav M. Zubok, "Gorbachev and the End of the Cold War: Perspectives on History and Personality," *Cold War History*, II (January, 2002), 63. See also Anatoly Chernyaev, *My Six Years with Gorbachev*, translated and edited by Robert English and Elizabeth Tucker (University Park, Pennsylvania: 2000), p. 32, for an early indication of the extent to which Reagan's rhetoric placed Gorbachev and his advisers on the defensive.

81. Reagan, *An American Life*, p. 567.

82. Shultz, *Turmoil and Triumph*, pp. 600–2.

83. Reagan, *An American Life*, p. 635.

84. Gorbachev, *Memoirs*, p. 408. See also Dobrynin, *In Confidence*, pp. 592–93.

85. Shultz, *Turmoil and Triumph*, p. 700; Reagan, *An American Life*, p. 657.

86. Chernyaev diary, January 16, 1986, in Chernyaev, *My Six Years with Gorbachev*, pp. 45–46.

87. Shultz, *Turmoil and Triumph*, pp. 700–1. See also Matlock, *Autopsy on an Empire*, pp. 93–94; and Lettow, *Ronald Reagan*, pp. 137, 199–200.

88. Gorbachev, *Memoirs*, pp. 189–93. See also Chernyaev, *My Six Years with Gorbachev*, pp. 66–67; and Reagan, *An American Life*, pp. 676, 710.

89. My account here follows that in the Reagan, Shultz, and Gorbachev memoirs, as well as Oberdorfer, *From the Cold War to a New Era*, pp. 189–209; Jackson, "Soviet Reassessment of Reagan," pp. 629–34; Lettow, *Ronald Reagan*, pp. 223–31; Raymond L. Garthoff, *The Great Transition: American-Soviet Relations at the End of the Cold War* (Washington: 1994), pp. 285–291; and Jack F. Matlock, Jr., *Reagan and Gorbachev: How the Cold War Ended* (New York: 2004), pp. 215–37.

90. Gorbachev, *Memoirs*, p. 419.

91. Dobrynin, *In Confidence*, p. 610. See also the comments of Anatoly Chernyaev, in William C. Wohlforth, ed., *Witnesses to the End of the Cold War* (Baltimore:1996), p. 109.

92. Reagan, *An American Life*, pp. 679, 683.

93. Margaret Thatcher, *The Downing Street Years* (New York: 1993), p. 471.

94. Gorbachev report to the Politburo, December 17, 1987, quoted in Chernyaev, *My Six Years with Gorbachev*, pp. 142–43.

95. Kennan diary, December 9, 1987, quoted in George F. Kennan, *Sketches from a Life* (New York: 1989), p. 351.

96. Speech at Notre Dame University, May 17, 1981, *RPP: 1981*, p. 434.

97. Shultz, *Turmoil and Triumph*, p. 586.

98. *Ibid.*, p. 591; Dobrynin, *In Confidence*, p. 583.

99. Shultz, *Turmoil and Triumph*, pp. 700–1. See also *ibid.*, pp. 716–17. For more on monodimensionality, see John Lewis Gaddis, *We Now Know: Rethinking Cold War History* (New York: 1997), pp. 283–84.

100. Shultz, *Turmoil and Triumph*, p. 711.

101. *Ibid.*, pp. 892–93; Oberdorfer, *From the Cold War to a New Era*, pp. 223–24. See also Chernyaev, *My Six Years with Gorbachev*, p. 142; and Fred I. Greenstein, "Ronald Reagan, Mikhail Gorbachev, and the End of the Cold War: What Difference Did They Make?" in Wohlforth, ed., *Witnesses to the End of the Cold War*, p. 217.

102. Mikhail Gorbachev, *Perestroika: New Thinking for Our Country and the World* (New York: 1987), p. 135.

103. Shultz, *Turmoil and Triumph*, p. 1098. See also, for Gorbachev's subsequent acknowl-

edgment of the economic superiority of market capitalism, Mikhail Gorbachev and Zdeněk Mlynář, *Conversations with Gorbachev: On Perestroika, the Prague Spring, and the Crossroads of Socialism*, translated by George Shriver (New York: 2002), p. 160.

104. Reagan speech at Moscow State University, May 31, 1988, *RPP: 1988*, p. 684.
105. See above, pp. 41–46.
106. For more on this, see pp. 287–88, 341–42, above; also Henry A. Kissinger, *Diplomacy* (New York: 1994), p. 714, and John Lewis Gaddis, "Rescuing Choice from Circumstance: The Statecraft of Henry Kissinger," in Gordon A. Craig and Francis L. Lowenheim, eds., *The Diplomats: 1939–1979* (Princeton: 1994), pp. 585–87. Kissinger's own account of the Helsinki Conference is in his *Years of Renewal* (New York: 1999), pp. 635–63.
107. Gates, *From the Shadows*, pp. 142–53, 161–69.
108. NSDD 75, "U.S. Relations with the U.S.S.R.," January 17, 1983, p. 4.
109. Reagan, *An American Life*, p. 569.
110. Shultz, *Turmoil and Triumph*, 323–45.
111. Reagan state of the union address, February 6, 1985, *RPP: 1985*, p. 136.
112. Speech to the Commonwealth Club of San Francisco, quoted in Shultz, *Turmoil and Triumph*, p. 525. Chernyaev describes the "panic" this speech caused in Moscow in *My Six Years with Gorbachev*, pp. 16–17. For more on the Reagan Doctrine, see Smith, *America's Mission*, pp. 297–304.
113. Reagan to Gorbachev, February 6, 1986, quoted in Reagan, *An American Life*, pp. 654–55.
114. Reagan, *An American Life*, p. 639. For Gorbachev's reservations about the war in Afghanistan, see also Chernyaev, *My Six Years with Gorbachev*, pp. 42–43, 89–90, 106.
115. Shultz, *Turmoil and Triumph*, p. 987.
116. *Ibid.*, p. 1003.
117. The evidence is laid out in detail in Ouimet, *The Rise and Fall of the Brezhnev Doctrine*.
118. Gorbachev, *Memoirs*, p. 465.
119. Reagan, *An American* Life, p. 683. Reagan's speech, delivered at the Brandenburg Gate on June 12, 1987, is in *RPP: 1987*, p. 686. For Gorbachev's response, see Garthoff, *The Great Transition*, pp. 316–18.
120. Bill Keller, "Gorbachev, in Finland, Disavows any Right of Regional Intervention," *New York Times*, October 26, 1989.
121. Gorbachev, *Memoirs*, p. 522.
122. See above, p. 48.
123. Reagan, *An American Life*, pp. 707–8.
124. See, for example, Peter Schweizer, *Victory: The Reagan Administration's Secret Strategy That Hastened the Collapse of the Soviet Union* (New York: 1994) and *Reagan's War: The Epic Story of His Forty Year Struggle and Final Triumph Over Communism* (New York: 2002).
125. Gorbachev, *Memoirs*, p. 457.
126. The evidence for Gorbachev's evolving views—and, as time went on, his increasingly desperate improvisation—is now overwhelming. See Arbatov, *The System*, pp. 330–35; and especially Chernyaev, *My Six Years with Gorbachev*, who documents the process throughout his book.
127. Reagan, *An American Life*, p. 267.
128. See, on this point, Lettow, *Ronald Reagan*, pp. 125, 130.
129. I owe this argument to Zakaria, "The Reagan Strategy of Containment," especially pp. 374, 387. For more on the cost versus risk dilemma, see John Lewis Gaddis, "Containment and the Logic of Strategy," *The National Interest*, #10 (Winter, 1987/88), 27–38.
130. Kissinger, *Diplomacy*, pp. 764–65.

131. Jeremi Suri, "Explaining the End of the Cold War: A New Historical Consensus?" *Journal of Cold War Studies*, IV (Fall, 2002), 92, emphasizes the joint responsibility of both leaders for bringing about the end of the Cold War.

132. Interview with George F. Kennan, June 10, 1996.

133. George Bush and Brent Scowcroft, *A World Transformed* (New York: 1998), pp. 13–14.

134. *Ibid.*, p. 9. For the Bush review and its follow-up, see Garthoff, *The Great Transition*, pp. 375–89.

135. See, for example, Georgii Arbatov, "The Limited Power of an Ordinary State," *New Perspectives Quarterly*, V (Summer, 1988), 31; also Charles Paul Freund, "Where Did All Our Villains Go?" *Washington Post*, December 11, 1988.

136. Philip Zelikow and Condoleezza Rice, *Germany Unified and Europe Transformed: A Study in Statecraft* (Cambridge, Mass.: 1995), pp. 127–31. See also, for background on these events, Michael R. Beschloss and Strobe Talbott, *At the Highest Levels: The Inside Story of the End of the Cold War* (Boston: 1993), pp. 3–171.

137. James M. Goldgeier and Michael McFaul, *Power and Purpose: U.S. Policy toward Russia after the Cold War* (Washington: 2003), p. 20.

138. Bush national radio and television address, December 25, 1991, *Public Papers of the Presidents: George Bush, 1991*, pp. 1654–55.

TWELVE. *Epilogue*

1. Kennan, *Memoirs: 1925–1950*, pp. 308, 310. See also Giles D. Harlow and George C. Maerz, eds., *Measures Short of War: The George F. Kennan Lectures at the National War College, 1946–47* (Washington: 1990).

2. Kennan, *Memoirs: 1925–1950*, p. 367.

3. *Ibid.*, p. 356.

4. Kennan, "The Sources of Soviet Conduct," pp. 574–75. For the extent to which Hitler believed the opposite, see Ian Kershaw, *Hitler: Nemesis, 1936–1945* (New York: 2000), pp. 207, 228.

5. Michael Howard, *The Lessons of History* (New Haven: 1991), p. 75. See also, on this "bellicist" mentality, Howard, *The Causes of War*, second edition, enlarged (Cambridge, Massachusetts: 1983), especially pp. 7–22.

6. This was the title of Kennan's first National War College lecture, delivered on September 16, 1946, published in Harlow and Maerz, eds., *Measures Short of War*, pp. 3–17. For the argument that great power war had by then become unfeasible, see John Mueller, *Retreat from Doomsday: The Obsolescence of Major War* (New York: 1989), pp. 3–92.

7. For more on this point, see Gaddis, *The Long Peace*, pp. 215–45.

8. Carl von Clausewitz, *On War*, edited and translated by Michael Howard and Peter Paret (Princeton: 1976), p. 87.

9. For the manner in which the Clausewitzian consensus crossed Cold War boundaries, see Martin van Creveld, *The Transformation of War* (New York: 1991), pp. 34–35.

10. *Ibid.*, pp. 36–37.

11. I have discussed this strategy at greater length in *Surprise, Security, and the American Experience* (Cambridge, Massachusetts: 2004). The Bush administration's strategy is most clearly expressed in *The National Security Strategy of the United States of America: September 2002* (Washington: 2002).

12. See, on this point, Melvyn P. Leffler, "9/11 and the Past and Future of American Foreign Policy," *International Affairs*, LXXIX (2003), 1051–54.

13. For more on this, see Gaddis, *Surprise, Security, and the American Experience*, p. 99.

14. I have written more about this in *The United States and the End of the Cold War*, pp. 193–216; and "Living in Candlestick Park," *The Atlantic*, CCLXXXIII (April, 1999), 65–74.

15. The term comes from Melvyn P. Leffler, *A Preponderance of Power: National Security, the Truman Administration, and the Cold War* (Stanford: 1992); but see also Gaddis, *We Now Know*, p. 284; and, for post–Cold War American predominance, Niall Ferguson, *Colossus: The Price of America's Empire* (New York: 2004), pp. 14–19.

16. Geir Lundestad, "Empire by Invitation? The United States and Western Europe, 1945–1952," *Journal of Peace Research*, XXIII (September, 1986), 263–77.

17. See Robert Kagan, *Of Paradise and Power: America and Europe in the New World Order* (New York: 2003), pp. 42–53; also Philip H. Gordon and Jeremy Shapiro, *Allies at War: America, Europe, and the Crisis Over Iraq* (Washington: 2004), pp. 37–39.

18. Gaddis, *Surprise, Security, and the American Experience*, pp. 100–1. For the decline in support for American foreign policy, see the Pew Research Center for the People & the Press report, "A Year After Iraq War: Mistrust of America in Europe Even Higher, Muslim Anger Persists," March 16, 2004, available at: http://people-press.org/reports/print. php3?PageID=795.

19. Kennan, "The Sources of Soviet Conduct," p. 582.

20. See, for example, Sun Tzu, *The Art of War*, translated by Samuel B. Griffith (New York: 1963), p. 77; Clausewitz, *On War*, p. 384; and on Marx and Lenin, Tony Smith, *Thinking Like a Communist: State and Legitimacy in the Soviet Union, China, and Cuba* (New York: 1987), pp. 24, 45, 48. Kennan discusses this Marxist-Leninist idea in "The Sources of Soviet Conduct," pp. 566–67.

21. *Ibid.*, p. 580.

22. For more on this, see John Lewis Gaddis, *The Landscape of History: How Historians Map the Past* (New York: 2002), especially p. 11.

23. The most comprehensive attempt to treat Kennan as a theorist is Richard L. Russell, *George F. Kennan's Strategic Thought: The Making of an American Political Realist* (Westport, Conn.: 1999). For Kennan's long-time aversion to theory, see his *Around the Cragged Hill: A Personal and Political Philosophy* (New York: 1993), p. 11.

Bibliography

Archives and Manuscript Collections

Acheson, Dean. Papers. (Harry S. Truman Library)

Ayers, Eban A. Diary. (Harry S. Truman Library)

Dulles, John Foster. Papers. (Seeley Mudd Library, Princeton University)

Eisenhower, Dwight D. Ann Whitman File.

————. Papers, 1916–52.

————. White House Office Files: Office of the Special Assistant for National Security Affairs. (Dwight D. Eisenhower Library)

Forrestal, James V. Papers. (Seeley Mudd Library, Princeton University)

Hagerty, James. Diary. (Dwight D. Eisenhower Library)

Johnson, Lyndon B. National Security Files.

————. Vice Presidential—Security File. (Lyndon B. Johnson Library)

Kennan, George F. Papers. (Seeley Mudd Library, Princeton University)

Kennedy, John F. National Security Files.

————. Pre-Presidential Files (John F. Kennedy Library)

Naval War College. Archives. (Naval War College Library)

Reagan, Ronald. Executive Secretariat, NSC: Records. (Ronald Reagan Library)

Roosevelt, Franklin D. President's Personal File.

————. President's Secretary's File. (Franklin D. Roosevelt Library)

Truman, Harry S. President's Secretary's File. (Harry S. Truman Library)

U.S. Department of Defense, Army Staff Records. Record Group 319. (Modern Military Records Branch, National Archives)

————. Joint Chiefs of Staff Records. Record Group 218. (Modern Military Records Branch, National Archives)

U.S. Department of State. Office of Intelligence Research Files. Record Group 59 (Diplomatic Branch, National Archives)

U.S. National Security Council. File of Recently Declassified National Security Council Records (Modern Military Records Branch, National Archives)

Other Unpublished Material

Carlson, Allen C. "Walt Rostow's World View," Seminar Paper, Ohio University, 1974.

DeLaurier, Craig. "The Ultimate Enemy: Kennedy, Johnson and the Chinese Nuclear Threat, 1961–1964," Senior Essay, Department of History, Yale University, April, 2000.

Eagles, Keith David. "Ambassador Joseph E. Davies and American-Soviet Relations, 1937–1941," Ph.D. Dissertation, University of Washington, 1966.

Ferraro, Matthew. "Going M.A.D.: Morality, Strategy, and Mutual Assured Destruction, 1957 to 1986," Senior Essay, Department of History, Yale University, April, 2004.

Igarashi, Takeshi. "George F. Kennan and the Redirection of American Occupation Policy for Japan: The Formulation of National Security Council Paper 13/2," paper prepared for the Amherst College Conference on the Occupation of Japan, August 20–23, 1980.

Kennan, George F. Interview, Washington, D.C., October 31, 1974.

————. Interview, Princeton, N.J., June 10, 1996.

————. Letter, September 4, 1980.

Rostow, W.W. Letter, September 22, 1980.

Schouten, Schuyler. "Kissinger's Realist Ethics: Morality and Pragmatism in American Foreign Policy," Senior Essay, Department of History, Yale University, April, 2003.

Published Documents

Documents on American Foreign Relations (Boston: 1939–53; New York: 1953–).

Etzold, Thomas H., and John Lewis Gaddis, eds. *Containment: Documents on American Policy and Strategy, 1945–1950* (New York: 1978).

Harlow, Giles D., and George C. Maerz, eds. *Measures Short of War: The George F. Kennan Lectures at the National War College, 1946–47* (Washington: 1990).

Karalekas, Anne. "History of the Central Intelligence Agency," in U.S. Congress, Senate, Select Committee To Study Government Operations with Respect to Intelligence Activities, *Final Report: Supplementary Detailed Staff Reports on Foreign and Military Intelligence: Book IV* (Washington: 1976).

Kornbluh, Peter, ed. *The Pinochet File: A Declassified Dossier on Atrocity and Accountability* (New York: 2003).

————, and Malcolm Byrne, eds. *The Iran-Contra Scandal: The Declassified History* (New York: 1993).

Public Papers of the Presidents: Dwight D. Eisenhower, 1953–1961 (Washington: 1960–61).

————: *George Bush, 1989–1993* (Washington: 1990–1994).

————: *Harry S. Truman, 1945–1953* (Washington: 1961–1966).

————: *Jimmy Carter, 1977–1981* (Washington: 1978–1981).

————: *John F. Kennedy, 1961–1963* (Washington: 1962–1964).

————: *Lyndon B. Johnson, 1963–1969* (Washington: 1965–1969).

————: *Richard M. Nixon, 1969–1974* (Washington: 1970–1975).

————: *Ronald Reagan, 1981–1989* (Washington: 1982–1990).

Ruffner, Kevin C., ed. *CORONA: America's First Satellite Program* (Washington: 1995).

Skinner, Kiron K., Annelise Anderson, and Martin Anderson, eds. *Reagan In His Own Hand* (New York: 2001).

The State Department Policy Planning Staff Papers, 1947–1949 (New York: 1983). 3 volumes.

Steury, Donald P., ed. *Intentions and Capabilities: Estimates on Soviet Strategic Forces, 1950–1983* (Washington: 1996).

U.S. Bureau of the Census: *Historical Statistics of the United States, Colonial Times to 1970* (Washington: 1975).

————. *Statistical Abstract of the United States: 1979* (Washington: 1979).

U.S. Congress. House of Representatives. Committee on Armed Services. [Hearings] *Unification and Strategy* (Washington: 1949).

————. ————. Committee on Foreign Affairs. [Hearings] *Assistance to Greece and Turkey* (Washington: 1947).

————. ————. Committee on House Administration. *The Presidential Campaign, 1976* (Washington: 1979).

————. Senate. Committee on Foreign Relations. [Hearings] *Assistance to Greece and Turkey* (Washington: 1947).

————. ————. ————. [Hearings in Executive Session] Economic Assistance to China and Korea (Washington: 1974).

————. ————. ————. [Hearings in Executive Session] *83rd Congress, 1st Session* (Washington: 1977).

————. ————. ————. [Hearings] *European Recovery Program* (Washington: 1948).

————. ————. ————. [Hearings in Executive Session] *Foreign Relief Assistance Act of 1948* (Washington: 1973).

————. ————. ————. [Hearings in Executive Session] *Legislative Origins of the Truman Doctrine* (Washington: 1973).

————. ————. ————. [Hearings in Executive Session] *Reviews of the World Situation, 1949–1950* (Washington: 1974).

————. ————. ————. [Hearings] *Supplemental Foreign Assistance Fiscal Year 1966—Vietnam* (Washington: 1966).

————. ————. ————. [Hearings in Executive Session] *The Vandenberg Resolution and NATO* (Washington: 1973).

————. ————. Committees on Armed Services and Foreign Relations [Hearings] *Military Situation in the Far East* (Washington: 1951).

————. ————. Select Committee To Study Governmental Operations with Respect to Intelligence Activities. *Alleged Assassination Plots Involving Foreign Leaders* (Washington: 1975).

————. ————. ————. *Covert Action in Chile, 1963–1973* (Washington: 1975).

————. ————. ————. *Foreign and Military Intelligence, Book 1, Final Report* (Washington: 1976).

[U.S. Department of Defense]. *The Pentagon Papers (Senator Gravel Edition): The Department of Defense History of the United States Decision-Making on Vietnam* (Boston: 1971). 4 volumes.

U.S. Department of Defense. *United States-Vietnam Relations, 1945–1967.* (Washington: 1971). 12 volumes.

U.S. Department of State. American *Foreign Policy, 1950–1955: Basic Documents* (Washington: 1957).

————. *Department of State Bulletin.*

————. *Foreign Relations of the United States, 1942–1964/68* (Washington: 1961–2003).

————. ————: *The Conference of Berlin (The Potsdam Conference), 1945.* (Washington: 1960). 2 volumes.

————. ————: *The Conferences at Cairo and Tehran, 1943* (Washington: 1961).

————. ————: *The Conferences at Malta and Yalta, 1945* (Washington: 1955).

————. ————: *The Conferences at Washington and Quebec, 1943* (Washington: 1970).

U.S. Office of Management and Budget: *The Budget for Fiscal Year 2005* (Washington: 2004).

U.S.S.R. Ministerstvo innostrannykh del SSSR. *Dokumenty vneshnei plitiiki SSSR* (Moscow: 1967–).

Vital Speeches of the Day.

Warner, Michael, ed. *CIA Cold War Records: The CIA under Harry Truman* (Washington: 1994).

Books

Acheson, Dean. *Present at the Creation: My Years in the State Department* (New York: 1969).

Alexander, Charles C. *Holding the Line: The Eisenhower Era, 1952–1961* (Bloomington: 1975).

Aliano, Richard A. *American Defense Policy from Eisenhower to Kennedy: The Politics of Changing Military Requirements, 1957–1961* (Athens, Ohio: 1975).

Allison, Graham T. *Essence of Decision: Explaining the Cuban Missile Crisis* (Boston: 1971).

Ambrose, Stephen E. *Eisenhower: Soldier, General of the Army, President-Elect, 1890–1952* (New York: 1983).

————. *Eisenhower: The President* (New York: 1984).

————. *Rise to Globalism: American Foreign Policy, 1938–1970* (Baltimore: 1970).

Anderson, Martin. *Revolution: The Reagan Legacy*, expanded and updated edition (Stanford: 1990).

Andrew, Christopher, and Oleg Gordievsky. *KGB: The Inside Story of Its Foreign Operations from Lenin to Gorbachev* (New York: 1990).

Arbatov, Georgii. *The System: An Insider's Life in Soviet Politics* (New York: 1992).

Arkes, Hadley. *Bureaucracy, the Marshall Plan, and the National Interest* (Princeton: 1974).

Backer, John H. *The Decision to Divide Germany: American Foreign Policy in Transition* (Durham: 1978).

Barber, James David. *The Presidential Character: Predicting Performance in the White House* (Englewood Cliffs, N.J.: 1972).

Barnet, Richard J. *Roots of War* (Baltimore: 1972).

Bassford, Christopher. *Clausewitz in English: The Reception of Clausewitz in Britain and America, 1815–1945* (New York: 1994).

Bell, Coral. *The Diplomacy of Détente: The Kissinger Era* (New York: 1977).

————. *Negotiation from Strength: A Study in the Politics of Power* (New York: 1963).

Berding, Andrew H. *Dulles on Diplomacy* (Princeton: 1965).

Beschloss, Michael R. *Mayday: Eisenhower, Khrushchev, and the U-2 Affair* (New York: 1986).

————, and Strobe Talbott. *At the Highest Levels: The Inside Story of the End of the Cold War* (Boston: 1993).

Bill, James A. *The Eagle and the Lion: The Tragedy of American-Iranian Relations* (New Haven: 1988).

Blouet, Brian W. *Halford Mackinder: A Biography* (College Station, Texas: 1987).

Blum, John Morton, ed. *The Price of Vision: The Diary of Henry A. Wallace, 1942–1946* (Boston: 1973).

Bohlen, Charles E. *Witness to History, 1929–1969* (New York: 1973).

Bowie, Robert R., and Richard H. Immerman. *Waging Peace: How Eisenhower Shaped an Enduring Cold War Strategy* (New York: 1998).

Brezhnev, Leonid. *On the Policy of the Soviet Union and the International Situation* (Garden City, N.Y.: 1973).

Brinkley, Douglas. *Dean Acheson: The Cold War Years, 1953–71* (New Haven: 1992).

Brown, Robert McAfee, ed. *The Essential Reinhold Niebuhr* (New Haven: 1986).

Brown, Seyom. *The Crises of Power: An Interpretation of United States Foreign Policy During the Kissinger Years* (New York: 1979).

Brzezinski, Zbigniew. *Power and Principle: Memoirs of the National Security Adviser, 1977–1981* (New York: 1983).

Bullitt, Orville H., ed. *For the President: Personal and Secret: Correspondence Between Franklin D. Roosevelt and William C. Bullitt* (Boston: 1972).

Bundy, McGeorge. *Danger and Survival: Choices About the Bomb in the First Fifty Years* (New York: 1988).

Bundy, William. *A Tangled Web: The Making of Foreign Policy in the Nixon Presidency* (New York: 1998).

Burns, James MacGregor. *Roosevelt: The Soldier of Freedom* (New York: 1970).

Bush, George, and Brent Scowcroft. *A World Transformed* (New York: 1998).

Callahan, David. *Dangerous Capabilities: Paul Nitze and the Cold War* (New York: 1990).

Campbell, Thomas M., and George C. Herring, Jr., eds. *The Diaries of Edward R. Stettinius, Jr., 1943–1946* (New York: 1975).

Cannon, Lou. *President Reagan: The Role of a Lifetime* (New York: 1991).

Carter, Jimmy. *Keeping Faith: Memoirs of a President* (New York: 1982).

Chen Jian. *Mao's China and the Cold War* (Chapel Hill: 2001).

Chernyaev, Anatoly. *My Six Years with Gorbachev*, translated and edited by Robert English and Elizabeth Tucker (University Park, Pa.: 2000).

Churchill, Winston S. *The Grand Alliance* (Boston: 1950).

Clausewitz, Carl von. *On War*, edited and translated by Michael Howard and Peter Paret (Princeton: 1976).

Collins, John M. *American and Soviet Military Trends Since the Cuban Missile Crisis* (Washington: 1978).

Conrad, Joseph. *Heart of Darkness*, edited by Robert Kimbrough (New York: 1970).

Corson, William R. *The Armies of Ignorance: The Rise of the American Intelligence Empire* (New York: 1977).

Craig, Campbell. *Destroying the Village: Eisenhower and Thermonuclear War* (New York: 1998).

Craig, Gordon A., and Francis L. Lowenheim, eds. *The Diplomats: 1939–1979* (Princeton: 1994).

Cullather, Nicholas. *Operation PBSUCCESS: The United States and Guatemala, 1952–1954* (Washington: 1994).

Cumings, Bruce. *The Origins of the Korean War: The Roaring of the Cataract, 1947–1950* (Princeton: 1990).

Dallek, Robert. *Franklin D. Roosevelt and American Foreign Policy, 1932–1945* (New York: 1979).

Davis, Lynn Etheridge. *The Cold War Begins: Soviet-American Conflict over Eastern Europe* (Princeton: 1974).

Davis, Rex Harry, and Robert Crocker Good, eds. *Reinhold Niebuhr on Politics* (New York: 1960).

Dawson, Raymond H. *The Decision to Aid Russia, 1941: Foreign Policy and Domestic Politics* (Chapel Hill: 1959).

Deane, John R. *The Strange Alliance: The Story of Our Wartime Cooperation with Russia* (New York: 1947).

DeSantis, Hugh. *The Diplomacy of Silence: The American Foreign Service, the Soviet Union, and the Cold War, 1933–1947* (Chicago: 1980).

Dickson, Peter W. *Kissinger and the Meaning of History* (New York: 1978).

DiLeo, David L. *George Ball, Vietnam, and the Rethinking of Containment* (Chapel Hill: 1991).

Dinerstein, Herbert S. *The Making of a Missile Crisis: October, 1962* (Baltimore: 1976).

Divine, Robert A. *Blowing on the Wind: The Nuclear Test Ban Debate, 1954–1960* (New York: 1978).

———. *Foreign Policy and U.S. Presidential Elections: 1960–1960* (New York: 1974). 2 volumes.

Dobrynin, Anatoly. *In Confidence: Moscow's Ambassador to Six Cold War Presidents (1962–1986)* (New York: 1995).

Dockrill, Saki. *Eisenhower's New-Look National Security Policy, 1953–61* (New York: 1996).

Donovan, Robert J. *Conflict and Crisis: The Presidency of Harry S. Truman* (New York: 1977).

Drew, Elizabeth. *American Journal: The Events of 1976* (New York: 1977).

Dulles, John Foster. *War or Peace* (New York: 1950).

Duric, Mira. *The Strategic Defense Initiative: US Policy and the Soviet Union* (Aldershot, England: 2003).

Edmonds, Robin. *Soviet Foreign Policy, 1962–1976: The Paradox of Super Power* (London: 1975).

Edwards, Lee. *The Conservative Revolution: The Movement That Remade America* (New York: 1999).

Eisenhower, Dwight D. *The White House Years: Mandate for Change, 1953–1956* (Garden City, N.Y.: 1963).

––––––––. *The White House Years: Waging Peace, 1957–1961* (Garden City, N.Y.: 1965).

El-Khawas, Mohamed A., and Barry Cohen, eds. *The Kissinger Study of Southern Africa: National Security Study Memorandum 39* (Westport, Conn.: 1976).

English, Robert D. *Russia and the Idea of the West: Gorbachev, Intellectuals, and the End of the Cold War* (New York: 2000).

Enthoven, Alain C., and K. Wayne Smith. *How Much Is Enough: Shaping the Defense Program, 1961–1969* (New York: 1971).

Feis, Herbert. *Contest over Japan.* (New York: 1967).

Ferguson, Niall. *Colossus: The Price of America's Empire* (New York: 2004).

Ferrell, Robert H., ed. *The Eisenhower Diaries* (New York: 1981).

Fischer, Beth A. *The Reagan Reversal: Foreign Policy and the End of the Cold War* (Columbia, Mo.: 1997).

Fischer, David Hackett. *Historians' Fallacies: Toward a Logic of Historical Thought* (New York: 1970).

FitzGerald, Frances. *Fire in the Lake: The Vietnamese and the Americans in Vietnam* (Boston: 1972).

FitzSimons, Louise. *The Kennedy Doctrine.* (New York: 1972).

Flash, Edward S., Jr. *Economic Advice and Presidential Leadership: The Council of Economic Advisers* (New York: 1965).

Fleming, D. F. *The Cold War and Its Origins, 1917–1960,* 2 volumes (Garden City, N.Y.: 1961).

Ford, Gerald R. *A Time to Heal* (New York: 1979).

Freedman, Lawrence. *Kennedy's Wars: Berlin, Cuba, Laos, and Vietnam* (New York: Oxford University Press, 2000).

Friedberg, Aaron L. *In the Shadow of the Garrison State: America's Anti-Statism and Its Cold War Strategy* (Princeton: 2000).

Gaddis, John Lewis. *The Landscape of History: How Historians Map the Past* (New York: 2002).

––––––––. *The Long Peace: Inquiries into the History of the Cold War* (New York: 1987).

––––––––. *Russia, the Soviet Union, and the United States: An Interpretive History,* second edition (New York: 1990).

––––––––. *Surprise, Security, and the American Experience* (Cambridge, Mass.: 2004).

––––––––. *The United States and the End of the Cold War: Implications, Provocations, Reconsiderations* (New York: 1992).

––––––––. *The United States and the Origins of the Cold War, 1941–1947* (New York: 1972).

––––––––. **We Now Know: Rethinking Cold War History** (New York: 1997).

Gaiduk, Ilya V. *The Soviet Union and the Vietnam War* (Chicago: 1996).

Gallucci, Robert L. *Neither Peace Nor Honor: The Politics of the American Military in Viet-Nam* (Baltimore: 1976).

Garthoff, Raymond L., *Détente and Confrontation: American-Soviet Relations from Nixon to Reagan*, revised edition (Washington: 1994).

————. *The Great Transition: American-Soviet Relations at the End of the Cold War* (Washington: 1994).

Gates, Robert M. *From the Shadows: The Ultimate Insider's Story of Five Presidents and How They Won the Cold War* (New York: 1996).

Gavin, Francis J., *Gold, Dollars, and Power: The Politics of International Monetary Relations, 1958–1971* (Chapel Hill: 2004).

Gelb, Leslie, and Richard K. Betts. *The Irony of Vietnam: The System Worked* (Washington: 1979).

George, Alexander L., and Richard Smoke. *Deterrence in American Foreign Policy: Theory and Practice* (New York: 1974).

Gittings, John. *Survey of the Sino-Soviet Dispute, 1963–1967* (London: 1968).

————. *The World and China, 1922–1972* (New York: 1972).

Gleijeses, Piero. *Conflicting Missions: Havana, Washington, and Africa, 1959–1976* (Chapel Hill: 2002).

Goldgeier, James M., and Michael McFaul. *Power and Purpose: U.S. Policy toward Russia after the Cold War* (Washington: 2003).

Gorbachev, Mikhail. *Memoirs* (New York: 1995).

————. *Perestroika: New Thinking for Our Country and the World* (New York: 1987).

————, and Zdeněk Mlynář. *Conversations with Gorbachev: On Perestroika, the Prague Spring, and the Crossroads of Socialism*, translated by George Shriver (New York: 2002).

Gordon, Philip H., and Jeremy Shapiro. *Allies at War: America, Europe, and the Crisis Over Iraq* (Washington: 2004).

Graebner, Norman A. *The New Isolationism: A Study in Politics and Foreign Policy Since 1950* (New York: 1956).

Graubard, Stephen. *Kissinger: Portrait of a Mind* (New York: 1973).

Greenfield, Kent Roberts. *American Strategy in World War II: A Reconsideration* (Baltimore: 1963).

Greenstein, Fred I. *The Hidden-Hand Presidency: Eisenhower as Leader* (New York: 1982).

————, ed. *Leadership in the Modern Presidency* (Cambridge, Mass.: 1988).

Griffith, William E. *The Sino-Soviet Rift* (Cambridge, Mass.: 1964).

Guhin, John Michael. *John Foster Dulles: A Statesman and His Times* (New York: 1972).

Halberstam, David. *The Best and the Brightest* (New York: 1972).

Haldeman, H.R. *The Ends of Power* (New York: 1978).

————. *The Haldeman Diaries: Inside the Nixon White House* (New York: 1994).

Hall, R. Cargill, and Clayton D. Laurie, eds. *Early Cold War Overflights, 1950–1956*, 2 volumes (Washington: 2003).

Halle, Louis J. *Civilization and Foreign Policy: An Inquiry for Americans* (New York: 1955).

————. *The Cold War as History* (New York: 1967).

Hamby, Alonzo L. *Beyond the New Deal: Harry S. Truman and American Liberalism* (New York: 1973).

————. *Man of the People: A Life of Harry S. Truman* (New York: 1995).

Hanhimäki, Jussi. *The Flawed Architect: Henry Kissinger and American Foreign Policy* (New York: 2004).

Harriman, W. Averell, and Elie Abel. *Special Envoy to Churchill and Stalin, 1941–1946* (New York: 1975).

Harris, Seymour E. *The Economics of the Political Parties* (New York: 1962).

Heller, Walter W. *New Dimensions of Political Economy* (Cambridge, Mass.: 1966).

Herring, George C., Jr. *Aid to Russia, 1941–1946: Strategy, Diplomacy, the Origins of the Cold War* (New York: 1973).

————. *America's Longest War: The United States and Vietnam, 1950–1975*, second edition (New York: 1986).

Hexter, J.H. *On Historians* (Cambridge, Mass.: 1979).

Hilsman, Roger. *To Move a Nation: The Politics of Foreign Policy in the Administration of John F. Kennedy* (New York: 1967).

Hitchens, Christopher. *The Trial of Henry Kissinger* (New York: 2001).

Hixson, Walter L. *George F. Kennan: Cold War Iconoclast* (New York: 1989).

Hoffmann, Stanley. *Primacy or World Order: American Foreign Policy Since the Cold War* (New York: 1978).

Hogan, Michael J. *A Cross of Iron: Harry S. Truman and the Origins of the National Security State, 1945–1954* (New York: 1998).

————. *The Marshall Plan: America, Britain, and the Reconstruction of Western Europe, 1947–1952.* (New York: 1987).

Holloway, David. *Stalin and the Bomb: The Soviet Union and Atomic Energy, 1939–1956* (New Haven: 1994).

Hoopes, Townsend. *The Devil and John Foster Dulles* (Boston: 1973).

Hoover, Herbert. *Addresses upon the American Road: 1950–1955* (Stanford: 1955).

Horelick, Arnold, and Myron Rush. *Strategic Power and Soviet Foreign Policy* (Chicago: 1966).

Hough, Jerry F., and Merle Fainsod. *How the Soviet Union Is Governed* (Cambridge, Mass.: 1979).

Howard, Michael. *The Causes of War*, second edition, enlarged (Cambridge, Mass.: 1983).

————. *The Lessons of History* (New Haven: 1991).

Hughes, Emmet John. *The Ordeal of Power: A Political Memoir of the Eisenhower Years* (New York: 1963).

Huntington, Samuel P. *The Common Defense: Strategic Programs in National Politics* (New York: 1961).

Isaacson, Walter. *Kissinger: A Biography* (New York: 1992).

Johnson, Lyndon B. *The Vantage Point: Perspectives of the Presidency, 1963–1969* (New York: 1971).

Kahan, Jerome H. *Security in the Nuclear Age: Developing U.S. Strategic Arms Policy* (Washington: 1975).

Kagan, Robert. *Of Paradise and Power: America and Europe in the New World Order* (New York: 2003).

Kaplan, Fred. *The Wizards of Armageddon* (New York: 1983).

Kaufman, William W. *The McNamara Strategy* (Washington: 1964).

Kearns, Doris. *Lyndon Johnson and the American Dream* (New York: 1976).

Kendrick, Alexander. *The Wound Within: America in the Vietnam Years, 1945–1974* (Boston: 1974).

Kennan, George F. *American Diplomacy: 1900–1950* (Chicago: 1951).

————. *Around the Cragged Hill: A Personal and Political Philosophy* (New York: 1993).

————. *The Cloud of Danger* (Boston: 1977).

————. *The Decline of Bismarck's European Order: Franco-Russian Relations, 1875–1890* (Princeton: 1979).

————. *Memoirs: 1925–1950* (Boston: 1967).

————. *Memoirs: 1950–1963* (Boston: 1972).

————. *The Realities of American Foreign Policy* (Princeton: 1954).

————. *Sketches from a Life* (New York: 1989).

Kennedy, John F. *The Strategy of Peace*, edited by Allan Nevins (New York: 1960).

Kershaw, Ian. *Hitler: Nemesis, 1936–1945* (New York: 2000).

Khong, Yuen Foong. *Analogies at War: Korea, Munich, and the Vietnam Decisions of 1965* (Princeton: 1992).

Khrushchev, Nikita. *Khrushchev Remembers: The Last Testament*, translated and edited by Strobe Talbott (Boston: 1974).

Kimball, Warren F. *Swords or Ploughshares? The Morgenthau Plan for Defeated Nazi Germany, 1943–1946* (Philadelphia: 1976).

Kinnard, Douglas. *President Eisenhower and Strategy Management: A Study in Defense Politics* (Lexington: 1977).

Kissinger, Henry A. *American Foreign Policy*, third edition (New York: 1977).

———. *Crisis: The Anatomy of Two Major Foreign Policy Crises* (New York: 2003).

———. *Diplomacy* (New York: 1994).

———. *Nuclear Weapons and Foreign Policy* (New York: 1957).

———. *The Troubled Partnership: A Reappraisal of the Atlantic Alliance* (New York: 1965).

———. *White House Years* (Boston: 1979).

———. *A World Restored* (New York: 1957).

———. *Years of Renewal* (New York: 1999).

———. *Years of Upheaval* (Boston: 1982).

Kistiakowsky, George B. *A Scientist at the White House* (Cambridge, Mass.: 1976).

Kolko, Joyce and Gabriel. *The Limits of Power: The World and United States Foreign Policy, 1945–1954* (New York: 1972).

Korb, Lawrence J. *The Fall and Rise of the Pentagon: American Defense Policies in the 1970's* (Westport, Conn.: 1979).

Kotkin, Stephen. *Armageddon Averted: The Soviet Collapse, 1970–2000* (New York: 2001).

Krock, Arthur. *Memoirs: Sixty Years on the Firing Line* (New York: 1968).

Kuklick, Bruce. *American Policy and the Division of Germany: The Clash with Russia over Reparations* (Ithaca: 1972).

Kuniholm, Bruce R. *The Origins of the Cold War in the Near East: Great Power Conflict and Diplomacy in Iran, Turkey, and Greece* (Princeton: 1980).

Lake, Anthony. *The "Tar Baby" Option: American Policy Toward Southern Rhodesia* (New York: 1976).

Lees, Lorraine M. *Keeping Tito Afloat: The United States, Yugoslavia, and the Cold War* (University Park, Pa.: 1997).

Leffler, Melvyn P. *A Preponderance of Power: National Security, the Truman Administration, and the Cold War* (Stanford: 1992).

Lettow, Paul. *Ronald Reagan and His Quest to Abolish Nuclear Weapons* (New York: 2005).

Levering, Ralph B. *American Opinion and the Russian Alliance, 1939–1945* (Chapel Hill: 1976).

———, Vladimir O. Pechatnov, Verena Botzenhart-Viehe, and C. Carl Edmondson. *Debating the Origins of the Cold War: American and Russian Perspectives* (New York: 2002).

Levin, N. Gordon. *Woodrow Wilson and World Politics* (New York: 1968).

Lewy, Guenter. *American in Vietnam* (New York: 1978).

Lilienthal, David E. *The Journals of David E. Lilienthal: The Atomic Energy Years, 1945–1950* (New York: 1964).

Lippmann, Walter. *The Cold War: A Study in U.S. Foreign Policy* (New York: 1947).

Loewenheim, Francis L., with Harold D. Langley and Manfred Jonas, eds. *Roosevelt and Churchill: Their Secret Wartime Correspondence* (New York: 1975).

Louis, William Roger. *Imperialism at Bay: The United States and the Decolonization of the British Empire, 1941–1945* (New York: 1978).

Lundestad, Geir. *America, Scandinavia, and the Cold War 1945–1949* (New York: 1960).

——. *The American Non-Policy Towards Eastern Europe, 1943–1947* (Oslo: 1978).

Luttwak, Edward N. *The Grand Strategy of the Roman Empire* (Baltimore: 1976).

Lyon, Peter. *Eisenhower: Portrait of a Hero* (Boston: 1974).

Maddux, Thomas R. *Years of Estrangement: American Relations with the Soviet Union, 1933–1941* (Tallahassee: 1980).

Mao Tse-tung. *Selected Military Writings of Mao Tse-tung* (Peking: 1967).

Mastny, Vojtech. *The Cold War and Soviet Insecurity: The Stalin Years* (New York: 1996).

——. *Russia's Road to the Cold War: Diplomacy, Warfare, and the Politics of Communism, 1941–1945* (New York: 1979).

Matlock, Jack F., Jr. *Autopsy on an Empire: The American Ambassador's Account of the Collapse of the Soviet Union* (New York: 1995).

——. *Reagan and Gorbachev: How the Cold War Ended* (New York: 2004).

May, Ernest R. *"Lessons" of the Past: The Use and Misuse of History in American Foreign Policy* (New York: 1973).

——, ed. *American Cold War Strategy: Interpreting NSC 68* (Boston: 1993).

Mayers, David. *George F. Kennan and the Dilemmas of US Foreign Policy* (New York: 1998).

McLellan, David S. *Dean Acheson: The State Department Years* (New York: 1976).

McNamara, Robert S. *In Retrospect: The Tragedy and Lessons of Vietnam* (New York: 1995).

Millis, Walter, ed. *The Forrestal Diaries* (New York: 1951).

Miroff, Bruce. *Pragmatic Illusions: The Presidential Politics of John F. Kennedy* (New York: 1976).

Miscamble, Wilson D., C.S.C. *George F. Kennan and the Making of American Foreign Policy, 1947–1950* (Princeton: 1992).

Morris, Roger. *Uncertain Greatness: Henry Kissinger and American Foreign Policy* (New York: 1977).

Moulton, Harland B. *From Superiority to Parity: The United States and the Strategic Arms Race, 1961–1971* (Westport, Conn.: 1973).

Mueller, John. *Retreat from Doomsday: The Obsolescence of Major War* (New York: 1989).

Murphy, Robert. *Diplomat Among Warriors* (Garden City, N.Y.: 1964).

Nash, Philip. *The Other Missiles of October: Eisenhower, Kennedy, and the Jupiters, 1957–1963* (Chapel Hill: 1997).

Newhouse, John. *Cold Dawn: The Story of SALT* (New York: 1973).

Ninkovich, Frank. *Modernity and Power: A History of the Domino Theory in the Twentieth Century* (Chicago: 1994).

Nitze, Paul H., with Ann M. Smith and Steven L. Rearden. *From Hiroshima to Glasnost: At the Center of Decision: A Memoir* (New York: 1989).

Nixon, Richard M. *RN: The Memoirs of Richard Nixon* (New York: 1978).

Oberdorfer, Don. *From the Cold War to a New Era: The United States and the Soviet Union, 1983–1991*, updated edition (Baltimore: 1998).

——. *Senator Mansfield: The Extraordinary Life of a Great American Statesman and Diplomat* (Washington: 2003).

Odom, William E. *The Collapse of the Soviet Military* (New Haven: 1998).

Olson, Keith W. *Watergate: The Presidential Scandal That Shook America* (Lawrence, Kans.: 2003).

Osborne, John. *White House Watch: The Ford Years* (Washington: 1977).

Ouimet, Matthew J. *The Rise and Fall of the Brezhnev Doctrine in Soviet Foreign Policy* (Chapel Hill: 2003).

Pach, Chester J., Jr., and Elmo Richardson. *The Presidency of Dwight D. Eisenhower*, revised edition (Lawrence, Kans.: 1991).

Palmer, Dave Richard. *Summons of the Trumpet: U.S.-Vietnam in Perspective* (San Rafael, Calif.: 1978).

Parmet, Herbert S. *Eisenhower and the American Crusades* (New York: 1972).

Paterson, Thomas G. *Soviet-American Confrontation: Postwar Reconstruction and the Origins of the Cold War* (Baltimore: 1973).

Patterson, James T. *Mr. Republican: A Biography of Robert A. Taft* (Boston: 1972).

Peterson, Peter G. *U.S.-Soviet Commercial Relations in a New Era* (Washington: 1972).

Pipes, Richard. *Vixi: Memoirs of a Non-Belonger* (New Haven: 2003).

Pogue, Forrest C. *George C. Marshall: Organizer of Victory* (New York: 1973).

Powers, Thomas. *The Man Who Kept the Secrets: Richard Helms and the CIA* (New York: 1979).

Prados, John. *The Soviet Estimate: U.S. Intelligence Analysis and Russian Military Strength* (New York: 1982).

Pruessen, Ronald W. *John Foster Dulles: The Road to Power* (New York: 1982).

Quandt, William B. *Decade of Decisions: American Policy Toward the Arab-Israeli Conflict, 1967–1976* (Berkeley: 1977).

Quester, George H. *Nuclear Diplomacy: The First Twenty-Five Years*, second edition (New York: 1973).

Ranelagh, John. *The Agency: The Rise and Decline of the CIA* (New York: 1986).

Reagan, Ronald. *An American Life* (New York: 1990).

Roman, Peter J. *Eisenhower and the Missile Gap* (Ithaca: 1995).

Roosevelt, Elliott, ed. *F.D.R.: His Personal Letters: 1928–1945*, 2 volumes (New York: 1950).

Rosenman, Samuel I., ed. *The Public Papers and Addresses of Franklin D. Roosevelt*, 13 volumes (New York: 1938–1950).

Rostow, W.W. *The Diffusion of Power: An Essay in Recent History* (New York: 1972).

———. *The Stages of Economic Growth: A Non-Communist Manifesto* (New York: 1960).

Russell, Richard L. *George F. Kennan's Strategic Thought: The Making of an American Political Realist* (Westport, Conn.: 1999).

Safire, William. *Before the Fall: An Inside View of the Pre-Watergate White House* (New York: 1975).

Sanders, Jerry W. *Peddlers of Crisis: The Committee on the Present Danger and the Politics of Containment* (Boston: 1983).

Schaller, Michael. *The U.S. Crusade in China, 1938–1945* (New York: 1979).

Schandler, Herbert Y. *The Unmaking of a President: Lyndon Johnson and Vietnam* (Princeton: 1977).

Scheer, Robert. *With Enough Shovels: Reagan, Bush, and Nuclear War* (New York: 1983).

Schell, Jonathan. *The Fate of the Earth* (New York: 1982)

———. *The Time of Illusion* (New York: 1976).

Schick, Jack M. *The Berlin Crisis, 1958–1962* (Philadelphia: 1971).

Schlesinger, Arthur M., Jr. *Robert Kennedy and His Times* (Boston: 1978).

———. *A Thousand Days: John F. Kennedy in the White House* (Boston: 1965).

Schnabel, James F. *The Joint Chiefs of Staff and National Policy, 1945–1947* (Wilmington: 1979). "History of the Joint Chiefs of Staff."

———. *Policy and Direction: The First Year* (Washington: 1972). "The U.S. Army in the Korean War."

Schweizer, Peter. *Reagan's War: The Epic Story of His Forty Year Struggle and Final Triumph Over Communism* (New York: 2002).

———. *Victory: The Reagan Administration's Secret Strategy That Hastened the Collapse of the Soviet Union* (New York: 1994).

Shawcross, William. *Sideshow: Kissinger, Nixon, and the Destruction of Cambodia* (New York: 1979).

Sheehan, Edward R.F. *The Arabs, Israelis, and Kissinger: A Secret History of American Diplomacy in the Middle East* (New York: 1976).

Sherwin, Martin J. *A World Destroyed: The Atomic Bomb and the Grand Alliance* (New York: 1975).

Shultz, George P. *Turmoil and Triumph: My Years as Secretary of State* (New York: 1993).

Sick, Gary. *All Fall Down: America's Tragic Encounter with Iran* (New York: 1985).

Sivachev, Nikolai V., and Nikolai N. Yakovlev. *Russia and the United States*, translated by Olga Adler Titelbaum (Chicago: 1979).

Smith, Bradley F., and Elena Agarossi. *Operation Sunrise: The Secret Surrender* (New York: 1979).

Smith, Gaddis. *American Diplomacy During the Second World War, 1941–1945* (New York: 1965).

————. *Morality, Reason, and Power: American Diplomacy in the Carter Years* (New York: 1986).

Smith, Tony, *America's Mission: The United States and the Worldwide Struggle for Democracy in the Twentieth Century* (Princeton: 1994).

————. *Thinking Like a Communist: State and Legitimacy in the Soviet Union, China, and Cuba* (New York: 1987).

Sorensen, Theodore C. *Kennedy* (New York: 1965).

Sorley, Lewis. *A Better War: The Unexamined Victories and Final Tragedy of America's Last Years in Vietnam* (New York: 1999).

Spykman, Nicholas John. *America's Strategy in World Politics: The United States and the Balance of Power* (New York: 1942).

Stearns, Monteagle. *Entangled Allies: U.S. Policy Toward Greece, Turkey, and Cyprus* (New York: 1992).

Stebbins, Richard P. *The United States in World Affairs: 1956* (New York: 1957).

————. *The United States in World Affairs: 1958* (New York: 1959).

Stein, Herbert. *The Fiscal Revolution in America* (Chicago: 1969).

Steiner, Zara S. *The Foreign Office and Foreign Policy, 1898–1914* (London: 1969).

Stephanson, Anders. *Kennan and the Art of Foreign Policy* (Cambridge, Mass.: 1989).

Stoessinger, John G. *Henry Kissinger: The Anguish of Power* (New York: 1976).

Stoler, Mark A. *Allies and Adversaries: The Joint Chiefs of Staff, the Grand Alliance, and U.S. Strategy in World War II* (Chapel Hill: 2000).

Stone, I.F. *The Hidden History of the Korean War* (New York: 1952).

Stueck, William. *The Korean War: An International History* (Princeton: 1995).

————. *Rethinking the Korean War: A New Diplomatic and Strategic History* (Princeton: 2002).

Sulzberger, C.L. *A Long Row of Candles: Memoirs and Diaries, 1934–1954* (New York: 1969).

Sun Tzu. *The Art of War*, translated by Samuel B. Griffith (New York: 1963).

Suny, Ronald Grigor. *The Soviet Experiment: Russia, the U.S.S.R., and the Successor States* (New York: 1998).

Suri, Jeremi. *Power and Protest: Global Revolution and the Rise of Détente* (Cambridge, Mass.: 2003).

Szulc, Tad. *The Illusion of Peace: Foreign Policy in the Nixon Years* (New York: 1978).

Taft, Robert A. *A Foreign Policy for Americans* (Garden City, N.Y.: 1951)

Talbott, Strobe. *Endgame: The Inside Story of SALT II* (New York: 1979).

Taubman, William. *Khrushchev: The Man and His Era* (New York: 2003).

Taylor, Maxwell. *Swords and Ploughshares* (New York: 1972).

————. *The Uncertain Trumpet* (New York: 1959).

Thatcher, Margaret. *The Downing Street Years* (New York: 1993).

Thorne, Christopher. *Allies of a Kind: The United States, Britain, and the War Against Japan, 1941–1945* (New York: 1979).

Trachtenberg, Marc. *A Constructed Peace: The Making of the European Settlement, 1945–1963* (Princeton: 1999).

————. *History and Strategy* (Princeton: 1991).

Truman, Harry S. *Memoirs: Year of Decisions* (Garden City, N.Y.: 1955).

————. *Memoirs: Years of Trial and Hope* (Garden City, N.Y.: 1956).

Truman, Margaret. *Harry S. Truman* (New York: 1973).

Tucker, Nancy Bernkopf. *Patterns in the Dust: Chinese-American Relations and the Recognition Controversy, 1949–1950* (New York: 1983).

Ulam, Adam B. *The Rivals: America and Russia Since World War II* (New York: 1971).

Van Creveld, Martin. *The Transformation of War* (New York: 1991).

Vance, Cyrus. *Hard Choices: Critical Years in America's Foreign Policy* (New York: 1983).

Walton, Richard J. *Cold War and Counterrevolution: The Foreign Policy of John F. Kennedy* (New York: 1972).

Ward, Patricia Dawson. *The Threat of Peace: James F. Byrnes and the Council of Foreign Ministers, 1945–1946* (Kent, Ohio: 1979).

Weart, Spencer R. *Nuclear Fear: A History of Images* (Cambridge, Mass.: 1988).

Weil, Martin. *A Pretty Good Club: The Founding Fathers of the U.S. Foreign Service* (New York: 1978).

Weinberg, Gerhard L. *A World at Arms: A Global History of World War II* (New York: 1994).

Weinberger, Caspar W. *Fighting for Peace: Seven Critical Years in the Pentagon* (New York: 1990).

Wenger, Andreas. *Living With Peril: Eisenhower, Kennedy, and Nuclear Weapons* (Lanham, Md.: 1997).

Whitworth, William. *Naive Questions About War and Peace* (New York: 1970).

Williams, William Appleman. *The Tragedy of American Diplomacy* (New York: 1962).

Wohlforth, William C., ed. *Witnesses to the End of the Cold War* (Baltimore: 1996).

Wohlstetter, Roberta. *Pearl Harbor: Warning and Decision* (Stanford: 1962).

Wolfe, Thomas W. *Soviet Power and Europe, 1945–1970* (Baltimore: 1970).

Wright, Gordon. *The Ordeal of Total War: 1939–1945* (New York: 1968).

Yaqub, Salim. *Containing Arab Nationalism: The Eisenhower Doctrine and the Middle East* (Chapel Hill: 2004).

Yergin, Daniel. *Shattered Peace: The Origins of the Cold War and the National Security State* (Boston: 1977).

Zagoria, Donald S. *The Sino-Soviet Conflict, 1956–1961* (Princeton: 1962).

Zelikow, Philip, and Condoleezza Rice. *Germany Unified and Europe Transformed: A Study in Statecraft* (Cambridge, Mass.: 1995).

Zhai, Qiang. *China and the Vietnam Wars, 1950–1975* (Chapel Hill: 2000).

Articles

Akins, James E. "The Oil Crisis: This Time the Wolf Is Here," *Foreign Affairs*, LI (April 1973), 462–90.

Arbatov, Georgii. "The Limited Power of an Ordinary State," *New Perspectives Quarterly*, V (Summer, 1988), 31.

Bender, Gerald J. "Angola, the Cubans, and American Anxieties," *Foreign Policy*, #31 (Summer, 1978), 3–30.

Bernstein, Barton J. "The Quest for Security: American Foreign Policy and International Control of Atomic Energy, 1942–1946," *Journal of American History*, LX (March 1974), 1003–44.

————. "Roosevelt, Truman, and the Atomic Bomb, 1941–1945: A Reinterpretation," *Political Science Quarterly*, XC (Spring, 1975), 23–69.

Brown, Seyom. "An End to Grand Strategy," *Foreign Policy*, #32 (Fall, 1978), 22–47.

Brzezinski, Zbigniew. "The Balance of Power Delusion," *Foreign Policy*, #7 (Summer, 1972), 54–59.

————. "The Deceptive Power of Peace," *Foreign Policy*, #14 (Spring, 1974), 35–56.

Buchan, Alastair. "A World Restored?" *Foreign Affairs*, L (July 1972), 644–59.

Bull, Hedley. "A View from Abroad: Consistency Under Pressure," *Foreign Affairs*, LVII ("America and the World: 1978"), 441–62.

Burr, William. "Avoiding the Slippery Slope: The Eisenhower Administration and the Berlin Crisis, November 1958–January 1959," *Diplomatic History*, XVIII (Spring, 1994), 177–205.

Caldwell, Dan. "US Domestic Politics and the Demise of Détente," in Odd Arne Westad, ed., *The Fall of Détente: Soviet-American Relations during the Carter Years* (Oslo: 1997), pp. 95–117.

Chace, James. "The Five-Power World of Richard Nixon," *New York Times Magazine*, February 20, 1972, pp. 14ff.

Chang, Gordon H. "JFK, China, and the Bomb," *Journal of American History*, LXXIV (March, 1988), 1287–1310.

Coogan, John W., and Michael H. Hunt. "Kennan and Containment: A Comment," Society for Historians of American Foreign Relations *Newsletter*, IX (March 1978), 23–25.

Costigliola, Frank. " 'Unceasing Pressure for Penetration': Gender, Pathology, and Emotion in George Kennan's Formation of the Cold War," *Journal of American History*, LXXXIII (March, 1997), 1309–39.

Davis, Nathaniel. "The Angola Decision of 1975: A Personal Memoir," *Foreign Affairs*, LVII (Fall, 1978), 109–24.

DeSantis, Vincent P. "Eisenhower Revisionism," *Review of Politics*, XXXVIII (April 1976), 190–207.

Divine, Robert A. "War, Peace, and Political Parties in 20th Century America," Society for Historians of American Foreign Relations *Newsletter*, VIII (March 1977), 1–6.

Drew, Elizabeth. "A Reporter at Large: Brzezinski," *New Yorker*, LIV (May 1, 1978), 90–130.

————. "A Reporter at Large: Human Rights," *New Yorker*, LII (July 18, 1977), 36–62.

Dulles, John Foster. "A Policy of Boldness," *Life*, XXXII (May 19, 1952), 146–60.

————. "Policy for Security and Peace," *Foreign Affairs*, XXXII (April 1954), 353–364.

Farnham, Barbara. "Reagan and the Gorbachev Revolution: Perceiving the End of Threat," *Political Science Quarterly*, CXVI (Summer, 2001), 225–52.

Freund, Charles Paul. "Where Did All Our Villains Go?" *Washington Post*, December 11, 1988.

Fromkin, David. "The Great Game in Asia," *Foreign Affairs*, LVII (Spring, 1980), 936–951.

Gaddis, John Lewis. "Containment: A Reassessment," *Foreign Affairs*, LV (July 1977), 873–87.

————. "Containment and the Logic of Strategy," *The National Interest*, #10 (Winter, 1987/88), 27–38.

————. "Grand Strategy in the Second Term," *Foreign Affairs* LXXIV (January/ February, 2005), 1–15.

————. "Harry S. Truman and the Origins of Containment," in Frank J. Merli and Theodore A. Wilson, eds., *Makers of American Diplomacy* (New York: 1974), pp. 189–218.

————. "Korea in American Politics, Strategy, and Diplomacy, 1945–50," in Yonosuke Nagai and Akira Iriye, eds., *The Origins of the Cold War in Asia* (New York: 1977), pp. 277–98.

————. "Living in Candlestick Park," *The Atlantic*, CCLXXXIII (April, 1999), 65–74.

————. "Rescuing Choice from Circumstance: The Statecraft of Henry Kissinger," in Gordon A. Craig and Francis L. Lowenheim, eds., *The Diplomats: 1939–1979* (Princeton: 1994), pp. 564–92.

————. "Was the Truman Doctrine a Real Turning Point?" *Foreign Affairs*, LII (January 1974), 386–402.

Gati, Charles. "What Containment Meant," *Foreign Policy*, #7 (Summer, 1972), 22–40.

George, Alexander L. "Case Studies and Theory Development: The Method of Structured, Focused Comparison," in Paul Gordon Lauren, ed., *Diplomacy: New Approaches in History, Theory, and Policy* (New York: 1979), pp. 43–68.

————. "The 'Operational Code': A Neglected Approach to the Study of Political Decision-Making," *International Studies Quarterly*, XII (June 1969), 190–222.

Gershman, Carl. "The Rise & Fall of the New Foreign Policy Establishment," *Commentary*, LXX (July 1980), 13–24.

Greenstein, Fred I. "Eisenhower as an Activist President: A New Look at the Evidence," *Political Science Quarterly*, XCIV (Winter, 1979–80), 575–99.

————. "Ronald Reagan, Mikhail Gorbachev, and the End of the Cold War: What Difference Did They Make?" in William H. Wohlforth, ed., *Witnesses to the End of the Cold War* (Baltimore: 1996), pp. 199–219.

Hammond, Paul Y. "NSC-68: Prologue to Rearmament," in Warner R. Schilling, Paul Y. Hammond, and Glenn H. Snyder, *Strategy, Politics and Defense Budgets* (New York: 1962), pp. 267–378.

Henrikson, Alan K. "America's Changing Place in the World: From 'Periphery' to 'Centre'?" in Jean Gottmann, ed., *Centre and Periphery: Spatial Variation in Politics* (Beverly Hills, Cal.: 1980), pp. 73–100.

Hoffmann, Stanley. "Choices," *Foreign Policy*, #12 (Fall, 1973), 3–42.

————. "The Hell of Good Intentions," *Foreign Policy* #29 (Winter, 1977–78), 3–26.

————. "Muscle and Brains," *Foreign Policy* #37 (Winter, 1979–80), pp. 3–27.

————. "The View from at Home: The Perils of Incoherence," *Foreign Affairs*, LVII ("America and the World: 1978"), 463–91.

————. "Weighing the Balance of Power," *Foreign Affairs*, L (July 1972), 618–48.

Holloway, David. "Research Note: Soviet Thermonuclear Development." *International Security*, IV (Winter, 1979–80), 192–97.

Hudson, Daryl J. "Vandenberg Reconsidered: Senate Resolution 239 and American Foreign Policy," *Diplomatic History*, I (Winter, 1977), 46–63.

Immerman, Richard H. "Confessions of an Eisenhower Revisionist: An Agonizing Reappraisal," *Diplomatic History*, XIV (Summer, 1990), 319–42.

————. "Eisenhower and Dulles: Who Made the Decisions?" *Political Psychology*, I (Autumn, 1979), 3–20.

Jackson, William D. "Soviet Reassessment of Ronald Reagan, 1985–1988," *Political Science Quarterly*, CXIII (Winter, 1998–99), 617–44.

Jessup, Philip C. "The Berlin Blockade and the Use of the United Nations," *Foreign Affairs*, L (October 1971), 163–73.

Kaplan, Fred M. "Our Cold-War Policy, Circa '50," *New York Times Magazine*, May 18, 1980, pp. 34ff.

Keller, Bill. "Gorbachev, in Finland, Disavows any Right of Regional Intervention," *New York Times*, October 26, 1989.

[Kennan, George F.] "X." "The Sources of Soviet Conduct," *Foreign Affairs*, XXV (July 1947), 566–82.

Kirkpatrick, Jeane. "Dictatorships and Double Standards," *Commentary*, LXVIII (November, 1979), 34–45.

Kissinger, Henry A. "Central Issues in American Foreign Policy," in Kermit Gordon, ed., *Agenda for the Nation* (Washington: 1968), pp. 585–614.

————. "Domestic Structures and Foreign Policy," *Daedalus*, XCV (Spring, 1966), 503–29.

————. "The White Revolutionary: Reflections on Bismarck," *Daedalus*, XCVII (Summer, 1968), 888–924.

Knight, Jonathan. "George Frost Kennan and the Study of American Foreign Policy: Some Critical Comments," *Western Political Quarterly*, XX (March 1967), 149–160.

Kruszewski, Charles. "The Pivot of History," *Foreign Affairs*, XXXII (April 1954), 388–401.

Lange, Peter. "What Is To Be Done—About Italian Communism," *Foreign Policy*, #21 (Winter, 1975–76), 224–40.

Lees, Lorraine. "The American Decision To Assist Tito, 1948–1949," *Diplomatic History*, II (Fall, 1978), 407–22.

Leffler, Melvyn P. "9/11 and the Past and Future of American Foreign Policy," *International Affairs*, LXXIX (2003), 1051–54.

Leighton, Richard M. "The American Arsenal Policy in World War II: A Retrospective View," in Daniel R. Beaver, ed., *Some Pathways in Twentieth Century History: Essays in Honor of Charles Reginald McGrane* (Detroit: 1969), pp. 221–52.

Lundestad, Geir. "Empire by Invitation? The United States and Western Europe, 1945–1952," *Journal of Peace Research*, XXIII (September, 1986), 263–77.

Mandelbaum, Michael. "Coup de Grace: The End of the Soviet Union," *Foreign Affairs*, LXXI ("America and the World, 1991/1992"), 164–83.

Marcum, John A. "Lessons of Angola," *Foreign Affairs*, LIV (April 1976), 407–425.

Mark, Eduard. "The Question of Containment: A Reply to John Lewis Gaddis," *Foreign Affairs*, LVI (January 1978), 430–40.

————. "What Kind of Containment?" in Thomas G. Paterson, ed., *Containment and the Cold War* (Reading, Mass.: 1973), 96–109.

Matloff, Maurice. "The 90-Division Gamble," in Kent Roberts Greenfield, ed., *Command Decisions* (Washington: 1960), pp. 365–81.

Matray, James I. "Truman's Plan for Victory: National Self-Determination and the Thirty-Eighth Parallel Decision in Korea," *Journal of American History*, LXVI (September 1979), 314–33.

May, Ernest R. "The United States, the Soviet Union, and the Far Eastern War, 1941–1945," *Pacific Historical Review*, XXIV (May 1955), 153–74.

[Morgan, George Allan] "Historicus." "Stalin on Revolution," *Foreign Affairs*, XXVII (January 1949), 175–214.

Morton, Louis. "Soviet Intervention in the War with Japan," *Foreign Affairs*, XL (July 1962), 653–62.

Muir, William K., Jr. "Ronald Reagan: The Primacy of Rhetoric," in Fred I. Greenstein, ed., *Leadership in the Modern Presidency* (Cambridge, Mass.: 1988), pp. 260–95.

Nitze, Paul. "The Development of NSC 68," *International Security*, IV (Spring, 1980), 170–76.

Nixon, Richard M. "Asia After Vietnam," *Foreign Affairs*, XLVI (October, 1967), 111–125.

Pearcy, G. Etzel. "Geopolitics and Foreign Relations," *Department of State Bulletin*, L (March 1964), 318–30.

Pechatnov, Vladimir O., and C. Carl Edmondson. "The Russian Perspective," in Ralph B. Levering, Vladimir O. Pechatnov, Verena Botzenhart-Viehe, and C. Carl Edmondson, *Debating the Origins of the Cold War: American and Russian Perspectives* (New York: 2002), pp. 85–151.

Quester, George H. "Was Eisenhower a Genius?" *International Security*, IV (Fall, 1979), 159–79.

Rabe, Stephen G. "Eisenhower Revisionism: A Decade of Scholarship," *Diplomatic History*, XVII (Winter, 1993), 97–115.

Reichard, Gary W. "Eisenhower as President: The Changing View," *South Atlantic Quarterly*, LXXVII (Summer, 1978), 265–81.

Rosenberg, David Alan. "American Atomic Strategy and the Hydrogen Bomb Decision," *Journal of American History*, LXVI (June 1979), 62–87.

Szalontai, Balázs. " 'You Have No Political Line of Your Own': Kim Il Sung and the Soviets, 1953–1964," Cold War International History Project *Bulletin*, #14/15 (Winter, 2003–Spring, 2004), 87–137.

Schilling, Warner R. "The Politics of National Defense: Fiscal 1950," in Warner R. Schilling, Paul Y. Hammond, and Glenn H. Snyder, *Strategy, Politics, and Defense Budgets* (New York: 1962), pp. 1–266.

Schlesinger, Arthur M., Jr. "Origins of the Cold War," *Foreign Affairs*, XLVI (October 1967), 22–52.

Serfaty, Simon. "Brzezinski: Play It Again, Zbig," *Foreign Policy*, #32 (Fall, 1978), pp. 3–21.

Shepley, James. "How Dulles Avoided War," *Life*, XL (January 16, 1956), 70–80.

Sidey, Hugh. "Assessing a Presidency," *Time*, CXI (August 18, 1980), 10–15.

Snyder, Glenn H. "The 'New Look' of 1953," in Warner R. Schilling, Paul Y. Hammond, and Glenn H. Snyder, *Strategy, Politics, and Defense Budgets* (New York: 1962), pp. 379–524.

Stern, Laurence. "Bitter Lessons: How We Failed in Cyprus," *Foreign Policy*, #19 (Summer, 1975), 34–78.

Suri, Jeremi. "America's Search for a Technological Solution to the Arms Race: The Surprise Attack Conference of 1958 and a Challenge to Eisenhower Revisionists," *Diplomatic History*, XXI (Summer, 1997), 417–51.

―――――. "Explaining the End of the Cold War: A New Historical Consensus?" *Journal of Cold War Studies*, IV (Fall, 2002), 60–92.

Szulc, Tad. "Lisbon & Washington: Behind the Portuguese Revolution," *Foreign Policy*, #21 (Winter, 1975–76), 3–62.

Ullman, Richard H. "Washington, Wilson, and the Democrat's Dilemma," *Foreign Policy*, #21 (Winter, 1975–76), 97–124.

Urban, George. "A Conversation with George F. Kennan," *Encounter*, XLVII (September 1976), 10–43.

Wells, Samuel F., Jr. "Sounding the Tocsin: NSC 68 and the Soviet Threat," *International Security*, IV (Fall, 1979), 116–38.

Westad, Odd Arne. "The Fall of Détente and the Turning Tides of History," in Westad, ed., *The Fall of Détente: Soviet-American Relations during the Carter Years* (Oslo: 1997), pp. 3–33.

Wohlstetter, Albert. "Is There a Strategic Arms Race?" *Foreign Policy*, #15 (Summer, 1974), 3–20.

―――――. "Rivals But No Race," *Foreign Policy*, #16 (Fall, 1974), 48–81.

Wright, C. Ben. "Mr. 'X' and Containment," *Slavic Review* XXXV (March 1976), 1–31.

Zakaria, Fareed. "The Reagan Strategy of Containment," *Political Science Quarterly*, CV (Autumn, 1990), 373–95.

Zubok, Vladislav M. "Gorbachev and the End of the Cold War: Perspectives on History and Personality," *Cold War History*, II (January, 2002), 61–100.

Index